HANDBOOK OF
WOMEN
BIBLICAL
INTERPRETERS

HANDBOOK OF
WOMEN
BIBLICAL
INTERPRETERS

A Historical and Biographical Guide

MARION ANN TAYLOR, EDITOR

AGNES CHOI, ASSOCIATE EDITOR

ℬ
Baker Academic
a division of Baker Publishing Group
Grand Rapids, Michigan

© 2012 by Baker Publishing Group

Published by Baker Academic
a division of Baker Publishing Group
P.O. Box 6287, Grand Rapids, MI 49516-6287
www.bakeracademic.com

Printed in the United States of America

Library of Congress Cataloging-in-Publication Data
Handbook of women Biblical interpreters : a historical and biographical guide / Marion Ann Taylor, editor; Agnes Choi, associate editor.
    p. cm.
Includes bibliographical references and index.
ISBN 978-0-8010-3356-8 (cloth)
    1. Women Biblical scholars. 2. Bible—Criticism, interpretation, etc.—History. I. Taylor, Marion Ann. II. Choi, Agnes.
BS501.A1H36 2012
220.6092′52—dc23   2012009033

In keeping with biblical principles of creation stewardship, Baker Publishing Group advocates the responsible use of our natural resources. As a member of the Green Press Initiative, our company uses recycled paper when possible. The text paper of this book is composed in part of post-consumer waste.

12 13 14 15 16 17 18   7 6 5 4 3 2 1

To Glen, David, Catherine, and Peter
And in memory of my parents, Archie and Mary Finlayson

Contents

Preface

The concept of a dictionary of women interpreters of the Bible was born out of a conversation with Dr. Carey Newman in 2000. The idea gradually took shape as I focused my research interests and teaching on women interpreters of the Bible. In 2001, my search for women interpreters of the Bible began in earnest. Dr. Renata Koke created the first chart of the names and publications of women interpreters, and I began to collect the writings of women on the Bible. When I realized that the number of women who had published on the Bible exceeded all my expectations, I focused my research on women interpreters of the nineteenth century.[1] In time and with the help of dedicated research assistants, students, and colleagues, the quest to find the writings of forgotten interpreters of the Bible in the nineteenth century was extended to include women interpreters throughout history.

1. Publications that grew out of this research include Marion Ann Taylor and Heather E. Weir, *Let Her Speak for Herself: Nineteenth-Century Women Writing on Women in Genesis* (Waco: Baylor University Press, 2006); Christiana de Groot and Marion Ann Taylor, eds., *Recovering Nineteenth-Century Women Interpreters of the Bible*, SBL Symposium Series 38 (Atlanta: Society of Biblical Literature, 2007); Marion Ann Taylor, "The Psalms outside the Pulpit: Applications of the Psalms by Women of the Nineteenth Century," in *Interpreting the Psalms for Teaching and Preaching*, ed. Herbert W. Bateman IV and D. Brent Sandy (St. Louis: Chalice, 2010), 219–32, 284–86; idem, "Cold Dead Hands upon Our Threshold: Josephine Butler's Reading of the Story of the Levite's Concubine. Judges 19–21," in *The Bible as a Human Witness to Divine Revelation: Hearing the Word of God through Historically Dissimilar Traditions*, ed. Randall Heskett and Brian P. Irwin, Library of Hebrew Bible / Old Testament Studies 469 (London: T&T Clark, 2010), 259–73; idem, "The Resurrection of Jephthah's Daughter: Reading Judges 11 with Nineteenth-Century Women," in *Strangely Familiar: Protofeminist Interpretations of Patriarchal Biblical Texts*, ed. Nancy Calvert-Koyzis and Heather E. Weir (Atlanta: Society of Biblical Literature, 2009), 57–73; idem, "Anglican Women and the Bible in Nineteenth-century Britain," *Anglican and Episcopal History* 75 (2006): 527–52.

This book is the culmination of years of collaborative research. I want to thank everyone who has supported the vision of creating a one-volume reference tool that introduces readers to women interpreters of the Bible throughout the history of Christianity. Dr. Heather Weir was in the first class I taught on women interpreters of the Bible in 2002 and has worked tirelessly with me on this project. Dr. Agnes Choi has been involved in the project since 2006, and her gifts of organization and attention to detail have made her an ideal associate editor. Thanks also to Dr. Meredith Donaldson Clark and my students who joined the quest to find forgotten women interpreters, especially to Isa Hauser for her diligence in finding German interpreters of the Bible and for her translation of German entries; to David Horrocks for his diligent work on issues related to genealogies; to Eleanor Clitheroe and Renee Kwan Monkman for commenting on an early draft of the book; and to Chris Dowdeswell, David Karram, Nola-Susan Crewe, and Maureen Teixeira for their research. Thanks to Dr. Robert Derrenbacker, treasurer and membership secretary for the Canadian Society of Biblical Studies, and Navar Steed, membership coordinator for the Society of Biblical Literature, for the statistics they provided regarding female membership in the CSBS and SBL. My colleague Dr. Michael Kolarcik deserves special thanks for his translation of Italian materials.

I want to express my gratitude to the scholars whom I consulted for ideas about which women should be included in this book, especially Kirsi Stjerna, Joy Schroeder, Timothy Larsen, Cynthia Scheinberg, Peter Erb, Michaela Sohn-Kronthaler, Ruth Albrecht, Pamela Nadell, and John Sandys-Wunsch. I bear the final responsibility for selecting the women interpreters included in this book.

I am grateful to the staff and board of Wycliffe College at the University of Toronto for their encouragement and support. I want to thank especially Wycliffe's principal, Dr. George Sumner, for his continued support of my research. My colleague Dr. Thomas Power deserves special mention for his help in tracking down primary sources and bibliographic material related to this project. The librarians at the interlibrary loan office at Robarts Library who tracked down the often hard-to-find books of women interpreters were very helpful. Thanks also to Brian Bolger, Jim Kinney, and Rachel Klompmaker at Baker for their guidance, support, and encouragement.

Funding for research on nineteenth-century women interpreters was generously provided by an ATS Lilly theological research grant in 2002–3, a Louisville Summer Stipend in 2004, an ATS Lilly research grant for the fall of 2004 and for the fall of 2007, an Ontario Government grant for a summer student in 2006, and a Stanford and Priscilla Reid Trust grant for 2010–11.

Finally I want to thank my husband and colleague, Glen Taylor, for supporting my work, and our children, David, Catherine, and Peter, who spent their adolescence patiently listening to me talk with excitement about my latest discovery of the writings of yet another woman who dared to interpret Scripture.

Marion Ann Taylor

List of Contributors

Acosta, Ana M. PhD, Columbia University. Associate Professor, Brooklyn College, City University of New York. **Mary Wollstonecraft**

Aelst, José J. van. PhD, Utrecht University, Medieval Literature. PhD mentor, Research Institute for History and Culture. **Berta Jacobs**

Albrecht, Ruth. PhD, Universität Erlangen. apl. Prof. für Kirchengeschichte, Fachbereich Evangelische Theologie, Universität Hamburg. **Jeanne-Marie de Chesnoy Guyon; Johanna Eleonora Petersen**

Batten, Alicia. PhD, St. Michael's College, University of Toronto. Associate Professor of Religious Studies, University of Sudbury. **Margaret Dunlop Gibson and Agnes Smith Lewis**

Becker, Elaine. PhD, Trinity Evangelical Divinity School. **Henrietta C. Mears**

Beilin, Elaine V. PhD, Princeton University. Professor of English, Framingham State University. **Anne Askew**

Bélanger, Stéphanie. PhD, University of Toronto. Assistant Professor, Royal Military College of Canada. **Marie Guyart**

Benckhuysen, Amanda. PhD, St. Michael's College, University of Toronto. Assistant Professor of Old Testament, University of Dubuque Theological Seminary. **Josephine Elizabeth Grey Butler; An Collins**

Blyth, Caroline. PhD, University of Edinburgh. Lecturer, University of Auckland. **Mary E. Simpson**

Bodner, Keith. PhD, University of Manchester. Professor of Religious Studies, Crandall University. **Elizabeth Singer Rowe**

Brandt, Eric. MA, Wheaton College (Illinois). **Amanda Berry Smith; Maria W. Miller Stewart**

Brown, Phyllis R. PhD, University of Oregon. Associate Professor, Santa Clara University. **Hrotsvit of Gandersheim**

Calvert-Koyzis, Nancy. PhD, University of Sheffield, England. **Anna Brownell Jameson**

Caron, Ann Marie, RSM. PhD, Drew University. Associate Professor and Chairperson of the Religious Studies Department, St. Joseph College. **Elisabeth of Schönau**

Chen, Sophia H. Y. MDiv, Tyndale Seminary. ThD candidate, Wycliffe College. **Elizabeth Smith**

Cho, Nancy Jiwan. PhD, Durham University. Assistant Professor of English, Seoul National University. **Dorothy Newberry Gott; Sophia Wigington Hume**

Choi, Agnes. PhD, St. Michael's College, University of Toronto. Assistant Professor of New Testament, Pacific Lutheran University. **Gracilla Boddington; Francis Egerton; Lucy Rider Meyer**

Conway, Mary. MTS, McMaster Divinity College. PhD candidate, McMaster Divinity College. **Ann Murry**

Crouch, Patricia. PhD, Temple University. Framingham State University. **Lucy Hutchinson**

D'Amico, Diane. PhD, University of Wisconsin–Madison. Professor of English, Allegheny College. **Christina Georgina Rossetti**

Davis, Elizabeth M. MA, University of Notre Dame. ThD candidate, Regis College, University of Toronto. **Elizabeth Bowerman; Catherine McAuley; Kathryn Lois Sullivan**

de Groot, Christiana. PhD, University of Notre Dame. Professor, Calvin College. **Annie Wood Besant; Florence Nightingale**

Delmonico, Betsy. PhD, University of Notre Dame. Professor of English, Truman State University. **Jane Anger; Ester Sowernam**

Demers, Patricia. PhD, University of Ottawa. University Professor, University of Alberta. **Hannah More**

Dickens, Andrea J. PhD, University of Virginia. Assistant Professor of Early and Medieval Church History, United Theological Seminary. **Beatrice of Nazareth**

Ditmore, Michael G. PhD, University of Texas at Austin. Professor of English, Pepperdine University. **Anne Hutchinson**

Donaldson Clark, Meredith. PhD, McGill University. Instructor, Nipissing University. **Margaret Beaufort; Mary Sidney Herbert; Margaret More Roper**

Doriani, Beth Maclay. PhD, University of Notre Dame. Dean of the College of Arts and Sciences and Professor of English, Eastern University. **Anne Bradstreet**

Dowd, Sharyn. PhD, Emory University. Pastor for Spiritual Formation and Mission Engagement, First Baptist Church of Decatur. **Helen Barrett Montgomery**

Dowdeswell, Krista M. MRel, Wycliffe College, University of Toronto. PhD student, Wycliffe College, University of Toronto. **Elizabeth Rundle Charles**

Du Mez, Kristin Kobes. PhD, University of Notre Dame. Associate Professor of History, Calvin College. **Katharine C. Bushnell; Lee Anna Starr**

Duquette, Natasha. PhD, Queen's University. Associate Professor and Chairperson of the English Department, Biola University. **Anna Barbauld; Elizabeth Carter; Felicia Hemans**

Erb, Peter C. PhD, University of Toronto. Professor Emeritus, Wilfrid Laurier University (Waterloo, Canada). **Charlotte Mary Yonge**

Evans, Paul S. PhD, St. Michael's College, University of Toronto. Assistant Professor of Old Testament, McMaster Divinity College. **Anne Wharton**

Felch, Susan M. PhD, The Catholic University of America. Professor of English, Calvin College. **Anne Vaughan Lock**

Fentress-Williams, Judy. PhD, Yale University. Associate Professor of Old Testament, Virginia Theological Seminary. **Jarena Lee**

Feroli, Teresa. PhD, Cornell University. Associate Professor of English, Polytechnic Institute of NYU. **Eleanor Davies**

Flynn, Shawn. PhD, University of Toronto. Assistant Professor of Theology and Religious Studies, St. Mark's Theological College. **Beatrice Laura Goff**

German, Igal. MA, Haifa University (Israel). PhD candidate, Wycliffe College, University of Toronto. **Katie Magnus**

Giere, Samuel D. PhD, University of St. Andrews, Scotland. Associate Professor of Homiletics, Wartburg Theological Seminary. **Helen Spurrell**

Gill, Catie. PhD, Loughborough University. **Katherine Evans and Sarah Cheevers**

Gordon, J. Dorcas. ThD, Knox College. Principal, Knox College. **Mary Douglas**

Griffiths, Valerie. ThM, Regent College (Vancouver, Canada). **Joyce Baldwin**

Guðmundsdóttir, Arnfríður. PhD, Lutheran School of Theology at Chicago. Professor of Systematic Theology, University of Iceland. **Briet Bjarnhjedinsdottir**

Hamilton, Michael. ThM, Princeton Theological Seminary. Assistant Professor of Religion and Philosophy, Principia College. **Mary Baker Eddy**

†Hardesty, Nancy A. PhD, University of Chicago. Professor of Religion, Clemson University. **Frances Elizabeth Willard**

Hauser, Isa. MTS, Wycliffe College, University of Toronto. ThM candidate, Wycliffe College, University of Toronto. **Regina Jonas; Justitia Sengers**

Helleman, Wendy Elgersma. PhD, Free University of Amsterdam. Visiting Professor, University of Jos, Nigeria. **Macrina the Younger**

†Hirst, Julie. PhD, Centre for Women's Studies, University of York, UK. **Jane Leade**

Hobby, Elaine. PhD, Birmingham University, UK. Professor of Seventeenth-Century Studies, Loughborough University. **Hester Biddle**

Hofman, Marina H. PhD candidate, University of Toronto. **Mary Ellen Chase**

Humphrey, Edith M. PhD, McGill University. William F. Orr Professor of New Testament, Pittsburgh Theological Seminary. **Elizabeth Stuart Bowdler**

Idestrom, Rebecca G. S. PhD, Sheffield University. Associate Professor of Old Testament, Tyndale Seminary. **Elizabeth Wordsworth**

Irwin, Brian P. PhD, St. Michael's College, University of Toronto. Associate Professor of Old Testament/Hebrew Scripture, Knox College. **Ada Ruth Habershon**

Irwin, Joyce. PhD, Yale University. Research Affiliate, Colgate University. **Anna Maria van Schurman**

Irwin, M. Eleanor. PhD, University of Toronto. Associate Professor Emerita, Department of Humanities, University of Toronto Scarborough. **Aelia Eudocia Augusta; Melania the Elder; Faltonia Betitia Proba**

Johnson, Ella. PhD, St. Michael's College, University of Toronto. Assistant Professor of Systematic Theology, St. Bernard's School of Theology and Ministry. **Gertrude the Great; Mechthild of Hackeborn; Mechthild of Magdeburg**

Jones, Arun. PhD, Princeton Theological Seminary. Dan and Lillian Hankey Associate Professor of World Evangelism, Candler School of Theology, Emory University. **Pandita Ramabai**

Jørstad, Mari. MRel, Wycliffe College, University of Toronto/Toronto School of Theology. PhD student, Duke University. **Birgitta of Sweden; Anne Docwra**

Keesmaat, Sylvia C. DPhil, Oxford University. Adjunct Professor of Biblical Studies, Institute for Christian Studies and Trinity College, University of Toronto. **Dorothy Leigh Sayers**

Kim, Brittany. MA, Wheaton College. PhD candidate, Wheaton College. **Jessie Penn-Lewis**

King, Margaret L. PhD, Stanford University. Professor of History, Brooklyn College and the Graduate Center, City University of New York. **Isotta Nogarola**

Kirk Rappaport, Pamela. DrTheol, University of Munich. Professor, St. John's University–NYC. **Juana Inés de la Cruz**

Knetsch, Robert. PhD candidate, St. Michael's College, University of Toronto. **Mary Cary; Elizabeth Hands**

Knowles, Michael P. ThD, University of Toronto/Toronto School of Theology. Professor and Hurlburt Chair of Preaching, McMaster Divinity College. **R. Roberts**

Ko, Grace. PhD, St. Michael's College, University of Toronto. Adjunct Instructor, Tyndale Seminary. **Louise Pettibone Smith**

Kwan Monkman, Renee. MDiv Hons., Providence Theological Seminary. PhD candidate, Wycliffe College, University of Toronto. **Phoebe Palmer**

Kydd, Roseanne. PhD, York University. **Suzanne de Dietrich**

Lee, Bernon. PhD, St. Michael's College, University of Toronto. Associate Professor of Biblical Studies, Bethel University. **Sarah (Ewing) Hall; Mary Inda Hussey**

Levarie Smarr, Janet. PhD, Princeton University. Professor, University of California–San Diego. **Olympia Morata**

Macumber, Heather. MDiv, Tyndale Seminary. PhD candidate, St. Michael's College, University of Toronto. **Sarah Hale**

McKee, Elsie. PhD, Princeton Theological Seminary. Archibald Alexander Professor of Reformation Studies and the History of Worship, Princeton Theological Seminary. **Katharina Schütz Zell**

McKinley, Mary B. PhD, Rutgers University. Douglas Huntly Gordon Professor of French, University of Virginia. **Marie Dentière**

Mealey, Mark. PhD, St. Michael's College, University of Toronto. **Susanna Wesley**

Michelson, Michal. PhD, Bar-Ilan University. Lecturer, Bar-Ilan University. **Mary Astell**

Miller, Shannon. PhD, University of California–Santa Barbara. Chair and Professor of English, Temple University. **Lucy Hutchinson; Rachel Speght**

Morrow, William S. PhD, University of Toronto. Associate Professor, Queen's University. **Margaret Brackenbury Crook**

Mueller, Janel. PhD, Harvard University. William Rainey Harper Professor Emerita, University of Chicago. **Katherine Parr**

Neel, Carol. PhD, Cornell University. Professor of History, Colorado College. **Dhuoda of Septimania**

Nevitt, Marcus. PhD, Sheffield University. Senior Lecturer in Renaissance Literature, The School of English, University of Sheffield. **Katherine Chidley**

Noffke, Suzanne, OP. PhD, University of Wisconsin–Madison. **Catherine of Siena**

Noftsinger, Kathy A. MA, Asbury Theological Seminary. PhD candidate, Hebrew Union College. **Kathleen M. Kenyon**

O'Dell Bullock, Karen. PhD, Southwestern Baptist Theological Seminary. Professor of Christian History and Director of the PhD Program, B. H. Carroll Theological Institute. **Anne Dutton**

Oeste, Gordon. PhD, St. Michael's College, University of Toronto. Associate Professor of Old Testament and Hebrew, Heritage Theological Seminary. **Louise Seymour Houghton**

Peterson, Brian. PhD, St. Michael's College, University of Toronto. Assistant Professor of Old Testament/Hebrew Bible, Lee University (Cleveland, TN). **Laura Huldah Wild**

Pope-Levison, Priscilla. PhD, University of St. Andrews (Scotland). Professor of Theology and Assistant Director of Women's Studies, Seattle Pacific University. **Elizabeth Cady Stanton; Sojourner Truth**

Potter, Elizabeth. MA, Queen's University. **Margaret Brackenbury Crook**

Pryds, Darleen. PhD, University of Wisconsin–Madison. Associate Professor of History and Spirituality, Franciscan School of Theology/Graduate Theological Union. **Angela of Foligno; Clare of Assisi**

Rex, Michael. PhD, Wayne State University. Associate Professor of English, Cumberland University. **Amey Hayward; Mary Scott**

Ritch, Janet. PhD, Centre for Medieval Studies, University of Toronto. Adjunct Professor, York University. **Marguerite de Navarre; Marguerite Porete**

Robertson, Beth. MA, University of Guelph. PhD candidate, Carleton University. **Phebe Ann (Coffin) Hanaford; (Frances) Julia Wedgwood; Mary L. T. Witter**

Robinson, Barbara. PhD, University of Ottawa. Rector, St. Paul's Anglican Church, Brockville. **Catherine Mumford Booth**

Rowland, Christopher. PhD, University of Cambridge. Dean Ireland's Professor of the Exegesis of Holy Scripture, University of Oxford. **Joanna Southcott**

Sancken, Joni. PhD, Toronto School of Theology. Assistant Professor, Eastern Mennonite Seminary, Eastern Mennonite University. **Elizabeth Dawbarn; Mary Deverell**

Scheinberg, Cynthia. PhD, Rutgers University. Professor, Department of English, Mills College. **Grace Aguilar**

Schroeder, Joy A. PhD, University of Notre Dame. Professor of Religion at Capital University and Professor of Church History at Trinity Lutheran Seminary. **Rebecca Cox Jackson; Bathsua Makin; Arcangela Tarabotti; Lucrezia Tornabuoni**

Selinger, Suzanne. PhD, Yale University. Theological Librarian Emerita, Drew University. **Charlotte von Kirschbaum**

Selvidge, Marla. PhD, St. Louis University. Professor and Director of the Center for Religious Studies, University of Central Missouri. **Julia Evelina Smith**

Sider Hamilton, Catherine. MA, Queen's University. PhD candidate, St. Michael's College, University of Toronto. **Egeria; Marcella; Paula**

Skemp, Sheila L. PhD, University of Iowa. Clare Leslie Marquette Chair in American History, University of Mississippi. **Judith Sargent Murray**

Slade, Carole. PhD, New York University. Adjunct Associate Professor of English and Comparative Literature, Columbia University. **Teresa of Avila**

Smith, Julia J. DPhil, Somerville College, University of Oxford. Independent scholar. **Susanna Hopton**

Smith, Mitzi Jane. PhD, Harvard University. Associate Professor of New Testament and Early Christianity, Ashland Theological Seminary/Detroit. **Zilpha Elaw**

Staley, Lynn. PhD, Princeton University. Shirley and Harrington Drake Professor of the Humanities in the Department of English, Colgate University. **Margery Kempe**

Stjerna, Kirsi. PhD, Boston University. Professor of Reformation Church History and Director of the Institute for Luther Studies, Lutheran Theological Seminary at Gettysburg. **Argula von Grumbach; Helena Konttinen**

Sutherland, Annie. DPhil, University of Oxford. Tutor in Old and Middle English, Somerville College, Oxford. **Julian of Norwich**

Suydam, Mary. PhD, University of California–Santa Barbara. Assistant Professor of Religious Studies, Kenyon College. **Hadewijch of Antwerp**

Tait, Rebecca. BA, Briercrest College and Seminary. MA candidate, Institute for Christian Studies. **Susan Bogert Warner and Anna Bartlett Warner**

Taylor, Marion Ann. PhD, Yale University. Professor of Old Testament, Wycliffe College. **Elizabeth Baxter; Mary Louisa Georgina Carus-Wilson; Marie Françoise Catherine Doetter Corbaux; Mary Cornwallis; Katie Magnus; Justitia Sengers; Harriet Beecher Stowe**

Thickstun, Margaret. PhD, Cornell University. Jane Watson Irwin Professor of English, Hamilton College. **Elizabeth Bathurst; Margaret Askew Fell**

Thompson, Alden. PhD, University of Edinburgh. Professor of Biblical Studies, Walla Walla University. **Ellen Harmon White**

Tonkiss Cameron, Ruth. MA, Sheffield University Postgraduate School of Library and Information Science; MCLIP, UK. Archivist for Union Theological Seminary and Burke Library Collections, The Burke Library (Columbia University Libraries). **Emilie Grace Briggs**

Trautwein, Sherri. MTS, McMaster Divinity College. ThD candidate, Wycliffe College. **Hannah Adams; Jane T. Stoddart**

Unterman, Yael. MA, Bar-Ilan University and Touro College. **Nehama Leibowitz**

Valerio, Adriana. ThD, University of Naples "Federico II" (Italy). Professor of Church History, Faculty of Lettere and Philosophy. **Domenica Narducci da Paradiso**

Vearncombe, Erin. MA, St. Michael's College, University of Toronto. PhD candidate, University of Toronto. **Harriet Livermore; Elizabeth Stuart Phelps**

Walton, Brad. ThD, Wycliffe College, University of Toronto. Robarts Library, University of Toronto. **Elizabeth I; Moderata Fonte; Gertrude More**

Wang, Lisa. PhD, University of London. Priest Associate, Cathedral Church of St. James. **Thérèse of Lisieux**

Warner, Laceye. PhD, University of Bristol, UK. Associate Professor of the Practice of Evangelism and Methodist Studies, Duke University Divinity School. **Sarah Grimké and Angelina Grimké Weld**

Weaver, Elissa B. PhD, University of California–Los Angeles. Professor Emerita of Italian Language and Literature, University of Chicago. **Antonia Pulci; Maria Clemente Ruoti**

Weddle Irons, Kendra. PhD, Baylor University. Visiting Assistant Professor of Religion and Philosophy, Texas Wesleyan University. **Mabel Madeline Southard**

Weir, Heather. ThD, Wycliffe College, University of Toronto. Independent Scholar. **Esther Beuzeville Hewlett Copley; Charlotte Elizabeth Tonna; Sarah Trimmer; Charlotte Maria Tucker**

Winston-Allen, Anne. PhD, University of Kansas. Professor, Southern Illinois University, Carbondale. **Magdalena Beutler**

Wisman, Josette A. PhD, The Catholic University of America. Associate Professor Emerita of French Studies, American University. **Christine de Pizan**

Wolters, Al. PhD, Vrije Universiteit (Amsterdam). Professor Emeritus of Religion and Theology/Classical Languages, Redeemer University College. **Ann Francis**

Woods, Susanne. PhD, Columbia University. Visiting Distinguished Scholar, University of Miami. **Aemilia Lanyer**

Wray Beal, Lissa M. PhD, St. Michael's College, University of Toronto. Associate Professor of Old Testament, Providence Theological Seminary. **Mary Anne Schimmelpenninck**

Young, Abigail. PhD, University of Toronto. Research Associate, University of Toronto. **Hildegard of Bingen**

Zink-Sawyer, Beverly. PhD, Vanderbilt University. Samuel W. Newell Jr. Professor of Preaching and Worship, Union Presbyterian Seminary. **Elizabeth Rice Achtemeier; Antoinette Louisa Brown Blackwell**

Introduction

MARION ANN TAYLOR

Are There Women Interpreters?

A Nobel Prize laureate in Literature, Shmuel Yosef Agnon (1888–1970), opens his story "The Wisdom of Women" as follows:

> In the city was an important Woman from a good family, who would read the Bible and study Mishnah and midrash and *halakhot* and *aggadot* and have learned discussions with the scholars in the *beit midrash*. There were those who esteemed her and sang her praises, and there were those who looked at her resentfully, saying that it is not suitable for a woman to study Torah, for a woman is only for children and there is no wisdom for a woman except at the spindle.[1]

As Agnon's short story continues, the men in the study hall, resentful of her presence, place a beautifully bound, dark red leather volume titled *The Book of the Wisest of Women* on the bookshelves. When the woman finds the book, she discovers its pages are blank. She is angry but acknowledges that the men are right to think, "We have no book that a woman authored."[2] She decides that her foremothers bear some responsibility for failing to leave a written legacy of Jewish wisdom.[3]

---

1. This story was first published in the Israeli newspaper *Ha'aretz*, Nov. 13, 1943. It was republished as "Ḥakhmot nashim," in *Me'atzmi'el 'atzmi*, ed. Emunah Yaron (Jerusalem: Schocken, 1976), 294–98. See Brenda Socachevsky Bacon, "'The Wisdom of Women': From Epstein to Agnon," *Nashim: A Journal of Jewish Women's Studies and Gender Issues* 15 (2008): 30.
2. Bacon, "'The Wisdom of Women,'" 32.
3. I wish to thank Yael Unterman for introducing me to Agnon's short story.

This story resonates with the experience of anyone who has tried to find women interpreters of Scripture from the past.[4] Standard histories of the interpretation of the Bible provide little help: they focus on the history of biblical scholarship, highlighting the lives and work of the most significant and authoritative voices of the academy, church, and synagogue. In his impressive *Dictionary of Major Biblical Interpreters*, Donald K. McKim chose to highlight "leading biblical interpreters by virtue of their particular approaches. . . . Some who are included have pioneered distinctive viewpoints. Others have engaged in thorough expositions of Scripture over a long period of time. Still others had made particular advances in some aspect that shapes the interpretive process."[5] Only three out of the more than two hundred biblical interpreters included in McKim's *Major Biblical Interpreters* are women (Julian of Norwich [1342–ca. 1416], Phyllis Trible [b. 1932], and Elisabeth Schüssler Fiorenza [b. 1938]).[6] Gerald Bray's history of biblical interpretation similarly focuses on credentialed scholars and theologians; at the same time he admits that the "*systematic* learned interpretation" of Scripture stands in tension with "unsystematic" or "popular" uses of the Bible.[7] Ironically, however, it is often "popular" interpreters who have had more impact on a generation than academic and scholarly interpreters, and since most women interpreters of Scripture used the Bible in an unsystematic or popular way, they have not been included in histories of the interpretation of the Bible.[8] Women had neither the academic training nor the status that allowed them to be heard in the university, church, synagogue, or even the press.[9] This book argues that women deserve inclusion in histories of the interpretation of the Bible.

Several important recent developments in scholarship suggest that future histories of the interpretation of Scripture will be more inclusive of popular voices in general,[10] and the voices of women in particular. Popular and

4. This handbook is more than a collection of the lives of women; it is part of a larger quest to recover the voices and lives of women by scholars in many fields and disciplines. Alison Booth suggests that the effect of supplementary canons of histories "may be corrosive rather than a slow water-drop effect; . . . many collective biographies undermine the order of monumental history, disrupting the small circles of icons in the temple of greatness." Alison Booth, "The Lessons of the Medusa: Anna Jameson and Collective Biographies of Women," *Victorian Studies* 42, no. 2 (2000): 258.

5. Donald K. McKim, ed., *Dictionary of Major Biblical Interpreters* (Downers Grove, IL: InterVarsity, 2007), ix.

6. William Yarchin includes samples of the interpretive work of Phyllis Trible and Elisabeth Schüssler Fiorenza in his reader in the history of biblical interpretation. William Yarchin, *History of Biblical Interpretation: A Reader* (Peabody, MA: Hendrickson, 2004).

7. Gerald Bray, *Biblical Interpretation: Past and Present* (Downers Grove, IL: InterVarsity, 2000), 40.

8. Ibid., 40, 360.

9. As a number of entries in this book will show, some exceptional women deserved inclusion in "traditional" histories of the interpretation of the Bible.

10. For a discussion of the revisionist approach to writing history, see Sabyasachi Bhattacharya, "History from Below," *Social Scientist* 11, no. 4 (April 1983): 3–20.

marginalized voices are now included in studies of the reception history of the Bible. David Gunn's commentary on Judges models such an inclusive approach.[11] Scholars draw on the pioneering work of Patricia Demers, Gerda Lerner, Elisabeth Gössman, and Marla Selvidge, which called attention to the work of women interpreters of Scripture, highlighting especially examples of protofeminist writings.[12] Their work of recovering and analyzing the work of women interpreters continues.[13] Joy Schroeder includes women's interpretations in her masterful work on the history of Christian interpretations of sexual violence.[14] Timothy Larsen's 2011 publication, *A People of One Book: The Bible and the Victorians*, signals a shift toward the inclusion of women's voices in historical works that consider the impact of the Bible on life and culture.

This volume continues the task of recovering and analyzing the writings of women interpreters of the Bible. It offers scholars and graduate students the challenge mentioned in many entries that the interpretive work of a particular female interpreter has not yet been fully studied. It provides a resource for those wanting to include the writings of women in courses on Scripture, theology, history, religious formation, and preaching.

The Women Interpreters of the Bible

"Are there any lives of women?"

"No, my dear," said Mr. Sewell; "in the old times, women did not get their lives written, though I don't doubt many of them were much better worth writing than the men's."

Harriet Beecher Stowe, The Pearl of Orr's Island

11. David M. Gunn, *Judges through the Centuries*, BBC (Oxford: Blackwell, 2005). The Blackwell series of commentaries focuses on the reception history of individual biblical books.

12. Patricia Demers, *Women as Interpreters of the Bible* (Mahwah, NJ: Paulist Press, 1992); Gerda Lerner, "One Thousand Years of Feminist Biblical Criticism," in *The Creation of Feminist Consciousness from the Middle Ages to Eighteen-Seventy* (New York: Oxford University Press, 1993), 138–66; Elisabeth Gössman, "History of Biblical Interpretation by European Women," in *Searching the Scriptures: A Feminist Introduction*, ed. Elisabeth Schüssler Fiorenza (New York: Crossroad, 1993), 27–40; Marla Selvidge, *Notorious Voices: Feminist Biblical Interpretation, 1500–1920* (New York: Continuum, 1996).

13. The Canadian Society of Biblical Studies (CSBS) and the Society of Biblical Literature (SBL) have supported this work by including sections on recovering female interpreters of the Bible. Papers from these meetings continue to generate considerable interest. See Christiana de Groot and Marion Ann Taylor, eds., *Recovering Nineteenth-Century Women Interpreters of the Bible*, SBL Symposium Series 38 (Atlanta: Society of Biblical Literature, 2007); Nancy Calvert-Koyzis and Heather E. Weir, eds., *Strangely Familiar: Protofeminist Interpretations of Patriarchal Biblical Texts* (Atlanta: Society of Biblical Literature, 2009); Nancy Calvert-Koyzis and Heather E. Weir, eds., *Breaking Boundaries: Female Biblical Interpreters Who Challenged the Status Quo* (London: T&T Clark, 2010).

14. Joy A. Schroeder, *Dinah's Lament: Sexual Violence in Christian Interpretation* (Minneapolis: Fortress, 2007).

The question of where to begin this biographical history of women interpreters is important. God's chosen people and their prophets and priests interpreted God's words from the earliest days. Perhaps Huldah, the prophetess (2 Kings 22:14–20) who delivered God's judgment on the legitimacy of the words on the scroll found in the temple during the period of Josiah, was interpreting Scripture. The New Testament contains a number of stories of women who encountered Jesus and interpreted his words and their experiences with Jesus for others. The stories of the woman of Samaria (John 4) and the women who were witnesses to the resurrection and interpreted it (Luke 24:10), for example, have empowered many women throughout history to interpret their own encounters with Jesus and the Scriptures.[15] Perhaps Mary, the mother of Jesus, should be considered an interpreter of Scripture since she pondered the events surrounding the birth of Jesus (Luke 2:19). A long tradition of understanding the Virgin Mary as an ideal reader or interpreter of Scripture is attested in the history of art and literature.[16] In her book for children on the life of Jesus, popular evangelical writer Hesba Stretton (1832–1911) wondered if Mary might have pondered the meaning of Jeremiah's prophecy about Rachel's voice of lamentation, weeping, and great mourning for her children (Jer. 31:15) when she passed Rachel's tomb on the way to Jerusalem for the presentation of Jesus at the temple (Luke 2:22–40).[17] Other women in the New Testament, including Eunice and Lois (Timothy's mother and grandmother), may be considered interpreters of Scripture since they taught the Christian faith to others (2 Tim. 1:2–5).[18]

Although it is possible to find women interpreters within the Bible, this book begins with women interpreters from the period of the early church and focuses primarily on the lives of women whose writings on the Bible are extant.[19] Of course women also used other media such as embroidery, music, and art to interpret Scripture, but their stories are left for others to tell. Of the hundreds of women who left records of their interpretations of the Bible, I

15. M. Marsin (fl. 1696–1701) emphasized the importance of Jesus's birth by a woman and his postresurrection appearance to women, and argued uniquely that Jesus's second coming should also be declared by a woman. M. Marsin, *The Womans Advocate* (London: J. Clark, 1697), 2–3.

16. See David L. Jeffrey, *People of the Book: Christian Identity and Literary Culture* (Grand Rapids: Eerdmans, 1996), 215–24, 228–30.

17. Hesba Stretton, *The Wonderful Life of Christ* (London: Religious Tract Society, 1899), 27.

18. Christina Rossetti cited Lois and Eunice as examples of female teachers to justify her authorship of a commentary on Scripture: *Face of the Deep: A Devotional Commentary on the Apocalypse* (London: SPCK, 1892), 195.

19. In cases where women's interpretive work has not survived the ravages of time (e.g., the writings of Marcella [ca. 327–410] and Paula [347–404]), was accidentally destroyed (e.g., many of Susanna Wesley's [1669–1742] writings were burned), or was intentionally eradicated (inquisitors thought they had destroyed Teresa of Avila's [1515–82] *Meditations on the Song of Songs*, but other copies survived the purge)—in such cases descriptions of their interpretive work are based on the witness of others to their contributions.

chose to highlight women whose interpretations were influential,[20] distinctive, or unique in terms of ideas[21] or interpretive genre,[22] or representative of the kind of interpretive writings done by a number of women at a certain period of time.

The availability of women's writings on the Bible has changed over time. In the first twelve hundred years of the Christian era, few records remain of women's interpretive work; no women interpreters from the first, second, third, sixth, seventh, and eighth centuries are included in this collection. In the post-Reformation period, women's writings on the Bible increased; in the eighteenth and nineteenth centuries, for example, hundreds of women published their writings on Scripture. Some of them published books that were more academic than popular, including commentaries on Scripture; others published dozens of popular books on the Bible. There are many reasons for the increase in women's writings, including such factors as women's increased literacy and education and access to the Bible and the publishing world. In addition more recent writings are more easily found and accessed.

Given the significant increase in women interpreters of the Bible in the late twentieth and twenty-first centuries, a decision had to be made as to when to end this biographical history of women interpreters. Since the names and publications of contemporary women are easily accessed and disproportionate in terms of sheer numbers in comparison to women from earlier periods in history,[23] I limited the number of post-nineteenth-century entries by using three criteria: the woman had to be deceased,[24] her work had to be representative,[25]

20. For example, Phoebe Palmer's arguments for the legitimacy of women's preaching convinced many, including Catherine Booth. Phoebe Palmer, *The Promise of the Father, or, A Neglected Specialty of the Last Days* (Boston: Henry V. Degen, 1859); Catherine Booth, *Female Ministry; or Woman's Right to Preach the Gospel* (London: Morgan & Chase, ca. 1870).

21. Amanda Berry Smith's justification for her public ministry was based in part on her unique reading of 1 Cor. 14:34–35 KJV: "Let your women keep silence in the churches; . . . and if they would learn anything, let them ask their husbands at home." "As I had no husband at home to ask, I thought according to my orders in John [15:16], I had my authority from the words of the Master." Amanda Smith, *An Autobiography: The Story of the Lord's Dealings with Mrs. Amanda Smith, the Colored Evangelist* (Chicago: Meyer & Brother, 1893), 431.

22. In *The Story of Jesus Christ: An Interpretation* (1897), Elizabeth Phelps crafts an interpretive approach that implicitly criticizes traditional male approaches. Erin Vearncombe, "Elizabeth Stuart Phelps and the 'Laws of Narrative Expression,'" in *The Story of Jesus Christ: An Interpretation*," paper presented at the Canadian Society of Biblical Studies, June 2007.

23. The number of female members of the largest professional societies devoted to the study of biblical literature is impressive. For example, in 2011 the SBL boasted over 8,534 members, and current data show that 23 percent of the SBL members are female; also, more than one-quarter of the more than 400 members of the CSBS are women.

24. This criterion meant that Leona Glidden Running (b. 1916), whose noteworthy career as a biblical scholar and teacher of biblical languages began in the early 1950s and continued into the twenty-first century, had to be excluded from this book.

25. For example, representing distinguished twentieth-century biblical scholars are Kathryn Sullivan (1905–2006) and Elizabeth Achtemeier (1926–2002); representing female scholars in social sciences whose work impacted biblical studies are archaeologist Kathleen Kenyon (1906–78) and

and her primary publications had to predate the globalization of the profession of biblical studies and the significant expansion in the involvement of women and ethnic minorities in professional biblical studies in the 1970s and '80s.[26] Thus missing from this book are entries on second-wave feminist biblical scholars (e.g., Phyllis Trible and Elizabeth Schüssler Fiorenza), feminist historians (e.g., Carol Meyers and Naomi Steinberg), feminist literary critics (e.g., Mieke Bal and Cheryl Exum), and womanist biblical scholars (e.g., Renita Weems), as well as biblical scholars who bring new feminist multicultural perspectives to biblical interpretation (e.g., Mercy Amba Oduyoye, Elsa Tamez, and Kwok Pui Lan). Also omitted are the many contemporary biblical scholars whose specialties in biblical interpretation include such classic disciplines as text criticism, source criticism, form criticism, redaction criticism, and tradition criticism, and more recent literary approaches including structuralism, deconstructionism, narrative criticism, and reader-response criticism. Not included are present-day women specializing in the history of the interpretation of the Bible and reception history and female scholars working in ancillary disciplines such as archaeology, Near Eastern languages and literature, and the social sciences as they relate to the Bible. Popular voices from this period are also missing.

I attempted to be inclusive in terms of religious, cultural, racial, and geographical diversity; however, Catholic female voices from Western Europe dominate until the time of the Reformation, after which point diverse Protestant voices prevail. British and American voices dominate the modern period, and non-Western and nonwhite voices are unrepresented in the book. Jewish women, representatives of various non-Christian and sectarian groups, and idiosyncratic writers are included. Women living in many different countries have interpreted Scripture: early women interpreters resided in such diverse places as Cappadocia, Antioch, Rome, and Bethlehem; medieval women tended to live in Continental Europe and England; the late eighteenth and nineteenth centuries witnessed increased numbers of women writers in North America, though women in Britain and other parts of Europe continued to publish on Scripture. Living in the dominant culture of the day seemed to provide opportunities for women in that culture to write.

---

anthropologist Mary Douglas (1921–2007); representing the popular voice is Dorothy Sayers (1893–1957); representing the work of religious educators are ecumenical lay leader Suzanne de Dietrich (1891–1981) and Jewish Bible interpreter Nehama Leibowitz (1905–97).

26. For a discussion of recent trends in biblical studies, see Richard N. Soulen and R. Kendall Soulen, *Handbook of Biblical Criticism* (Louisville: Westminster John Knox, 2001), 21–22. For a helpful discussion of the history of feminist biblical interpretation, see Elizabeth Schüssler Fiorenza's *Sharing Her Word: Feminist Biblical Interpretation in Context* (Boston: Beacon, 1998). The volumes on feminist biblical studies in the twentieth century (ed. Elisabeth Schüssler Fiorenza) and on current trends (eds. Maria Cristina Bartolomei and Jorunn Økland) in the much-anticipated multivolume international, interdenominational, and multidisciplinary history of the Bible and women—these works promise to fill out what is missing in this book.

Most of the women in this book published under their given names, though there are a few women whose identities are questioned (e.g., the English pamphleteer Ester Sowernam [fl. 1615–17]). Many nineteenth-century authors published as Mrs. X, with X representing her husband's name (e.g., English writer, Elizabeth Baxter [1837–1926], wife of Michael Baxter, published as either Mrs. Michael Baxter or Mrs. M. Baxter). Some women published pseudonymously. Several works of Italian author Arcangela Tarabotti circulated pseudonymously under anagrams such as Galerana Baritotti (or Baratotti). After her marriage, Mary Petrie published as "Mrs. C. Ashley Carus-Wilson," though she published as Helen Macdowall with *The Sunday at Home*. Charlotte Tucker (1821–93) wrote under the pseudonym A. L. O. E. (A Lady of England). To hide their identities, some women omitted their surnames or used their initials when publishing; Charlotte Elizabeth Tonna (1790–1846) published simply as Charlotte Elizabeth so that her estranged husband would have no claim on the income from her books, and English commentator Gracilla Boddington (1801–87) published as G. B. The identities of many women who published without revealing their full names are now lost. A surprising number of women were identified in print simply as "the author of X," with X representing the author's first or most famous book (e.g., Susan Warner published as "the author of *The Wide Wide World*," and Elizabeth Rundle Charles as "the author of *The Chronicles of the Schönberg-Cotta Family*).

A Typical Entry

Each of the 180 entries contains a short biography of a female interpreter of the Bible, where possible including factual details about her birth, family, education, and formative influences. Such information provides the context for her interpretive work. Her work is then analyzed, focusing on her approach and methods of biblical interpretation and highlighting key themes and providing examples. Attention is given to evidence of gendered exegesis, especially when a woman's experiences shaped her interpretation or when she addressed traditionally problematic passages (e.g., Gen. 1–3; 1 Cor. 11 and 14; 1 Tim. 2) or discussed female biblical figures. Entries include comments on the interpreter's significance and legacy and include a bibliography of primary and secondary sources. The entries vary in length, and the length generally reflects the person's significance as an interpreter of the Bible.

Calling Up the Spirits of the Dead

There have been pens enough, Heaven knows, to chronicle the wrongs, the crimes, the sorrows of our sex: why should I add an echo to that voice, which from the beginning has cried aloud in the wilderness of this world, upon women betrayed, and betraying in self-defence? A nobler and more grateful task be mine, to show them how much of what is most fair, most excellent, most sublime among the productions of human genius, has been owing to their influence, direct or indirect; and call up the spirits of the dead,—those who from their silent urns still rule the pulses of our hearts—to bear witness to this truth.

> Anna Jameson, *The Romance of Biography or Memoirs of Women Loved and Celebrated by Poets, from the Days of the Troubadours to the Present Age; A Series of Anecdotes Intended to Illustrate the Influence which Female Beauty and Virtue have Exercised over the Characters and Writings of Men of Genius*

This book features both famous and forgotten figures in the history of women interpreters. The famous women include queens, noblewomen, abbesses, founders and cofounders of sects and denominations, wives of famous church leaders, martyrs, preachers, authors, and scholars. The seventh-century bishop Isidore of Seville, for example, recognized Proba's (ca. 320–ca. 370) importance by including her among the illustrious *men* (!) of the church.

Many female interpreters were highly regarded in their circles of influence. Their writings on Scripture empowered them privately in terms of their own spiritual devotion, and publicly, bringing them renown, financial gain, and occasionally persecution or death (e.g., French mystic Marguerite Porete [d. 1310] and English Protestant Anne Askew [ca. 1521–46]). Some women gained notoriety through their writings alone (e.g., German commentator Justitia Sengers[27] [fl. 1585]); others, like Italian preacher Domenica Narducci (1473–1533) and English prophet Joanna Southcott (1750–1814), were involved in polemical public discourse and preaching. Some women were renowned in other contexts (e.g., Elizabeth I [1533–1603] was Queen of England; Florence Nightingale [1820–1910] was remembered as the lady with the lamp; Josephine Butler [1828–1906] worked to repeal the Contagious Diseases Laws), but their work as biblical interpreters has not yet been fully recognized. Lesser-known women include those whose biographies are lost to time or whose importance was recognized by only a few. However, as F. Digby Legard has recognized, "Woman's sphere is wider than we think and women's influence is perhaps stronger than we like to allow."[28]

---

27. Some scholars remember her as Justitia Sanger. William L. Holladay mentions a commentary on 96 psalms by Justitia Sanger, but her commentary is only on Ps. 69. *The Psalms through Three Thousand Years: Prayerbook of a Cloud of Witnesses* (Minneapolis: Fortress, 1993), 198.

28. F. Digby Legard was the editor of Mary Simpson's seemingly unimportant writings for young poorly educated farm laborers. Mary E. Simpson, *Ploughing and Sowing; or, Annals of an Evening School in a Yorkshire Village, and the Work that Grew Out of it, From Letters and Private Notes By a Clergyman's Daughter*, ed. F. Digby Legard (London: J. & C. Mozley, 1861), vi.

The biographies of individual women interpreters attest to their uniqueness, though patterns are seen in their lives. Women writers were married, divorced, widowed, or single. Some had children, some gave up their children. Many women gave up family, including young children, to follow their call or sense of vocation, which included interpreting Scripture. Marie of the Incarnation (1599–1672), founder of the Ursuline order in Canada, left her young son in the care of her sister when she entered the novitiate. A number of women gave up their wealth and privilege to live ascetic or monastic lifestyles. Paula (347–404) forfeited a life of privilege in Rome to live in utter poverty in a monastic cell in Bethlehem. Not all interpreters adopted unconventional lifestyles, however. A number of nineteenth-century interpreters lived conventional family lives, but changes to family life brought on by a financial crisis, illness, or death pushed them to publish for profit to provide for their own needs and those of others. Examples include authors Charlotte Elizabeth Tonna (1790–1846), Harriet Beecher Stowe (1811–96), Elizabeth Rundle Charles (1828–96), and Susan (1819–85) and Anna Warner (1827–1915).

Most women who interpreted Scripture were well educated. Many from privileged families were given the finest education available. Women like the erudite Elizabeth Carter (1717–1806) and scholar and poet Ann Francis (1738–1800) learned from their fathers and brothers; Anna Maria van Schurman (1607–78) attended lectures at the University of Utrecht, though she was hidden from the male students; English poet Elizabeth Hands (ca. 1746–1815) likely received her exposure to literature in the home of her employer. Some, such as Elizabeth Smith (1776–1806), were self-taught scholars; however, even self-educated women needed access to books.

Many women lamented their lack of formal education. English devotional writer Susanna Hopton (1627–1709) bewailed the defects of her education, especially in classical and biblical languages, though her knowledge of Scripture and theology was recognized by many. Some interpreters, including African American Sojourner Truth (ca. 1791–1883), were illiterate. Many published interpreters advocated for women's equal access to education. Mexican nun Sor Juana Inés de la Cruz (1651–95) and English philosopher Mary Astell (1666–1731) were both early advocates of women's rights to higher education, including the study of Scripture. Beginning in the middle of the nineteenth century, a number of women were granted the kind of equal access to education that their foremothers only dreamed of. Reverend Antoinette Brown Blackwell (1825–1921), lay biblical scholar Emilie Briggs (1867–1944), and ordained rabbi Regina Jonas (1902–44) had access to theological education; Elizabeth Achtemeier (1926–2002) and Sister Kathryn Sullivan (1905–2006) were theological educators who participated fully in the academy and church, though Sullivan was not allowed to do advanced Scripture studies in the 1950s, and full participation in the church included ordination only for Achtemeier, a Presbyterian; a priestly vocation was not an option for Sister Sullivan, RSCJ.[29]

Women interpreters gained access to Scripture in various ways, depending on such factors as religious affiliation, cultural and social location, education, and financial resources. Many early interpreters, even highly educated women, only prayed and memorized the Scriptures they heard recited in the liturgy and preached on by clergy. Doctor of the Church Catherine of Siena (1347–80) was so familiar with the words of Scripture that its words became her words. In contrast, some post-Enlightenment women had direct access to multiple versions of the Bible. Text critics Agnes Smith Lewis (1843–1926) and Margaret Dunlop Gibson (1843–1920) discovered, photographed, deciphered, and published early manuscripts. Generally speaking, women gained greater access to the Bible over time.

Women's access to academic and theological resources for the study of Scripture similarly was uneven and related to such factors as religious affiliation, cultural and social location, education, and financial resources. Paula (347–404) studied with Jerome and provided him with the reference tools needed to translate the Scriptures into Latin. Mary Cornwallis (1758–1836) shared her husband's theological library and had the financial resources to buy any books she needed. Similarly, Harriet Beecher Stowe (1811–96) accessed the theological resources provided first by her father and then by her husband, whose love for books put great financial strain on the family. In general, nineteenth-century British interpreters had greater access to scholarly resources, including artifacts in the British Museum, than did American and Canadian interpreters. The interpretive work of Florence Nightingale (1820–1910), (Frances) Julia Wedgwood (1833–1913), and Mary Carus-Wilson (1861–1935) was indelibly shaped by the critical scholarly resources they used to aid their study of Scripture.

Throughout history a surprising number of women recognized the importance of studying the original languages of Scripture. Paula (347–404) was certainly not the only woman to learn Greek and Hebrew so that she could read the Scriptures in the original languages. In her *Epistle* of 1539, Genevan reformer Marie Dentière (1495–ca. 1561) mentions that her young daughter had written a Hebrew grammar for young girls from whom Scripture had been concealed. In 1841, an introduction to the basics of reading Hebrew was included in *The Christian Lady's Magazine*, edited by Charlotte Elizabeth Tonna (1790–1846), to encourage lay Anglican women to study the Old Testament in Hebrew. Artist and musician Helen Spurrell (1819–91) learned Hebrew after she turned fifty and went on to publish a translation of the Old Testament from an unpointed or consonantal Hebrew text. Catholic educational writer Elizabeth Bowerman (1852–1930) studied Greek as she prepared to write commentaries on the Gospels.

29. RSCJ is an acronym for the religious order Religious of the Sacred Heart of Jesus.

Women who translated and paraphrased Scripture often became aware of gender bias in translations of texts relating to women. Mary Astell (1666–1731) was convinced that men used "their skill in Language and the Tricks of the Schools" to change the original meaning of texts to limit women's voice and role.[30] Women's rights activist, minister, and biblical scholar Lee Anna Starr (1853–1937) believed that the King James Version and Revised Version were tainted with masculine bias and argued that the Scripture—correctly translated—authorized the liberation of women. Julia Smith's (1792–1886) translation of the Bible was used by the compilers of *The Woman's Bible*, who commended this first American translation of the Bible by a woman. Medical doctor and social reformer Katharine Bushnell (1855–1946) believed that women's suffering would be allayed and gender equality secured when prejudice in translation was removed.

Many women interpreters were connected to men in positions of power in their families, communities of faith, the academy, or publishing world. Macrina (ca. 330–379), the elder sister of Basil the Great and Gregory of Nyssa, and Melania (ca. 340–ca. 410), whom Palladius named "man of God," had a significant influence on men in positions of power. Marriage brought Agnes Smith Lewis (1843–1926) closer to the heart of Cambridge University and the resources she needed to carry out her work as a text critic. Marriage to Michael Baxter, owner of the Christian Herald Publishing Company, facilitated Elizabeth Baxter's (1837–1926) extensive publishing career (she published at least forty books and a great number of smaller pamphlets). The Rev. E. H. Bickersteth, a prolific author and father of Charlotte Bickersteth Ward (1822–96), nurtured his daughter's significant writing career. A number of women worked collaboratively with relatives; handwritten entries for the renowned *Brown-Driver-Briggs Hebrew Lexicon* indicate that Emilie Briggs (1867–1944) did much more work for her father than their coauthored book on the Psalms suggests. Further, women often sought endorsements from recognized and credentialed male authorities for their publications on Scripture. Joana Julia Greswell (1838–1906), author of the *Grammatical Analysis of the Hebrew Psalter* (1873), sought the endorsement of the famous scholar-churchmen J. J. S. Perowne and R. Payne Smith for her Hebrew textbook for divinity students at Oxford and elsewhere.[31] Some women worked in the shadow of men; Charlotte von Kirschbaum (1899–1975), Karl Barth's assistant, was herself an independent and significant biblical interpreter. Beatrice Goff (1903–98), who defended her doctoral thesis on the J Document in the

30. Mary Astell, *Some Reflections upon Marriage*, in *Astell, Political Writings*, ed. Patricia Springborg (Cambridge: Cambridge University Press, 1996), 14.

31. J. Glen Taylor, "'Miss Greswell Honed Our Hebrew at Oxford': Reflections on Joana J. Greswell and Her Book *Grammatical Analysis of the Hebrew Psalter* (1873)," in *Breaking Boundaries: Female Biblical Interpreters Who Challenged the Status Quo*, ed. Nancy Calvert-Koyzis and Heather E. Weir (London: T&T Clark, 2010), 83–106.

Hexateuch at Boston University in 1933, spent her career assisting male colleagues in various research projects, yet also published several major works of her own.

Women interpreters of the Bible were not disinterested readers of Scripture. Most brought to their interpretive work theological presuppositions about the nature of Scripture. They read, studied, and meditated on Scripture, using various spiritual disciplines and an assortment of interpretive methods and study guides. They produced a variety of written responses to Scripture, including paraphrases, hymns, poetry, diaries, autobiographies, dramas, letters, tracts, diatribes, study guides, commentaries, sermons, and spiritual writings. Anglican Elizabeth Rundle Charles (1828–96) published poetry, hymns, essays, scriptural reflections, historical fiction, a travel journal, and commentaries. The plays, poetry, tracts, essays, and novel of English writer and social reformer Hannah More (1745–1833) reveal her profound engagement with the Bible. Some genres used by women had a limited life: the Latin Cento, which retold salvation history by using lines from Latin poets, flourished for a time, as did biblical epics in the seventeenth century and instructional literature in the eighteenth and early nineteenth centuries. Many women interpreters would have agreed with the sentiments of learned Reformed gentlewoman Anne Lock (1534–ca. 1602), who felt constrained "by reason of [her] sex" and yet did what she could to bring her "poore basket of stones to the strengthening of the walles of that Jerusalem, whereof (by grace) we are all both Citizens and members."[32]

Women interpreters inspired, educated, and entertained a range of audiences: the young, other women, mixed audiences, the uneducated, the unconverted, the unenlightened, and even authorized experts. Herrad of Hohenbourg (fl. 1176–96) wrote *Hortus deliciarum* (*Garden of Delights*), a synthesis of twelfth-century monastic and scholastic learning specifically for the women of Hohenbourg. A number of women wrote for a variety of audiences: the prolific author Charlotte Yonge (1823–1901) founded and edited *The Monthly Packet of Evening Readings for Younger Members of the English Church* (1851–99) and published educational resources for Sunday school and catechism classes, novels, poetry, history, biographies, and commentaries on biblical themes and texts for adult audiences.[33] As education became more available to women and academic disciplines became more specialized, the writings on the Bible by credentialed women became more focused and often addressed colleagues in the academy, a relatively new primary audience for female writers. A recent example is the work of anthropologist Mary Douglas

32. Anne Vaughan Lock, *The Collected Works of Anne Vaughan Lock*, ed. Susan M. Felch (Tempe: Arizona Center for Medieval and Renaissance Studies, 1999), 77.

33. The most exhaustive, but incomplete, list of Charlotte Yonge's works is found in Georgina Battiscombe and Marghanita Laske, eds., *A Chaplet for Charlotte Yonge* (London: Cresset, 1965), 204–16.

(1921–2007) on the doctrine of defilement in the book of Numbers, written specifically for scholars.

The Question of Authorization

When gender, lay status, historical moment, and even Scripture itself as traditionally interpreted precluded women from formally expounding and interpreting the Bible, women felt they had to justify their interpretive acts. Typically women who dared to interpret Scripture claimed some type of divine authorization for their work. Visionary Hadewijch of Antwerp (fl. 1250s) claimed divine approval for her work. Validation for the work of Gertrude the Great (ca. 1256–1302) came not only from a command from Christ but also from a charge from her superiors, who asked that she write religious instructions on parchment. Italian scholar and writer Olympia Morata (ca. 1526/27–55) felt that God spoke through her and that her readers were to ignore the fact that she was a woman. African American interpreter Maria Stewart (1803–79) appealed to her spiritual calling as the basis for her authority.

Women claimed other sources of authority to justify their work as interpreters of Scripture. Like many early Protestants, Katharina Schütz Zell (ca. 1498–1562) based her right to teach on her knowledge of the Bible and contemporary Reformed theology. In her quest for authority, devotional poet An Collins (ca. 1653) appealed to her intellect, vocation, gifts, experiences, and divine inspiration. Pietism provided a foundation for Johanna Petersen (1644–1724) to interpret and teach Scripture with confidence and authority. Margaret Fell (1614–1702) drew support from the Quaker belief in the continuing revelation of God to lambast priests who decried that women should not speak and yet preached sermons based on women's words in Scripture. Anne Docwra (ca. 1624–1710) cleverly justified her expositions of biblical prophecy by citing the Church of England's Thirty-Nine Articles of Religion. Education and access to scholarly resources enabled women like Mary Astell (1666–1731) to put forward the notion of an independent religious scholar. Changing perceptions of women's spirituality enabled a number of British and American nineteenth-century authors to speak from their positions of domestic power as angels or priests of the home.[34] Because opportunities for graduate education and positions of leadership in many religious institutions opened for women in the twentieth century, women did not have to justify themselves in the same ways that their foremothers did. Still, many women faced and continue to face the challenge of gaining full-time tenured teaching and research positions in the academy and employment in senior leadership positions in the church and synagogue.

34. See Marion Ann Taylor and Heather E. Weir, *Let Her Speak for Herself: Nineteenth-Century Women Writing on Women in Genesis* (Waco: Baylor University Press, 2006), 2–10.

Favorite Bible Books

Women's interpretive writings on Scripture through the ages have manifested great diversity in subject matter. Some women wrote on particular biblical books or chapters within books (e.g., Justitia Sengers's 1585 commentary on Ps. 69); some reflected thematically across texts (e.g., Elizabeth Stuart Phelps, *The Story of Jesus Christ: An Interpretation*, 1897); some studied particular characters in Scripture (e.g., Grace Aguilar, *The Women of Israel*, 1845). Women seemed especially drawn to comment on Genesis, Song of Songs, Psalms, the Gospels, the Epistles (esp. texts about women), and Revelation. The stories in Genesis about the creation and fall and those featuring female characters elicited reflections on woman's nature and role in the family, in communities of faith, in society at large, and also on women's rights.[35] Venetian writer Moderata Fonte (1555–92) challenged the traditional understanding that Adam's creation before Eve signaled his superiority, arguing instead for his inferiority, since the order of creation moved from lower to higher beings.

Women's writings on the Song of Songs and Psalms focused on the life of devotion, prayer, and worship. *Meditations on the Song of Songs*, by beatified and canonized Teresa of Avila (1515–82), primarily explored the allegory of the Song as it related to her own mystical marriage to God. The sonnet sequence on Ps. 51 by Anne Lock (1534–ca. 1602), however, not only engaged the heart but also critiqued contemporary politics and theology, including eucharistic theology. English Moravian ecumenist Mary Anne Schimmelpenninck's (1778–1856) detailed spiritual exposition of the Psalms was influenced by the authors from the Cistercian convent of Port-Royal, France.

The Gospels allowed women to reflect on Jesus's relationships with women and on particular figures who not only modeled female devotion and discipleship but also public leadership, specifically preaching, prophesying, and evangelism. In her polemic against those who suggested that women lacked the academic credentials needed for preaching, English Elizabeth Baxter (1837–1926) held out the woman of Samaria as an example of a woman who preached based on her experience of Jesus and not on her academic qualifications. Methodist Episcopal preacher Mabel Madeline Southard (1877–1967) used historical criticism and cultural studies to shed light on Jesus's revolutionary treatment of women, a conclusion that settled her own sense of call to ministry.

Robert Kachur's study of women's devotional writings on Revelation lists a surprising number of commentaries by women in the second half of the nineteenth century.[36] These commentaries suggest that the book of Revelation

---

35. Ibid.

36. Robert Kachur, "Envisioning Equality, Asserting Authority: Women's Devotional Writing on the Apocalypse, 1845–1900," in *Women's Theology in Nineteenth-Century Britain: Transfiguring the Faith of Their Fathers*, ed. Julie Melnyk (New York: Garland, 1998), 3–36.

inspired women to reflect on the notion of a new heaven and a new earth, where the injustices of this world would be rectified. English poet and devotional writer Christina Rossetti (1830–94) looked forward to the equality that women would find in heaven.

Key Biblical Texts

Many women specifically addressed biblical texts that traditionally interpreted defined women's roles in marriage and in communities of faith (e.g., Gen. 1–3; 1 Cor. 11:3; Eph. 5:21–33; Col. 3:18–19; 1 Tim. 2:11–15; 5:14; 1 Pet. 3:1–7). Mary Astell (1666–1731) included a detailed exegesis of relevant New Testament texts in her *Reflections upon Marriage*, arguing for mutuality of human dependency on God and submission to God. Itinerant preacher Zilpha Elaw (ca. 1790–fl. 1846), who believed Scripture taught submission to fathers and husbands and prohibited women from teaching or preaching in church, argued that these principles could be revoked in extraordinary cases like hers. Lee Anna Starr (1853–1937) challenged Paul's authority, noting that he himself considered some of his comments to be "uninspired" (1 Cor. 7:12, 25); she suggested that Jesus's teachings be given priority over Paul's. American social activist Elizabeth Cady Stanton (1815–1902) rejected the authority of the Bible's teachings that prescribed women's subordination and circumscribed their roles. She encouraged women to rebel against the custom of head coverings at church as a sign of subordination (1 Cor. 11:2–16) and encouraged women to use common sense when interpreting difficult passages.

Stories about Women

Women were also especially interested in stories about women and family life. They often brought a female perspective to their reading of these and other texts. English linguist Elizabeth Smith (1776–1806) revealed her particular interest in the character of Job's wife, whom she redeemed through her translation of Job 2:9–10 and 19:17. Mary Cornwallis (1758–1836) and Sarah Trimmer (1741–1810) read proverbs about the disciplining of children (e.g., Prov. 13:24; 29:15) through the lens of their experiences as mothers. Cultural sensibilities often influenced women's ability to engage issues related to sexuality. Trimmer, for example, refused to comment on the Song of Songs in her biblical commentary and notes only that the story of Tamar in Gen. 38 features "some very irregular conduct in Jacob's sons, which every true Christian must abhor, as contrary to the pure law of the gospel."[37] Other in-

---

37. Sarah Trimmer, *A Help to the Unlearned in the Study of the Holy Scriptures* (London: F. C. & J. Rivington, 1805), 38.

terpreters openly discussed the biblical stories of women as victims of sexual violence. Italian nun Arcangela Tarabotti (1604–52) courageously challenged traditional readings of the story of Dinah's rape in Gen. 34, which blamed Dinah's inquisitiveness and not Shechem's sexual desires for the violent act. Josephine Butler (1828–1906) read the story of the Levite's concubine (Judg. 19) through the lens of her own work with prostitutes as a prophetic call to women and men of England to hear the cries of England's oppressed and to work for social change. In their quest to understand Scripture's teachings about women, many women interpreters intuitively or intentionally followed the hermeneutical principle of common sense articulated by the American Methodist Frances Willard: "A pinch of common-sense forms an excellent ingredient in that complicated dish called Biblical interpretation, wherever it is set forth at the feast of reason, especially if it is expected at all to stimulate the flow of soul!"[38]

Most women interpreters paid special attention to both what the Bible said and did not say about women. Those using literary genres that encouraged imagination often filled in perceived gaps in Scripture's portrayal of figures, adding names, dialogue, and details. English educator Bathsua Makin (ca. 1600–after 1675) added to the information given in Scripture about the learning of such women as Miriam, Deborah, the Queen of Sheba, and Huldah to support her argument for female education. In her drama that retold the story of Moses's birth with an all-female cast, writer Hannah More (1745–1833) embellished the character of Pharaoh's daughter, suggesting that she empathized with Hebrew women suffering under her father's cruel edict:

> Unhappy mothers! Oft my heart has bled
> In secret anguish o'er your slaughter'd sons;
> Powerless to save, yet hating to destroy.[39]

Catholic educator Elizabeth Bowerman (1852–1930) was sensitive to both the presence and absence of women in Scripture; she named unnamed women and added women to stories where she felt they should have been mentioned but were not (Acts 4:23; 5:14).

Reading the Bible like a Man

Not all women read the Bible through the lens of their experiences as women, highlighting stories and texts relevant to women's lives or addressing polemical issues relating to woman's nature and role. Many women's writings are indistinguishable from men's. Educator Bathsua Makin (ca. 1600–after 1675)

---

38. Frances E. Willard, *Woman in the Pulpit* (Boston: D. Lothrop, 1888), 26.
39. Hannah More, *The Works* (London: T. Cadell, 1830), 1:13.

adopted a male persona when she published *An Essay to Revive the Ancient Education of Gentlewomen* (1673). For a variety of reasons, a number of women authors did not address issues related to women. Florence Nightingale (1820–1910) showed little interest in texts related to women in the Bible; she found the image of the Suffering Servant in Isa. 49:3–4 to be a compelling model for her life of service.[40] Julia Wedgwood (1833–1913) regularly signed her name to her work yet rarely mentioned her sex; she even assumed a male persona in her article on the boundaries of science. The study materials Mary Carus-Wilson (1861–1935) prepared specifically for women made no mention of the women in the Bible. Nehama Leibowitz (1905–97), regarded by some as the first significant female Jewish Bible interpreter,[41] opposed feminism and feminist readings of biblical texts.

It is not surprising that when women drew on the resources of the male academy, church, or synagogue and used the methods of interpretation honed in these centers, their interpretive work resembled that of their male contemporaries. Thus Fanny Corbaux (1812–83), a self-taught scholar, was invited to lecture and publish her work in historical geography, Semitic philology, and history of religions. A number of female advocates of biblical criticism in nineteenth-century Britain incorporated critical ideas into the educational materials they authored for children and young people.[42] Julia Wedgwood popularized criticism in her book *The Message of Israel in the Light of Modern Criticism* (1894).

Women and Social Justice

In their teaching, preaching, theological reflection, and exposition, many women addressed issues of social justice. They wrestled with the inequities they saw regarding poverty, slavery, homelessness, education, and gender. Mary Cary (b. 1620/21, fl. 1647–53), a leading member of a militant, millenarian sectarian group, boldly advised the British government following the execution of Charles I. English commentator Elizabeth Bowdler (ca. 1717–79) engaged in social and religious commentary on such issues as slavery, suicide, purgatory, free will, and providence. Women's concerns for social justice often went beyond the printed page. Some actively engaged in social and political movements intent on changing social conditions and

---

40. *Florence Nightingale's Spiritual Journey: Biblical Annotations, Sermons and Journal Notes*, vol. 2 of *The Collected Works of Florence Nightingale*, ed. Lynn McDonald (Waterloo: Wilfred Laurier Press, 2001), 201.

41. Arguably, nineteenth-century British writer Grace Aguilar (1816–47) deserves that title.

42. See Barbara MacHaffie's excellent study of how Old Testament criticism was taught to Victorian children in "Old Testament Criticism and the Education of Victorian Children," in *Scottish Christianity in the Modern World*, ed. Stewart J. Brown and George Newlands (Edinburgh: T&T Clark, 2000), 91–118.

standards. Nineteenth-century activists Sarah and Angelina Grimké wrote and spoke against slavery and in favor of women's rights. Amanda Berry Smith (1837–1915) was an outspoken promoter of both holiness and temperance. Josephine Butler (1828–1906) campaigned on behalf of prostitutes in Britain and internationally. American Louise Pettibone Smith (1887–1981) was not only a credentialed biblical scholar, professor, translator, and author but also a woman whose social activism was rooted in her understanding of Old Testament law (e.g., Lev. 24:22–24).

Women as Theologians, Pastors, Religious Educators, and Preachers

[Gertrude] became a student of theology and tirelessly ruminated on all the books of the Bible she could obtain. The basket of her heart she packed to the very top with more useful, and honey-sweet texts of holy Scripture, so that she always had at hand an instructive and holy quotation.

Gertrude the Great, *The Herald of God's Loving Kindness: Books One and Two*

The quest for the writings of forgotten women interpreters of the Bible revealed that many women interpreters were also lay theologians, religious educators, pastors, or preachers. Marcella's (ca. 327–410) passion for biblical exegesis was related to her interests in the theological implications of Scripture, which in turn led to her leadership in the anti-Origenist movement in Rome. The highly venerated Hildegard of Bingen (1098–1179) authored a visionary work of moral theology (*Liber vitae meritorum*) and another that showcases her work in exegesis, theology, and spiritual anthropology (*Liber divinorum operum*). Franciscan mystic Angela of Foligno's (ca. 1248–1309) contemporaries designated her *Magistra theologorum*, master of theologians. Reformed Church Mother Katharina Schütz Zell (ca. 1498–1562) entwined her extensive knowledge of Scripture, pastoral sensitivities, and theology. Pietist Johanna Petersen's (1644–1724) theological treatises on millennialism and the idea of universal salvation also exhibit her work as a biblical interpreter. Irish nun Catherine McAuley's (1778–1841) *Cottage Controversy* features theological conversations between a Roman Catholic cottager and a Protestant lady of the manor. Not all female-authored theological writings gained ecclesiastical approval: French mystic Marguerite Porete (d. 1310) was burned at the stake for her heretical notion of a feminized Trinity and her call for salvation by faith alone.

Since many women's writings on Scripture are educationally focused, they shed considerable light on the history of women as religious educators. The letters of the pilgrim Egeria (fl. 380s) brought the Scriptures to life for her readers. Like many mothers throughout history, ninth-century noblewoman Dhuoda of Septimania (fl. 841) instructed her son in the basics of the Christian life. Sarah Trimmer's (1741–1810) experiences of teaching her own children became the basis for her later career as a religious educator of children and adults. Women continued to play important roles in religious education in the twentieth century. Catholic biblical scholar Kathryn Sullivan (1905–2006), Reformed Old Testament scholar Elizabeth Achtemeier (1926–2002), and Jewish religious educator Nehama Leibowitz (1905–97) used their scholarship to inform their work as religious educators.

The numbers of women who preached in public or with the pen throughout history are surprising.[43] In her sermon on 1 Cor. 14:34, Italian preacher Domenica Narducci (1473–1533) challenged traditional ecclesial exegesis that prohibited women from preaching. Genevan Marie Dentière (1495–ca. 1561) opposed traditional readings of Paul and Calvin in her defense of women's right to interpret, teach, and preach Scripture. English Puritan Katherine Evans (ca. 1618–92) was publicly whipped and imprisoned for her preaching. Anglican writer Mary Deverell (fl. 1774–97) wrote and published a series of sermons on a dare. Author Esther Copley (1786–1851) wrote sermons for her alcoholic husband, enabling him to carry out his Sunday preaching obligations at the Baptist church in Kent. Finnish sleep preacher Helena Konttinen (1871–1916) delivered sermons in a sleeplike state. The numbers of women engaged in preaching ministries increased significantly in the nineteenth and twentieth centuries.[44]

Moreover, women's interpretive writings on Scripture often contained pastoral insights for their readers. Women's letters to family members and friends often addressed pastoral care issues. German Reformer Katharina Schütz Zell (ca. 1498–1562) offered effective pastoral advice to those under her care. In her novel *Minister's Wooing*, Harriet Beecher Stowe (1811–96) advocated for female pastors. In her commentaries, Mary Cornwallis (1758–1836) offered practical and moral counsel to those facing life's challenges.

That the search for women interpreters brought to light female theologians, religious educators, preachers, and pastors is to be expected. Most of the women interpreters featured in this collection did not separate out the theological disciplines. They read Scripture in light of their experiences, questions, and needs; they expected Scripture to speak into their lives.

43. Beverly Mayne Kienzle and Pamela J. Walker, eds., *Women Preachers and Prophets through Two Millennia of Christianity* (Berkeley: University of California Press, 1998); Mary Kim Eunjoo, *Women Preaching: Theology and Practice through the Ages* (Cleveland: Pilgrim, 2004).

44. Christine Krueger, *The Reader's Repentance: Women Preachers, Women Writers, and Nineteenth-Century Social Discourse* (Chicago and London: University of Chicago Press, 1992); Bettye Collier-Thomas, *Daughters of Thunder: Black Women Preachers and Their Sermons, 1850–1979* (San Francisco: Jossey-Bass, 1998); Catherine A. Brekus, *Strangers and Pilgrims: Female Preaching in America, 1740–1845* (Chapel Hill: University of North Carolina Press, 1998); Priscilla Pope-Levison, *Turn the Pulpit Loose: Two Centuries of American Women Evangelists* (New York: Palgrave, 2004).

The Cloud of Witnesses

> Wherefore seeing we also are compassed about with so great a cloud of witnesses, let us lay aside every weight, and the sin which doth so easily beset [us], and let us run with patience the race that is set before us.
>
> Heb. 12:1

Agnon's story of the beautifully bound but blank book of women's wisdom reminds us that for much of our history the wisdom of our foremothers was not passed on from one generation to the next. Instead of building on the wisdom of foremothers regarding biblical interpretation, faith, and tradition, each generation of interpreters confronted issues related to women and the Bible anew. What would it have meant for women in the eighteenth, nineteenth, and even twentieth centuries to have had before them Mary Astell's (1666–1731) reading of Paul and women? Would history have been different if Johanna Petersen's (1644–1724) empowering theology of women had been passed on to subsequent generations of Pietists? What would it mean today for women studying theology to know that their foremothers of faith also wrestled with how to balance family life and professional life?[45]

Of course some women in history did have access to the wisdom of other women.[46] A number chose to live in community with other women, where they discussed religious matters and shared their ideas and writings. Women living in the intellectual and mystical center of the Benedictine-Cistercian monastery at Helfta (in Saxony) often had contact with other religious: Mechthild of Hackeborn (1240–98) learned from the prolific authors Mechthild of Magdeburg (ca. 1208–ca. 1282/94) and Gertrude the Great (ca. 1256–1302). Some Protestant writers shared their wisdom with other women (and sometimes men) who encouraged them intellectually, emotionally, and financially. Mary Astell (1666–1731) had the companionship and patronage of female neighbors and friends; Elizabeth Carter (1717–1806) and Hannah More (1745–1833) were members of an association of women known as The Blue Stocking Society. Some women shared their wisdom with other women through the written word: Egeria (fl. 380s) wrote an account of her travels in the Holy Land for a community of women at home who shared her passion for the Scriptures; the writings of Joanna Southcott (1750–1814) influenced the early twentieth-century English prophetic figure Mabel Barltrop.[47] The wisdom of Madame Guyon (1648–1717) continues to influence a number of religious communities

---

45. Elizabeth Stuart Phelps and Harriet Beecher Stowe specifically wrote about the tension between professional and domestic self-fulfillment.

46. The influence of men's wisdom on women is assumed here. Harriet Beecher Stowe, for example, constantly drew on the expertise of her husband, renowned biblical scholar Calvin Stowe.

47. Jane Shaw, *Octavia, Daughter of God: The Story of a Female Messiah and Her Followers* (London: Jonathan Cape; New Haven: Yale University Press, 2011).

today.[48] As the writings of women are studied more fully, the patterns of influence will become clearer, including the transatlantic cross-pollination of women's wisdom. For example, Harriet Beecher Stowe wrote the introduction to Charlotte Elizabeth Tonna's (1790–1846) *Collected Works*; Sophia Ashton (1819–72) borrowed heavily from the writings of Grace Aguilar (1816–47).[49]

Conclusion

This book shows that Agnon's suggestion that *The Book of the Wisest of Women* is empty is wrong. The wisdom of many women was written down and shared with individuals and communities of listeners and readers. Women's interpretations of the Bible did not, however, become part of the great-book tradition; as a result their influence was circumscribed, and their writings were lost or forgotten.

This book remembers women interpreters and suggests that what they wrote is important. It speaks of women who felt called to study, write, teach, and preach Scripture. It tells how Scripture inspired women to live lives of sacrifice and devotion, to daringly engage their culture and challenge tradition. It reveals patterns of interpretation, including a focus on female characters in Scripture and questions related to women's nature and place. It also shows that women did not all interpret Scripture in the same way: their interpretations were shaped by their experiences, culture, questions, and interpretive methods.

Discovering what the Bible meant to women in the past helps us in our quest to discover its meaning for today. As John Thompson states: "We don't fully know what the Bible *means* until we know something about what the Bible *has meant.*"[50] Reading Scripture through the eyes of women can open us to hear the Scripture in new ways. As John Goldingay suggests, one generation's blindness to the meaning of a text can be corrected by reading through the eyes of interpreters from another generation or context: "There are certain aspects of this written witness [canon of Scripture] which one generation can 'hear' in the way that another cannot, so that interpreters who want to appropriate the text's significance as fully as possible are willing to look at it through the eyes of other generations' exegesis as well as of their own, which are inevitably blinkered in certain respects."[51]

48. Patricia A Ward, *Experimental Theology in America: Madame Guyon, Fenélon, and Their Readers* (Waco: Baylor University Press, 2009).

49. Taylor and Weir, *Let Her Speak for Herself*, 10, 149–50.

50. John L. Thompson, *Reading the Bible with the Dead: What You Can Learn from the History of Exegesis That You Can't Learn from Exegesis Alone* (Grand Rapids: Eerdmans, 2007), 11.

51. John Goldingay, *Theological Diversity and the Authority of the Old Testament* (Grand Rapids: Eerdmans, 1987), 41–42.

Women's wisdom through the ages deserves careful consideration. And as educator and social activist Frances Willard (1839–98) recognized, it is important to listen to both male and female perspectives on texts: "And the truth of God, a thousand times repeated by the voice of history, science, and every-day experience[,] resounds louder to-day than in all preceding ages: 'It is not good for man to be alone!'"[52]

52. Frances E. Willard, *Woman in the Pulpit* (Boston: D. Lothrop, 1888), 45.

Achtemeier, Elizabeth Rice (1926–2002)

Elizabeth Rice Achtemeier was born in Bartlesville, Oklahoma, on June 11, 1926. Her strong faith and her love for the church were instilled in her by the example of her mother, the daughter of a Presbyterian minister, and by the worship and Christian education offered at the First Presbyterian Church of Bartlesville. The church was the center of the family's life. Particularly meaningful to the young Elizabeth were the hymns and music of the church, through which, she recalled, she came to know the language of faith. She also developed an appreciation for good preaching and sound biblical scholarship at an early age. Faith, she learned, was "to be informed by sound and diligent learning" (*Not Til I Have Done*, 11), a commitment that shaped her life and her career as a biblical scholar.

Achtemeier was raised with a belief in the equality of women and was supported by her parents in her academic pursuits. She completed her undergraduate work at Stanford University, where she was encouraged to attend seminary by a university chaplain whom she credited with shaping her religious thought and her academic future. In the fall of 1948, Achtemeier entered Union Theological Seminary in New York with plans to become a Christian educator. After some congregational experience, however, she discerned a call to ordained ministry. She noted the influence on her life of many outstanding theologians and church leaders who taught at Union Seminary in the mid-twentieth century, including Reinhold Niebuhr, Paul Tillich, John Bennett, Paul Scherer, George Buttrick, and James Muilenburg.

While a divinity student at Union, Elizabeth Rice met Paul J. Achtemeier, a fellow student. They married on her birthday in June 1952 and became partners in marriage and in scholarship, raising two children and coauthoring several articles and books. Together they traveled to Europe on fellowships to study with Gerhard von Rad in Germany and Karl Barth in Switzerland. Barth's teaching on the Word of God in Jesus Christ and transcendence in Scripture inspired Achtemeier's own lifelong emphasis on the Word of God, especially as it is made manifest in preaching. After returning to the United States, Achtemeier entered the PhD program at Columbia University in conjunction with Union Theological Seminary, focusing her work in the area of Old Testament, under the direction of Professor James Muilenburg, who had inspired her academic interest and her commitment to "solid scholarship with revelatory insight into the Word of God" (*Not Til I Have Done*, 40).

While completing her doctoral work, Achtemeier joined her husband on the faculty of Lancaster Theological Seminary in Pennsylvania, where she taught Old Testament as a visiting professor. She also traveled to teach at Gettysburg and Pittsburgh seminaries. As she moved from teaching Old Testament theology to content, she adopted the methodology she had learned under Gerhard von Rad in Heidelberg, "dividing the Old Testament into three Heilsgeschichte (salvation history) units, each with its own major theological testimony" (*Not Til I Have Done*, 81). She was thereby able to organize and teach the vast amount of diverse material found in the Old Testament. In the process of working with Old Testament texts, Achtemeier also discerned a pattern of promise and fulfillment in the activity of God as revealed in both the Old and New Testaments. On examining specific texts more closely, the Scriptures became for her "a unified story" that defined much of her future work as a biblical scholar. Her understanding of God's ongoing divine activity by means of the continuity of both Testaments was set forth in her first book, *The Old Testament Roots of Our Faith*.

In 1973 the Achtemeiers moved to Richmond, Virginia, where Paul joined the all-male faculty of Union Theological Seminary as a professor of New Testament. Despite gender bias and an unwritten policy forbidding the hiring of faculty wives, Elizabeth was offered an appointment as a visiting and, later, adjunct professor of Old Testament. The need on the faculty at the time, however, was for a homiletics professor, and Achtemeier was asked to serve as a visiting professor of homiletics. She had recently published what would become one of her most popular works, *The Old Testament and the Proclamation of the Gospel*, making her the ideal choice for the appointment. She welcomed the opportunity, having embraced the field of homiletics as the ultimate venue for her biblical work, and she focused many of her subsequent publications on various aspects of preaching.

Achtemeier's joint appointment in Bible and homiletics led to one of her greatest and most important contributions to the field of biblical scholarship: bridging the worlds of biblical scholarship and Christian preaching. Throughout her life, Achtemeier had been inspired by good preaching and came to see its importance for the life and work of the church. Because of her belief in the centrality of preaching, she lamented what she perceived to be a decline in the quality of preaching in many churches by the 1970s. In *The Old Testament and the Proclamation of the Gospel*, she addressed what she discerned to be one of the primary reasons for that decline: the loss of the Bible and a disregard for biblical authority in the church. Mainstream Protestantism, she lamented, had strayed from its biblical foundations, resulting in preaching that was little more than feel-good therapy or personal opinion, worship that reflected the congregation and its culture more than the Bible and the heritage of the church, and pastoral ministry shaped by the ideas and practices of secular psychology and social agendas. "The Bible is that which creates the church," she stated in an interview in 1989. "It is that story that sustains the church's life. As soon as the church wanders away from the biblical story, it ceases to be the Christian church. It becomes something else—a social society, a good works agency, an ideological group, etc."

Part of the reason for the loss of the Bible in the church, Achtemeier maintained, was Christianity's abandonment of the Old Testament. Restoring the Bible and its story to a central place in the church meant acknowledging the *whole* story, including the Old Testament, as necessary for the life of the Christian church. The Old Testament's understanding of God and God's activity "forms the basis of the New Testament's view of Jesus Christ and his church," she wrote in *The Old Testament and the Proclamation of the Gospel*. "When the church lost the Old Testament, it therefore lost the Bible—and the Christian faith—as a whole," leaving it "to carry on its life apart from the totality of its Scripture" (44). To that end, the majority of Achtemeier's interpretive work was focused on the Old Testament and its use in Christian preaching.

Achtemeier entered the professional worlds of both the church and the academy at a time when feminism was on the rise. She played an interesting and important role in the evolving debate over feminist theologies and approaches to Scripture. After years of encountering feminist ideology, she wrote her definitive statement on feminism in an article for the journal *Interpretation*: "The Impossible Possibility: Evaluating the Feminist Approach to Bible and Theology" (1988). She concluded that "there is no one feminist approach to Bible and theology," a field that embraces a multitude of views and is constantly changing (45). The question, she stated, was "not *if* women should enjoy equal status, personhood, and discipleship in the church but *how* that God-given freedom is to be gained—or perhaps better, regained." She affirmed the work of biblical scholars in the 1970s and 1980s showing evidence in Scripture that women "enjoyed equal discipleship and service in the company of Jesus and in the earliest New Testament Church" (46). Over the centuries of the church, much of that freedom had been lost, she observed, making the question not one of "*if* women should enjoy equal freedom in Christ but *how* to reclaim it. How can the church in our time become the *whole* people of God? How can it be the one Body of Christ in which there is neither Jew nor Greek, slave nor free, male nor female?" (46).

The question of "How?" is the point at which Achtemeier diverged from other feminist scholars. She acknowledged the discrimination against women that persisted to some degree in all Christian communions, even those that ordained women as clergy, but the remedy for that discrimination lay in a deeper look at the Bible rather than in noncanonical resources such as personal experience or non-Christian religious traditions. She condemned the feminist approach that abandoned the authority of Scripture and claimed the Bible to be "a totally androcentric book, compiled and interpreted through the centuries solely by men, and therefore useless for evaluating feminist positions" ("The Impossible Possibility," 48). She also feared that in such an interpretive stance, "the basis for deciding what is or what is not the Word of God has been shifted from the givenness of the canonical whole to the subjective position of the reader" (49). Such a "standpoint-dependent" theology is open to distortion, she believed. One the one hand, "When our own experience is the criterion, what overcomes our tendencies to self-interest, to pride, to rationalization, and to sin? What becomes the measure of what is just and unjust?" On the other hand, "there is a 'givenness' to the canon. It has been assembled and handed down to us; it contains words that stand over against us and judge us; and we have to come to grips with it," including its demands and call to obedience (51).

Countering the claims of some feminist scholars, Achtemeier argued that the texts they sought to "exorcize" from the Bible were neither as numerous nor as problematic as those scholars portrayed them to be. The Pauline strictures against women's participation in the church found in 1 Cor. 14, she maintained, "are clearly contradicted by his assumption in 1 Corinthians 11 that women will prophesy and pray in worship, and chapter 14 is therefore historically conditioned." Another seemingly problematic text, Eph. 5, was certainly "written out of a patriarchal setting," but it "overcomes its own culture with the love of God: Husband and wife are to be *subject to one another* in Christ, acting toward each other as if toward the Lord (symbolized for the husband in Christ's body, the church) and rendering to each other that sacrificial love with which Christ loves his own" ("The Impossible Possibility," 53). There is nothing demeaning in that portrait, Achtemeier wrote. Texts about women found in the Pastoral Epistles "reflect the struggle of the church to set its own house in order, in the face of Gnostic asceticism and libertinism." The "weak women" in 2 Tim. 3:1–9 had been led astray by gnostic teaching. The portrayal of women in that text "vividly illumines the problems that the church was up against, if it does not excuse the surrender to patriarchal culture that the church adopted" (53).

Rather than "throwing out portions of the canon," especially in an age when many have questioned biblical authority and abandoned the Scriptures, Achtemeier advocated accepting the Bible as a whole and applying "the Reformation principle of letting the Scriptures interpret the Scriptures to understand rightly any particular passage" ("The Impossible Possibility," 53). She maintained that at the very beginning of the sacred history, there is the affirmation of female equality: "our equal creation in the image of God, our mutual helpfulness and companionship with our mates, and the affirmation that male domination over female is the result of our sin." At the end of that sacred history in Jesus Christ, "there is the defeat of that domination and the ringing affirmation that we are all one in our Lord, an affirmation acted out so vividly in Jesus' own attitudes and actions toward every sort of woman" (52). Christ is "the final reinterpretation of the whole sacred history" (53), making the ultimate message of the Bible a "liberating message, in which in fact countless Christian men and women have found their one source of true freedom in the service of their Lord" (54).

In addition to her contributions to the fields of biblical scholarship and homiletics, Achtemeier sought the Bible's authoritative word on what she called "burning issues" of her time, including marriage and family, sexuality, abortion, and environmental issues. Above all else, she was a biblical scholar in and for the church, evidenced by more than twenty books and many articles. In addition, she was a popular preacher and lecturer, preaching from many of the best-known pulpits in churches and university chapels across the United States and Canada and giving several major lectureships. She was a frequent speaker at conferences for clergy and laity. All of her life's work—writing, teaching, and preaching—reflects her passion for understanding and responding to God's Word in Jesus Christ.

Bibliography

Achtemeier, Elizabeth. *The Committed Marriage*. Philadelphia: Westminster, 1976.

———. *Creative Preaching*. Nashville: Abingdon, 1980.

———. "The Impossible Possibility: Evaluating the Feminist Approach to Bible and Theology." *Interpretation* 42 (Jan. 1988): 45–57.

———. *Nature, God, and Pulpit*. Grand Rapids: Eerdmans, 1992.

———. *Not Til I Have Done: A Personal Testimony*. Louisville: Westminster John Knox, 1999.

———. *The Old Testament and the Proclamation of the Gospel*. Philadelphia: Westminster, 1973.

——— (with Paul J. Achtemeier). *The Old Testament Roots of Our Faith*. Nashville: Abingdon, 1962.

———. *Preaching about Family Relationships*. Philadelphia: Westminster, 1987.

———. *Preaching from the Old Testament*. Louisville: Westminster John Knox, 1989.

Transcript of an unpublished interview. Elizabeth Achtemeier Papers, William Smith Morton Library, Union Presbyterian Seminary. December 1989.

—BEVERLY ZINK-SAWYER

Adams, Hannah (1755–1831)

Hannah Adams was born in 1755 in Medfield, Massachusetts. She was the second of five children born to Thomas Adams and Elizabeth Clark. Her mother died when she was twelve years old, and her father, a failed farmer and an unsuccessful merchant, was unable to provide financial security for his children, though his love for books translated into an extensive library. This access to books allowed Hannah to develop her appetite for literature. She committed large portions of poetry to memory and concentrated her reading on novels and devotional reflections. Due to poor health, she was unable to attend school and other social functions as a child, but this did not prevent her from learning all she could. When her father took in boarders for tutoring, Adams received her own education from them in the areas of Latin, Greek, geography, and logic. Soon she was taking on her own pupils. Adams's personal reflections on her early love of learning prompted this revealing, if unusual, memory from her childhood: "The first strong propensity of my mind which I can recollect, was an ardent curiosity, and a desire to acquire knowledge. I remember that my first idea of the happiness of Heaven was, of a place where we should find our thirst for knowledge fully gratified" (*Memoir*, 4).

Adams also confessed an enduring disappointment at not having had the benefit of a systematic education. She felt that the loss of her mother at such an early age deprived her of maternal direction, and too much time spent reading novels in isolation from the wider world allowed her to commit errors in understanding. Despite these challenges, Adams estimated that by the age of twenty she had read more books than other women her age. Although her physical fragility resulted in an isolation that led to social awkwardness, it afforded her the luxury of committing the majority of her time to literary pursuits. Adams died in 1831, at the age of seventy-six, in Brookline, Massachusetts. In time, history would remember her as the first American woman to earn her living solely from writing.

It was in her early twenties that Adams's intellectual interests took a decided turn. While studying Greek and Latin with a gentleman boarder, she came into contact with a copy of Thomas Broughton's *An Historical Dictionary of All Religions from the Creation of the World to This Perfect Time* (1742). His work on various Christian and non-Christian sects piqued her curiosity, and she began to pursue any work that made reference to denominations. Disgusted with the biased and unfair treatments that she found in these works, she set to compiling her own "unprejudiced" collection of reference material. At first the work went slowly, since Adams was forced to set her intellectual interests aside in order to support herself financially. She sought work in traditional spheres, but her physical ailments limited her ability to bring in sufficient funds. Out of desperation, Adams determined to translate her love for books and learning into financial gain and ventured into the male-dominated realm of publication for profit. This resulted in her first and perhaps most well-known publication, *A View of Religions*, which appeared in four American editions in 1784, 1791, 1801, and 1817.

Though Adams toiled to support herself, she had to rely more on the patronage of wealthy supporters of her work than on the profit garnered from the works themselves. Still, she pursued literary projects that she believed would provide her with a livelihood and serve the needs of the reading public. In addition to her principal work on comparative religion, Adams engaged in local history with *A Summary History of New England* (1799), adding to it a companion volume, *An Abridgement of the History of New England* (1805); then she found her true calling in her extensive engagement with historical Judaism in *The History of the Jews* (1812). These longer works, coupled with a few shorter publications on the Christian religion, the Gospels, and her own memoir, testify to her commitment to research and the care with which she approached all her work.

Adams's writing on the history of religion and even her rendering of local history were colored by her theological assumptions and in certain cases punctuated by Scripture. In *A View of Religions*, a project of compilation in service of various sects, she provided theological counsel for her readers, shaping their opinions (Schmidt 34). *An Abridgement of the History of New England* led to a legal controversy with the Rev. Jedidiah Morse that was, in part, fueled by a clash of theological assumptions present in the documenting of local history. *The History of the Jews*, a massive work chronicling the historical suffering of the Jewish people, included two Old Testament quotations that provided interpretive keys for the historical analysis that followed. Volume 1, opening with Deut. 28:64–65, focused on the prophecies of destruction and the dispersion of the people. Volume 2, opening with Jer. 31:10, 28, focused on the future ingathering of the Jewish people: their conversion to the Christian faith. Gary Schmidt's analysis of Adams's use of Scripture in these volumes suggests that her pattern of weaving together the events of history and the unfolding work of God is an underlying, if unacknowledged, aspect of her writing: "What Adams wanted to do with these Old Testament passages was to set Jewish history within the supernatural, prophetic context so that history became . . . not simply the working out of events within time but the working out of spiritual directions" (246). In each case, Adams's theological concerns and the authority of Scripture gave shape to her research and guided her analysis of historical events and diverse faith communities.

As she neared the end of her life, Adams endeavored to publish a work on the New Testament. Her initial intention was to provide a historical background for each book. In preparation, she immersed herself in various scholarly works of the period, focusing on geography, archaeology, natural history, linguistics, and Gospel harmonization. In time, however, she accepted that this larger work would never be accomplished, and instead she produced a series of letters to her nieces, complemented by an appendix of study questions. She wanted her work to enable young people to "read the New Testament with more pleasure and advantage, and that they may be induced to make the sacred Scripture the object of their daily study, the rule of their life, and their guide to everlasting happiness" (*Letters*, iii). *Letters on the Gospels* (1824, with a second edition appearing in 1826) is Adams's most sustained treatment of biblical literature. She works diligently to build a bridge between history and biblical study, alerting her nieces and other young readers to the importance of understanding the cultural context of a biblical passage before one could capably render an interpretation. Schmidt argues that in this work Adams demonstrates her belief that the Bible is not only a "spiritual text" but also a book "whose historical context, if properly studied, could complement and even clarify the text's theological meanings" (321). Whereas Scripture had informed her treatment of history, now history would serve to inform her treatment of the text.

Throughout her letters, Adams attends to the historical setting of Jesus's life and ministry, his teachings, certain miracles, and several well-known parables. Her analysis of Scripture grows out of two convictions: (1) that historical context informs understanding of the biblical content, and (2) that biblical content is intended to inform virtuous living in the present time. Adams begins with historical reconstruction, utilizing both biblical and secondary sources to weave a coherent picture of the first-century world. Attention is given to the Roman occupation of Judea (*Letter* 2), the state of the Jewish nation (*Letter* 3), the religious sects within Judaism (*Letter* 4), the geographical locations named in connection with Jesus (*Letter* 5), and the particular history of Jerusalem (*Letter* 6). With this foundation secured, Adams goes on to treat portions of the Gospel narratives.

One example, taken from the Sermon on the Mount (*Letter* 7), explores Jesus's challenge to the historical expectations of first-century Judaism. In her reading of Matt. 5:1–11, Adams argues that Jesus's enlightened teachings ("Blessed are the poor in spirit. . . . Blessed are the meek") upset Jewish hopes for the establishment of an earthly messianic kingdom through the military overthrow of Rome. His words reveal the way of God's kingdom, in contrast to earthly kingdoms, and in all times provide all people with the moral teaching they need to purify their hearts and acknowledge Jesus as Lord (*Letter* 7.44). In a second example, Adams considers a miracle of Jesus, the healing of the centurion's servant found in Matt. 8 and Luke 7 (*Letter* 12). Her interpretation conflates details from both accounts and explores the necessity of posting Roman soldiers in conquered Judea, the reported relationship between a Roman centurion and Jewish elders, and the evils of slavery in the Roman world. These historical insights inform her interpretation and application of the miracle text. For Adams, *Christian virtue* is evidenced in the concern this centurion shows for his dying servant. *Piety* and *generosity* replace the often-strained relations between Jews and Romans in the building of a synagogue at his own expense. *Humility* takes the place of Roman arrogance in the centurion's deferential request for Jesus's help. *Faith* marks the climax of the episode, where, faced with the miraculous and authoritative person of Jesus, the centurion is unable to resist surrendering to his divinity.

As Adams reflected on her life, she cited the New Testament as her foremost guide in pursuing the truth. Among her personal papers was found a list of seven serious resolutions, believed to have been penned during the early years of her writing career. The first resolution is this: "I resolve to read the Bible more attentively; and diligently, and to be constant and fervent in prayer for divine illumination and direction" (*Memoirs*, 72). She honored this commitment throughout her life, and the development of her methodology is evidenced in her writing. Adams stands as an early example of the American shift toward the use of historical-critical methods of biblical interpretation.

Bibliography

Adams, Hannah. *An Abridgement of the History of New England, for the Use of Young Persons.* Boston: B. & J. Homans, and John West, 1805.

———. *A Dictionary of All Religions and Religious Denominations: Jewish, Heathen, Mahometan, Christian, Ancient, and Modern.* New York: James Eastburn, 1817. Repr., Introduced by Thomas A. Tweed. Classics in Religious Studies 8. Atlanta: Scholars Press, 1992.

———. *The History of the Jews from the Destruction of the Temple to the Nineteenth Century.* 2 vols. Boston: John Eliot, 1812.

———. *Letters on the Gospels.* Cambridge, MA: Hillard & Metcalf, 1824.

———. *A Memoir of Miss Hannah Adams, Written by Herself with Additional Notices by a Friend.* Boston: Gray Bowen, 1832.

———. *Narrative of the Controversy between the Rev. Jedidiah Morse, D.D. and the Author.* Boston: John Eliot, 1814.

———. *A Summary History of New England, from the First Settlement at Plymouth, to the Acceptance of the Federal Constitution.* Dedham, MA: H. Mann & J. H. Adams, 1799.

———. *The Truth and Excellence of the Christian Religion.* Boston: John West, 1804.

Schmidt, Gary D. *A Passionate Usefulness: The Life and Literary Labors of Hannah Adams.* Charlottesville: University of Virginia Press, 2004.

Tweed, Thomas A. "An American Pioneer in the Study of Religion: Hannah Adams (1755–1831) and Her *Dictionary of Religions.*" *Journal of the American Academy of Religion* 60, no. 3 (1992): 437–64.

Vella, Michael W. "Theology, Genre, and Gender: The Precarious Place of Hannah Adams in American Literary History." *Early American Literature* 28 (1993): 21–41.

— SHERRI TRAUTWEIN

Aguilar, Grace (1816–47)

Grace Aguilar, born in England, was one of the most famous Jewish woman theologians and Jewish writers in nineteenth-century England, America, and much of Europe. In her short life she produced writings on Jewish topics in genres including biblical commentary, fiction, poetry, and theology. Though minimal critical attention has been paid to her work, literary or theological, much of her writing offers a clear precedent and connection to other European Enlightenment approaches to Judaism, as well as later feminist Jewish approaches to Jewish texts. In addition, it is possible to trace Aguilar's links to other important Jewish movements of her day. While her primary audience was the Jewish community of England and America, she was also widely read by Christian readers and sought to publish in mainstream non-Jewish publications.

Aguilar was born in the London suburb of Hackney on June 2, 1816, to Emanuel (1787–1845) and Sarah (1787–1854) Aguilar. The Aguilar family stemmed from Portuguese Jews who had fled to England to escape the Inquisition, and where they remained active in the Sephardic community. Aguilar was never healthy and suffered from a series of both diagnosed and undiagnosed illnesses from a young age until her death at age thirty-one. In addition, when Aguilar was twelve, her father contracted tuberculosis, prompting the family's move to the coast in Devon; Aguilar would serve as nurse to her mother even while in ill health herself.

Both Aguilar's mother and father participated in her religious education. In Devon and later Brighton, the Aguilar family was somewhat isolated from an active urban Jewish community. As a result, Aguilar developed many non-Jewish friendships. On occasion she attended Protestant church services, and the experiences of alienation and otherness that she experienced were recorded in a number of published and unpublished poems. These experiences seemed to give her important insights later reflected in writing designed to battle Jewish women's conversion to Christianity.

By the time she was twenty-four (1840), Aguilar was drafting a number of literary and theological works, many of which would be published near the end of her life or posthumously. About this same time, Aguilar and her family moved back to London, and Aguilar began to work seriously toward publishing, successfully enlisting Benjamin Disraeli (1804–81) and his father, Isaac Disraeli (1766–1848), to help her find a publisher. She also contacted Isaac Leeser (1806–68), the editor of the American Jewish periodical *The Occident*, who agreed to publish *The Spirit of Judaism*, Aguilar's first major theological work. The 1840s became Aguilar's most productive period, in which she wrote historical fiction, the first novella to describe nineteenth-century Anglo-Jewish life, and in 1845 *Women of Israel*, arguably her most influential work of biblical interpretation. In 1847 Aguilar's final illness prompted a trip to Germany to visit her brother and to recover her health; she died in Frankfurt on September 16. She was buried in the Frankfurt Jewish Cemetery, and her death was noted on the front pages of Jewish newspapers in England and the United States. In addition, Jews from France, Jamaica, and Germany wrote tributes and poems in commemoration of her. Her mother continued to publish and promote her works after her death, and some of these works remained in print well into the twentieth century; the twenty-first century has seen a rebirth of interest in her work. In 1996 Michael Galchinsky published *The Origin of the Modern Jewish Woman Writer: Romance and Reform in Victorian England*, highlighting Aguilar as a central figure in the Anglo-Jewish literary world and bringing Aguilar's importance to contemporary readers; other critical works followed into the twenty-first century.

Nevertheless, most of the recent criticism of Aguilar's writing has concerned her historical and domestic fiction, with less attention being given to her religiously focused writings and poetry. Most startling, she is rarely included in historical accounts of the development of Jewish theology or the development of Jewish feminist theology—this even though she published two works of distinctly feminocentric biblical and religious writing. One reason for this might be that Aguilar's approach is not overtly feminist as defined by standards of the twentieth century and beyond; students often find her work difficult to reconcile with current assumptions that feminist must mean *public* female religious empowerment. Yet her biblical interpretation is striking not only for its originality and comprehensiveness. Also of note is Aguilar's oft-stated purpose for her writing: to connect Jewish women to their scriptural heritage and to render this heritage relevant for the lives of Jewish women in the nineteenth century. While not claiming public roles for Jewish women in Jewish life, Aguilar certainly believed that the Jewish woman had centrally important functions in Jewish history and religion. Paradoxically, her own identity as an unmarried woman who was one of the most public advocates of Judaism in nineteenth-century England challenged, to some degree, the lack of emphasis she placed on Jewish women's public identity in her work as well as her emphasis on the role of the mother in Jewish acculturation. In addition, as suggested below, Aguilar used her biblical interpretation to challenge conventional Jewish and Christian male clerical readings of Jewish Scripture.

Aguilar's *Women of Israel* (1845) is her most direct work of biblical interpretation and offers an excellent window into her larger approach to biblical commentary. In her introduction, Aguilar observes that there is a distinct need for a work of biblical interpretation specifically for Jewish women, one that does not share the explicit or implicit thesis that she sees in so many Christian women's writings on the Bible, "that the value and dignity of woman's character would never have been known but for the religious doctrine of Jesus" (2). Aguilar explicitly aims to show Jewish women how "the Bible" speaks directly to them as Jewish women: "The Bible must become indeed the book of life to the female descendants of that nation whose earliest history it so vividly records; and be regarded, not as merely political or religious history, but as the voice of God, speaking to each individual, giving strength to the weak, encouragement to the desponding, endurance to the patient, justice to the wronged, and consolation unspeakable as unmeasurable to the afflicted and the mourner" (7).

Aguilar also states that a careful understanding of the Bible and Jewish law demonstrates, despite Christian interpretations to the contrary, how woman has never been "degrade[d]" (4) in Jewish law, and that this work aims to "lead them to look earnestly and believingly into the history of every woman in the Bible, and trace there the influence of God's holy and compassionate love" (8).

With these goals in mind, Aguilar's readings in *Women of Israel* are often quite striking, original, and ambitious. The volume begins with Eve and interprets all passages related to women up through Maccabees. These include women mentioned in the Pentateuch and in prophetic and historical biblical texts, as well as Esther, Mariamne, Helena, and Berenice; Aguilar also includes more general comments about Jewish women's history in the period of the Second Temple and concludes with the chapter "Women of Israel of the Present, as Influenced by the Past," which includes commentary on Talmudic sources as well. This section begins by recognizing that women have generally been "debarred" from the study of the Talmud and that her work in this area has been facilitated by the kindness of a (male) friend. Aguilar goes on to argue that the talmudic rabbis support one of her main arguments in *Women of Israel*, that Jewish women have always been understood as having equal spiritual stature with men—thus refuting a number of nineteenth-century Christian commentators who claimed that only after the inception of Christianity could women claim equal spiritual status with men.

Aguilar's primary approach in this text is to connect her readings of biblical women to contemporary women's concerns; in so doing, she often makes important distinctions about different historical practices in Judaism and produces unique readings of texts about Jewish biblical women. For example, in her reading of Sarah in *The Women of Israel*, Aguilar aligns emotional and spiritual narratives as she works to explain how Sarah could have ordered the expulsion of Hagar and Ishmael (Gen. 21:8–21). Aguilar writes, "In a mere superficial reading, we acknowledge [that] Sarah does appear in rather an unfavorable light" (58). Aguilar suggests that Sarah obviously loves Hagar and Ishmael, that her first demand that they leave is borne out of anger, but that even after that moment Sarah is compelled by God to recognize that Ishmael has another historical role to play outside Abraham's family. Thus Aguilar observes that even Sarah knew, as "we" do, that "there are times when we feel urged and impelled to speak that which we are yet conscious will be productive of pain and suffering to ourselves" (58).

Similarly, in her lengthy discussion of Miriam's various roles in both Exodus and Numbers, Aguilar strips Miriam of the prophetic or heroic status often granted to her by other women biblical commentators. Instead, Miriam's Song of the Sea (Exod. 15:20–21) becomes an example not of "true piety" but rather a show of the "mere enthusiasm of the moment." Here Miriam becomes an example, often echoed by nineteenth-century detractors of women's literary agency, of women who voice poetry out of vanity rather than more virtuous didactic or prophetic motives. Aguilar's interpretation makes more sense when read with her interpretation of Miriam's later punishment by God for speaking against Moses (Num. 12). Miriam's ejection from the camp and her leprosy are read as "undeniably proving that woman must be quite as responsible a being as man before the Lord, or He certainly would not have deigned to appear Himself as her judge" (*Women of Israel*, 195). Because the goal of the text is to prove how well-respected women have always been in Judaism, Aguilar refuses to cast Miriam as a heroic figure, but rather as an example of a woman judged as having full responsibility before God for her seemingly faulty actions. Indeed, Aguilar goes so far as to suggest that Miriam speaks against Moses (and his relationship with his wife, Zipporah) because as a single woman she harbors jealousy. Aguilar's psychological reading of Miriam may strike contemporary women as harsh, but it is an excellent example of the ways she connects the women of the Jewish Scriptures to situations and emotions she deems relevant to her contemporary readers. This approach often leads Aguilar to suggest that the biblical women she interprets are never what they might appear to be on the surface; Sarah's seemingly cruel demand is actually a reflection of divine prophecy, while Miriam's appearance of prophetic song is read as evidence of her misplaced vanity about her own poetic powers.

In *Women of Israel* and other texts such as *Jewish Faith*, Aguilar is also highly cognizant of the need to connect contemporary Jewish readers to specifically Jewish ideas and belief, particularly because of the many pressures toward Christian conversion that Jewish women, in particular, faced in Christian culture. Thus, when interpreting the Jewish scriptural events that might seem far from the experience of nineteenth-century Jewish women, Aguilar often includes a comment on the cultural differences in women's opportunities that mark different moments in Jewish history. In her reading of Deborah, in *Women of Israel*, Aguilar notes that Deborah's role as judge might be perceived as a potential model for contemporary Jewish women's larger roles in the public sphere; yet as her interpretation continues, Aguilar is careful to suggest that Deborah's important public role can also be understood more figuratively for women in Aguilar's day: "Deborahs in truth we cannot be; but each and all have talents given, and a sphere assigned them, and, like her, all have it in their power, in the good performed toward man, to use the one, and consecrate the other to God" (211).

Aguilar's insistence on maintaining the separate gendered spheres that organized her own cultural and historical moment has perhaps most harmed her legacy for twenty-first-century readers and likewise limited her influence in liberal Jewish circles. Yet Aguilar's theological approach, not only to the Bible but also to Judaism itself, should not be reduced to this simple conclusion. Indeed, in *Spirit of Judaism* she spends much time suggesting that the problems for women in Judaism come either from specific historical oppression of Jews more generally, or stem from the oral (rabbinic) rather than written tradition, a position for which her editor, Rabbi Isaac Leeser, censors her repeatedly in his notes to her text. Likewise, in her novella *Perez Family*, she positions the mother as a key transmitter of Jewish values through her interpretation of the biblical portion of the week.

Other writings also offer challenges to Christian interpretations of Jewish prophetic texts, taking on the power of Christian rhetoric so dominant in nineteenth-century England. Because she did not avoid having Christian contact, both with friends and even through listening to Christian sermons, Aguilar understood the sheer power that Christian interpretations of the Jewish Bible held in her historical moment. While honoring her friends' beliefs in what seems to be a remarkable model of interfaith tolerance, she often took direct aim at Christian interpretations of Jewish Scripture in order to reinforce a specifically Jewish reading. In a typical example from an essay titled "Sabbath Thoughts on a Lecture on the Twenty-second Psalm by the Reverend R. S. Anderson 9th Nov. 1836," Aguilar explains:

> I cannot esteem my friends for following up their faith, unless I know what they are taught, and, when I do know that, and see how exactly they obey the dictates of their law, I must esteem them, however mistaken that law may appear to me; but I am more convinced in my own belief, because all that the Christian preaches, of portions of the Old Testament being typical of the sufferings of Christ, is to me clearly illustrative of the sufferings of my own loved nation. Now Mr. Anderson took for his lecture on Wednesday, the 22nd Psalm, as being equally descriptive of the sufferings of Christ, as the 53rd chapter of Isaiah; but as I believe, that same chapter is most beautifully and clearly prophetic of the miseries of the Jewish nation in the time of their captivity, I cannot but also believe if the 22nd Psalm is indeed prophetic, it is typical of the same subject. (*Essays*, 20–21)

In essay after essay, Aguilar insists that Jewish Scripture contains specifically Jewish religious truth, rather than being only a springboard for Christian typological prophecy; though this may seem obvious today, Aguilar's approach to the shared scriptural heritage of Christians and Jews shows remarkable courage for her historical moment. While there is a longer legacy of women commentators in Christian culture, Aguilar should be considered as one of Jewish history's most important figures.

Bibliography

Aguilar, Grace. *Essays and Miscellanies: Choice cullings from the manuscripts of Grace Aguilar: Selected by her mother, Sarah Aguilar*. Philadelphia: A. Hart, 1853.

———. *The Jewish Faith: Its Spiritual Consolation, Moral Guidance and Immortal Hope*. Edited by I. Leeser. Philadelphia: [L. Johnson], 1864 [1846].

———. *The Perez Family*. In *Grace Aguilar: Selected Writings*. Edited by Michael Galchinsky. Peterborough, ON: Broadview, 2003.

———. *The Spirit of Judaism*. Edited by Isaac Leeser. Philadelphia: Sherman, 1842.

———. "The Wanderers." *Occident* 3 (Oct. 1845): 330–32. http://www.jewish-history .com/occident/volume3/oct1845/wanderers.html.

———. *The Women of Israel*. New York: D. Appleton, 1901 [1845].

Galchinsky, Michael. "Grace Aguilar." In *Jewish Women: A Comprehensive Historical Encyclopedia*. 2005– [updated online]. Jewish Women's Archive: http://jwa.org/encyclopedia/article/aguilar-grace.

———, ed. *Grace Aguilar: Selected Writings*. Peterborough, ON: Broadview, 2003.

———. *The Origin of the Modern Jewish Woman Writer: Romance and Reform in Victorian England*. Detroit: Wayne State University Press, 1996.

Harris, Daniel A. "Hagar in Christian Britain: Grace Aguilar's [1838 Poem] 'The Wanderers.'" *Victorian Literature and Culture* 27 (1999): 143–69.

Scheinberg, Cynthia. *Women's Poetry and Religion in Victorian England*. Cambridge: Cambridge University Press, 2002.

Valman, Nadia. *The Jewess in Nineteenth-Century British Literary Culture*. Cambridge: Cambridge University Press, 2007.

— CYNTHIA SCHEINBERG

Angela of Foligno (ca. 1248–1309)

Angela of Foligno was a lay Franciscan mystic who gained unlikely fame and influence as a spiritual teacher; she became known by her contemporaries as *Magistra theologorum* (master of theologians) after a midlife conversion abruptly changed her affluent life. Living in the heart of Umbria (Italy), Angela was married with children when she experienced a passionate religious conversion that was deepened by the sudden death of all the members of her family. Released from domestic responsibilities, Angela followed a guilt-ridden spiritual path that focused on the incarnation and suffering of Christ. This spiritual path, supported by Franciscan friars, catapulted her into a career of spiritual teaching and charity.

As a laywoman, her education would have been "informal," limited to listening to sermons preached especially by friars, and participating in conversations with her confessor, known only as "a Franciscan." Supported by her confessor, who transcribed and in all likelihood edited her writings, Angela dictated a spiritual memoir, known as the *Memorial*, and a series of letters offering spiritual, pastoral, and theological advice, which have become known as her *Instructions*. In both works, Angela reveals her skill at offering both analytical biblical interpretations and what one could call visceral biblical interpretations, with special attention consistently given to the suffering and passion of Christ.

Angela's mixed audience of laity and clergy is clear from her writings, which include both scholastic analysis of Scripture and more emotionally evocative descriptions of scriptural, mainly New Testament, themes. In her *Instructions*, for example, she discusses the meaning of the suffering of Christ through an analysis of Matt. 27:46, "My God, my God, why have you abandoned me?" in a format that resembles traditional scholastic exposition. Christ cried out for three reasons: that God would become manifest, that the unspeakable suffering Christ endured would be known, and that people would have hope and be comforted (Lachance 233). But Angela subsequently describes (in third person) her visceral experience of Christ's suffering: "After her absorption into the fathomless depths of God and while she was still under the impact of this continuing vision, the image of the blessed crucified God and man appeared to her, looking as if he had just been taken down from the cross. His blood flowed fresh and crimson as if the wounds had just recently been opened" (Lachance 245).

Her graphic descriptions illustrate the kind of theological and spiritual study that she supported and the form of theological and spiritual teaching that she offered. Hers was a visceral form of study and understanding of Scripture. In turn, this is the kind of active engagement she encouraged in her followers, who included both laity and clergy. Angela exhorted her followers that the book they study and from which they preach should be the "God-man" (Lachance 262). While she was not anti-intellectual in her approach to Scripture, she advised her followers to be always willing to give up their books so that their preaching would not be dry.

Angela's impact on her immediate contemporaries was profound, especially among those affiliated with the Spirituals, a rigorous movement within the Franciscans that was condemned. Through the centuries, Angela's writings circulated in limited circles since they were often linked to suspicions of heresy. Nevertheless, she has influenced mystical writers, including the Catholic saint Francis de Sales (d. 1621), the German Pietist Johann Arndt (d. 1621), and, more recently, Thomas Merton (d. 1968), as well as such French feminist writers as Simone de Beauvoir (d. 1986) and Julia Kristeva (b. 1941).

Bibliography

Lachance, Paul, trans. *Angela of Foligno: Complete Works*. New York: Paulist Press, 1993.

Menestò, Enrico, ed. *Angela da Foligno, terziaria francescana: Atti del Convegno storico nel VII centenario dell'ingresso della beata Angela da Foligno nell'Ordine francescano secolare (1291–1991), Foligno, Nov. 17–19, 1991*. Spoleto: Centro italiano di studi sull'alto Medioevo, 1992.

Mooney, Catherine. "The Authorial Role of Brother A in the Composition of Angela of Foligno's Revelations." Pages 34–63 in *Creative Women in Medieval and Modern Italy*, edited by E. Ann Matter. Philadelphia: University of Pennsylvania Press, 1994.

Pryds, Darleen. *Women of the Streets: Early Franciscan Women and Their Mendicant Vocation*. St. Bonaventure, NY: Franciscan Institute Pubs., 2010.

Their, Ludger, OFM, and Abele Calufetti, OFM, eds. *Il libro della beata Angela da Foligno*. Spicilegium Bonaventurianum 25. Critical edition. Grottaferrata: Editiones Collegii S. Bonaventurae ad Claras Aquas, 1985.

—DARLEEN PRYDS

Anger, Jane (fl. 1589)

Jane Anger her Protection for women: To defend them against the scandalous reportes of . . . Venerians was published in London in 1589. About a dozen Jane (or Joan) Angers were active in England at that time (Foster 384), but nothing certain is known about the author except what the pamphlet itself reveals. Some scholars regard the name as an apt pseudonym for a choleric author who "rages" against misogynists. Anger's reputation comes from her being the first Englishwoman to publish a defense of women. Her learning is obvious from the style of her writing and the range—from Ariadne to Zenobia—of the characters she discusses.

She opens with an apologetic preface to English gentlewomen, but a second preface, addressed to "all women," takes a different tone, cursing false men to be blown by Boreas from "Paul's steeple . . . to the devil's haven." Her purpose is to rebut a now-lost work by Thomas Orwin titled *Boke His Surfeit in Love, with a farwel to the folies of his own phantasie* (1588). Poking good satiric and sometimes even bawdy fun, Anger cites cases from Menelaus onward in which men have proved to be lustful hypocrites. Typical is her version of the famous "cuckold's horns": the merciful gods had set horns upon men's foreheads not to make their cuckolding obvious but to break the falls that bruise their pates when they trip while chasing women (B2). She argues that though Boke, "the Surfeiter," probably had experiences with "Italian Curtizans" (C3), he had been rejected by many virtuous women and now projects his own lustful desires on them. Anger admits that a few women, like "Cletemnestra, Dalila and Jesabel," were "spotted" (B3), but identifies many more virtuous women, mostly classical, some Christian. As Anger portrays them, "most men" are animals, such as cock, scorpion, snake, eel, dog, wolf, horse. And they disguise the mile markers to the "Labyrinth" at the end of life's path in order to lure women from redemption. Thus "Follie, Vice, Mischiefe, Lust, Deceite, and Pride" are made to look like "Fancie, Virtue, Modestie, Love, Truemeaning, and Handsomnes" (D1).

Anger rarely cites Scripture directly, preferring to address "goddesses" interchangeably with "God," and to assign Apollo and Olympus the same rhetorical reality as Lucifer or Revelation's "lake of destruction." However, scattered references do prove her to be a protector of Christian women, as when she sees "GOD making woman of mans fleshe, that she might bee purer than he." The fruitfulness of women's bodies is especially noted as the source of man's salvation. Moreover, she asserts that "a woman was the first that believed, a woman likewise the first that repented of sin" (C1). Those who "snarle . . . that only God is good, and therfore women are ill" are trying to "correct Magnificat," forgetting that men are worse than women (C2).

While it might be stretching a point to say that "Jane Anger" was a significant interpreter of the Bible, she does attack misogynist interpretations, using a knowledge of the classics, a wicked sense of humor, a logician's flair, and all the rhetorical skills that her generation of English writers possessed.

Bibliography

Anger, Jane. *Jane Anger her Protection for women: To defend them against the scandalous reportes of a late surfeiting lover, and all otherlike Venerians that complaine so to bee overcloyed with women's kindnesse.* London: Richard Jones & Thomas Orwin, 1589. Pages A1–D4 in *Defences of Women: Jane Anger, Rachel Speght, Ester Sowernam and Constantia Munda,* selected by Susan G. O'Malley. The Early Modern Englishwoman: A Facsimile Library of Essential Works; Series 1, Printed Writings, 1500–1640; Part 1, vol. 4. Aldershot, UK: Scolar, 1996.

———. "Jane Anger her Protection for women." Pages 29–52 in *The Women's Sharp Revenge: Five Women's Pamphlets from the Renaissance,* edited by Simon Shepherd. New York: St. Martin's Press, 1985.

Foster, Donald W. "Commentary: In the Name of the Author." *New Literary History* 33, no. 2 (2002): 375–96.

Henderson, Katherine U., and Barbara F. McManus. *Half Humankind: Contexts and Texts of the Controversy about Women in England, 1540–1640.* Urbana: University of Illinois Press, 1985.

Martin, Randall, ed. *Women Writers in Renaissance England.* New York: Longman, 1997.

Shepherd, Simon. "Introduction." Pages 9–23 in *The Women's Sharp Revenge: Five Women's Pamphlets from the Renaissance.* New York: St. Martin's Press, 1985.

—Betsy Delmonico

■ Askew, Anne (ca. 1521–46)

Anne Askew, a Lincolnshire gentlewoman and an early convert to Reformation doctrine, was accused of heresy, imprisoned, examined, tortured, and finally burned at the stake in London in 1546. During the last years of her life, she wrote an account of her interrogations, letters, and statements of her faith; these documents were collected and published in 1546–47 in the Duchy of Cleves by the exiled Reformer John Bale, who added his "elucidation" to her texts. Askew's significance as a Tudor evangelical and martyr is reflected in the seven editions of *The first examinacyon* and *The lattre examinacyon* in print by 1585; John Foxe also included these works in *Actes and Monuments,* ensuring that they would never be out of print. The woodcut on the title page of the first edition features a radiant female figure, holding a martyr's palm frond in one hand and a book titled *Biblia* in the other as she tramples a beast wearing a papal crown. Clearly, the image contributed to contemporary antipapal propaganda, but it also suggests that Scripture is the source of Askew's evangelical power.

Askew was born in about 1521 to Sir William Askew and Elizabeth Wrottesley Askew of Stallingborough in Lincolnshire. After her mother died, her father married Elizabeth Hutton Hansard, and the family moved to South Kelsey, closer to Lincoln. Although Bale is vague about his sources, he offers some details about Askew's life. He claims that after the death of her older sister, Askew's father forced her to marry her sister's fiancé, Master Kyme, that they had two children, and that her frequent Bible reading led to her conversion to a Reformed faith and to Master Kyme's expelling her violently from their home. According to Bale, Askew sought a divorce, and it is possible that her failure to gain approval for the divorce in the bishop's court in Lincoln brought her to the Court of Chancery in London. Several documents attest to Askew's presence in London, including City of London records reporting that she was detained on March 10, 1545, "for certeyn matters concernying the vi Articles" (C.L.R.O. Repertory 11, fo. 174v). The Six Articles delineated orthodox doctrine as the law of the land in an attempt to curtail the spread of the English Reformation.

In her account of her examinations, Askew details questions asked by clerical and secular officials and her answers; these dialogues indicate that Askew was accused of being a Sacramentarian who denied the doctrine of transubstantiation and affirmed that the sacrament of the altar was either symbolic or a remembrance, and that Christ was not really present. Perhaps because of her evasive or ambiguous responses, Askew was eventually bailed from prison by her cousin Master Brittayne. She was arrested again in June 1545 but released because of a lack of witnesses. In June 1546 Askew and her husband were summoned to appear before the Privy Council, and although he was dismissed, she was detained and questioned, finally being sent to Newgate Prison (in London). She was then condemned as a heretic at the Guildhall without the jury required by law. Her examinations by officials of church and state continued out of the public eye, culminating with her questioning in the Tower of London about her connections to some of the women associated with Queen Katherine Parr (the last wife of Henry VIII), who might also be evangelicals and might have supported her.

On June 29, after her denials of such connections, and after the lieutenant of the Tower refused to cooperate, Sir Richard Rich and Lord Chancellor Wriothesley themselves tortured her on the rack, an act expressly against the law. She apparently gave no information and writes that she told the chancellor that she "wolde rather dye, than to breake my faythe" (Askew, ed. Beilin, 132). Finally, on July 16, 1546, when she was about twenty-five, Askew was taken to Smithfield, just outside London Wall; still refusing to recant, she was burned as a heretic in the presence of City of London officials as well as the lord chancellor, the duke of Norfolk, and other members of the Privy Council.

Just as the woodcut in *The Examinations* represents the Bible as the foundation of Askew's strength, her text confirms the centrality of Scripture to her life and work. As she reveals in one of her dialogues with Bishop Bonner, she had once journeyed to Lincoln Cathedral to read the Bible in public, claiming that the priests of Lincoln approached her but did not speak to her. One priest finally spoke to her, she tells Bonner, but "hys words were of so small effecte, that I ded not now remember them" (56–57). Her dismissive tone clearly marks her choice of Scripture over priestly words, but even more, as it is likely that Askew went to the cathedral after the 1543 Act for the Advancement of True Religion, she would have knowingly defied the section of the law prohibiting gentlewomen from reading the Bible in public. Continually Askew asserts that Scripture is the ultimate authority on all matters of faith, including the contentious—and dangerous—debate on the sacraments.

Indeed, as she reconstructs the dialogues between herself and her examiners, scriptural allusion and exegesis are at the heart of almost every sentence of her text, even though she appears to understand clearly the risks of her insisting on the primacy of Scripture over ecclesiastical tradition. During her first examination, for instance, to answer a question, she shows her interrogator biblical chapters; when asked to interpret them, she replies with Matt. 7:6, "I would not throwe pearles amonge swyne for acornes were good ynough" (21). Her insult may be brave, but it also shows Askew's equivocation in refusing to assume the role of exegete while yet quoting Scripture. Askew writes here as if she thinks through scriptural language. In *The lattre examinacyon*, when she writes her confession, she asserts her version of *scriptura sola*: "And for so moch as I am by the lawe unryghtouslye condemned for an evyll doer concernynge opynyons, I take the same most mercyfull God of myn, whych hath made both heaven and earthe, to recorde, that I holde no opynyons contrarye to hys most holye worde" (138).

And when Bonner informs her that she will be burned, she tells him that she "had searched all the scriptures yet coulde I never fynde there that eyther Christ or hys Apostles put anye creature to deathe" (98). Not only is the Bible the source of her faith and the basis of her defense against her accusers, but implicit in her advocacy of Scripture as solely and totally sufficient for salvation is an attack that evangelicals directed against the "unwritten verytees" (143), their term for traditional doctrine and practices.

Addressing the inevitable problem of a woman's citing Scripture publicly, at an early point in her text, Askew includes a dialogue with the bishop's chancellor, who tells her that the apostle Paul "forbode women to speake or to talke of the worde of God." Askew provides an exegesis of the Pauline text decidedly in her favor: "I knew Paules meanynge so well as he, whych is, i. Corinthiorum xiii. That a woman ought not to speake in the congregacyon by the waye of teachynge. And then I asked hym, how manye women he had seane, go into the pulpett and preache. He sayde, he never sawe non. Then I sayde, he ought to fynde no faute in poore women, except they had offended the lawe" (29–30).

By claiming that Paul's injunction is actually against women preaching, Askew represents herself as clarifying Scripture and exonerated from wrongdoing. As Gertz-Robinson shows, Askew evades any accusation that she is a preacher even as she adopts the persona and rhetoric of an instructor in the faith. Similarly, when asked later to explain the same passage from Paul, she responds with an ironic barb that asserts her knowledge of Scripture while hedging against further trouble: "I answered, that it was agaynst saynt Paules lernynge, that I beynge a woman, shuld interprete the scriptures, specyallye where so manye wyse lerned men were" (54).

As ironic and forceful as Askew can be in defending herself as a female evangelical, she invariably turns to male prophets and saints to elucidate her struggles and beliefs. As scholars have noted, Askew's biblical models include Stephen, David, Daniel, and Job, and these figures may have formed for her, as Linton suggests, a "scriptural community" (140). Stephen—represented in Acts 7 as preacher, adversary of evil rulers, victim of false witnesses, and the first martyr—is Askew's first choice of role model. Twice, when she is questioned about the sacrament, she asks her interrogator why Stephen was stoned to death. She writes that her questioner did not know why, but she refuses to tell him the answer, citing only the text associated with Stephen from Acts 7:48 and Paul in Acts 17:24, "That God dwelleth not in temples made with handes" (49). David the psalmist also appears at crucial moments in *The Examinations*, providing Askew with the language for her struggle, as in her allusion to Ps. 69: "O lorde, I have more enemyes now, than there be heeres on my heade" (146). Her interest in the Psalms appears most fully in her paraphrase of Ps. 54, "For thy names sake, be my refuge" (72). In Daniel, she finds the prophet who criticizes and teaches a powerful ruler, perhaps a glance at Henry VIII; in "pacyent Job" (132), she calls on a model of fortitude after she has been tortured on the rack.

In *The lattre examinacyon*, Askew responds much more directly to questions about her faith, citing the basis of her Sacramentarianism in Christ's words from Matt. 26; Luke 22; and 1 Cor. 11: "Take, eate. Thys is my bodye whych is geven for yow . . . as an outwarde sygne. Thys do ye, in remembraunce of me" (88–89). Such open declarations led inevitably to Smithfield: with three other Sacramentaries, she was burned there. In his edition of her work, Bale includes "The Balade which Anne Askewe made and sange whan she was in Newgate." Each verse reflects Askew's scripturalism, from the initial simile of the "armed knyght" with a shield of faith to the final prayer for forgiveness for "these men."

See also Parr, Katherine (1512–48)

Bibliography

Askew, Anne. *The Examinations of Anne Askew*. Edited by Elaine V. Beilin. Oxford: Oxford University Press, 1996.

———. *The first examinacyon of Anne Askewe*. Edited by John Bale. Wesel: D. van der Straten, 1546.

———. *The lattre examinacyon of Anne Askewe*. Edited by John Bale. Wesel: D. van der Straten, 1547.

———. *The two examinations of the worthy servant of God, Maistris An Askew*. In *Actes and Monuments*, by John Foxe. London: John Day, 1563.

Beilin, Elaine V. "Anne Askew's Dialogue with Authority." Pages 313–22 in *Contending Kingdoms: Historical, Psychological, and Feminist Approaches to the Literature of Sixteenth-Century England and France*, edited by Marie-Rose Logan and Peter L. Rudnytsky. Detroit: Wayne State University Press, 1991.

Betteridge, Thomas. *Tudor Histories of the English Reformations, 1530–83*. Pages 80–119. St. Andrews Studies in Reformation History. Aldershot, UK: Ashgate, 1999.

Gertz-Robinson, Genelle. "Stepping into the Pulpit? Women's Preaching in *The Book of Margery Kempe* and *The Examinations of Anne Askew*." Pages 459–82 in *Voices in Dialogue: Reading Women in the Middle Ages*, edited by Linda Olson and Kathryn Kerby-Fulton. Notre Dame, IN: University of Notre Dame Press, 2005.

Hickerson, Megan. "Negotiating Heresy in Tudor England: Anne Askew and the Bishop of London." *Journal of British Studies* 46 (2007): 774–95.

Linton, Joan Pong. "Scripted Silences, Reticence, and Agency in Anne Askew's *Examinations*." *English Literary Renaissance* 36 (2006): 3–25.

Monta, Susannah Brietz. "The Inheritance of Anne Askew, English Protestant Martyr." *Archiv für Reformationsgeschichte* 94 (2003): 134–60.

Snook, Edith. "Gendering the English Reformation: The Vernacular Reader in Anne Askew's *Examinations* and Katherine Parr's *Lamentacion of a Synner*." Pages 25–56 in *Women, Reading, and the Cultural Politics of Early Modern England*. Burlington, VT: Ashgate, 2005.

Watt, Diane. *Secretaries of God: Women Prophets in Late Medieval and Early Modern England*. Pages 81–117. Cambridge: D. S. Brewer, 1997.

— ELAINE V. BEILIN

■ Astell, Mary (1666–1731)

Mary Astell was born to a merchant family in Newcastle-upon-Tyne but spent her adult life as a single woman in London, writing and publishing treatises on educational, theological, philosophical, and political issues. She became an integral member of the city's intellectual set, interacting with Archbishop William Sancroft, John Norris, Richard Steele, Daniel Defoe, the Earl of Shaftesbury, Damaris Masham, and John Locke, among others. She was educated at home by a curate uncle who introduced her to the classics, poetry, and the theosophical ideas of the Cambridge Platonists, and was self-taught thereafter. As an ardent Anglican, Astell pursued a life of devout scholarship with the companionship and patronage of her aristocratic neighbors Lady Catherine Jones, Lady Elizabeth Hastings, and Lady Ann Coventry, with whose aid she established a girls' charity school in her later years.

A recurrent theme in Astell's writings is God's dispensation granting to women minds and souls equal to men's. The main concern of her tracts on women's education, *A Serious Proposal to the Ladies: By a Lover of Her Sex*, in two parts (*SP 1* and *SP 2*), is facilitating women's development of their God-given rational aptitude by training their intellect and focusing on virtuous concerns worthy of their attention. Along with her critique of the inequitable status of married women, *Some Reflections on Marriage* (*SRM*), these works have earned Astell modern recognition as a prominent early feminist. They also gained her a popular following in her day, though her overtly religious works, *Letters concerning the Love of God* (*L*) and *The Christian Religion as Profess'd by a Daughter of the Church of England* (*CR*), bypassed in her modern reception, were central to her reputation among her contemporaries. Upholding the parity of men and women's reason and worth by citing select biblical verses and highlighting their espousal of gender equivalency is an underlying motif throughout her corpus. Her exegesis is based on a straightforward, rational reading of texts alongside stringent attention to the historicity of biblical accounts, employing a "hermeneutics of suspicion" that privileges her reason over traditional male erudition (Thickstun 151).

Women's pursuit of spiritual knowledge was a core concern of Astell. As a young woman, she exchanged meditations on the nature of love that humanity owes the Divine with the Malebranchean theologian John Norris, a divine she deemed "not so narrow-Soul'd as to confine Learning to his own Sex, or to envy it in ours" (*L* 1). Norris's publication of their correspondence established Astell's early reputation as a serious philosophical theoretician. In her *Serious Proposal*, she posited a method to amend the educational gender disparity by establishing a "*Religious* Retirement," wherein women could develop and direct the divine gift of sense in communal study (*SP* 1:20). Proclaiming that "religion is the adequate business of our lives. . . . Nothing being a fit employment for a rational Creature, which has not either a *direct* or *remote* tendency to this great and *only* end," Astell cites biblical precedent to authorize her project (*SP* 1:21). She points out that "the Holy Ghost" has "left it on record, that *Priscilla* as well as her Husband, catechiz'd the eloquent *Apollos*," citing a woman who presumed to teach a prominent man (Acts 18:26; *SP* 1:24). Paul, "the great Apostle," she writes, "found no fault" in this but rather commended the couple as "my helpers in Christ Jesus" (Rom. 16:3; *SP* 1:24). The Bible, she points out, thus explicitly demonstrates that women are "as capable of Learning as Men are, and that it becomes them as well" (*SP* 1:24). Divine support for women's scholarship, including their teaching of men, is a documented reality that the contemporary paucity of learning opportunities for her gender did not reflect. When her proposed institution failed to come to fruition, Astell outlined a program of solitary study in *Part II, Wherein a Method is offer'd for the Improvement of their Minds*. That improvement, she asserts, will enable "these Clouds that hide the most adorable Face of GOD from us" to disperse, with the result that women "shall no more dispute his Will, nor seek exemption from it, but with all Sincerity of Heart, and ardent Desire cry out, *Lord, what wilt thou have me to do? Not my Will, Lord, but thine be done!*" (Luke 22:42; *SP* 2:160–61). She concludes that "the business of our Lives will be to improve our Minds and to stretch our Faculties to their utmost extent" so that woman may "declare the Wisdom, Power and Goodness, of that All-Perfect Being from whom we derive *All* our Excellencies, and in whose Service, they ought *Wholly* to be employ'd" (*SP* 2:161, 96). Intellectual and devout, Astell's writings evidence effective employment of her encyclopedic knowledge of Scripture to support her own construal of a gender-inclusive virtuous community.

Astell's most detailed biblical exegesis is to be found in the preface to the third edition of *Reflections upon Marriage*, a text occasioned by the particularly scandalous divorce case of her neighbor the duchess of Mazarin. She added the prologue to refute critics of earlier editions, who claimed that the pro-woman sentiments that she had posited "were not agreeable to scripture." What constitutes the biblical message, she points out, is a matter of interpretation. "Scripture is not always on their side who make parade of it," she declares, and men, "thro' their skill in Languages and the Tricks of the Schools," often attempt to "wrest it from its genuine sense to their own Inventions" (*SRM* 14). She methodically forefronts her own textual analysis of passages traditionally cited to limit women's voice and role.

Astell first examines Paul's meditations on women's standing in the church and the right to prophesy. She specifies that in his restrictive pronouncements, the apostle "argues only for decency and Order, according to the present Custom and State of things" (1 Cor. 11; *SRM* 11). She points out that in the full citation, "Praying and Prophesying in the Church are allow'd the Women" provided that they, as well as the men, observe proper standards of dress, assuring her readers that "no inequality can be inferr'd from hence" (1 Cor. 11:8; *SRM* 11). The juxtaposition of this directive with the verse attesting to the man as head of the woman shows only that "it is not so much a Law of Nature, that Women shou'd Obey Men, as that Men shou'd not wear long Hair," she argues (*SRM* 12). Additionally, the parallelism of the designated hierarchies between man and woman and that of Christ and God testifies that as the latter denotes "no natural Inferiority among the Divine Persons, but that they are in all things Coequal," so the two genders are "on a Level" (1 Cor. 11:8; *SRM* 11). In pronouncing the mutuality of human dependency on God, 1 Cor. 11:12 signifies that "the Relation between the two Sexes is mutual, and the Dependance Reciprocal, both of them Depending intirely upon GOD, and upon Him only" (*SRM* 13). Her reading counters accepted interpretations subjugating women by attention to textual detail and prioritization of the clearly stated equivalency of shared human subordination to God, which concludes the verse.

The Bible does, Astell acknowledges, write of women "as in a State of Subjection," but so too does it tell "of the Jews and Christians when under the Dominion of the Chaldeans and Romans" "requiring" in both cases a "quiet submission to them under whose Power they liv'd" (Jer. 40; *SRM* 14). Submission is necessary for social order, she admits, but denies that requisite temporal deference suggests inferiority: "Will any one say" that these ruling political authorities "had a Natural Superiority and Right to Dominion . . . or any Pre-eminence, except what their greater Strength acquir'd," as is claimed in gender hierarchy (*SRM* 14–15)? While women have been "kept in Ignorance of the Original, wanting Languages and other helps to Criticise on the Sacred Text," men merely "shew their desire to maintain their Hypotheses, but by no means their Reverence to the Sacred Oracles" with their imprecise scholarship (*SRM* 14). Extrapolating generic woman's subservience from a particular historical necessity is clearly, she claims, a misreading of the holy account.

Astell reinterprets passages in Genesis that have been used to support contentions of women's lesser status. She paradoxically cites 2:21–22 rather than the more egalitarian 1:27, refuting the notion that gender inequality is inherent in the order of creation by invoking a parallel analogy. Any sensible reader must agree, she maintains, that "Earthly Adam's being Form'd before Eve, seems as little to prove her Natural Subjection to him, as the Living Creatures, Fishes, Birds and Beasts being Form'd before them both, proves that Mankind must be subject to these Animals" (1:20–28; *SRM* 21). As for the first couple's proportional responsibility for the fall and resultant sinfulness, she clarifies Pauline intention: "Nor can the Apostle mean that *Eve* only sinned; or that she only was *Deceiv'd*," since the words specify that it was "*Adam*" who "sinn'd willfully and knowingly," and so "became the greater Transgressor" (3:1–6; *SRM* 21). In Astell's account, close reading of Scripture in context leads to its intended egalitarian connotation.

Womankind's gender subordination was routinely justified by citing the pronouncement that after the fall, Adam will have dominion over Eve; Astell reveals that those who make this analogy inaccurately interpret the biblical text. Just as God informs Eve that her husband will rule over her (Gen. 3:16), Astell notes, likewise Esau is told that he will serve his younger brother (27:40). It is unreasonable to conclude that "one Text shou'd be a Command any more than the other, and not both of them be Predictions only," since "the Text in both Cases" is merely "foretelling what wou'd be; but, neither of them determining what ought to be," she writes (*SRM* 19, 20). Astell's interpretive strategy negates restrictive decrees drawn from Scripture by identifying citations with analogous language and circumstances that support the logic of her reading.

The predominance of intelligent and active female biblical paragons serve as proof texts for Astell's contention that God chooses women as well as men to fulfill his plan and act in the world. She specifically cites the national leader Deborah, whose narrative contests the "pretence of *Natural Inferiority*" of women, since "it was GOD who Inspir'd and Approv'd that great Woman, raising her up to Judge and to Deliver His People Israel," and "the Law of Nature is the Law of GOD, who cannot contradict Himself" (Judg. 4–5; *SRM* 24). Her treatise enumerates prominent visionary women from the Old and the New Testaments as evidence that God "did not deny Women that Divine Gift the Spirit of Prophecy, neither under the Jewish nor Christian Dispensation" (*SRM* 26). She lists the daughters of Zelophehad, Ruth, Esther, Rebecca, Miriam, Abigail, the wise woman of Tekoa, the Queen of Sheba, the Shunammite, and Huldah—alongside the daughters of Philip, Mary, Mary Magdalene, the Syrophoenician, Elizabeth, Martha, Tabitha, Anna, and the women who bore witness to the resurrection. Through these examples, Astell underscores the message that *"there is neither Bond nor Free, Male nor Female, but they are all one in Christ Jesus"* (Gal. 3:28, cf. KJV; *SRM* 26). As is characteristic of emerging eighteenth-century interpretive methodology, she supports her arguments through reason and empirical (textual) evidence.

In her magnum opus, *Christian Religion*, Astell outlines the rational principles upholding conservative Anglican orthodoxy in order to inform women of the grounds on which their religion is based and the duties incumbent on its adherents. She bases women's obligation to study and to personally ascertain the correctness of the Christian message on "that Command of Christ's, *Call no Man master upon Earth*" (Matt. 23:9; *CR* 1). Her synthesis of biblical commands leads her to conclude, "If GOD had not intended that Women shou'd use their Reason, He wou'd not have given them any, for He does nothing in vain" (*CR* 5). She encourages women to defend their own interpretation of God's Word by citing the biblical decree: "A Woman may put on the whole Armour of GOD without degenerating into a Masculine Temper; she may take the Shield of Faith, the Sword of the Spirit, the Helmet of Salvation, and the Breastplate of Righteousness without any offence to the Men" (Eph. 6:11–17; *CR* 72). Her tract is replete with marginal notes referring to the verses that corroborate her more generalized reflections and exegesis.

Astell's hermeneutics synthesize languages of rationality and religion as she systematically refutes accepted custom and interpretive traditions that repudiate women's equivalency. She upholds the authority of church doctrine as she calls for women's independence of mind through her forthright biblical interpretations. While commending those who accept a traditional domestic role for suffering a "continual Martyrdom to bring Glory to GOD and Benefit to Mankind" (*SRM* 78), Astell exemplifies and promotes an alternative, or at least additional option, that of independent religious scholar. A well-known figure during her lifetime, Astell was quickly forgotten after her death. The impetus for her twentieth-century revival was a 1916 monograph, but her manuscripts began to be retrieved from rare book libraries only in the 1970s. Since then, a biography, modern editions of her treatises, critical articles, and numerous anthologies containing selections from her works have been published. She is now included in the canon of early modern women writers, and recent work has just begun to recognize the spiritual emphasis and biblical roots of her corpus as a foundation of her feminism rather than a foil for it; yet her legacy as a biblical exegete still awaits sufficient acknowledgment.

Bibliography

Astell, Mary. *The Christian Religion as Profess'd by a Daughter of the Church of England*. 3rd ed. London: Wilkin, 1717.

———. *A Serious Proposal to the Ladies: Parts I and II* [1st ed., 1694]. Edited by Patricia Springborg. London: Pickering & Chatto, 1997.

———. *Some Reflections upon Marriage* [1700]. Pages 2–80 in *Astell: Political Writings*, edited by Patricia Springborg. Cambridge: Cambridge University Press, 1996.

Astell, Mary, and John Norris. *Letters concerning the Love of God*. Edited by E. Derek Taylor and Melvyn New. Aldershot, UK: Ashgate, 2005.

Kolbrener, William, and Michal Michelson, eds. *Mary Astell: Reason, Gender, Faith*. Aldershot, UK: Ashgate, 2007.

Michelson, Michal. "Our Religion and Liberties: Mary Astell's Christian Political Polemics." Pages 123–36 in *Virtue, Liberty, and Toleration: Political Ideas of European Women, 1400–1800*, edited by Jacqueline Broad and Karen Green. Dordrecht: Springer, 2007.

Perry, Ruth. *The Celebrated Mary Astell: An Early English Feminist*. Chicago: University of Chicago Press, 1986.

Reuther, Rosemary Radford. "Prophets and Humanists: Types of Religious Feminism in Stuart England." *Journal of Religion* 70, no. 1 (1990): 1–18.

Springborg, Patricia. *Mary Astell: Theorist of Freedom from Domination*. Cambridge: Cambridge University Press, 2005.

Thickstun, Margaret Olofson. "'This Was a Woman That Taught': Feminist Scriptural Exegesis in the Seventeenth Century." *Studies in Eighteenth Century Culture* 21 (1991): 149–58.

— Michal Michelson

Baldwin, Joyce (1921–95)

Joyce Baldwin was born in Essex County, England, into a Christian family. The family moved to Nottingham in 1937, where during the war years Baldwin earned an honors degree in French and German (1942) and a Cambridge postgraduate certificate in education (1943). She was involved in the university's Christian Union and felt called to serve in China. Since mission work in China was not possible in 1943, Baldwin taught French. In 1947 she began her training with the China Inland Mission and, sensing that her future might include teaching Scripture, she completed course work at the London Bible College and acquired a diploma in theology from the University of London. Baldwin reached China in 1949, just as the Communists gained control. Two years later she returned to Britain, permanently weakened by amoebic dysentery, with the door closed to further service overseas.

In 1956, after regaining a measure of health, Baldwin began teaching Old Testament at Dalton House, Bristol, an Anglican center for training women as parish workers and missionaries. While preparing lectures and teaching, she upgraded her own qualifications with a bachelor of divinity degree from the University of London (1958). She encouraged her students to undertake academic study, and with support from the faculty of the neighboring Tyndale Hall, they began to acquire degrees in theology.

Eager to enhance her teaching, Baldwin attended the Tyndale House Summer Schools for Old Testament Study in Cambridge, where she met leading evangelical scholars who encouraged her to pursue her academic gifts. In 1962, Donald Wiseman invited her to give a paper on "*Semah* as a Technical Term in the Prophets." She later became a member of the Society for Old Testament Studies (SOTS).

Baldwin's career as a published interpreter of Scripture began in 1966, when Inter-Varsity Press (UK) asked her to contribute several articles to the new edition of the *New Bible Commentary Revised* (1970), and Wiseman asked her to write a commentary on Haggai, Zechariah, and Malachi for the Tyndale Old Testament Commentaries series. Despite her physical frailties and responsibilities as vice principal and later principal of Dalton House, Baldwin accepted these challenges, and the commentary was published in 1972. The editorial policy of this series was to give college students and church lay leaders access to the latest academic knowledge, helping them to understand the Bible in its original context before exploring its relevance for today. Baldwin's commentary was generally well received. Her colleagues were astonished at the breadth and depth of her study and her meticulous exegesis. J. I. Packer referred to her "computer mind, . . . tenacious for Biblical truth—with a gift for analyzing evidence with luminous clarity" (personal interview, July 1995). Her approach to Zechariah, in particular, elicited the attention of biblical scholars. Influenced by the literary approach of Paul Lamarche, who used chiastic patterns to interpret Zech. 9–14, Baldwin presented the book "as an artistic whole, with an over-all plan and unity of message" (*Haggai, Zechariah, and Malachi*, 70). Her primary interest was not the reconstruction of the book's prehistory; rather, she argued for what would later be called a canonical approach: "Whether the unity results from the master mind of one prophet or from a redactor or redactors is in the last analysis immaterial. What is urgent is that the whole book, after being fragmented for so long, should once again make its full impact on the church" (70). In 1977, Brevard Childs judged her work to be "the best all-round commentary on these three prophets for the pastor" (Childs 77–78).

Baldwin went on to write three other commentaries in this series (*Daniel* [1978], *Esther* [1984], *1 and 2 Samuel* [1988]), as well as *Lamentations–Daniel* for the Bible Study Commentary series (1984); *The Message of Genesis 12–50* for the series The Bible Speaks Today (1986); "Jonah" in *The Minor Prophets: An Exegetical and Expository Commentary* (1993); a number of smaller articles on subjects related to the Old Testament; and several books on women and ministry.

Baldwin's commentary on Daniel drew a more critical response from many in the academy as she defended dating the book to the sixth century BCE. Still, reviewer John Gammie judged her book as "at once scholarly, irenic, highly readable and convincing of the reasonableness, if not the correctness, of the evangelical approach to the Book of Daniel, . . . a work sufficiently open and irenic to suggest that the day may be arriving when meaningful dialogue can transpire between evangelical and higher critics" (453). Baldwin was a conservative evangelical scholar, but she was not dogmatic; her sensitivity to rhetorical features and structures of texts pushed her to consider questions related to the final form and message of biblical books. Her interests included discerning the message of Scripture for readers. She was convinced, for example, of the value of apocalyptic texts for the contemporary church: "The whole church needs the kind of reassurance that a study of this book can bring, not least in view of Marxist claims to hold the key to history and to be able by human strategy to introduce a utopian world government. No wonder the church becomes defeatist if it sets on one side an important part of the Bible's understanding of history. Moreover its evangelism becomes ineffective without the message of the apocalyptic books" (*Daniel*, 17).

The 1970s saw an escalating debate on women's ordination in the Church of England, and Trinity College, with its evangelical foundation, included women and men both for and against this. For Baldwin, the publication of her first commentary was God's seal on her gifts and ministry. In the culturally separated worlds of men and women in China, the pastors had to keep their distance from the women church members. Chinese and missionary women, married and single, were responsible for women in the churches. Baldwin had seen women using their spiritual gifts and knew they were as capable as men. When the moderate Movement for the Ordination of Women started in Britain in 1979, Baldwin became a member and helped to organize two of their conferences in Bristol. She was ordained a deacon in 1987, but did not seek full ordination in 1994, feeling that her gifts and calling had already been recognized.

Although Baldwin did not embrace radical feminist theology, she was interested in female figures in Scripture and sometimes allowed her experience as a woman to influence her reading of Scripture. She firmly rejected the concept of a "Creation Ordinance" in Gen. 1–2, which supposedly authorized patriarchy and asserted the authority and leadership of men and the subordination of women. She produced two booklets on the subject for Anglican women and defended this view more fully in a debate on *The Role of Women*. She argued that patriarchy was instituted as a result of the fall and had no place in a Christian community. This meant that she interpreted such difficult texts as 1 Tim. 2:12 in accordance with the wider principles and examples found in the rest of Scripture.

Baldwin's commentary on Esther provides many examples of how she read Scripture with a female lens. Commenting on the institution of the king's harem, for example, Baldwin observes, "The prestige of living in the royal palace was small compensation for the king's neglect, though girls with a passion for luxury could no doubt indulge it to the full" (*Esther*, 68). Moreover, sensitive to the complexity of relationships between husbands and wives, she commented on Esther's relation to Ahasuerus: "Other people often have easier access to her husband than a wife, who has sometimes to reckon with volatile feelings and relations, in so sensitive a relationship" (79).

Baldwin was a quiet person, and her health prevented her from accepting engagements outside the college, so she was not widely known. She lived in college accommodations for twenty-five years and, in addition to her teaching, spent many meals discussing women's ministry in the church with a succession of students struggling with the idea.

In 1981, her final year before retirement, she was invited to become acting principal of Trinity Theological College. Nine years earlier, Dalton House had joined Bristol's two Anglican theological colleges for men to form Trinity Theological College, and Baldwin had become dean of women, retaining her "principal" status, but essentially functioning as a dean. However, for the sake of Anglican women who were still denied ordination, she suggested now to the board that the word "acting" be dropped from the title, and they agreed. Baldwin became principal of a coed Anglican Theological College in 1981, six years before women were allowed to become deacons and thirteen years before they could be ordained to the priesthood.

Baldwin was succeeded by George Carey, who later became archbishop of Canterbury. In 1982 she married an old friend, Jack Caine, who helped her to continue her writing. Baldwin is remembered as a pioneer, a quiet woman in a man's world where she held her own. She was a conservative evangelical scholar who worked within a modern framework, using all the tools of the academy to come to conservative conclusions about questions of history and authorship, on the one hand, and to a realization of the importance of the final shape of a text in terms of determining meaning and significance, on the other.

Bibliography

Baldwin, Joyce. *Daniel: An Introduction and Commentary*. Tyndale Old Testament Commentary. Leicester, UK: Inter-Varsity, 1978.

———. *Esther: An Introduction and Commentary*. Tyndale Old Testament Commentary. Leicester, UK: Inter-Varsity, 1984.

———. *Haggai, Zechariah, Malachi: An Introduction and Commentary*. Tyndale Old Testament Commentary. London: Tyndale, 1972.

———. "*Semah* as a Technical Term in the Prophets." *Vetus Testamentum* 14 (1964): 93–97.

———. *Women Likewise*. London: Falcon, 1973.

———. "Women's Ministry: A New Look at the Biblical Texts." Pages 158–75 in *The Role of Women*, edited by Shirley Lees. Leicester, UK: Inter-Varsity, 1984.

———. *You and the Ministry*. London: Church Pastoral Aid Society, 1979.

Childs, Brevard. S. *Old Testament Books for Pastor and Teacher*. Philadelphia: Westminster, 1977.

Gammie, John G. Review of *Daniel: An Introduction and Commentary*, by Joyce G. Baldwin. *Journal of Biblical Literature* 99 (1980): 453.

Griffiths, Valerie. "Joyce Baldwin-Caine." Pages 329–43 in *Bible Interpreters of the Twentieth Century*, edited by Walter A. Ewell and J. D. Weaver. Grand Rapids: Baker Books, 1999.

———. "Mankind: Male and Female." Pages 72–95 in *The Role of Women*, edited by Shirley Lees. Leicester, UK: Inter-Varsity, 1984.

— VALERIE GRIFFITHS

Barbauld, Anna (1743–1825)

Anna Barbauld was a British writer of poems, hymns, and essays that draw on biblical texts to focus the reader's attention on the maternal aspects of an affectionate and relational God. Her parents, John Aikin, DD, and Jane Aikin were Presbyterians. She was primarily homeschooled by her mother, whose "mind had been cultivated and her principles formed, partly by the society of the celebrated Dr. Doddridge" (Aikin 14), a famous eighteenth-century dissenting minister. Barbauld's father also contributed to her education—by teaching her Greek and Latin—but she had to "convince" him to "let" her read in these languages (14). As a child,

> the love of rural nature sunk deep into her heart; her vivid fancy exerted itself to colour, to animate, and to diversify all the objects which surrounded her: the few but choice authors of her father's library, which she read and re-read, had leisure to make their full impression, —to mould her sentiments and form her taste; the spirit of devotion, early inculcated upon her as a duty, opened to her by degrees an exhaustless source of tender and sublime delight; and while yet a child she was surprised to find herself a poet. (Aikin 15)

Her literary reflections on God's sublimity in both poetry and prose blend complex and multifaceted biblical quotations and allusions with keen observations of the natural world, reflecting both the biblical knowledge and scientific curiosity of eighteenth-century dissenting communities. She also brought strong emotions to her reading of Scripture, which at times set her at odds with the very same intellectual communities that initially encouraged and enabled her to publish.

The poems and hymns that Anna Barbauld first published contain repeated biblical and maternal metaphors for divine love and compassion. Thankfulness for God's playful creativity and soothing care is expressed in Barbauld's early poetry, where she reimagines God's act of creation:

> Earth's blooming face with rising flowers he drest,
> And spread a verdant mantle o'er her breast;

53

Then from the hollow of his hand he pours
The circling waters round her winding shores,
The new-born world in their cool arms embracing,
And with soft murmurs still her banks caressing.
At length she rose complete in finish'd pride,
All fair and spotless like a virgin bride;
Fresh with untarnish'd lustre as she stood
Her Maker blest his work, and call'd it good.
("Hymn I," in *Poems*, lines 25–34)

Her "Hymns I–V" were first included in William Enfield's collection *Hymns for Public Worship* (1772) before they were reprinted along with additional devotional verse in her single-authored collection *Poems* (1773). "Hymn I" alludes to the maternal, generative imagery of Gen. 1:2, in the original Hebrew (*Strong's Dictionary*, 518), as Barbauld contemplates the beginning of the world, when "struggling beams of infant light" (*Poems*, line 13) were hushed by the Holy Spirit, who "brooded o'er the kindling seeds of life" (line 16). Later she directly quotes Ps. 110:3 to craft a feminine, birthing simile for the creation of the stars: "Ten thousand glittering lamps the skies adorning, / Numerous as dew drops from the womb of morning" (lines 23–24). This generative imagery of God's creative power continues into the concluding poem of her collection, "A Summer's Evening Meditation," when Barbauld imagines a place in the universe beyond astronomical knowledge: "Where embryo systems and unkindled suns / Sleep in the womb" (lines 97–98). Barbauld's early poems also express a willingness to submit to the "gentle sway" ("To Wisdom," line 5) of the Holy Spirit and to accept the "strong compassion" ("Hymn III," line 18) of "Jesus, the friend of human kind" ("Hymn III," line 17). Throughout these early poems—even as she engages with difficult concepts, such as original sin, "the traitor in thy heart" ("Hymn V," line 16), and militant biblical metaphors, such as the "immortal shield" (line 18) and "armour from above" (line 19)—Barbauld maintains an emphasis on divine love. Her *Poems* went into four editions in 1773 alone, proof of their popularity. Barbauld's entry into the publishing world was largely facilitated by her familial connections. The dissenting publisher Joseph Johnson published her first collection of poetry. Johnson came to be known for his encouragement of women writers, and in the 1770s he was actively publishing writings arising out of the Warrington Academy, where Barbauld's father taught.

Barbauld's next significant publication, *Devotional Pieces Compiled from the Psalms and the Book of Job: To Which Are Prefixed Thoughts on the Devotional Taste, on Sects, and on Establishments* (1775), addresses questions of biblical interpretation more directly; she challenges the sometimes detached intellectualism of the dissenting Warrington Academy. In the prefatory essay on "Devotional Taste," Barbauld, as a poet, defines the biblical psalms as emotive, communal odes. She explains: "After all, it is not in reading alone these noble pieces that will give us their full force: they must be really used in acts of worship. It was not in so cold, so unaffecting a manner, that the Psalms of David were first exhibited. The living voice of the people, the animating accompaniments of music, . . . the exalting movements of pious joy, all conspired to raise, to touch, to subdue the heart" (52).

Barbauld dedicated *Devotional Pieces* to her father, John Aikin, a classicist and theologian at the dissenting Warrington Academy, and she published the book with Joseph Johnson, a radical bookseller known for fostering radical inquiry. However, despite her dissenting academic allegiances, Barbauld questions overly analytical approaches to Scripture that seek an Enlightenment disinterestedness detached from communal, emotional experiences of God. She argues that the psalms, in particular, can be fully appreciated only when they are used in living, corporate prayer and praise closer to their original context in the Israelite community. After her essay, she presents the reader with alternating passages from Psalms and the book of Job, grouped into three sections: "Moral Psalms"; "Psalms of Praise, Penitence, and Prayer"; and "Prophetic Psalms."

In her prefatory essay on "Devotional Taste," Barbauld critiques what she sees as the overuse of Enlightenment rationalism in dissenting biblical interpretation, which she believes can turn the reading of Scripture into a purely intellectual exercise devoid of reverent emotion. This critique led to her *Devotional Pieces* being largely dismissed within her community, and she turned next to the less threatening vehicle of children's literature. Her *Hymns in Prose for Children* (1781) was written for the youngest of the boys she taught at Palgrave School, an institution she established with her husband, Rochemont Barbauld (Aikin 26). Prominent themes of the hymns are the wonder of creation and the providential and maternal care of the Creator. In order to set up her maternal simile for God, Barbauld alludes to Christ's statement that he has longed to gather the children of Jerusalem together "as a hen doth gather her brood under her wings" (Luke 13:34). In her *Hymns in Prose*, Barbauld speaks of evening as a time when "the chickens are gathered under the wings of the hen and are at rest" (26) and "the child sleeps upon the breast of its mother" (29). She then moves on to assert that in the evening, just "as the mother moveth about the house with her finger on her lips, and stilleth every little noise, that her infant be not disturbed; as she draweth the curtains around its bed, and shutteth out the light from its tender eyes, so God draweth the curtains of darkness around us; so he maketh all things to be hushed and still, that his large family may sleep in peace" (32–33). Barbauld's *Hymns in Prose* also refers to the second coming of "Jesus, the Son of God, . . . the friend of the good" (88). Barbauld borrows imagery from Rev. 17:14 and then adds the concept of friendship in order to depict the return of Jesus Christ as a sublimely joyous rather than primarily terrifying event.

In the revolutionary period of the 1790s, Barbauld wrote literature of social consciousness and political protest and continued to draw on her biblical knowledge in doing so. Her "Epistle to William Wilberforce, Esq., on the Rejection of the Bill for Abolishing the Slave Trade" (1791) laments the distortion of biblical texts by those who were quoting Scripture in defense of slavery. The young radical female abolitionist Helen Maria William was spending time with Barbauld at this point, causing the conservative Horace Walpole to derisively compare Barbauld to Deborah and Williams to Jael, in the book of Judges (Walpole 11:320). For Barbauld, social justice and biblical interpretation are indeed linked; in her "Hymn: Ye are the salt of the earth" (1797), she draws on Matt. 5:13 to advocate active compassion for the poor and imprisoned. Committed to issues of social justice, Barbauld could still be conservative on the question of equal education for women. Her poem "The Rights of Women" (1792) rebuts Mary Wollstonecraft's more radical *Vindication of the Rights of Woman* (1792) by suggesting the relative unimportance of individual rights within the mutuality of marriage. When bluestocking Elizabeth Montagu invited Barbauld to start a girls' school with her, Barbauld quickly and firmly declined the invitation.

However, Lucy Aikin reports that her aunt Anna Barbauld

> was acquainted with almost all the principal female writers of her time; and there was not one of the number whom she failed frequently to mention in terms of admiration, esteem, or affection, whether in conversation, in letters to her friends, or in print. To the humbler aspirants in the career of letters, who often applied to her for advice or assistance, she was invariably courteous, and in many instances, essentially serviceable. . . . Children and young persons, especially females, were accordingly large sharers of her benevolence: she loved their society and would often invite them to pass weeks or months in her house, when she spared no pains to amuse and instruct them. (xxxiv)

One such young woman, Mary Anne Galton, spent a month at Barbauld's home in 1798, went on to marry and change her name to Mary Anne Schimmelpenninck, and then published prolifically in the fields of aesthetic theory and biblical commentary in the nineteenth century (Duquette 67–75). Another nineteenth-century woman writer influenced by Barbauld was Elizabeth Barrett Browning, who read and loved Barbauld's *Hymns in Prose for Children* from her youth (McCarthy 85). Despite Barbauld's resistance to starting a formal, institutionalized girls' school, she served as a strong female mentor for a new generation of women writing biblical interpretation, in both prose and verse, through the Romantic period and into the Victorian era.

See also Schimmelpenninck, Mary Anne (1778–1856); Wollstonecraft, Mary (1759–97)

Bibliography

Aikin, Lucy. "Memoir." Pages 13–50 in vol. 1 of *The Works of Anna Laetitia Barbauld: With a Memoir by Lucy Aikin*. London: Longman, 1825. New York: Carvill, Bliss & White, 1826.

Barbauld, Anna. *Devotional Pieces Compiled from the Psalms and the Book of Job: To Which Are Prefixed Thoughts on the Devotional Taste, on Sects, and on Establishments*. London: Joseph Johnson, 1775.

———. *Hymns in Prose for Children*. London: Joseph Johnson, 1781.

———. *Poems*. London: Joseph Johnson, 1773.

Duquette, Natasha. "Anna Barbauld and Mary Anne Schimmelpenninck on the Sublimity of Scripture." Pages 62–79 in *Sublimer Aspects: Interfaces between Literature, Aesthetics, and Theology*, edited by Natasha Duquette. Newcastle upon Tyne: Cambridge Scholars Pub., 2007.

McCarthy, William. "Mother of All Discourses: Anna Barbauld's Lessons for Children." Pages 85–112 in *Culturing the Child, 1690–1914: Essays in Memory of Mitzi Myers*, edited by Donelle Ruwe. Lanham, MD: Children's Literature Association and Scarecrow, 2005.

The New Strong's Complete Dictionary of Bible Words. Edited by John Kohlenberger. Vancouver: Thomas Nelson, 1996.

Walpole, Horace. *Horace Walpole's Correspondence*. Edited by W. S. Lewis and Warren Hunting Smith. 34 vols. New Haven: Yale University Press, 1939.

— Natasha Duquette

Bathurst, Elizabeth (fl. 1678–85)

Elizabeth Bathurst, eldest daughter of Charles Bathurst, joined the Religious Society of Friends (Quakers) in 1678. Her father's testimonial describes a young woman who had "great Weakness of Body" but "large Endowments of Mind" and devoted herself to studying Scripture from childhood. At some point after her conversion, Bathurst journeyed from London to Bristol to spread Quaker doctrine. Two well-known Friends—George Whitehead (1636–1723) and Charles Marshall (1637–98)—praised her effectiveness as a preacher on that journey and in London, where she was then imprisoned. Bathurst's first work—*Truth's Vindication* (1679)—defends Quaker principles successfully enough to have been reprinted in three editions in 1683. She also published *An Expostulatory appeal to the Professors of Christianity, Joyned in Community with Samuel Ansley* (1680) and *The Sayings of Women, which were spoken upon sundry Occasions, in several Places of the Scriptures, &c.* (1683). A posthumous collection—*Truth vindicated* (1691)—included, in addition to the above works, "An Introduction by way of Preface to the Ensuing Treatise," and two epistles, one addressed to non-Quakers, the other to those newly convinced. This commemorative volume may explain the assertion in Joseph Smith's *A Descriptive Catalogue of Friends' Books* (1867) that she died early in 1691. Her own testimony about the 1678 date of her convincement, combined with her father's claim that she converted "not above seven years before the Lord was pleased to take her to himself," suggests that she died in about 1685.

Although Bathurst claims that she intended *The Sayings of Women* to present passages about women prophets and disciples, she frames her digest with the assertion that "women receive an Office in the Truth as well as Men, and they have a Stewardship, and must give an Account of their Stewardship to their Lord, as well as the Men." Occasionally she points to the moral of her excerpts, as with the case of Huldah: "Now here, neither King nor Priest, despised a Woman's Speech."

In *Truth's Vindication*, Bathurst asserts that Quaker principles "are all consonant and agreeable to the Records of Scripture," but her position on Scripture's authority is not likely to have satisfied her critics. She approaches the Scriptures as "Declarations of Divine Things," but warns that "there is good Reason to distinguish between the written Words, the Writing or Letter, and the Living Word, which is the quickning Spirit." Because Jesus himself is the Word of God, she reasons that when, for example, Jeremiah says, "Hear the word of the LORD" (Jer. 7:2), he is asking the Hebrews to recognize the Word, not suggesting that the words that follow are *themselves* "the Word of the LORD." She rejects the idea that access to Scripture provides the only means to discover Jesus or to attain salvation, reading them instead as "the Records of so many Prophecies and Testimonies of his primitive Servants."

Bathurst demonstrates a broad control of scriptural proof texts and forestalls her critics with gestures such as "the word Original be not found in Scripture" or "I find not the word Sacrament in all the Scripture." She occasionally interrupts her explanations to exclaim, "But I know I will be expected I should prove this by Scripture," and then quotes chapter and verse. She tends to read Scripture metaphorically: "The one Baptism necessary to Salvation, I do believe is inward and spiritual, being that of the Holy Ghost"; Jesus's promise in John 14:18, "I will come to you," means "an inward Coming, see Verse 20, of the same Chapter: At that Day ye shall know that I am in my Father, and ye in me, and I in you, saith Christ"; when Adam was evicted from Eden, "Death came over his Soul, though he lived outwardly, yet did he die as to that inward Principle of Divine Life."

Representatively, Bathurst argues in "An Introduction" that Abel expressed a "living faith" through his offering because he "looked beyond the Firstlings of his own Flock, to Christ the First-born of God, who was to be made an Offering for Sin." Abel required no "Scripture-Revelation" of Christ, but acted "by the Manifestation of [God's] Spirit" in him, "flying on the Wing of Faith to Christ, the one Offering." Bathurst treats all scriptural sources with absolute evenhandedness because she believes that "True Religion is of great Antiquity" and available to all humans, past, present, and future, through the direct revelation of Christ within the individual heart.

Bibliography

Bathurst, Elizabeth. *Truth vindicated by the faithful testimony and writings of the innocent servant and hand-maid of the Lord.* London: T. Sowle, 1705. First printing, [London,] 1679. All citations here are from the 3rd ed., London: Mary Hinde, 1773. http://esr.earlham.edu/dqc/.

— MARGARET THICKSTUN

Baxter, Elizabeth (1837–1926)

Elizabeth (Foster) Baxter was the third daughter of eight children born to Thomas Nelson Foster (1799–1858), a Quaker manufacturer of agricultural fertilizers, and his second wife, Elizabeth Gibbs. Baxter was educated at home in Evesham, England, by a governess and then, at the age of eleven, was sent to a boarding school in Worcester for five years. She had a conversion experience as a teenager and associated herself with the evangelical wing of the Anglican church. As a young adult, Baxter worked among the poor, published a weekly commentary on the Sunday lections, and was in charge of the Mildmay home for deaconesses, where she designed the Mildmay bonnet and deaconess dress. In 1868 she married the Rev. Michael Paget Baxter (1834–1910), an unconventional end-times lecturer whose book *Louis Napoleon: The Infidel Antichrist* (1861) went through many editions. The Baxters spent the first fifteen years of marriage traveling throughout Britain, as Michael gave lectures about Christ's second coming and Elizabeth preached the gospel. The Baxters were involved in the evangelistic crusades that Dwight L. Moody (1837–99) and Ira D. Sankey (1840–1908) led in Britain. Elizabeth read and expounded Scripture to thousands of women. In February 1875 *The Yorkshire Post* reported on Baxter's meetings, describing her as a compelling and charismatic Bible expositor:

> Mrs. Baxter's Scripture readings every afternoon for ladies [in Leeds], which have been carried on in connection with St. James Mission, have had an extraordinary success. Had as many as 1,500 ladies listening to her with most rapt attention. Most of audience women of middle class. The portion of Scripture read and expounded by Mrs. Baxter was that found in the 33rd chapter of Exodus beginning at the 11th vs. with elegance and diction, precision of language, and earnestness of manner, [she] laid the grand lesson drawn from these works. (Wiseman 101)

Elizabeth Baxter was also involved in both the writing and business sides of her husband's newspaper and publishing house, *The Christian Herald*. In 1876 Baxter took her son and his caregiver to Europe, where she recovered from a work-related breakdown and again became involved in preaching, teaching, and evangelism. In 1882 she became interested in healing ministries, which led to the publication of a monthly paper and the establishment of the Bethshan home for divine healing. In 1886 Baxter established a missionary training home and several foreign missions. In 1894 she participated in a mission tour of the world.

Elizabeth Baxter was a prolific author, publishing some forty books and a great number of smaller booklets, tracts and brief appeals, expositions, and weekly Sunday school lessons. Her published works most often grew out of her teaching and preaching ministries. They include commentaries on Old and New Testament books, including *Proverbs* (1891), *Job* (1894), *Mark* (1896), *Revelation* (1896), and *Ezekiel* (1902), as well as thematic studies, including *The Women in the Word* (1897) and *The School of the Patriarchs* (1903). Baxter also published on such topics as the Anglican Book of Common Prayer (1871), the second coming (1893), and divine healing (1900).

Baxter was a popular noncredentialed interpreter of Scripture. She had no formal theological training, though she read widely and knew Greek very well. She made few references to scholars and theologians in her publications. She felt the opinions of all experts, as well as her own, needed to be examined carefully. In the preface to *Divine Healing*, Baxter sets out her grandmother's hermeneutical principle of testing opinions by using "much prayer and waiting upon the Holy Spirit for light, taking nothing from a fallible human being, but comparing Scripture with Scripture to see if these things really are so" (intro). In her comments on the Samaritan woman (John 4), she encourages women without formal theological training to use their spiritual experiences as interpretive guides. A female preacher need not become "a doctor of divinity"; instead, like the woman of Samaria, she should base her preaching on her experiences of Jesus, leaving "the knotty points which scholars wrangle over to others" (*Women*, 228).

Baxter did not focus her interpretive work particularly on issues related to women. However, like many female interpreters, Baxter had a particular interest in the Woman Question—what the Bible had to say about women's nature and place. Her personal stance on the Woman Question was complicated. On the one hand, Baxter herself was a public figure, a pioneer in women's ministries, called as God's prophet to teach, preach, and evangelize. On the other hand, she advocated for the ideology of separate spheres, stressing women's roles as helpmates, their spiritual superiority, and their propensity to sin. In her commentary on the book of Ezekiel, Baxter writes at length on the false female prophets. Like Calvin, she argues: "Women are more susceptible than men to spiritual influences, bad and good. 'Adam was first formed; then Eve; and Adam was not beguiled, but the woman being beguiled hath fallen into transgression' (1 Tim. 2:13, 14)" (*Ezekiel*, 129). She then countered this negative teaching, pointing out that "it was a woman who 'sat at the Lord's feet and heard His Word' (Luke x.39), and she alone, of all the disciples of Jesus, so understood His coming sufferings and death, that she could anoint Him for His burial (Mark xiv.1–9; John xii.1–8). The apostles could not understand the lesson of the cross (Luke ix:44, 45; xviii:34); it was reserved for a woman to anoint the great Sin-offering" (129–30). Baxter then defended the idea of "true prophetesses, co-existent with the true prophets of Jehovah," citing the examples of Miriam, Deborah, Hannah, Huldah, Mary the mother of Jesus, Anna, the daughters of Philip the evangelist, and the women who worked alongside Paul (130). True prophets, both male and female, Baxter avers, spoke not by human will, but by the power of the Holy Spirit (2 Pet. 1:21) to build up, encourage, and console (1 Cor. 14:3; *Ezekiel*, 131). Baxter believed that God honors the ministry of women, but cautions that women are "in greater danger than men whenever they are pushed forward . . . into publicity" (133). Baxter did not support the growing number of women taking up prominent positions "in the forefront of the battle in matters of social purity, sobriety, and benevolence" (135). Men, she argues, should take the lead: "Was it not a keen reproof to Barak that God must needs raise up Deborah to judge Israel (Jud. iv.1–16)? If men took the lead in all these things, women might and would stand at their side and help them, without running the risk of the special temptations into which positions of prominence may bring them" (135).

Baxter judged the female characters in Scripture on the basis of how they lived up to her own understanding of woman's nature and calling. She judged that Sarah, for example, "very frequently and very signally failed" as helpmeet to Abraham. Baxter held Sarah responsible for Abraham's bad decision to go down to Egypt during the famine, although the biblical text itself does not speak of Sarah's role in the decision-making process: "Sarah was at this juncture no real help to her husband. She failed in being a helpmeet. If she had had the confidence to remain in the land of Canaan, and had said, 'Our God, who has led us thus far, will never fail us in a time of famine,' Abraham might have been spared the failure and the disgrace with which he a witness for God, afterwards returned from the land of Egypt" (*Women*, 10). Similarly, Baxter viewed Abraham's request that Sarah hide the fact that they were married as a reversal of Eve's temptation by Adam and suggested that Sarah could have stopped the wife-sister ruse by reminding Abraham of God's great promises of blessing: "How she might have encouraged her husband's faith! But instead of looking at things with the eye of faith, Sarah comes down to earthly combinations, and falls into Abraham's plans to deceive Pharaoh; . . . they were made no blessing [in Egypt]" (11–12). Baxter also interprets Sarah's plan for having a child through Hagar as an incident in which "Sarah was no helpmeet to her husband. She acted selfishly and cruelly, because she considered herself rather than her God" (13). Baxter's negative assessment of Sarah conflicts with that of the writer of Hebrews (11:11), so she imagines that with time Sarah's "germ of faith" produced the kind of faithfulness that the New Testament writer extols: "All the great imperfections of her life had been forgiven and blotted out, and nothing was remembered against her" (9). Using the rhetoric of the pulpit, she admonishes readers to take courage from Sarah's character change: "Let us trust our God to show us our failure, shortcoming, and sin, in many of our household and family relations; let us trust Him to show us where we are wrong, to purify us, and work in us that life of faith which shall be to His glory, that sin may cease and the life of Christ be formed in us" (15).

Elizabeth Baxter was an Anglican who used her sense of call to prophetic ministry to justify her extensive teaching and preaching ministries. Her approach to interpreting Scripture was popular and devotional. Her extensive writings provide an important window into Victorian culture as she brings distinctive presuppositions shaped by her social setting to her reading of texts. Her views on the nature and role of women are especially important since they reveal the struggles of a woman living in a period of transition that allowed her both to embody traditional male roles (i.e., preaching, teaching, and interpreting Scripture) and to preach separate-spheres ideology that restricts the roles of women. Through her various public ministries and her publications, Baxter influenced a wide audience.

Bibliography

Baxter, Elizabeth. *Divine Healing*. London: Christian Herald, 1900.

———. *Ezekiel, Son of Man: His Life and Ministry*. London: Christian Herald, 1902.

———. *His Last Word: Readings in Revelation*. London: Christian Herald, 1896.

———. *Job*. London: Christian Herald, 1894.

———. *The Lord's Coming: A Few Hints to the Children of God*. London: Christian Herald, 1893.

———. *Portraits from Proverbs*. London: Christian Herald, 1891.

———. *The School of the Patriarchs*. London: Christian Herald, 1903.

———. *Teachings from St. Mark's Gospel*. London: Christian Herald, 1896.

———. *Thoughts for Worshippers: Suggestive Hints on the Book of Common Prayer*. London: J. Snow, 1871.

———. *The Women in the Word*. London: Christian Herald, 1897.

Wiseman, Nathaniel. *Elizabeth Baxter: Saint, Evangelist, Preacher*. London: Christian Herald, 1928.

— MARION ANN TAYLOR

■ Beatrice of Nazareth (ca. 1200–1268)

Beatrice of Nazareth, a Cistercian nun and author of *Seven Manners of Loving*, was born in Tirlemon in the Low Countries in about 1200 and died on August 29, 1268. She was placed with the beguines at Lieu (Léau/Zoutleeuw, Belgium) as a young girl, and from there she was later transferred to Bloemendaal, a Cistercian nunnery founded by her father. Eventually she was made prioress of the Cistercian house at Notre Dame de Nazareth (Belgium) and remained there the rest of her life.

Beatrice wrote about her own mystical and ascetical experiences, and some of her diaries were published as short texts on the spiritual life. Although her work did not circulate widely beyond the Low Countries, her work was important to the convents in that area. In particular, she is considered to be a major translator of the bridal mysticism of Bernard of Clairvaux to women's communities. After her death, the notes that she left were translated and edited by a Cistercian monk to form a hagiographic *Life* illuminating her work as a spiritual leader among women of the Cistercian order. Part of the significance of Beatrice's work is its use of the vernacular Old Flemish, and her work is among the oldest extant in that dialect.

Her early education provided her with a solid theological and scriptural basis and also showed that she had some unique talents with regard to learning. Her education included both the liberal arts and specialized training in manuscript copying. *The Life of Beatrice of Nazareth* reports that by age five she could recite the entire Psalter (1.19). Scripture continued to have a central place in Beatrice's life in the convent, where Scripture was read, recited, and prayed within the context of the daily offices and in her private prayers. Familiarity with Scripture and an interest in interpreting it appear as more than casual references in the *Life* and in the shape of the *Life*, as her hagiographer reports it. Scripture is identified in her *Life* as occupying first place in her spiritual life, as going in front of the faithful, directing her steps homeward, and dispelling error (2.84).

Beatrice also turned to Scripture to answer questions of both a concrete and an abstract nature. For instance, she asked Scripture for guidance in what to do in her daily life; she also sought out answers to more abstract theological questions, such as the nature of the human experience of God in mystical rapture. An example of this is when she drew on Scripture to come to an understanding of God's relationship to creation (2.84–86). Beatrice's writings also reveal that she looked to Scripture to provide rules for right living, presumably in addition to the Rule of Benedict that she and her sisters followed (2.86). Scripture was the basis for her fervent devotion. Scripture consoled her and kindled a fire of devotion in her. She also referred to Scripture as a weapon with which to attack vices and as a garden from which she could collect fruits (2.85, 103). As the *Life* reports: "She looked to her accustomed helper, and the Most High had hidden his face, not openly helping her in the fight, nor himself fighting for her, as he did yesterday through windows or through lattices. . . . Wisely she stored in the house of her heart whatever she could collect here and there from the Scriptures and the examples of the saints, in order to fight back" (2.135).

The *Life* reports that she received a special gift through divine grace that opened her mind to understanding Scripture (2.85–86). Her methods of understanding Scripture included the exegetical techniques of her time, involving multiple levels of meaning for the interpretation of Scripture, focusing, as the *Life* says, on the mystical meanings of Scripture: "From everything she used to read or hear, she carefully sought with her enlightened mind to draw the wheat from the chaff, that is, now the moral and now the mystical meaning from the hull of the letter" (2.85).

Beatrice interpreted the Scriptures in light of her own experiences. For instance, her life in the convent, with its community life, its opportunities for teaching the other sisters, and Beatrice's own sickness and frailty and experiences of penitential prayer—all form aspects of her probing of Scripture. Beatrice interpreted Scripture by using all her senses: in the *Life*, she tastes, loves, savors, and sees. Her interpretation of Scripture is further driven by her deepening mystical union with God. This union came about through contemplation and was aimed at wisdom, not knowledge. Her favorite topics in Scripture were the boyhood and infancy of Christ, the election of the gentiles, and the eternal predestination of the faithful. In the *Life* that was written about her, the Scriptures most often referred to are Matthew, Paul, and the Psalms, although there are some references to other books such as Job, Isaiah, and the other prophets. When she was not expounding Scripture to others, she was ruminating on what she read in Scripture in private (52.26).

As the 1993 Dutch translation of Beatrice's earlier Flemish work shows, her writings continue to be regarded as an important witness to a type of spirituality that was based on a synthesis of the Bernardine mystical interpretation of Scripture and bridal mysticism that was important in her own community and those associated with Cistercian reform.

Bibliography

Anonymous Cistercian monk. *The Life of Beatrice of Nazareth, 1200–1268.* Translated by Roger de Ganck and J. B. Hasbrouck. Kalamazoo, MI: Cistercian Pubs., 1991.

———. *Vita Beatricis.* Translated into Dutch as *Hoezeer heeft God mij bemind: Beatrijs van Nazareth (1200–1268).* Edited by H. W. J. Vekeman. Kampen: Kok, 1993.

Beatrice of Nazareth. *Seven menieren van minne.* Edited by L. Reypens and J. van Mierlo. Leuven: De Vlaamsche Boekenhalle, 1926.

Ganck, Roger de. *Beatrice of Nazareth in Her Context.* 2 vols. Kalamazoo, MI: Cistercian Pubs., 1991.

Lewis, G. J. *Bibliographie zur deutschen Frauenmystik des Mittelalters.* Berlin: E. Schmidt, 1989.

— ANDREA J. DICKENS

Beaufort, Margaret (1443–1509)

Pious widow, powerful matriarch, woman of letters, sinister political operative, and generous patroness of education—Lady Margaret Beaufort's legacy has ebbed and flowed with the tides of history. Margaret Beaufort was the only daughter of John Beaufort, and was the great-granddaughter of John of Gaunt, the duke of Lancaster and son of Edward III. Yet the Beaufort family's position in the order of succession remained uncertain, for they comprised an illegitimate branch. Dynastically a Lancastrian, and at one time a potential heiress to the throne, Beaufort spent much of her life weathering the turmoil of the War of the Roses. She suffered similar turmoil in her private life, being left fatherless as an infant and a pregnant widow by the age of thirteen. As mother to Henry Tudor, her sole child, Beaufort played a significant role in finally uniting the warring Houses of Lancaster and York: her son's coronation as Henry VII and marriage to Elizabeth of York established the Tudor line.

Her role as the king's mother granted her not only power and respect, but also an independence rarely enjoyed by late-medieval women. Declared a *femme sole*, an unprecedented status for a monarch's mother that granted her legal autonomy and the right to hold property, Beaufort directed her energies toward, among other endeavors, the academic study of Scripture. She served as patroness to numerous clergy, academics, and fraternities; she founded chantries, university colleges, and professorships; she oversaw the production of devotional books and actively worked to promote the cult of the Holy Name of Jesus. By supporting academic work and making scholarly books accessible, such patronage allowed her to participate indirectly in theological study and interpretation. Moreover, Beaufort made use of the recent invention of the printing press to publish her own translations of theological works. While these works are not Beaufort's own interpretations of Scripture, her choice of what to translate and her decision to publish her translations under her own name, rather than anonymously or under a male pseudonym, are both in themselves interpretive actions. What is remarkable about Beaufort's translations is that rather than preparing them for private use, she chose to make them public and available to a wide readership. At a time when writing and publishing were avenues closed to most women, Beaufort's name and role as the king's mother appeared clearly at the beginning of both works, advertising not only her skill as a translator, but also her status as the "excellent princess" (*Mirror*, sig. A2r).

Her first and most famous translation was book 4 of *The Imitation of Christ*, by the monk and priest Thomas à Kempis (d. 1471), which she completed despite knowing little Latin by working from a French translation. Beaufort's decision to translate this book, which is a meditation on and exhortation to the taking of communion, reflects her own devotion to the Eucharist. Beaufort's translation was published in 1504, together with the translation of the first three books of the *Imitation*, which she had commissioned from Cambridge scholar William Atkinson. Unlike Atkinson, Beaufort takes little license with her translation, except possibly in one place, where à Kempis's "Proni enim sunt sensus *hominis* ad malum ab adolescencia sua" becomes, in Beaufort's rendering, "For the wit of man *and woman* from their childhood be inclined unto all evil" (265, emphasis added). Because of both her own devotion to Christ and her own experience of being a teenage mother to a son who would hold the divine right of kingship, the translation of lines such as "I desire to receive thee with such affection, reverence, praising, honour, worthiness, and love, and such faith, hope and purity as thy right holy mother and glorious virgin Mary conceived thee, when she answered meekly and devoutly unto the angel that showed unto her the holy mystery of the incarnation of thee, the son of God" (281) must have held particular significance for Beaufort.

Beaufort's other translation was of the *Mirror of Gold for the Sinful Soul*, a treatise on spiritual discipline by the Carthusian Jacobus de Gruitroede (d. 1475), which she ordered published in 1506. The book, which incorporates scriptural, patristic, and philosophical writings, is divided into seven chapters, one for each day of the week, "to the intent that the sinful soul soiled and defouled by sin may in every chapter have a new mirror wherein he may behold and consider the face of his soul" (sig. A2v). What is striking about the treatise, particularly in light of Beaufort's decision to translate it, is its denigration of the female body: "Certainly thou hast been from thy beginning a thing vile, stinking, detestable and abominable conceived in filthy rottenness of flesh and stinking filthy concupiscence: and in the embracement of stinking lechery . . . conceived in the unclean spot of sin" (sig. A4r). "Lechery" is the only sin to receive its own section, where abuses against Dinah, the Levite woman, Tamar, and Rizpah are all cited as examples. The purpose of the treatise is to convict readers of their sin, encourage them to repentance and penance, and prepare them for death and judgment, heaven or hell.

Beaufort commissioned the printing of many other books, both devotional and secular, working closely with the printers Thomas Caxton, Wynkyn de Worde, and Richard Pynson. Her account books indicate that she took a role in distributing printed devotional works throughout her own households. In his sermon "A Morning Remembrance," preached one month after Beaufort's death, John Fisher, Beaufort's confessor and spiritual guide, made clear that Beaufort's scholarly projects and patronages extended from her own deep faith. He compared Beaufort's nobility, self-discipline, piety, and hospitality to Martha in John's Gospel, a model for active and devout female agency. Although recent scholarship has tempered Fisher's hagiographical portrait, Beaufort was long known for her piety, "the diligent order of her soul to God" (sig. 4r). This included her personal devotions: Fisher records that she would rise at five in the morning to pray, hear four or five Masses, and visit three altars daily. Her piety was more publicly demonstrated by her patronage of theological education, for "she was as a mother," Fisher writes, to "students of both the universities" (sig. 7r). Finally, perhaps as part of her own spiritual discipline, and "for the profit of others she did translate divers matters of devotion out of French into English" (sig. 2r). In these translations, Beaufort "facilitate[d] the circulation of devotional material from the enclosed orders into the wider world" (Powell 225). Beaufort stands as an early example of a woman who promptly recognized the advantageous possibilities of the new technology of print, harnessing its capacity to disseminate throughout England newly translated Continental devotional material.

Bibliography

Beaufort, Lady Margaret. "*De imitatione Christi*, Book IV." Pages 259–83 in *Middle English Translations of De imitatione Christi*, edited by John K. Ingram. London: Early English Text Society, 1893.

———. *Mirroure of golde for the synfull soule*. London: Richard Pynson, 1506.

Collinson, Patrick, Richard Rex, and Graham Stanton. *Lady Margaret Beaufort and Her Professors of Divinity at Cambridge, 1502–1649*. Cambridge: Cambridge University Press, 2003.

Fisher, John. *Here after foloweth a mornynge remembraunce had at the moneth mynde of the noble prynces Margaret countesse of Rychmonde et Darbye*. London: Wynkyn de Worde, 1509.

Hogrefe, Pearl. *Women of Action in Tudor England: Nine Biographical Sketches*. Ames: Iowa State University Press, 1977.

Jones, Michael K., and Malcolm G. Underwood. *The King's Mother: Lady Margaret Beaufort, Countess of Richmond and Derby*. Cambridge: Cambridge University Press, 1992.

Powell, Susan. "Lady Margaret Beaufort and Her Books." *The Library*, 6th ser., 20, no. 3 (Sept. 1998): 197–240.

Simon, Linda. *Of Virtue Rare: Margaret Beaufort, Matriarch of the House of Tudor*. Boston: Houghton Mifflin, 1982.

— Meredith Donaldson Clark

Besant, Annie Wood (1847–1933)

Annie Besant was raised in the Church of England, became a freethinker, then an adherent of socialism, and finally a convert to Theosophism. She lived in England for the first half of her life, and then moved to India. In England she was widely known as an exceptional orator and a prolific writer; with Charles Bradlaugh, she founded the Freethought Publishing Company. Her personal life involved much hardship. She married an Anglican clergyman and quickly gave birth to a son and daughter. She began to have serious doubts about her faith, questioning the goodness of God and the divinity of Jesus, and felt she could no longer take communion. Her husband gave her the ultimatum to take communion or leave; she chose to leave. She and her husband separated, and she was granted custody of her daughter, but not her son. Her speaking and writing skills, as well as her venture into editing and publishing, sustained her and her daughter. However, when she and Bradlaugh decided to reprint a book on birth control, they were charged with obscenity. Although the charges were ultimately dropped, her husband used the incident to claim that she was an unfit mother, and she lost custody of their daughter. Annie Besant personally experienced the application of England's laws on marriage and divorce, as well as laws regulating a wife's earnings and women's rights in the legal system. In her speaking and writing, she protested against their injustice.

Besant wrote extensively on many topics, but her writings focusing on the interpretation of Scripture include only two brief pamphlets, *Woman's Position according to the Bible* (1885) and *God's Views on Marriage* (1890), both published by the Freethought Publishing Company. In both pamphlets, Besant argues that the Bible is not inspired and that the injustices experienced by women in the patriarchal society of Victorian England are due to Scripture and the Christian faith. She agrees with the views promoted by Bradlaugh in *The Bible: What It Is* (1870). She quotes from this work and accepts Bradlaugh's position that the Bible promotes questionable morality, reflects primitive science, presents a God whose character is despicable, and contains many errors and inconsistencies. They both measured the Bible by using the standards of nineteenth-century history, science, and morality, and they found it wanting.

The first pamphlet, *Woman's Position according to the Bible*, engages the position prevalent in this age of discovery that the role and status of women were much better in Christian lands than in heathen lands. Besant begins by making an important distinction not usually noticed in the nineteenth century: she claims that the comparison must consider class as well as gender. Rather than compare the life of an English aristocrat to an Australian savage, she suggests that the comparison be made between that of an Indian squaw and a married factory hand, "who toils all day at the factory, and returns home at night to clean the house, wash, mend and make the children's clothes, cook the supper, etc." (1).

Besant claims that civilization—by which she means the triumph of justice, not religion—is the reason for women's improved status. She does recognize some progression within Scripture, but not enough to rid women of the oppression of patriarchy. For example, she documents the development in marriage customs from women being captured as spoils of war, to women being purchased, both of which involve polygyny. In the New Testament, marriage becomes monogamous, but it is monogamy in servitude. The Bible stops short of monogamy with equality since it retains women's submission to men in marriage. Besant exposes the injustices in the marriage laws in England and traces their roots to the inequality and double standard found in Scripture. She concludes that justice in marriage will be achieved when women and men throw off the chains of the Christian religion and embrace the liberation found in Freethought.

The second essay, *God's Views on Marriage*, was published five years later and expounds the same themes. It is dedicated to the bishop of Manchester, James Fraser (1818–85), and is ostensibly a rebuttal to his attack on secularism. However, the bishop had died five years earlier, so it is difficult to explain the urgency and shrill tone of the pamphlet. The issue at hand is the bishop's claim that secularists teach that "a man might live tally with a woman [in companionate/common-law marriage], and send her away if she became sick or otherwise unpleasant" (3). Besant surveys the marriages recorded in Genesis, studies the marriage laws in the Pentateuch, and finds much to bolster her thesis that Christianity, not secularism, should be of concern to the bishop. She observes that Abraham and Sarah committed incest since Sarah was his sister (Gen. 20:12), that Abraham sent Hagar away when he was finished with her (21:8–14), that the laws allowed a father to sell his daughter into concubinage (Exod. 21:7–11), that women were acquired as spoils of war (Deut. 21:10–14), and that it was very easy for a man to divorce his wife (24:1). She contrasts the low moral standards promoted by Scripture with the enlightened views of secularists that marriage should be the lifelong union of equals based on love and respect, that divorce could be initiated by either partner, and that the grounds for divorce would be the same for each spouse.

In both pamphlets Besant advocates that those who support equality between women and men need to leave the Bible and the Christian faith. She does not treat the Bible as complex or ambiguous. She did not find that its message was sometimes liberating and sometimes oppressive. For Besant, the Bible is shot through with patriarchy, and there is no point in trying to tease out a message that would empower women. For this reason, she calls for an exodus from the Bible and Christianity.

Bibliography

Besant, Annie. *Autobiographical Sketches.* London: Freethought Pub., 1885.

———. *God's Views on Marriage.* London: Freethought Pub., 1890.

———. *Woman's Position according to the Bible.* London: Freethought Pub., 1885.

Bradlaugh, Charles. *The Bible: What It Is.* London: Austin, 1870.

de Groot, Christiana. "Annie Besant: An Adversarial Interpreter of Scripture." Pages 201–15 in *Recovering Nineteenth-Century Women Interpreters of the Bible*, edited by Christiana de Groot and Marion Taylor. Atlanta: Society of Biblical Literature, 2007.

Nethercot, Arthur. *The First Five Lives of Annie Besant.* Chicago: University of Chicago Press, 1960.

———. *The Last Four Lives of Annie Besant.* Chicago: University of Chicago Press, 1964.

Taylor, Anne. *Annie Besant: A Biography.* Oxford: Oxford University Press, 1992.

— CHRISTIANA DE GROOT

Beutler, Magdalena (1407–58)

Magdalena Beutler was born in 1407 to a wealthy family in Kenzingen, Germany. Her father died when she was four. His widow, Margareta, gave away her fortune and devoted herself to a life of radical asceticism and reform, eventually becoming a well-known mystic in Basel. Beutler, who at the age of five had begun to have visions and suffered from catalepsy, was placed in the care of the Clarissan Sisters in nearby Freiburg.

Like her mother, Beutler devoted herself to vigils and fasting, but at the age of twenty-two she mysteriously "disappeared" from her cloister for three days. On the third day, she was found lying before the altar, apparently unconscious. On recovering from her ordeal, she explained that God had shown her a vision of what would be the fate of those who refused to accept a life of voluntary poverty. Moved by her account, the sisters in the convent gave up material possessions and agreed to hold all goods in common. Having succeeded in the monetary reform of her cloister, Beutler continued to influence the sisters spiritually through her visions.

Her vita, composed by a confessor or possibly by Clarissan sister Elisabeth Vogtin, is extant in five complete and fragmentary versions. It relates Beutler's homilies for sisters in the cloister on topics such as "How the Body of Our Lord Pays for All Our Sins" or "How [the Sisters] Should Pray Devoutly." The homilies convey Beutler's insights informed by her mystical visions.

Although it is not known who recorded her homilies, it appears that Beutler herself composed a 337-page meditation on the Lord's Prayer ("Erklärung des Vaterunsers"), a work of improvisations on the text of the Lord's Prayer by using a kind of rhythmic free association of meditations, petitions, epithets, and praises of God the Father and Christ. The work contains three sets of over one hundred variations on the Lord's Prayer, as well as other Paternoster meditations in praise of the Trinity, on the wounds of Christ, and "for penitence," composed in order that those who repeat them might be forgiven of sins (Greenspan 105–298). Beutler's "Interpretation of the Lord's Prayer," forms a stream-of-consciousness devotional monologue, consisting of repetitive, affective responses to the Lord's Prayer. She repeatedly stresses the warm filial praise and love of God and Christ, incorporating lists of divine attributes and allusions to or quotes from the Bible that are interspersed with ecstatic comments. Intertwining her own voice with that of God or Christ, she recalls Jesus's suffering during his passion. Rather than detailing the brutality of the scene, however, she recalls it most often with gratitude and a kind of eucharistic devotion focused on the theme of healing. Beutler's writing offers a window on the kinds of texts that women could still produce under the eyes of censors.

Beutler's vita was composed in the vernacular and continued to circulate in German-speaking regions of the Middle and Upper Rhine as late as the seventeenth century.

Her meditation on the Lord's Prayer survives in only two manuscripts, but Karen Greenspan has identified a similar one, "Die Guldene Litanei" ("The Golden Litany"), also attributed to Beutler, that is extant in over forty manuscripts and eleven printed copies (2n3).

Throughout the High and late Middle Ages, women had been prohibited from publicly preaching or expressing theological views, yet some women, like Beutler, continued to write their revelations and visions. While these writings lent authority by marking a person as chosen by God to receive his special grace and recognition, they were also dangerous, since this kind of direct line to God bypassed the church's hierarchy. Accordingly, church councils of the fifteenth century prohibited them.

The interesting thing about Beutler's case is the way that she, by employing her revelatory writing in the service of the Observant reform, was still able to use her visions to acquire influence and the right to speak with authority. Although rejected by the leaders of the reform movement, Beutler was revered as a mystic in her own convent, and her vita, along with the writings attributed to her, were copied and circulated.

Unlike women who wrote on the Bible in the sixteenth century, Beutler was clearly aware of the writings of her foremothers, such as the earlier mystics Hildegard of Bingen and one of the Mechthilds of Helfta, whose excerpted works circulated in anthologies of devotional texts that were read in cloisters throughout Germany and the Low Countries. It was after such women that Beutler patterned herself. Her devotional meditations thus form a bridge between the texts of visionary female writers of earlier centuries and the doctrinal tracts produced by women in the sixteenth century, although they remain within the conventions of medieval mystical writing.

See also Hildegard of Bingen (1098–1179); Mechthild of Hackeborn (von Hackeborn) (1240–98); Mechthild of Magdeburg (von Magdeburg) (ca. 1208–ca. 1282/94)

Bibliography

Backes, Martina. "Zur literarischen Genese frauenmystischer Viten und Visionstexte am Beispiel des Freiburger 'Magdalenenbuches.'" Pages 251–60 in *Literarische Kommunikation und soziale Interaktion: Studien zur Institutionalität mittelalterlicher Literatur*, edited by Beate Keller et al. Bern: Peter Lang, 2001.

Dinzelbacher, Peter, and Kurt Ruh. "Magdalena von Freiburg." Columns 1117–21 in vol. 5 of *Die deutsche Literatur des Mittelalters: Verfasserlexikon*, edited by Kurt Ruh et al. 2nd ed. Berlin: de Gruyter, 1985.

Greenspan, Karen. "Erklärung des Vaterunsers: A Critical Edition of a Fifteenth-Century Mystical Treatise by Magdalena Beutler of Freiburg." PhD Diss., University of Massachusetts, 1984.

Schleussner, Wilhelm. "Magdalena von Freiburg: Eine pseudomystische Erscheinung des späteren Mittelalters, 1407–1458." *Der Katholik* 87 (1907): 15–32, 109–27, 199–216.

Winston-Allen, Anne. *Convent Chronicles: Women Writing about Women and Reform in the Late Middle Ages*. University Park: Pennsylvania State University Press, 2004.

— ANNE WINSTON-ALLEN

Biddle, Hester (1629/30–97)

According to brief references in her own writings, Hester (sometimes Ester or Esther) Biddle spent her childhood in Oxford, England, and was raised a

Protestant. In her late teens, when still a committed Protestant, she moved to London, but a crisis of faith followed the execution of Charles I in 1649. Having heard the preaching of Edward Burrough and Francis Howgill, she became convinced that Quakers understood God's will, and by May 24, 1655, when she published her two broadsides, "Wo to thee City of Oxford" and "Wo to thee Town of Cambridge," she was explicitly identifying as a Friend. Quaker archives record her ministry in the 1650s in Newfoundland, the Netherlands, Barbados, and Alexandria. Two longer analytical writings then followed: A Warning from the Lord God of Life and Power unto Thee O City of London (1660), and The Trumpet of the Lord Sounded forth unto These Three Nations (1662). During this same period she married Thomas Biddle, a shoemaker (d. 1682), and gave birth to four sons (three of them born 1660, 1663, 1668; only the death date of the other, in 1666, is known). There are no further extant publications after 1662, but state records show that in 1694 she obtained a license from Mary II to go to France for an audience with Louis XIV.

From the appearance of her first 1655 broadsides, it is clear that Biddle had engaged closely with the Scriptures, and that, modeling herself on Old Testament prophets, especially Ezekiel, and drawing widely on New Testament books, she believed that she had a duty to explain the Bible's true meaning. In her last published pamphlet, she explains of herself and fellow believers: "We are not like the World, who must have a Priest to Interpret the Scriptures to them, and when he is removed, they are scattered and knows not what to do; but my friends, we witness the Scriptures fulfil'd, who hath said in the latter days, He would pour out of his Spirit upon Sons and Daughters and they should Prophesie [Acts 2:17]."

Central to her interpretation is a conviction that social and economic inequality must end. In "Wo to thee City of Oxford" and in the near-identical "Wo to thee Town of Cambridge," for instance, she echoes Ezekiel (esp. chaps. 16 and 22) as she threatens the two university towns with destruction by fire if they do not abandon their exploitative practices and realize that instead of enclosing common land and demanding tithes, they should feed the poor. In The Trumpet she again reproaches the "high and lofty ones! who spendeth God's Creation upon your lusts," asking them, "Did not the Lord make all men and women upon the earth of one mould?" and calling them to "cloath the naked, and feed the hungry, and set the oppressed free" (12). "The Lord is no respecter of persons," she adds (22).

It is also evident that Biddle, like many Quakers of this period, sought to develop a much more positive understanding of God's plan for womankind than that traditionally preached. In her writings, allusions to the Whore of Babylon, who "sitteth as a Queen" (cf. Rev. 18:7; Trumpet, 6), are used to criticize the powerful—mostly men. Isaiah's condemnation of the daughters of Zion for their haughtiness (3:16–26) is embroidered upon, so that the faces "decked with black spots" are clearly evocative of the fashions of wealthy Restoration Londoners (*Warning*, 11), rather than seeming to refer to women in general. By contrast, whenever she alludes to God's promises to his people, the phrase "sons and daughters" appears, including when making use of passages that in the Bible refer only to "sons." Preferring the first creation story (Gen. 1:26–27) to the second, she reflects that God "created *Adam* in innocency, and *Eve* of the Dust of the Earth" (*Trumpet*, 20).

Just how consciously developed her perspective was, and something of her live preaching voice, is demonstrated in the account that survives of her confrontation in court with Alderman Richard Brown in 1662. She had been arrested for preaching before a meeting of two hundred to three hundred people. Challenged by the court that "*They never heard of a woman to speak before,*" she marshaled her evidence:

> She asked them, if they had not read the scriptures, she told them, *Phoebe was a Prophetesse* [Rom. 16:1] and *Philip had four Daughters that prophesied* [Acts 21:9], and *Paul* wrote to his Brethren that they should take care of *the women that were fellow labourers with him in the Gospel* [Phil. 4:3]. The Judge said, That was a great while agoe; she told him, It was when the Church was in her Beauty and Glory, but since darknesse had covered the Earth, and grosse darknesse hath vailed the Kings and Rulers, so that it is become a strange thing to the Apostates *to hear of a Daughter to prophesie*. (Society of Friends 1662)

Although Biddle's writings and those of her fellow Quaker women preachers indeed became engulfed by the "grosse darknesse" that is lamented here, copies of all these pamphlets and broadsides survive, most being held in London in the British Library and Friends' Library, and in the United States at the Folger Shakespeare Library. Further study could lead to a radical revision of some present-day assumptions about the range and depth of women's work as interpreters of the Bible.

Bibliography

Biddle, Hester. *Oh! Wo, Wo from the Lord God of Heaven and Earth, Be unto ye Inhabitants of the Town of Dartmouth*. London: For Thomas Simmons, 1659.

———. *The Trumpet of the Lord Sounded forth unto These Three Nations*. London: n.p., 1662.

———. *A Warning from the Lord God of Life and Power unto Thee O City of London*. London: Robert Wilson, 1660.

———. "Wo to thee City of Oxford." [London?]: n.p., [1655?].

———. "Wo to thee Town of Cambridge." [London?]: n.p., [1660–69?].

Hobby, Elaine, and Catie Gill. "Biddle, Hester (1629/30–1697), Quaker Minister and Writer." Pages 668–69 in vol. 5 of *Oxford Dictionary of National Biography*, edited by H. C. G. Matthew and Brian Harrison. Rev. ed. Oxford: Oxford University Press, 2004–11.

[Society of Friends]. *The Third Part of the Cry of the Innocent for Justice*. London: n.p., 1662.

— ELAINE HOBBY

Birgitta of Sweden (1302/3–73)

Saint Birgitta of Sweden (Birgitta Birgersdotter) was born in 1302/3 in Finsta, Sweden. She married Ulf Gudmarsson in 1316, and the couple had eight children. Ulf died in about 1344, and Birgitta experienced her first revelation shortly afterward. From 1344 to 1349, Birgitta lived in Alvastar, Sweden, and during this time she received a number of revelations. These were recorded with the help of her confessor, Master Mathias Ovidi. From 1350 until her death in 1373, Birgitta lived in Rome. While in Rome, Birgitta continued to receive revelations, worked to establish her order (the Birgittine Order), and petitioned the papacy to return to Rome from Avignon. Birgitta was canonized in 1391.

Birgitta's revelations were primarily auditory and were dictated to various confessors; these were recorded in Latin and collected in eight books. Birgitta's revelations called people—individuals as well as civic and clerical authorities—to repentance; thus Birgitta's role resembled that of the Old Testament prophets (Hidal 90). Piltz (181) also reports that Birgitta was called the "channel of Christ."

Birgitta's revelations were filled with allusions to Scripture, and these allusions took multiple forms. When admonishing or encouraging, Birgitta frequently compared and referred her contemporaries to such scriptural figures as Haman (1.17), Peter and Paul (2.7), Elijah (3.1), the Centurion (3.26), and Jonah (3.33). Birgitta also used literary forms found in Scripture, such as prophetic language and parables. A vivid example of prophetic language is found in the prologue to book I, which decrees judgment on the proud noblemen of Sweden, using language that echoes such prophetic indictments as Isa. 56:9; Jer. 5:17; 15:3; and Ezek. 39:4: "Those bodies of which they are so proud will be struck down by the sword, lance, and hatchet. Beasts and birds will tear to pieces those lovely limbs in which they glory. Others will carry away the riches they gather against my will, and they themselves will be in want."

Parables written by Birgitta include "Judges, Defenders and Laborers" (1.55), "Savaged Sheep and Negligent Shepherd" (1.59), "A Beekeeper" (2.19), and "A Prudent Canon" (3.4). This use of literary forms shows that Birgitta's understanding of Scripture went beyond recitation.

Birgitta also employed symbolic readings of Scripture, using allegory and typology, to apply the biblical text to her contemporary situation, and in contemplation of Christ and Mary. When using allegory to shed light on her present context, Birgitta's aim was often to illuminate sin and idolatry, as when Christians were compared to the Israelites' fashioning the golden calf (1.48;

Exod. 32). When allegory and typology are used devotionally, the aim is to create a deeper understanding of Christ and Mary and to show their prefiguration in Scripture. For example, Mary is compared to the ark of the covenant, and its contents (the staff, manna, and tablets of the law) are compared to Christ (1.53). A reading of Solomon as a prefiguration of Christ demonstrates that deeper knowledge of Christ and admonition against sin are not separate, but connected themes (2.5). Solomon and his wisdom represent Christ, whereas the Queen of Sheba represents the pagans, who will receive Christ's gifts due to the ingratitude of Christians:

> I [Jesus] am prefigured by Solomon, although I am far richer and wiser than Solomon was, inasmuch as all wisdom comes from me and anyone who is wise gets his wisdom from me. . . . I promised and offered these goods to Christians as to my own children, in order that they might possess them forever, if they imitate me and believe in my words. But they pay no attention to my wisdom. . . . Surely, if the sons do not want their inheritance, then strangers, that is, pagans, will receive it.

Finally, Birgitta had visions of scriptural events, especially the nativity (Harris 7.21–24) and the passion (7.15; see also 1.10). Their visual nature distinguishes them from her auditory revelations. The visions interpret Christ's birth and death through the lens of a fourteenth-century understanding of these events, focusing on Mary's virginity and her lack of pain in childbirth, and on the gruesome nature of Christ's crucifixion. Mary's lack of pain in childbirth may suggest a devaluation of the body, but writings such as Birgitta's third and fourth prayers highlight the importance of the body in her devotion to both Christ and Mary.

Birgitta's writings were preserved primarily by her order, the first printed edition appearing in 1492. During the Reformation the order became almost extinct, but today three branches of the Birgittine Order exist, including two reformed branches established in the seventeenth and twentieth centuries. Birgittine houses are located primarily in Europe, but can also be found in the United States, Mexico, and India. These orders preserve Birgitta's legacy of active mysticism, focusing both on apostolic ministry and ascetic devotion. Birgitta has experienced a renaissance of wider interest in the twentieth and twenty-first centuries, with extensive scholarship produced on her life and writings.

Bibliography

Birgitta of Sweden. *The Revelations of St. Birgitta of Sweden*. Vol. 1, *Liber caelestis, Books I–III*. Vol. 2, *Liber caelestis, Books IV–V*. Translated by Denis Searby. New York: Oxford University Press, 2006–8. Vols. 3–4, projected.

Harris, Marguerite Tjader, ed. *Birgitta of Sweden: Life and Selected Revelations*. Translated by Albert Ryle Kezel. Mahwah, NJ: Paulist Press, 1990.

Hidal, Sten. "'Jag är den Gud som gav lagen åt Mose': Birgitta och Gamla tesamentet." Pages 89–98 in *Heliga Birgitta—budskapet och förebilden: Föredrag vid jubileumssymposiet i Vadstena 3–7 oktober 1991*, edited by Alf Härdelin and Mereth Lindgren. Kungliga Vitterhets, historie och antikvitets akademien: Konferenser 28. Stockholm: Almqvist & Wiksell, 1993.

Klockars, Birgit. *Birgitta och böckerna: En undersökning av den heliga Birgittas källor.* Kungliga Vitterhets, historie och antikvitets akademien: Historiske serien 11. Stockholm: Almqvist & Wiksell, 1966.

Morris, Bridget. *St. Birgitta of Sweden.* Woodbridge, UK: Boydell, 1999.

Piltz, Anders. "Revelation and the Human Agent: St. Birgitta and the Process of Inspiration." Pages 181–88 in *Tongues and Texts Unlimited: Studies in Honour of Tore Janson on the Occasion of His Sixtieth Anniversary*, edited by Hans Aili and Peter af Trampe. Stockholm: Stockholms Universitet, Institutionen för klassiska språk, 2000.

— MARI JØRSTAD

Bjarnhjedinsdottir, Briet (1856–1940)

Briet Bjarnhjedinsdottir, a leader of the Icelandic suffrage movement and spokesperson for women's rights, was born into a poor family in the northern part of Iceland. Like most Icelanders, her family belonged to the Evangelical Lutheran Church and followed the custom of rural Icelanders of reading pietistic literature in the evening. Her knowledge of the Christian faith and the Scriptures was undoubtedly based on those readings, as well as her reading of a catechism (most likely based on Luther's *Small Catechism*) in preparation for her confirmation. Though her formal education was limited, she was able to support herself as a young adult by teaching children in their homes. Her experience of being paid only half the amount that men were paid for the same job made her aware of the need to address publicly the issue of gender inequality. Bjarnhjedinsdottir went on to pursue further education, studying English and Danish, which allowed her to become involved in women's international movements. In 1888, Bjarnhjedinsdottir married Valdimar Ásmundsson (1852–1902), who was the editor of one of Iceland's few journals, an important social critic of his time, and a genuine supporter of women's rights. When he died at the age of fifty, Bjarnhjedinsdottir became a single mother of two young children and the family's sole breadwinner.

As a writer, public speaker, and political advocate, Bjarnhjedinsdottir promoted women's rights and education. In 1885 her article on women's rights and education won her recognition as the first woman to have an article published in an Icelandic journal. In December 1887 Bjarnhjedinsdottir became the first woman to give a public lecture in Reykjavík, Iceland's capital, speaking to a packed audience on the same subject. Her lecture was published in a monograph a few months later. Bjarnhjedinsdottir founded *Women's Magazine* in 1895 and was its editor and main contributor until 1919. After attending a congress of the International Women's Suffrage Alliance in Copenhagen in

1906, she initiated the foundation of the Icelandic Women's Rights Association in 1907 and chaired the association for twenty years. In 1907 Icelandic women were granted universal municipal suffrage and eligibility. Together with three other women, Bjarnhjedinsdottir became a member of the Reykjavík city council, elected on a nonparty women's list supported by all of the women's organizations of the town. She continued her work in politics as a member of the town council from 1908 to 1911, and again from 1913 to 1919.

Like many other women who fought for women's rights, Bjarnhjedinsdottir recognized that the Bible had played an important role in preventing women from gaining full equality with men. In her public lecture of 1887, Bjarnhjedinsdottir called particular attention to the history of interpreting the story of woman's creation in Gen. 2, to misogynist Old Testament laws and narratives, and to some of the teachings of the apostle Paul. She observed how the account of woman's creation out of the man's rib had been used to argue for women's subordination, claiming it was God's intention that woman, being created out of man's rib, be subordinate to man. She judged that those who "blame it on God" had simply used the Bible to "trash human goodness and sense of justice" (*Fyrirlestur um hagi og rjettindi kvenna*, 334).

Furthermore, Bjarnhjedinsdottir drew attention to misogyny in many Old Testament texts, such as the rules regarding women's cultic purity in Leviticus, and the lack of women's rights in the ancient Hebrew world. Specifically, she cited the account of the daughters of Zelophehad (Num. 27), who were initially denied their inheritance because of their gender, and various accounts in Judges that featured husbands and fathers who exercised unlimited authority over their wives, mistresses, and daughters and were allowed to abuse or even kill them without any repercussions.

Bjarnhjedinsdottir also thought that Paul's view of women was problematic. She suggested that Paul was following the creation story in his instructions to women to be submissive, forbearing, and obedient to their husbands. She highlighted as problematic Paul's instructions to women to cover their heads in church and public gatherings, and to remain silent in meetings (1 Cor. 11:5–6; 14:33b–35). Bjarnhjedinsdottir stated, "This teaching of the apostle Paul has to some extent been the cause of the cruelty and oppression women have had to suffer after Christianity came about, on behalf of their fathers, husbands, and other men who have ruled over them" (*Fyrirlestur um hagi og rjettindi kvenna*, 335). While Bjarnhjedinsdottir certainly found Paul's message problematic, she held his interpreters to be even more culpable. She suggested that interpreters had used the instructions to husbands and wives in Eph. 5:22–33 to justify male headship, rather than focusing on the significance of the comparison Paul drew between the relationship of husband and wife, and between Christ and the church. She opined that interpreters had either simply forgotten about this comparison, or they had found it an unimportant and inconvenient hindrance to their domination.

Bjarnhjedinsdottir argued further that Christianity had weakened women's rights in the Nordic countries since men were able to use Scripture to justify their oppression of women. She drew a parallel between the use of the Bible in the debate over slavery and women's rights, insisting that in both cases the apostles had adjusted their teaching to the customs and practices of those to whom they were preaching, in order to guarantee a successful mission. If they had insisted on the transformation of social structures and practices, such as the end of slavery and the equal status of women and men, their mission of spreading the gospel was unlikely to have succeeded (341–42).

In her fight for the equality of women and men, Bjarnhjedinsdottir addressed not only problematic biblical texts, but also the history of their interpretation. Her approach was similar to that found in the *Woman's Bible*, which was first published seven years after she delivered her lecture on women's freedom and education in 1887. It is important to recognize, however, that Bjarnhjedinsdottir was familiar with the writings of those on either side of the Atlantic. In her 1887 lecture, Bjarnhjedinsdottir cited a public lecture "on women's freedom and education" delivered and printed in 1885 in Reykjavík by a young lawyer educated in Copenhagen, who had based his lecture on Elizabeth Cady Stanton, Susan B. Anthony, and Mathilda Gage's *History of Woman Suffrage*, and John Stuart Mill's *The Subjection of Women*. Although Bjarnhjedinsdottir was most likely indebted to the scholarship of other interpreters of the Bible, her own experience of inequities in education and employment was undoubtedly the main force behind her lifelong effort to promote gender equality.

See also Stanton, Elizabeth Cady (1815–1902)

Bibliography

Auður Styrkársdóttir. *From Feminism to Class Politics: The Rise and Decline of Women's Politics in Reykjavík, 1908–1922.* Umeå: Umeå University, Department of Political Science, 1998.

———. "Wahlrecht mit einem Haken: Der bemerkenswerte Fall Islands." Pages 28–37 in *Mit Mach zur Wahl: 100 Jahre Frauenwahlrecht in Europa.* Vol. 1, *Geschichtlicher Teil.* Bonn: Frauenmuseum, 2006.

Bjarnhjedinsdottir, Briet. *Fyrirlestur um hagi og rjettindi kvenna* [*A Lecture on the Status of Women and Their Rights*]. Original, Reykjavík: Sigurður Kristjánsson, 1888. Republished in a collection of writings with an Icelandic translation of John Stuart Mill's *On the Subjection of Women*. In *Kúgun kvenna* [Oppression of Women]. Reykjavík: Hid islenska bokmenntafelag [Icelandic Literary Society], 1997.

Sigríður Dúna Kristmundsdóttir. *Doing and Becoming: Women's Movement and Women's Personhood in Iceland, 1870–1990.* Félagsvísindastofnun Háskóla Íslands [Social Science Research Institute, University of Iceland]. Reykjavík: University of Iceland Press, 1997.

— ARNFRÍÐUR GUÐMUNDSDÓTTIR

Blackwell, Antoinette Louisa Brown (1825–1921)

Antoinette Louisa Brown was born on May 20, 1825, in Henrietta, New York, in the heart of the "burned-over district" of upstate New York. Blackwell's parents were Congregationalists, but the family had little formal religious life until her father's conversion under revivalist Charles Grandison Finney. Antoinette Blackwell requested membership in the Congregational Church of Henrietta at the age of nine and from then on envisioned a religious vocation. Her family and church recognized her gifts, allowing her to speak and pray in public and encouraging her to become a missionary or minister's wife. By the time she reached young adulthood, however, Blackwell knew that her call was to ordained ministry even though no woman had yet been ordained as a pastor in a Congregational church. After completing elementary and secondary schools and earning money as a teacher, she enrolled in the Ladies Literary Course at Oberlin Collegiate Institute in Ohio in the spring of 1846. She graduated in the summer of 1847 and returned to Oberlin that fall to study theology. Because of her gender, she was granted only semiofficial status as a student, but she completed the degree in 1850 and was qualified to serve as pastor of a church.

Blackwell's career as a biblical interpreter began out of necessity when an Oberlin professor who opposed her desire for a theological education challenged her to write an essay on 1 Cor. 14:34–35 and 1 Tim. 2:11–12, the Pauline texts commanding women's silence in church. Rather than being intimidated, Blackwell regarded the assignment as an opportunity to state the claim for women's right to a public role in the church. After translating the texts from the Greek and doing extensive research on them, she produced an essay deemed worthy of publication in the *Oberlin Quarterly Review*.

Like other nineteenth-century feminist exegetes such as Harriet Livermore, Phoebe Palmer, and Catherine Booth, Blackwell in this essay argues that the words of Paul, the attributed author of the texts, were not meant to limit the participation of women in the church but to warn against "excesses, irregularities, and unwarrantable liberties" ("Exegesis," 362) evident in some of the New Testament churches. In making her case, Blackwell points to places in Scripture where God had called and empowered women, including "the ancient prophetesses [who] were called of the Lord to become teachers of Israel" (358). She cites texts such as Acts 2:16–17; 21:9; and 1 Cor. 11:5 to show "that females were accustomed to act as prophetesses in those days, evidently too, under the direct sanction of the apostles." From these references she concludes that it was *not* "inexpedient and therefore unlawful for the women of that age to speak in the church." Not only that, but "it has become at the present day entirely proper, right, and even necessary to the promotion of the best interests of society" (360).

Blackwell states that the assigned texts address not the permissibility of women's public leadership in the church but the style and content of their proclamation and the ways in which they exercise their leadership. She carries out an extensive study of the use of the word *lalein* (to speak) in classical as well as in New Testament Greek and discovers that the term "came to be used in reference to idle talk, chattering, babbling" (362). A similar study of the term *sigatōsan* (to keep silent), as used in 1 Cor. 14:34, refers not to "absolute stillness, or cessation from all sound," but commands refraining from "some kind of talking which was not profitable to the church" (366). Neither passage, she states, was meant to silence women in either the New Testament or the modern church, for Scripture reveals that women, "being taught by the Spirit of the Mighty God," did actually take part in public ministries, including "the work of instructing the church, of speaking," and "doing anything else which they had the wisdom and ability to do." Instead, her exegesis of these texts leads her to conclude that women "were reproved for nothing but pernicious customs which existed among them, and they were commanded to abstain from nothing except those practices which were not calculated to cause 'all things to be done decently and in order'" (368). In conclusion, Blackwell asks, "in what portion of the inspired volume do we find any commandment forbidding woman to act as a public teacher, *provided* she has a message worth communicating, and will deliver it in a manner worthy of her high vocation? Surely nowhere" (372–73).

What Blackwell could not have realized at the time was that the Oberlin assignment would give rise to one of her greatest legacies: that of foremost exegete for the budding American women's rights movement. While at Oberlin, Blackwell was introduced to liberal religious approaches and reform ideology, including the movement for greater rights for women, which began with the first national gathering focused on women's rights in Seneca Falls, New York, in the summer of 1848. As one of the first women theologically trained in the United States and a gifted orator, Blackwell offered a unique theological perspective on a movement that was often criticized as devoid of any religious dimension and hostile to the church. In the fall of 1850 she was invited to give a speech at the First National Woman's Rights Convention. Her speech was a reworking of her Oberlin paper setting forth a biblical justification for greater rights for women. The secretary of the convention recorded that "Antoinette L. Brown, a graduate of Oberlin College, and a student in Theology, made a logical argument on woman's position in the Bible, claiming her complete equality with man, the simultaneous creation of the sexes, and their moral responsibilities as individual and imperative" (Stanton, Anthony, and Gage 224).

Following her theological education Blackwell traveled across central New York State, preaching in churches and speaking on behalf of women's rights, abolition, and temperance. She was determined to imbue the women's rights movement with a religious dimension and convinced the leaders to open and close the conventions with prayer. At the 1852 National Woman's Rights

Convention, Blackwell introduced a resolution declaring "that the Bible recognizes the rights, duties, and privileges of woman as a public teacher, as every way equal with those of man; . . . and that it truly and practically recognizes neither male nor female in Christ Jesus" (Stanton, Anthony, and Gage 535). She argues that "God created the first human pair equal in rights, possessions, and authority. He bequeathed the earth to them as a joint inheritance; gave them joint dominion over the irrational creation; but none over each other (Gen. 1:28)." As they ruled over creation jointly, so they sinned jointly and were both consigned to live with the consequences of their sin. Her exegesis of the Hebrew text led her to conclude that God placed no unique punishment upon women. Instead, "the two who are one flesh have an identity of interests, therefore if it is a curse or evil to woman, it must be so to man also" (535).

She goes on to address the New Testament texts that mandate the submission and silence of women. "The submission enjoined upon the wife in the New Testament," she states, "is a Christian submission due from man towards man, and from man towards woman" (535). Any interpretation of Eph. 5:22–24 that suggests man as literally the head of the woman she decries as "blasphemous," for man then would be exercising over woman "all the prerogatives of God Himself." Instead, "the mystical Head and Body, or Christ and His Church, symbolize oneness, union" (536). She then reiterates her earlier work on the Epistle texts that appear to command women's silence. In 1 Cor. 14:34, "woman is merely told not to talk unless she does teach," and in 1 Tim. 2:12, women are prohibited from "dogmatizing, tutoring, teaching in a dictatorial spirit, . . . both in public and private." "The Bible tells us of many prophetesses approved of God," she concludes. "The Bible is truly democratic. Do as you would be done by, is its golden commandment, recognizing neither male nor female in Christ Jesus" (536).

A small Congregational church in South Butler, New York, in which Blackwell had preached during her travels, was seeking a pastor and invited her to fill the position. Pleased with her work as a pastor, the church raised the issue of ordination and arranged an unprecedented service, the first ordination of a woman in the Congregational Church, on September 15, 1853. After just eighteen months as pastor of the South Butler church, however, Blackwell resigned her position to devote herself to work for women's rights. A few years after her marriage to Samuel Blackwell, she presented what was described as a "sermon" defending the sanctity of marriage during a debate over more liberal divorce laws at the 1860 Woman's Rights Convention. Her understanding of Scripture undergirded her words when she declared: "I believe that God has so made man and woman, that it is not good for them to be alone, that they each need a coworker. There is no work on God's footstool which man can do alone and do well, and there is no work which woman can do alone and do well. We need that the two should stand side by side everywhere" (Stanton, Anthony, and Gage 727).

Blackwell continued to do some speaking and preaching as a minister in the Unitarian Church after her marriage but devoted most of her time to writing. She published numerous articles and ten books addressing subjects such as philosophy, metaphysics, gender, and theology, as well as a novel and a book of poetry. She was one of the few "old pioneers" of the suffrage movement to both participate in the First National Woman's Rights Convention and cast her ballot in the first national election open to women in 1920. By the time of her death in 1921, she had reshaped the landscape of American religion and politics with her biblical arguments for women's rights in both church and society.

See also Booth, Catherine Mumford (1829–90); Livermore, Harriet (1788–1868); Palmer, Phoebe (1807–74)

Bibliography

Blackwell, Antoinette Brown. "Exegesis of I Corinthians, XIV, 34, 35; and I Timothy II, 11, 12." *Oberlin Quarterly Review* 4, no. 3 (July 1849): 358–73.

———. *The Physical Basis of Immortality.* New York: G. P. Putnam's Sons, 1876.

———. *The Sexes throughout Nature.* New York: G. P. Putnam's Sons, 1875.

———. *The Social Side of Mind and Action.* New York: Neale Pub., 1915.

———. *Studies in General Science.* New York: G. P. Putnam's Sons, 1869.

Cazden, Elizabeth. *Antoinette Brown Blackwell: A Biography.* Old Westbury, NY: Feminist Press, 1983.

Kerr, Laura. *Lady in the Pulpit.* New York: Woman's Press, 1951.

Spies, Barbara S. "Antoinette Brown Blackwell." Pages 63–75 in *Women Public Speakers in the United States, 1800–1925,* edited by Karlyn Kohrs Campbell. Westport, CT: Greenwood, 1993.

Stanton, Elizabeth Cady, Susan B. Anthony, and Matilda Joslyn Gage, eds. *History of Woman Suffrage.* Vol. I. Rochester, NY: National American Woman Suffrage Association; New York: Fowler & Wells, 1881.

Zink-Sawyer, Beverly. *From Preachers to Suffragists: Woman's Rights and Religious Conviction in the Lives of Three Nineteenth-Century American Clergywomen.* Louisville: Westminster John Knox, 2003.

— BEVERLY ZINK-SAWYER

Boddington, Gracilla (1801–87)

Gracilla Boddington was born March 27, 1801, the second child of Benjamin Boddington (1773–1853) and his wife, Grace (d. Feb. 10, 1812). Three younger sisters did not survive infancy, but her younger brother, Thomas, eventually became an Anglican priest. She spent much of her life in Titley, Herefordshire, and never married.

Boddington wrote numerous works on the Bible and Christian life. In addition to commentaries on every book of the New Testament, she also published four other works: *Family Prayers for Cottagers* (1851), *A Solemn Warning on a Serious Subject* (1874), *A Few Words of Counsel on the Subject of the Sacrament of the Lord's Supper* (1875), and *Morning and Evening Prayers* (3rd ed., 1868).

Like many devotional commentators, Boddington paraphrased the biblical text, discussed its moral significance and ethical applications, and often included a closing prayer that grew out of her reflections on the text. Although brief historical comments can be found in her commentaries, Boddington's primary interest was for her readers to develop a deeper religious commitment. For example, in her discussion of 1 Cor. 1:1–3, she inquires what it means to call on Christ:

> Surely it means something more than merely saying prayers addressed to His name. When we call a person by his name, it is because we wish him to attend to something we are going to say. But many people call upon the name of God, who do not wish Him to attend to them; they are not attending themselves to what they are saying; they forget to whom they are speaking, and are thinking of something else all the time. What a mockery of God is this! Yet there are those who feel satisfied that this is calling upon the name of Jesus Christ; and because they say a prayer in this careless manner night and morning, they give themselves credit for being the disciples of Christ, and think themselves very religious people. (*First Corinthians*, 3)

While Boddington typically explored the spiritual significance of a biblical text, she also commented on passages that raised issues related to such debates as women's place and nature. Her comments reveal her traditional position on the place of women in the home and in society. In her discussion of 1 Cor. 11:2–16, for example, she affirms the inferiority of women. She observes in nature "one unbroken chain of gradation, leading from the simplest up to the most complicated of His works," and draws the analogy that "among the creatures whom God has endued with the blessing of life, there is every sort of rank from the worm that crawls in the dust up to the Cherubim and Seraphim who surround His throne. And again, there are gradations in station, and degrees in glory, belonging to each division" (139–40). Thus she concludes, "The doctrine which St. Paul has laid down in the passage before us, is the inferiority of women to men" (141). She condemns resistance to this divinely ordained hierarchy as "pride of heart" (140) and affirms that "as a Christian duty, we are bound to conform to our station, whether in regard to our age, our sex, or our outward condition" (141).

Boddington also calls for the subordination of women in the context of marriage. She frames her discussion of Eph. 5:21–33 with the question of submission: "The Holy Spirit here teaches us that we should submit ourselves one to another in the fear of the Lord. But the language we too commonly hear among us at the present day is, that all men are equal, and therefore why should one submit to another[?]" (*Ephesians . . . Colossians*, 72). Boddington asserts that just as one ought to submit to the authority of the church and the state, wives should submit to their husbands (72). She likens insubordination to an infection: "All evil is contagious, and none more so than the spirit of insubordination and rebellion; like an infectious disorder, it spreads from one to another, till a whole neighbourhood is infected" (73).

Boddington casts the subordination of wives to their husbands in a more positive light in her discussion of Col. 3:18–25:

> Passive obedience is what neither wives nor children, nor servants, like to hear of. But this is required of them by God, and it would be greatly for their happiness to obey. Those who are not led astray by a wilful temper, would consider it a great privilege to have a wiser head than their own to look up to for guidance and direction. . . . Doubt and fearfulness must often distress those, who are left altogether alone to act upon their own responsibility. How thankfully, then, would every humble, teachable mind, that desires to do right, bend to these rules. So far from thinking it a burthen [*sic*], or a duty only, every woman should count it a privilege and pleasure to submit in all things to her own husband, if the Lord, who has seen fit to require this subjection, has also seen fit to give her a husband to rule over her. . . . Oh, how tenderly compassionate is God in all His laws! They are all, one and all, intended only to make us happy. His commandments are holy, just, and good; and in keeping of them there is great reward. (*Ephesians . . . Colossians*, 215–16)

A similar argument is found in Boddington's discussion of husbands and wives in 1 Pet. 3:1–7:

> However little our corrupt hearts may relish the duty of submission, as taught us in the Scriptures, it is nevertheless true, that if we would be happy we must comply with it; for in every society of human beings, great or small, confusion will reign, if there is no head. When all think that they have an equal right to manage, and none are willing to submit, things can never go on well. Pride makes subjection painful; but submission with humility brings peace. Wisdom, therefore, as well as duty, teaches us to cultivate an humble spirit, so that we may be ready, when required to yield obedience to our superiors. (*Epistles of . . . St. Peter*, 106–7)

Although Boddington was not the first English woman to comment on all the books of the New Testament (Sarah Trimmer and Mary Cornwallis had preceded her), she was the first woman to publish multiple volumes on the books of the New Testament, explaining the biblical text in "simple and familiar language," a task in which she engaged over the course of more than forty years. It is curious that Boddington called for the submission of women while at the same time writing and publishing commentaries, an activity that was not socially acceptable for a submissive woman of this period. Nevertheless, her work was well received, as evidenced by the reprinting of a number of her works during her own lifetime.

See also Cornwallis, Mary (1758–1836); Trimmer, Sarah (1741–1810)

Bibliography

Boddington, Gracilla. *The Epistles of St. James, St. Peter, St. John, and St. Jude, explained in simple and familiar language*. London: James Nisbet, 1852.

———. *Family Prayers for Cottagers*. 2nd ed. London: Wertheim & Macintosh, 1851.

———. *A Few Words of Counsel on the Subject of the Sacrament of the Lord's Supper*. London: James Nisbet, 1875.

———. *Morning and Evening Prayers*. 3rd ed. London: William Macintosh, 1868.

———. *A Practical Commentary on the Acts of the Apostles, in simple and familiar language*. London: James Nisbet, 1876.

———. *A Practical Commentary on the Gospel of St. John, in simple and familiar language*. London: James Nisbet, 1870.

———. *A Practical Commentary on the Gospel of St. Luke, in simple and familiar language*. London: James Nisbet, 1869.

———. *A Practical Commentary on the Gospel of St. Mark, in simple and familiar language*. London: James Nisbet, 1863.

———. *A Practical Commentary on the Gospel of St. Matthew, in simple and familiar language*. London: James Nisbet, 1861.

———. *The Revelation of St. John the Divine, practically considered in simple and familiar language*. London: James Nisbet, 1881.

———. *The Sacrament of the Lord's Supper, explained in simple language, with meditations and prayers*. London: James Nisbet, 1843.

———. *A Solemn Warning on a Serious Subject*. Edinburgh: D. Grant, 1874.

———. *St. Paul's Epistles to the Ephesians, Philippians, and Colossians, explained in simple and familiar language*. London: James Nisbet, 1847.

———. *St. Paul's Epistle to the Hebrews, explained in simple and familiar language*. London: James Nisbet, 1846.

———. *St. Paul's Epistle to the Romans, explained in simple and familiar language*. London: James Nisbet, 1837.

———. *St. Paul's Epistles to the Thessalonians, Timothy, Titus, and Philemon, explained in simple and familiar language*. London: James Nisbet, 1846.

———. *St. Paul's First Epistle to the Corinthians, explained in simple and familiar language*. London: James Nisbet, 1839.

———. *St. Paul's Second Epistle to the Corinthians, and the Galatians, explained in simple and familiar language*. London: James Nisbet, 1841.

— AGNES CHOI

Booth, Catherine Mumford (1829–90)

Catherine Booth, cofounder of the Salvation Army and influential British "holiness" preacher, was born on January 17, 1829, in Ashbourne, Derbyshire. Her parents, John and Sarah Milford Mumford, were conscientious members of a Wesleyan Methodist chapel, and her father, a coach builder by trade, was a Methodist lay preacher. Although a vocal temperance crusader, John began to drink heavily, compromising both his employment and his influence within the chapel and family. Sarah Mumford, determined to shield the young Catherine from "worldly influences" and nurture her in the serious piety of nineteenth-century Wesleyanism, homeschooled her daughter, primarily utilizing a curriculum of spiritual biography, the published sermons of John Wesley, the commentaries of Methodist interpreter Adam Clarke, and the regular reading of Scripture.

In 1855 Catherine married William Booth, a Methodist lay preacher whom she had met three years earlier in the home of a man who would later become a major supporter of her husband's mission in East London. William Booth was ordained to the Methodist ministry on May 27, 1858, but resigned three years later from the Gateshead circuit in a dispute with the Methodist New Connexion Conference over his conviction that he was called to the work of itinerant evangelism. It was during William's incumbency at Gateshead that Catherine commenced her own public preaching ministry. At the congregation's invitation, she provided pulpit coverage during the months that her husband was recovering from ill health. Thus a preaching career was launched that spanned two decades: Catherine preached regularly in the homes, auditoriums, and churches of London's West End and in the English seaside towns. In this way she supplemented the family income needed to support the Booths' eight children and offset the financial precariousness of her husband's work among the "poorest."

Catherine Booth quickly gained renown for her ability to combine authoritative spiritual presence with the gentle "womanly" bearing and demeanor so admired by West End society. Her vast popularity as a preacher is nonetheless surprising in that her rhetoric, published sermons, and lectures were consistently combative and polemical vis-à-vis the Victorian churches. Her sermons were rigorous appeals for a recognition of the demands of the radical reign of God to which the Gospels witnessed. The Booths and their followers called their brand of cross-centered evangelicalism "Aggressive Christianity," and Catherine's lectures consistently contrasted what she understood as the rigor of the kingdom of God with the trivial aspirations and lifestyles of the middle-class English women of her time. Too often women were culturally locked in what she called the "ordinary, silly sickly circles of gossip and croquet, . . . drawing room occupations considered most respectable and satisfactory in the case of young girls" (*Popular Christianity*, 107). According to Booth, the failure of the church to affirm and utilize the gifts of women had resulted in women's consignment to an irrelevant round of daily tasks and, more tragically, to a dilettante spirituality. For example, she states:

> They have no personal participation in the Spirit or purposes of their professed Lord, no realization of His presence, and no glowing anticipation of His predicted triumphs. But watch the change when the time for dismissal comes; see the rush of acquaintances at the church or chapel doors to shake hands with one another; listen to the rush of tongues; —there is plenty of enthusiasm now! Frank's prizes at school or honours at College. . . . Lizzie's new baby,—these are topics in which the heart is interested, and so the tongue is inspired, and the soul comes forth from its lethargy! (111)

It is indisputable that the theology and pastoral practice of William and Catherine Booth were profoundly influenced by the writings of the American lawyer Charles Finney and the evangelistic campaigns of James Caughey, as well as Walter and Phoebe Palmer. In response to a pamphlet written and circulated by the Rev. Arthur Augustus Rees, opposing the ministry of Mrs. Palmer in Britain, Catherine in 1859 anonymously wrote and published her first spirited defense of women's right to preach. It was titled *Female Teaching; or, The Rev. A. A. Rees versus Mrs. Palmer, being a reply to a pamphlet by the above named gentleman of the Sunderland revival.* Almost twenty years before the formal constitution of the Salvation Army, this tract articulated the position that the denomination would adopt with respect to women in ministry. In 1870 the pamphlet was republished as *Female Ministry; or, Women's Right to Preach the Gospel,* an edition in which direct references to the catalyzing Rees-versus-Palmer controversy were omitted, and which has remained the definitive Salvation Army authorization for women's ministry.

In this work, Booth maintains that the "consistent interpretation" of Scripture demonstrates that "not only is the public ministry of women unforbidden but absolutely enjoined by both precept and example in the Word of God" (*Female Ministry,* 136). She asserts that examples of women assuming leadership roles are plentiful and obvious in biblical narrative, highlighting not only the charismatic exceptionality of Miriam, Huldah, and Deborah's prophetic roles, but also their political and military leadership (in Deborah's case, an army of ten thousand men; Judg. 4:10).

Booth argues that the relevant supportive "precepts" for women's ministry can be determined by an approach to biblical interpretation that she terms the "commonsense reading" of Scripture. She structures her apologetic around two central themes. The first is her explication of the account of woman's position in the created order (Gen. 1:27–31), before and after the fall, and her understanding of the mitigation of the Genesis "curse" through the redemptive work of Christ. For Booth, the Genesis account indicates that the subordination of woman with the attendant implications for ministry is neither natural nor eternal, but tragic. "By nature . . . God has given to women a graceful form and attitude, winning manners, persuasive speech and above all, a finely-tuned emotional nature, all of which appear to us eminent natural qualification for public speaking. We admit that want of mental culture, the trammels of custom, the force of prejudice and one-sided interpretations of Scripture have hitherto almost excluded her from this sphere" (133).

Booth does not doubt that women's subjection to their husbands as a consequence of primal disobedience remains an enduring aspect of the human social order. She concedes that the sole legitimate restraint on a woman's voice is that imposed by a husband, but she cannot resist questioning what kind of Christian husband would be so bold as to stand in the way of God's call on the heart of a wife he has pledged to cherish.

Booth's second interpretive focus is the examination of those texts in the New Testament Epistles conventionally read as prohibiting or proscribing women's sphere of active public engagement in church life. For example, Paul's language in such passages as 1 Cor. 11:4–5 would have no meaning if women had not been both edifying and exhorting under the influence of the Holy Spirit. Furthermore, she asserts that an accurate understanding of the nature of biblical prophetic utterance categorically circumvents issues of gender. The prophetic utterances of either men or women in no way imply the assumption of authority. To prophesy is to humbly deliver the message of the gospel, a mental and spiritual stance requiring obedience, subjection, and responsibility, rather than authority and power. In her comment on 1 Tim. 2:12–13, Booth asserts that "we have never met with the slightest proof that this text has any reference to the public exercise of women" (149). Rather, she claims, the epistle is referring entirely to the private life and character of women.

Booth lacked formal academic training, but she made extensive, at times ponderous, use of the popular, published lexographical or biblical word studies of her time to further her arguments. For example, in the later editions of *Female Ministry*, she extensively cites the research of lexicographers—such as Edward Robinson; Liddell and Scott; Schleusner and Parkhurst—pertaining to the Greek word *lalein* (to speak). Their recognition that the word was frequently used to mean "prattle, chatter, or loquaciousness" supports her dismissal of 1 Cor. 14:34–35 as in any sense referring to the thoughtful, godly teaching of Spirit-empowered women (159).

Throughout her life, Catherine Booth remained an uncompromising advocate for women's biblical right and missional responsibility to preach. She made sure that such a right was formally entrenched in the 1870 conference policy minutes of the Christian Mission, the revivalist ministry she cofounded with her husband William, which in 1878 was restructured and renamed "The Salvation Army." Both through her prolific popular writing and by her vocational mentoring and example, Booth has ensured that women's preaching became the standard expectation and enduring practice of the denomination.

See also Palmer, Phoebe (1807–74)

Bibliography

Booth, Catherine. *Aggressive Christianity*. London: S. W. Partridge, 1880.

———. *Female Teaching; or, the Rev. A. A. Rees versus Mrs. Palmer, being a reply to a pamphlet by the above named gentleman of the Sunderland revival. 1859.* 2nd ed., enlarged. London: G. J. Stevenson, [1961]. Revised as *Female Ministry; or, Women's Right to Preach the Gospel*. London: Morgan & Chase, [1870]. In Papers on Practical Religion. London: S. W. Partridge, [1878]. Rev. ed. as Practical Religion. London: Salvation Books, 2008.

———. *Popular Christianity*. London: Salvation Army, 1887.

Keinze, Beverly M., and Pamela J. Walker, eds. *Women Preachers and Prophets through Two Millennia of Christianity*. Berkeley: University of California Press, 1998.

Walker, Pamela. *Pulling the Devil's Kingdom Down: The Salvation Army in Victorian Britain*. Berkeley: University of California Press, 2001.

— BARBARA ROBINSON

Bowdler, Elizabeth Stuart (ca. 1717–97)

Elizabeth Stuart Bowdler (née Cotton) is intriguing, both in her own right and as a portal into the mores of the eighteenth century. Though anything but "typical," some of what she has written is intelligible only in terms of her context as an educated Anglican woman living at the culmination of the Enlightenment. Her passion for Anglicanism was moderated by sympathy for those with other convictions; doubtless she was influenced by her father and grandfather, who suffered exile as Jacobites. The choice of the fourth-century St. Pancras Old Church (Middlesex) for her marriage to Thomas Bowdler was apt for a woman who took the "long view" of the church, and who dreamed about God's will for all of Christendom. Her interest in the Scriptures was matched with a love of letters that she passed on to her children, especially Jane Bowdler (1743–84), whose writings were celebrated. The family lived in Bath and Ashley (Somerset) and had concourse with writers and those who supported the arts.

Only one piece is confidently known to be from her hands, *Practical Observations on the Revelation of St. John*, written in 1775, published anonymously in 1787, and published under her own name in 1800. She has been proposed as the author of *The Song of Solomon Paraphrased: With an Introduction Containing Some Remarks on a Late New Translation of this Sacred Poem; Also, a Commentary and Notes Critical and Practical*, written in 1769 and published 1775. (The work is held in the New York Public Library and St. Andrew's, Scotland, but is attributed to Bowdler only in the New York Collection.) An examination of the two works reveals similar approach, themes, and interests.

There is a note to "The Right Reverent Dr. Robert Lowth" at the head of *Song of Solomon Paraphrased*. By this, the "most humble servant" (*Song*, vi) commends her handiwork to one whose fame for criticism of the Hebrew

Scriptures was established. Bishop Lowth, onetime professor in Oxford, hailed from Hampshire (a stone's throw from Bath, where the Bowdlers lived) and held positions in Hampshire (priest in Ovington, 1735; archdeacon of Winchester, 1750) before becoming bishop at St. David's, Wales (1766). Despite the author's reserve in her note, the Bowdlers therefore may have known Lowth personally before his move to Oxford later in 1766. A subscription list for a poetic publication names the famous Bath families of Montagu and Miller, who knew both the Bowdlers and the Lowths. Since the author of *Song of Songs Paraphrased* was seeking to critique another writer's translation of that biblical poem, her appeal to Lowth (who had translated the Bible and systematized the dualisms of Hebrew poetry) would have been a natural or even bold move. Bowdler herself had a great facility with languages—French, Latin, and if the Song of Songs commentary is her work, Hebrew (and perhaps Greek).

Bowdler's "practical commentary" on the book of Revelation is true to its description. Written for the nonspecialist, it is not sensationalist, though a later editor considered it predictive of the French Revolution: "a great and enlightened nation would in a few years renounce the religion of Christ" (8). Bowdler herself is not consumed with the predictive aspect of the Apocalypse. She calls any thoroughly futurist reading "surely very much mistaken" (110) and makes no claims to definitively decode its symbols. Though she details some of the mid-eighteenth-century landscape, she does not name France, but envisions a general apostasy. The editorial preface leads us to anticipate an eccentric interpretation, a seventeenth-century *Late Great Planet Earth.* Instead, Bowdler eschews "the rash interpretation of enthusiasts, whether Papists or Protestants" (6), and shows literary sensibility and attention to genre, even though she occasionally strays into speculation. Of particular note is her quaint interpretation of the two witnesses in Rev. 11 (51–57), as the Roman and Orthodox churches, flawed yet proclaiming the gospel, and once revived, useable by God. Only an Anglican would intuit such a meaning! This, coupled with the author's constant search for a via media (middle way), illuminates her specific religious, social, and historical context.

Bowdler cannot resist social and religious commentary. Treated are the advances and challenges of the Enlightenment, "modern" philosophy ("under the pretended banner of reason" [76]), slavery, suicide, Confucian morality, Islam and Judaism, Socinianism, the truth of "Free-Will" and "Providence" over Reprobation and Deism, "the heathen notion" of purgatory, and "the late revived error of" soul sleep (181), the ecclesial "high pretensions" (59) of Rome and Constantinople, denominationalism, apostolic succession, the branch theory of Christendom, and the glory of primitive Christianity.

Chiefly she aims to "clear up the literal sense" (esp. the literary structure of Revelation) so as "to make the practical part more apparent" (4). Thus she highlights worship of the Trinity and the communion of saints, commends humility and duty, rejects any view of the Apocalypse as violent, sounds the call to suffering (during which believers should remain "calm" and "cheerful" [113–14]), and delights in divine mystery. Throughout she straddles precritical and newly emerging methods of reading Scripture, respecting ancient approaches (e.g., typological, and literal vs. spiritual meanings) as well as historical context (Domitian) and authorial intent.

Bowdler's appreciation of startling metaphors (e.g., "stars falling" read as social disaster), her avoidance of common exegetical errors (e.g., "the sea" recognized as the basin of the temple, not the ocean), her appeal to intertextual echoes, and her tracing of two synchronic visions of the text in chapters 5 and 11 (21 and passim)—these are generally sophisticated. Today's readers will be refreshed by her insistence on the body's dignity, over against the spiritualized hope more common in her day. Admittedly dependent on a secondary source ("Mr. Mede"), she is not slavish, nor does she commit herself to a particular school of interpretation (e.g., millennialism or the appearance of a particular antichrist). Only occasionally does she abandon her historical ("antiquarian" [39]), literary, and practical method, as when she toys with reading Revelation's 1,260 days as years, so as to reach her own day. As a female in a conservative context, she does not style herself a teacher, but as one who has merely committed her instruction to writing for the benefit of her own children and other "young minds" (x–xii), that they may objectively assess it, with the help of others. Her disavowal proves unnecessary since her writing compares well with male authors of her own era and perspective.

Turning to *The Song of Solomon Paraphrased*, one sees from the subtitle (*Commentary and Notes Critical and Practical*) that its purpose is more elevated than the first piece. Bowdler introduces her method, critiques a newly authored translation of the Song of Solomon, provides a paraphrase (with critical comments) on the seven parts of the scriptural book, and offers practical instruction. Both the introduction and the conclusion are embroidered by poetry in Arabic, English, and French. Evident throughout is her facility in Hebrew and interaction with several commentators, alongside the anonymous author whose translation she is critiquing. She mounts her argument with awareness of textual difficulties, literary judgment, care for the original language, and discernment concerning the appeal to historical and contemporary analogues. Her judgment is unfortunately flawed by fancies regarding the poem's origin (written by the "virgin bridegroom" Solomon [2]) and by an exaggerated sense of propriety. Indeed, it is her "rule . . . to take every word in the most modest sense it will bear, because I believe that was the sense intended" (5). The book, she believes, is transparent only to one who has "the chaste ideas of an angel, with a tenderness even passing the love of women" (subjective genitive) "whose ideas have not been sullied by improper books, or foolish conversations" (2). Men of her licentious day may possess "an improved education, . . . carried even as far as the knowledge of the original language," yet are "incapable of a proper command over their imaginations" and "inclined to indulge a ludicrous wantonness of expression." Thus they "are most unfit to render" the human "sentiments" of "this beautiful Poem," let alone "to express the love of God, which passes all knowledge" and "of Christ, the heavenly Bride-groom, whom Solomon in this Poem is certainly meant to represent" (2).

Her scruples notwithstanding, one finds remarkable observations, as well as a self-conscious approach to reading that is still worth consideration. In concert with the commentary on Revelation are the intertwining themes of humility, duty, and practicality. Found in both commentaries are attention to the literal and symbolic (or typical) sense; close attention to genre and structure; discernment of intertextual echoes (esp. Ezekiel); a concern for morals and meditation on mystery; caution over enthusiasm and the unbridled imagination; breadth of interest and cross-disciplinary references; and homey illustrations. Such common themes, methods, and strategies make ascription of common authorship nearly irresistible, not to mention characteristic turns of phrase: "I am sensible (of/that)"; "received" traditions/interpretations; "supposed to have/to be" (a phrase used when she or someone else has made a judgment call); and the concluding "having thus taken/completed." Finally, both scriptural books present the same challenge, acknowledged in both commentaries: they have been abused in enthusiasm, fueled by speculation or by licentiousness. In the italicized phrases below, we hear the same female voice, inviting the ordinary reader, and calming those pedants who fear that these symbolic books ought not to be read by the *hoi polloi* (the common folk):

> It is a matter of amazement, that they who profess to study the Bible, and acknowledge it to be the word of God, should think any part of it unfit to be read. . . . Ought not [the most ignorant] *be instructed* to read these, as well as *the other parts of scripture, with advantage*? For I will venture to say, there is not a chapter in the Bible from which a modest humble Christian may not gather useful knowledge. . . . (*Revelation*, 1–2)

> But the abuse of a thing is not a reason for condemning it. Give me a heart capable of the tender sensations expressed in this book, and a mind untainted by vice, . . . and such a one will read the Song of Solomon, not only without danger, but *with great advantage*, and find here, as *in every part* of the Sacred Writings, *solid instruction*. (*Song*, 166)

Bowdler's "trademark" is that she "intends" to "attend to the literal sense" while remaining aware of the symbolic (*Revelation*, 4; *Song*, 26, 38–39). The same justification for this method is expounded thoroughly in the popular commentary and with flair in her academic offering: without understanding the literal, one cannot understand the higher sense. Bowdler's use of the word "literal" is nuanced, referring to the whole structure and the generic signals that indicate a "poetic fiction," such as a vision in the case of Revelation or a pastoral drama in the Song of Solomon (*Revelation*, 5; *Song*, 8). In her Song of

Solomon commentary, she illustrates her method by means of an illustration from fine art (38–39): she is like a generalist, with the ability to step back from the detailed task of restoring an ancient painting so she can see the whole. Synthesis is her goal, though she cares also about "every nicety of grammar" (39) and of translation, whether by the Masoretes or in the Septuagint! Yet again she turns her gender to good use, exploiting a posture of humility: in *Revelation*, she speaks maternally, as the simple but perspicacious generalist.

These works demonstrate both the constraints of context and the magnificence of an independent mind. Elizabeth Bowdler, if the author of both, shows a remarkable facility to address the modestly educated and an elite audience. She sets forth a consistent method, adapted to her readerships, and shows sensitivity to the mores and concerns of the time, while also displaying awareness of the intricacies of history. Though she concentrates overtly on duty, morals, and the practical, her real interest is transparent: to delight in literature and to meditate on Christ and the mystery of redemption. Without apology, she inhabits the maternal and spousal imagery in a manner annoying to the present age and scandalous to hers. In her commentary on Revelation, she would, "like Mary, . . . have laid [these things] in [her] heart and taught them to [her] children" (*Revelation*, 5). Pity that her own son, Thomas, inherited her reserve but without the underlying passion. One suspects he might have been tempted to bowdlerize the passionate language by which his mother closes what seems clearly to be her other work: "Let Him kiss me with 'the kisses of his mouth.'"

Bibliography

Bowdler, Elizabeth Stuart. *Practical Observations on the Revelation of St. John.* Printed at Bath: Cuttwell; sold at London: G. G. & J. Robinson, and J. Hatchard, 1800.

———— [?]. *The Song of Solomon Paraphrased: With an Introduction Containing Some Remarks on a Late New Translation of this Sacred Poem; Also, a Commentary and Notes Critical and Practical.* Edinburgh: Drummond; London: Hay, 1775.

Bowdler, Jane. *Poems and Essays.* Bath: Cruttwell, 1787.

Major, Emma. "Bowdler [née Cotton] Elizabeth Stuart." Page 887 in vol. 6 of *Oxford Dictionary of National Biography*, edited by H. C. G. Matthew and Brian Harrison. Rev. ed. Oxford: Oxford University Press, 2004–11.

Pickering, Amelia. "The Sorrows of Werter." With a list of subscribers, including the Rev. Robert Lowth and Lady Miller (of Bath). London: T. Cadell, 1788. http://www.archive.org/stream/sorrowsofwerterp00pickuoft/sorrowsofwerterp00pick uoft_djvu.txt.

— EDITH M. HUMPHREY

Bowerman, Elizabeth (Madame Cecilia) (1852–1930)

Elizabeth Bowerman, born to a Protestant family in England in 1852, was educated as a social worker. In 1874 she entered the Roman Catholic Church, and in 1875 the religious congregation of Les Religieuses de Saint-André. She took the religious name "Cecilia" along with the title "Madame" given to members of that congregation. She ministered through teaching, instruction of catechumens, and religious writing, first in an elementary school on the Isle of Jersey and later at St. Andrew's Convent in Streatham, London. She studied Greek to prepare herself to write commentaries on the Gospels. She wrote devotional works, school and home plays for girls, Scripture manuals, and the *Catholic Scripture Manual Atlas* (published to complement the manuals), and she translated several theological works from French into English.

Bowerman's scriptural interpretation is most evident in the Scripture manuals written to prepare young Catholics for the university local examinations. Each manual (one book for the Gospel of Mark; two books for each of the Gospels of Matthew, Luke, and John as well as the Acts of the Apostles) contains the complete Latin Vulgate and English (Douay-Rheims) versions of the text, annotations for individual verses, additional notes on selected texts, and "Side-Lights" (notes on the temple, Jewish worship, the Jewish priesthood, synagogues, Jewish history, the Jewish calendar, etc.). Bowerman paid attention to the nuances of the Greek language as well as Hebraisms, noted variant wording among the various manuscripts, and included extensive notes on history, culture, and geography. In her words, "The great work of critical exegesis is to establish, as far as possible, the original text, and this we know to be inspired. It is worthy of remark, however, that the Holy Spirit leaves to the speaker or writer his own peculiar style" (*Acts*, I.153). Her diverse sources included Roman Catholic, Protestant, and Jewish theological works.

Bowerman frequently comments on passages related to women and points out whenever women should be mentioned but are not. In Acts 4:23, she observes, "They went to the place, possibly to the Cenacle, where the other apostles and disciples were assembled, and along with these we may include the holy women" (*Acts*, I.121). She speaks of Acts 5:14 as "one of St Luke's characteristic references to womanhood, and, with the exception of the ministering women, the first distinct allusion to the conversion of women, although the 'five thousand' mentioned in iv.4 doubtless includes both sexes" (*Acts*, I.132). In commenting on Acts 1:14, she says, "We know the names of a few [ministering women]—St. Mary Magdalene, Salome, Joanna, Susanna, Martha, Mary of Cleophas. There were probably many others" (*Acts*, I.67).

Bowerman gives unnamed women the names assigned them in the tradition: thus in Acts 7:21 Pharaoh's daughter is named Thermuthis, according to Josephus (*Acts*, I.164); in Mark 5:25, the woman with the issue of blood is named Veronica, according to Eusebius, who relates that "she erected at the gate of her house a bronze image representing Jesus standing, while a woman knelt before Him with outstretched hands" (*Mark*, 131); the tradition gives the woman of Canaan in Matt. 15:21–28 the name Zulusta or Justa, and "at the present day a mosque (formerly a Christian chapel) opposite the eastern gate of Sidon, stands in commemoration of the miracles worked in her favour" (*Mark*, 159).

Bowerman praises women beyond the words used in the texts. In Mark 7:29, she directs, "Notice that the faith of the mother saved the child" (*Mark*, 160). Quoting Trench, she states that "the case of this lonely woman not suffering our Lord 'to go' until He had blessed her is the greatest of the three ascending degrees of faith. The paralytic broke through *outward hindrances*, blind Bartimeus through the *opposition of his fellows*, but this woman triumphed over the apparent refusal of our Lord Himself" (*Mark*, 347). She says of Priscilla: "Her name generally precedes that of Aquila, and commentators have therefore inferred that she was a Roman and of a higher social position than Aquila, and connected with the family of the Prisci, which gave many famous consuls and propraetors to Rome. As she instructed Apollo, it is evident that she was a woman of culture, and well instructed in the Old Testament, since she was able to teach one mighty in the Scriptures" (*Acts*, I.337). Bowerman reads the New Testament in light of the Old Testament, using stories of women in the Old Testament to explain events in the New Testament. Concerning the naming of John the Baptist, she explains that "in the earliest ages children were named from some circumstance concerned with the birth of their parents, e.g., *Anna called his name Samuel because she had asked him of the Lord*" (1 Sam. 1:20). "So Pharaoh's daughter called her adopted son *Moses, saying: Because I took him out of the water*" (Exod. 2:10) (*Luke*, I.99). When discussing the Magnificat, she notes that "Debbora [*sic*], Judith, and Anna had sung a canticle to the Lord" (*Luke*, II.14).

In her devotional works with meditations for Lent and Easter, Bowerman includes comments on topography and Jewish customs. So she writes: "The Author has endeavoured to bring these sacred subjects before her readers as practically and realistically as possible—to let them see these events as they probably occurred—and at the same time, to refrain from freely indulging in pure conjectures. To this end the 'side lights' of topography and Jewish customs have been thrown on the Gospel narratives as far as possible" (*From the Sepulchre*, xi).

Madame Cecilia's works were used extensively in Catholic schools in both the United Kingdom and North America until the 1950s. Given her other ministries, the amount and depth of material she produced in one decade of her life are remarkable. Her attention to detail, her focus on women, her openness to a wide range of biblical authorities, and her ability to produce both critical works and devotional works influenced by biblical interpretation—all these have left the legacy of a rare woman's voice in biblical interpretation for Roman Catholic laity.

Bibliography

Cecilia, Madame. *Acts of the Apostles: Books I and II*. London: Kegan Paul, Trench, Trübner, 1908.

———. *Catholic Scripture Manual Atlas Specially Prepared with Reference to the Catholic Scripture Manuals*. London: Kegan Paul, Trench, Trübner, 1905.

———. *From the Sepulchre to the Throne*. New York: Benziger Brothers, 1914.

———. *The Gospel according to St. John, with Introduction and Annotations: Books I and II*. London: Burns, Oates & Washbourne, 1923.

———. *The Gospel according to St. Luke, with Introduction and Annotations: Books I and II*. London: Kegan Paul, Trench, Trübner, 1905–6.

———. *The Gospel according to St. Mark, with Introduction and Annotations*. London: Kegan Paul, Trench, Trübner, 1904.

———. *The Gospel according to St. Matthew, with Introduction and Annotations: Books I and II*. London: Burns, Oates & Washbourne, 1906.

———. *Looking on Jesus, the Lamb of God*. London: R & T Washbourne, 1911.

—ELIZABETH M. DAVIS

■ Bradstreet, Anne (1612–72)

Anne Bradstreet was born as Anne Dudley in England to a former soldier of Queen Elizabeth I. She sailed with her parents and husband of two years, Simon Bradstreet, to America in 1630 with the Massachusetts Bay Company, led by the esteemed Puritan John Winthrop. In the late 1630s or early '40s, the Bradstreets made Andover, Massachusetts, their permanent home. Bradstreet became the first published American poet when her brother-in-law, apparently without her knowledge, took her poems to England and had them published in 1650 under the title *The Tenth Muse, Lately Sprung Up in America*. The first American edition of *The Tenth Muse* was published in 1678, posthumously, as an expanded collection called *Several Poems Compiled with Great Wit and Learning*. Her long poem, "Contemplations," was included in the second edition.

Bradstreet's home and living conditions form important contexts for understanding her art. The Bradstreets had been a leading, wealthy family in aristocratic England. Now, in America, she and her extended family were living in one of the most remote settlements, where all the colonists focused on survival and daily needs. Thus the frontier brought some limited egalitarianism (both among social groups and between the sexes) since all made significant sacrifices to survive. Yet the colonies' male leaders retained social and ecclesiastical power and, important for understanding Bradstreet's poetry, the family (including Bradstreet herself) espoused conservative theology, politics, and social views. In Bradstreet's poetry, both frontier egalitarianism and Puritan conservatism are evident, with the latter stance much more frequent.

Bradstreet's egalitarianism can be direct or, more often, veiled, with the poet often relying on irony or simply gentle teasing in the poetic lines. For instance, in "The Prologue," (found in *The Tenth Muse*) she defends women—herself and her own talents—when she writes, "I am obnoxious to each carping tongue / Who says my hand a needle better fits" (lines 27–28; see *Works*). Yet in the remainder of the poem she disparages women's attempts at art: "Men have precedency and still excel, / It is but vain unjustly to wage war; / Men can do best and women know it well" (40–42). The length, detail, and sheer artistry of this section lead the reader to interpret the lines as ironic. Her poetry is hardly the "mean and unrefined ore" she describes it to be (49); it is certainly not art that will make "your [i.e., men's] glist'ring gold but more to shine" (50). Poetic lines such as these show her carefully maneuvering between an acceptable conservative theology, which saw women as weaker vessels and therefore less capable of good art, and a sense of her own calling as a poet.

In her specifically religious poetry, Bradstreet generally expresses conservative theology that does not challenge her contemporaries' views of women or of God. The majority of the religious poems were published posthumously (the exceptions are "David's Lamentation for Saul and Jonathan," "The Flesh and the Spirit," and "The Vanity of All Worldly Things," which were printed in the first two editions of her poetry). Those published in her lifetime, like her other early poetry, exhibit an impersonal tone and content while reflecting the Elizabethan literary tradition. The early "David's Lamentation," written on 2 Sam. 1:19, is an expansion of the idea of "How [in battle] did the mighty fall!" (line 4, echoed in 34), as the speaker mourns the deaths of Saul and Jonathan in a formal, impersonal approach. The more famous "The Flesh and the Spirit" and the "Vanity of All Worldly Things" are focused on specific theological concepts. "The Flesh and the Spirit," for instance, illustrates the Augustinian (and potentially gnostic) notion that the spirit is superior to the body: the poem deprecates the body as a "foe" to be "combat[ted]" (lines 41–42) and ultimately as "unclean" (107), apparently unable to be sanctified.

In a notebook of poems called the Andover Manuscript poems, Bradstreet turns to the Bible for content, as well as for specific literary models, as found in the book of Psalms and specifically in the Psalter she knew best, the *Bay Psalm Book* (*BPB*). Bradstreet explicitly identifies with David ("Then have I . . . said with David," she states in the letter that opens the notebook), but more important, she closely follows the psalms' literary features (*Works*, 242). David was understood by the Puritans to be the writer of the psalms as well as a sanctified, suffering servant; by imitating the psalms, Bradstreet tries to present to her children (her primary audience for the notebook) psalms of her own—poetry acceptable to God.

In these poems Bradstreet expresses her struggles with doubt and faith, her deep affection for her family, and her grappling with loss and suffering. She intends to teach her children that all her afflictions "have made me . . . search [my soul for] what was amiss," with the result that she has discovered that "the Lord hath manifested the most love to me" (*Works*, 242). She looks to God to heal and encourage her and to keep her family safe, at times wrestling with God to understand the hardship in her life. Her struggle and psalmic diction are seen when she writes, "O stay my heart on Thee, my God, / Uphold my fainting soul" ("In My Solitary Hours in My Dear Husband His Absence" [*sic*], lines 19–20). Another characteristic poem shows a celebratory tone, as she adopts the diction, tone, parallelism, and metrics of the *BPB*:

> My soul, rejoice thou in thy God
> Boast of Him all the day,
> Walk in His law, and kiss His rod,
> Cleave close to Him always.
>
> (untitled; 253)

Bradstreet's adoption of rhetorical techniques is comprehensive: she does not simply express psalmic diction and imagery, as many Christian poets have done (e.g., God as light, strength, shelter, and protective bird) or the metrics of the *BPB*; she also draws on the devices, structural technique (Hebrew synonymous parallelism), and genres, along with the meters and rhyme schemes, as specifically captured in the *BPB*. The psalmic genres themselves form a frame for Bradstreet's Andover poems, as she closely follows the psalms' forms for thanksgiving, prayers of supplication, and lament, all of which have detailed structures. The biblical texts offer her models of a sanctified poetics through which she teaches others how to live a life faithful to God amid the extremes of existence wrought by the unique challenges of her American setting.

See also Elizabeth I (1533–1603)

Bibliography

Craig, Raymond A. *A Concordance to the Complete Works of Anne Bradstreet.* Lewiston, NY: Edwin Mellen, 2000.

———. "Singing with Grace: Allusive Strategies in Anne Bradstreet's 'New Psalms.'" *Studies in Puritan American Spirituality* 4 (1993): 1–24.

Doriani, Beth M. "'Then Have I . . . Said with David': Anne Bradstreet's Andover Manuscript Poems and the Influence of the Psalm Tradition." *Early American Literature* 24 (1989): 52–69.

Hensley, Jeannine, ed. *The Works of Anne Bradstreet.* Cambridge, MA: Harvard University Press, 1967.

Piercy, Josephine K. *Anne Bradstreet.* New York: Twayne Pub., 1965.

—BETH MACLAY DORIANI

Briggs, Emilie Grace (1867–1944)

Emilie Grace was born in Berlin, Germany, the eldest daughter of intellectual and musician Julia Valentine and theologian Charles Augustus Briggs. Briggs's formative years were spent in her father's Presbyterian church community in Roselle, New Jersey, and from 1874 among the faculty and students of Union Theological Seminary (UTS), New York, where her father taught Hebrew before becoming a controversial Old Testament scholar and advocate for higher criticism. Following her father's heresy trials, Briggs joined the Episcopal Church.

Leading the way for women in theological scholarship, Briggs was the first woman to earn a diploma from UTS in 1897; at the same ceremony she received the first bachelor of divinity degree, summa cum laude. She was featured in newspaper headlines but does not appear in any known graduation photographs. In 1897 she gained membership in the Society of Biblical Literature and Exegesis and was elected to the American Oriental Society in 1920.

From 1896 to 1916 Briggs used her facility with languages to teach New Testament from the Greek text at the Episcopal New York Training School for Deaconesses. She also published a number of articles and used her theological and linguistic skills and training primarily to assist her father in his scholarly work. Manuscript entries submitted by Charles Briggs for *The Brown-Driver-Briggs Hebrew and English Lexicon* reveal significant numbers from the hand of Emilie. The joint authorship by father and daughter of *A Critical and Exegetical Commentary on the Book of Psalms* is stated by Charles Briggs to be simple justice for their joint labor on both the lexicon and commentary.

While she was teaching, Emilie Briggs worked toward a doctorate of philosophy, producing a dissertation titled "The Deaconess in the Ancient and Mediaeval Church." This consisted of a broad and scholarly analysis of biblical (notably 1 Cor. 11 and 1 Tim. 3), patristic, and other sources bearing witness to and defining the role of deaconesses from the apostolic age onward. More specifically, Briggs traced innumerable women undertaking priestly or diaconal duties from earliest Christian times forward. Texts are interpreted not only to secure a continuous historic basis for the newly revived tradition of the women's diaconate, but also to establish it as an ordained order in the modern church. Briggs aimed to counter the late-nineteenth-century view of the deaconess as an "experiment in modern philanthropy" ("Deaconess," 598) and provided evidence that the role of a deaconess should include teaching and working in a support role alongside a priest. She concluded: "The service of the diaconate is one of assistance both to the people and to the ministry. . . . This distinguishes it from all other branches of the Christian ministry. Bishop and presbyter also serve the people; the deacon serves both the people and their ministers" (536).

By 1913 Briggs had fulfilled all conditions for the doctoral degree with the exception of the publication of her thesis. After an initial publisher's rejection, she set this aside in order to complete and publish her late father's unfinished works. *The History of the Study of Theology* was published in 1916, although a commentary on Lamentations was rejected. In the 1920s Briggs undertook further unsuccessful attempts to publish her dissertation.

Although one of the few women of this period to publish scholarly theological articles, Briggs's final years were spent preparing her father's archival papers in order to write his biography. Briggs's legacy was the inspiration behind the founding of the Archives of Women in Theological Scholarship.

Bibliography

Briggs, Charles A. "Hebrew-English Lexicon Notes." Charles A. Briggs Papers, Series 4, Union Theological Seminary Archives, The Burke Library (Columbia University Libraries), Union Theological Seminary, New York, pre-1906.

————. *The History of the Study of Theology*. Union Theological Seminary Lectures, 1912–13. Prepared for publication by Emily Grace Briggs. New York: C. Scribner & Sons, 1916.

Briggs, Charles A., and Emilie Grace Briggs. *A Critical and Exegetical Commentary on the Book of Psalms*. International Critical Commentary. New York: C. Scribner's Sons, 1906–7.

Briggs, Emilie Grace. "The Date of the Epistle of St. Paul to the Galatians." *The New World: A Quarterly Review of Religion, Ethics and Theology* 9, no. 33 (May 1900): 115–29.

————. "The Deaconess in the Ancient and Mediaeval Church." PhD diss. [unpublished, so degree denied], Union Theological Seminary, 1913. Emilie Grace Briggs Papers, Series 2, Box 2, Union Theological Seminary Archives / Archives of Women in Theological Scholarship, The Burke Library (Columbia University Libraries), Union Theological Seminary, New York.

————. "The Restoration of the Order of Deaconesses." *Biblical World* 41, no. 6 (June 1913): 382–90.

————. "סֶלָה [Selah]." *American Journal of Semitic Languages and Literatures* 16, no. 1 (Oct. 1899): 1–29.

—Ruth Tonkiss Cameron

Bushnell, Katharine C. (1855–1946)

A leading nineteenth-century social reformer, Katharine (Kate) Bushnell believed that male-biased biblical translations and interpretations bore substantial responsibility for the subjugation of women. As a young woman, Bushnell studied classics at Northwestern University (Chicago) for two years before switching to the study of medicine; after her graduation in 1879, she served for three years as a missionary in Kiukiang, China, under the auspices of the Women's Board of the Methodist Episcopal Church. When she returned to the United States, she accepted a position with the social purity department of the Woman's Christian Temperance Union. She set up a home for "fallen women" in Chicago, lectured nationwide on social purity topics, and in the summer of 1888 helped to mobilize American social purity forces by undertaking a highly publicized investigation of prostitution in the lumber and mining camps of northern Wisconsin and Michigan.

Following the success of this campaign, she conducted a series of investigations of British army brothels in India, serving under the direction of Josephine

Butler. Her social purity work heightened her sensitivity to women's suffering, yet she was repeatedly alarmed to find "respectable" Christians resisting her efforts. While in China, she had been shocked to discover a "sex-biased" Chinese translation of the Bible, accepted and endorsed by Western missionaries, and she soon suspected that male prejudice might have warped English translations of the Bible as well. She devoted herself to a critical study of the Hebrew and Greek Scriptures to expose and to undo this prejudice, optimistic that by revising traditional Christian teachings concerning women and sexuality she would be able to alleviate women's suffering and bring about true equality for women.

In 1908 Bushnell began a correspondence course for women, and beginning in 1910 she periodically published portions of her work. Her studies culminated in the publication of *God's Word to Women* in 1923. The book contains one hundred "Lessons" demonstrating how centuries of male translation and interpretation have distorted the Bible into a misogynistic text. Well-read in modern biblical scholarship but rejecting "destructive" higher criticism, she instead turned to Hebrew and Greek texts to demonstrate how the Bible, rightly interpreted, establishes women's equality. Her seemingly conservative methods produced radical results.

Perhaps most dramatically, through her retranslation of the early chapters of Genesis, she argues that God expelled Adam only—and not Eve—from Eden. Although both had eaten the forbidden fruit, Bushnell explains, Adam had blamed God for his sin, while Eve rightly blamed the serpent. Eve, however, eventually chose to follow her husband out of Eden, as Bushnell demonstrates through her analysis of the Hebrew word *tĕshûqâ* in Gen. 3:16. The term had traditionally been translated as "desire," reading "Thy desire shall be to thy husband, and he shall rule over thee"—or even worse, as "lust." Translated in this way, the verse had "been the cause of much degradation, unhappiness and suffering to women," and had instigated "much immorality among men, in the cruelty and oppression they have inflicted upon their wives," Bushnell declares. The translation composed "the very keystone of an arch of doctrine subordinating woman to man, without which keystone the arch itself falls to pieces" (*God's Word*, paragraph 139). Bushnell argues that *tĕshûqâ* should instead be rendered "turning away"; according to her revised translation, God prophesied that Eve would turn away from her Creator in sinful submission to her husband. The fulfillment of this prophecy could be seen in the centuries-long oppression of women that has ensued.

According to Bushnell's translation of Genesis, then, the man's sin was the sin of pride and domination, while the woman's sin was her turning from God and submitting to man. With this framework, Bushnell examines the rest of the Scriptures. For example, by analyzing the Old Testament Scriptures—particularly Gen. 2:24—and utilizing the work of nineteenth-century anthropologists such as J. J. Bachofen, J. F. McLennan, L. H. Morgan, J. Lubbock,

W. Robertson Smith, E. B. Tylor, E. A. Westermarck, and J. G. Frazer, Bushnell argues that God had initially established a matriarchal order; patriarchy ensued after humanity's fall into sin. Bushnell believed that man's sinful oppression of women was particularly evident in the sexual double standard, which held women to far higher standards of morality than men, and which had been perpetuated by centuries of "sex-biased" translations of the Bible.

The clearest example of this bias could be found in English translations of the Hebrew *hayil*, which had been translated to connote "force, strength, or ability" in the over two hundred times it appears in the Hebrew Bible, according to Bushnell, except in four cases where it refers specifically to a woman (Ruth 3:11; Prov. 12:4; 31:10, 29). In each of these cases, translators had rendered the term as "'virtue'—i.e., chastity." She detected an "instinctive distaste" among male translators for praising a "strong" woman; although Bushnell agrees that virtue is "a quality of great importance to women," she suggests that women would be better "equipped to guard their virtue" if they were correctly taught from the pulpit "to be strong, in body, mind and spirit" (*God's Word*, paragraphs 623–33). Defending the authenticity of the story of the woman caught in adultery (John 8:2–11) was also central to Bushnell's efforts to challenge the sexual double standard.

Bushnell's theological explorations were wide-ranging; in addition to writing extensively on Eve, she carefully considered other women appearing in the biblical narrative, including Miriam, Sarah, Hagar, Rebekah, Deborah, Jael, Ruth, Hannah, Esther, Mary the mother of Jesus, Mary Magdalene, Phoebe, and Priscilla. Her analysis of Sarah is particularly revealing. She argues that, in accordance with matriarchal custom—and likely because Sarah's judgment surpassed Abraham's—God ordained Sarah the head of her tribe and commanded Abraham to obey her (Gen. 21:12). Abraham and Sarah constituted the "first Christian family," according to Bushnell, and demonstrated how leadership "turned not upon sex, but upon which one, husband or wife, knew best what to do" (*God's Word*, paragraphs 520, 550). Bushnell also defends the virgin birth of Christ and refutes traditional interpretations of Pauline texts on women's power and male headship (1 Cor. 11:2–16; 14:34; Eph. 5:21–33; 1 Tim. 2:8–15). She argues, for example, that when Paul wrote about a husband's headship over his wife, he was describing the conditions only at that time, and that he believed men should work to elevate women, who had suffered centuries of oppression. Additionally, Bushnell insists that all discussions of male headship should be placed in the context of Matt. 6:24, "No one can serve two masters." As Bushnell explains, Paul "would never encourage the husband to imitate Adam and antichrist in trying to be '*as* God,' to woman, and to interfere with Christ's authority over His own servant,—woman" (*God's Word*, paragraphs 291, 303).

Although it received a number of favorable reviews, *God's Word to Women* failed to find a wide readership. As a self-published book, it bore the unmistakable imprint of Bushnell's style; untouched by an editor's hand, it was a remarkable but fairly unorganized collection of densely argued propositions, supported by frequent references to Hebrew and Greek texts and extensive citation of both biblical and secular scholars, and marked by Bushnell's engaging and at times sarcastic voice. By the time she published the book, she appeared increasingly out of step with developments within modern Protestantism and the women's movement, and she found few allies in her attempts to bring about women's rights through theological reform.

By the time of her death at the age of ninety-one, her work seemed to have faded into oblivion. But her work *God's Word to Women*, quietly handed down from generation to generation and summarized in part in Jessie Penn-Lewis's *The "Magna Charta" of Woman according to the Scriptures* and Lee Anna Starr's *The Bible Status of Woman*, would continue to find a small but committed readership. A number of Bushnell's writings are now available online, where they are accessible to an increasingly global audience. Nearly a century after its publication, Bushnell's *God's Word to Women* continues to offer intriguing glimpses into one woman's attempt to reconcile a deep respect for the authority of the Scriptures with a far-reaching feminist commitment.

See also Butler, Josephine Elizabeth Grey (1828–1906); Penn-Lewis, Jessie (1861–1927); Starr, Lee Anna (1853–1937)

Bibliography

Bushnell, Katharine C. *Dr. Katharine C. Bushnell: A Brief Sketch of Her Life Work.* Hertford, UK: Rose & Sons, 1932.

———. *God's Word to Women: One Hundred Bible Studies on Woman's Place in the Divine Economy.* Oakland, CA: The author, 1923. Many reprints, such as Minneapolis: Christians for Biblical Equality, 2003. http://godswordtowomen.org/gwtw.htm.

———. *The Vashti-Esther Bible Story.* Piedmont, CA: privately printed, 1945.

Bushnell, Katharine C., and Elizabeth Andrew. *The Queen's Daughters in India.* London: Morgan & Scott, 1899.

Du Mez, Kristin Kobes. *The Forgotten Woman's Bible.* PhD diss., University of Notre Dame, 2004. http://etd.nd.edu/ETD-db/theses/available/etd-09212004-131917/. Louisville: Westminster John Knox, 2012.

Hardwick, Dana. *Oh Thou Woman That Bringest Good Tidings: The Life and Work of Katharine C. Bushnell.* Kearney, NE: Morris Pub., 1995. Repr., St. Paul: Christians for Biblical Equality, 1995.

Penn-Lewis, Jessie. *The "Magna Charta" of Woman according to the Scriptures.* Bournemouth, UK: Overcomer Book Room, 1919.

Starr, Lee Anna. *The Bible Status of Woman.* New York: Fleming H. Revell, 1926. Repr., Zarephath, NJ: Pillar of Fire, 1955.

— KRISTIN KOBES DU MEZ

Butler, Josephine Elizabeth Grey (1828–1906)

Josephine Butler is well known for her social activism in advocating for the rights of women, particularly the growing numbers of women in nineteenth-century Britain who resorted to prostitution for survival. To these "outcasts" Butler devoted her life, campaigning for the repeal of the Contagious Diseases Acts; advocating for women's rights to education, property, and the vote; and creating awareness of the dark world of human trafficking of women in Europe.

Less known is the role that Butler's religious convictions played in her life and her advocacy work. Evident from her writings is an evangelical Christian faith that served as a constant companion and a source of empowerment for her work with the poor and the marginalized. Much of her writing was devoted to social reform rather than exegesis proper. However, she found the Bible to be a powerful weapon in her arsenal against those who would oppose her. For Butler, Old Testament narratives served as a prophetic call to the middle class to join her cause (e.g., *Lady of Shunem*, 91–92). The Gospels beckon its readers to follow a Jesus who treated women with equality and respect and who liberated them from the social and religious constraints that marginalized them (*Woman's Work*, lix). Though Pauline texts spoke of the subjection of women to men, Butler contextualized and dismissed them as specific applications of biblical principles not readily transferable to today (xlviii–xlix). "This apostle spoke for the exigencies of a given period," Butler explains, "and from the point of view of a man born under limitations of vision and judgment, but enabled by a divine insight to apply with wisdom the essential teaching of his Master to the accidents of the time and society in which he lived" (xlix). For Butler, the overriding witness of the whole canon of Scripture testifies to a gospel that has positive social implications for women and, more particularly, for oppressed and impoverished women.

In 1894, toward the end of her life, Butler wrote *The Lady of Shunem*, a book devoted to sustained reflection on select stories and passages in Scripture that provide instruction and encouragement for parents and particularly for mothers (1). Different from her other works, *Lady of Shunem* has a pastoral quality, inviting parents to follow the examples of various biblical characters (both men and women) in entrusting themselves and their children to the care and love of God. In working with the biblical passages, Butler exhibits a familiarity with critical approaches to Scripture, but summarily dismisses them in favor of a more theological reading. Typology (the conviction that Old Testament characters and events anticipate persons or features of life in the Christian dispensation), figuration (the notion that words, characters, and events point beyond the literal sense to convey spiritual and moral instruction or truth), and intertextuality (examining one part of Scripture in terms of its interrelationship with other parts) all play a significant role in her interpretation and appropriation of these stories for her readership.

Butler also draws heavily on her own experiences as a mother in her engagement with the biblical text. At times her use of experience is explicit as she invites her readers to employ the knowledge and wisdom they have gained as parents to identify, empathize with, and interpret the characters in the biblical stories. At other times, her motherly experience forms the backdrop to her reading of a story. For example, Butler's grief over the tragic death of her six-year-old daughter is evident in the pathos that characterizes her reflections on the death of the son of the lady of Shunem (2 Kings 4:8–37; 12–13). Though Butler employs experience as a means to identify with the characters of Scripture, her goal is not to valorize them. Instead she seeks to point her readers beyond the human role models to "the attitude of God towards parents and families, and especially to remind mothers of what the Saviour is, what he has shown himself in the Scripture to be and what he will ever be, to *Mothers*" (3). While Butler clearly admires the faith and wisdom of the lady of Shunem, her emphasis is on the love and faithfulness of the God "who created the mother's heart and who knows how to deal with it" (27). For Butler, this testimony is both biblical and personal. The lady of Shunem experienced God's love and faithfulness in the revival of her child. For Butler, God's faithfulness would take another form—opening her eyes to see the troubled young women whose grief was greater than her own and blessing her work among them.

In many respects, Butler assumes rather than establishes the biblical message of social equality. For her, the class and gender hierarchy that characterized nineteenth-century Britain demonstrated that the teachings and principles of Jesus had been largely ignored. In some respects, *The Lady of Shunem* is Butler's effort to direct her readers back to God, in the hopes that the rekindling of faith would result in the social reform to which she devoted her life.

Bibliography

Boyd, Nancy. *Three Victorian Women Who Changed Their World: Josephine Butler, Octavia Hill, Florence Nightingale.* New York: Oxford University Press, 1982.

Butler, Josephine. *The Lady of Shunem.* London: H. Marshall, 1894.

———, ed. *Women's Work and Women's Culture.* London: Macmillan, 1869.

Jordan, Jane. *Josephine Butler.* London: John Murray, 2001.

Mathers, Helen. "The Evangelical Spirituality of a Victorian Feminist: Josephine Butler, 1828–1906." *Journal of Ecclesiastical History* 52, no. 2 (April 2001): 282–312.

— Amanda Benckhuysen

Carter, Elizabeth (1717–1806)

In early to mid-eighteenth-century England, Elizabeth Carter learned nine languages, including biblical Greek and Hebrew, translated classical Greek literature and philosophy, and published two volumes of poetry. After her death, her "Notes on the Bible" were published, transcribed from the handwritten comments in the margins of her Bible. These notes reveal the depth of Carter's biblical interpretation, as she corrects mistranslations of the Greek and Hebrew, quotes biblical scholars such as Robert Lowth, and adds important details about the position of women in the Bible.

Elizabeth Carter was born on December 16, 1717, in the village of Deal in Kent, the eldest child of the Rev. Dr. Nicholas Carter and Margaret Carter (née Swayne). Her father preached in Canterbury Cathedral, and his position brought his daughter into contact with Dr. Lynch, dean of Canterbury, and Dr. Secker, archbishop of Canterbury. Peltz notes that Elizabeth "Carter was the daughter of a cleric who, rather unusually, educated both his sons and daughters to a high level" (68). Elizabeth's mother, known for her wit, knew Latin, French, Greek, Italian, and Hebrew. Carter grew up in an erudite home where biblical study and language acquisition were highly valued.

Though as a child she was initially slow in acquiring knowledge of ancient languages from her father, Carter showed perseverance. Her biographer, the Rev. Pennington, reports that early on she "formed a resolution, or at least an intention, which she was enabled to keep, of devoting herself to study, and living a single life" (Carter and Pennington 1:8). She became a very disciplined reader: "Her general rule, when in health, was to read before breakfast two chapters in the Bible, a sermon, . . . some Hebrew, Greek, and Latin" (1:140). She was also fond of geography, history, and astronomy, and eventually learned French, Italian, Spanish, German, Portuguese, and Arabic.

Carter is known primarily for her translations of Greek texts and for her poetry. At the age of seventeen she had her first poem published by her father's friend Edward Cave in his *Gentleman's Magazine*. Through Cave, Carter met "many authors and scholars of note" (1:39), such as Samuel Johnson. Though she published her first work anonymously, she was attaching her name to publications by 1735. Lonsdale argues, "Elizabeth Carter did much to make the woman writer 'respectable,' taking advantage of the new opportunities in the periodical press" (166). In 1738, Carter published a collection of poems, printed by Cave, that address theological topics. Her birthday poem "In Diem Natalem" expresses her gratitude to God for creating her "elemental clay" (line 9) from "heaps of matter" (8) and protecting her with his "providential care" (33).

Wisdom, like Providence, is a theme throughout Carter's poetry. Anne Hunter's elegiac "Lines to the Memory of Mrs. Elizabeth Carter, Feb. 28, 1806" observe of Carter: "By praise undazzl'd, humble, tho' admired, / She tur'd her lyre to Wisdom's moral lay" (lines 9–10). Line 10 alludes to Carter's "Ode to Wisdom" (1746). Carter draws on Proverbs to personify Wisdom as female, writing, "She loves the cool, the silent eve, / Where no false shows of life deceive" (13–14). At the end of her poem, after having considered Greek mythological figures such as Pallas (Minerva) and philosophers such as Plato, she addresses the biblical God:

> No more to fabled names confin'd,
> To Thee! Supreme, all-perfect mind,
> My thoughts direct their flight:
> Wisdom's thy gift, and all her force
> From Thee derived, unchanging source
> Of intellectual light!
>
> (lines 79–85)

In her "Notes on the Bible," Carter uses the term "Divine Wisdom" in reference to the agency of God. Remarking on God's command that Abraham sacrifice Isaac (Gen. 22:2), she writes: "The repeated trials with which it pleased Divine Wisdom to exercise the faith and obedience of Abraham, served to prove the excellence of his character, and how he deserved the glorious title of 'friend of God'" (2:188).

Carter's "Notes on the Bible" convey her views on Christian men and women serving together as brothers and sisters under the authority of Christ. Pennington argues, "Though she detested the principles displayed in Mrs. Woolstonecraft's [sic] wild theory concerning the 'Rights of Women,' and never wished them to interfere with the privileges and occupations of the other sex, yet she thought that men exercised too arbitrary a power over them, and considered them as too inferior to themselves" (1:448). Carter even corrected Dr. Secker, archbishop of Canterbury, on the original Greek of 1 Cor. 7:12–13. Pennington narrates:

> She was complaining to him one day in the palace at Lambeth of the unfair manner in which our translators have rendered the 12th and 13th verses of the viith chapter of the first Epistle of the Corinthians; that for the evident purpose of supporting the superiority of the husband, they had translated the same verb (ἀφιέτω and ἀφιέτω) as applied to the husband, *put away*, and as applied to the wife, *leave: Let him not put her away,* and *Let her not leave him.* The Archbishop denied the fact, and asserted that the words in the original were not the same; but finding his antagonist obstinate, "Come with me, Madam Carter," said he at length, "to my study and be confuted." They went, and his Grace, on consulting the passage, instead of being angry that he was found to be in the wrong, said with the utmost good humour, "No Madam Carter, 'tis I that must be confuted, and you are in the right." (161–62)

Carter draws on 1 Corinthians to envision men and women cooperating together in mutual submission to Christ. She writes of 1 Cor. 9:5: "Brothers and sisters was the term by which the first Christians expressed their affection and relation to each other as members of the same common family, of which our Saviour was the head" (2:303).

In her "Notes on the Bible," Carter also points out mistranslations in the KJV, where more gender-neutral ideas were suggested in the original. For example, she wrote of Jer. 49:2, "*Daughters*, rather *villages*" (2:251); of Heb. 3:4, "*By some man*, rather, *By some person*" (2:310); and of James 3:1, "*Masters* is too general a word; it ought to be translated *teachers*, which exactly answers the original" (2:312). In each of these cases a gender bias is conveyed by the perceived mistranslation, which Carter, with her knowledge of the biblical languages, seeks to rectify.

Finally, Carter's "Notes on the Bible" bring women characters from Scripture into the foreground. For example, she writes of Exod. 24:14, "According to Josephus, *Hur* was the husband of Miriam" (2:194); of 2 Chron. 8:6, which concerns the royal burial places, "In Jerusalem was no other sepulchre but that of the house of David, and of Huldah the prophetess" (2:212); of 2 Chron. 11:20, "As Maachah, or Michaiah, is in the following chapter called the daughter of Uriel, she might probably be the grand-daughter of Absalom" (2:212). Carter also reads Old Testament passages as prophetic of Mary's pregnancy and the birth of Christ. She writes of Ps. 110:3, "The whole psalm is a prophecy of the Messiah. . . . *The womb of the morning* is probably a poetical figure of the East; and the whole verse a prophetic description of the adoration and offerings of the wise men" (2:223); and of Isa. 7:14, "This prophecy; which had its full completion in the birth of our blessed Saviour, seems, in this primary signification, to relate to the son of Isaiah. The virgin here mentioned was probably the same person who, in the third verse of the next chapter, is called the prophetess, and who was perhaps taken to wife by Isaiah" (2:233). In writing her notes on the Old Testament, Carter foregrounds women's cultural roles, not only as wives, daughters, and granddaughters, but also as wise prophetesses.

In her notes on the New Testament, Carter continues to give identities to nameless women in Scripture; for example, she writes of Mark 14:3, "*A woman*, &c.—Mary, the sister of Lazarus" (2:287). When Carter focuses on another Mary, Mary Magdalene, she characterizes her as a solitary contemplative. In Carter's notes on Mark 16:1–2, she argues that Mary Magdalene did not initially recognize the resurrected Jesus because she had come alone to the empty tomb "by the dawning of the day, and not after the sun was risen" (2:288). Carter reemphasizes this view of Mary Magdalene as the lone pilgrim at dawn within her note for John 20:1 (2:296–97) and in her apologetics ("Objections against the New Testament with Mrs. Carter's answers to Them," 2:368–69).

Later in life, Carter lived out her Christian faith in tangible ways, following the tradition of community and encouragement that she had experienced through her connection to the bluestockings. From 1780 onward, she belonged to a ladies' society for relieving the poor. A monument to her in the village of Deal is engraved with the words: "In deep learning, genius, and extensive knowledge, she was equaled by few; in piety, and the practice of every Christian duty, excelled by none." Carter died on February 19, 1806, and is buried in the grounds of Grosvenor Chapel, London.

See also Wollstonecraft, Mary (1759–97)

Bibliography

Backscheider, Paula. *Eighteenth-Century Women Poets and Their Poetry: Inventing Agency, Inventing Genre*. Baltimore: Johns Hopkins University Press, 2007.

Carter, Elizabeth, and Montagu Pennington. *Memoirs of the life of Mrs. Elizabeth Carter, with a new Edition of her Poems; to which are added some miscellaneous essays in prose, together with her notes on the Bible, and answers to objections concerning the Christian religion*. Edited by Montagu Pennington. London: F. C. & J. Rivington, 1807. 4th ed. in 2 vols., London: James Cawthorn, 1825.

Guest, Harriet. *Small Change: Women, Learning, Patriotism, 1750–1810*. Chicago: University of Chicago Press, 2000.

Lonsdale, Roger. *Eighteenth-Century Women Poets*. Oxford: Oxford University Press, 1990.

Peltz, Lucy. "Living Muses: Constructing and Celebrating the Professional Woman in Literature and the Arts." Pages 56–93 in *Brilliant Women: 18th-Century Bluestockings*, by Elizabeth Eger and Lucy Peltz. New Haven: Yale University Press; London: National Portrait Gallery Pubs., 2008.

— NATASHA DUQUETTE

Carus-Wilson, Mary Louisa Georgina (Petrie) (1861–1935)

Mary (Petrie) Carus-Wilson was born in Surrey, England, to Colonel Martin Petrie and Eleanor Grant Macdowall Petrie. She received a fine education, including a bachelor's degree from University College, London. In 1881, while still a student, she became involved in establishing a correspondence school for women that grew to be staffed by two hundred university-educated women and boasted more than three thousand students worldwide in the 1890s. In addition to her work with The College by Post, she taught English, Greek, and French at a number of small colleges. She also lectured to predominantly female audiences on such subjects as critical and devotional Bible study, suffrage, world religions, and medicine. Her extant journals record the titles of her lectures and such details as the date, place, sponsoring organization, and the remuneration received (Carus-Wilson Papers, MSS 018, Box 3, Folder 28, 95 pages). In 1892 she married Charles Ashley Carus-Wilson, a professor of engineering at McGill University in Montreal. She resigned her position at The College by Post when she moved to Canada. She had three children before returning to England, where she continued to write and lecture. After her marriage, she published under the name "Mrs. C. Ashley Carus-Wilson," though she published as Helen Macdowall with *The Sunday at Home*. During her lifetime Carus-Wilson published nine books and hundreds of articles for magazines, journals, and papers.

Carus-Wilson published extensively on subjects related to the Bible and missions. Her experiences of teaching gave rise to two books specifically on the Bible, *Clews to Holy Writ* (1892) and *Unseal the Book* (1899), and several books on missions in the New Testament, including *Redemptor Mundi: A Scheme for the Missionary Study of the Four Gospels* (1907). She also published *Irene Petrie, Missionary to Kashmir* (1900), the life story of her only sister, who died in Kashmir in 1897; *The Expansion of Christendom: A Study in Religious History* (1910); and a collection of poetry that includes *Poems* written from the perspective of female biblical characters (1895). Carus-Wilson's writings on the Bible reveal a confident, well-educated evangelical Anglican shaped by a changing face of biblical studies in the late nineteenth century in England.

Carus-Wilson's commitment to reading Scripture "in the fullest light our own age can throw upon it" (*Clews*, 7) is evident in her book, which aimed at teaching students to read the Scriptures "critically, devotionally, and practically in order to know what to believe, whom to love, and how to live" (15). *Clews to Holy Writ* set out a three-year scheme for studying the Bible "in the chronological order of the events it relates and the books it contains, so far as that can be ascertained" (ix). Each chapter summarizes the history, geography, theology, and lessons of the historical period under discussion, and includes a reading list and questions. In *Clews to Holy Writ*, students are introduced to such ancient and classical scholars as Josephus, Chrysostom, Rabbi Ishmael, Luther, and Calvin, as well as nineteenth-century scholars including Westcott, Liddon, Ewald, Kuenen, and Blunt. They also learn about such scholarly debates as the relationship of science and the Bible, whether Deuteronomy was written and not merely discovered in the reign of Josiah, and the idea of a second, exilic Isaiah. Students were to buy *The Oxford Revised Version Study Bible*, a Bible dictionary, the Speakers Commentary Series, a concordance, and various Bible handbooks (15–16).

Carus-Wilson's approach to Genesis illustrates her willingness to blend new ideas with traditional presuppositions about the nature of Scripture. Her commitment to reading the Bible in its ancient Near Eastern context convinced her that in the early chapters in Genesis, "there is nothing distinctively Hebrew, their simplicity of treatment and subject belongs to the dawn of civilisation, and they have interesting features in common with the earliest Egyptian and Chaldean literature" (*Clews*, 21). At the same time, she reads Genesis as more than "a mere compilation of old annals, but a religious history, whose unity and symmetry show that it was penned throughout with a definite design" (21). She argues for the literary unity of Genesis based in its "twelve natural divisions," which, with the exception of Gen. 1:1, are marked by the formulaic phrase, "These are the generations . . . of . . ." (21).

110

In her discussion of the book of Isaiah in *Clews*, Carus-Wilson similarly engages complex critical issues around the book's prehistory. She describes the book as having two parts that differ in terms of contents, style, and subject matter (122). She explains the theory of dual authorship, setting out a number of counterarguments to this theory, including the inconclusive nature of the literary argument from alleged differences of vocabulary and style (122–23). She ostensibly defends the traditional notion of unity; however, her propensity toward historicism pushed her to read Isa. 40–66 in connection with the later age it describes and for which "it was no longer a sealed book (Dan. xii.9)" (123). She presents Isa. 40–66 as "a legacy to posterity rather than a gift to contemporaries (Isa. xlvi.4–7)" (123). Her ambivalence on the issue of authorship is evident in the questions she asks students. They are first asked to work through the evidence for dual authorship based on differences in historical setting: "Prove by quotations that Isaiah xl–lxvi speaks of Judah's Captivity as past and not future, and account for this." However, they are then asked to observe thematic unity illustrating how "the word *peace* runs as a golden thread throughout the tissue of the whole Book of Isaiah" (135).

Carus-Wilson's *Unseal the Book: Practical Words for Plain Readers of Holy Scriptures* (1899) focuses more on hermeneutical issues with a view to encouraging a thoughtful, reasonable, and faithful reading of Scripture. The book addresses "seven seals" that block the meaning and message of Scripture for modern readers. Carus-Wilson highlights problems with the text of Scripture, translation, and canonical ordering on the one hand, and problems with the reader on the other. She advocates strongly for the superiority of the Revised Version (1885) over the King James Version (1611), providing examples of its better arrangement and greater accuracy, its discrimination of literary forms, its use of headings and helpful marginal notes, and its correction of obscure and incorrect renderings (51).

In this later work Carus-Wilson again promotes an approach to Scripture that uses all the available methods and tools of scholarship, including a historical approach, arguing that "the Book of Books is first of all an historical work, it must be read in the historical spirit" (*Unseal the Book*, 80). She encourages readers to determine the text's literal/historical sense—what it conveyed to its first audience—before determining its "fuller" meaning for the present, a meaning that "grows out of the plain original meaning, and cannot be taken independently" (76). She includes many examples of how reading a text in its original context solves credibility issues for readers. For example, she suggests that a knowledge of local geography will help a reader who finds "little warrant . . . for the picture of Absalom suspended by the flowing locks of which he was so proud." On the basis of information gleaned from a contemporary traveler, she clarifies: "What actually happened, as a traveller through the Wood of Ephraim can perceive today, was that his head was caught in the low forked branches of the trees, a catastrophe which the rider there is warned against now" (107).

While Carus-Wilson believed that reading Scripture in its original context solved many problems faced by readers, she also thought that understanding the nature of the biblical texts themselves was important. In particular, she places considerable weight on the notions of spiritual and natural progression. Just as "Adam's communion with God differed from that of St. Paul, . . . the revelation to each age was perfect for its own time, but not for future times" (103). She asks: "What meaning would Gen. i have had for any one in past ages, or for the mass of unscientific Bible readers of our own age, had it been expressed in the precise terminology of the scientist?" (103–4). She also addresses the doubts of many regarding the question of the extent of the flood in Gen. 6–9, reasoning that while the flood story was "universal as regards the human race," the Bible does not demand that the flood be regarded as "universal as regards the globe and all other creatures" (106). She advocates a "sanctified common-sense approach" to Scripture, drawing an analogy between Christ and the Bible: as Christ was both "perfect God and perfect Man," so Scripture is "not partly divine and partly human but wholly or perfectly human, and wholly or perfectly divine" (155).

Carus-Wilson places the burden for responsible biblical interpretation on the reader. She criticizes both dogmatic and superficial readers. She advocates serious study of the Bible, and sees value in commentaries, but warns against overreliance on them: "Too much commentary is . . . thought-saving pious meditation, rather than thought-stimulating suggestion; . . . we should gain far more for ourselves by writing our own commentary" (111). The intelligent reader needs to read the Bible as more than a human book, to include a spiritual reading of the Bible that grows out of its literal/historical sense and combines "study and prayer" and "knowledge and faith" (134).

Even though Carus-Wilson's guidebooks to the study of Scripture were written for women, they did not give women a prominent place. In Clews, she simply acknowledges that the Old Testament contains examples of women's "striking character and influence," suggesting that their "true exaltation" is in connection to Jesus and their "large and fruitful share" in the work of the church (297). Her views on women do surface in other writings, however. For example, in a published missionary Bible study on the parable of the kingdom that likens it to a woman who mixed yeast into three measures of flour (Luke 13:20–21), Carus-Wilson counters traditional readings of the significance of the number three, arguing that the parable is about women's "subtle" yet "all-pervading influence in the home and the woman who makes the home" ("Extension and Energy"). She cites Anna and Mary Magdalene as examples of women "sent forth as the first preachers of the incarnation and the resurrection," who filled "an all-important though not a conspicuous place in church history" ("Extension"). Then beginning with Priscilla, she names women "utterly unknown to fame" throughout history, including women in British history (Hilda, Bertah, and Etheolburga) and on the mission field who worked to expand God's kingdom ("Extension"). The clearest examples of Carus-Wilson's gendered exegesis are found in her poetry, where she reads biblical narratives through the lens of the female characters. Her lengthy poem "Michal," for example, explores Saul's daughter's feelings for David:

> Lost! From clinging arms and straining gaze my lord is fled and gone:
> . . . Now I live upon those kisses till his lips are mine again,
> Press my lips upon his pillow in the darkness, and see plain
> David, all his face aglow while women pour the joyous song.
> ("Michal," in *Tokiwa*, lines 191–99)

Similarly, in her poem "The Blessed Mother," Carus-Wilson explores Mary's reflections on "he who leaned on my love / In childhood, and on whose strong love I leaned" ("The Blessed Mother," in *Tokiwa*, lines 239–42). Her own experiences as a wife and mother and her presuppositions about the question of woman's nature and place have shaped her recasting of these biblical characters.

Carus-Wilson was an influential popularizer of an approach to the study of the Bible that assumed an organic view of biblical history and an openness to biblical criticism insofar as its results were consonant with an evangelical version of progressive revelation. Her confidence lay not only in the Bible, but also in scientific research, historicism, evolution, human development, and the human mind. She was one of many women who had an important role in paving the way for the relatively easy acceptance of higher criticism in England.

Bibliography

"Carus-Wilson, Mary Louisa Georgina Petrie, Papers, 1840–1932." Pitts Theological Library, Archives and Manuscripts. Emory University, Atlanta.

Carus-Wilson, [Mary] Mrs. Ashley. *The Expansion of Christendom: A Study in Religious History*. London: Hodder & Stoughton, 1910.

———. "Extension and Energy: Missionary Bible Study on Two of Christ's Parables." *The Church Missionary Gleaner*, Aug. 1898, 123.

———. *Irene Petrie, Missionary to Kashmir*. London: Hodder & Stoughton, 1900.

———. *Redemptor Mundi: A Scheme for the Missionary Study of the Four Gospels*. London: Hodder & Stoughton, 1907.

———. *Tokiwa and Other Poems*. London: Hodder & Stoughton, 1895.

———. *Unseal the Book: Practical Words for Plain Readers of Holy Scriptures*. London: Religious Tract Society, 1899.

Petrie, Mary Louisa Georgina. *Clews to Holy Writ; or, The Chronological Scripture Cycle: A Scheme for Studying the Whole Bible in Its Historical Order during Three Years*. London: Hodder & Stoughton, 1892.

— MARION ANN TAYLOR

■ Cary, Mary (b. 1620/21, fl. 1647–53)

Mary Cary lived during the time of the English Civil War and the Cromwellian Interregnum. She consorted with the Fifth Monarchists, a militant, millenarian sectarian group that saw itself as shaped by biblical prophecy. Along with other women in the movement, such as Anna Trapnel, she was a leading member because of her intense prophetic writings. Yet little is known of the details of Cary's life outside these works: she was married, changed her name to Rande, and wrote numerous works that commented on biblical prophecy, but it is unknown when she died and what happened to her after the monarchy was restored. As a Fifth Monarchist group leader, she and her fellow agitators defined themselves in prophetic terms, basing the group's name on the prophecies in the Old Testament. In Dan. 7, four beasts are seen coming out of the sea, each representing an earthly kingdom. The "fifth kingdom" was seen by the Fifth Monarchists as the established kingdom of Jesus Christ on earth. They saw the events of the English Revolution as propitious for such an event and worked with fervor to see it come to fruition. This movement and Cary's role within it, therefore, were based on radical scriptural exegesis. The nature of the kind of interpretation in which the Fifth Monarchists were engaging and the unstable position of the British government at the time also meant that they were a radically political movement. Mary Cary's works particularly reflect these characteristics.

Cary's central works are scriptural commentaries, specifically on the prophetic books of the Bible. Most notable and largest are *The Little Horns Doom & Downfall*, which was combined with *A New and More Exact Mappe; or, Description of New Jerusalems Glory*, both published in April 1651. She also published tracts such as *A word in season to the kingdom of England* (1647) and *The Glorious Excellencie of the Spirit of Adoption* (1645), all of which, to varying degrees, display her millenarian enthusiasm and radical apocalypticism in the context of Cromwellian England. In the preface to her work *The resurrection of the witnesses; and, Englands fall from (the mystical Babylon) Rome* (1648), she states that at the age of sixteen she felt moved "by the Spirit of God" to study the Scriptures, particularly the books of the prophets and Revelation. There is no other known indication of any theological or biblical training. Unlike the mystical trances of Anna Trapnel that gave rise to prophetic utterances, Cary worked strictly on bringing biblical prophecies to life, applying them directly to the context of her own time. She saw herself as an inspired exegete, and her fellow Fifth Monarchists also saw her as a prophetess.

Much of her exegetical work is highly imaginative, but it also displays much boldness in her polemical aims to advise the new government in power after the execution of Charles I. She uses various exegetical strategies such as mathematical manipulation and drawing on recent English history as illustrating scriptural prophecy—in support of the regicide (the end of the "fourth kingdom") and to hail the new millennial age. In some ways many of her interpretations are not new, and many are repeated even today, in new contexts by current millenarian groups; what makes her unique is how she sees the new age as bringing in a time that will give a new dignity to the role of women. Her two largest works (*Little Horns* and *New and More Exact Mappe*) are dedicated to several "Vertuous, Herioicall, and Honourable Ladies," which included wives of various members of parliament, including Elizabeth Cromwell. The walls of the New Jerusalem, described in Rev. 21:19–21, are adorned with "all manner of precious stones," and her novel interpretation of this passage is that these gems are godly women who serve as the foundation of the new kingdom. Moreover, she uses Joel 2:28–29 (and its restatement in Acts 2:17–21), where it is said that "on my handmaidens I will pour out in those days of my Spirit; and they shall prophesy," to validate her right as a woman in "the last days" to assert her visionary zeal.

The leaders of the Fifth Monarchy also acknowledged Cary's interpretive skill and saw her as a prophetess inspired by the Spirit of God. They looked to her for her imaginative interpretation not only of Scripture, but also of the events to which the English people were subjected. She was unafraid to disdain earthly power and to cut across gender barriers to speak to the events of her time; she did not simply participate in the Fifth Monarchy movement, but contributed to the shaping of it.

Bibliography

Baston, Jane. "History, Prophecy, and Interpretation: Mary Cary and Fifth Monarchism." *Prose Studies* 21, no. 3 (1998): 1–18.

Capp, Bernard. "Cary, Mary (b. 1620/21)." Pages 445–46 in vol. 10 of *Oxford Dictionary of National Biography*, edited by H. C. G. Matthew and Brian Harrison. Rev. ed. Oxford: Oxford University Press, 2004–11.

Cary, Mary. *The Glorious Excellencie of the Spirit of Adoption*. London, 1645.

———. *The Little Horns Doom & Downfall; and, A New and More Exact Mappe; or, Description of New Jerusalems Glory*. Early English Books Online. London: The author, 1651.

———. *The resurrection of the witnesses; and, Englands fall from (the mystical Babylon) Rome*. Early English Books Online. London: Giles Calvert, 1648.

———. *A word in season to the kingdom of England; or, A precious cordiall for a distempered kingdom*. Early English Books Online. London: Giles Calvert, 1647.

Cohen, Alfred. "The Fifth Monarchy Mind: Mary Cary and the Origins of Totalitarianism." *Social Research* 31, no. 2 (Summer 1964): 195–213.

———. "Mary Cary's The glorious excellencie discovered." *British Studies Monitor* 10, nos. 1–2 (1980): 4–7.

Gillespie, Katharine. *Domesticity and Dissent in the Seventeenth Century: English Women Writers and the Public Sphere*. Cambridge: Cambridge University Press, 2004.

Hobby, Elaine. *Virtue of Necessity: English Women's Writing, 1649–88*. Ann Arbor: University of Michigan Press, 1989.

Lowenstein, David. "Scriptural Exegesis, Female Prophecy, and Radical Politics in Mary Cary." *Studies in English Literature* 46, no. 1 (Winter 2006): 133–53.

Wiseman, Sue. "Unsilent Instruments and the Devil's Cushions: Authority in Seventeenth-Century Women's Prophetic Discourses." Pages 180–85 in *New Feminist Discourses: Critical Essays on Theories and Texts*, edited by Isobel Armstrong. London: Routledge, 1992.

—ROBERT KNETSCH

■ Catherine of Siena (1347–80)

Caterina di Giacomo di Benincasa (Catherine of Siena) was born in Tuscan Siena in 1347, the twenty-fourth of twenty-five children of a wool dyer and a poet's daughter. Though she had no formal schooling and lived a mere thirty-three years, she became a significant force in late fourteenth-century Italian church and society and now bears the titles of saint (1461), patron of Italy (1960), and doctor of the Roman Catholic Church (1970). She became a Dominican lay tertiary (a *Mantellata*) when she was about eighteen and began to be active in ecclesiastical and political spheres when she was about twenty-seven. As a young adult, she had learned to read and later learned to write, though probably in a quite elementary way; with a few possible exceptions, she dictated all her works to a variety of scribes. She was the first woman to have her works disseminated in any of the Tuscan dialects. She died in Rome on April 29, 1380.

In about 1370 Catherine began to use letter writing as one of her favored means to reach out to, advise, and influence others. About 385 of these letters (most of them dating from 1374 until her death in 1380) have been discovered and published to date. They address a remarkably wide variety of her contemporaries: popes, cardinals and bishops, royalty and public officials, family and friends and disciples, and an assortment of others, including allies and opponents, a mercenary captain, a prostitute, a homosexual, and political prisoners. Her purpose, however, is always deeper than the merely social or informational; she is interested primarily in the eternal dimension of personal lives and societal affairs. The letters bear a particular added interest because her activity extends so far beyond the normal feminine bounds of her time and her status.

A collection of twenty-six of Catherine's spontaneous prayers, all from the last four years of her life and most from her final seventeen months, were also preserved. Her crowning work is *The Dialogue*, which she called simply "the book." In it she endeavors to share with her disciples and others her vision of life with God in Christ, composed in the form of a conversation between herself and God the Father.

It is clear from her writings that Catherine's theology and spirituality grew out of a faith solidly grounded in the Christian gospel. Yet she surely never studied the Bible with the critical insights and tools today's interpreters take so much for granted. Nor did anyone else in her era, not even the best of scholars, though in the thirteenth century biblical commentary had dominated the theological curriculum in European universities, and in Catherine's own fourteenth century mystical writers were again contributing significantly to the exposition of the Scriptures. Yet even these works generally reached Catherine only secondhand and thirdhand.

Latin Bibles designed for personal use and reference appeared for the first time in Italy in the mid-thirteenth century but these also were mainly in the hands of preachers and scholars. Manuscripts with parts of the Bible such as Psalters, single Gospels, or collections of the readings for Sunday liturgies proliferated. Bibles and selections in the vernacular also existed but were largely suspect because most of those who had translated and promoted them, especially for lay use, had been excommunicated as heretics.

Catherine had learned to read when she was about twenty precisely because she desired personal access to the psalms of the Divine Office. She became sufficiently familiar with Latin to ask a Dominican friar friend about the precise reading of the second verse of Ps. 131—whether, in that verse, "I have calmed and quieted my soul, like a weaned child with its mother," the expression was *sicut adlactatus* (like a nursing child) or *sicut ablactatus* (like a weaned child [Vulgate])—because it would make a difference in how she interpreted the psalm as well as in God's relationship with humankind (Noffke 40). If Catherine were indeed *reading* the psalms of the Office regularly or even had easy access to a Psalter or breviary, she could and probably would have checked the word herself. It is more likely, however, that she simply listened and prayed along as the friars sang the hours, certainly memorizing a good deal of the text eventually.

Thus hearing is likely the mode through which Catherine was most exposed to the Scriptures. One is led to this conclusion not only by the example just related but also by the ways that her use of biblical passages sometimes reflect an obvious mishearing rather than a misreading. For example, she repeatedly calls Paul a "vessel of love," apparently having heard *vasello di dilectione* (or the Latin *vas delectionis*) rather than the actual *vasello d'electione* (Latin *vas electionis*, "chosen vessel," or literally, "vessel of election" in Acts 9:15). And when she counsels "not looking back at what you have already plowed," it is because she heard *l'arato* (what has been plowed) rather than *l'aratro* (the plow) in Luke 9:62.

And how did she hear? Among her friends and disciples were theologians, lawyers, politicians, and poets. She associated with Dominicans, Franciscans, Benedictines, Carthusians, and Augustinians. She listened to the scholarly preaching that was the chief ministry of the friars at the Church of San Domenico, up the hill from her home in Siena, as they preached within the liturgy, outside the church in the piazza, and in instructional sessions held weekly for the *Mantellate*. She read the popular spiritual works of fellow Dominican

Domenico Cavalca. She sat for hours at the feet of her Augustinian mentor, William Flete, and corresponded with both him and the Vallombrosan Benedictine Giovanni dalle Celle, both theologically astute. She was, besides, a tireless conversationalist, bringing to her encounters a barrage of questions, observations, and conclusions of her own, and chiding those who wearied of her intensity. The theological leanings of her mentors, particularly Augustinian and Thomistic, are reflected in her writings.

In the liturgy of the Mass and Divine Office, which she attended almost daily, she would hear in Latin the psalms and readings incorporated there. In sermons, instructions, and conversations, she would hear isolated passages in whatever translation and with whatever interpretation the speaker would give them. Her biblical allusions are drawn almost entirely from these sources. Catherine certainly never read the Bible, or even any individual biblical book, as a whole. She seldom "cites" passages, as medieval writers so commonly did to support what they were saying, as "proof texts." Instead biblical expressions flow through her sentences as naturally as if they are her own—sometimes intact, sometimes rephrased, sometimes in new and different combinations. These are not references made simply out of a phenomenal memory, or with a concordance or "book of quotations" at her elbow. They are her very vocabulary—in letters and reflections and prayers dictated or overheard in the rush of life or in withdrawn quiet or ecstasy. They are not appliqués on the surface of her works but threads without which the whole fabric of her thought would disintegrate.

Quite early in her life, John and Paul had become Catherine's favorite saints. Just when and how is not known, but clearly they were kindred spirits, and she finds in their writings a voice for her own convictions. Their themes and expressions sing through her writings more than any others of the Scriptures. For example, Christ as a vine with branches, but also as a fire generating sparks (John 15:5); Christ (and God) as thirsty (John 19:28); God as desiring nothing else but that one be made holy (1 Thess. 4:3); that in Christ, who strengthens, one can do anything (Phil. 4:13). She speaks more of Paul than she does of John, yet when she chooses a nickname for her dearest friend, Raimondo da Capua, it is "my very special John," *mio Giovanni singolare*. Catherine's spirit was nourished by the Word as truly as her blood was revivified by the air she breathed. For her the Word *is* eternal Wisdom, *is* Jesus Christ, *is* Way and Truth and Life. And the Word is in every human attempt to express and witness to this one Word. This is well illustrated in a letter of hers (T226) to Raimondo da Capua and another disciple, Papo:

> I long to see you true sons and trumpeters of the incarnate Word, God's Son, not only with your voices but [also] in your actions. Learn from the Master of Truth, who preached virtue only after he had practiced it [Acts 1:1]. . . .
>
> It is impossible for us either to learn about or to have the good life, or to be hungry for God's honor and the salvation of souls, unless we go to the school of

the Word, the Lamb slain and abandoned on the cross, because it is there that the true teaching is found. This is what he said: "I am Way and Truth and Life." No one can go to the Father except through him [John 14:6]. Let your mind's eye be opened to see, and unplug your ears and listen to the teaching he gives you. Look at yourselves, for in him you will find yourselves, and in yourselves, him. What I mean is that you will find yourselves in him in that he is creating you in his own image and likeness—as a free gift, and not because he owes it to you [Gen. 1:26; Rom. 4:4–5]. And within yourselves you will discover God's boundless goodness in having taken on *our* likeness by the union the divine nature has effected with our human nature. . . .

Wisdom, the incarnate Word, saw and knew that [suffering] was the better part, and so he loved it and clothed himself in it. . . . Wrap this garment round you, and make it so much part of yourself that it will never be lifted from you except when life is, when we will leave behind the garment of suffering, and will stand there clothed in the garment of delight. . . . This is what the dear trumpeter Paul did. He was stripped of the joy of [seeing] the divine Essence [1 Cor. 13:12, 2 Cor. 12:2–7] and clothed himself in Christ crucified. He clothed himself in the human Christ—that is, in the sufferings and humiliations of Christ crucified, and wanted no other joy. He even said, "I refuse to glory except in the cross of Christ crucified" [Gal. 6:14]. . . . The gentle Paul seemed truly to have studied this teaching. He knew it so thoroughly that he became . . . like a sponge absorbing water, so that as he traveled along the way of humiliation, he absorbed the boundless charity and goodness with which God supremely loves us creatures. He saw that [Christ's] will is for the eternal Father's honor and our salvation and holiness (1 Thess. 4:3), and that he gave himself up to death in order to realize this holiness in us. Paul grasped and understood this. . . . And he became a vessel of love filled with fire, to carry and preach God's Word (Acts 9:15).

One can begin from practically any of the Pauline and Johannine texts that were so central for Catherine and connection by connection reconstruct the entire tapestry of her thought and spirituality. This is exactly the sort of thing she does for others in her *Dialogue* and letters and expresses so intimately in her recorded prayers. She did not nor could she have engaged in the sort of exegetical and hermeneutical study that modern scholarship would exact, but she presents an example of that integration of the Word into life in which the biblical message becomes, as it were, one's very "vocabulary." The perennial relevance of her commonsense and practical spirituality, enlivened by her saturation with the Word, has kept her writings alive through more than six centuries and through translation into every major language of the world; in recent decades this ongoing relevance has called forth a resurgence of interest in this fourteenth-century mystic and activist.

Bibliography

Caterina da Siena. *Il Dialogo della Divina Provvidenza ovvero Libro della Divina Dottrina*. 2nd ed. Edited by Giuliana Cavallini. Roma: Edizioni Cateriniane, 1995. E-book of the 1912 ed., released 2008: http://www.gutenberg.org/files/26961/26961-h/26961-h.htm.

―――. *The Dialogue of Catherine of Siena.* Translated by Suzanne Noffke. New York: Paulist Press, 1980.

―――. *Lettere.* Edited by Antonio Volpato. In *Santa Caterina da Siena: Opera Omnia: Testi e Concordanze.* Edited by Fausto Sbaffoni. Pistoia: Provincia Romana dei Frati Predicatori, 2002. Compact disk and manual.

―――. *The Letters of St. Catherine of Siena.* Translated by Suzanne Noffke. 4 vols. Tempe, AZ: Medieval & Renaissance Texts & Studies, 2000–2001, 2007–8.

―――. *The Prayers of Catherine of Siena.* Translated by Suzanne Noffke. New York: Paulist Press, 1983. 2nd ed., San Jose: iUniverse.com, 2001.

―――. *S. Caterine da Siena: Le Orazioni.* Edited by Giuliana Cavallini. Rome: Edizioni Cateriniane, 1978.

Noffke, Suzanne. *Catherine of Siena: Vision through a Distant Eye.* Collegeville, MN: Liturgical Press, 1996.

—SUZANNE NOFFKE, OP

Charles, Elizabeth Rundle (1828–96)

Elizabeth Rundle Charles was born in Tavistock, Devonshire, England, and enjoyed a relatively privileged childhood. She was an only child, and her parents' liberal approach to education led to her extensive instruction in numerous languages, history, and the liberal arts. The Rundles stressed to their daughter the importance of responsible social commitment and charity to the poor. Though Charles was a member of the Church of England throughout her life, she believed that her early exposure to a variety of denominational traditions had been to her benefit, and many of her writings strongly reflect what today might be called an "ecumenical spirit." She showed early promise as an author and received praise from Lord Alfred Tennyson and J. A. Froude for her early work. When her close but childless marriage ended with the early death of her husband shortly following the death of her father, it fell on her to support her aging mother. With little inheritance, she turned to her writing and successfully provided for both her mother and herself for the remainder of their lives.

Charles was an influential and prolific author in Victorian England. She wrote over fifty volumes, and her publishing career spanned over thirty years. Charles's work as a biblical interpreter is historically significant because developments in her own thought resulted in significant differences between her earlier and later writings, with the latter reflecting a shift in the larger culture regarding the spheres of influence deemed appropriate for women. Charles believed that writing was her vocation and a part of her Christian duty. She used her work to advocate for several social-change movements, including the abolitionist movement, the British campaign against sati (or suttee—widow-burning) in India, and the Christian missionary movement (esp. in its emphasis on the educational rights of women).

In 1862 Charles published what became her best-known book, *The Chronicles of the Schönberg-Cotta Family*, a work of historical fiction examining the life and personal influence of the young Martin Luther on the family of his printer. It went through many editions, was widely translated, and cemented Charles's reputation as a novelist. Charles followed *Chronicles* with over twenty works of religious historical fiction; although none achieved the same level of acclaim as the first, her Christian historical novels were some of the most popular works of religious fiction in nineteenth-century England. The wide reception of her fiction, however, has somewhat obscured her extensive work in other genres.

Charles also published collections of Christian poetry, hymns, essays, scriptural reflections on various themes or biblical books, a travel journal, and teaching resources intended for use by those involved in the catechesis of children or adult converts. Charles's earlier writings tend to take the form of traditional "devotional" writings, but they almost always examine biblical texts and themes and thus are interpretive texts. As time went on, however, Charles engaged more openly in the work of biblical and theological interpretation; near the end of her career, she published two works that clearly belong in the genre of biblical commentaries.

Two prominent features of her work as a biblical interpreter are the way she seeks to read the Bible as living history and her gendered exegetical style. In her interpretive efforts, Charles seeks to bring the biblical narratives to life. She believes that for Scripture to be "of its true use, the readers and writers must not be primarily 'scribes,' whose object is to multiply copies, or to utter repetitions of the books, but teachers whose purpose is to translate the letter into life" (*By the Coming*, 80). Hence, while always following the text closely, Charles often uses her gifts as an author of historical fiction to fill out the biblical account in a way that illuminates the text and serves to support the point she is making. For example, in her travel journal *Wanderings over Bible Lands and Seas* (1862), she engages in a creative imagining of what it might have been like in biblical times, based on her knowledge both of history and the scriptural text as she records her personal impressions of the geography on a trip through the Holy Land. Her method is effective at drawing the reader into the text and helps to illustrate her belief that Scripture, as the living Word of God, acts to evoke a lived experience in those who truly receive it.

A second characteristic of Charles's biblical interpretation is that she unabashedly reads the Bible through the lens of her experience as a woman. One example of the kind of gendered exegesis common in Charles's writings is the theme of the "veil." In *Sketches of the Women of Christendom* (1880), a text written to serve as a resource for female missionaries educating women in India, Charles interprets the biblical stories of important female figures in Scripture, including Eve, Mary (the mother of Jesus), Mary Magdalene, the sisters Mary and Martha, Dorcas, Lois and Eunice, Lydia, and Priscilla. She anticipates that women hearing the New Testament for the first time might find it lacking in female exemplars or question the way some of the female characters seem to prematurely disappear from the narrative. She uses the theme of the veil as an interpretive tool to explain these absences and to challenge the assumption that because there were more male-focused biblical narratives in Scripture, women are ultimately less important in the story and to God. Referencing a "veil of light [that] shines on us for a time, in some deed of sacrifice and service, and then [is] lost to sight again" (2), she draws a parallel with the "veiling" of women in Scripture and the way Jesus's divine nature was "veiled" in his humanity, suggesting that these women's narratives testify all the more so to the holy and blessed character of these female subjects. Far from indicating their unimportance, Charles interprets the silence of Scripture in relation to the stories of these women as evidence of their ultimate value as Christian models. According to Charles, these women prove more Christlike as they direct attention away from themselves and toward Christ.

This veiling theme proves to be important for Charles, and she returns to it in several other works, including both of her full-length biblical commentaries. Significantly, both commentaries were written near the end of her career and examine Hebrews and Revelation, books with a history of allegorical interpretation. This allows her to interpret them "apocalyptically," emphasize the present order as contrasted with a particular vision of the coming order, and advocate to her readers their resistance of oppressive social and ecclesiastical systems. In one of these, she even goes so far as to suggest that her "devotional" approach to biblical interpretation is more valid than the traditional "academic" and male-dominated approach (Kachur 21–22).

Charles's interpretive style is engaging and compelling, in large part because she uses many different lenses to inform her reading of the biblical text. Above all, Charles desired to help her audience (most of whom she presumed to be women) to better understand the Bible and to find points of connection between it and their own experiences. One contemporary of Charles claimed that "her gifts of expression and of awakening dormant and unsuspected powers in others, has profoundly influenced the religious life of many of the best and noblest leaders of women workers, in this age of women's work and influence" (*Our Seven Homes*, 221). While her own influence may have been great, she remained nameless in the minds of countless readers since many of her texts were credited only to "the author of 'The Chronicles of the Schönberg-Cotta Family.'" The veiled nature of her authorship appears not to have troubled Charles, who lived in the promise of a coming order where there was to be "neither male nor female" and where "the religious barriers between man and woman" would prove "mere obsolete walls, meaning nothing" (*Within the Veil*, 50–51).

Bibliography

Charles, Elizabeth Rundle. *The Book of the Unveiling: Studies in the Revelation of S. John the Divine.* London: SPCK, 1892.

—————. *By the Coming of the Holy Ghost: Thoughts for Whitsuntide; By the Author of "Chronicles of the Schonberg-Cotta Family."* London: SPCK, 1888.

—————. *Our Seven Homes: Autobiographical Reminiscences of Mrs. Rundle Charles, Author of "The Schonberg-Cotta Family."* London: John Murray, 1896.

—————. *Sketches of the Women of Christendom: By the Author of "Chronicles of the Schonberg-Cotta Family."* New York: Dodd, Mead, 1880.

—————. *Wanderings over Bible Lands and Seas.* London: T. Nelson, 1862; New York: Robert Carter & Brothers, 1866.

—————. *Within the Veil: Studies in the Epistle to the Hebrews.* London: SPCK, 1888.

Jay, Elisabeth. "Charles, Elizabeth Rundle." Pages 160–61 in vol. 11 of *Oxford Dictionary of National Biography*, edited by H. C. G. Matthew and Brian Harrison. Rev. ed. Oxford: Oxford University Press, 2004–11.

Kachur, Robert M. "Envisioning Equality, Asserting Authority: Women's Devotional Writings on the Apocalypse, 1845–1900." Pages 3–36 in *Women's Theology in Nineteenth-Century Britain: Transfiguring the Faith of Their Fathers*, edited by Julie Melnyk. New York: Garland, 1998.

Taylor, Marion Ann. "Elizabeth Rundle Charles: Translating the Letter of Scripture into Life." Pages 149–64 in *Recovering Nineteenth-Century Women Interpreters of the Bible*, edited by Christiana de Groot and Marion Ann Taylor. Atlanta: Society of Biblical Literature, 2007.

— Krista M. Dowdeswell

Chase, Mary Ellen (1887–1973)

Regarded as one of the most important literary figures in New England in the early twentieth century, Mary Ellen Chase was a distinguished teacher, writer, and scholar. She earned a doctorate in English from the University of Minnesota in 1922, then taught English there for four years, and later held positions at the College of St. Catherine and Smith College. The collection of her vast writings includes fiction for adults and children, nonfiction, biography, academic texts, essays, magazine articles, and biblical commentary.

Chase's beloved home of Maine, featured in many of her writings, gained her a reputation as a renowned author in the region. She documented her love for the heritage, history, and traditions of New England through novels. These stories held a positive view of American culture, which often received criticism. Imbued in her stories is a deep spirituality, born out of her own strong Christian faith commitments and the influence of her religious Protestant upbringing. In some way, all her works reflect the strong Puritan values her parents esteemed. Chase wrote for the general populace and avoided both scholarly jargon and controversial theological matters. Although historical criticism reigned in the academy, she instead chose a more accessible literary approach to reading Scripture.

Though her most famous works—*Mary Peters* (1934), *Silas Crockett* (1935), *Windswept* (1941), and *Edge of Darkness* (1957)—are novels that chronicle the life and times of New England, she also wrote five books on the Bible. *The Bible and the Common Reader* (1944) shows her special interest in illuminating the history of Israel as indispensible to understanding the biblical text. She provides historical background in a personal way by focusing on individuals and relationships between people and places. In this work, Chase brings the biblical text and times to life with personal anecdotes, scholarly insights, and devotional reflections. Her writing is influenced by her tendency toward storytelling, and her lively writing style made her book very popular in her community, raising interest in the biblical text and making it understandable to the average person.

Life and Language in the Old Testament (1955) is a follow-up to *The Bible and the Common Reader*. Also intended for the common reader, it was an attempt "to supply some of the keys which will open the doors to a vast and rich treasure house of language and of life" (11). The book begins with an examination of the ancient Hebrew mind—its identity, individuality, and historical journey. Chase then moves to imagination in the Old Testament and addresses how the Hebrew people perceived life, the world, and God. Finally, Chase examines the language of the Old Testament by analyzing its usage and salient peculiarities. Chase's work focuses on the main components of the biblical text, so Moses, Jacob, Abraham, David, and the prophets receive the greatest attention, but she also provides commentary on lesser recognized characters, including women.

Other books that Chase wrote demonstrate her enthusiasm for the Bible and a desire to make it accessible to the average person. These include *Readings from the Bible* (1952), *The Psalms for the Common Reader* (1962), and *The Prophets for the Common Reader* (1963).

To her work of biblical interpretation, Chase brings an expertise in reading literature. She highlights many literary features of the biblical text and notices the unique role of land, the playful use of time, and the meaning, spirit, and symbolism of place. Well before the development of modern literary criticism, she proposes that language is key to the meaning and significance of the narratives. For Chase, the directness, strength, simplicity, and charm of the narratives are brought to life by various narrative techniques, like the powers of association and suggestion, repetition, and omissions.

The language which they employed for their stories was sharp and quick, unfinished, inflexible, fragmentary in comparison; the emotions which it suggested were never fully described. And yet, through its very brevity and bareness and through its empty silences, its writers were able to evoke responses and even understandings impossible to the writers of the epics. (*Life and Language*, 117)

As a careful reader of texts, Chase asks questions that anticipate those of many contemporary narrative critics:

> Who were the "wise ladies" of Sisera's mother? Did they sit like the ladies in *Sir Patrick Spens*, waiting for tidings, with their gold combs in their hair? Did Uriah the Hittite have the least suspicion that he bore his own death concealed in David's letter to Joab? What did Heber the Kenite say to Jael, his wife, when he learned of her terrible act against his new allies? What had been the deeply laid plans between the desperate mother of Moses and his frightened sister, who stood afar off and watched the baby in his cradle of bulrushes? What did Joseph's half-brothers say about him around their sheepfolds by night? (114)

Chase's writings set the groundwork for future scholarship on type-scenes by discussing the technique of repetition of objects and motifs, and the symbolism imputed to common items, such as body parts. Importantly, Chase recognizes the use of dialogue: "It served not only to move events onward, but often to take the place of both description and exposition. Characters are left to reveal themselves largely in their speech since . . . they are rarely portrayed or explained by their creators or recorders" (153).

In her day, Chase's novels had great appeal, especially in Maine and the greater New England area, but today these works reside on history shelves of Maine libraries. Her books on the Bible reached their intended popular audience but were not acknowledged in the academic community. The time is ripe for acknowledging Chase not only as a precursor of contemporary narrative criticism but also as an insightful interpreter of biblical texts.

Bibliography

Chase, Evelyn Hyman. *Feminist Convert: A Portrait of Mary Ellen Chase*. Santa Barbara, CA: John Daniel, 1988.

Chase, Mary Ellen. *The Bible and the Common Reader*. New York: Macmillan, 1944.

———. *Life and Language in the Old Testament*. New York: W. W. Norton, 1955.

———. *The Prophets for the Common Reader*. New York: W. W. Norton, 1963.

———. *The Psalms for the Common Reader*. New York: W. W. Norton, 1962.

———. *Readings from the Bible*. New York: Macmillan, 1952.

"Mary Ellen Chase (1887–1973)." Pages 9–30 in vol. 124 of *Twentieth-Century Literary Criticism*, edited by Janet Witalec. Detroit: Gale, 2002.

Orlando, Linda M. "Mary Ellen Chase: Storyteller." May 22, 2003. http://www.suite 101.com/article.cfm/maine_people/100445.

Squire, Elienne. *A Lantern in the Wind: The Life of Mary Ellen Chase*. Santa Barbara, CA: Fithian, 1995.

— MARINA H. HOFMAN

▉ **Cheevers, Sarah** *See* Evans, Katherine (ca. 1618–92) and Sarah Cheevers (Chevers) (ca. 1608–ca. 1664)

▉ **Chidley, Katherine** (fl. 1616–53)

Katherine Chidley, seamstress and sometime Leveller (English dissenters who promoted radical social democracy, including human equality before God), was a leader of one of London's burgeoning Nonconformist congregations during the middle decades of the seventeenth century. She was the sole author of three texts—*The Justification of the Independent Churches of Christ* (1641), *A New Yeares Gift* (1645), and *Good Counsel to the Petitioners for Presbyterian Government* (1645)—each of which offers a vociferous challenge to Presbyterian ecclesiology. She also organized and contributed to the Leveller women's petitions of the 1640s and early '50s, key texts in the history of women's radical collective action, making compelling cases for the involvement of nonaristocratic women in the period's politics.

Chidley's pamphlets combine eloquent defenses of religious toleration with calls for women's rights within marriage and the household. Thus at the same time as she asserts the propriety of sectarian congregations being led by individuals without university education, she also exposes the economic oppressions of women under prelacy. She derides the issue of churching (the public appearance of women at church to return thanks after childbirth) in particular for the way it constrains women to be passive and superstitious, inveighing against ministers, who "must have another patrimony for the birth of [a] childe, for before the mother dare go abroad, shee must have their blessing that the Sun shall not smite her by day nor the Moone by night" (Chidley, *Justification*, 57).

An important biblical text for Chidley's pro-toleration perspective in the face of Presbyterian opposition to it was 1 Cor. 7:12–14, concerning the liberty of conscience regarding "unbelieving" husbands and wives. Chidley connects what she perceives as the inalienable Protestant right to freedom of worship with the intellectual and spiritual autonomy of both marriage partners, wondering "what authority [the] unbeleeving husband hath over the conscience of his believing wife. It is true he hath authority over her in bodily and physical respects, but not be a Lord over her conscience" (26).

On several occasions Chidley confronted Presbyterian ministers in person and in print on these issues. Her chief antagonist was the period's most noted heresiographer, Thomas Edwards, author of *Gangraena* (1646). Chidley's first pamphlets are point-by-point refutations of Edwards's writings; she refuses to accord him the doctrinal and gender authority he thought due to him and continues to animadvert his works even when he claims (paradoxically) that she is beneath his notice. The title page to her *Justification* gives the clearest sense of the ways that she uses biblical passages for polemical ends, to shape public response to her work and to deflate the male authority of Edwards's brand of Presbyterianism. She opens her adversarial polemical encounter with a quotation from 1 Sam. 17:45: "Thou comest unto me with a Sword and Speare and with a Shield, but I come to thee in the name of the LORD of Hoasts." As if styling Edwards as an oversized Goliath doomed to defeat by a physically unimpressive opponent is not enough, she then quotes Judg. 4:21, likening her intervention to that of Jael, "who tooke a naile of the tent, and tooke an hammer in hand, and went softly unto [Sisera], and smote the naile into his temples and fastened it to the ground." If Chidley was clear about the penetrating acuity of her arguments, she was also certain that women had a vital role to play in the toleration debates of revolutionary England.

Bibliography

Chidley, Katherine. *The Justification of the Independent Churches of Christ*. London: William Lahrner, 1641.

Gillespie, Katharine. *Domesticity and Dissent in the Seventeenth Century*. Cambridge: Cambridge University Press, 2004.

———, ed. *Katherine Chidley*. Early Modern Englishwoman: A Facsimile of Essential Works; Series 2, Printed Writings, 1641–1700; Part 4, vol. 4. Aldershot, UK: Ashgate, 2009.

Hinds, Hilary. *God's Englishwomen: Seventeenth-Century Radical Sectarian Writing and Feminist Criticism*. Manchester, UK: Manchester University Press, 1996.

Nevitt, Marcus. *Women and the Pamphlet Culture of Revolutionary England, 1640–1660*. Aldershot, UK: Ashgate, 2006.

— MARCUS NEVITT

Christine de Pizan (ca. 1364–ca. 1430)

Christine de Pizan (Pisan) was born in Venice and came to Paris as a child to reunite with her father, a physician/astrologer of King Charles V. She was educated by her father and first used his library to carry out her research (later she was given access to libraries owned by the king and his kin). The deaths of her father and her husband when she was about twenty-five left her almost destitute. She began writing in about 1393 to support herself and her family, and thus can be called the first professional woman writer in Europe. Her first works—courtly poetry, very much in fashion at the time—guaranteed her the patronage of powerful people at court. The important value of human love was one of the three great foci of her literary inspiration. The second was her defense of the French monarchy and her denunciation of the Hundred Years' War and the civil war that ensued. The third was her defense and praise of women.

Christine's prodigious writings include many poems and more than a dozen long treatises. Although a deeply religious woman, she wrote only a few religious works. Nevertheless, her spirituality can be found in all her writings. She was a literary interpreter of the Bible. In about 1402 she wrote her first religious works in verse: *L'Oroyson Nostre Dame*, *Les XV joyes Nostre Dame* and *Une Oroyson de Nostre Seigneur* (*Oeuvres*, 1:1–26). The first of these is composed in stanzas separated by the litany "Ave Maria." It is a prayer that does not follow any model, but Christine uses the names of SS. Bernard, Augustine, Ambrose, Jerome, and Anselm, plus Cassiodorus, as famous theologians who had written on Mary's unique virtues. Christine requests that the Virgin protect the French nobility, particularly the queen, and all the women of the kingdom.

The second work retells fifteen happy episodes of Mary's life. This is not a new theme, but what distinguishes Christine's work from the other "Joies de la Vierge" is that it is written in verse, which makes it more refined for courtly readers and less monotonous than the prose versions. Christine stresses that Mary is the one person who can procure salvation for all sinners, and she puts a strong emphasis on the maternal vocation of the Virgin. As one critic wrote: "The joys signify the happiness that motherhood brings through the definitive triumph of life" (Gros 106).

The third poem is based on the lessons found in Scripture. In sixty stanzas separated by the litany "Pater Noster," it recalls the life of Christ and in particular his passion as witnessed through his mother's sensibility (Gros 109). Again, Christine's brand of early feminism can be seen in her stressing throughout the poem the unbearable pain felt by the mother during the various stages of her son's passion.

Most of Christine's work was not written for explicitly religious purposes, yet her writings have a great deal of biblical content, thus she draws examples of famous women from the Bible. In *Le Livre de la cité des dames* (1405), for instance, Christine builds a pantheon of famous women. The first part celebrates famous women from antiquity or Greek mythology for their accomplishments; in the last two parts, Christine comments on several women who "will forever be praised in the Holy Scriptures" (*Ladies*, 107). She reminds her readers that there were women prophets in the Bible (not following their chronological appearances in the Bible): Deborah, in the time when the judges ruled over Israel; Elizabeth, who recognized her cousin as the Mother of God; Anna, who announced that the infant Jesus would save the world; and the Queen of Sheba, who prophesied upon seeing a long board lying over a mud puddle that whoever (and it was to be Christ) destroyed the law of the Jews would die on the wood of this plank (106). This last example is not found in the Old Testament; Christine may have read this story of the Queen of Sheba as a prophet in the *Golden Legend*, a text that she knew quite well. Christine provides examples of good that has come into the world due to the actions of women: she comments on the stories of Judith and Esther, who both delivered their people from slavery. Judith, though young and beautiful, was chaste and virtuous, and she prayed day and night to the Lord to help her enslaved people. She killed Holofernes, and her people were freed by her, "the honest woman who will forever be praised on this account in the Holy Scriptures" (145). Christine writes that God saved his people through another woman, Esther, who persuaded her husband, King Ahasuerus, to have Haman, his adviser who had plotted to have her people killed, taken prisoner and hanged for his crimes.

Christine argues against men who say that there are few chaste women by giving examples of women pure in their bodies and thoughts, like Susanna, who was ready to die rather than sin with the old men who coveted her body. Pharaoh lusted after the chaste Sarah, but God punished him with such terrible diseases of mind and body that he never touched her. Rebecca, the wife of Isaac, behaved with such humility toward her husband that God granted her his grace and love, and although she was barren, he gave her two children, one of whom became a patriarch of Israel. Although Christine notes that for brevity she has to omit many virtuous and chaste women from her narrative, she provides one last example: Ruth, who was "quite chaste during her marriage as well as during her widowhood" (*Ladies*, 157). She infers that Ruth was chaste since her mother-in-law loved her for her kindness to her dead husband and herself, and Boaz also recognized that Ruth had not gone after men. Christine had carefully chosen her biblical heroines since for many centuries some of them had been thought to prefigure Christ: like him, they suffer, they are tried in public, they defeat evil, they are saviors.

On the basis of her female-centered theology, she understands creation not as gendered bodies but as ungendered souls. Her argument is as follows: "Some men are foolish enough to think, when they hear that God made men in His image, that this refers to the material body. This was not the case, for God had not yet taken a human body. The soul is meant, the intellectual spirit which lasts eternally just like the Deity. God created the soul and placed wholly similar souls, equally good and noble in the feminine and in the masculine bodies" (*Ladies*, 23). On the creation of the body, she writes that "woman was made by the Supreme Craftsman. In what place was she created? In the terrestrial paradise. From what substance? Was it vile matter [implying that such was the case with Adam]? No, it was from the noblest substance which had ever been created: it was from body of man from which God made woman" (24). When God formed the body of woman out of one of Adam's ribs, he signified that "she should stand at his side as a companion and never lie at his feet like a slave and also that he should love her as his own flesh" (24). Christine also writes that women should be glad for Eve's misdeed since they gained more through Mary the redeemer than what they lost through Eve. Therefore, "for as low as human nature fell through this creature woman, was human nature lifted higher by this same creature" (24). To men who attack women by saying that "God made women to speak, weep, and sew," Christine retorts that Jesus himself shed tears "from the eyes of his worthy and glorious body when he saw Mary Magdalene and her sister Martha weep for their dead brother

Lazarus the leper and then resurrected him" (27). Christine reminds her readers that Jesus was moved by a woman in tears because she had lost a child, and he resurrected him (Luke 7:11–17). To men who attack women because they talk too much, Christine writes that if women's language had been so blameworthy, "our Lord Jesus Christ would never have deigned to wish that so worthy a mystery as His most gracious resurrection be first announced by a woman, just as He commanded the blessed Magdalene, to whom He first appeared on Easter, to report and announce it to His apostles and to Peter. Blessed God, may You be praised, who, among the other infinite boons and favors which You have bestowed upon the feminine sex, desired that woman carry such lofty and worthy news" (28). As for sewing, Christine writes that "God desired that this be natural for women, for it is an occupation necessary for divine service" (30).

Les Sept psaumes allégorisés (1409) is Christine's commentary on the seven Penitential Psalms. Each psalm verse is followed by a personal commentary interlaced with biblical quotations or allusions from the fathers of the church, contemporary theologians like Jean Gerson, or historical events. For example, Ps. 102 in Christine's text reads:

> XVII. **He regarded the prayer of the destitute and did not despise their supplication.** Dear sweet Jesus Christ, who heard the prayers of the destitute and did not despise them, I beg you, in memory of the day when you were led to the high priest Caiaphas at daybreak to be accused and struck harshly, to hear my voice that asks you again in the name of the Catholic Church, which you had seemingly given up a while ago, to grant your shepherd Alexander, your newly elected vicar, and to all who will succeed him, understanding, power, strength, and the desire to rule over the holy papal office to their souls' profit, to the increase of the holy faith, to the Christendom's salvation, and to the repair made to the past ruin. Keep them especially free from evil vainglory, pride, and lust. I beg of you to grant the same to all prelates, priests, and people who take care of souls, to all the clergy. Give me the virtue of compassion so that I am inclined to help the destitute as best I can. (127, my trans.)

"Allégorisés" means several things in this work: it is, of course, the interpretation of these Old Testament texts on the basis of Christian doctrines, but it also means, as Rains puts it, "any kind of picturesque, symbolic or metaphorical interpretation of words or larger units of thought, including number symbolism, typology, etc." (43). The psalms are also "the basis for extended moral commentary on the speaker's vices and virtues" (Walters 145). Psalm 51 follows the Athanasian Creed, which enumerates the seven deadly sins, the five bodily senses, the Ten Commandments, the twelve articles of faith, and the seven gifts of the Holy Spirit. In it, Christine prays to Christ that he understand the sins of humankind. Psalm 130 contains new petitions in honor of the seven last words of Christ: Christine makes them on behalf of the lower classes of society and on behalf of all pious women, whatever class they come from, to help them realize their salvation. The image of the sufferings of the body politic is inspired by the sufferings of Christ. Psalm 143 invokes the death of Christ and his last words, and Christine prays that all Christians go safely through the pilgrimage of human life to reach the repose of the heavens. She even prays for miscreants, Saracens, pagans, and the blind Jews to be led back to God's holy law.

In her *Épistre de la prison de vie humaine* (1418), a letter addressed as a consolation to noble women who have lost relatives at the famous battle of Agincourt, Christine comments on the cryptic words of Paul in 1 Cor. 15 regarding the resurrection. Refusing to follow Benedict XII's doctrine proclaiming that the worthy dead will possess the beatific vision immediately after their demise (Wisman 340), Christine asserts that body and soul will be reunited on judgment day. In this work uniquely dedicated to a feminine audience, she describes how they will find their loved ones on this day. They will be able to live their eternal life in the same material body that they had before, but it will be a body glorified by the traditional four *dotes* (which are the gifts of *claritas*, *agilitas*, *subtilitas*, and *impassibilitas*), and so they will be able to embrace their loved ones, talk to them, and live in their company in the celestial court.

Christine wrote her last commentary on the Bible in about 1420: *Les Heures de contemplacion sur la Passion de Nostre Seigneur*. Its structure is borrowed from the Divine Office celebrated seven times a day in monasteries, and it relates the passion of Christ in eight sections. The modern critics Boulton and Dulac have noticed how the author encourages her readers to take an active role in her representation of the passion; at times she also seems to be like a disciple in the presence of Christ. They also remark on the countenance and dignity of Christ's mother in comforting the apostles. This text was written in the abbey of Poissy, where Christine had retired by then and where she died.

Until the French Revolution, Christine was often referenced in a generally laudatory manner. But in the nineteenth century, when literature became an object of study in schools and universities, her name seemed to have almost completely disappeared. At the beginning of the last century, her works were rediscovered. Her unique defense of women and her statement that they are intellectually equal to men, her love for her country, and her efforts to put a stop to all wars, always accompanied by a deep spirituality—all these features have nowadays made her one of the most studied medieval writers and interpreters of Scripture.

Bibliography

Boulton, Maureen. "Christine's *Heures de contemplacion de la Passion* in the Context of Late-Medieval Passion Devotion." Pages 99–113 in vol. 1 of *Contexts and Continuities*, edited by Angus J. Kennedy with Rosalind Brown-Grant, James C. Laidlaw, and Catherine M. Müller. Glasgow: University of Glasgow Press, 2002.

Christine de Pizan [Pisan]. *The Book of the City of Ladies.* Translated by Earl Jeffrey Richards. 2nd ed. New York: Persea Books, 1982. Repr., 1998.

―――. *The Epistle of the Prison of Human Life . . .* Edited by Josette A. Wisman. New York: Garland, 1984.

―――. *Les Sept psaumes allégorisés.* Edited by Ruth Ringland Rains. A critical ed. from the Brussels and Paris MSS. Washington, DC: Catholic University of America Press, 1965.

―――. *Oeuvres poétiques de Christine de Pisan.* Published by Maurice Roy. 3 vols. Paris: Firmin Didot, 1886–96.

Dulac, Liliane. "Littérature et dévotion: À propos des *Heures de contemplacion sur la Passion de Nostre Seigneur* de Christine de Pizan." Pages 475–84 in vol. 1 of *Miscellanea mediaevalia,* edited by J. Claude Faucon, Alain Labbé, and Danielle Quéruel. Paris: Honoré Champion, 1998.

Gros, Gérard. "'Mon oroison, entens . . .' Étude sur les trois opuscules pieux de Christine de Pizan." *Bien dire et bien apprendre* 8 (1990): 99–112.

Walters, Lori J. "The Royal Vernacular: Poet and Patron in Christine de Pizan's *Sept Psaumes allégorisés* and *Charles V.*" Pages 145–82 in *The Vernacular Spirit: Essays on Medieval Religious Literature,* edited by Renate Blumenfeld-Kosinski, Duncan Roberston, and Nancy Bradley-Warren. Basingstoke, UK: Palgrave Macmillan, 2002.

Wisman, Josette. "The Resurrection according to Christine de Pizan." *Religion and the Arts* 3–4 (2000): 337–59.

—JOSETTE A. WISMAN

■Clare of Assisi (1193/94–1253)

Known as the founder of the female branch of the Franciscan order, Clare pioneered the religious way of life for monastic women within the Franciscan family. Clare was born into an affluent family in Assisi and therefore was presumed to marry. Hagiographic accounts, however, highlight that Clare was already widely recognized as pious and unusually gifted spiritually by her contemporaries when she was a girl. Dedicated to a life of prayer and self-mortification even in her youth, she would have encountered the charismatic Francis when she was in her early teens, although their first actual meeting was probably in 1211, when she was seventeen. Clare is said to have heard Francis of Assisi preach a series of Lenten sermons during 1212 at the church of St. Giorgio in Assisi, and was thereby inspired to lead a form of vowed religious life modeled on Francis's path. At the age of eighteen, on the evening of Palm Sunday 1212, Clare left her family, chaperoned by an aunt, and met Francis and his companions at the Portiuncula, where Francis cut her hair in a tonsure symbolizing her entry into vowed religious life (Carney 37). To prevent rumors of unseemly relations between Clare and the male band of Franciscans, she was delivered to a nearby Benedictine monastery of San Paolo. Eventually, after volatile efforts by Clare's relatives to force her to return to fulfill family obligations, Clare persevered in her vow, joined by her sister Agnes and eventually many other women. In time, they moved to San Damiano, where she lived out the rest of her life, diligently providing leadership to her growing group of followers and crafting reasoned arguments to secure for them the life dedicated to gospel living that they desperately sought. They were known by contemporaries as the "Poor Ladies" and are generally referred to as "Poor Clares," "Clarisses," or the second order of the Franciscans.

While most of the details of Clare's life after she entered vowed religious life remain secret behind the monastic walls she accepted, it is clear that from within the cloister, Clare diligently supervised and administered her community of sisters as their abbess, a position she reluctantly accepted from Francis, but one that she mastered, despite chronic illness. Her leadership periodically leaked out beyond the walls, as in an episode of her life that took place in 1240 and that has become an iconic scene: Clare faced down approaching enemy forces by standing at an exterior window of San Damiano, holding a monstrance bearing the holy sacrament as her only defense (Peterson 222). The scene, depicted by many artists, encapsulates Clare's faith and, more important, her life: armed with nothing but Christ, she could withstand even the strongest of enemies.

After a life dedicated to protecting her community both physically and spiritually, Clare died on August 11, 1253, just two days after the Rule that she had written to protect the primacy of poverty in the lives of the Poor Ladies finally received papal approval.

Clare's extant written work is limited to one Rule and four letters addressed to Agnes of Prague. Other works attributed to her, including a testament, blessing, and another letter, are of contested authenticity. The paucity of her writing, much like that of Francis, reflects the nature of her religious vocation. Rather than serving a public with copious spiritual teachings, Clare served her immediate community through leadership, through private teachings that do not remain extant, and through her life as a role model of her understanding of gospel living.

The four letters to Agnes of Prague reflect development of Clare's spiritual interests and concerns over time since they were written over a nineteen-year span. But these letters are not exactly Clare's own spiritual reflections. Written to advise the royal princess Agnes on the rigors of religious life, the letters reflect Clare's wise and gentle counsel as a spiritual adviser to Agnes, and they should be read in this light. The letters reflect Clare's mastery of the use of biblical sources to support her understanding of the Franciscan life.

Letter 1 offers a contrast of the secular and spiritual life for Agnes before the latter entered religious life in 1234. In between paragraphs of exposition on the religious life, heavily referenced with passages from the New Testament, Psalms, and liturgies, Clare offers poetic summaries of main points, especially related to poverty, Clare's more fervently contested spiritual vow:

O, blessed poverty,
Who bestows eternal riches on those who love and embrace her!
O holy poverty,
To those who possess and desire you,
God promises *the kingdom of heaven* [Matt. 5:3]
And offers, indeed, eternal glory and blessed life!
O God-centered poverty,
Whom the Lord Jesus Christ,
Who ruled and now rules heaven and earth,
Who spoke and things were made [cf. Pss. 33:9; 148:5],
Condescended to embrace before all else!

(Armstrong 192)

In Letter 2, written between 1235 and 1236, Clare encourages Agnes in her vowed life and grounds the central tenet of lived poverty in the practice of contemplation. Clare's style of argument remains the same, with a carefully woven persuasive exposition punctuated by scriptural passages for support. Letter 3 focuses specifically on answering Agnes's concern about the practice of fasting and abstinence following a papal declaration in 1237 mandating total abstinence from meat. In a response similar to her previous letter, Clare encourages Agnes to rest her concerns on higher, more nourishing issues:

Place your mind before the mirror of eternity!
Place your soul in *the brilliance of glory*. [cf. Heb. 1:3]
Place your heart in *the figure of the* divine *substance*! [cf. Heb. 1:3]
And *transform* your whole being *into the image* of the Godhead Itself through contemplation. [cf. 2 Cor. 3:18]

(Armstrong 200)

In the final letter, written at an unknown date but certainly much later, most likely near the end of Clare's life in 1253, Clare writes of the joy and, interestingly enough, wealth that she has experienced while living a vowed religious life, and she encourages Agnes once again to persevere in her faith:

Happy, indeed, is she to whom it is given to share this sacred banquet,
To cling with all her heart to Him
Whose beauty all the heavenly hosts admire unceasingly,
Whose love inflames our love,
Whose contemplation is our refreshment,
Whose graciousness is our joy. . . .

(Armstrong 204)

Inasmuch as this vision is *the splendor of eternal glory* [Heb. 1:3], *the brilliance of eternal light and the mirror without blemish* [Wis. 7:26], look upon that mirror each day, O queen and spouse of Jesus Christ, and continually study your face within it, so that you may adorn yourself within and without with beautiful robes and cover yourself with the flowers and garments of all the virtues as becomes the daughter and most chaste bride of the Most High King. (Armstrong 204)

The other writing attributed to Clare is the Rule, which she worked on and fought for through much of her religious life. Having been given guidelines for the religious life by Francis when she entered into vows, Clare accepted the Benedictine Rule for the Poor Ladies in 1217. A new Rule was written for them in 1247 by Innocent IV. In neither Rule is the practice of poverty, so central to the Franciscan understanding of gospel living, included. Clare began writing her own version of a Rule that received papal approval on August 9, 1253. While this Rule is, interestingly enough, not peppered with as many scriptural passages or references as her letters, it is based on Clare's understanding of how the Poor Ladies could live scripturally, that is, according to the gospel: "The form of life of the Order of the Poor Sisters which the Blessed Francis established, is this: to observe the holy Gospel of our Lord Jesus Christ, by living in obedience, without anything of one's own, and in chastity" (Armstrong 211). Where possible, scriptural foundation is given to support the tenets of the Rule. For example, when entering the community, a woman is to "let the words of the holy Gospel be addressed to her: that she should *go and sell* all that she has and take care to distribute the proceeds *to the poor* [cf. Matt. 19:21]" (Armstrong 212). In stipulating the appropriate dress for the sisters, Clare affirms, "And for the love of the most holy and beloved Child Who *was wrapped* in the poorest of *swaddling clothes and laid in a manger* [cf. Luke 2:7–12] and of His most holy Mother, I admonish, entreat, and exhort my sisters that they always wear the poorest of garments" (Armstrong 213). In much of the remainder of the Rule, Clare turns to the Later Rule of Francis for referencing. Nevertheless, the premise of the Rule is gospel living.

Like many medieval women, Clare's understanding of Scripture is perhaps found reflected more in her way of life than in her extant writings. To understand how Clare commented on Scripture, one really needs to examine how she lived out a life of poverty and, equally important, how she fought for that life of poverty against contemporary assumptions that women were too frail to endure the rigors of material poverty, which their male counterparts purported to embrace. For Clare, living the gospel life clearly included a patient willingness to persevere in claiming the right to live with personal integrity as well as obedience to hierarchical authorities. Thus Clare's most important contribution in biblical commentary is found more in the accounts of her life, even though these accounts are shrouded in hagiographic myth. And in the end, much of her life remains unknown precisely because of the poverty she lived in. As Armstrong writes, "This poverty of sources . . . is very much in keeping with the life of Clare, for it reflects her total absorption in the mystery of Christ and her desire to imitate Him in poverty and humility."

Thus the few writings of Saint Clare are eloquent reminders to everyone who is curious about her place in the Franciscan heritage of her total commitment to its ideals" (174).

Recent scholarship has reshaped our understanding of Clare and her contributions to Franciscan spirituality. Far from being a passive recipient of Francis's influence and tutelage, Clare likely in turn influenced Francis in her own experiences and teachings, and certainly displayed strong leadership in carving out a way of life for women that held true to the Franciscan ideals of gospel living. As Margaret Carney writes, "She dared to synthesize the evangelical ideals of Francis, the new forms of urban female religiosity, and the best wisdom of the monastic tradition to create a new and enduring order in the Church" (19). Nevertheless, the attention she receives as the founder of the female branch of Franciscans tends to unduly overshadow the women who followed in the Franciscan tradition, but outside monastic walls (Pryds passim).

Bibliography

Armstrong, Regis J., OFM, and Ignatius Brady, OFM., trans. *Francis and Clare: The Complete Works*. New York: Paulist Press, 1982.

Bartoli, Marco. *Chiara d'Assisi*. Rome: Instituto Storico dei Cappucini, 1989.

Carney, Margaret, OSF. *The First Franciscan Woman: Clare of Assisi and Her Form of Life*. Quincy, IL: Franciscan Press, 1993.

Clare of Assisi. "Epistolae ad b. Agnetem." Edited by W. Seton. *Archivum Franciscanum historicum* 17 (1924): 513–19.

———. "Regula." Pages 49–75 in *Seraphicae legislationis textus originales*. Claras Aquas, Quaracchi: Collegium S. Bonaventurae, 1897.

Mooney, Catherine M. "*Imitatio Christi* or *Imitatio Mariae?* Clare of Assisi and Her Interpreters." Pages 52–77 in *Gendered Voices: Medieval Saints and Their Interpreters*, edited by Catherine M. Mooney. Philadelphia: University of Pennsylvania Press, 1999.

Mueller, Joan. *The Privilege of Poverty. Clare of Assisi, Agnes of Prague, and the Struggle for a Franciscan Rule for Women*. University Park, PA: University of Pennsylvania Press, 2006.

Peterson, Ingrid, OSF. *Clare of Assisi: A Biographical Study*. Quincy, IL: Franciscan Press, 1993.

Pryds, Darleen. *Women of the Streets: Early Franciscan Women and Their Mendicant Vocation*. St. Bonaventure, OK: Franciscan Institute Pubs., 2010.

— DARLEEN PRYDS

Collins, An (ca. 1653)

Little is known about the woman who composed the slim volume of devotional material titled *Divine Songs and Meditations*. The title page of the last extant copy (now housed at the Huntington Library in San Marino, CA) attributes the collection to An Collins, a seventeenth-century woman who is now known only through her published work. In this collection of religious verse, Collins presents herself as a woman who, if not formally educated, delights in learning and the pursuit of knowledge. She read widely from "pleasant histories" and "profane discourses" ("The Discourse," in Collins 106–19) and "became affected to Poetry, insomuch that I proceeded to practice the same" ("To the Reader," 1). Of greater value to Collins, however, than these secular works was the enlightening of her mind by the Spirit and the revelation of "Divine Truth" through meditation on Scripture and the study of theology ("A Song demonstrating the vanities of Earthly things," 21–36). Collins considered her intellectual curiosity and ability a gift from God and best employed when placed in the service of the study of God and his ways in the world. Religiously, the language and themes of her poetry associate her with Protestantism and suggest sympathies with more radical groups like the Quakers (Gottlieb, in Collins xvii–xviii). References to the English Civil War (1642–51) and other political controversies and religious debates of her day date the writing of her poetry to the 1640s and early '50s. When she was born, where she lived, whether she was married—this information is lost to history.

Divine Songs and Meditations is comprised of a prose epistle to the reader, a verse preface, an extended discourse in which Collins outlines her spiritual autobiography, thirteen poems, five meditations, and concluding verses paraphrasing Eccles. 12. Her stated goal for the volume is to bring the comfort of God's grace to Christians who are "of disconsolate Spirit." The experience of suffering and vulnerability was central to Collins's life and forms a dominant theme in many of her poems. For Collins, pain is not purposeless, but rather it nudges us back to God, in whose presence and care we experience true contentment and joy. Although Protestantism provided the background for her convictions about the sovereignty and goodness of God, Scripture supplied her with the language and imagery for interpreting and describing her own spiritual life. For Collins, the words of Scripture are not so much to be interpreted as internalized and appropriated so as to lend divine perspective on human experience and to direct the hearts and minds of God's people toward God. Though Collins's writing incorporates allusions and key phrases from the full range of Scripture, she is particularly attentive to the Song of Songs, adopting the cadences and rhythm of the Song for her own poetry. The lush, Eden-like garden of the Song, in all its serenity and fecundity, functions as both the counterpoint to Collins's state of mind and soul in the midst of her suffering as well as a metaphor for the transforming power of God's healing and restoring activity in her life when "the Spring succeedeth Winter, and Day must follow Night" ("Another Song exciting to spirituall Mirth," 12–13).

Throughout her poetry, Collins does little to focus attention on her gender, preferring instead to represent her experiences as common to human existence. While she occasionally mentions or alludes to women of the Bible, she rarely lingers over their stories. Whether she hoped by this to have wider appeal to mixed audiences is not clear. However, she seems keenly aware of the need to establish her legitimacy as a devotional poet, appealing to her robust intellect; the calling, gifts, and opportunities granted her by God; her own experience in suffering; and the imposition of divine truth on her mind. In large measure the authority of her voice is achieved by association with traditional Christian doctrine and her employment of the words of Scripture. However, Collins also regularly underscores her own significant contribution and ample qualifications for the task, refusing to downplay her own agency in the exposition of truth reflected in her poetry.

Collins has been compared to well-known religious poets like George Herbert for her wit, her literary skill and innovation in wielding poetic forms, and the depth of her spiritual integrity. In the development of her personal theodicy throughout this devotional work, she offers her readers the firm ground of faith on which to stand while she wrestles with, questions, and ponders the meaning of suffering in the Christian life. Among other virtues, the richness of her theological reflection and authenticity of her writing render this work of abiding value and ensure her place among other devotional interpreters of Scripture.

Bibliography

Collins, An. *Divine Songs and Meditations*. Edited by Sidney Gottlieb. Tempe, AZ: Medieval Renaissance Texts & Studies, 1996.

Gottlieb, Sidney. "An Collins and the Experience of Defeat." Pages 216–26 in *Representing Women in Renaissance England*, edited by Claude J. Summers and Ted-Larry Pebworth. Columbia: University of Missouri Press, 1997.

Hobby, Elaine. *Virtue of Necessity: English Women's Writing, 1649–88*. London: Virago, 1988.

Norcliffe, Mary. "An Collins (FL. 1653): Mistress of Religious Verse." PhD diss., University of Massachusetts, 1998.

Wilcox, Helen. "My Soule in Silence?" Pages 9–23 in *Representing Women in Renaissance England*, edited by Claude J. Summers and Ted-Larry Pebworth. Columbia: University of Missouri Press, 1997.

— AMANDA BENCKHUYSEN

■ Copley, Esther Beuzeville Hewlett (1786–1851)

Esther Copley was born Esther Beuzeville, the daughter of Peter (Pierre) Beuzeville (1741–1812), a silk manufacturer, and his wife, Mary (Marie) Griffith Meredith (1744–1811). Following her father's retirement from business, the Beuzevilles settled at Henley-on-Thames, where they worshiped in a dissenting church; a plaque commemorating the family can be found at the United Reformed Church in Henley-on-Thames.

Esther Beuzeville married James Philip Hewlett (1779/80–1820) in 1809, and the couple lived in Oxford, where Hewlett was an Anglican clergyman.

It is not known if Esther attended her husband's church during their marriage; certainly she worshiped at the Baptist chapel in Oxford following his early death. The Hewletts had three sons and two daughters. Esther began publishing in 1815; following her husband's death in 1820, her writing was the primary means of support for herself and her children.

In 1827 Esther Beuzeville Hewlett married William Copley (d. 1857). At that time William Copley was the minister at the Baptist chapel in Oxford. The Copleys moved from Oxford following William Copley's career, living first in St. Helier on the island of Jersey, then at Eythorne, Kent, when William Copley was called to be the minister of the Baptist chapel there. William Copley was an alcoholic, and his wife apparently wrote his sermons and ensured that he performed his Sunday duties. Eventually William Copley resigned his post and left Eythorne and his wife in 1847. Esther Copley remained in Eythorne until her death in 1851. She is buried in the Baptist churchyard there.

Esther Copley was a prolific author. She began publishing as Esther Hewlett in 1815. One of her early efforts, *Cottage Comforts* (1825), a domestic economy, was also one of her most successful works, still in demand more than a decade after her death. Copley's writings were primarily directed to the young and the poor. She tried to inculcate in her readers good moral principles in addition to providing them with some understanding of the world. Four of her works for youth focus on the Bible: *Scripture Natural History for Youth* (1828), *Scripture History for Youth* (1828), *A Brief View of Sacred History from the Creation of the World to the Destruction of Jerusalem by the Romans* (1831), and *Scripture Biography* (1835). *A Brief View of Sacred History* was written to fill a perceived need for an affordable textbook that could be used for Christian education. Copley presented the other three works as a collection, providing different kinds of information that would assist maturing readers in understanding the Bible better.

Scripture Natural History for Youth describes the natural objects found in the Bible. These "natural productions" are organized by the familiar categories "Animal, Vegetable, and Mineral" (1). The book appears to use the Bible as a starting point for a discussion of the natural world, with biblical references taking up little of the space given to each natural object. For example, in the section on the lion, which leads the "Animal" category, most space is given to a description of lions and anecdotal reports of their behavior; relatively little space is given to biblical references to lions, with emphasis on the fact that the lion was the symbol of the tribe of Judah. While this kind of discussion may not seem to be biblical interpretation, it is important to realize that readers are left with the firm impression that the creatures, plants, and minerals of the biblical world are a part of the real world of sense experience. This book anchors the Bible in the reality of the world around young readers and dispels any notion that the biblical world might be a fantasy realm.

Scripture History for Youth, the second of the three works intended to aid the youthful reader in understanding the Bible, provides "a connected view of Scripture History" (1:iii). Where *Scripture Natural History* anchors the biblical world in the world of her readers' experience, *Scripture History* anchors the biblical story in world history. For her retelling of the story of the Bible, Copley consulted "standard biblical writers" to ensure that her explanations of "Oriental Customs" are correct (1:iii–iv). While Copley wants her readers to understand the general history of the Bible, she also hopes to "promote the growth of early piety" (1:iv). Copley promotes piety by applying the biblical stories to the lives of her readers. For example, after the story of the fall, Copley comments that "clothing was rendered necessary by sin," and admonishes her readers to let this fact be "a check upon pride of apparel" (1:37).

Copley's third volume on the Bible for older youth, *Scripture Biography*, provides the biographical details of biblical characters left out of the general history found in *Scripture History* (*Scripture History*, 2:iii). (For a comparison of the two works, see the excerpts on the creation of woman and the biographical entry on Eve found in Taylor and Weir 33–37.) In Copley's view, biography provides more obvious examples and applications than the general history, and she hoped it would aid readers "in the pursuit of whatsoever things are lovely and of good report" (*Scripture Biography*, iv). Copley's view of piety, particularly for women, was influenced by her nineteenth-century context. This is clearly seen in the discussion of Deborah in *Scripture Biography*. While readers can "admire the splendid and high achievements of Deborah," they are reminded "that woman's truest excellence in general consists of the gentler virtues of humility, meekness, patience, self-denial, industry, prudence, and benevolence" (167).

Scripture Biography is more than a book to introduce youth to the characters of the Bible. It also contains alphabetically arranged entries for every person named in the Bible. Each entry provides background information on the character and the major events of that life as recorded in the Bible. The entries on major figures, such as Jesus, Moses, Paul, or David, extend over several pages, with shorter entries of a paragraph or two for minor characters. This substantial work of scholarship has not yet been studied in any detail. Along with Copley's other works that engage the Bible (including *A History of Slavery and Its Abolition*, 1836), *Scripture Biography* needs further study in the twenty-first century.

Bibliography

Copley, Esther Hewlett. *Scripture Biography: Comprehending All the Names Mentioned in the Old and New Testaments*. London: Sunday School Union, 1835.

———. *Scripture History for Youth*. 2 vols. London: H. Fisher, Son & P. Jackson, 1828.

———. *Scripture Natural History for Youth*. 2 vols. London: H. Fisher, Son & P. Jackson, 1828.

Mitchell, Rosemary. "Copley, Esther." Pages 343–44 in vol. 13 of *The Oxford Dictionary of National Biography*, edited by H. C. G. Matthew and Brian Harrison. Rev. ed. Oxford: Oxford University Press, 2004–11.

Taylor, Marion Ann, and Heather E. Weir. *Let Her Speak for Herself: Nineteenth-Century Women Writing on Women in Genesis*. Waco: Baylor University Press, 2006.

— HEATHER WEIR

Corbaux, Marie Françoise Catherine Doetter (Fanny) (1812–83)

Fanny Corbaux was born in 1812 to the well-known English statistician and mathematician Francis Corbaux, who spent much time abroad. Fanny and her sister Louisa (b. 1808) were both talented artists, but since women were unable to study at the Royal Academy Schools until 1861, they were self-taught. Fanny taught herself to paint by copying works in the National Gallery and the British Institution for Promoting the Fine Arts. When her father experienced financial distress and health problems in 1827, Fanny Corbaux's artistic talents supplied the family with needed income. Corbaux's miniature portraits were very popular; her larger watercolors regularly featured literary and biblical heroines including Hagar, Miriam, Leah, Naomi, Ruth, and Hannah. Gold medals and honorary membership in the Society of British Artists and the New Society of Painters in Water-Colour followed.

Corbaux also developed interests in biblical scholarship and became a distinguished self-taught biblical scholar. Captivated by the early history of Israel and biblical languages, she mastered Greek and Hebrew, traveled extensively in the Holy Land, and entered into scholarly discussions about historical geography, Semitic philology, and the history of Israel. She lectured in various academic societies, published in scholarly periodicals, and was well received in the academic community. In 1843 *The Edinburgh New Philosophical Journal* published her lengthy article "On the Comparative Physical Geography of the Arabian Frontier of Egypt, at the Earliest Epoch of Egyptian History and at the Present Time." A series of articles on the geography of the exodus published in *The Athenaeum* in 1848–50 featured again her expertise in historical geography. Corbaux's philological work was featured in "The Rephaim, and Their Connection with Egyptian History," in the renowned *Journal of Sacred Literature* (1851). Her identification of the Egyptian gods An, On, or Onnos with the Chaldean god Oannes and with the Philistine god Dagon elicited considerable scholarly debate.

Corbaux's acceptance into the guild of biblical scholars was exceptional. Scholarly confidence in her abilities as a scholar peaked when she was asked to write the historical and chronological introduction to Heath's *The Exodus Papyri* (1855). Corbaux deserves to be recognized as one of England's first accepted female lay biblical scholars. She died in Brighton on February 1, 1883.

Bibliography

Corbaux, Miss F. "Geography of the Exodus." *The Athenaeum*, Oct. 21, 1849, 1048, 1053–54; March 23, 1850, 311–12; April 27, 1850, 449–50.

———. "On the Comparative Physical Geography of the Arabian Frontier of Egypt, at the Earliest Epoch of Egyptian History and at the Present Time." *Edinburgh New Philosophical Journal* 44 (1848): 13–42, 209–31.

———. "The Rephaim, and Their Connection with Egyptian History." *Journal of Sacred Literature*, NS, 1 (1851): 151–72.

Yeldham, Charlotte. "Corbaux, Marie Françoise Catherine Doetter [Fanny], (1812–1883)." Pages 381–82 in vol. 13 of *Oxford Dictionary of National Biography*, edited by H. C. G. Matthew and Brian Harrison. Oxford: Oxford University Press, 2004–11.

— MARION ANN TAYLOR

Cornwallis, Mary (1758–1836)

Little is known about the author Mary Cornwallis (née Harris) before her marriage in 1778 to William Cornwallis, an Oxford fellow and for over fifty years Anglican priest of the parish of Elham and Wittersham, Kent. The Cornwallises had two daughters: Sarah (1779–1803) married James Trimmer, the son of the renowned author and educator Sarah Trimmer, then died after giving birth to James Cornwallis Trimmer; Caroline (1786–1858) was a writer, scholar, feminist, and social advocate.

As part of her spiritual discipline, Mary Cornwallis studied Scripture assiduously. She made careful notes, using the books found in the family's extensive library and buying any other books she needed. She was well educated and knew French and Hebrew and likely Greek and Latin. When teaching her children, she used her study notes and later reworked them into a Scripture commentary for her grandson. His untimely death at age twelve inspired Cornwallis to publish her four-volume, two-thousand-page work, *Observations, Critical, Explanatory, and Practical, on the Canonical Scriptures* (1817; 2nd ed., 1820), as the means of endowing a free primary school in her husband's parish in memory of her grandson. Caroline Cornwallis helped her mother prepare the manuscript for publication. In 1826, Cornwallis published a second book, *A Preparation for the Lord's Supper, with a Companion to the Altar, Intended for the Use of Ladies.*

Cornwallis patterned *Observations* on standard biblical commentaries of her time and addressed textual, interpretive, and practical issues arising out of a careful study of Scripture. She referenced and quoted at length a remarkably wide array of commentaries, sermons, and essays on such topics as travel, Oriental customs, and theology. Most of the authors she cited were eminent Anglican scholars, though she also included female authors such as Sarah Trimmer, whose son James had married Cornwallis's daughter Sarah, and dissenter Thomas Williams, whose 1801 translation and commentary on Song of Songs influenced her own approach to the book. Cornwallis's summaries and quotations provide an important window into her intellectual world, and her personal comments on Scripture reflect her social location as a mother, grandmother, clergy-wife, and lay theologian.

Cornwallis's motherly voice rings out in her comments on 1 Cor. 6 when she warns against marrying a "libertine, who, restless and uneasy in himself, is incapable of tasting the tranquil pleasures of domestic life" (IV.297). With vehemence she declares: "Woe be to the thoughtless and unprincipled female who embraces the fatal maxim that a reformed rake makes the best husband!" (IV.297). Similarly in her commentary on 1 Pet. 3:1–7, Cornwallis counsels a woman to examine the "principles and temper" of the man she marries because he would become "her master" (IV.438). She offers advice on how submission in marriage can work to the advantage of both husband and wife. Believing that a woman whose "strength is inferior" would not be successful in "disputes and clamours" because a man's "ardent nature" disposes him "to resist opposition," she counsels every woman to "secure [her husband's] confidence by upright conduct, and his affection by kind compliance; that he, finding her always actuated by right motives, may listen to her counsels in matters of importance" (IV.438). Her motherly comments on scriptural teachings about marriage grow out of the text and her life experiences.

Cornwallis's motherly/grandmotherly voice also resounds in her commentary on Proverbs, a book directed particularly to young men. Commenting on the series of warnings against the infamous "strange woman" in Prov. 5:1–14, Cornwallis counsels that "the youth who, with the desire to preserve his innocence, seeks shelter in the bosom of his own family; who cherishes a taste for useful study and occupation, and the society of the wise and good; shall escape from the snares of the wicked, and enjoy the peace which springs from an approving conscience" (III.9). Unlike traditional male commentators, Cornwallis does not blame female seducers; instead, she reproaches men for corrupting "the unhappy woman" in the first place. Taking on the mantle of a preacher, she strongly exhorts men to educate women properly:

> Would men for a moment consider the extent of the mischief done to themselves by undermining and subverting the good principles of women, they would, upon motives of self-interest, pursue a different course. Where are they to find domestic comfort but in the integrity of those who constitute their families as wives, sisters, daughters, or servants? What madness therefore is it in them to enter as it were into a conspiracy against their own happiness, by sowing the seeds of vanity in the female mind, by unsettling its religious principles, by breaking down the fence of natural modesty, by encouraging those Christian graces which render women useful members of society, and a blessing in the domestic circle! (III.5)

Cornwallis recognizes that men's attitudes toward women and sexuality have shaped society's values. She calls attention to society's double standards for women and sexuality.

Cornwallis's experiences as mother of the parish also inform her reading of Scripture. Her commentary on 1 Tim. 3, which sets out the qualifications for bishops and deacons, reveals not only her own sense of vocation as a clergy wife, but also points toward her latent feminism. Cornwallis wonders why the apostle, who mandates that deacons' wives are to be "grave, not slanderers, sober, faithful in all things" (III.11), neglects to characterize a bishop's wife. Her explanation reveals her own understanding of a clergy-wife's powerful role as mother of the parish:

> We may conclude the omission to arise from the idea, that if the latter [deacons' wives] were so responsible, the former [clergy wives] could not fail to consider themselves as much or more so. Every good woman will gladly conform to the character given, ver. 11; she will take pleasure in assisting her husband in the lesser duties of his ministry. While he acts as the father, she will prove a mother to the parish; and we know that a tender mother delights to instruct, to guide, to comfort, to protect, the children of her love, and if compelled to reprove, she will do it with gentleness. (IV.386–87)

Cornwallis identifies herself as the mother of the parish Elham and Kent, and her commentary shows her fulfilling that role: she instructs, guides, comforts, protects, and reproves.

Cornwallis comments further on the mandate that wives be "grave" (1 Tim. 3:11), suggesting that this directive does not mean that wives are to be gloomy or morose, but rather free "from all levity in dress or manner: for without a certain dignity of character, all attempts to reform others would be fruitless and ridiculous" (IV.387). She further elevates the role of clergy-wife, mandating that a priest's wife "must therefore be considered as more responsible than other women, even in things apparently trifling" (IV.387). For her hard work and faithfulness in this life, Cornwallis offers "recompense in the world to come" (IV.387).

One of the many places where Cornwallis's voice as an Anglican lay theologian resounds is in her commentary on Song of Songs. Cornwallis follows a traditional typological/allegorical reading of the Song as a picture of Christ and the church, but she finds the notion of intimacy with God difficult. She is deeply concerned that many readings of the Song of Songs encourage religious enthusiasm practiced by the Moravians and other sects. To prove her point, she cites the respectful and reverent responses of Thomas and Mary Magdalene to meeting the risen Christ, the one exclaiming, "My Lord, and my God," the other simply, "Master" (III.67). Cornwallis also worries that interpreting the bride in Song of Songs as a type of an individual believer rather than the church blurs the lines of distinction between human and divine. Accordingly, she sets out her doctrine of God: "Let us remember that all familiarity between God and his creatures is entirely unbecoming; and that he who came in our nature to die for us, will come again to be our judge" (III.67).

Mary Cornwallis was a woman who entered into the male world of commentary-writing rather unintentionally. Her work is impressive. The sections that read more like the compilations of the works of the great Anglican divines disclose what Cornwallis viewed to be important resources in the interpretive task. Her more personal observations on Scripture demonstrate that in addition to reading Scripture with the aid of great books, she also read through the lens of her experiences as wife, mother, clergy-spouse, and informed Anglican, aware of the theological and moral issues of her day.

See also Trimmer, Sarah (1741–1810)

Bibliography

Cornwallis, Mary. *Observations, Critical, Explanatory, and Practical, on the Canonical Scriptures.* London: Baldwin, Cradock & Joy, 1817. 2nd ed., 1820.

———. *A Preparation for the Lord's Supper, with a Companion to the Altar, Intended for the Use of Ladies.* London: Baldwin, Cradock & Joy, 1826.

Taylor, Marion Ann. "Words of a Mother: Mary Cornwallis, Nineteenth-Century Biblical Interpreter." Pages 39–44 in *Recovering Nineteenth-Century Women Interpreters of the Bible,* edited by Christiana de Groot and Marion Ann Taylor. SBL Symposium Series 38. Atlanta: Society of Biblical Literature, 2007.

— MARION ANN TAYLOR

Crook, Margaret Brackenbury (1886–1972)

Margaret Brackenbury Crook was born in England on May 5, 1886. She attended college at St. Anne's School at Oxford, receiving her bachelor of arts with first-class honors in philosophy in 1913, followed by the diploma in anthropology with distinction in 1914. By 1917 she had graduated first in her class with a certificate in theology from Manchester College, resulting in her admission to the Unitarian ministry. That same year her first book was published: *The Track of the Storm: Tales of the Marne, the Meuse, and the Aube* (1917), a collection of stories and vignettes from the front lines of World War I, some of which had previously appeared in the *Manchester Guardian*. In 1921 she was appointed associate professor in the Department of Religion and Biblical Literature at Smith College, Northampton, Massachusetts. She taught at Smith for thirty-three years, retiring in 1954. During her time there and following her retirement, Crook published a number of devotional poems, over thirty articles and reviews in the field of Old Testament studies, and two monographs: *The Cruel God: Job's Search for the Meaning of Suffering* (1959) and *Women and Religion* (1964). She was also the editor of and primary contributor to *The Bible and Its Literary Associations* (1937). She died on May 24, 1972.

The Bible and Its Literary Associations was the product of a joint effort by the faculty at Smith College. Written in connection with a course offered at Smith, the book seeks to give readers knowledge of the development and production of the Bible and an understanding of its lasting influence and presence in Western culture. It also covers the development of a number of translations of the Bible and emphasizes the spread and influence of the Bible and its various translations as products of a living chain of readers and writers leading to contemporary times. Crook wrote eight of its twenty essays.

In her contributions, Crook provides an introduction to the biblical text, discussing the context in which its various parts were formed. Particularly in her essay on the Pentateuch and former prophets, Crook draws connections with other ancient stories, including those of Egypt and Babylon. As a result she places biblical narratives in the context of polytheistic cultures, which used various kinds of ritual observances. Her work demonstrates how elements of the biblical text show both a departure from these traditions and their continuation or appropriation in the development of Jewish festivals and rituals. One example of this is the story of the sacrifice of Jephthah's daughter (Judg. 11). Crook argues that through this story, "the Hebrew teachers transmuted the pagan ceremonies; and henceforth the Hebrew women could wail at the high places in the fall of the year—not for the dying god of vegetation—but for the heroine of Israel" (38).

Crook's essays also cover the development of the Hebrew Bible in relation to the history of Israel as well as the creation of the New Testament and the emergence of Christianity. In her discussion of the formation of the Christian canon, Crook describes the variety of writings from this time period, stressing the number and range of available texts that were not included in the New Testament. Crook's final contribution is an essay describing the creation of the King James Version (KJV) of the Bible. She focuses on the issues involved in translation by explaining the method used by those who produced it. This discussion highlights her claims about the Bible as a product of a living chain of readers and writers: the process of translation is ongoing, and the KJV's translators had no sense of finality in their work. This book of essays was welcomed as a useful outline for the literary history of the Bible, particularly for students. Reviews described it as effective and comprehensive, with important implications for interdisciplinary studies.

The Cruel God pays particular attention to the burgeoning knowledge of ancient Near Eastern (ANE) literature in the postwar period. Crook proposes that one should imagine the writer of Job in the context of an ANE scribal school, likely situated in Babylon during the first half of the fifth century BCE. In Job, the writer (whom Crook calls "the Poet") addresses problems raised by his students, using the standard teaching of the scribal schools. Basing himself on a preexisting legend alluded to in the prose prologue and epilogue, the Poet uses the dialogue form to explore the problems of human suffering, especially when they are exacerbated by unexamined systems of human thought. Moreover, the final product then gave the students a written record of the debate to guide their memory of what had been said.

Knowledge of the polytheistic background of the ANE helps to contextualize the dilemma and approach of the book of Job. As Crook reconstructs the original story alluded to in the prose narrative, Job's friends and his wife criticize his single-minded devotion to the god known as Yahweh. They recommend that he find a more compassionate deity. Relevant parallels include the Akkadian poem "I will praise the lord of wisdom" and the Ugaritic tale of Aqhat (written in an ancient Semitic language related to biblical Hebrew, the poem tells the story of a king who is blessed by the god El with a son, Aqhat; tragically, Aqhat offends the goddess Anat). In both cases the polytheistic context of these poems allows the protagonists to find a benevolent deity in a situation where they are confronted by a hostile divine power. But in the Poet's revision of this old story, the three friends now have become spokesmen for Israel's ethical monotheism. Within this context, Crook interprets the thrust of Job's dilemma as a question: "Can it be that God is cruel and that He does not care?" The argument of the dialogues (including the speeches of Yahweh in Job 38–41) focuses on this issue. Job's friends are startled by the question since they support the optimistic appraisal of God implicit in traditional wisdom teaching, which Job himself would like to do if it were not so contrary to his own experience. Crook's resolution of the book interprets Yahweh's speeches as upholding God's sovereignty as Creator and Lord of history. This leads to the rejection of false questioning on the part of Job and a response of confession and praise. But Job's expression of deference in 42:1–6 is neither a matter of passive acquiescence nor penitent humiliation; it is motivated by a joyful vision of a Deity who is not bound by human categories of thought.

According to Crook, contemporary readers of Job are to imagine that the Poet wrote down his dialogues as they were developed with his students. The book shows signs of intermittent composition as well as explicit influence from cuneiform sources. One sign that the book was written over a period of time is the disorder of the third speech cycle in Job 22–27. For Crook, the simplest explanation is that the third speech cycle was never completed. Finally, there is the problem of several endings to the book of Job. While Crook follows an opinion shared by many that the Elihu speeches in Job 32–37 are a later addition, her solution for the presence of the poem on wisdom in Job 28 is more novel. It is an incomplete supplement to the poetic dialogues made by the Poet in his old age, after the first form of the book was finished.

Crook's contribution to the scholarship on Job is not often cited. This is unfortunate, for her method of approach bears reflection. Crook tries to solve issues involved in the coherence of the book with regard to a particular model of ANE book production. Though the model she espouses has a number of difficulties, her approach to the composition of Job by appealing to practices of ancient bookmaking is one on which contemporary Joban scholarship could well reflect.

In *Women and Religion*, Crook provides a broad survey of women's roles in religion from ancient times to her day. She introduces her work by stating, "Women have a heritage in religion to regain, develop, and carry forward. This is not a feminist movement; it concerns men as well as women and offers benefits to both" (1). Crook views this work as a process of rectifying the lack of knowledge of women's roles in religion historically. Despite its title, *Women and Religion* focuses on Judaism, Christianity, and Islam—especially on Christianity. The book is divided into seven sections, which trace the development of the Bible and women's position according to its content and interpretation over time. Throughout the work, Crook draws connections to the status of women in contemporary Western society.

The first section describes the background to the creation of the earliest parts of the Hebrew Bible. Crook argues that early forms of human religion held female deities in high regard and that the Hebrew Bible records the usurpation of these deities by the formation of a patriarchal religion dedicated to the worship of one god. She identifies this shift as having a number of consequences: among them are the lessening of women's roles in public religious practices and the general relegation of women to the private realm. Through a close reading of the Bible, the loss of women's roles becomes evident: "Israel's story yields the most dramatic and consistent account the world has ever known of the loss of woman's ancient official share in the public observance of religion" (56).

With this background established, Crook begins her look at the Bible by addressing the legacy of Eve, the first woman. Eve is seen to have both triumphs and disabilities. Her triumph is the appropriation of the ability to create life independently of God. Her disabilities (such as childbirth pains), however, have constituted the major focus in the history of interpretation, and she has often been remembered as the originator of sin and a temptress. Moving beyond Genesis, Crook discusses a number of female characters in the Hebrew Bible. The marginalization of persons such as the Witch of Endor (1 Sam. 28) is viewed as an indication of how alternate forms of religion are denounced within the Hebrew tradition, which ultimately denies women the roles of power they once held.

In the second half of the book, the focus shifts to early Christianity and the New Testament. Arguing that early Christianity also held many opportunities for women that were later eliminated, Crook points to a number of women mentioned in the New Testament who clearly had important roles in the early church. She discusses the scholarship surrounding Paul's Letters and considers Paul's intentions to have been to allow women greater power and equality within Christian communities, although his words have been misconstrued to produce the opposite effect and repress women's participation: "[His] knowledge of the teachings of Jesus, including those concerning women, comes from . . . Jesus' followers after the crucifixion. Though he very seldom quotes Jesus, Paul treats women according to his teachings" (136). She defends this viewpoint with the proposal that many of Paul's Letters have been added to and elaborated on before they reached the product found in the New Testament. Crook argues of these embellishments, "Those who mention the place of women in the church fail to follow up Paul's generous point of view" (137).

In addition, Crook explores the characterization of the church in feminine terms and the development of Marianism, which reveres Mary but leaves her conspicuously absent from the Trinity. In this regard she remarks: "In spite of popular adoration of Mary the basic nature of divinity is securely masculine" (218). Crook acknowledges that there were some attempts in early Christianity to identify Mary with a personification of God's wisdom but suggests that Thomas Aquinas's assertion that the Father, Son, and Holy Spirit are one essence put the matter above debate, allowing no room for the feminine in the Trinity and thus in the power structure of the church.

Crook also explores women's roles in Protestant Christianity by examining a few key figures such as the wife of Luther, Susanna Wesley, and Antoinette Brown, the first ordained female Congregationalist minister in the United States (1853). *Women and Religion* ends by expressing a need to rethink contemporary concepts of God and humanity to allow for a more inclusive experience and practice of religion. She writes: "We take God too much for granted, and have looked upon God as a perfectly finished entity, complete and all-sufficing, with little left for the role of humanity beyond repentant obedience" (248).

The reception of *Women and Religion* was mixed. Elements of Crook's approach and exegesis were appreciated with regard to the discussion of women biblical characters, but the utility of her broad survey of the history of women's roles in religion following the formation of the Bible was questioned. Despite these criticisms, Crook should be remembered as a female scholar who addressed the androcentric tendencies of both the biblical text and its interpretations. This has been recognized by Elisabeth Schüssler Fiorenza, who appreciates Crook's insistence that "the masculine monopoly in biblical religions must be broken and that women must participate in shaping religious thought, symbols and traditions" (8). Although little contemporary scholarship refers to Crook's work, her analysis of women's roles in the development of biblical religion is a noteworthy contribution from this time period.

See also Blackwell, Antoinette Louisa Brown (1825–1921); Wesley, Susanna (1669–1742)

Bibliography

Crook, Margaret Brackenbury, ed. *The Bible and Its Literary Associations*. New York: Abingdon, 1936.

————. *The Cruel God: Job's Search for the Meaning of Suffering*. Boston: Beacon, 1959.

————. *The Track of the Storm: Tales of the Marne, the Meuse, and the Aube*. London: Headley Brothers, 1917.

————. *Women and Religion*. Boston: Beacon, 1964.

Giele, J. Z. Review of *Women and Religion*, by Margaret Brackenbury Crook. *Journal for the Scientific Study of Religion* 5, no. 2 (Spring 1966): 308–10.

Margaret Brackenbury Crook Papers. Biographical Note. Smith College Archives. http://asteria.fivecolleges.edu/findaids/smitharchives/manosca51_bioghist.html.

Muilenburg, James. Review of *The Bible and Its Literary Associations*, by Margaret Brackenbury Crook. *Journal of Bible and Religion* 6, no. 2 (Spring 1938): 98–99.

Robbins, Howard C. Review of *The Bible and Its Literary Associations*, by Margaret Brackenbury Crook. *Religion in Life* 7, no. 3 (Summer 1938): 469–70.

Schüssler Fiorenza, Elisabeth. "The Ethics of Biblical Interpretation: Decentering Biblical Scholarship." *Journal of Biblical Literature* 107 (1988): 13–17.

Thelen, Mary Frances. Review of *The Cruel God: Job's Search for the Meaning of Suffering*, by Margaret Brackenbury Crook. In *Journal of Bible and Religion* 28, no. 3 (July 1960): 371–73.

—ELIZABETH POTTER AND WILLIAM S. MORROW

■ Davies, Eleanor (1590–1652)

Lady Eleanor Davies, whose prophetic career spanned the years between 1625 and 1652, possessed one of the most distinctive literary and theological voices of the English Revolution (1640–60). During the course of twenty-six years, she published some sixty-nine treatises, spent years in jail, and made astonishing predictions on subjects ranging from the coming of the end of time to the death of her first husband. She emerges from her writings as a satirist of the follies of her age who combines scriptural exegesis and cultural commentary to proclaim the fast approach of the last days.

Lady Eleanor was born in 1590 to George Touchet, the eleventh Baron Audley, and his wife, Lucy. In 1609 her father arranged her first marriage to the poet and prominent barrister Sir John Davies. She bore three children, only one of whom survived to adulthood. Her life took a dramatic turn in 1625: by her account, a "Heavenly voice" told her, "There is Ninteene yeares and a halfe to the day of Judgement, and you as the meek Virgin" (Davies, *Her Appeale* [1641] in Cope, *Writings*, 81). Shortly thereafter, she published her first tract, *A Warning to the Dragon*.

The early years of her prophetic career were particularly difficult. Neither her two husbands nor the king of England, Charles I, received her prophecies well. After her first husband, Davies, burned her prophetic writings, Lady Eleanor told him "within three years to expect the mortal blow"; he died shortly afterward, in 1626. Her second husband, the professional soldier Sir Archibald Douglas, likewise burned her books. In 1633, at the prompting of

Charles, the ecclesiastical courts found her guilty "of unlawful printing & publishing of books," for which she spent two years in the Gatehouse prison (Davies, *The Blasphemous Charge Against Her* [1649], in Cope, *Writings*, 253). She was jailed again—this time in Bedlam (the prison for the insane)—in late 1636 or early 1637 for literally occupying the bishop's throne at the Cathedral of Litchfield, declaring herself "primate and metropolitan," and defacing the cathedral's tapestries (Cope, *Handmaid*, 84). She spent additional time in jail later in her career, but she did so more sporadically—in parts of 1646, 1647, 1648, 1650, and 1651. Financial debts rather than her prophetic activities per se appear to have caused these later periods of imprisonment. She died in July of 1652.

Lady Eleanor identified as a prophet in the sense that she deemed herself to be an inspired reader of Scripture. In particular, she saw herself as a gifted interpreter of the apocalyptic books Daniel and Revelation. She attributed her capacity to decipher the complex imagery of these and other biblical texts to her possession of "the Spirit of God" and insisted that her prophecies were consistent with Scripture: "saying no other things then [than] the Prophets and Apostles did say should come to passe, that yee might know the certainty of those things" (Davies, *A Warning to the Dragon*, in Cope, *Writings*, 56, 2–3). Thus, based on Daniel, she determined that the last judgment was sure to occur in the winter of 1644–45; this did not happen, but in making such a calculation she participated in the English Reformed tradition of using the apocalyptic books to predict the time of the end. Lady Eleanor's prophecies also shared with radical Protestant exegetes of her period an emphasis on typological readings of Scripture. In her 1633 broadside *Woe to the House*, she presents Charles as a type of Ahab, who in 1631 sanctioned the execution of her brother, Mervin, Earl of Castlehaven, after he was convicted on charges of rape and sodomy. She, in turn, portrays Mervin as a type of Naboth and insists that his wife, Anne Stanley, acted as a type of the duplicitous Jezebel and betrayed him.

Lady Eleanor's was an age of prophecy and radical religious fervor, but she stands out from her fellow visionaries because she was not affiliated with a religious sect nor did she adhere exclusively to Anglicanism or Puritanism, the period's dominant Christian traditions. Instead, she incorporated elements of both in her writings. In keeping with Anglican practice, she subscribed to the feast days of the traditional liturgical calendar. Yet her tract *For Whitson Tyds Last Feast* (1645) marries this traditional feast day with her more radical (in the sense of more typical of Puritan belief) claims of the coming of the apocalypse: as her title suggests, she believes the Whitsunday (Pentecost) of 1645 to be the last, and she further adds that this is fitting because "the second *Comming* of the *holy Ghost*" will arrive, as prophesied in Joel, just before the last judgment (Davies, *For Whitson Tyds Last Feast*, in Cope, *Writings*, 158).

A further instance of Lady Eleanor's polyglot theology is her belief, after the early Christian theologian Origen, in apocatastasis. This is the doctrine, predicated in part by Paul in 1 Cor. 15:54–57, that Christ's victory over death results in salvation for all, even the damned. Apocatastasis (see its only occurrence in Acts 3:21) does not deny punishment for sins but rather maintains that such punishment cannot be eternal. Lady Eleanor dedicated four treatises—*The Restitution of Reprobates* (1644), *Je le tien* (1646), *The Mystery of General Redemption* (1647), and *The Writ of Restitution* (1648)—to expounding a doctrine that she hoped might mitigate her readers' anxiety about eternal life and the second coming. Indeed, she denounces the "illegal constructions and terrification of that uncharitable nature" that deny the "worlds general pardon" (*General Redemption*).

Not surprisingly, given the era in which she lived, Lady Eleanor never made explicit feminist avowals. Rather, she insists that the depravity of her age has compelled God to select a woman as his prophet: "The weaker *Sex* preferred more proper for them, requisit for former days neither" (Davies, *The Restitution of Prophecy* [1651] in Cope, *Writings*, 365). Even when she presents more positive claims for female prophetic authority, she does so in terms of patriarchal power. Throughout her career, she invokes her maiden name to insist that her noble patronymic (Audley or Audeley) identifies her with the prophet Daniel. She uses the anagram "ELEANOR AUDELEY / REVEALE O DANIEL" as a signature on many of her tracts (Davies, *A Warning*, in Cope, *Writings*, 6). At one point she asserts that the circumstances surrounding Jezebel's burial prove that all women, even those who marry, retain a claim to the authority of the paternal signifier: "But because the *Daughter of a King . . . buryed in silence*, for so births PREROGATIVE *surmounts* or *goes* before *that gain'd* by Marrage *as descent* and *blood*" (Davies, *From the Lady Eleanor, Her Blessings to Her Beloved Daughter* [1644], in Cope, *Writings*, 121). From this, she deduces, women maintain a kind of psychic virginity that gives them a unique relationship to God's Word. Thus, in *The Everlasting Gospel* of 1649, she mentions her flight to Amsterdam to publish her 1633 tracts and compares it to the Virgin Mary's flight to Egypt to protect her newborn son.

From the moment of her calling in 1625, Lady Eleanor steadfastly sought to publicize the broader political meaning of her interpretations of Daniel and Revelation for her contemporaries. Her unwavering commitment to her prophetic vocation is perhaps best documented by her daughter, Lucy, in the epitaph she wrote for her mother: "In a woman's body a man's spirit, In most adverse circumstances a serene mind, In a wicked age unshaken piety and uprightness" (Cope, *Handmaid*, 162).

Bibliography

Cope, Esther S. *Handmaid of the Holy Spirit: Dame Eleanor Davies, Never So Mad a Ladie.* Ann Arbor: University of Michigan Press, 1992.

————. ed. *Prophetic Writings of Lady Eleanor Davies.* New York: Oxford University Press, 1995.

Davies, Lady Eleanor. *The Mystery of General Redemption*, n.p., 1647.

Feroli, Teresa. *Political Speaking Justified: Women Prophets of the English Revolution.* Newark: University of Delaware Press, 2006.

————. "The Sexual Politics of Mourning in the Prophecies of Eleanor Davies." *Criticism* 36 (1994): 359–82.

————. "Sodomy and Female Authority: The Castlehaven Scandal and Lady Eleanor's *The Restitution of Prophecy.*" *Women's Studies* 24 (1994): 31–49.

Hawes, Clement. *Mania and Literary Style: The Rhetoric of Enthusiasm from the Ranters to Christopher Smart.* Cambridge: Cambridge University Press, 1997.

Hindle, C. J. "A Bibliography of the Printed Pamphlets and Broadsides of Lady Eleanor Douglas, the Seventeenth-Century Prophetess." *Edinburgh Bibliographical Society Transactions* 1, no. 1 (1936): 65–98.

Mack, Phyllis. *Visionary Women: Ecstatic Prophecy in Seventeenth-Century England.* Berkeley: University of California Press, 1992.

Matchinske, Megan. "Holy Hatred: Formations of the Gendered Subject in English Apocalyptic Writing, 1625–51." *English Literary History* 60 (1993): 349–77.

————. *Writing, Gender and State in Early Modern England: Identity Formation and the English Subject.* Cambridge: Cambridge University Press, 1998.

— TERESA FEROLI

Dawbarn, Elizabeth (fl. 1794–1816)

Elizabeth Dawbarn lived in Wisbech, England. Her interpretive writings were addressed both to children and to adults and focused on the Old Testament, which she read in both a detailed literal and a theologically symbolic sense. She used the Bible to explain and defend doctrine and was concerned with demonstrating the historical and symbolic connection between the Old and the New Testaments.

The eternal existence of the Son of God (1800) exemplifies Dawbarn's literal and symbolic approaches to Scripture as she seeks to prove the eternal existence of Jesus Christ. She posits through a verse-by-verse theological exposition that Wisdom in Prov. 8 is a type of Christ, building her case by citing other Scriptures with similar language that speak of God or Jesus. Once she has established that Wisdom in Prov. 8 is God and therefore has eternal existence, she builds a scriptural bridge to prove that the Son also has eternal existence. For example, in Isa. 54:8 God is called the "Redeemer," and Gal. 3:13 refers to Christ as the one who redeems as only God can redeem. Thus the Son is God and therefore eternal (19–21).

While privileging a literal approach, Dawbarn also adopts a deeper spiritual or theologically symbolic interpretive lens to the Bible, writing,

A superficial reading [of] them will avail nothing. The divine Revelation is one entire system, and can never be understood if read only in a broken and

unconnected manner. If we do not search the scriptures with a child-like simplicity, accompanied with fervent prayer to the Lord for his Spirit to illuminate our
understandings, so that we may enter into the sublimity of the Sacred Records,
we certainly never shall know any thing to any good purpose, concerning the
great Author of them who is the One living and true God, the great Creator
and Preserver of all things, in "whom we live, move, and have our being [Acts
17:28]." (30)

In *The Young Person's Assistant in reading the Old Testament* (1806, 1816),
Dawbarn uses the format of a mother writing letters to her children to communicate educational material about the Bible and to implicitly reinforce the role
of a mother in instilling Christian knowledge into her children. Throughout
this work, she defines biblical or theological terms—such as "figure," "dispensation," and "abomination"—that might be hard for children to understand
(19, 20, 45). She also clarifies interpretively difficult passages, such as Mal.
1:2–3, where God does not hate Esau but loves him differently than Jacob (47).
    As in her other work, Dawbarn reads the Bible as a unified whole, apply-
ing a detailed literal approach to the text and using resources such as Brown's
Bible Chronology to generate a time line of the books of the Old Testament,
thus helping readers study the Bible in a way that makes narrative sense (6,
41–42). For example, she suggests that 2 Kings 25; 2 Chron. 36; and Jer. 39
should be read together (41–42). She also advocates figural readings of texts,
seeing patterns of Christian worship, for example, in Exodus, Leviticus, and
Numbers. She writes, "All the Jewish worship, and every thing pertaining to it
was shadowy, figurative, typical, or symbolical, and all had a special reference
to Christ; he being the *sum* and *substance* of all the shadows, figures, types
and symbols" (13). She offers the example of Old Testament anointing as a
"symbolic representation of the gift of the Holy Spirit," noting that Jesus's
being called "Messiah," "Christ," or "anointed one" testifies to the unity of
the Bible (22). Further, Solomon's temple itself is a type of Christ (28), the
Song of Solomon is an allegory of the relationship between Christ and the
church (34), and many of the psalms refer to Christ, "the spiritual David"
(31). At times Dawbarn's interpretations are anti-Semitic. For example, the
"slaughtered Jews" in Zeph. 1:7 are interpreted as a sacrifice to "God's just
vengeance," with the Chaldeans or Babylonians as divinely appointed guests
"to slay them" and "feed upon and devour their substance" (41). However,
she is also clear that God has set Israel apart and continues to care for the
Jewish Diaspora (58).
    Dawbarn's other major interpretive writing is a political essay, *A dialogue
between Clara Neville and Louisa Mills on loyalty, &c.: Recommended to the
attention of every female in Great Britain* (1794), written as a dialogue between
two women. It uses Bible passages such as Isa. 49:23; Rom. 13:1; and 1 Pet.
2:17 to encourage women to be loyal to the British monarchy (6, 17–18, 20–22).

Although Dawbarn's personal history has largely been forgotten, her literary writings are significant examples of the work of a Christian educator, lay theologian, and political activist in this period.

Bibliography

Blain, Virginia, Patricia Clements, and Isobel Grundy, eds. "Dawbarn, Elizabeth." Page 272 in *The Feminist Companion to Literature in English: Women Writers from the Middle Ages to the Present*. New Haven: Yale University Press, 1990.

Dawbarn, Elizabeth. *A dialogue between Clara Neville and Louisa Mills on loyalty, &c.: Recommended to the attention of every female in Great Britain*. Wisbech, UK: John White, 1794.

———. *The eternal existence of the Son of God, shewn to be a doctrine of scripture, in a short exposition of the eighth chapter of Proverbs*. Wisbech, UK: John White, 1800.

———. *The Young Person's Assistant in reading the Old Testament; In a series of letters from a mother to her children, relative to divine truth*. 2nd ed. Wisbech, UK: John White, 1816.

— JONI SANCKEN

Dentière, Marie (1495–ca. 1561)

Born in 1495 to a noble family (d'Ennetières) in Tournai, Marie Dentière left her Augustinian convent in that city in the early 1520s for Strasbourg to find refuge among German sympathizers of church reform. They welcomed French reformers known as "evangelical," from the French word for Gospel, *évangile*. Dentière married Simon Robert, a former priest from Tournai, and together they joined Guillaume Farel in preaching reform in the Swiss Valais. They were the first French married couple to accept a pastoral assignment for the Reformed Church. In 1533, after being widowed with children, she married Antoine Froment, a disciple of Farel, and moved to Geneva, where the couple participated in the struggles to win that city for the Reformed Church. In August 1535 she exhorted nuns in the Poor Clares convent to leave their order and renounce celibacy.

After the Council of 200 banished Farel and John Calvin in 1538, a pamphlet titled *A Very Useful Epistle Composed by a Christian Woman of Tournai* was printed in Geneva in 1539. Addressed to Marguerite, queen of Navarre and sister of the French King Francis I, the four hundred printed copies were clearly meant for a broader public in both France and in French-speaking Switzerland. The salutation identifies the author either as "Marie Dentière" or, in some printings, by the initials "M. D." The pamphlet attacks members of the Council of 200, yet it mainly targets the Roman Catholic clergy and those in power in France who did not challenge Rome. The edition was quickly confiscated, and only two copies are known to have survived. They show over two hundred biblical references in the margins of the sixty-five-page pamphlet.

The *Epistle* consists of three parts. The dedicatory salutation to Marguerite deplores Calvin and Farel's expulsion and the general corruption of the times. Dentière asks Marguerite to urge King Francis to intervene. She identifies two groups of women in her intended audience: those "in captivity," where the Reformed religion was persecuted, and "poor little women" wanting to know the truth (53). She acknowledges 1 Tim. 2, but insists "even though we are not permitted to preach in public in congregations and churches, we are not forbidden to write and admonish one another in all charity" (53). She mentions a Hebrew grammar that her young daughter has written in order to help other little girls, for "until now scripture has been so hidden from them" (53).

The second section is a "Defense of Women," following the tradition of works by Boccaccio, Christine de Pizan, and Cornelius Agrippa in praising illustrious women. The "Defense" continues the *querelle des femmes*, a polemic beginning in the fourteenth century that either defended or excoriated women. Dentière rejects the misogynist side of that debate that presented all women as inherently evil, a view based on the claim that Eve was the temptress who had led Adam into sin. Dentière invokes only biblical women:

> Several women are named and praised in holy scripture, as much for their good conduct, actions, demeanor, and example as for their faith and teaching: Sarah and Rebecca, for example, and first among all the others in the Old Testament, the mother of Moses, who, in spite of the king's edict, dared to keep her son from death; . . . and Deborah, who judged the people of Israel in the time of the Judges, is not to be scorned. Judges 4. Must we condemn Ruth, who even though she was of the female sex, had her story told in the book that bears her name? . . . What wisdom had the Queen of Sheba, who is not only named in the Old Testament, but whom Jesus dared to name among the other sages! (54)

Dentière goes on to praise New Testament women:

> If we are speaking of the graces that have been given to women, what greater grace has come to any creature on earth than to the virgin Mary, mother of Jesus, to have carried the son of God? It was no small grace that allowed Elizabeth, mother of John the Baptist, to have borne a son miraculously after having been sterile. What woman was a greater preacher than the Samaritan woman, who was not ashamed to preach Jesus and his word, confessing him openly before everyone? . . . Who can boast of having had the first manifestation of the great mystery of the resurrection of Jesus, if not Mary Magdalene, . . . and the other women, to whom, rather than to men, he had earlier declared himself through his angel and commanded them to tell, preach, and declare it to others? (55)

Dentière uses the model of biblical women to reject the notion that women are the source of evil and insists that they are able and entitled to interpret Scripture and teach one another. She calls on biblical authority to defend women's right to a public voice in religious matters. She counters Paul's injunction *tacient* [Vulgate: *taceant*] *mulieres* (Let the women be silent [1 Cor. 14:34]), by invoking John 4 and Mark 16. She reminds the reader first that in John 4:28–29 the Samaritan woman, after her encounter with Jesus at the well, goes back into town and urges the people to come out and listen to him; she goes on to recall Mark 16, where Jesus's resurrection is first revealed to women by an angel and where Jesus himself appears to a woman, Mary Magdalene, and instructs her to announce the news to the apostles. Dentière uses the terms "preach" (*prescher*) and "woman preacher" (*prescheresse*), conveying her conviction that women should not simply teach doctrine to other women in private, but should preach to both men and women, "openly before everyone" (55).

For Dentière, the sole authority and source of Christian doctrine is the Bible. Marginal biblical references become more frequent in the long third section, the epistle proper (56–87). It affirms that faith in Christ alone is the Christian's sole means of salvation, and it warns against false prophets who have tried to replace him. Dentière decries devotion to images, veneration of the saints, pilgrimages, and indulgences—all practices that have no authority in the Bible. She attacks the Catholic Mass, particularly the doctrine of transubstantiation, the conversion of the bread and wine into the substance of the body and blood of Christ in the Eucharist. In her arguments, she often paraphrases the passages from Scripture that are indicated in the margins. The *Epistle* closes with spirited attacks, not only on the papacy and the French court and clergy, but also on the Genevan officials who had expelled Calvin and Farel. A final reference to Rev. 18 portrays the Catholic Church as the great Babylon (87).

After the *Epistle*'s publication, Dentière appears only fleetingly in history, usually identified through her husband. In September 1546, Calvin, in writing to Farel, describes a confrontation with "Froment's wife." As "a funny story," he introduces a scene of Dentière preaching on the street corners and in taverns. When challenged by Calvin, she criticizes him and his associates for wearing long garments and accuses them of being like the scribes in Luke 20:46, "who want to walk about in long robes." She complains of the leaders' tyranny in suppressing open speech. Calvin dismisses her derisively.

That hostile encounter did not prevent a subsequent meeting of Calvin and Dentière, this time in print. Calvin preached a series of fifty-four sermons on Paul's First Epistle to Timothy in 1554–55; these were published in Geneva by Conrad Badius in 1561, the year of Dentière's death. Soon thereafter the seventeenth of these, a *Sermon on the Modesty of Women in Their Dress*, on 1 Tim. 2:9–11, was published separately in two editions. Both carried a preface addressed "to the Christian reader" and signed only with the initials "M. D." Those initials, recalling the initials on the Geneva copy of the *Epistle*, have led scholars to identify the author of the preface as Marie Dentière. She reinforces

Calvin's message about modesty in clothing, but she adds an additional lesson against women's use of cosmetics: "Now among the vices that reign today, makeup and excessive finery in clothing win the prize. . . . Saint Cyprian . . . cannot hold back from saying that all makeup by which the facial features are corrupted is the work of the devil, . . . for after the makeup has faded, the women seem more like a corpse, or a painted idol in a temple, long covered with dust, than a live creature" (92). The word *froment* (wheat) at the end of both the preface (93) and the *Epistle* (87) links the two texts, a punning signature relating both works to Marie Dentière and her husband, Antoine Froment.

Marie Dentière all but disappeared from notice after her death; in the 1860s, however, Swiss scholar A.-L. Herminjard revived her memory, though with great antipathy, in his *Correspondance des Réformateurs*. He includes excerpts from her *Epistle* (V.295–304), omitting the "Defense of Women." He refers to her as "Froment's wife" and portrays her as a "proud and vindictive woman [who] was, in spite of her intelligence, a bad counselor for her new husband, whom she dominated absolutely." He adds that "she prepared his moral downfall" (VI.173–74n28) and calls her an "ambitious and scheming woman" (VIII.106nn14–15). By implying that Dentière was the cause of her husband's immorality, Herminjard perpetuates the misogynist notion that Eve caused Adam's fall and that, since then, women have been responsible for leading men into sin.

In 2002 Marie Dentière received belated recognition when her name was added to the Wall of the Reformers in Geneva, the major monument to the Reformation in that city. That acknowledgment was due to the efforts of the Rev. Isabelle Graesslé, the first woman moderator of the Reformed Church of Geneva's Company of Pastors and the director of the Museum of the Reformation in Geneva. In the face of ridicule and suppression, Marie Dentière found in Scripture the models of courageous women who empowered her. She dared to challenge Paul and Calvin, and she called on Christ's words to women to support her conviction that women could preach God's Word.

See also Christine de Pizan (ca. 1364–ca. 1430)

Bibliography

Denommé, I. "La vision théologique de Marie d'Ennetières et le 'groupe de Neuchâtel.'" Pages 179–97 in *Le livre évangélique en français avant Calvin*, edited by Jean-François Gilmont and William Kemp. Turnhout: Brepols, 2004.

Dentière, Marie. *Epistle to Marguerite de Navarre; and, Preface to a Sermon of Calvin.* Translated and edited by Mary B. McKinley. The Other Voice in Early Modern Europe. Chicago: University of Chicago Press, 2004.

———. *Epistre tres utile faicte et composée par une femme chrestienne de Tornay, envoyée à la royne de Navarre seur du roy de France. Contre les Turcz, Juifz, infideles, faulx chrestiens, anabaptistes, et Lutheriens. Lisez et puis jugez.* Geneva: Jean

Gérard, 1539. Copies at Geneva: Musée Historique de la Réformation; and Paris: Bibliothèque Mazarine. Repr., Geneva: Bibliothèque publique et universitaire, 1999.

————.*Les conditions et vertus requises en la femme fidèle et bonne mesnagere: Contenues au xxxi. Chapitre des Prouerbes de Salomon. Mis en forme de Cantique, par Théodore de Besze. Plus, un Sermon de la modestie des femmes en leurs habillemens, par M. Iean Calvin. Outre, plusieurs chansons spirituelles, en Musique.* M.D.LXI. Copies at Lunel: Bibliothèque municipale, Fonds Médard; and Geneva: Musée Historique de la Réformation.

Douglass, J. D. "Marie Dentière's Use of Scripture in Her Theology of History." Pages 227–44 in *Biblical Hermeneutics in Historical Perspective: Studies in Honor of Karlfried Froehlich on His Sixtieth Birthday.* Grand Rapids: Eerdmans, 1991.

Graesslé, Isabelle. "Vie et légendes de Marie Dentière." *Bulletin du Centre Protestant d'Études* 55, no. 1 (March 2003): 1–31.

Head, T. "A Propagandist for the Reform: Marie Dentière." Pages 260–83 in *Women Writers of the Renaissance and Reformation*, edited by Katharina M. Wilson. Athens: University of Georgia Press, 1987.

————. "The Religion of the Femmelettes: Ideals and Experience among Women in Fifteenth- and Sixteenth-Century France." Pages 149–75 in *That Gentle Strength: Historical Perspectives on Women in Christianity*, edited by Linda Coon, Katherine Haldane, and Elisabeth Sommer. Charlottesville: University Press of Virginia, 1991.

Herminjard, A.-L., ed. *Correspondance des Réformateurs dans les pays de langue française: Recueillie et publiée avec d'autres lettres relatives à la Réforme et des notes historiques et biographiques.* 9 vols. Geneva: H. Georg, 1866–97. Repr., Nieuwkoop: B. De Graaf, 1965.

Kemp, W., and D. Desrosiers-Bonin. "Marie d'Ennetières et la petite grammaire hébraïque de sa fille d'après la dédicace de l'*Epistre* à Marguerite de Navarre." *Bibliothèque d'Humanisme et Renaissance* 60, no. 1 (1998): 117–34.

McKinley, Mary B. "The Absent Ellipsis: The Edition and Suppression of Marie Dentière in the Sixteenth and the Nineteenth Century." Pages 85–99 in *Women Writers of the Ancien Régime: Strategies of Emancipation*, edited by Colette Winn. New York: Garland, 1997.

Skenazi, C. "Marie Dentière et la prédication des femmes." *Renaissance and Reformation / Renaissance et Réforme* 21, no. 1 (1997): 5–18.

Thompson, John Lee. "Calvin and Marie Dentière." Pages 40–45 in *John Calvin and the Daughters of Sarah: Women in Regular and Exceptional Roles in the Exegesis of Calvin, His Predecessors, and His Contemporaries.* Geneva: Droz, 1992.

— Mary B. McKinley

■ Deverell, Mary (fl. 1774–97)

Mary Deverell, likely born at Minchinhampton, Gloucestershire, was an Anglican writer who, along with Hannah More, was mentored by Bristol heiress Ann Lovell Gwatkin. One of her better-known works, a collection of eight sermons, demonstrates her skill as a biblical interpreter and originated with a clergyman friend's "dare" for her to write a sermon he could preach (Blain,

159

Clements, and Grundy 286; *European Magazine*). Although it is unknown which, if any, of Deverell's published sermons were orally preached, a written sermon collection was a common and respected literary genre in its own right during the eighteenth century (Edwards 400). Nevertheless, to assign the title of "sermons" to a woman's work was unusual and possibly contested in her day (Blain, Clements, and Grundy 287). Deverell claimed to be of low social standing, but she loved reading and had enough connections to secure subscriptions for her writings and enjoy modest notoriety (*European Magazine*). She acknowledged her unique position in an "apology" in the introduction to *Sermons on the Following Subjects* (1774), noting that she did not intend to give the title of "sermons" to her compositions but conceded to do so because her subscribers (including clergy) felt that this title was the most fitting due to their "form and nature" (iv–v). *Sermons* was published in Bristol by a newspaper owner, Sarah Farley, and enjoyed a wide subscription base with second and third editions (1776, 1777), which Deverell expanded with an additional sermon.

Sermons is typical of eighteenth-century Protestant homiletics in Deverell's use of straightforward language to appeal to both the intellect and hearts of her readers (Edwards 400). In contrast to the "*explicatory*" or "*observatory*" styles, which closely follow a selected passage of Scripture, Deverell primarily writes in the "*applicative*" style (Lessenich 89–91). Thus her use of Scripture serves her interest of applying biblical and moral subjects to the lives of her readers. She uses a specific biblical text as a starting point for her reflection, reading the Bible as a seamless whole and allowing the New and Old Testaments to illuminate each other and her topic. For example, in her sermon on "Mercy," which begins with Jesus's "kind reproof" of the woman caught in adultery in John 8:11, she cites other passages (Matt. 12:20; Luke 7:40–48; 11; 15) to show Christ's forgiving and kind character toward sinners; the example of David and Bathsheba shows the depths of pain caused by adultery (63, 66–67, 71, 72–74, 76–81). Although she does not generally focus on women's concerns in the text or among her readers, she writes sympathetically about the woman caught in adultery in John 8, addressing male bias or "vile partiality" on the part of the accusers as they make no mention of the adulterous man. She writes, "It would have been incompatible with the divine wisdom and goodness to have condemned the woman, the *weaker* vessel, and to have freed the man, who was made the *stronger*" (65). She later observes that women "sadly" behave in the opposite manner, lenient toward male indiscretions and strict toward other women (70).

Deverell's sermons display a thorough knowledge of Scripture, the classics, and her own culture (including anti-Catholic rhetoric [82]), as well as a remarkable ability to compose sermons, all without formal credentials. Her deep knowledge of biblical texts, including apocryphal writings, allows her to apply biblical truths to the lives of her readers. She makes strong connections between reason and revelation in her interpretive approach, demonstrating that following biblical dictates makes rational sense (34). To that end, she draws examples from classical history, such as using the friendship of Augustus and Maecenas to support her exposition of 1 Sam. 18:3–4 (20–21), as well as the lives and sayings of well-respected British religious, political, and scientific figures such as Bishop John Tillotson, Edward VI, Lady Jane Gray, and Sir Isaac Newton. In one footnote she defends her use of an apocryphal text, Sir. 10:18: "As our church has allow'd the Apocryphal writings to be publickly read for edification, on account of the many excellent moral observations contained in them, I have therefore thought myself sufficiently authorized [to use them]" (84). Throughout her sermons, the Bible is her central source of authority, and she uses a variety of methods of interpretation to serve her purposes, including an interpretation of Joseph as a "type" of Jesus Christ in her sermon on "Afflictive Providence" (153).

In a later, less conventional publication, *Miscellanies* (1781), Deverell comments on the discomfort some have showed with *Sermons*: "They themselves approve of my writings, . . . but the title of *Sermons* from a woman startles them! And must not be encouraged in our sex" (110). She defends her work through her immersion in the Bible: "The wisdom that [the Bible] imparts, is not confined to sex or colleges"(110). Deverell was ahead of her time in her desire to interpret Scripture and "preach" in a public context. Her efforts reached an audience more than two hundred years before the Anglican Church ordained women in England.

See also More, Hannah (1745–1833)

Bibliography

Blain, Virginia, Patricia Clements, and Isobel Grundy, eds. "Deverell, Mary." Pages 286–87 in *The Feminist Companion to Literature in English: Women Writers from the Middle Ages to the Present*. New Haven: Yale University Press, 1990.

Deverell, Mary. *Miscellanies in Prose and Verse*. 2 vols. [London]: J. Rivington, 1781.

———. *Sermons on the Following Subjects*. 1st ed. Bristol: S. Farley; London: Carnan & Newbery, 1774.

Edwards, O. C., Jr. *A History of Preaching*. Nashville: Abingdon, 2004.

Lessenich, Rolf P. *Elements of Pulpit Oratory in Eighteenth-Century England (1660–1800)*. Cologne: Böhlau, 1972.

Philological Society of London. Review of *Miscellanies in Prose and Verse, Mostly Written in the Epistolary Style: Chiefly upon Moral Subjects and Particularly Calculated for the Improvement of Younger Minds, Anecdotes of the Author, by Mary Deverell. European Magazine, and London Review: Containing the Literature, History, Politics, Arts, Manners, and Amusements of the Age* 2 (Sept. 1782): 199.

Stott, Anne. "Deverell, Mary (fl. 1774–1797)." Pages 942–43 in vol. 15 of *Oxford Dictionary of National Biography*, edited by H. C. G. Matthew and Brian Harrison. Oxford: Oxford University Press, 2004–11.

—Joni Sancken

▨ Dhuoda of Septimania (fl. 841)

The sole extant work of the ninth-century noblewoman Dhuoda, wife of the Frankish warlord Bernard of Septimania, is a Latin book for their young son William, titled *Liber manualis*, turned into English as *Manual* or *Handbook*. This small text instructs the absent fourteen-year-old William in his comportment as a Christian nobleman. In the mother-author's tone, in her attention to Scripture, and in her sense of history, Dhuoda's work is framed by the collapse of Charlemagne's pan-European Empire.

Dhuoda composed her text in the early 840s at Uzès, near Avignon, during the civil wars first separating Germany and France at the end of the reign of Louis the Pious, Charlemagne's son. Her husband, Bernard, was a leading participant in that conflict, supporting and then betraying Louis's youngest heir, Charles the Bald, on whom the West Frankish kingdom eventually devolved. During Bernard's apparently lengthy absences, Dhuoda herself served as steward of his broad dominions on the southern limit of Frankish territory. She had likely been educated in Charlemagne's palace school as a member of his kinship group; she reminds her son that she and his father were married in the palace at Aachen. Her work thus offers evidence for the level of scriptural learning and the character of religious practice among Carolingian elites at the moment of Charlemagne and Alcuin's educational program's fullest achievement, but while its ruin was imminent outside the monastic context. Her modestly presented *Handbook* is the only book-length work to have survived from the hand of a European woman between the fourth-century pilgrimage record of the Spanish Egeria and the tenth-century dramas of the canoness Hrotsvit. Dhuoda's work thus holds unique importance in the histories of Latin literature, women's literary activity, parenting, and exegesis by lay commentators. Although her *Handbook* is explicitly written for her elder child, Dhuoda clearly intended for him eventually to share it with his younger brother, and in several passages she suggests that in time it may come to a wider audience among William's noble companions—perhaps even the young king Charles the Bald.

Recent editors have arranged Dhuoda's *Handbook* in eleven "books" of varying length, most of them fewer than ten printed pages long. Such biographical information about her as survives is all contained within her prologue and several chapters of the tenth book. Dhuoda's opening passages are marked by the emotional intensity she maintains throughout the remaining sections of the work. The first two of her work's brief books call her primary reader, William, to understand a Christian person's obligations both to love God and to understand the central mystery of the Trinity: "God must be loved and praised—not only by powers on high, but also by every human creature who walks upon the earth and reached toward heaven" (1.1, trans. Neel 7). The later books address ethics, religious practice, and scriptural interpretation: "In holy reading you will learn how you must pray and what you should avoid, be wary of, or seek out—what you should do in all matters" (8.1, trans. Neel 83).

Dhuoda's moral theology resonates clearly with the ideas of contemporaries such as Jonas of Orléans, indicating the extent to which the lay Carolingian nobility was informed by ecclesiastical teaching known to modern scholars from many monastic and clerical sources, but hers remains an emphatically lay and feminine voice. Her *Handbook*'s lengthiest books, the third and fourth, express her concerns and sensibility as a laywoman and a mother. Here Dhuoda advises her son that self-consciously Christian deportment will enhance his safety and success as a secular nobleman; she exhibits powerful maternal authority even as she supports patriarchy within the family and in imperial leadership.

Throughout the scriptural examples from which she constructs her teaching for her young son, Dhuoda demonstrates a deep concern with the historical-literal sense of Scripture, as well as with its contemporary relevance. She understands her own time to be a period of spiritual travail analogous to the Hebrews' during Absalom's rebellion against David (3.7). In this context of a civil war's disordering right relations among the Frankish magnates, across their society and within their families, Dhuoda warns her son that spiritual practice grounded in the Psalms and moral actions informed by the Beatitudes are the appropriate means to the establishment of peace between father and son, king and warrior: "May you strive to act so peacefully that you may be found worthy to share the lot of blessedness with those of whom it is written, *Blessed are the peacemakers* (Matt. 5:9)" (4.8, trans. Neel 55). Her addressee, William, as other primary sources reveal, is at the time of the *Handbook*'s composition a hostage to the West Frankish king to retaliate for his father's contumacy. The young nobleman would have done well to heed his mother's counsel. Seven years later he would be executed by the same Carolingian heir for following his father in rebellion, but Dhuoda likely never knew of her beloved child's end. In her *Handbook*, she speaks of her own fragility and illness, and she seems to have died soon after she set it aside in 843.

Although Dhuoda's work survives in only a few medieval manuscripts, it may have been known to her younger son, ancestor of the medieval dukes of Aquitaine. Copies of Dhuoda's *Handbook* date from the tenth and fourteenth centuries. In the nineteenth century it received a modern edition, but the text was better established on the basis of newly discovered manuscript evidence in Pierre Riché's edition for Sources chrétiennes. Recent translations by Carol Neel and Marcelle Thiébaux have brought Dhuoda's compelling work to a wide English-speaking audience. Meanwhile, basic to further study of this important woman author are the works of Marie Anne Mayeski on Dhuoda as theologian and exegete, and of Rosalind McKitterick on its context in Carolingian letters.

See also Egeria (fl. 380s); Hrotsvit of Gandersheim (ca. 935–ca. 975)

Bibliography

Dhuoda. *Handbook for Her Warrior Son: Liber manualis.* Translated by Marcelle Thiébaux. Cambridge Medieval Classics 8. Cambridge: Cambridge University Press, 1998.

———. *Handbook for William: A Carolingian Woman's Counsel for Her Son.* Translated by Carol Neel. Rev. ed. Washington, DC: Catholic University of America Press, 1999.

———. *Manuel pour mon fils.* Edited by Pierre Riché. Translated by Bernard de Vrégille and Claude Mondésert. Sources chrétienne 225. Paris: Cerf, 1975.

Dronke, Peter. *Women Writers of the Middle Ages.* Cambridge: Cambridge University Press, 1984.

Mayeski, Marie Anne. *Dhuoda: Ninth Century Mother and Theologian.* Scranton, PA: University of Scranton Press, 1995.

McKitterick, Rosalind. *The Carolingians and the Written Word.* Cambridge: Cambridge University Press, 1989.

— CAROL NEEL

Dietrich, Suzanne de (1891–1981)

How did a small woman, crippled by congenitally dwarfed arms and legs, the seventh daughter born to a noble industrialist family in Alsace, rise to become a highly published international interpreter of the Bible for laypeople? Several strands became prominent in the weaving of Suzanne de Dietrich's work. Her groundbreaking leadership as a woman, first in engineering studies and later in international Christian movements, meshed well with her commitment to the role of laity in religious life. Her involvement in international Christian student movements; her elevation of group Bible studies to a central place; and her lifetime dedication to ecumenical work—all of these contributed to her reputation as "the greatest lay theologian of our time" (Weber 130).

With no male heirs to continue the Dietrich line of industrialists, the young and intelligent Suzanne de Dietrich was presented with the proposal to study engineering. It was in meeting the arduous entrance requirements for engineering and in the long hours of taxing study that she cultivated the habits of discipline and concentration that would serve her well in her life's vocation. She graduated as the second French woman in engineering in Europe in 1913, only to leave the promising prospects offered her in the field to pursue a life of studying the Scriptures. Dietrich heralded feminism as a great wave of potential social change, one that she hoped would nonetheless respect the qualities unique to women's nature.

Whether as a young leader in the burgeoning student Christian campaigns, a visionary pioneer in the global ecumenical movement, or a seasoned biblical interpreter and lecturer, Dietrich placed the Scriptures at the heart of all her public and personal activities. In addition to producing commentaries on specific New Testament books, she wrote how-to sections within her books: how to organize group Bible study, her special area of expertise; how to approach the Bible's large collection of smaller books; how to trace themes, such as liberty or salvation history, through the Old and New Testaments.

As an interpreter of biblical texts, Dietrich was clear about her basic assumptions. The Bible is to be studied for its uniqueness, not only as a book that reveals God to us but also as a book in which God speaks to us about his plan of salvation. She understood the Bible to be an organic whole, with each of the parts a necessary element that illuminates our understanding of its central message, which is the Word made flesh in Christ. Each part was to be seen first as an expression of its own time and then potentially as a revelation of a deeper truth that reverberates into the reader's time. For example, the root story of the exodus, while historical through and through, transcends its original context to connect with Christ as the true Passover Lamb. Dietrich also sees the journey of each individual as an exodus from captivity to freedom in Christ. But the Bible is not just a message for the individual; it is also the testimony of an original community speaking to the church community and all the communities of generations to come. A special blessing is reserved for those who gather in Christ's name to hear this Word spoken in public worship.

Dietrich readily admitted that the Bible was not always an easy book to comprehend. In addition to one's diligence in thoughtful reading, prayer and the work of the Holy Spirit must accompany Bible study. It is the Spirit who testifies to the truth of Christ in the Scriptures. In meditating and puzzling on its message, all must obey what they do understand and place themselves under the teaching of the church and other believers from whom they can learn.

Dietrich herself was a meticulous, dedicated, and gifted student of the Bible. While not a Greek scholar, she knew her way in Greek and read voraciously in the biblical scholarship of her day. Her colleague W. A. Visser 't Hooft describes her as "the interpreter *par excellence* of the 'Biblical renewal' of the 30s and 40s," who carried the thinking of such eminent theologians and biblical scholars as K. Barth, E. Thurneysen, E. Brunner, J. Schniewind, J. Jeremias, C. H. Dodd, E. C. Hoskyns, P. Bonnard, and F. Leenhardt to the laity (186). Nor were the new schools of historical criticism and higher criticism outside her purview. In her book *Discovering the Bible* (1952), Dietrich offers an adept analysis of Bible study and historical criticism, sifting through its positive and more questionable contributions. She concludes that historical criticism, within certain limits, offers a blessing with its emphasis on historical concreteness, reminding us that God is no abstract being speaking in generalities, but a living God who is talking to living people (12–14).

Another principle of interpretation that Dietrich stressed was her contention that the Bible is its own interpreter, thus various parts of the Bible written by different authors will shed light on the obscure meanings of other parts (*Free Men*, 8). This is an outgrowth of her emphasis on the organic wholeness of the book (*Witnessing*, 169). For example, she describes the book of Deuteronomy as a commentary on the laws of Exodus, and understands 1 and 2 Chronicles as a partial reinterpretation of the books of Kings (*Discovering*, 15). She offers the person of Christ in the New Testament as the most striking example of the fulfillment of Old Testament prophecies (*Discovering*, 17–21, 25; *Witnessing*, 166). Thus, for Dietrich, the enigma of Isa. 53 is answered by Jesus.

Dietrich's Bible commentaries put her interpretive principles into practice. Her writings explicating biblical texts are extensive, some found within works addressing the Bible as a whole, such as in her best-known book, *God's Unfolding Purpose: A Guide to the Study of the Bible* (1960), and others in publications devoted to biblical commentary on specific books of the New Testament.

Her commentary on Matthew (vol. 16 [London: SCM, 1962] of the 25-vol. set of *The Layman's Bible Commentary*), a thorough and precise treatment of Matthew, reflects Dietrich's exemplary knowledge of the full biblical composition. In drawing out the traditional Jewish slant of Matthew, Dietrich mentions a few lesser-known details. Jesus, like all pious Jews, wears fringes on his clothing as a reminder of the commandments of the Lord (Num. 15:38–39). It is this hem or fringe that the woman with the issue of blood touches and is made well (Matt. 9:20; *Saint Matthew*, 8).

Matthew's Gospel provides a rich resource for excavating Old Testament proofs as apologetics for his new revelation. It fits naturally with Dietrich's strong commitment to the unity of the two Testaments. Under the heading "The Flight into Egypt" (Matt. 2:13–23), a number of comparisons connect Jesus to the exodus event as a recapitulation (19). Like the patriarch Joseph, Jesus's earthly father, Joseph, receives his directions from God via a dream. Like Abraham, Jacob, and his sons, this Joseph flees to Egypt when refuge is needed. Jesus is taken into exile as an infant for protection from King Herod in a flight across the desert until God leads the family back "to the land of Israel" (19). The words of Hosea describe this event: "Out of Egypt have I called my son" (Hos. 2:15; 11:1).

Dietrich was no radical feminist, but her eye to the circumstances of women in 1961 predates much feminist biblical criticism. In the genealogies of Matthew, she examines the women in the enumeration and does not find Sarah, Rebecca, or Rachel there. Instead, she sees Tamar, Rahab, Ruth, and Bathsheba—all women marked by unconventional encounters with men. Dietrich comments that this line of ancestors is "not a line of moral saints but of forgiven sinners," a reminder of the covenant of grace: "In opening the Kingdom to prostitutes and pagans, Jesus could declare himself the bearer of the divine initiative to which the Old Testament testifies" (16).

And He Is Lifted Up: Meditations on the Gospel of John (1969) was Dietrich's last major commentary. As always, her writing is concise and clear, but this commentary offers some unusual stylistic features that have made it more obscure and therefore less well-received by readers. The verses are paraphrases of the original text in the form of poetic prose intermingled with her commentary, also in blank verse. It is sometimes as jarring as it is thought provoking and always aesthetically engaging. The story of Jesus's first miracle at the wedding in Cana is particularly poignant. An excerpt from John 2 reads as follows:

> Mother, what are you asking of me?
> My hour is not yet come.
> The hour of the blood-filled wedding, of the eternal wedding,
> when my blood will flow like generous wine,
> The jars for purification rites. The free wine flowing strong like a river:
> two dispensations;
> two covenants;
> two baptisms,
> Lustral water changed into wine for the supper.
> The church's Husband participating in this village wedding blesses the
>   human couple and their earthly joy with a simple act; in his eyes
>   their joy is healthy and legitimate.
> Human love sanctified, transfigured by the divine Presence.
>
> *(And He Is Lifted Up, 27)*

In a few lines, Dietrich identifies the sign of the jars of water for purification as the new wine, the flowing blood of the new covenant. She makes the connection with Jesus as the "Husband," the future head of the church, once again linking the archetypical root metaphor of God and his people Israel as marriage. It elevates marriage into much more than a social construct: it is a major conveyor of the timeless relationship of the love and fruitfulness of God/Christ and his people/church, imperfectly mirrored in the marriage of man and woman.

Suzanne de Dietrich was an outstanding lay theologian who rubbed shoulders with some of Europe's finest philosophers, theologians, and ecumenists of the twentieth century. She inspired generations of students across the globe. Eschewing a narrow dogmatism, she nonetheless insisted that there was no substitute for good exegesis, that the text itself operated like a fermenting agent, capable of energy-producing transformations that yielded new life.

On January 24, 1981, Suzanne de Dietrich died in the presence of devoted family and friends, five days short of her ninetieth birthday. On her simple flat tombstone inscribed with a cross are the psalmist's words, "Praise the Lord, my soul."

Bibliography

Dietrich, Suzanne de. *And He Is Lifted Up: Meditations on the Gospel of John.* Translated by Dennis Pardee. Philadelphia: Westminster, 1969.

———. *Discovering the Bible: A Practical Handbook for Bible Study.* Geneva: World Council of Churches, 1952; Nashville: Source Pub., 1952/53.

———. *Free Men: Meditations on the Bible Today.* Translated by Olive Wyon. London: SCM, 1961.

———. *God's Unfolding Purpose: A Guide to the Study of the Bible.* Translated by Robert McAfee Brown. Philadelphia: Westminster, 1960.

———. *The Gospel according to Matthew.* Translated by Donald G. Miller. Richmond: John Knox, 1961.

———. *Rediscovering the Bible: Bible Study in the World's Student Christian Federation.* Geneva and Toronto: World's Student Christian Federation, 1942.

———. *Toward Fullness of Life: Studies in the Letter of Paul to the Philippians.* Philadelphia: Westminster, 1946, 1966.

———. *The Witnessing Community: The Biblical Record of God's Purpose.* Philadelphia: Westminster, 1958.

Hall, Douglas John. *Remembered Voices: Reclaiming the Legacy of "Neo-Orthodoxy."* Louisville: Westminster John Knox, 1998.

Visser 't Hooft, W. A. "Suzanne de Dietrich, 1891–1981: A Tribute by W. A. Visser 't Hooft." *Ecumenical Review* 33 (1981): 186–87.

Weber, Hans-Ruedi. *The Courage to Live: A Biography of Suzanne de Diétrich.* Geneva: WCC Pubs., 1995.

— ROSEANNE KYDD

■ Docwra, Anne (ca. 1624–1710)

Anne Docwra was an English Quaker who wrote several works in support of the practices of the Friends. The eldest daughter of Sir William Waldegrave of Bures, Suffolk, Docwra moved to Cambridge after her marriage to James Docwra and lived there until her death in 1710.

Anne Docwra used biblical interpretation to defend Quaker beliefs and practices. Her defense consisted of two elements: a hermeneutic drawn from articles of the Church of England and the citation of scriptural examples of the practice in question. This method of argument is seen in Docwra's defense of female participation in worship and of inspiration or enthusiasm.

In *An epistle of love and good advice*, Docwra argues that "[the] Light, Power and Spirit of the Lord God is tendred to all mankind, as well Women as Men" (3), and she supports this by biblical illustrations of women in religious roles. Examples include "the believing Woman of *Samaria*, that carried the Tidings of the *Messiah* to the *Samaritans*"; Jesus's postresurrection appearance to two women, who were sent "to carry the Glad-tidings of his Resurrection to his Disciples"; Peter's sermon on the prophet Joel (Acts 2:14–21); and Paul's statement, "There is neither Jew nor Greek, Bond nor Free, Male nor Female, but are all one in Christ" (Gal. 3:28; *Epistle*, 4). Acknowledging that Paul elsewhere forbids women to teach and exercise authority over men (1 Tim. 2:11–12), Docwra downplays the importance of this contradiction by citing the twentieth of the Thirty-Nine Articles of Religion of the Church of England: "The Protestant-Religion forbids the expounding one place of Scripture to make it repugnant to another" (4). Drawing on the authority of the Church of England, Docwra tries to establish the legitimacy of an interpretation of Scripture that permits a level of female participation in worship unusual for her time.

In "A Treatise concerning Enthusiasm, or Inspiration, of the Holy Spirit of God," Docwra uses the same line of argument to defend inspiration. Citing the thirty-ninth article of the Church of England, "The Scriptures are a sufficient Rule both of Faith and Manners" (41), Docwra argues that all instances of inspiration found in the Bible are from God, and that contemporary inspiration should therefore not be rejected. Particular emphasis is given to Isa. 54:13 (though Docwra erroneously refers to 45:13): "And thy Children shall be taught of the Lord" (44), to the promise of a new covenant found in Jer. 31:31–34, and to repetitions of these promises in the New Testament. Docwra's use of these texts allows her to read the enthusiasm of Quakers as evidence that "they are come under the New Covenant, to be taught by God" (47).

Anne Docwra saw Scripture as "a good Witness against any Opposers" ("Treatise," 39) and used it in defense of a movement outside the established religious order of seventeenth-century England. In an effort to lend weight to her interpretations, Docwra adopted a hermeneutic drawn from an authority recognized by conformists: the Church of England.

Bibliography

Booy, David, ed. *Autobiographical Writings by Early Quaker Women*. Early Modern Englishwoman, 1500–1750: Contemporary Editions. Aldershot, UK: Ashgate, 2004.

Docwra, Anne. *An epistle of love and good advice to my old friends & fellow-sufferers in the late times, the old royalists and their posterity: And to all others that have sincere desires towards God*. London: [A. Sowle?], 1683.

———. "A Treatise concerning Enthusiasm, or Inspiration, of the Holy Spirit of God." In *The second part of An apostate-conscience exposed being an answer to a scurrilous pamphlet, dated the 11th of April, 1699: Written and published, by F. Bugg, intituled, Jezabel withstood, and her daughter Ann Docwra reproved for her lies and lightness, in her book, stiled, An apostate conscience exposed, &c*. London: T. Sowle, 1700.

Mullett, Michael. "Docwra, Anne (c. 1624–1710)." Pages 375–76 in vol. 16 of *Oxford Dictionary of National Biography*, edited by H. C. G. Matthew and Brian Harrison. Rev. ed. Oxford: Oxford University Press, 2004–11. http://dx.doi.org/10.1093/ref:odnb/45813.

— Mari Jørstad

Douglas, Mary (1921–2007)

Born Mary Margaret Tew, Mary Douglas's background is described as unique among British anthropologists of this era. Commenting on many factors—her gender (female), her ethnic and religious identity (English Catholic and part Irish), her family background (her father served in the Indian Civil Service in Burma; her mother died when she was young), her education (an ultramontane convent school run by the Dames du Sacré Coeur)—one biographer states that it is not remarkable that she "should become particularly sensitive to social differences, to marginality, and to exclusion. Her commitments—among others to hierarchy, authority, structured organization, difference and its incorporation and to ritual—all seem to stem from this early period" (Fardon 22).

As an anthropologist and scholar, her career took her from Oxford to East Africa, to University College London, to New York, and finally to Northwestern University in Chicago. Her publications are extensive: traditional writings on the Nuer in East Africa and eclectic works such as *Risk and Culture* (1982), which in its analysis of risk and ecological issues in the contemporary United States, gave rise to charges of "cultural relativism, sociological reductionism or, even, un-American character of her arguments" (Fardon 145).

Douglas's intellectual career stands out in terms of the frequency with which she crossed disciplinary boundaries, and also in the ways in which her work sought to construct rather than deconstruct. Foremost, however, is her belief in the ability of the social sciences to contribute a positive perspective on problems that may seem irresolvable (Fardon 44).

Her contribution to the work of biblical interpretation, theology, and even liturgy (Bradshaw and Melloh) has been her explicit investigation of the ways that method in anthropology could assist in rereading biblical sources as cultural texts. Spanning the entirety of her academic career, this commitment is a twofold contribution: first, her own interpretation of biblical texts from the perspective of anthropological (cross-cultural) theory, and second, her influence in expanding the interpretive breadth of biblical scholars for whom her theories have provided another lens into reading particularly challenging texts.

First is her own reading of biblical texts. *Purity and Danger: An Analysis of the Concepts of Pollution and Taboo* (1966) situates dirt and pollution as cultural concepts related to the total structure of social life, a structure that depends on a clear definition of roles and allegiances. Beliefs about pollution function as a society's attempt to influence behavior and as a way to guard against disturbances of the social order. An illustration includes a reading of the abominations of Leviticus (and Deuteronomy) and the dietary rules enshrined there. Her insights on Leviticus were expanded in 1999 to a work titled *Leviticus as Literature*.

As well as writing and lecturing on biblical texts, Douglas sought to engage in discussion with biblical scholars. In 1995 she was instrumental in setting up a colloquium devoted to scholarly questions about Leviticus, its structure, whether it could be read as a separate book apart from some larger literary structure, the relationship of Leviticus to the Pentateuch, to Chronicles, and so forth. Unusual was the interdisciplinary focus of this event, including not only biblical scholars but also anthropologists, specialists in comparative literature, and lawyers.

Her work on the book of Numbers (1993) is dedicated to opening a place for a new reading of Numbers because of her surprise at how "the book was dismissed" or how biblical scholars apologized for "its disorderliness, its chaotic constructions" (Wachtel 346). In the introduction she wonders if she is producing a "smart Alec" statement, which could be construed to say that "all have been marching out of step, except our Mary" (*In the Wilderness*, 16). Nevertheless she proceeds to produce a reading premised on her conviction that the priestly editors were not only neglected and misinterpreted but also contrasted unfavorably with the prophets. In privileging the first words of Numbers, "in the wilderness," Douglas uses the anthropological lens of defilement and magic as she lays out a structure of alternating sections of story and law arranged in a circle, arguing that "the prophets and priests were one religious community, and the religion a whole" (17).

Her second contribution to biblical scholarship acknowledges the way that her work has influenced and been used by biblical scholars. In the 1980s biblical scholars began conversational partnerships with sociology, anthropology (particularly cultural anthropology as represented by Mary Douglas, Clifford Geertz, and Victor Turner), and to a much lesser extent psychology. Douglas's work on theories of the body as a natural and social symbol and her work on group and grid have provided a cultural lens for reading biblical texts, long viewed by scholars as presenting thorny problems of interpretation. In their use of her models for analyzing culture, New Testament scholars, for example, have renewed confidence as they claim reconstructions of earliest Christianity in terms of community-formation issues such as authority, group cohesion, and boundary concerns.

Mary Douglas was an anthropologist who viewed religion as a critical lens for the development of her cultural models and theories. Her work is important not just for the fresh insight it brings to reading biblical texts, but also for the way her theories provide a useful tool for biblical interpreters who seek a broader methodological framework within which to probe biblical texts. Douglas models a female interpreter who uses insights from the social sciences to shed light on the ancient text.

Bibliography
Bradshaw, Paul F., and John Allyn Melloh, eds. *Foundations in Ritual Studies: A Reader for Students of Christian Worship*. Grand Rapids: Baker Academic, 2007.

Douglas, Mary. *In the Wilderness: Doctrine of Defilement in the Book of Numbers.* Journal for the Study of the Old Testament: Supplement Series 158. Sheffield: Sheffield Academic, 1993.

———. *Leviticus as Literature.* Oxford: Oxford University Press, 1999.

———. *Natural Symbols: Explorations in Cosmology.* New York: Pantheon Books, 1973.

———. *Purity and Danger: An Analysis of the Concepts of Pollution and Taboo.* London: Routledge & Kegan Paul, 1966. Repr., London: Routledge, 2003.

Fardon, Richard. *Mary Douglas: An Intellectual Biography.* London: Routledge, 1999.

Sawyer, John F. A., ed. *Reading Leviticus: A Conversation with Mary Douglas.* Journal for the Study of the Old Testament: Supplement Series 227. Sheffield: Sheffield Academic, 1996.

Wachtel, Eleanor. *Original Minds: Conversations with CBC Radio's Eleanor Wachtel.* Toronto: HarperFlamingo Canada, 2003.

— J. DORCAS GORDON

■ Dutton, Anne (ca. 1692–1765)

Anne Williams Cattel Dutton—theologian, writer, spiritual director, interpreter of Scripture, and contemplative Calvinistic Baptist leader—was born in Northampton, England, to parents of devout faith. A sober-minded child who memorized Scripture early, she attended the Independent Congregational Church at Castle Hill, where at age thirteen she was converted under the ministry of John Hunt (1698–1709), and five years later was baptized by the Rev. John Moore. As she matured, several religious movements influenced Dutton's spiritual growth, including biblical experientialism, hyper-Calvinism, evangelical revivalism, and missionary zeal.

Anne Williams married Thomas Cattel, a fellow church member, on January 4, 1715, and the same year moved to London, where she attended the Cripplegate Baptist Church under the ministry of John Skepp (1715–21). In 1719, after Thomas died unexpectedly of a stroke, Anne returned to Northampton. The next year, Anne married Benjamin Dutton (1691–1747) of Bedfordshire, the youngest son of a Baptist minister. In 1732 Benjamin became pastor of the Baptist church in Great Gransden, Huntingdonshire, about the time Anne began to write. By 1740, as the Evangelical Awakening was sweeping across England, Anne had published seven theological works.

The church grew rapidly under the Duttons' leadership. New meeting and minister's houses were built by 1743, by which time Anne was corresponding with leaders of the revival, had published fourteen more books, and Benjamin had traveled to America to solicit funds both for publishing Anne's new work and for building projects at the Great Gransden church. Benjamin raised sufficient funds by 1747 and turned homeward, but he drowned in a shipwreck on his return voyage. Left a widow and childless at age fifty-five, Anne remained in Great Gransden, continuing to write. Supported by transatlantic evangelical leaders, her ministry widened until, at the time of her death in 1765, Anne

Dutton was one of the most prolific woman writers of the eighteenth century and had nurtured thousands of individuals in spiritual development.

Comprising some fifty volumes, Dutton's published works include theological essays and letters, poetry, hymns, and an autobiography written in three parts. The first and second parts relate her early years and conversion, the "special providences of God," and her formative opportunities for worship, spiritual growth, and the life of holiness, despite afflictions. The third part describes her work in detail, much of which was published under the initials A. D.; attached to it is a cogent defense of the right of women both to write and to publish.

Laboring under prevailing eighteenth-century social, historical, and religious role constraints, Dutton's letters and transatlantic correspondence are replete with allusions to the weakness of her sex, even though she was well aware that she was an exceptional case, as she stated in *A Brief Account III*: "[God] shew'd me, how he had distinguish'd *me* from most of my *Sex:* That he had not dealt with *many*, as he had dealt with *me*" (18). Dutton developed a strong ego and felt divinely called; however, she carefully situated her ministry of writing and spiritual direction as *private* teaching and counsel. She saw her role as feeding "weak lambs," most of whom were laypeople needing nurture, encouragement, clarification, or correction in their spiritual walks of faith ("Letter 5," in *Honourable Gentleman I*, 113). Dutton calls her readers to imagine that when her books come into their houses, it is Dutton herself who is coming to sit and chat. Through these visits from a "Babe," God might give readers "Strength" and "a Visit *Himself*, by so weak a *Worm*, to [their] strong Consolation." According to Dutton, God can work as easily "by Worms, as by Angels" ("Lawfulness Letter," in *Brief Account III*, 10).

Two of Dutton's most important theological treatises are *A Discourse on Walking with God* (1735) and *On God's Act of Adoption*, published with *On the Inheritance of the Adopted Sons of God* (1737). In these works she evinces a Puritan spirituality and biblical experientialism that was attractive to Calvinist Methodists like Howell Harris and George Whitefield, the latter of whom circulated them in the *London Weekly Papers* beginning in August 1741. Most of her letters were couched as specific responses to readers' questions, yet there were times when Dutton addressed entire works to the "lambs of Christ" or to "babes in Christ," such as *Thoughts on the Lord's Supper* (1748) and *Hints on the Glory of Christ* (1748). Her popularity exploded as her letter books and treatises were published and read aloud in churches, societies, and Bible study and prayer groups as public teaching beneficial to spiritual growth.

Employing primarily a nonliteral exegetical approach to Scripture, Dutton's interpretation at times was more allegorical than not as she applied passages to herself and others. For example, in April 1743, while confessing that she had not specifically sought God's direction in the publication of *A Brief*

Account II, she relates that several biblical texts "broke in upon [her] heart" (Isa. 49:3; Rev. 12:6, 14). Through the Revelation passage that speaks of "the Woman [who] fled into the Wilderness," Dutton believes that God gave her "a sweet Hint, *Where* my poor Books were to be *us'd*, even in the *American* Wilderness." The "Face of the Serpent" in Revelation had "forc'd [her] out of *England*," but God still had a use for her. Immediately another "Word dropt upon [her] heart, *And* there *will I nourish thee*, Gen. 45:11." Writing of this experience in her journal, Dutton uses what she calls the "application of the Word" to provide herself spiritual self-direction in this imagery of the Woman of Revelation (*Brief Account III*, 87–91).

Dutton appropriates images from Scripture as well. Using "the barren woman" and childbirth imagery, Dutton communicates her own struggle with childlessness, but rejoices that her books and letters have become her children:

> Long have I look'd upon my poor *Books* as my *Children*, by which I hop'd to serve and glorify GOD. And having conceiv'd Hopes that the Lord would bring them out, and use them; when the Time drew nigh, I have *cried, travailing in Birth, and pained to be deliver'd*. And when opprest with Fear that they would not come forth, and so all my Labour be in vain; the Lord has comforted me with this Word, "Shall I bring to the *Birth*, and not cause to *bring forth*? Saith the LORD." And when any of them have been brought out, and I have been ready to think, that one, and another of them would be the *last*; the Lord hath said unto me, "Shall I cause to bring forth, and *shut the Womb*? (Shall I do this, and no more for thee?) Saith *thy* GOD." By which He has sweetly encourag'd me to hope in his Mercy; and upon me it has been, according as I hoped and trusted in HIM. For most of my books are now brought forth, and all the rest are coming out. *Oh what a Good, Gracious, Wonder-working, and All-performing GOD, have I!* (*Brief Account III*, 88–89)

Less often, she uses the "widow" and her "mite," as when she describes her books as gifts that she places in the hands of Christ as a "legacy for His weak children" (*Brief Account III*, Appendix, 109, 119).

Dutton's ministry was not always well received, as seen in her published disagreements with John Wesley and Ralph Cudworth, and with the Moravian Brethren over variant understandings of salvation, humanity's responsibility under God's sovereignty, and the sometimes adverse reactions to her female voice. In response to those who sought to silence her, Dutton argues in the "Lawfulness Letter" that all believers were both gifted and commanded to be useful in the body of Christ (1 Cor. 12), and that for their building up and edification, believers are compelled to share with others how Christ has nourished them. She reminds her readers that Satan uses any means at his disposal to thwart Christians from being useful in the Lord's service, suggesting that Satan even employs other faithful Christians to do his bidding, as in the case of Peter (Matt. 16:23) and the disciples when they grumbled over the woman who anointed Christ (26:8). Dutton warns that all Christians need to *"watch over [their] spirit[s] and against the Suggestions of Satan"* lest they unwillingly serve Christ's enemy. What matters is not a person's self-perceived strength or weakness, but Christ's call. Dutton declares, "If any person is fully persuaded in his own Mind, from the Word and Spirit of Christ, that it is his Duty to engage in any Piece of Service for God; it is sufficient Warrant for him to do so" (*Brief Account III*, 10).

Dutton died at Great Gransden on November 17, 1765, bequeathing her Bible to her friend and hymnist Ann Steele (1717–78) and leaving sacks full of letters from England, Wales, Scotland, America, the Netherlands, and elsewhere. She had endowed the church with houses, land, an annual sum of twenty-five pounds and five shillings, and her library of 212 volumes. In recent years, Dutton has received much attention for her role as a link in the chain of noteworthy spiritual directors in Christian history. Scholars today recognize the distinguished career of Anne Dutton, who was perhaps the most theologically capable and influential woman of her era, an uncommon interpreter of Scripture, and an obedient servant of Christ.

Bibliography

Dutton, Anne Williams Cattell. *A Brief ACCOUNT of the Gracious Dealings of GOD with a Poor, Sinful, Unworthy Creature, Relating to Some particular EXPERIENCES of the LORD'S Goodness, in bringing out several little TRACTS, to the Furtherance and Joy of Faith. With an APPENDIX, And a LETTER prefix'd on the Lawfulness of a Woman's Appearing in Print. PART III.* By A. D. London: J. Hart, sold by J. Lewis, 1750.

———. *A Brief ACCOUNT of the Gracious Dealings of GOD with a Poor, Sinful, Unworthy Creature, Relating to A Train of special PROVIDENCES attending Life, by which the Work of Faith was carried on with Power. Part II.* By A. D. London: J. Hart, sold by J. Lewis and E. Gardner, 1743.

———. *A Brief ACCOUNT of the Gracious Dealings of GOD with a Poor, Sinful, Unworthy Creature, Relating to The Work of Divine Grace on the Heart, in a saving Conversion to CHRIST, and to some Establishment in HIM. PART I.* By A. D. London: J. Hart, sold by J. Lewis and E. Gardner, 1743.

———. *Letters sent to an honourable gentleman, for the encouragement of faith: By one who has tasted that the Lord is gracious.* London: J. Hart, sold by J. Lewis and E. Gardner 1743.

———. *Thoughts on the Lord's Supper. Published with Hints of the Glory of Christ: As the Friend and Bridegroom of the Church; From the Seven Last Verses of the Fifth Chapter of Solomon's Song; In a Letter to a Friend.* London: J. Hart, sold by J. Lewis, 1748.

Sciretti, Michael, Jr. "'Feed My Lambs': The Spiritual Direction Ministry of Calvinistic British Baptist Anne Dutton during the Early Years of the Evangelical Revival." PhD diss., Baylor University, 2009.

—KAREN O'DELL BULLOCK

Eddy, Mary Baker (1821–1910)

Mary Baker Eddy was an American religious leader and author of the book *Science and Health with Key to the Scriptures*. Known to her followers as the "Discoverer and Founder of Christian Science," Eddy claimed to have discovered the Principle of Christ Jesus's healing in 1866; she spent the rest of her life establishing Christian Science as a system of healing and founding a church to promote and extend it.

Eddy understood herself as both the discoverer of a scientific truth and the founder and leader of a Christian church. Her work as an interpreter of the Bible was central to both enterprises. Controversial from the beginning of her career to its end, and beyond, Eddy insisted that her writings on the Scriptures were the result of a tripartite synergy between "revelation, reason, and demonstration" (*Science and Health*, 109). Her basis for this claim is rooted in her life experience.

Born Mary Morse Baker on a farm at Bow, New Hampshire, as the youngest of six children, she was intelligent, lively, attractive, and chronically ill. Her father, Mark Baker, was a staunch orthodox Calvinist; her mother, Abigail Ambrose Baker, was a gentler influence. Both were active in the Congregational Church. Eddy later described herself as "early a child of the Church" (*Message to the Mother Church*, 32). This affinity was tested when she was examined for membership during her adolescence and withstood the minister on the subject of predestination; she was admitted to membership, maintaining that affiliation for over thirty years until she founded a church of her own.

Eddy's regular schooling was limited by bad health, yet her older brother, Albert Baker, tutored her during his vacations from Dartmouth College. However, it was life experience, including a series of personal disasters, that had the greatest impact on Eddy's emerging approach to scriptural study and interpretation.

Widowed during her first year of marriage, Eddy returned home pregnant in 1844. She was too sick to care for her child, and the boy was eventually taken from her. She remarried in 1853, principally to regain custody, but instead found herself in a precarious marriage plagued by financial setbacks. She was bedridden much of the time, and the Bible was her primary source of comfort, encouragement, and insight.

During these difficult decades, Eddy studied homeopathy, becoming convinced of the mental nature of disease, but she was unable to find permanent health. She tried different therapies, finally making her way to Portland, Maine, in 1862 for treatment by Phineas Quimby, a self-taught healer who used no drugs but talked to his patients about their ills and rubbed their heads, controlling them mentally without placing them in a trance state. At first Eddy improved dramatically under Quimby's supervision and interrogated him about his theory, associating it with Christianity, which was basically incompatible with Quimby's ideas but congenial to her own religious sensibilities.

However, she relapsed when she returned to Lynn, Massachusetts, where she and her husband had recently moved. She became dependent on Quimby but did not regain her health.

The year 1866 began on a dismal note. Eddy's father died, predeceased by her mother. Her husband's infidelities became increasingly embarrassing. Quimby's death early in the year must have darkened the bleak picture. On a bitterly cold night in February, she was on her way with friends to a temperance meeting when she fell on the icy pavement, striking her head. By turns unconscious and in agony, she was soon moved to a nearby house, and the next day to her own apartment on a stretcher. She was sedated by her doctor, and the local paper reported her condition as "critical." It was then that she asked for her Bible and turned in the Gospels to one of Jesus's healings. At that moment, she writes, a powerful spiritual insight welled up in her: "That short experience included a glimpse of the great fact that I have since tried to make plain to others, namely, Life in and of Spirit; this Life being the sole reality of existence" (*Miscellaneous*, 24). She got up, dressed, and told her friends what had happened. She had launched out on a new life.

Eddy spent the next three years immersed in biblical study. At first she planned to write a book titled "The Bible in Its Spiritual Meaning." Her husband left her; almost destitute, Eddy moved from one boardinghouse to another, reading and writing all day in her room, talking to others about her ideas at meals, and taking cases for healing, not as a homoeopathist or a hypnotist, but under the newfound regime of her discovery.

Eddy began her scriptural research in Genesis. According to her emerging theology, Gen. 1:1–2:3 contains the spiritual, true account of God's "very good" creation, whose elements are to be interpreted metaphysically. In contrast, Gen. 2:4–4:26, narrating the fall and its aftermath, represents an allegory based on matter, the reverse of creation by God, who is Spirit. In Eddy's dialectic, if the first account is true, then the second is false, including its implications of humankind's doomed subjection to evil, sin, sickness, and death. She believed that the Hebrew prophets glimpsed this distinction, and that Christ Jesus, born of a virgin in contravention of material law, fully embodied it as the Son of God. He healed the sick, raised the dead, cleansed the sinful, and ratified his mission to humanity through his crucifixion, resurrection, and ascension.

The terms that Eddy uses for God—Father-Mother, Divine Principle, Love, Mind, Spirit, Soul, Truth, and Life—are intended to be synonymous and emerged from her study and interpretation of the Bible. Convinced that a spiritual understanding of God would heal people, she taught Christian Science to others, moving into the roles that would define her for the next two decades: author and teacher.

In this matrix of research, teaching, healing, and the emerging criticism of her ideas, *Science and Health* was born, published in 1875. Eddy's most enduring relationship was to her book. She revised and refined it for thirty-five years, sometimes alone, sometimes in consultation with editors. Hundreds of scriptural quotations, references, metaphors, themes, and paraphrases pack the text. Eddy intended her book to induce readers to study the Bible, as well as to regain physical and mental health or to let go of chronic sin. She added the section "Key to the Scriptures" in 1883; it included metaphysical exegeses of Genesis and Revelation, along with a glossary of biblical terms.

For example, her "spiritual interpretation" of Gen. 1:1, "In the beginning God created the heaven and the earth," explains: "The infinite has no beginning. This word beginning is employed to signify the only—that is, the eternal verity and unity of God and man, including the universe. . . . There is but one creator and one creation. This creation consists of the unfolding of spiritual ideas and their identities, which are embraced in the infinite Mind and forever reflected. These ideas range from the infinitesimal to infinity, and the highest ideas are the sons and daughters of God" (502–3).

Science and Health attracted little public attention until the 1880s, when Eddy and her third husband, Asa "Gilbert" Eddy, relocated to Boston. Ministers denounced Eddy and her interpretation of the Bible; physicians charged that she was a fraud. However, the Christian Science Church, established in 1879, began to put down roots and grow. Eddy "retired" to New Hampshire in 1889 but was more engaged than ever with her church and the world. She became a public figure whose views on the Bible, religion, and national and international affairs were published and dissected in the newspapers. Her development as a religious leader culminated in the unique form of government she developed in her *Church Manual* and in her founding of *The Christian Science Monitor* in 1908. The newspaper, although not "religious" in the conventional sense, was a manifestation of Eddy's conviction that Christian Science was designed to heal collective as well as individual ills. Her death in 1910 transferred the responsibility for the business of her church, including the publishing of *Science and Health*, to the Christian Science board of directors.

Mary Baker Eddy's career spanned a tumultuous period of combat between traditional Christianity and the physical sciences. Her provocative interpretation of the Bible offered a unique critique of the conflict between science and religion, challenging what she saw as the materiality of both systems. She claimed a spiritual origin for humanity and the universe, articulated in a metaphysics designed to heal. Her writings continue to shape the practice of Christian Science and her church.

Bibliography

Eddy, Mary Baker G. *Church Manual*. Boston: Christian Science Board of Directors, 1936.

———. *Message to the Mother Church: Boston, Massachusetts, June, 1901*. Boston: Christian Science Board of Directors, 1929.

———. *Miscellaneous Writings, 1883–1896*. Boston: Christian Science Board of Directors, 1924.

———. *Prose Works Other than Science and Health*. Boston: Christian Science Board of Directors, 1953.

———. *Science and Health with Key to the Scriptures*. Boston: Christian Science Board of Directors, 1934.

Gill, Gillian. *Mary Baker Eddy*. Reading, MA: Perseus Books, 1998.

Gottschalk, Stephen. *Rolling Away the Stone: Mary Baker Eddy's Challenge to Materialism*. Bloomington: Indiana University Press, 2006.

Huff, Barry. "Mary Baker Eddy: Liberating Interpreter of the Pauline Corpus." Pages 245–58 in *Strangely Familiar: Protofeminist Interpretation of Patriarchal Biblical Texts*, edited by Nancy Calvert-Koyzis and Heather Weir. Atlanta: Society of Biblical Literature, 2009.

McDonald, Jean A. "Mary Baker Eddy and the Nineteenth-Century 'Public' Woman: A Feminist Reappraisal." *Journal of Feminist Studies in Religion* (1986): 89–111.

Peel, Robert. *Mary Baker Eddy: The Years of Authority*. New York: Holt, Rinehart & Winston, 1977.

———. *Mary Baker Eddy: The Years of Discovery*. New York: Holt, Rinehart & Winston, 1971.

———. *Mary Baker Eddy: The Years of Trial*. New York: Holt, Rinehart & Winston, 1966.

— Michael Hamilton

Egeria (fl. 380s)

Egeria is known only through her account of her travels in the Holy Land in 381–84. No other work by her, and virtually no information about her, survives. Her "travel diary" is untitled and unattributed, perhaps because it survives only as a fragment; the beginning and end have been lost. It is, however, priceless: colorful, lively, simply written but powerful, opening to the contemporary reader the world of early Christian Bible-centered piety that drove the fourth century's explosion of pilgrimage and rediscovery of the Holy Land. It is also crucial for the window it opens on the thriving fourth-century circles of women devoted to celibacy and biblical scholarship, women who often, like the company of virgins and widows who accompanied Paula on her travels through the Holy Land, were committed to tracing scriptural history in the places where it happened.

Egeria hailed from "the ends of the earth," as the bishop of Edessa puts it (*Itinerarium Egeriae* [*It. Eg.*] 19.5, in Maraval; or in Wilkinson): probably from Galicia, in northern Spain, though a reference to the Rhone in her letter suggests that an origin in Gaul is also possible. Her name is known because of Valerius of Bierzo, a seventh-century monk who praises to his brothers a "fragile woman's" difficult journey through the Holy Land toward spiritual transformation. The journey Valerius describes is clearly the same one recorded in her diary; he names this woman "most blessed Egeria" (*Ep.* 1). She writes of her journey to a group of women back home—"venerable lady

179

sisters" (*It. Eg.* 3.8; 20.5), she calls them, "ladies of my soul" (19.19), "my light" (23.10)—who are united with her in a passion for the Scriptures and a habit of communal Bible reading. This may be an early monastic community, as Valerius suggests in calling her *sanctimonialis*, meaning "holy," "religious" (a term used in later Latin specifically for monks and nuns); it may be a group of women who gather to read the Bible and pray together, like the virgins and widows who gathered around Marcella and Paula in Rome in the mid-fourth century. Egeria writes simply and in a rather strange Latin. Unlike Marcella, she does not seem to know Greek (let alone Hebrew) and shows no knowledge of the Latin classics; thus she may have had a limited education. She writes, however, with an impressive narrative clarity and power, and with considerable rhetorical skill: her journey and the scriptural narrative it traces come to life in the pages of her letter. What is known incontrovertibly about her is that she was wealthy enough to afford a three-year journey and to hire mules and a retinue, and important enough to be greeted by bishops everywhere she went.

Egeria's account of her travels through the Holy Land begins "in the middle of things [*in medias res*]," with words that capture the essence of the letter and point to Egeria's particular genius as an interpreter of Scripture: "*Ostendebantur iuxta scripturas*: [the places] were shown according to the Scriptures." In Egeria's "travel diary," Scripture and the land are intimately interwoven. Scripture shapes her journey so thoroughly as to transform the fourth-century landscape: current events, local customs, politics on the edges of a weakening Roman Empire, the daily life of a busy city like Jerusalem—none of this interests her. Mount Sinai is the place where Moses talked to God; the plain in front of it is the place where the Israelites sojourned. In the whole course of her travels, she offers only one name that is not that of a biblical personage: Marthana, deaconess and monastic, her dear friend, whom she is greatly delighted to meet outside Jerusalem. It is not that she meets no other people. She meets many: Roman soldiers in their forts, monks in their caves, the people of Faran and their camels, the pagans who throng Edessa. Who they are, however, does not matter. What matters is only that in their various ways they show her "the things according to the Scriptures." Scripture thus renders the world: what Egeria sees is the story of Moses and the Israelites, of Melchizedek and the vine-filled valley, of Jesus and the cross and empty tomb—not the contemporary exotica of a foreign land. Further, the land thus mapped by Scripture is a land transformed: all the people are holy, and all the valleys "very beautiful."

And yet the land, the place itself, is crucial. Egeria seeks only one thing, her desire (*desiderium*), as she calls it, to trace on the Holy Land the stories of the Holy Scriptures. Here in the places where it happened, biblical history comes alive. Indeed, to walk in the places where the holy people of Scripture walked, where holy monks now live, is to be drawn into the story. Whereas the Pilgrim of Bordeaux (333 CE) simply lists sites as they occur—Zacchaeus's tree standing next to Elisha's spring and Rahab's house—so that biblical references are jumbled together in rich confusion, in Egeria a narrative emerges (3.2; cf. 2.5; 2.6). In the journal's first twelve chapters, readers walk with her through the book of Exodus, in its broad outline and in detail. "They showed us also the place where the calf was made—for in that place is fixed, even today, a great stone. As we were going we saw the summit of the mountain . . . from which place holy Moses saw the children of Israel dancing in those days when they made the calf. They showed us even the huge rock in the very place where holy Moses . . . 'enraged, broke the tablets' [Exod. 32:19] which he was carrying" (5.3–4). As the apostasy of the Israelites comes to life on the plain, so Moses's ascent to the glory of God becomes Egeria's own, in her ascent of Mount Sinai. A hard coming she has of it—straight up the outlying mountains, "as if up a wall," and straight down again, on foot because it is too steep for a mount—but she does not feel the pain because, she says, "the desire which I had, God willing, I saw being fulfilled" (3.2). At the top, "where the glory of God descended in that day when the mountain smoked" (3.2; cf. 2.5; 2.6), *ecce!* Look! A priest—a whole company of priests—appears from nowhere, and they celebrate the Eucharist and see, from the mountaintop, the kingdoms of the world, from Egypt to Palestine and the Mediterranean: "You will scarcely believe it!" she says to her "sisters" of the view—and indeed scholars do not believe her. When she descends, she sees from afar the mountaintop that before was invisible to her eyes.

Egeria's journey through the biblical story taken as literal history becomes a journey of spiritual transformation, the soul's journey into the presence of God. In the intersection between Scripture and the land, the biblical story comes alive; Egeria's vivid telling of her journey—in its intertwining of ancient story and present place, holy Moses and holy monks, the literal and the spiritual—becomes a narrative of transformation, inviting the reader to come in.

Over the years, Egeria's account of her travels has been of immense importance to liturgists and Latinists alike. In it she describes in detail the daily and weekly liturgies of Lent and Holy Week as they were conducted in the late fourth century in Jerusalem, opening thereby a window on to the worship practices and the piety of the early church. Similarly, her journal reveals to scholars a European form of late Latin as it might have been used popularly in the far reaches of the Roman Empire. Her letter is perhaps most valuable, however, as a record of two things. First, it reveals the vitality and importance of biblical interpretation by and among women in the early church. Second, it paints a striking picture of the nature of that interpretation: at once literal and spiritual, finding a present spiritual power in the biblical history read with an intense literalism. As Egeria climbs the mountain in Moses's footsteps, she also knows the majesty of God that descended there upon Moses long ago.

See also Marcella (ca. 327–410); Paula (347–404)

Bibliography

Campbell, Mary. *The Witness and the Other World: Exotic European Travel Writing, 400–1600*. Ithaca, NY: Cornell University Press, 1988.

Frank, Georgia. *The Memory of the Eyes: Pilgrims to Living Saints in Christian Late Antiquity*. Berkeley: University of California Press, 2000.

Hunt, E. David. *Holy Land Pilgrimage in the Later Roman Empire, AD 312–460*. Oxford: Clarendon, 1982.

Maraval, Pierre, ed. *Egérie: Journal de voyage et lettre sur la Bse. Egérie*. Sources chretiennes 296. Paris: Cerf, 1982.

Sivan, Hagith. "Holy Land Pilgrimage and Western Audiences: Some Reflections on Egeria and Her Circle." *Classical Quarterly* 38 (1988): 528–35.

Wilken, Robert. *The Land Called Holy: Palestine in Christian History and Thought*. New Haven: Yale University Press, 1992.

Wilkinson, John. *Egeria's Travels*. 3rd ed. Warminster, UK: Aris & Phillips, 1999.

— CATHERINE SIDER HAMILTON

Egerton, Francis (Harriet Catherine) (1800–1866)

Harriet Catherine Egerton (née Greville) was the only daughter of Charles Greville and Charlotte, the eldest daughter of William, third duke of Portland. On June 18, 1822, she married Francis Leveson-Gower (1800–1857), who assumed the Egerton surname and arms on his father's death in 1833. They had five sons and two daughters.

Egerton published a number of works. These included *Outlines of Irish History* (1829); commentaries on all the Pauline and General Epistles (1832–38); *The Believer's Guide to the Holy Communion* (1849); a translation of the French work by Jean Henri Grand Pierre; and *Journal of a Tour in the Holy Land, in May and June, 1840* (1841), a work containing excerpts from the journal that she kept during her journey through Palestine, as well as drawings by Lord Egerton.

Egerton had an extensive knowledge of Scripture. This can be observed in her *Journal* as well as in her commentaries. Throughout her *Journal*, Egerton draws connections between her travels and the Bible. For example, in an entry concerning her time in Jerusalem, she observes that the roofs of the houses are flat: "Thus David had the misfortune to see Bathsheba" (2 Sam. 11:2; *Journal*, 18). In another entry, this one describing her time in Bethlehem, she wonders whether the surrounding fields are "perhaps, the very fields where the angels announced to the shepherds the birth of the Saviour of the world" (Luke 2:8–14; *Journal*, 32). In yet another entry, she recalls the parable of the good Samaritan as she describes her visit to Jericho (Luke 10:30–35; *Journal*, 36).

Egerton's commentaries on the Pauline and General Epistles are intended to be resources for teachers and parents in the instruction of children. Since the content level is quite advanced, it is likely that Egerton had older children in view. She observes that children are familiar with the Old Testament and the Gospels, but unfamiliar with the Epistles, which are mistakenly considered "too difficult for their [the children's] understandings, and, therefore, seldom form a part of early education" (*Romans*, iii). She argues, however, that the doctrinal teachings of the Epistles are too important to be overlooked: "These doctrines, as they are of the utmost importance to the present and future happiness of man, so ought they to be impressed with care and diligence on the youthful mind; and, as their exposition is chiefly to be found in the Epistles, thither must attention be turned by all, who would wish to come to the knowledge of the truth" (iv).

Each commentary is organized in a similar fashion. The preface of each commentary provides information concerning the date of the epistle, the author's location and circumstances at the time of writing, and the character of the recipients of the epistle. The discussion of each chapter contains a brief summary, questions about each verse, and in many cases, answers to the questions. Cross-references to relevant biblical texts are found throughout these commentaries.

Egerton's comments on several passages shed light on her views concerning the place of women. From a spiritual standpoint, Egerton holds men and women to be equal: "There is no discrimination from . . . sex; but . . . all are equally accepted in Christ, if sincere believers" (*Galatians*, 54). Nevertheless, she accepts the superiority of men: "Both men and women may be alike renewed after the image of God in righteousness and true holiness. But the woman is the glory of the man, that is, it is the glory and honour of man that God hath given him superiority over so excellent a creature as the woman, a creature endued with reason like himself" (*First Corinthians*, 50). Although Egerton acknowledges biblical prophetesses, including Deborah (Judg. 4–5), Huldah (2 Kings 22:14–20), Anna (Luke 2:36–38), the daughters of Philip (Acts 21:8–9), and some Corinthian women (1 Cor. 11:5), she asserts that women ought not to speak in the public assembly because "these cases of extraordinary inspiration do not warrant an infraction of the Apostle's rule, 'Let your women keep silence in the Churches'" (50). Further, "the Apostle laid it down as a general rule, that women must not be allowed to speak in the public congregation, or to assume the office of teachers or disputants" (70). Egerton's comment on 1 Tim. 2:12 confirms this position; yet in citing Priscilla as an example, she allows that women might teach in private settings: "It is only women's *public* teaching that is forbidden. They may privately instruct, as Priscilla did Apollos (Acts xviii. 26); and a believing wife is bound to instruct an unbelieving husband, when he requires a reason of her faith: but she must not teach or preach in public, or pretend to any authority over man" (*1 Timothy*, 33, italics original).

Although Egerton did not disclose her religious affiliation in her writings, her Protestant commitment can be inferred from several comments concerning Roman Catholicism. In her *Journal*, for example, one learns of her support of the Ladies' Hibernian Female School Society, a group involved in the education of "the *female* population of Ireland, by uniting a Scriptural education with those necessary arts of domestic and humble life" ("Notice," italics original). In particular, she praises their work since it extends to "a great proportion of whom are the children of Roman Catholics, who thankfully avail themselves of the instruction afforded them in these Protestant schools" (*Journal*, "Notice"). One finds a critique of Roman Catholicism in her comments on glossolalia (1 Cor. 14): "The Apostle not only dislikes, but [also] plainly forbids, preaching, praying, and all other offices being performed in the Church in a language not understood; so that the practice of the church of Rome in their Latin prayers is a contradiction to the whole of this chapter" (*First Corinthians*, 66). And again: "Had the Apostle lived about the era of the Reformation, and written expressly against the Church of Rome, he could not more emphatically have exposed the absurdity and wickedness of worshipping God and performing all public offices in Latin, of which the common people understand not one word. No wonder the rulers of that Church lock up the Scriptures also, seeing they must bear too evident a testimony against them" (68).

Egerton's influence was limited to her own lifetime: her works were not republished in later years. Nevertheless, the writings of this educated laywoman reveal her intimate knowledge of Scripture and her desire not only to transmit knowledge about the historical context of Scripture to subsequent generations but also to encourage them to engage with its meaning.

Bibliography

Boase, G. C. "Francis Egerton." Pages 993–94 in vol. 17 of *Oxford Dictionary of National Biography*, edited by H. C. G. Matthew and Brian Harrison. Rev. ed. Oxford: Oxford University Press, 2004–11.

Egerton, Lady Francis. *Journal of a Tour in the Holy Land, in May and June, 1840*. London: Harrison, 1841.

———. *Outlines of Irish History: Written for the Use of Young Persons*. London: John Harris, 1829.

———. *Questions on St. Paul's Epistles to the Ephesians, Philippians, and Colossians, With Practical and Explanatory Observations Suited to the Capacity of Children: Upon the Plan of Mr. Fuller's Scripture Examiner*. London: Samuel Holdsworth, 1837.

———. *Questions on St. Paul's Epistles to the I. & II. Thessalonians, and I. & II. Timothy, With Practical and Explanatory Observations Suited to the Capacity of Children: Upon the Plan of Mr. Fuller's Scripture Examiner*. London: Samuel Holdsworth, 1838.

———. *Questions on the Epistles General of St. James and St. Peter, Upon the Plan of Mr. Fuller's Scripture Examiner*. London: Samuel Holdsworth, 1836.

———. *Questions on the Epistles General of St. John and St. Jude, Upon the Plan of Mr. Fuller's Scripture Examiner*. London: Samuel Holdsworth, 1836.

———. *Questions on St. Paul's Epistles to the Hebrews, With Practical and Explanatory Observations Suited to the Capacity of Children: Upon the Plan of Mr. Fuller's Scripture Examiner*. London: Samuel Holdsworth, 1837.

———. *Questions on St. Paul's Epistle to the Romans, With Practical and Explanatory Observations Suited to the Capacity of Children: Upon the Plan of Mr. Fuller's Scripture Examiner*. London: Holdsworth & Ball, 1832.

———. *Questions on St. Paul's First Epistle to the Corinthians, With Practical and Explanatory Observations Suited to the Capacity of Children: Upon the Plan of Mr. Fuller's Scripture Examiner*. London: Samuel Holdsworth, 1836.

———. *Questions on St. Paul's Second Epistle to the Corinthians and the Epistle to the Galatians, With Practical and Explanatory Observations Suited to the Capacity of Children: Upon the Plan of Mr. Fuller's Scripture Examiner*. London: Samuel Holdsworth, 1837.

— AGNES CHOI

Elaw, Zilpha (b. 1790, fl. 1846)

Zilpha Elaw was born free near Philadelphia. Her mother died while giving birth to her twenty-third child (only three survived) when Elaw was twelve years old. Since her father was unable to care for her and her younger sister, Hannah, Elaw was placed with a Quaker family until she turned eighteen. Her father died a year and a half later. Elaw's brother, the oldest child, had been taken by his maternal grandparents years earlier. While in her father's house, Elaw learned the spiritual disciplines of morning and evening family devotions and prayer. In 1808, Elaw joined the Methodist Episcopal Society when the movement entered her part of the country. The very personal and demonstrative religion developed in her father's house, the contemplative spirituality of the Quakers, and the Methodist emphasis on the Spirit, forgiveness of sins, and sanctification all shaped Elaw's religious perspective.

In her autobiography, *Memoirs of the Life, Religious Experience, Ministerial Travels, and Labours of Ms. Zilpha Elaw, an American Female of Colour; Together with Some Account of the Great Religious Revivals in America [Written by Herself]* (1846), Elaw records details of her personal life and public ministry, including her spiritual journey, God's distinct callings, and her experiences as an itinerant preacher. None of Elaw's sermons have survived. Her book demonstrates an affinity for Paul and the Pauline Letters, which she interprets through the lens of her lived experiences. Elaw recalls a certain slave driver who attended one of her meetings in the Antebellum South. She writes, "Like Paul for the Galatians, I travailed in birth for him" (Gal. 4:19; *Memoirs*, in *Sisters of the Spirit*, 101).

In a fashion similar to that of other female spiritual autobiographers, God revealed God's self to Elaw in visions (through her own and her sister Hannah's) that strikingly resemble Paul's Damascus road epiphany (Acts 9). In 1817 Elaw received her first vision while attending a camp meeting in Burlington, New

Jersey. She writes, "I sank down upon the ground, and laid there for a considerable time [and] surrounded and engulphed [*sic*] in the glorious effulgence of [God's] rays, I distinctly heard a voice. . . . 'I will show thee what thou must do.' I saw no personal appearance" (*Sisters*, 66–67). God informed Elaw that God had separated her for house ministry or exhortation. Like Phoebe (Rom. 16:1–2), Elaw would travel to homes to speak to families about their salvation, visit the sick, and perform other "errands and services" for the Lord (*Sisters*, 67). Elaw expresses her personal sanctification and preparation for service as being "made meet for the master's use." Invoking Pauline language, she writes: "Whether I was in the body, or whether I was out of the body, on that auspicious day, I cannot say" (cf. 2 Cor. 12:3; *Sisters*, 66). After a brief illness that Elaw attributes to God's "rod" because of her reluctance to preach publicly, she appropriated Phil. 1:20–23, stating that she was "willing either to live or die as [God] thought best, though I could rather have preferred to depart and be with Christ, which is far better" (75–77).

As an itinerant preacher, Elaw traveled throughout the United States and England, even though the Methodists had denied full ordination credentials to female preachers like Elaw and her contemporary Jarena Lee. As she preached, Elaw discursively constructed an identity and vocational legitimacy for herself as a woman called by God and not by any mortal. She employed Pauline language from Gal. 1–2 to legitimate her divine call "not from mortal man, but from the voice of an invisible and heavenly personage sent from God" (*Sisters*, 82).

In light of God's inescapable call, Elaw struggled with her own socialization that women belonged in the home, caring for husband and children. Elaw's need to care for her only child (a daughter born in 1811, the year after she married; the child is not named in Elaw's book), overwhelming debt, and discouragement sometimes interrupted Elaw's preaching activities. During one such hiatus, she established a school for female "coloured" children who were refused admittance to white "seminaries." To begin her itinerant preaching in Philadelphia, Elaw closed that school two years after she opened it and left her child with a relative.

Elaw "surrendered" herself in marriage to Joseph Elaw in 1810. Mr. Elaw was one of the last to discover that Zilpha had been preaching publicly. Zilpha prayed that he would accept and support her call, but Mr. Elaw could not make peace with the thought of his wife becoming a "laughing stock." Elaw chose God's commission to preach over submission to her husband's "flesh and blood," despite her general belief that women should submit to their fathers before marriage and to their husbands in marriage (*Sisters*, 84). Although Elaw believed the wife was "destined to be the help-meet" of her husband, a wife "dare not" submit to a "worldly man" (62). Paradoxically, Elaw reaffirmed Paul's prohibition against women's teaching or preaching in church (1 Cor. 14:33b–35; 1 Tim. 2:11–12) while defending her own call as extraordinary. She argued that the Pauline proscription did not apply to "the extraordinary directions of the Holy Ghost in reference to female Evangelists, or oracular sisters; nor to be rigidly observed in *peculiar* circumstances" (*Sisters*, 124). According to Elaw, when Paul spoke the church was experiencing disorder and excess, and the brethren were all extensively gifted with utterances. Elaw interpreted Paul's injunction for women to learn privately and in silence through the lens of her own "peculiar" experience.

Elaw's autobiography demonstrates her audacity to name and claim her own experiences as God's revelations. She interpreted and appropriated biblical texts and images as validations and expressions of her call even as she wrestled with that call in light of conventional understandings of women's limited roles in the home and church. Elaw determined that her calling as an itinerant preacher was legitimate despite Pauline proscriptions against it. In order to appease Paul and to obey God, Elaw viewed her calling as the extraordinary gift of God's Spirit.

See also Lee, Jarena (1783–ca. 1849)

Bibliography

Cullen, Margaret. "Holy Fire: Biblical Radicalism in the Narratives of Jarena Lee and Zilpha Elaw." Pages 143–63 in *The Force of Tradition: Response and Resistance in Literature, Religion, and Cultural Studies*, edited by Donald G. Marshall. Lanham, MD: Rowman & Littlefield, 2005.

Elaw, Zilpha. *Memoirs of the Life, Religious Experience, Ministerial Travels, and Labours of Ms. Zilpha Elaw, an American Female of Colour; Together with Some Account of the Great Religious Revivals in America [Written by Herself]*. London: The author, 1846. Reissued as pages 49–160 in *Sisters of the Spirit*, edited by William L. Andrews. Bloomington: Indiana University Press, 1986.

Haywood, Chanta M. "Prophesying Daughters. Nineteenth-Century Black Religious Women, the Bible, and the Black Literary History." Pages 355–66 in *African Americans and the Bible: Sacred Texts and Social Textures*, edited by Vincent L. Wimbush. New York: Continuum, 2003.

McKay, Nellie Y. "Nineteenth-Century Black Women's Autobiographies: Religious Faith and Self-Empowerment." Pages 139–54 in *Interpreting Women's Lives: Feminist Theory and Personal Narratives*, edited by The Personal Narratives Group. Bloomington: Indiana University Press, 1989.

Smith, Mitzi Jane. "'Unbossed and Unbought': Zilpha Elaw and Old Elizabeth and a Political Discourse of Origins." *Black Theology* 9.3 (2011): 287–311.

— MITZI JANE SMITH

Elisabeth of Schönau (1129–65)

Elisabeth of Schönau was born near Bonn, Germany, in 1129. Her family, of Rheinisch nobility, had strong connections to the church. When Elisabeth was twelve years old, her family presented her to the Benedictine double monastery at Schönau, in the diocese of Trier, not far from Cologne and the Rhine. This foundation was part of a spiritual renewal that encompassed a commitment to women's monastic life. Young Elisabeth attended the monastery school and joined the community of nuns. In 1147 she made her monastic profession as a Benedictine nun, and ten years later the nuns elected her magistra, or superior, of the women's monastery.

An official vita was never written for Elisabeth of Schönau. The little that is known about her life comes from her own writings and from her brother Ekbert's work, *De obitu*, written after her death on June 18, 1165. She was a spiritual adviser within her community, a powerful intercessor, as well as a preacher to both clergy and laypeople. Today Elisabeth of Schönau is most remembered as a twelfth-century visionary, not a mystic. She is often referred to as a protégé of Hildegard of Bingen and compared with her as visionary and prophet.

Elisabeth's visionary experiences began when she was twenty-three years old, just five years after the visions of Hildegard of Bingen were authenticated by Pope Eugenius II. At the time (1152), Elisabeth was coping with a severe bout of depression and in poor health. As early as March 1154 she began having regular visions of the angel who lifted her soul up to the heavens and mediated divine revelation from God to herself. She relates the experience: "After a little while, the angel of the Lord came, and quickly raised me up and stood me on my feet saying: 'O person, rise and stand on your feet and I will speak with you, and do not be afraid, because I am with you all the days of your life. . . . Say to the apostates on earth . . .'" (*First Book of Visions*, chap. 67, in *Works*). Just as the angel mediated between her and God, Elisabeth saw herself as a mediator between heaven and earth, bringing a message of God's judgment and a call to conversion, especially to the clergy of her day. She was called by God like the Old Testament prophets, the apostle Paul, and the seer of the Apocalypse.

Her works are collections of her pronouncements about what she saw and heard in ecstatic trances. Elisabeth's visionary experiences usually occurred in the context of the liturgical cycle, as part of her ongoing prayer life and nurtured by her monastic milieu. At the celebration of the Eucharist or during the Hours of the Divine Office, she might experience rapture or ecstasy. Sometimes she would behold the saint being honored or some symbolic manifestation relevant to the season in the liturgical calendar. For example, in her vision one Christmas Eve, recorded in chapter 4 of the *Third Book of Visions*, as she and the sisters were celebrating the vigil of Christ's nativity, Elisabeth "remained awake in prayer" when "around the hour of the divine sacrifice, (i.e., the Mass) . . . she came into a trance," and saw

as it were a sun of marvelous brightness in the sky. In the middle of the sun was the likeness of a virgin whose appearance was particularly beautiful and desirable to see. She was sitting with her hair spread over her shoulders, a crown of the most resplendent gold on her head, and a golden cup in her right hand. A splendor of great brightness came forth from the sun, by which she was surrounded on all sides, and from her it seemed to fill first the place of our dwelling, and then after a while spread out little by little to fill the whole world. (*Works*, 123–25)

As the vision continued, Elisabeth saw a dark cloud obscure the sun, and the virgin "appeared to weep copiously, as if grieving much on account of the earth's darkness" (123). Perplexed, Elisabeth asked "the holy angel of the Lord what kind of vision it could be and what meaning it might have" (123). His response:

> The virgin you see is the sacred humanity of the Lord Jesus (*domini Jesu sacra humanitas*). The sun in which the virgin is sitting is the divinity that possesses and illuminates the whole humanity of the Savior. The dark cloud that intermittently blocks the brightness of the sun from the earth is the iniquity which reigns on the earth. . . . There is no joy now in the Son of Man for this generation of those who have enraged Him, and great is His regret about those who do not give thanks for his benefits. This is the lamentation of the virgin who cries in the face of the cloud. (123–24)

Thus far this example illustrates the contexts of the liturgical season of Christmas as celebrating the incarnation, the communal celebration of Mass, the fact that Elisabeth's visionary trance occurs "while she is awake," the role of the angel, and an allegorical interpretation that identifies the moral tenor of the times. As the text continues, her initial understanding is deepened when "three days later the glorious Queen of Heaven" appears to Elisabeth along with John the Evangelist. Elisabeth questions him about the interpretation of her vision. She wants to know why "the humanity of the Lord Savior [was] shown to me in the form of a virgin and not in a masculine form?" (124). John answers: "The Lord willed it to be done in this way so that the vision could so much more easily be adapted to also signify His blessed mother" (124–25). The contemporary reader of this vision might immediately think of the image of Mary in the Apocalypse, "the woman clothed with the sun" (Rev. 12:1); yet Rachel Fulton points out that in the twelfth century the conventional reading of the "woman clothed with the sun" would be the church and not Mary, suggesting that there is something of novelty in Elisabeth's vision (Fulton 410). There is also complexity.

Elisabeth's visionary experiences (simple visions, raptures, and ecstasies) continued at intervals until her death in 1165. Eight works comprise the collection of visionary works associated with Elisabeth. These are her three visionary works: *First Book of Visions*, *Second Book of Visions*, and *Third Book of Visions* (*Libri visionem primus, secundus, tertius*), parts of which circulated during her lifetime. She also wrote three thematic works: *The Book of the*

189

Ways of God (*Liber viarum Dei*, 1157), her longest work; *Vision about the Resurrection of the Blessed Virgin Mary* (*Visio de resurrectione Beate Virginis Marie*, 1159), in which Elisabeth describes the responses of Mary and an angel to the question of whether Mary's body had gone to heaven with her soul at death, a point of doctrinal controversy in her day; and *The Book of Revelations*, about the Sacred Company of the Virgins of Cologne (*Revelatio de sacro exercitu virginum Coloniensium*, 1157), the most popular of her works in her own day. Since the introductions to Elisabeth's texts were written by her brother, Ekbert, they should not be assumed to reflect Elisabeth's view or to be the necessarily more accurate view of what happened at Schönau, for they simply reflect Ekbert's interpretation of Elisabeth (Clark, *Visionary*, 29).

Elisabeth's writings show her knowledge of the Bible as prayed in and through the round of the liturgy (day, week, seasons, and feasts), heard in sermons, and pondered in the monastic process called *lectio divina*, or divine reading. Visionary and apocalyptic books such as Ezekiel and Revelation provided topoi of visionary experiences. Yet Elisabeth's descriptions of her own visionary experiences do not exactly mirror biblical passages. Rather, with her imagination she transforms vivid biblical symbols into images that have meaning for her in an attempt to articulate what she believes she perceives. Early on she comes to recognize her call to be "a channel of communication and grace to others" (Clark, *Visionary*, 88; also see 74–88).

A century after her death, monastery libraries in Germany, France, and England housed copies of Elisabeth's works. An extensive circulation of her manuscripts (some 145 medieval manuscripts) beyond the walls of Schönau points to her reputation as a woman especially gifted by God and to the receptive audience of her readers. As visionary prophet, reformer, and teacher, Elisabeth of Schönau rightly finds a place within a tradition of vision and prophecy that formed part of the intellectual environment of the twelfth century, an era some historians view as one of the most critical periods of Western civilization. The corpus of her work needs further study in terms of her work as a biblical interpreter.

See also Hildegard of Bingen (1098–1179)

Bibliography

Beard, Anne, OSB. "The Visionary Life of Elisabeth of Schönau: A Different Way of Knowing." Pages 167–84 in *Medieval Women Monastics: Wisdom's Wellsprings*, edited by Miriam Schmitt, OSB, and Linda Kulzer, OSB. Collegeville, MN: Liturgical Press, 1996.

Clark, Anne L. *Elisabeth of Schönau: A Twelfth-Century Visionary*. Philadelphia: University of Pennsylvania Press, 1992.

———. "Why All the Fuss about the Mind? A Medievalist's Perspective on Cognitive Theory." Pages 170–82 in *History in the Comic Mode: Medieval Communities and the Matter of Person*, edited by Rachel Fulton and Bruce W. Holsinger. New York: Columbia University Press, 2007.

Elisabeth of Schönau. *Elisabeth of Schönau: The Complete Works*. Classics of Western Spirituality. Translated and introduced by Anne L. Clark. Preface by Barbara Newman. New York: Paulist Press, 2000.

Fulton, Rachel. *From Judgment to Passion: Devotion to Christ and the Virgin Mary, 800–1200*. New York: Columbia University Press, 2002.

McGinn, Bernard. *The Growth of Mysticism*. Vol. 2 of *The Presence of God: A History of Western Christian Mysticism*. New York: Crossroad, 1994.

— Ann Marie Caron, RSM

Elizabeth I (1533–1603)

Elizabeth I, queen of England from 1558 to 1603, received a thorough education in Scripture, Protestant theology, Latin, Greek, and the Romance languages. In adolescence she translated works by Margaret of Navarre, Katherine Parr, John Calvin, and Bernardino Ochino into various languages. She also translated Ps. 13 from the Vulgate. Her manner of interpreting Scripture is generally to be deduced from numerous references in her speeches, private prayers, and poems. Generally she reflects the conventional penitential piety of the sixteenth century and concentrates on scriptural passages dealing with the duties and dangers involved in a monarch's life.

Elizabeth's public utterances frequently contained direct references to Scripture. On hearing of her accession to the throne, she quoted Ps. 118:23; in reference to the burden of royalty, Luke 12:48. In comparing the smaller though voluntary subsidies granted her by the clergy to the larger though forced subsidies of the Commons, she commented, "I esteem more of their mites than of your pounds" (Mark 12:41–44). In answering the Commons' petition that Mary Queen of Scots be put to death, she takes Solomon as her model, citing 1 Kings 3:9. Her poem of thanksgiving for the defeat of the Armada analogizes the fleet's destruction to Pharaoh's in the Red Sea, and the English to the Israelites led out of danger (Exod. 13:21). Her subjects in turn compared Elizabeth sometimes to Deborah and sometimes to Theodosia, the eighth-century Byzantine anti-iconoclast.

Elizabeth composed many prayers in various languages. Extensive scriptural quotations indicate how she applied biblical passages and motifs to her own situation. A prayer written in the Tower of London, where she was confined for suspected disloyalty to her sister, Queen Mary I, alludes to Matt. 7:24–27. A published collection of her Latin *Precationes privatae* (Private Prayers, 1563) contains collects, thanksgivings, and petitions, prefaced with psalm quotations and versicles drawn from the Vulgate and adjusted in vocabulary, grammar, or phrasing to suit her peculiar circumstances, using feminine pronouns and adjectives throughout and often changing the third person to the first. For instance, "The king will hope in the Lord and not miscarry in the mercy of the Most High" (*rex sperat in domino, et in misericordia Altissimi non com-movebitur* [Ps. 21:7] becomes "I shall hope in the Lord and not miscarry in the mercy of the Most High" (*sperabo in domino et in misericordia Altissimi non commovebor*). There is some creative interpolation. For instance, the "living God" (*Deum vivum*) of Ps. 42:2 becomes "God, the living fountain" (*Deum fontem vivum*) of Jer. 2:13. There is also some rewriting, as when "All kings shall adore" (*Adorabunt omnes reges*) of Ps. 72:11 becomes "You have adorned all kings" (*Adornasti omnes reges*), and "The king shall rejoice" (*laetabitur rex*) of Ps. 21:1 becomes "Let kings rejoice" (*laetentur reges*).

Not surprisingly, many of the biblical quotations focus on the conditions and duties of monarchy, including the dispensation of justice and threats from enemies. A thanksgiving, written after recovering from a near-fatal case of smallpox, blurs the distinction between sickness of body and of soul, quoting Matt. 9:12. In a thanksgiving for many blessings received, she remembers Luke 12:48. Elizabeth also published a collection of original prayers in French, Italian, Spanish, Latin, and Greek (1569). A prayer in French "for the whole realm and body of the Church," is written from a sovereign's point of view and incorporates the whole of Ps. 101 (which Luther had called "David's mirror of a monarch") in Clement Marot's French metrical translation.

Many other prayers survive in manuscript, often in her own hand. Her English prayers use the language of the Book of Common Prayer and are dense with scriptural allusions. Some creativity is shown in her alteration of "I am a worm and no man" (BCP, Ps. 22:6) to "Thou made me not a worm, but a creature according to Thine own image." One prayer, written in Greek, includes an extensive list of repentant sinners, including the woman who bathed Christ's feet with her tears, Zacchaeus the tax collector, the crucified thief who acknowledged Christ's kingdom, and Saul the persecutor of the church.

In 1563, Elizabeth published her *Sentences sententiae*, a collection of pithy sayings drawn from biblical, classical, patristic, medieval, and humanist sources, on topics related to royal governance. Each section begins with a wide range of scriptural quotations, the majority derived from the Wisdom books (Proverbs, Ecclesiastes, Ecclesiasticus [Sirach], and Wisdom of Solomon). In her opening section on the duty of obedience to princes, she follows Luther in quoting extensively from Rom. 13. The quotations contain a few discrepancies with the scriptural originals, most of them very slight. She interjects an explicit reference to Christ into Tobit 4:19 (4:20, Vulgate): "Seek of God that He may direct thy ways, and that all thy counsels may abide in Christ."

In a letter to Henry IV of France, deploring his conversion, Elizabeth hopes that the hands of Esau (the Roman Church) may not spoil the blessings of Jacob (the Protestant Church), according to a common sixteenth-century allegory. A poem composed in French, in about 1590, discusses her spiritual struggles by using many Pauline concepts, such as the old-man-versus-new-man dichotomy (Eph. 4:22, 24; Col. 3:9–10); being a babe in Christ, not yet "capable" of adult food (1 Cor. 3:1–2); and the "seal of salvation" (2 Cor. 1:22; Eph. 1:13).

Elizabeth's interpretations and occasional allegorizations of Scripture seem generally to conform to the conventional readings of sixteenth-century Protestantism. Her references to and adaptations of biblical quotations, not only in her private prayers but also in her dry comments and witty ripostes, reflect that intimate knowledge of Scripture that was so conspicuous a feature of English culture in her time.

See also Marguerite de Navarre (1492–1549); Parr, Katherine (1512–48)

Bibliography

Elizabeth I. *Autograph Compositions and Foreign Language Originals.* Edited by Janel Mueller and Leah S. Marcus. Chicago: University of Chicago Press, 2003.

———. *Collected Works.* Edited by Leah S. Marcus, Janel Mueller, and Mary Beth Rose. Chicago: University of Chicago Press, 2000.

———. *The Poems of Queen Elizabeth I.* Edited by Lester Bradner. Providence: Brown University Press, 1964.

———. *Translations, 1544–1589.* Edited by Janel Mueller and Joshua Scodel. Chicago: University of Chicago Press, 2009.

Erickson, Carolly. *The First Elizabeth.* New York: Summit, 1983.

Neale, John E. *Queen Elizabeth I.* London: Jonathan Cape, 1934.

Prescott, Anne Lake. "The Pearl of the Valois and Elizabeth I: Marguerite de Navarre's *Miroir* and Tudor England." Pages 61–76 in *Silent but for the Word: Tudor Women as Patrons, Translators, and Writers of Religious Works*, edited by Margaret Patterson Hannay. Kent, OH: Kent State University Press, 1985.

Sanders, Seth. "Book of Translations Reveals Intellectualism of England's Powerful Queen Elizabeth I." *University of Chicago Chronicle* 22, no. 2 (Oct. 10, 2002), http://chronicle.uchicago.edu/021010/elizabeth.shtml.

— BRAD WALTON

Eudocia Augusta, Aelia (ca. 400–460)

Eudocia was born to non-Christian parents and named Athenais, "the Athenian," a name anticipating that she would become a cultured woman. She was baptized as a Christian in preparation for her marriage in 421 to the Eastern Roman Emperor Theodosius II. She gave birth to two daughters, of whom the elder and only survivor married the Western Roman Emperor Valentinian. In 438–39 she made a pilgrimage to Jerusalem with the encouragement of Melania the Younger and brought back relics to Constantinople. Shortly thereafter she returned to Jerusalem and lived there until her death. (For a discussion of her life and possible reasons for leaving the court, cf. Holum 112–18 and Cameron 112–30.)

She composed an encomium on her husband's victory over the Persians in 422 and may have been the power behind the throne in setting up the "university" of Constantinople (Holum 123–24). Eudocia had a particular interest in Antioch, her likely birthplace; she delivered a speech in hexameters when she stopped there on her pilgrimage to Jerusalem, and turned a prose account of a local saint, Cyprian, into hexameters.

During her exile in Jerusalem she composed hexameter paraphrases of the Octateuch (Genesis to Ruth) in eight books and the books of Daniel and Zechariah (all now lost). Photius, the ninth-century lexicographer, read all these poems and praised Eudocia's *Paraphrase of the Octoteuch* extravagantly: "The reader . . . has no need of the originals because the meaning is always preserved precisely without expansion or abridgement, and the wording too, wherever possible, preserves a close similarity" (*Bibliotheca,* 183, Wilson 174). Photius found "the same grace" in her Zechariah and Daniel (*Bibliotheca,* 184).

Her only surviving work on the Bible is *Homerocentones,* a cento of almost 2,400 lines, with a brief account of creation and the fall, plus a far more detailed account of the life of Christ, with a particular emphasis on his miracles. This poem was stitched together from the *Iliad* and *Odyssey* as Proba's cento was from Virgil. Eudocia's treatment of her material may be judged by her recasting the wedding in Cana as a Homeric feast, with dancing, a minstrel, acrobats, and animal sacrifices (Usher, *Stitchings,* 103–4), and by Mary's grief at the death of Christ as a Homeric lament, with borrowings from Briseis's mourning for Patroclus and Andromache's mourning for Hector (140–41).

Proba's influence on Eudocia is not known, though a copy of the *Cento Virgilianus* had been presented to Arcadius, Theodosius's father, and may have been read by Eudocia. Her starting point, as she explains in her introduction, was a Homeric cento by the (otherwise unknown) bishop Patricius, which she corrected and enlarged. Scholars disagree about the nature and extent of Eudocia's contribution. Usher ("Prolegomenon") has collated a neglected manuscript with the *editio princeps* (Aldus 1502, reissued by Peter Brubach 1541 and 1554, corrected by Stephanus 1578) to produce a longer, more complete text than the previous Teubner product (Ludwich) and argues (*Stitchings*) that Eudocia contributed two-thirds of the poem. Rey (Eudocia, *Centons*) takes Patricius as the main author, whose work Eudocia enlarged and rearranged. Schembra (Eudocia, *Homerocentones*) finds evidence of four recensions (Prima, Secunda, A, and B). Sections of the *Homerocentones* have been translated into English (Usher) and the whole into French (Rey). Because until recently a good text was hard to find, serious scholarly interest in her poem has been slow to develop. Usher's studies throw fresh light on Eudocia's retelling of Bible stories through Homeric themes.

Together with the lost paraphrases on various Old Testament books, the *Homerocentones* have made a significant contribution to Bible knowledge. It would, for example, have been easier to memorize hexameters than the mostly prose Septuagint. In the *Homerocentones,* Eudocia displays skill and an understanding of Homeric composition as well as knowledge of both Old and New Testaments.

See also Proba, Faltonia Betitia (ca. 320–ca. 370)

Bibliography

Cameron, Alan. "The Empress and the Poet." *Yale Classical Studies* 27 (1982): 217–89.

Eudocia Augusta. *Centons homériques.* Edited and translated by André-Louis Rey. Paris: Cerf, 1997.

———. *Homerocentones.* Edited by Rocco Schembra. Turnhout: Brepols, 2007.

———. *Homerocentones Eudociae.* Edited by M. D. Usher. Stuttgart: Teubner, 1998. This work collates Iviron MS with Aldus-Stephanus, replacing Arthur Ludwich, *Euodiciae Augustae . . .* (Leipzig: Teubner, 1897).

Holum, Kenneth G. *Theodosian Empresses: Women and Imperial Dominion in Late Antiquity.* Berkeley: University of California Press, 1982.

Usher, M. D. *Homeric Stitchings: The Homeric Centos of the Empress Eudocia.* Lanham, MD: Rowman & Littlefield, 1998.

———. "Prolegomenon to the Homeric Centos." *American Journal of Philology* 118 (1997): 305–21.

Van Deun, Peter. "The Poetical Writings of the Empress Eudocia: An Evaluation." Pages 273–82 in *Early Christian Poetry: A Collection of Essays,* edited by J. den Boeft and A. Hilhorst. Leiden: Brill, 1993.

Wilson, N. G., trans. *The Bibliotheca of Photius: A Selection.* London: Duckworth, 1994.

— M. Eleanor Irwin

Evans, Katherine (ca. 1618–92), and Sarah Cheevers (Chevers) (ca. 1608–ca. 1664)

Katherine Evans and Sarah Cheevers (or Chevers), English Quakers, wrote two collaborative works, *This is a short relation* (1662) and *A True Account* (1663), each of which is autobiographical, being a defense of liberty of conscience. They were part of the first wave of Quakerism, which spread its message abroad through lay preaching and the distribution of group members' printed religiopolitical writings. The women wrote and ministered and are best known for surviving a lengthy spell in a Maltese jail, where they had been detained by the Roman Catholic Inquisition.

Evans converted in the mid-1650s with her husband and children, having from this date preached in the Isle of Man, Ireland, the Isle of Wight, Portsmouth, Warminster, and Salisbury (Villani, "Evans"). In *A True Account,* Evans describes how she was publicly whipped after the locals of Salisbury turned against her (157). Cheevers, also married and with children, and ten years older than Evans (she was about fifty, Evans about forty), shared her

195

friend's commitment, and together they planned an expedition to Alexandria. They set out in 1658, and while docking at Malta had preached and distributed Quaker pamphlets, which led to their detention. The inquisitors on Malta, in discussion with the Roman authorities, kept the women first under house arrest, then in prison until late 1662, and thereafter under house arrest once more, until passage to England could be arranged. The inquisitor primarily sought to convert the women to Catholicism. In 1661 another Quaker, Daniel Baker, visited the women in prison, finding them in poor health though with a manuscript account of their experiences, even despite the friars having taken away their candles, ink, Bibles, and ransacked their room in the search for their papers. Baker, "unknown to the oppressors," as he puts it, and "through not a little difficulty," was able to keep most of the writing secret, meaning that once he was back in England, *A Short Relation* was published (64, 66).

Their collaboratively written texts show what an inquisitorial prison was like. *A Short Relation* (SR) was written with the women despairing of ever being freed, whereas the latter part of *A True Account* ends with descriptions of their release and homeward journey (207 pages merely reprint SR). The writers' intention was to maintain a posture of steadfastness through their plucky defense of the Quaker faith, even when mind and body were tested to the utmost during rigorous examinations and extended periods of solitary confinement. The women probably believed that they would die in Malta, either due to the unsanitary conditions in the prison, or because the inquisitors might indeed make true their threat to impose the death sentence. They were also weak because they fasted for weeks at a time, which they maintained was in obedience to their God's instructions (Gill 234–47). Even so, the Quaker women resolutely explained the central doctrines of their faith, insisting that all believers could open themselves to God and experience an immediate and direct oneness that Quakers referred to as a light within. As Sarah explains, "The Lord did count me Worthy to go and give in my Testimony for his Truth, the Word of his Prophesie, before the great and mighty ones of the Earth" (SR, 38).

They both spoke for their God and listened to him: "I heard a voice saying *ye shall not die*" (SR, 23). Their writing is biblically infused, dense with allusions, and these are seen to be directly relevant to their case; they lacked neither "revelations nor visions" (SR, 22). These visions include predicting an apocalyptic war in heaven and the firmament against the Dragon (i.e., the Catholics), as well as the insight that "*the Pope, he will not hurt thee*" (SR, 11–12, 33, 73, 82). The purpose, then, of using the language of Revelation is to paint God as their protector and avenger. The Bible also provides models of female religiosity: Daniel Baker's seeing Evans and Cheevers awaiting the bridegroom in the passage he labels a "vision of God," and the women's referring to themselves as the wise virgins who kept their lamps burning (Matt. 25:1–13; SR, 49, 70).

The records of the friars and the inquisitor who examined the women often show their opposition to lay preaching and to the ministry of women. For instance, their comments decry the women for their unlearnedness, specifically their noncomprehension of Latin, and the friars maintained that women should know God through an intercessor (*SR*, 13, 15). To the friars, the women's belief that they had felt the "living presence" of the Spirit of God and spoke on his behalf seems to have been unnerving; it led to the assertion that they were possessed, or witches (*SR*, 23). However, the women were also offered immediate freedom if they converted to Catholicism and joined the island's nunnery (Gill).

Within the dialogues ostensibly highlighting the differences between the Catholic and the Quaker faith, a commentary on their respective approaches to the position of women emerges. Evans and Cheevers's attitude was spiritual equality in action, with them bowing only to the authority of God while "opened" to the Spirit and in the prophetic mode. The Inquisition, meanwhile, used an authority that was institutionally hierarchical, which could not incorporate these women's versions of religiosity. Both faiths were condemnatory of the other.

Two other texts written from prison are of a more theological character. Evans's *A brief discovery* (1663) proposes that the believer who abides by God's rule is free from sin; a brief paragraph on the ministry argues that when speaking for God, the prophet is ungendered. This is in specific answer to Paul's objections to women's speaking in 1 Cor. 14:33b–35: "He that is born of God, whether in Male or in Female, Let him speak freely as his Father giveth him Utterance" (35). Cheevers's *To All People* (1663) depicts a loving God who brings universal salvation. The women are remembered for their stubborn adherence to their faith.

Bibliography

Cheevers, S. *To All People*. London: Printed for Robert Wilson, 1663.

Evans, Katherine. *A brief discovery of God's eternal truth*. London: Printed for Robert Wilson, 1663.

———. *A True Account of the Great Tryals*. Edited by S. Villani. Pisa: Scuola Normale Superiore, 2003.

———. *A true account of the great tryals and cruel sufferings*. Edited by Daniel Baker. New ed. of *This is a short relation*. London: Printed for Robert Wilson, 1663.

Evans, Katherine, and S. Cheevers. *This is a short relation of some of the cruel sufferings (for the truths sake) of K. E. and S. Chevers in the Inquisition in the Isle of Malta*. London: Printed for Robert Wilson, 1662.

Gill, C. "'Bad Catholics': Anti-Popery in *This Is a Short Relation* (Katherine Evans and Sarah Cheevers, 1662)." Pages 234–47 in *Expanding the Canon of Early Modern Women's Writing*, edited by P. Salzman. Newcastle, UK: Cambridge Scholars Pub., 2010.

Villani, S. "Katharine Evans." Pages 724–25 in vol. 18 of *Oxford Dictionary of National Biography*, edited by H. C. G. Matthew and Brian Harrison. Rev. ed. Oxford: Oxford University Press, 2004–11.

———. "Sarah Cheevers." Pages 288–89 in vol. 11 of *Oxford Dictionary of National Biography*, edited by H. C. G. Matthew and Brian Harrison. Rev. ed. Oxford: Oxford University Press, 2004–11.

— CATIE GILL

■ Fell, Margaret Askew (1614–1702)

Margaret Askew Fell, often called the Mother of Quakerism, was born in 1614 to Judge John Askew and his wife at Dalton-in-Furness, a small town in the north of England. In 1632 she married Thomas Fell, a barrister who served as a judge and as a member of Parliament for Lancashire. They raised eight children. Because of Margaret's expressed desire to serve the Lord, the Fell household frequently hosted traveling preachers, including George Fox in 1652. During that visit, Margaret and her daughters were convinced of the truth of his preaching and joined the Religious Society of Friends. From that point onward, Fell and her family formed an important center for the emerging Quaker movement, providing meeting space, lodging, and financial and political support from her home at Swarthmoor Hall. She coordinated the correspondence among itinerant preachers and far-flung meetings, preserved documents, and established the Kendal Fund for assisting Quaker missionaries and those in prison.

Although nothing specific is known about Fell's education, she was clearly taught both to read and to write and was encouraged to read Scripture. She must also have been trained to run a large household, since Swarthmoor Hall was on a substantial estate, and Thomas Fell traveled frequently as a judge for the Assizes. At Thomas Fell's death in 1658, their son George inherited the bulk of the estate, but Thomas left Swarthmoor Hall itself to Margaret and her daughters.

Throughout her fifty years as a convinced Friend, Fell conducted an extensive ministry through letters of encouragement and exhortation to Quakers throughout England. She also served as a spokeswoman for the Religious Society of Friends through published pamphlets and through letters to those in authority. In 1660 she composed a letter to King Charles II on his return to England, outlining the sufferings of the Quakers and assuring the king that the movement offered no political threat to his rule. That letter is consigned by Fox and twelve other Quaker men. Two of Fell's pamphlets, *For Manasseth Ben Israel* and *A Loving Salutation to the Seed of Abraham*, both initially published in 1656, were translated into Hebrew as part of the Quaker outreach to the Jews. Scholars now believe that the translator of the second piece was Benedictus de Spinoza, newly excommunicated from the Jewish community.

Because of her social status, Fell was able to intervene on behalf of Quakers imprisoned for their beliefs. She wrote prolifically to persons in power, to the nobility, and three times to King Charles II. In 1660 she traveled to London to intercede personally with the newly restored king on behalf of George Fox. She succeeded in freeing Fox and in securing a proclamation of freedom for the Quakers. Her position and favor with the king did not, however, exempt her from persecution: she was arrested in 1664 for providing meeting space in her home and, because she refused to take the Oath of Obedience, sentenced to praemunire: the forfeiture of her estates to the English Crown and indefinite imprisonment. She remained in prison for four and a half years, during which she wrote her most famous pamphlet, *Women's Speaking Justified, Proved and Allowed of by the Scriptures, All Such as Speak by the Spirit and Power of the Lord Jesus: And How Women Were the First That Preached the Tidings of the Resurrection of Jesus, and Were Sent by Christ's Own Command before He Ascended to the Father (John 20:17).*

Women's Speaking Justified continues the themes of Fell's earlier pamphlets: that God is no respecter of persons; that the Spirit continues to speak in this world through those who are open to its life and power; that the licensed clergy are hirelings, who may know the letter of Scripture but do not understand its spirit. Her argument demonstrates a strong control of Scripture and a healthy sense of her own authority to interpret it. In the pamphlet Fell sets out to demonstrate "how God himself hath manifested his Will and Mind concerning women, and unto women" (115). She employs the Quaker belief in continuing revelation to defend women's inspired speaking against the sermonizing of priests who "take Texts, and Preach Sermons upon Womens words, and still cry out, Women must not speak, Women must be silent" (124). This idea of continuing revelation imposes on Scripture an equality of authority despite historical order. Paul's revelation neither preempts Fell's nor overrides those in the Hebrew Scriptures.

In her reading of Genesis, Fell argues that "God hath put no such difference between the Male and the Female as men would make" (115), citing the first version of the Creation story (Gen. 1:27)—"So God created man in His own image, in the image of God created He him; male and female He created them"—and giving them joint responsibility over the earth. Reading the punishment and prophecy in Gen. 3 allegorically, Fell is able to set aside its apparent instantiation of sexual hierarchy: the enmity between the serpent and the woman represents the enmity between Satan and the Church: "If the Seed of the Woman speak not, the Seed of the Serpent speaks" (116). Fell interprets the Seed of the Woman both as the true Church and as the men and women within it. Any person objecting to "the Spirit of the Lord speaking in a woman, simply, by reason of her Sex" reveals himself to be "the Seed of the Serpent" (116). In this way, sexual hierarchy is itself sin, for men who oppose women's equal authority are trying to "limit the Power and Spirit of the Lord Jesus, whose Spirit is poured upon all flesh, both Sons and Daughters, now in his Resurrection" (121).

Fell praises Jesus's female followers not simply for their superior devotion, but also for their swift and early declarations of faith and for their active discipleship. She devotes a paragraph to the woman with the alabaster box of ointment (Matt. 26:7), who, she argues, "knew more of the secret Power and Wisdom of God, then [sic] his Disciples did" (117), and praises Martha among others for "her true and saving Faith, which few at that day believed so on him." Consistently, Fell weaves a story in which women rather than men recognize Jesus's divinity, and Jesus "manifested his love, his will, and his mind" (121) to women. Fell insists on Jesus's special ministry to women, pointing out instances when he explicitly reveals his messiahship. Of Jesus's acknowledging his divinity to the Samaritan woman at the well (John 4:1–42), Fell writes, "This is more than ever he said in plain words to Man or Woman (that we read of) before he suffered" (117).

Having established women's active discipleship during Jesus's life, Fell points to the centrality of women's ministry to Christianity. Demonstrating their superior devotion through their determination to prepare Jesus's body for burial, women are rewarded by becoming the first to spread the gospel of his resurrection. That Jesus entrusted women with this task, Fell argues, ought to stop the mouths of any critics of women's preaching: "What had become of the Redemption of the whole Body of Man-kind, if they had not believed the Message that the Lord Jesus sent by these women [?]" (118).

Fell sees such equal and active discipleship continuing in the New Testament record: she points out that Priscilla taught Apollos (Acts 18:26) and that Paul entreated the Philippians "to help those Women who laboured with him in the Gospel" (121; Phil. 4:3). In her discussion of the Pauline Epistles, Fell emphasizes the pastoral nature of the advice as Paul responds to particular incidents in the lives of the congregations he addressed. She reads the pronouncement of 1 Cor. 14:34—"Let your women keep silence in the churches, for it is not permitted unto them to speak"—as addressed to general confusion in the church at Corinth. She points out that, in the same epistle, "the Man is commanded to keep silence as well as the woman, when they are in confusion and out of order" (119). She also observes that Paul earlier specifies appropriate behavior for women when they are praying and prophesying (1 Cor. 11) and concludes that 1 Cor. 14:34 addresses women who are under the law, rather than women on whom God has poured out his Spirit. She handles 1 Tim. 2:11–12 in a similar manner, arguing that Paul addresses ignorant novices "such as he is teaching to wear their apparel, what to wear, and what not to wear" (12), rather than making a pronouncement forbidding women's preaching generally, and especially not prohibiting the speech of "such as have the Power and Spirit of the Lord Jesus poured upon them" (120).

Consistent with her belief in continuing revelation, Fell reaches back into the Old Testament to extend her distinction between women under the law and women led by the Spirit. She identifies a rich record of women who prophesied, including Huldah, Miriam, Hannah, the Queen of Sheba, Esther, Judith, and the women who praised Ruth. Whenever possible, Fell points out that men in authority encouraged women's speech. Fell also highlights the quality of each woman's utterance. After each extensive quotation, she challenges her readers: "Now let us see if any of you blind Priests can speak after this manner, and see if it be not a better Sermon than any you can make" (122). She accuses the clergy of "making a Trade of Womens words to get money by" (124) even as they denounce women for speaking. In this context, she addresses both Elizabeth's and Mary's "sermons" during their pregnancies, identifying them as "two women [who] prophesied of Christ" (123) and accusing the clergy of hypocrisy when they use Mary's Magnificat in their "Common Prayer" and yet forbid women to preach.

In 1669, Fell married George Fox, who continued to travel extensively in England, as well as to America and Holland. As a couple they continued to collaborate in shaping Quaker practice. Although Quaker Women's Meetings had begun in London during the late 1650s, Fell was instrumental in defining their role. The Women's Meetings engaged in work associated with traditional women's roles—the care of the sick, the elderly, the poor, the orphaned and imprisoned, and the instruction of younger women—but they also presided over marriage contracts and intervened in marital disputes, giving women specific authority over men in at least one area of their domestic lives. Fell has been criticized for participating in an organizational structure that defined men's and women's separate spheres of influence; she has also been criticized for emphasizing group cooperation over individual prophecy. Everyone agrees, however, that the activities of the Women's Meetings contributed to the stability of the Religious Society of Friends and to its survival.

Because of her central role among the founding members of the Religious Society of Friends, Fell's work has always been available. In 1712 her daughter published her collected writings. Substantial selections from her letters have been preserved in hagiographic treatments of Fell and of her second husband, George Fox. It is only from the 1990s onward, however, that Fell has begun to receive appropriate credit for her intellectual and organizational contributions to the founding of Quakerism.

Bibliography

Donawerth, Jane. "Women's Reading Practices in Seventeenth-Century England." In *Sixteenth Century Journal* 37, no. 4 (2006): 985–1005.

Fell, Margaret. *Undaunted Zeal: The Letters of Margaret Fell*. Edited and introduced by Elsa F. Glines. Richmond, IN: Friends United Press, 2003.

———. *Womens Speaking Justified*. London, 1667. Reprint as pages 115–26 in *First Feminists: British Women Writers 1578–1799*, edited by Moira Ferguson. Bloomington: University of Indiana Press, 1985.

Feroli, Teresa. *Political Speaking Justified: Women Prophets and the English Revolution*. Newark: University of Delaware Press, 2006.

Kunze, Bonnelyn Young. "Margaret Fell (1614–1702)." Pages 256–69 in vol. 19 of *Oxford Dictionary of National Biography*, edited by H. C. G. Matthew and Brian Harrison. Rev. ed. Oxford: Oxford University Press, 2004–11.

———. *Margaret Fell and the Rise of Quakerism*. Stanford, CA: Stanford University Press, 1994.

Luecke, Marilyn Serraino. "'God hath made no difference such as men would': Margaret Fell and the Politics of Women's Speech." In *Bunyan Studies* 7 (1997): 73–95.

Thickstun, Margaret Olofson. "Writing the Spirit: Margaret Fell's Feminist Critique of Pauline Theology." *Journal of the American Academy of Religion* 63, no. 2 (1995): 269–79.

— MARGARET THICKSTUN

Fonte, Moderata (1555–92)

Moderata Fonte was the pseudonym of Modesta Pozzo, a Venetian woman born to a wealthy though not aristocratic family. She not only wrote extensively but also distinguished herself in genres normally associated with male writers, such as the chivalric romance, verse narrative, and philosophical dialogue. This was quite unusual for a respectable wife and mother in Renaissance Venice, where married women were particularly secluded and among whom literary distinction was rare. Orphaned at an early age, she was adopted into the household of her grandparents. Her elementary education took place at the convent of Santa Marta, where her intellectual precocity and charm were quickly recognized. Her more advanced education was informally conducted under the guidance of her grandfather Prosperi Saraceni. At age twenty-one she came to live with her aunt Saracena Saraceni and uncle by marriage, Giovanni Doglioni, who gave her further mentoring in literature and who later wrote her biography. At twenty-seven, Fonte married Filippo Zorzi, a government lawyer three years her junior. He gave her control over her dowry and seems to have encouraged her literary activities. They had four children. Moderata Fonte died in childbirth at age thirty-seven.

In 1581 Fonte published her first work, a chivalric poem, *Tredici canti del Floridoro* (Thirteen Cantos on Floridoro). This was followed by *La feste* (The Celebration), a dramatic dialogue in which two philosophers, a Stoic and an Epicurean, discuss the purpose of human life. It was performed before the Doge of Venice in December 1581. In 1582 she published *La Passione di Christo* (The Passion of Christ), a narrative poem, written in octava rima, the verse form of chivalric romance. Ten years later she published another religious narrative poem, *La Resurrezione di Giesù Christo* (The Resurrection of Jesus Christ), also composed in the chivalric style. Both are written in a vivid, emotionally heightened style influenced by Petrarch and Ariosto. Narrative, meditative, and lyric passages are interspersed. Both poems are distinctive in emphasizing the roles played by female characters in the life of Christ, especially the Virgin Mary and Mary Magdalene.

Fonte is best known today for her discussion of feminist issues in *The Worth of Women: Wherein Is Clearly Revealed Their Nobility and Their Superiority to Men*, published posthumously in 1600. It is written in the form of a dialogue among seven women, each having a distinct personality and point of view. This work belongs to a genre of which the Renaissance produced a substantial number of examples, defending women from misogynistic prejudices and asserting their equality with men in most aspects of human life and their superiority in some, yet Fonte's work is remarkable for being less academically and rhetorically conventional. Indeed, Fonte is skeptical as to the utility of traditional intellectualist arguments for the female cause since men, while acknowledging them in theory, ignore them in practice. Consequently Fonte places a much greater emphasis on concrete examples of the appalling socioeconomic expressions of misogyny drawn from ordinary life; however, Fonte stops short of an explicit call to political action. Fonte's literary style is extensively marked by Renaissance conventions of rhetorical ingenuity, intellectual gamesmanship, and paradox. Consequently the reader is not always certain of the nature, or even the seriousness, of her intentions.

Fonte's interpretation of the Genesis story of Adam and Eve, given through the scholarly interlocutor Corinna, is part of a wider argument intended to show that male political superiority over women is based neither on nature nor on the divine will. In opposition to some traditional interpretations of Genesis, Corinna argues that the temporal priority of Adam's creation indicates not his superiority over Eve, but his inferiority, since the pattern of creation is from entities of lower value to those of higher. This position is not original to Fonte. She may have borrowed it, either directly or indirectly, from Cornelius Agrippa's *On the Nobility and Preeminence of the Female Sex* (ca. 1529).

Fonte not only asserts Eve's superiority to Adam, but also absolves her of blame for the fall. In a deconstruction of Genesis reminiscent of gnosticism, Corinna observes that Eve's tasting of the forbidden fruit was based on a morally acceptable motive, the acquisition of knowledge. However, Adam's eating the fruit was motivated by "greed," after hearing that he should eat it because it tasted good. Corinna supports this interpretation by observing that it was not on Eve's tasting but on Adam's eating of the forbidden fruit that the couple was expelled from Eden. It was therefore Adam's act, not Eve's, that was the first sin. As a balance to the Adam and Eve story, Corinna mentions Mary and recognizes her pivotal role in redemption, a role accorded to no male who, like Mary, was merely human. She observes that there is no man comparable to Mary in moral and spiritual qualities.

Fonte offers a list of women exemplifying a wide range of moral and intellectual virtues, as well as high achievement in literature, warfare, technology, statecraft, and devotion to community and family. Her examples are almost exclusively drawn from Greco-Roman history and mythology. The only biblical heroine she mentions is Judith.

In part 2 of *The Worth of Women*, Fonte returns to questions concerning the creation and the fall. The character Leonora comments that, in the subhuman world, all creatures recognize that women are the equals of men, if not their superiors. She compares examples of cooperation adduced from the nonhuman world to the general malice and enmity that men have for women, indicating that, through their fall, men have deprived women not only of the natural equality that God intended for them but also of the help and cooperation that men are intended to give women. By their fall, therefore, men have displaced women from their God-given place of equality in the created order.

Moderata Fonte's work was forgotten shortly after her death. It has been only from the 1980s onward that scholars have rediscovered her work, examined Fonte herself in her historical context, and recognized her for the bold and ingenious author that she is.

Bibliography

Cox, Virginia. "Moderata Fonte and *The Worth of Women*." Pages 1–10 in Moderata Fonte's *The Worth of Women*, edited and translated by Virginia Cox. Chicago: University of Chicago Press, 1997.

———. "Moderata Fonte (1555–1592)." In *University of Chicago Library: Italian Women Writers*. http://www.lib.uchicago.edu/efts/IWW/BIOS/A0016.html.

———. "The Single Self: Feminist Thought and the Marriage Market in Early Modern Venice." *Renaissance Quarterly* 48 (1995): 513–81.

Doglioni, Giovanni Niccolo. "Life of Moderata Fonte." Pages 31–40 in Moderata Fonte's *The Worth of Women*, edited and translated by Virginia Cox. Chicago: University of Chicago Press, 1997.

Finucci, Valeria. "When the Mirror Lies: Sisterhood Reconsidered in Moderata Fonte's *Thirteen Cantos of Floridoro*." Pages 116–28 in *Sibling Relations and Gender in the Early Modern World*, edited by N. J. Miller and N. Yavneh. Aldershot, UK: Ashgate, 2006.

Fonte, Moderata. *Floridoro: A Chivalric Romance*. Translated by Julia Kisacky. Chicago: University of Chicago Press, 2006.

———. *The Worth of Women: Wherein Is Clearly Revealed Their Nobility and Their Superiority to Men*. Edited and translated by Virginia Cox. Chicago: University of Chicago Press, 1997.

Maprezzi Price, Paola. *Moderata Fonte: Women and Life in Sixteenth-Century Venice*. Madison: Fairleigh Dickinson University Press, 2003.

———. "Venezia Figurata and Women in Sixteenth-Century Venice: Moderata Fonte's Writings." Pages 18–34 in *Italian Women and the City: Essays*, edited by J. L. Smarr and D. Valentini. Madison: Fairleigh Dickinson University Press, 2003.

Smarr, Janet Levarie. *Joining the Conversation: Dialogues by Renaissance Women*. Ann Arbor: University of Michigan Press, 2005.

— BRAD WALTON

Francis, Ann (1738–1800)

British scholar and poet Ann Francis was the author of *A Poetical Translation of the Song of Solomon, from the original Hebrew, with a Preliminary Discourse, and Notes, Historical, Critical, and Explanatory* (London, 1781). Although she lived her entire life in a village parsonage—first as a vicar's daughter in South Stoke, Sussex, and then as a vicar's wife in Edgefield, Norfolk—and therefore did not have the advantages of university training, she was well educated, participated actively in the literary culture of England in her day, and published several volumes of poetry. She was taught at home by her father, the Rev. Daniel Gittins, and acquired a good knowledge of Latin, Greek, and Hebrew. In 1764 she married the Rev. Robert Bransby Francis. The *Poetical Translation* was the first of five volumes of poetry that she published, and her only foray into biblical scholarship. The "List of Subscribers" that prefaces the book includes the names of some of the most eminent Old Testament scholars of the day, including Robert Lowth, Benjamin Kennicott, and John Parkhurst. It is to the latter, the author of a widely used dictionary of biblical Hebrew, that the work is dedicated. He was probably also the "learned friend" whom she thanks for his assistance (v). Besides Parkhurst, she acknowledges her indebtedness to Thomas Harmer and the anonymous author (now known to be Thomas Percy) of the 1764 *Song of Solomon, Newly Translated from the Original Hebrew*.

Although Francis does not reject the traditional interpretation of the Song as an allegory of Christ and the church, she focuses her attention on what she takes to be its literal meaning: a dramatic dialogue depicting the wedding between Solomon and the daughter of Pharaoh. Accordingly, she divides her *Poetical Translation* into seven cantos, corresponding to the seven days of a traditional Jewish wedding, beginning respectively with 1:2; 2:1; 3:1; 4:12; 5:2; 6:4; and 8:1. Following Harmer, Francis introduces a novel feature into the dramatic interpretation of the Song by distinguishing two female voices: those of the "Egyptian Spouse" and the "Jewish Queen." The latter, who is assumed to have been Solomon's previous primary wife, resents her new rival, who is not only a gentile but also is of higher social standing. By thus distinguishing between two female voices, Francis postulates a love triangle at the heart of the work, just as the better-known Shepherd Hypothesis does by distinguishing two male voices. In the final verse, after Solomon has married his Egyptian bride, the Jewish queen announces her intention to keep her distance from him. Throughout the work, in order to make the postulated dramatic action clear, Francis adds detailed stage directions to the Hebrew text.

The scholarly notes to the text deal mainly with ways that contemporary Oriental customs, largely drawn from the accounts of European travelers to the Middle East, are taken to illustrate specific details in the text. She takes these illustrations indiscriminately from travelers' accounts of Turks, Persians, Arabs, and Egyptians, assuming that modes of dress and other cultural practices have remained unchanged throughout "the East" since the days of Solomon (ix). Thus Francis explains the *shōr* (navel) of 7:2 as the kind of clasp that Lady M. W. Montagu describes as part of the dress of "a certain great Turkish lady" during Montagu's visit to Constantinople in 1718.

Francis's work is based on an independent study of the Hebrew text, but her "translation" is a flowery poetic paraphrase. Thus the three Hebrew cola of 1:2 become six English lines, beginning:

> Let him on me the balmy kiss bestow,
> With ruby mouth, whence honey'd accents flow:
> For ah! Those lips are fragrant as the rose,
> When on its head the purple orient glows.
>
> (*Poetic Translation*, 3)

Francis does not entirely ignore the Christian allegorical reading of the Song, but her distinction of two female voices, one gentile and one Jewish, gives it a distinctive twist. Since Solomon in this view is a type of Christ, the Egyptian spouse prefigures the gentile church, and the Jewish queen prefigures the Jewish people who reject Christ (v, 101).

Although Francis's *Poetical Translation* was initially politely received, it has since been largely forgotten. There are two noteworthy exceptions. The celebrated Baptist preacher Spurgeon said of it: "Framed on a fanciful theory. Verses flowing and feeble. Insignificant" (113). The contemporary scholar Dove, a specialist in the history of interpretation of the Song of Songs, writes: "[Francis's] insistence on bringing together learning and feeling, what she knew as male and female worlds, makes her Song of Songs an outstanding feminist moment" (161).

Bibliography

Dove, Mary. "'Merely a Love Poem'? Common Sense, Suspicion, and the Song of Songs." Pages 151–63 in *Feminist Poetics of the Sacred: Creative Suspicions*, edited by Frances Devlin-Glass and Lyn McCredden. Oxford: Oxford University Press, 2001.

Francis, Ann. A *Poetical Translation of the Song of Solomon, from the original Hebrew, with a Preliminary Discourse, and Notes, Historical, Critical, and Explanatory.* London: Printed for J. Dodsley, 1781.

Labbe, Jacqueline M. "Francis [née Gittins], Ann." Pages 733–34 in vol. 20 of *Oxford Dictionary of National Biography*, edited by H. C. G. Matthew and Brian Harrison. Rev. ed. Oxford: Oxford University Press, 2004–11.

Spurgeon, Charles H. *Commenting and Commentaries: Two Lectures Addressed to the Students of the Pastors' College, London Metropolitan Tabernacle, Together with a Catalogue of Biblical Commentaries and Expositions.* London: Passmore & Alabaster, 1876.

— AL WOLTERS

■ Gertrude the Great (Gertrud von Helfta) (ca. 1256–1302)

Gertrude was born in about 1256 and appeared on the doorstep of the Benedictine-Cistercian monastery at Helfta in Saxony only four years later. Since her birthplace and family of origin were unknown to the religious community and even to herself, one can only speculate reasons for her early entrance into the monastery. What is known, however, from the life (*Vita*) of Gertrude, written by her religious sisters, is that Gertrude soon distinguished herself as the brightest student that the Helfta nuns had ever known and that she became a scholar of liberal arts. This eventually led her to be tagged with the descriptor "the Great"—indeed, the only woman in Christian history thus far to be acclaimed in this way.

Gertrude's *Vita* relates that at the age of twenty-five she experienced her first of many visions of Jesus, which transformed her into an eloquent and insightful interpreter of Scripture. The Helfta nuns tell us: "She became a student of theology and tirelessly ruminated on all the books of the Bible which she could obtain. The basket of her heart she packed to the very top with more useful, and honey-sweet, texts of holy Scripture, so that she always had at hand an instructive and holy quotation" (Gertrude, *Herald of God's Loving Kindness*, 39). Gertrude's tireless devotion to teaching and interpreting the Bible apparently included a number of editorial tasks: "If she found anything useful in holy Scripture which seemed hard for the less intelligent to understand, she would alter the Latin and rewrite it in a more straightforward style, so that it would be more useful to those who read it. She spent her whole life in this way, from early morning until night, sometimes in summarizing lengthy passages, sometimes in commenting on difficulties in her desire to promote God's praise and her neighbor's salvation" (57–58).

Gertrude began to put her religious instruction to parchment in 1289 after receiving a command from Christ in a vision and a request from her superiors. She wrote extensively in Middle German and Latin, although only two of her Latin works remain: *The Memorial Herald of the Abundance of Divine Love* (*Legatus memorialis abundantiae divinae pietatis*), consisting of Gertrude's autobiography and visionary accounts, and *Teachings of Spiritual Exercises* (*Documenta spiritualium exercitionum*), containing seven liturgically based meditations. Indeed, both works reveal Gertrude's intimate familiarity with the biblical text; combined, they make nearly a thousand references to Scripture.

Like many other medieval women interpreters, including her religious sister Mechthild of Hackeborn and friend Mechthild of Magdeburg, Gertrude was most inclined to read the Bible in the moral sense. In the Scriptures she saw warnings and models of behavior, invitations to liturgical worship, and sustenance for faith. Particularly reminiscent of Mechthild of Hackeborn, Gertrude approaches the Bible with an eye for immediacy: she looks for texts that she can directly apply to her own and others' experiences of God. Gertrude certainly finds the psalmist's words particularly fruitful for her devotions, and she frequently places them on her own lips. For example, she petitions, "Gird my thigh with the sword of your Spirit (Ps. 45:3) . . . so that in all virtue I may act viriliously and energetically. . . . Look upon and see my battle; you yourself teach my hands to fight (144:1). If armies in camp should stand together against me, my heart will not fear (27:3)" (*Spiritual Exercises*, 87–88). In addition, New Testament maxims on love prominently figure in Gertrude's dialogues with God. Perhaps the most surprising and daring appropriation of them occurs when, expressing her impatient longing for divine union, Gertrude repeats back to Jesus the words he spoke to Judas: "Ah! Now O love, what you do, do quickly (John 13:27)" (95).

Gertrude not only prays but also *feels* scripturally. In contrast to more prosaic, schoolmen's discourse of exegesis, a major element of Gertrude's approach to the biblical text is her quest for imaginative and dynamic interaction with the Incarnate Word. The following autobiographical account from the *Herald* illustrates how Gertrude uses Scripture as a basis for her visionary style:

> On any one day . . . I recited five verses of the psalm "Bless the LORD, O my soul" [Ps. 103]. . . . At the first verse, "Bless the LORD, O my soul," I was granted to lay down upon the wounds of your sacred feet the scouring rust of sin and all attachments to the worthless pleasures of the world. Then, at the second verse, "Bless the Lord, O my soul, and never forget all that he has done for you," I was to wash away all the stains of fleshly and ephemeral pleasure in the fountain of your cleansing love, whence blood and water flowed for me. At the third verse, "Who forgiveth all thy iniquities," like the dove who builds her nest in the cleft of the rocks, I was to find rest for my soul (Song 2:14; Psalm 84:3–4) in the wound of your left hand. Then, at the fourth verse, "Who redeemeth thy life from destruction," approaching your right hand, I was to draw confidently from the treasures which it held all that I lacked for the perfection of every virtue. Thus honorably adorned, through the fifth verse, "Who satisfieth thy desire with good things," I was purged from the infamy of sin. My deficiencies were made good by your sweetest and most longed-for presence. (*Herald of Divine Love*, 101)

Indeed, for Gertrude, the biblical Word has the innate power to enlighten, to heal, to purify, and to renew. Its fecundity is to be felt and experienced in both the material and immaterial worlds. As she sees it, there is a profound interplay between God's self-revelation in the created world and in the Bible. Indeed, Gertrude's bodily senses often delight in both sources of divine revelation at the same time. For example, while reading the Bible beside a fishpond amid the idyllic landscape of Helfta, Gertrude reports the way her senses relish in the "crystalline water flowing through, the fresh green trees standing around, the freedom of the birds" and "the doves, wheeling in flight." She then aligns the experiences of her senses with corresponding biblical images and draws a moral lesson from them.

If I poured back like water the flowing streams of your graces with constant and proper thanksgiving, I would grow in a zeal for virtue like the trees and would blossom with a fresh flowering of good works (Psalm 1:3; Jer. 17:7–8). Moreover, if I looked down on the things of the earth and, in free flight like the doves (Ps. 55:6), sought the things of heaven, . . . my mind would be completely at your disposal and my heart would offer you a dwelling-place with all that is pleasant and joyful. (*Herald of God's Loving Kindness*, 105–6)

By praying and feeling the biblical text, and appropriating it in an extravagantly personal manner, Gertrude undoubtedly demonstrates original and creative dynamics in moral exegesis.

Thus Gertrude, like many other female authors in the Middle Ages, does not simply reproduce the interpretations of church fathers. Yet unlike medieval women interpreters, such as Mechthild of Magdeburg, Gertrude does not make an excuse for writing with an expression of modesty or a humility topos. Instead, she is serene about the implications of her learning, her contact with Christ, and her gender. Gertrude's self-confident reinterpretation of Scripture is especially clear in her claim to female priestly privileges.

To be sure, Gertrude opposes the writings of late thirteenth-century canonists and theologians, who had spoken repeatedly about the Scripture's teaching on the ineligibility of women for clerical roles. Therein, references to Gen. 3:16 and 1 Tim. 2:12 were frequently used to support the argument that woman's "natural" state of subjection prohibits her from preaching and teaching. Allusions to Matt. 16:18–19 also were employed to reinforce banning women from priestly ordination. To provide just one example, Pope Innocent III interpreted the fact that Christ bestowed the keys of the kingdom upon Peter, a *male* disciple, as the divine decision to limit priestly ministry to men.

Gertrude's interpretations of these difficult biblical passages, however, do not restrict women's discipleship. Regarding Eve's role in the fall and 1 Timothy's injunctions against women's teaching and preaching, she is eloquently silent. In addition, Gertrude reports a vision in which Christ has yet to learn of Pope Innocent III's interpretation of Matt. 16:18–19. Christ reassures Gertrude of her suitability for ecclesiastical ministry by speaking the same words to her that he spoke to Peter:

Does not the whole church possess what I promised only to Peter, when I said: "And whatsoever thou shalt bind upon earth, it shall be bound also in heaven"? (Matt. 16:19). The church believes that this same power still resides in all her ministers. Why do you not believe that, prompted by love, I can and will perform whatever I have personally promised to do? . . . Behold, I have given my words in thy mouth. . . . And whatsoever you promise on earth, relying on my goodness, I shall ratify in heaven. (*Herald of Divine Love*, 79–80)

Indeed, by faithfully relating the words of Christ in her ear, Gertrude interpreted the Bible both confidently and countertraditionally. In this way, Gertrude creatively and cleverly developed new dynamics in moral exegesis. Though there is little evidence to prove that Gertrude's work influenced later generations of women interpreters, the way Gertrude built on medieval women's hermeneutic of personal appropriation strikes out on its own in the history of biblical interpretation.

See also Mechthild of Hackeborn (von Hackeborn) (1240–98); Mechthild of Magdeburg (von Magdeburg) (ca. 1208–ca. 1282/94)

Bibliography

Forman, Mary. "Gertrud of Helfta's 'Herald of Divine Love': Revelations through *Lectio Divina.*" *Magistra* 3, no. 2 (Winter 1997): 3–27.

Gertrude the Great. *The Herald of Divine Love.* Translated and edited by Margaret Winkworth. Mahwah, NJ: Paulist Press, 1993.

———. *The Herald of God's Loving Kindness: Books One and Two.* Translated by Alexandra Barratt. Kalamazoo, MI: Cistercian Pubs., 1991.

———. *The Life and Revelations of Saint Gertrude: Virgin and Abbess, of the Order of St. Benedict.* Translated by M. Frances Clare. Westminster, MD: Newman, 1949.

———. *Spiritual Exercises.* Translated by Gertrud Jaron Lewis and Jack Lewis. Kalamazoo, MI: Cistercian Pubs., 1989.

Matter, E. Ann. "Innocent III and the Keys to the Kingdom of Heaven." Pages 145–51 in *Women Priests: A Catholic Commentary on the Vatican Declaration*, edited by Leonard Swidler and Arlene Swidler. New York: Paulist Press, 1977. http://www.womenpriests.org/classic/matter.asp.

———. "The Song of Songs in the *Exercitia spiritualia* of Gertrud the Great of Helfta." *Laurentianum* 31 (1990): 39–49.

McCabe, Maureen. "The Scriptures and Self-Identity: A Study in the Exercises of Saint Gertrude." Pages 497–507 in *Hidden Spring: Cistercian Monastic Women*, edited by John Nichols and Lillian Thomas Shank. Vol. 3 of *Medieval Religious Women.* Kalamazoo, MI: Cistercian Pubs., 1995.

Stephens, Rebecca. "The Word Translated: Incarnation and Carnality in Gertrud the Great." *Magistra* 7, no. 1 (Summer 2001): 67–84.

— ELLA JOHNSON

Gibson, Margaret Dunlop (1843–1920), and Agnes Smith Lewis (1843–1926)

Agnes Smith Lewis and Margaret Dunlop Gibson were born twin sisters in Irvine, Scotland, in 1843 to John and Margaret Smith. Despite their disadvantages—they were Scottish, Presbyterian, and female at a time when scholarly circles were dominated by English, Anglican men—these two women had a considerable impact on biblical studies and the study of ancient manuscripts.

Neither one ever received an official degree, but by the end of their lives they had earned honorary doctorates from some of the most prestigious universities in the United Kingdom and Europe, as well as a Gold Medal from the Royal Asiatic Society, awarded in 1915. Almost inseparable, these "accomplished sisters," as Joseph Henry Thayer referred to them (633), were "affectionately nicknamed" the "Giblews" (Reif 333), and today their portraits hang in the hall of Westminster College, Cambridge.

When the girls were three months old, Margaret Smith died and they were raised by their father, a solicitor in Irvine who inherited a large fortune from a relative. This money furnished them with an education at a private girls' school and later at a finishing school in Kensington. John Smith, who studied foreign languages as a hobby, inculcated this interest in his daughters (Price 15), as did a local minister of the United Presbyterian Church, William Robertson, who was cultured and multilingual and encouraged the twins to explore theological questions and to travel.

John Smith died when his daughters were twenty-three, and the women inherited his fortune, with the provision that they stay together. This wealth provided them with funds to go on expeditions and to spend time studying languages, writing, and painting. Agnes Lewis published a travel diary in 1870 that was based on her and Margaret's tour of Europe, parts of North Africa, and the Middle East (Cornick 3), as well as lengthy novels. Eventually both women were to publish more accounts of their adventures and various studies of ancient manuscripts (esp. Agnes Lewis), focusing particularly on Syriac and Arabic versions of both canonical and noncanonical documents.

In 1880 Margaret Smith wed James Gibson, a retired United Presbyterian minister, who sadly died only four years later. In 1888, Agnes Smith married an Anglican cleric and librarian at Corpus Christi named Samuel Lewis, who also died abruptly, in 1890. Although the sisters had developed reputations as skilled linguists and travelers before Agnes Smith's marriage to Lewis, the relationship gave the two women even greater intimacy with scholarly circles in Cambridge, where they had moved. This included the biblical scholar Rendel Harris, who had discovered a Syriac version of Aristides's *Apology* at St. Catherine's monastery in 1889. The twins had been intrigued by descriptions of the Egyptian desert that James Gibson had narrated, as well as by St. Catherine's and its reputation for housing ancient manuscripts. Encouraged by Harris, and seeking to recover from the sorrow of Samuel Lewis's death, they decided to visit the Sinai with the aim of photographing some of the manuscripts. They set forth in 1892 to make what was to be one of their most important discoveries.

Since Tischendorf's "borrowing" (Cornick 11) of the Codex Sinaiticus, a fourth century Greek manuscript that originally contained the entire Bible, from the monastery in 1844, the monks at St. Catherine's had become wary of Westerners who tried to infiltrate their precincts. Lewis and Gibson were well prepared, however, not only with letters of introduction but also with facility in modern Greek and Arabic (apparently the monks were impressed that the two women would speak Greek to each other), and much more than a superficial knowledge of the Greek Orthodox Church, Greek culture, and customs (the librarian at the monastery, Father Galaktéon, was delighted to read about his own birthplace in the Greek edition of Lewis's book *Glimpses of Greek Life and Scenery* [1884]; see *Shadow*, vi).

While at St. Catherine's, Lewis boldly requested to see the oldest Syriac manuscripts. The librarian obliged, and Lewis noticed that a particularly dirty specimen was actually a palimpsest: it contained one text written on top of an older one. In this case, stories of Christian women saints were written on top of what Lewis recognized to be a Syriac version of the Gospels. This proved to be the famous palimpsest that came to be known as the "Lewis Syriac Gospels," a complete copy of the Cureton Codex, which can be dated to the late fourth century. Using a steam kettle, the twins carefully pried apart the leaves that were stuck together, and later they photographed and transcribed the pages.

Lewis's major work on the palimpsest was published in 1913, in which she demonstrated her thoughts about scribal practices and the formation of the Gospels. She obviously promoted textual criticism for the establishment of the biblical text, and she acknowledged that the theory of verbal inspiration was no longer applicable, despite her commitment to the Bible as a source of divine revelation (Cressy 35). In her analysis of the textual variants posed by the palimpsest, she often incorporated her observations about the cultures and customs she had observed in her travels (see O'Neill 54); she argued that the Syriac translators sometimes imported their own information that had not been available to other scribes. Thus in John 4:27 she advanced the notion that the Syriac addition of Jesus as *standing* while speaking to the Samaritan woman was entirely appropriate because it was "quite in keeping with our Lord's character. . . . Standing is not the usual habit of the Jewish Rabbi when he is engaged in teaching, so it is all the more remarkable that our Lord should have shown so much courtesy to our sex in the person of one of its most degraded representatives" (*Light*, 148).

Another significant contribution was the discovery of a Hebrew fragment of Sirach, which until then had not been found, and which the sisters brought back from a Cairo synagogue along with many other texts. These manuscripts came to form the Lewis-Gibson Collection of Genizah fragments, now housed at Westminster College, Cambridge (Reif 341). The piece from Sirach was published by the twins' friend and great scholar Solomon Schechter. Although Lewis and Gibson viewed Ben Sira as a woman-hater, they recognized the tremendous value of the fragment. Lewis observed with some amusement: "It seems therefore a just judgment upon him [Ben Sira] that the Hebrew text of his book . . . should have practically disappeared for fifteen centuries, and should have been brought under the eyes of a European scholar [Schechter], I might say a scholar of his own nation, by two women" (*Shadow*, 180).

Often perceived as a pair of eccentrics, and denied formal studies or teaching posts at the university, Lewis and Gibson nonetheless created a legacy through their discoveries, their accounts of their travels, and their careful transcription, editing, and commentary on ancient texts. Despite remaining fiercely Presbyterian, these two women also demonstrated an openness to and respect for a variety of cultures and religions different from their own. Finally, they never wasted a moment. As one person wrote after having known the twins, "Since then we have learned to value time, and the way we use it, differently" (Klipstein 115).

Bibliography

Cornick, David. "Cambridge and Sinai." Pages 3–24 in *From Cambridge to Sinai: The Worlds of Agnes Smith Lewis and Margaret Dunlop Gibson*, edited by David Cornick and Clyde Binfield. Translated by John Proctor. London: United Reformed Church, 2006.

Cressy, Martin. "What Did the Giblews Believe?" Pages 25–37 in *From Cambridge to Sinai: The Worlds of Agnes Smith Lewis and Margaret Dunlop Gibson*, edited by David Cornick and Clyde Binfield. Translated by John Proctor. London: United Reformed Church, 2006.

Gibson, Margaret Dunlop. *How the Codex Was Found: A Narrative of Two Visits to Sinai from Mrs. Lewis's Journals, 1892–1893*. Cambridge: Macmillan & Bowes, 1893.

Klipstein, Editha. "The Learned Twin Sisters from Scotland." Pages 109–15 in *From Cambridge to Sinai: The Worlds of Agnes Smith Lewis and Margaret Dunlop Gibson*, edited by David Cornick and Clyde Binfield. Translated by John Proctor. London: United Reformed Church, 2006. First published as "Die gelehrten Zwillingsschwestern aus Schottland." *Schweizer Frauenblatt*, April 1934.

Lewis, Agnes Smith. *Glimpses of Greek Life and Scenery*. London: Hulst and Blackett, 1884.

———. *In the Shadow of Sinai: A Story of Travel and Research from 1895 to 1897 [1898]*. Cambridge: Macmillan & Bowes, 1898.

———. *Light on the Four Gospels from the Sinai Palimpsest*. London: William & Norgate, 1913.

O'Neill, J. C. "Agnes Smith Lewis as a Textual Critic." Pages 39–63 in *From Cambridge to Sinai: The Worlds of Agnes Smith Lewis and Margaret Dunlop Gibson*, edited by David Cornick and Clyde Binfield. Translated by John Proctor. London: United Reformed Church, 2006.

Price, A. Whigham. *The Ladies of Castlebrae*. London: Headline, 1985.

Reif, Stefan. "Giblews, Jews and Genizah Views." *Journal of Jewish Studies* 55 (2004): 332–46.

Soskice, Janet Martin. *The Sisters of Sinai: How Two Lady Adventurers Discovered the Hidden Gospels*. New York: Alfred A. Knopf, 2009.

Thayer, Joseph Henry. Review of *How the Codex Was Found: A Narrative of Two Visits to Sinai etc.*, by Margaret Dunlop Gibson. *Andover Review* 19 (1893): 632–33.

— ALICIA BATTEN

213

■ Goff, Beatrice Laura (1903–98)

Beatrice Goff was a multidisciplinary researcher in the Bible and the ancient Near East. She was born on December 14, 1903, in Andover, Massachusetts, and completed a master's of arts in biblical and religious studies at Wellesley College in 1928. She enrolled in doctoral studies at Boston University and completed her doctoral thesis in 1933, which was titled "The J-Document in the Hexateuch."

Despite her qualifications, Goff encountered some difficulty in obtaining a full-time teaching position at a major university. Instead, she worked as an assistant to various male counterparts. Even with this hurdle, both the quality and quantity of her scholarly work represent a significant achievement. In her publications, Goff did not engage with women's issues or focus on the interpretation of biblical texts concerning ancient women. Rather, Goff researched and published in the same areas as her male counterparts: in the fields of biblical studies, Assyriology, and Egyptology.

While working as an assistant to Professor Ropes at Harvard's Radcliffe College, Goff published part of her dissertation ("Lost Jahwistic Account"), and after leaving Radcliffe, she published on Israelite "Syncretism." She argued that syncretism was a more common phenomenon in ancient Israel than scholars of her time had thought, a position that is now a consensus in the field of Israelite religion.

Goff's work shifted to ancient Near Eastern studies when in 1936 she accepted a research position at Yale University under Professor Erwin Goodenough, who was known for his work on Jewish symbolism. Goff may have seen more opportunities for women in the field of Near Eastern studies. She had a good example at Yale in Assyriologist Ettalene Mears Grice, who in 1917 was the first woman at Yale to receive a degree in Semitics and was made head of the famous Yale Babylonian collection in 1925, when A. T. Clay died (Foster).

Unable to find a permanent position, Goff left Yale and studied library sciences. After teaching as an adjunct professor of religion at Randolph Macon Women's College in Virginia, she was appointed assistant professor at Mount Holyoke Women's College in Massachusetts. She broke her contract, citing lack of opportunities for women to carry out biblical scholarship there (Cohen). In 1946 she became the executive director of the YWCA in Springfield, Indiana. Perhaps knowing the difficulties of attaining a permanent position, she returned to Yale as Goodenough's assistant and engaged in serious work for twenty years, despite the lack of opportunities for female professorships. From 1956 to 1979 she published both major works and articles in this context.

At Yale, Goff undertook advanced training in Akkadian, Sumerian, and Egyptian, supplemented by research trips to Iraq in 1958 (to see the excavations at Nippur, Warka, and the Diyala region), followed by a research trip to Egypt in 1965–66. At this time her reviews demonstrate competence to critique current work in the field (Review of *Bauwerke*; "Observations"). The Yale years were foundational for her two major works; the first was a 276-page volume titled *Symbols of Prehistoric Mesopotamia* (1963), followed by *Symbols of Ancient Egypt in the Late Period* (1979). These works approached symbols "horizontally," in a given frame of time, rather than "vertically," over a larger span of time. Motivated to understand the relationship between symbols and literature, Goff tested three levels of symbolism across the ancient Near East: (1) symbols understood without words; (2) symbols requiring some explanations that occur in a variety of art forms; and (3) symbols that need extended elaboration in myth. Goff's first work, on Mesopotamian symbols that occurred before most writing forms, drew criticism since her interpretations of symbols could not always be tested (McGuire). Goff responded by exploring Late Egyptian sources in which her symbolic interpretations could be supported with textual evidence ("'Significance' of Symbols"; *Symbols of Ancient Egypt*). Although some of her assumptions about Egyptology were questioned, her analysis of Egyptian symbols was better received, filled a need in that field, and demonstrated the successes of her method (Niwinski).

Failing eyesight in her later years made more work difficult, yet Goff earned her place in scholarship by collaborating with her male colleagues (Goff and Buchanan) and equaling them in skill and contributions to the field. In 1981, at the age of seventy-eight, Goff married a widower, Mr. Dowell, and retired to the Boston area. On March 26, 1998, she died in Suffolk, Massachusetts, at the age of ninety-five.

Bibliography

Cohen, S. "Beatrice Laura Goff, 1903–." In *Breaking Ground: Women in Old World Archaeology*, edited by Martha Sharp Joukowsky and Barbra S. Lesko. Providence: Brown University Institute of Archaeology and the Ancient World, 2004–. Website continuously updated, http://www.brown.edu/Research/Breaking_Ground/.

Foster, Benjamin. "The Beginnings of Assyriology in the United States." Pages 44–73 in *Orientalism, Assyriology and the Hebrew Bible*, edited by Steven Holloway. Hebrew Bible Monographs 10. Sheffield: Sheffield Phoenix, 2007.

Goff, Beatrice L. "Books Suitable for Use in Undergraduate Courses in the Old Testament." *Journal of Bible and Religion* 6, no. 3 (1938): 140–43.

———. "The Lost Jahwistic Account of the Conquest of Canaan." *Journal of Biblical Literature* 53, no. 3 (1934): 241–49.

———. "Observations on Barnett's *A Catalogue of Nimrud Ivories*." *Journal of the American Oriental Society* 80, no. 4 (1960): 340–47.

———. Review of *Bauwerke in der altsumerischen Bildkunst*, by Ernst Heinrich. *Journal of Near Eastern Studies* 18, no. 3 (1959): 230–32.

———. "The 'Significance' of Symbols: A Hypothesis of Symbols Tested with Relation to Egyptian Symbols." Pages 476–505 in *Religions in Antiquity: Essays in Memory of Erwin Ramsdell Goodenough*, edited by Jacob Neusner. Leiden: Brill, 1968.

———. *Symbols of Ancient Egypt in the Late Period: The Twenty-First Dynasty.* New York: Mouton, 1979.

———. *Symbols of Prehistoric Mesopotamia*. New Haven: Yale University Press, 1963.

———. "Syncretism in the Religion of Israel." *Journal of Biblical Literature* 58, no. 2 (1939): 151–61.

Goff, Beatrice L., and Briggs Buchanan. "A Tablet of the Uruk Period in the Goucher College Collection." *Journal of Near Eastern Studies* 15, no. 4 (1956): 231–35.

McGuire, Gibson. Review of *Symbols of Prehistoric Mesopotamia*, by Beatrice L. Goff. *Journal of Near Eastern Studies* 31, no. 4 (1972): 382–84.

Niwinski, A. Review of *Symbols of Ancient Egypt in the Late Period*, by Beatrice L. Goff. *Orientalistische Literaturzeitung* 78 (1983): 325–32.

— SHAWN FLYNN

Gott, Dorothy Newberry (1747/48–1812)

Dorothy Newberry was born in Monks Kirby, Warwickshire. She was an ex-Quaker prophetess who self-published three millenarian pamphlets, all of which contain protofeminist interpretations of the Bible. Her relationship with the Society of Friends was formative in her theological development. She was introduced to Quaker principles by her mother (Mary) and brought up to believe that Quakers were God's chosen people. Despite disownment in 1773 for marrying outside the Society of Friends, she continued to privilege Quaker language and theology (esp. the practice of silent communion with God and the importance of Light) for the rest of her life. Indeed, all her publications may be read as attempts to justify herself to her human rejecters as one chosen and beloved by God.

Gott, an ex-servant who taught herself to write, entered the prophetic phase of her life when, after the death of her husband, Abraham Gott (ca. 1732–85), she began to see visions and hear God's voice. Her pamphlets are warnings to prepare for Christ's second coming and judgment: *The midnight cry* (1788) is directed to "Friends and Neighbours"; the conclusion of *Christ the standard* (1798?) addresses "the King, Bishops, Judges, Lords, and Commons of Great Britain, Jews, Dissenters, the World, True Believers, and Women"; and *The Noon-day sun* (1811) is directed to "The Reader." Gott's eschatology shares similarities with the interpretations of seventeenth-century Friends in that she understands the second coming initially as the enfolding of Christ's transforming Light within (Dandelion, Gwyn, and Peat), to be followed by the physical materialization of the heavenly Savior on earth at a later, unspecified date. There is no record of oral preaching by Gott.

Gott's autobiographical narratives suggest that her reflections on the Scriptures were related to her personal circumstances. In the face of her expulsion from the Quakers, she derives comfort from Christ's compassion for marginal women—specifically, the Samaritan woman (John 4:7–29) and the hemorrhaging woman (Matt. 9:20–22; Mark 5:25–34; Luke 8:43–48). In response to the brokenness of rejection, she writes about desiring to sit at Christ's feet in silence, like Mary of Bethany (Luke 10:38–42; *Midnight cry*, 9). In *The*

Noon-day sun, she returns to the story of Martha and Mary (Luke 10:38–42) to assert that "they were typical of the law and gospel," adding that Sarah and Hagar (Gen. 16) were also representatives of "the spirit and the letter" (16). To account for the period of Christ's death, she extends this idea of the disparity between pre-Christian legalism and post-Christian grace, claiming that he should have remained dead for six days to reflect the creation of the world, but "the shortness of the three days, [was] to show how much shorter the work of redemption could be performed, under the gospel dispensation, than under the law" (17).

Her protofeminism seems to have been a reaction to the cruelty suffered under her husband; she described Abraham as being an "Egyptian master," meaning that he was comparable to the oppressive Egyptian slave masters in the book of Exodus (*Midnight cry*, 5). From her belief that women have been maligned, she claims that Eve cannot be blamed for the fall (Gen. 3) because the paradise that Adam had been instructed to tend was "the woman's understanding; the garden part of the man; because she is the only part man can multiply by, to bring forth the Son of righteousness"; also, the "knowledge with which Adam was to have dressed Eve's mind was the knowledge of Christ" (*Christ the standard*, 36). This unusual allegorical reading of the garden in the story of the fall allows for an interpretation that, if Eve's mind had been cultivated, she would have been able to withstand the devil. Gott describes her reclamation of Eve as a search for the mother's dead body. When her body is eventually unearthed, "much putrified . . . in the grave of obscurity," Gott explains that Eve's resurrection is obtainable through a recovery of the knowledge of Christ, the "silver" that was lost in the fall (42).

Gott also reinterprets 1 Cor. 14:34–35. She asserts that when Paul forbids women from speaking in church and advises them to ask and learn from their husbands at home, he does not mean that they should apply to their earthly husbands, but to Christ—their true, heavenly husband. She explains that Christ "could not recommend the woman to [the human] man, that remains in the fall" (*Christ the standard*, 56). Gott may have extrapolated this idea from the early Quaker leader Margaret Fell's *Womens Speaking Justified*; in comments on the passage, Fell asserts that Christ "is the Husband, and his Wife is the Church" (4). Gott's implication is that only Christ, not fallen men, has authority over women; therefore the sexes are equal on earth. She repeats this idea in *The Noon-day sun*, a work that also drew from the "two seeds" motif of Gen. 3:15 to assert that women have a special role in the redemption of humanity through Mary's motherhood of Christ.

Gott may have been a rival of the more famous contemporary prophetess Joanna Southcott; Balleine explains that the two women's teachings were so similar that some people followed both prophets (51). At the first Swedenborgian conference held in London in April 1789, Gott met William Blake and may have influenced his understandings of female prophets and prophecy. She

217

is mentioned twice in David Rivers's *Literary Memoirs* (1798). With reference to another millennial writer, Richard Clarke, Rivers comments that his "writings may in truth be justly ranked with those of Jacob Behmen, Baron Swedenborg, and Dorothy Gott" (99), suggesting that he believed her writings to be important. However, Gott remained a minor prophet throughout her life, and her writings were never as widely read as those of the more charismatic contemporary prophets Joanna Southcott or Richard Brothers.

See also Fell, Margaret Askew (1614–1702); Southcott, Joanna (1750–1814)

Bibliography

Balleine, G. R. *Past Finding Out: The Tragic Story of Joanna Southcott and Her Successors.* London: SPCK, 1956.

Cho, Nancy Jiwon, and David Worrall. "William Blake's Meeting with Dorothy Gott: The Female Origins of Blake's Prophetic Mode." *Romanticism* 6 (April 2010): 60–71. http://www.euppublishing.com/doi/pdfplus/10.3366/E1354991X10000875.

Dandelion, Ben Pink, Douglas Gwyn, and Timothy Peat. *Heaven on Earth: Quakers and the Second Coming.* Kelso: Curlew Productions and Woodbrooke College, 1998.

Fell, Margaret. *Womens speaking justified, proved and allowed of by the Scriptures, all such as speak by the spirit and power of the Lord Jesus.* London, 1667.

Gott, Dorothy. *Christ the standard of truth set up, by the light of the morning star, the spirit of truth; and Satan, the son of perdition, revealed, by the same light. . . .* London: The author, [1796/98?].

———. *The midnight cry, "Behold, the bridegroom comes!" or, An order from God to get your lamps lighted. . . .* London: The author, 1788.

———. *The Noon-day sun; A revelation from Christ, to dispel the night of apostacy, to make an end to sin, to bring an everlasting righteousness, to seal up the visions and prophecies in oblivion, to anoint the most holy King. . . .* London: The author, 1811.

Rivers, David. *Literary Memoirs of Living Authors of Great Britain, Arranged According to an Alphabetical Catalogue . . . and Including a List of their Works. . . .* 2 vols. London: R. Falder, 1798.

—Nancy Jiwon Cho

■ Grimké, Sarah (1792–1873), and Angelina Grimké Weld (1805–79)

Sarah Moore and her younger sister Angelina Emily are well known for their pioneering work for abolition and women's rights. Sarah, the second daughter and sixth of fourteen children, and Angelina, the youngest, were born to John and Mary Grimké, respected and affluent members of Charleston society. The Grimké sisters received infant baptism in the Protestant Episcopal Church. Though thirteen years separated them, both experienced evangelical conversions in adolescence, facilitated by Presbyterian clergy. A growing maturity of faith, alongside disillusionment as a result of largely lukewarm responses to the sins of slavery, led both to engage the Society of Friends.

The emerging American Anti-Slavery Society (AASS) enlisted the Grimkés' participation. The Grimkés attended the New York gathering in 1836. The AASS, founded in December 1833, sponsored the Anti-Slavery Convention of American Women, which held three annual sessions from 1837 to 1839; the Grimkés attended each. Already beginning to write and speak publicly, the Grimkés significantly shaped the movement from the mid-1830s, remaining active until 1839.

During their brief careers as agents for the AASS, the Grimkés wrote copiously for the movement. Angelina Grimké wrote *Appeal to Christian Women of the South* (1836), the response to which was emphatic—from both supporters and detractors. Angelina was invited to attend the AASS Agents' Convention. Sarah later wrote *Letters on the Equality of the Sexes* (1838), the first American-authored, fully developed women's rights argument, ten years before the first women's rights convention in Seneca Falls, New York. Sarah's essay first appeared as a series of published pieces in the *New England Spectator* and the *Liberator* in 1837 and 1838, as a response to controversy ignited by a pastoral letter that the Congregational clergy circulated.

Angelina Grimké spends almost half of her *Appeal* in offering a biblical argument against slavery, drawn from both the Old and New Testaments. Giving considerable attention to Genesis, Exodus, Leviticus, and Deuteronomy to discern faithful practices of acquiring, protecting, and even releasing (e.g., Jubilee themes) servants, Angelina offers biblical contrasts to Southern slavery. Looking to Jesus's example in the Gospels as well as the witness of women throughout the Bible—such as Miriam, Deborah, Jael, Huldah, Esther, Elizabeth, Mary, Anna, and Mary Magdalene—Angelina presents obedience to God as "the doctrine of the Bible" and contrasts that with obedience to "man." "You must take it up on *Christian* ground, and fight against it with Christian weapons, whilst your feet are shod with the preparation of the gospel of peace" ("Appeal," 26; cf. Eph. 6:15). Upon this biblical foundation, Angelina appeals to women from their sense of Christian duty.

Sarah and Angelina's focus on the sin of slavery led them to uncover the related sin of woman's disenfranchisement. In her *Letters*, Sarah outlines a Christian theology and practice for women that includes (1) woman's reading and interpreting Scripture (preferably in its original languages); (2) an acknowledgment of woman's equality with man, thereby claiming her evangelistic ministry; (3) an acknowledgment of the oppression of woman, particularly white affluent women, that has resulted in her "vacuity of mind," necessitating her intellectual cultivation; (4) the notion that through (white affluent) woman's salvation and holiness, she may confess to her complicity in the sins of racism; and (5) her ministry to the spiritual and material welfare of others, especially slaves. Sarah emphasizes the need for women to read Scripture in the original languages for the purpose of interpreting the biblical texts for themselves, rather than relying on male clergy and other ecclesiastical leaders. Sarah's argument encourages women to read and interpret Scripture through the lens of Enlightenment ideology, specifically individualism, in response to a selective application of Scripture to the rights and social constructs attributed to women and people of African descent.

In her strategy to empower women, Sarah draws heavily from the creation and fall narratives in Genesis, offering alternative readings, yet surveying examples from throughout the Bible that emphasize woman's equality with man, beginning with Eve's infraction and Adam's subsequent sharing in the same sin. Woman's equality with man in the fall holds woman responsible with man for sins in the world. "The Lord Jesus defines the duties of his followers in his Sermon on the Mount. He lays down grand principles by which they should be governed, without any reference to sex or condition" (*Letters*, 38). For Sarah, women's empowerment requires their acknowledgment of complicity in the sins of racism on equal ground with men. Sarah also addresses woman's equal role in Christian community and marriage in response to 1 Cor. 7, 14; Eph. 5; and 1 Tim. 2.

The Grimkés are well known as the only Southern white women to become leading abolitionists. They also were advocates for women's rights, and their writings remain pertinent to contemporary feminist conversations. Foundational to their leadership for antislavery and feminist reforms was their commitment to a vital Christian faith. In response to their conversions, the Grimké sisters developed a significant ministry through publication and public speaking, all within the context of the Second Great Awakening. The Grimké sisters' careful and sometimes provocative biblical interpretation emphasizes a powerful message for liberation and social change in response to structures of systemic sin and injustice.

Bibliography

Barnes, Gilbert H., and Dwight L. Dumond, eds. *Letters of Theodore Dwight Weld, Angelina Grimké Weld, and Sarah Grimké, 1822–1844*. New York: D. Appleton-Century, 1934.

Brekus, Catherine. *Strangers and Pilgrims*. Chapel Hill: University of North Carolina Press, 1998.

Fox-Genovese, Elizabeth. *Within the Plantation Household: Black and White Women of the Old South*. Chapel Hill: University of North Carolina Press, 1988.

Grimké, Angelina E. "Appeal to Christian Women of the South." *The Anti-Slavery Examiner* 1, no. 2 (Sept. 1836). http://utc.iath.virginia.edu/abolitn/abesaegat.html. Repr., *Appeal to Christian Women of the South*. New York: American Anti-Slavery Society, 1836.

Grimké, Sarah. *Letters on the Equality of the Sexes, and the Condition of Woman: Addressed to Mary S. Parker*. Boston: I. Knapp, 1838. http://books.google.com/books/about/Letters_on_the_equality_of_the_sexes_and.html?id=6w0LbHT6Ei0C. Reissued in *Letters on the Equality of the Sexes and Other Essays*. Edited by Elizabeth Ann Bartlett. New Haven: Yale University Press, 1988.

Lerner, Gerda. *The Grimké Sisters from South Carolina: Rebels against Slavery*. Boston: Houghton Mifflin, 1967. Repr., Chapel Hill: University of North Carolina Press, 2004.

Warner, Laceye. *Saving Women: Retrieving Evangelistic Theology and Practice*. Waco: Baylor University Press, 2007.

—LACEYE WARNER

Grumbach, Argula von (1492–ca. 1563/68)

Bavarian noblewoman Argula von Grumbach (née von Stauff) was likely born in 1492. She read the Bible from a young age and at ten owned a valuable medieval Koberger Bible, which allowed her to read the Scriptures in her mother tongue. Her time as a teenage lady-in-waiting in Queen Kunigunde's court in Munich provided her with spiritual and intellectual stimulation and contacts with theologians like Johann Staupitz. Encouraged by her parents in her religious and intellectual ambitions, von Grumbach became an emancipated lay theologian whose published letters defended the "truth" she found from reading the Scriptures herself through the lenses offered by the evangelical faith, Luther's theology in particular. Her letters, which quoted Scripture extensively, proclaimed justice and Christian freedom and explored the implications of God's truth and providence in people's lives. She was one of the best-selling lay pamphleteers and rare female authors in Reformation Germany.

Born into the noble family of Bernardin von Stauff and Katherine Thering/Törring, von Grumbach was orphaned in 1509 by the plagues. After her then-guardian uncle Hieronymus was executed in 1516, she married Friedrich von Grumbach, a man who did not share her commitment to the Reformation. Although she raised their five children as Protestants, von Grumbach's zeal in promoting the Protestant faith had provoked animosity and abuse in the home and eventually resulted in Friedrich's loss of position and financial security. Her unhappy marriage ended with Friedrich's death in 1530. Von Grumbach's second marriage, in 1533 to Count von Schlick, a man in favor of the evangelical faith, ended in separation and widowhood in 1535. Von Grumbach likely died in 1554, but there is some evidence of a certain old woman "von Stauff" actively involved in Protestant gatherings and ceremonies until the 1560s.

Most of the information on von Grumbach comes from her published letters during 1523–24. Her first letter, dated September 20, 1523, was written in defense of an eighteen-year-old student accused of "Lutheran heresy." Von Grumbach demands that the faculty of the University of Ingolstadt demonstrate to her from the Scriptures where the boy—or Luther or Melanchthon, for that matter—has erred. Not calling herself a "Lutheran" but a "Christian woman," von Grumbach argues there is nothing heretical in the writings of Luther, whose translation of the Bible into German has proved his orthodoxy. Using close to a hundred biblical quotations, she argues that by attacking Luther, the university is clashing with the apostles and the Gospels.

On that same day von Grumbach sent the letter (*The Account*) to the university. Prince Duke Wilhelm received her "reformation proclamation" letter. Other letters on behalf of the Protestant faith followed. On October 27 or 28 she wrote to the city council and magistrates of Ingolstadt, and on December 1 to the Count Palatine Johann von Simmern and Prince Fredrick the Wise. That same month she sent a letter to her cousin Count Adam von Thering, and on June 29 in the next year, 1524, she sent her final letter to the people and the city council of Regensburg. She ended her writing career later that summer with a long poem in response to a misogynist anti-Argula poem, published anonymously by Johannes of Lanzhut. The poem slandered von Grumbach, calling her a whore and a heretic, making innuendos regarding her sexual attraction toward the student whom she defended and even toward Luther. Although her letter to the university was published fourteen times, von Grumbach never received a public response from the faculty.

Vilified by her opponents, von Grumbach won the admiration of reformers like Luther, who in his letters praised her as "God's daughter," Christ's valiant disciple, and a unique instrument in fighting monsters and Bavarian "pigs." She became a "lobbyist," attending the diets of Nuremberg, Regensburg, and Augsburg—significant assemblies of the Imperial Estates where the Protestants' fate in the German-speaking parts of the Holy Roman Empire was deliberated, visiting Luther in Coburg, and trying to mediate personally between different parties, especially on the debate over the Eucharist. Over the years, von Grumbach corresponded with Luther, who remained a major influence on her as she developed her own approach to biblical interpretation.

Von Grumbach's intimate familiarity with the Scriptures can be seen in her letters. She effortlessly draws from many memorized texts, mostly the Gospels (over thirty references to John and fifty-nine to Matthew, with Matt. 10 being her favorite), Paul's letters to the Corinthians (over twenty times), the Psalms (twenty times), and the prophets Isaiah and Jeremiah (thirty-four and twenty-eight references, respectively). Constantly lifting up the principle *sola scriptura* (Scripture alone), but without offering exegesis per se, von Grumbach uses biblical texts to support her arguments, typically citing verse after verse. For instance, her letter to the University of Ingolstadt begins with five unrelated verses (Ezek. 33:8; Matt. 10:32; 12:31; Luke 9:26; John 6:63) before denouncing the university's unjustified use of violence and defending Luther and Melanchthon (*The Account*, in Matheson 28–29, 75–76). Her letters are often filled with exhortations, as well as didactic and even apocalyptic overtones, as though she were delivering her words orally. She interprets life situations in light of the Scriptures, which provide her with models and appropriate language.

Von Grumbach's profound knowledge of the Bible was the basis of her unflappable self-confidence. She knew of the mandate in 1 Tim. 2:11–12, regarding women learning in silence in the church, but considered more important Isa. 3:4, 12, with its promise of God's calling children and women to lead and rule in particular times. Using Scripture, she set out norms for "right" teachings and teachers in accordance with God's Spirit (e.g., Isa. 54:13; Jer. 31:34 [though she erroneously referred to Jer. 3]; Matt. 16:17; John 6:45; 1 Cor. 12:3). Von Grumbach was not prepared to hide her gift because of her gender, and she did not see herself as a lonely woman on a mission. On the contrary, von Grumbach was prepared for martyrdom. Indeed, her husband "persecute[ed]" her at home, and her opponents contemplated the value of cutting off her fingers or strangling her. As a confident interpreter of Scripture, she signed her letters proudly as "countess, widow, née Baroness von Stauff." She justified her words: "Ah, but what a joy it is when the Spirit of God teaches us and gives us understanding, flitting from one text to the next—God be praised—so that I came to see the true, genuine light shining out." Her lack of standard credentials did not stand in her way: by the "grace of God," she believed that she had the right to "ask questions." She wrote even though "I have no Latin; but you have German, being born and brought up in this tongue. What I have written to you is no woman's chit-chat, but the word of God; and [I write] as a member of the Christian Church, against which the gates of Hell cannot prevail" (*The Account*, in Matheson 86–87, 89–90).

Von Grumbach stands among the most prolific women theologians of the German Reformation and distinguishes herself as a fearless and theologically sophisticated laywoman, involving herself at the center of the theological and political issues of the day. She defended Lutheran theology from Scripture, the source and justification for her authority and confidence.

Bibliography

Bainton, Roland H. "Argula von Grumbach." Pages 97–109 in *Women of the Reformation in Germany and Italy*. Minneapolis: Augsburg Pub. House, 1971. Repr., Lima, OH: Academic Renewal Press, 2001.

Classen, A. "Argula von Grumbach." Pages 487–88 in vol. 1 of *An Encyclopedia of Continental Women Writers*, edited by Katharina M. Wilson. New York: Garland, 1991.

Grumbach, Argula von. *[The Account of a Christian woman of the Bavarian nobility whose open letter, with arguments based on divine Scripture, criticizes the University of Ingolstadt for compelling a young follower of the gospel to contradict the word of God.]* Ingolstadt, 1523. In English in Matheson, *Argula von Grumbach*, 72–91.

Halbach, Silke. *Argula von Grumbach als Verfasserin reformatorischer Flugschriften*. Europäische Hochschulschriften: Series 23, Theologie 468. Frankfurt: Peter Lang, 1992.

Joldersma, H. "Argula von Grumbach (1492– after 1563?)." Pages 89–96 in *German Writers of the Renaissance and Reformation, 1280–1580*, edited by James Hardin and Max Reinhart. Vol. 179 of *Dictionary of Literary Biography*. Detroit: Gale Research, 1997.

Matheson, Peter, ed. and trans. *Argula von Grumbach: A Woman's Voice in the Reformation*. Edinburgh: T&T Clark, 1995.

Stjerna, Kirsi. "Argula von Grumbach, 1492 to 1563/68?—A Bavarian Apologist and a Pamphleteer." Pages 71–85 in *Women and the Reformation*. Malden, MA: Blackwell Pub., 2009.

— KIRSI STJERNA

Guyart, Marie (Marie of the Incarnation) (1599–1672)

In 1599 Marie Guyart was born in Tours, France, to devout parents, Florent Guyart, a master baker, and Jeanne Michelett, who provided their seven children with good educations. She died in Quebec, Nouvelle-France, in 1672. From a young age, Guyart was attracted to a cloistered life, but following her parents' wishes, she married a silk worker named Claude Martin in 1617. His death two years later followed a financial crisis, which left his wife a bankrupt widow and mother of a six-month-old son. The newly independent and administratively gifted Marie took over the business; after eliminating all the family debts, she closed the business and went to live with her sister's family. Again her business acumen was recognized, and in 1925 she was entrusted with her brother-in-law's business. During these years, her sense of call to a religious life continued and was encouraged by her confessor, Dom Raymond de Saint Bernard, a member of the Order of Feuillants, recently split from the Cistercians. She lived a rigorous religious life, which included wearing chains and a hair shirt under her clothes and sleeping on a plank with haircloth next to her flesh. She left her eight-year-old son with her sister and entered the novitiate of the Ursulines of Tours. The story is told of her young son, Claude Martin, screaming from the gates of the convent, "Give me back my mother!" Her son had a very hard time accepting his mother's decision but stayed in contact with her. Through correspondence, she provided him with inspiration and guidance during his own theological struggles, and eventually explained to him that she did not abandon him, but that she offered him to God. To his mother's delight, Claude Martin also followed a religious life, joining the Benedictines of Saint-Muir in 1641.

When Marie Martin became an Ursuline nun, she took the name "Marie of the Incarnation." She became the assistant mistress of novices and a teacher of Christian doctrine; at the same time, she experienced visions and dreams centered on her relationship with God. One of her visions was of the new world, known to her as paradise, which she understood to be a calling to found a convent in Canada. In 1639, after much preparation, she left for New France with several other Ursuline nuns and three nuns who were to found a hospital in Quebec City, which was little more than a village of a few houses at that time. It was there that Marie of the Incarnation founded the convent of the Ursulines, a congregation of nuns who, among other things, taught catechism to the Aboriginals and young girls who attended classes at the convent.

Marie of the Incarnation was a prolific writer, and a number of her writings are extant. These include several collections of letters that reveal her spiritual life and also invaluable information on everyday life, including business, history, and such personal issues as surviving cold, famine, loneliness, and menacing attacks by the Iroquois: "They took, once again, one of our Reverend fathers [F. Bressani, after F. Jogues]. They burned him slowly, we were told, and cut his flesh" (Écrits, 3:212). Her writings include spiritual notes from 1625–38 (Exclamations et élévations), which contain her personal addresses to God (published by her son in La Vie, 1677); an early autobiography (1633) and a later one (1654); theological reflections (École Sainte: Explications des mystères de la foi, 1633–35); a catechism; and Exposition du Cantique des Cantiques (1631–37, published in 1682). In 1647, in collaboration with the father Jérôme Lalement, she wrote the Constitutions et règlements des premières Ursulines de Québec. Her son published her biography by using fragments of her autobiography. A collection of her letters was published in 1681; a more complete collection of her religious writings and letters (Écrits spirituels et historiques, 1929–39) was reedited by Dom Jamet of the Congregation of France. Her writings show that she was mainly influenced by the Holy Scriptures, the writings of Teresa of Avila and Francis of Assisi, the catechism of the Council of Trent, the Jesuits with whom she was working in Canada, and several religious with whom she corresponded.

Marie of the Incarnation's correspondence is often used as a source for historical accounts. She mentions various historical "events" in her letters that are often read as "historical documents" and are considered significant writings regarding the customs in seventeenth-century Nouvelle-France (Brodeur 83). Her correspondence primarily describes her own spiritual journey, thus placing her in a category to be compared with Teresa of Avila (Bossuet 356). Her writing shows a unique and remarkable level of theological comprehension. Her main sources of inspiration were the Psalms, the Canticle of Canticles, and Paul, yet it is John who has the strongest influence on the tone of her writings. Her correspondence is embedded with not only the theological concept of God's love but also the inner mystical experience of God's love. Her belief that "God is love" (1 John 4:8, 16) stands behind all her theology and mystical experiences.

Marie of the Incarnation experienced three progressive trinitarian revelations: in 1625, 1627, and 1631. The first instructed and prepared her for what was awaiting her: her eyes were enlightened (Écrits, 2:233–35). The second was a more elevated sense of grace from God, experienced as a marriage with the incarnated Word, a union that directly affected her will: she felt embraced by God's love; she was living a martyrdom of love. It was not until after this second revelation that she began to express her relationship with God by using sacrificial vocabulary (Adriazola 69). From this point onward, her spirituality was focused on prayer and sacrifice. She believed that all she was, her entire being, even her own blood, was received from God, and that without blood, without the effusion of blood, there could be no remission of sin (Heb. 9:18–22). It was not until the third revelation, however, that she experienced an epiphany fundamental to the development of her inner being; she was then mystically transformed to a point where she could so profoundly feel the Trinity that she could almost touch it. What she experienced in her own life was a reflection of what was happening in eternity (Adriazola 230). After this, for Marie of the Incarnation living meant living for God (Phil. 1:21). For Marie of the Incarnation, the fact that "God is love" requires an understanding of the love shown through the sacrificial death of Christ on the cross and his love for humanity (Adriazola 73). God is love since God allowed his son to die because of love.

Christ's self-sacrifice for the reparation of sin was understood in a very specific way in the seventeenth century. The spiritual trend of the "École française" believed that it was central to religious belief to know and to assimilate the mystery of redemption by acknowledging the death of Christ—a death that was an act of salvation used to wipe out the sins of the world (Adriazola 246). After this mystical experience, Marie of the Incarnation's existence became an oblation: she must sacrifice her life so that a new nation could receive divine life through the knowledge and the assimilation of the mystery of redemption. She also understood her separation from her son as a sacrifice for a greater good, in the hopes that he would embrace religious life—which he did. In her everyday sacrifices and penances, she imitated Christ.

This conception of the reversibility of suffering, which insisted that Christians bear witness to God's love through their persecutions and sufferings (Matt. 5:11; Luke 6:22–23; 1 Pet. 4:14), was popular in seventeenth-century literature. The martyr is the one who defends justice by imitating the life of Jesus Christ, who was persecuted, to allow the coming of a new order of justice.

The quest to be persecuted, inseparable from the themes of the love of suffering and the need for mortification, is common in spiritual writings by martyrs who confess their most intimate desires of dying for their love of Jesus Christ. The writings of Marie of the Incarnation express these desires to unite the aspiration to death and the fervor of love: "And since this union, I suffered from a violent desire of dying that consumed me, that made me languish" (*Correspondance*, 6: "Et depuis cest union, j'ai pâti un désir viollant de mourir qui me consommoit, qui me faissoit languir"). As many of her contemporaries, Marie of the Incarnation was perfectly aware of the destiny of the Canadian martyrs whose faith she read in the *Relations*. Many, including her son, who was then a Benedictine monk, were inspired by their glorious actions and dreamed of imitating them. In 1641, she rejoiced when she read that her son wished to become a martyr (*Correspondance*, 133: "si l'on me venoit dire : 'vostre fils est martir' je panse que je mourrois de plaisir"). "To imitate Christ in his suffering is truly the greatest wish," she explained to her son; "Christ is the ultimate model and to be able to imitate him in his suffering brings intensive joy." She insisted on how she herself lived this desire of imitation of Christ: it was a desire that became the motivation to live a life of penance, of mortification, of steadiness (397: "Ce désir vous doit être un puissant aiguillon pour mener une vie pénitente, mortifiée, régulière").

After Marie of the Incarnation died in Nouvelle-France, her son published her autobiographies (which were both written after pressing requests from her son) despite her explicit instructions not to do so (Brodeur 83). Without Dom Claude's disobedience, not much would be known of Marie de l'Incarnation. She funded one of the oldest teaching institutes on the North American continent. At her death in 1672 she was venerated as a saint, and in 1980 she was beatified.

See also Teresa of Avila (1515–82)

Bibliography

Adriazola, María-Paul del Rosario. *La connaissance spirituelle chez Marie de l'Incarnation.* Sainte-Foy, QC: Anne Sigier; Paris: Cerf, 1989.

Bossuet, Jacques-Bénigne. *Instruction sur les états d'oraison.* Bk. 9 in vol. 27 of *Œuvres de Bossuet.* Versailles: J. A. Lebel, 1817.

Brodeur, Raymond. *Marie de l'Incarnation: Entre mère et fils; Le dialogue des vocations.* Sainte-Foy, QC: Presses de l'Université Laval, 2000.

Lalemant, Jérôme, s.j. *Constitutions and Regulations of the first Ursulines of Québec [Constitutions et règlements des premières Ursulines de Québec].* Paris: Veuve Louis Billaine, 1682 [orig. 1647].

Mahoney, Irene, ed. *Marie of the Incarnation: Selected Writings.* New York: Paulist Press, 1989.

Marie de l'Incarnation. *Catéchisme de la vénérable Mère Marie de L'Incarnation, fondatrice des Ursulines de Québec ou Explication familière de la doctrine chrétienne.* 3rd ed. Paris: Casterman, 1878.

———. *Correspondance.* New ed. Solesmes: Abbaye St.-Pierre, 1971.

———. *Dieu mon Amour: Extraits de la Relation de 1633.* Montreal: Bellarmin, 1972.

———. *L'École sainte ou Explication familière des Mystères de la Foy, pour toutes sortes de personnes qui sont obligées d'enseigner la doctrine chrétienne, par la Vénérable Mère Marie de l'Incarnation, religieuse ursuline.* Paris: Abbé Coignard, 1984.

———. *Écrits spirituels et historiques.* 4 vols. Paris: Desclée de Brouwer, 1929–39.

———. *Lettres de la Vénérable Mère Marie de l'Incarnation, Première Supérieure des Ursulines de la Nouvelle France, divisée en deux parties (1644).* Paris: Veuve Louis Billaine, 1681.

———. *Marie de l'Incarnation, Autobiographie, Extraits de la Relations de 1654.* Paris: Solesmes, 1976.

———. *Retraites de la Vénérable Mère Marie de l'Incarnation, Religieuse Ursuline, avec une exposition succincte du Cantique des Cantiques.* Paris: Veuve Louis Billaine, 1682.

———. *La Vie de la Vénérable Mère Marie de l'Incarnation, Première Supérieure des Ursulines de la Nouvelle-France, tirée de ses lettres et de ses écrits.* Paris: Veuve Louis Billaine, 1677.

— STÉPHANIE BÉLANGER

Guyon, Jeanne-Marie de Chesnoy (1648–1717)

Jeanne-Marie de Chesnoy, née de la Motte Guyon and best known as Madame Guyon, was born on April 13, 1648, in Montargis, between Paris and Orléans. The daughter of wealthy and devout Roman Catholic parents, she spent time in various convents during her childhood. At the age of sixteen she married Jacques Guyon, seigneur de Chesnoy, a man more than twenty years her senior. They lived together in Paris until her husband died in 1676, when she took a vow of chastity, devoted herself to raising her children, and intensified her previously begun search for a deeper spirituality. The writings of Francis de Sales and Jeanne de Chantal were especially formative. A number of clergy supported her on her spiritual journey, which diverged from the intellectual approach to faith favored by French Roman Catholicism.

Guyon lived in various places around Grenoble in the 1680s before moving to Paris in 1686. During this time she began to disseminate her mystical ideas, even influencing those in the circles around Madame de Maintenon, the secret second wife of Louis XIV. At the same time, she became involved in the debate over Quietism between the influential bishops Bossuet (1627–1704) and Fénelon (1651–1715). Aspersions were cast on her person and work because of her connections with a form of Quietistic Mysticism that focused on one's own inner experiences as the key to meeting God and that was associated with a neglect or a refusal of practicing good works and of celebrating the sacraments. In 1688 Guyon was arrested and interned in a convent for a few months; she was again punished with confinement to a convent in 1695 and with imprisonment in the Bastille from 1698 to 1703. Although Guyon was persecuted and imprisoned at the hands of her church, she agreed with all the teachings of the Roman Catholic tradition and refused to distance herself from the church. She lived in Blois, southwest of Orléans, where she taught a circle of pupils until her death on June 9, 1717.

Guyon's printed work, for the most part published posthumously, consists of more than forty volumes. Many of the themes present throughout her work already appear in the first of her published works, *Spiritual Torrents* (*Torrens spirituels*, 1682) and *A Short and Easy Method of Prayer* (*Moyen court et très facile de faire oraison*, 1685), which describe her own experiences that then become the basis for her teaching on how to structure one's prayer life. Her autobiography, begun during her first imprisonment in 1688 and completed in 1709, consists in great part of prayers and spiritual reflections. A large part of her printed works consists of her voluminous correspondence aimed at guiding readers into a deeper exercise of faith. Of special interest are her twenty volumes of commentary on the Bible, which, according to her own testimony, she recorded within a matter of months in 1684. With the exception of her commentary on the Song of Solomon, her commentaries received little attention during her lifetime; the Reformed theologian Pierre Poiret arranged for their printing near the end of her life (1713–15).

Guyon's biblical interpretation grew out of her mystical experiences. She saw herself as an instrument of the Holy Spirit, who communicated the words granted to her by divine grace. She described herself, among other things, as a "channel" through which the divine "Author and Originator" let his formulations flow (*L'Apocalypse* [1699], 78; in *Le Nouveau Testament*, 1713). She felt that God had commissioned her to interpret all of the Scriptures: "I had no book other than the Bible and I used it alone, without ever looking for anything else" ("Je n'avois aucun livre que la Bible et ne me suis servi que de celui-là, sans jamais rien chercher"; *La Vie* 1 [1791]: 222). In her introduction to the books of the Old Testament, she explains that although many distinguished men had undertaken to explain the Holy Scriptures, no one had yet tried to set out its mystical or inner sense: she felt that God had called her to this activity (*Les Livres de L'Ancien Testament* [1714–15], 48).

Guyon's biblical interpretations focused on the mystical teachings that emanated from individual works and phrases, rather than on the narrative flow of the text. She explains the creation of man and woman in Gen. 2 as a depiction of the relationship of Christ to the church as his bride. Thus the union of Adam and Eve points to the mystical marriage of the soul with Christ (*Les Livres de L'Ancien Testament*, vol. 1). She regarded the female figures Rebekah, Deborah, Ruth, Judith, and Esther as women "who had, like herself, walked the way of mysticism" (Le Brun, "Macht und Wissen," 157). Her attention to such themes as grief, weakness, or rejection as a way to God lends a specific profile to her interpretation of the female biblical protagonists. Patricia A. Ward characterizes her approach as "marked by none of the critical debates of the time, but by a hermeneutic of the inner life, based on her own experience, her reading of authors such as Saint John of the Cross, and her deep acquaintance with the Biblical text" (Ward, "Madame Guyon," 172).

As a Roman Catholic laywoman of the late seventeenth century who used the biblical text as the foundation for the formulation of her spiritual experiences, Guyon had far-reaching influence, crossing confessional boundaries and reaching into the nineteenth and twentieth centuries. German Pietists especially related to her. The most important witness to this connection is the Berleburger Bible, printed in Bad Berleburg between the years 1726 and 1742. Guyon's works counted as the most important reference for these Pietistic interpreters of the Bible, who were part of the radical wing of the church reform movement of Pietism and drew widely on her works in the production of their eight-volume folio. Despite the Berleburger Bible's programmatic support for women such as Jane Leade, Antoinette Bourignon, Johanna Eleonora Petersen, and Madame Guyon to have rights equal to men in interpreting the Bible, its influence was limited to the circle of radical Pietism, and thus it did not contribute to a change in the practice of biblical interpretation.

Guyon's long-term impact was strongly connected to her teaching and her life. Her way of suffering vouched for the authenticity of her faith. The deeper piety that she promoted represented—especially for the laity, both men and women—an understanding of Christianity, which was transferable to very diverse life and faith settings. The high level of Guyon's attractiveness is demonstrated by the countless reprints and translations of her works even to the present day. Guyon's importance rests, above all, on her role as a mystic teacher, who tirelessly appealed for an immersion in prayer, to thus experience the nearness and love of God. Her teachings are based on the mystic tradition of the *via negativa* and are only with difficulty classified by systematic criteria. Her extensive work as a biblical interpreter calls for more careful attention and analysis by biblical scholars.

See also Leade, Jane (1624–1704); Petersen, Johanna Eleonora (1644–1724)

Bibliography

Aegerter, Emmanuel. *Madame Guyon: Une aventurière mystique.* Paris: Librairie Hachette [Corbeil], 1941.

Guyon, Jeanne-Marie Bouvier de La Motte. *Les Livres de L'Ancien Testament: Avec des Explications & Reflexions qui regardent La Vie Interieure.* 12 vols. Cologne: Jean de la Pierre, 1714–15.

———. *Madame Guyon: An Autobiography.* Chicago: Moody, 1986.

———. *Le Nouveau Testament de Notre Seigneur Jesus-Christ: Avec des Explications & Reflexions qui regardent La Vie Interieure.* 8 vols. Cologne: Jean de la Pierre, 1713.

———. *A Short and Easy Method of Prayer.* Edited by Halcyon Backhouse. Hodder & Stoughton Christian Classics. London: Hodder & Stoughton, 1990.

———. *The Song of Songs of Solomon: With Explanations and Reflections Having Reference to the Interior Life.* Translated by James W. Metcalf. New York: A. W. Dennett, 1879.

———. *The Spiritual Teachings of Madame Guyon, Including Translations into English from Her Writings.* Translated by Nancy C. James. Foreword by John M. Graham. Lewiston, NY: Edwin Mellen, 2007.

———. *La Vie de Madame J. M. B. de la Mothe-Guyon, écrite par elle-même. . . .* Paris: Libraires Associés, 1791.

———. *The Way Out.* Translated by Ann Witkower. Gardiner, ME: Christian Books, 1985; Jacksonville, FL: SeedSowers Christian Pub., 1993. A translation of *Les Livres de L'Ancien Testament* and of *Le Nouveau Testament . . .* , both *Avec des Explications & Reflexions.*

Lagny, Anne. "Francke, Madame Guyon, Pascal: Drei Arten der 'écriture du moi.'" Pages 119–35 in *Jansenismus, Quietismus, Pietismus,* edited by Hartmut Lehmann et al. Göttingen: Vandenhoeck & Ruprecht, 2002.

Le Brun, Jacques. "Macht und Wissen der Frau nach dem Werk von Jeanne Guyon." Pages 156–76 in *Geschlechterperspektiven: Forschungen zur Frühen Neuzeit*, edited by Heide Wunder and Gisela Engel. Königstein/Taunus: Ulrike Helmer, 1998.

———. "Présupposées théoretiques de la lecture mystique de la Bible: L'example de 'La Sainte Bible' de Madame Guyon." *Revue de théologie et de philosophie* 133 (2001): 287–302.

Schrader, Hans-Jürgen. "Madame Guyon, Pietismus und deutschsprachige Literatur." Pages 189–225 in *Jansenismus, Quietismus, Pietismus*, edited by Hartmut Lehmann et al. Göttingen: Vandenhoeck & Ruprecht, 2002.

Ward, Patricia A. *Experimental Theology in America: Madame Guyon, Fénelon, and Their Readers*. Waco: Baylor University Press, 2009.

———. "Madame Guyon (1648–1717)." Pages 161–74 in *The Pietist Theologians: An Introduction to Theology in the Seventeenth and Eighteenth Centuries*, edited by Carter Lindberg. Malden, MA: Blackwell Pub., 2005.

— RUTH ALBRECHT

Habershon, Ada Ruth (1861–1918)

Ada Ruth Habershon was the youngest of four surviving children born into a wealthy Plymouth Brethren family in London, England. Her father, Samuel Osborne Habershon (1825–89), was a prominent physician who practiced and taught medicine and authored scores of articles and several monographs on medical subjects. In a manner atypical of most Plymouth Brethren, the Habershons afforded their daughter an exposure to the arts and the broader world of evangelicalism. In her youth, Habershon spent three and a half years studying at the Female School of Art (later to become part of the Royal College of Art) in South Kensington, London. While the family worshiped among the Brethren, they also frequented the Metropolitan Tabernacle of the Baptist preacher Charles H. Spurgeon, who became a close family friend. In 1884, Ada Habershon participated in the London evangelistic crusade of American evangelists D. L. Moody and Ira Sankey, and two decades later in that of R. A. Torrey and Charles Alexander (1905). When Alexander (the song leader in Torrey's crusade) asked Habershon to write hymns for him, she eventually provided him with just fewer than a thousand.

Despite intermittent periods of illness, Habershon was energetically involved in many areas of Christian ministry. Along with her parents, and following her formal education, she devoted herself to the work of Gray's Yard Ragged Church and Schools, one of the many charitable schools that offered free Christian and secular education to the poor in Victorian England. Following the death of her parents in 1889, Habershon's work expanded into other areas, including two North Sea voyages aboard Dr. Wilfred Grenfell's hospital ships. For a time she acted as the honorary finance secretary of the London YWCA, where she taught Bible studies and raised funds for the construction of the organization's headquarters. It was also during this period that she began to write and publish on biblical subjects.

At the Keswick Convention of 1892, Habershon was reintroduced to D. L. Moody, who asked her to annotate a Bible for him. This she did, basing her work on notes she had entered in the margins of her own Bible and those lent to her by other preachers and Bible teachers. What followed was a request from Moody to come to the United States, deliver the Bible, and give lectures to students at his Northfield Seminary for Young Ladies (Northfield, MA). In the summer and fall of 1895 Habershon spent three months living in Moody's home in Northfield and giving talks to the women of the seminary. In September she traveled to Chicago, where she spent time at Moody's Bible Institute for Home and Foreign Missions and lectured to women's groups at Moody's Chicago Avenue Church.

Returning to England, Habershon commissioned a model of the tabernacle and traveled with it, giving talks under the auspices of the YWCA. When poor health ended her itinerant speaking, she turned her attention to hymn writing, Bible study, and publishing. In the years that followed, she produced at least eight books and over a thousand hymns and poems, numerous articles in religious magazines, as well as booklets on such subjects as doctrinal error, dispensational eschatology, and the gospel message. In 1912, Habershon founded the Women's Branch of the Prophecy Investigation Society, regularly presenting papers at its twice-annual meetings and serving as its honorary secretary until her death in 1918.

Habershon's typological and intensely christocentric approach to interpreting Scripture limits the kinds of questions she asks of the text and the issues she sees it as raising. While the subjects she covers are wide ranging, Habershon focuses on genres where the typological approach is most fruitfully applied. Thus her works include studies on the priests and Levites, the tabernacle, parables, and the use of the Old Testament in the New. Conspicuously absent is any systematic treatment of Pauline material, Wisdom literature, or other plainly didactic genres. Even apocalyptic literature, fertile ground for geopolitical speculation by many within Habershon's dispensationalist circle, often receives a typological treatment at her hand. In her writing on Scripture, Habershon does not emphasize female characters or concerns, nor does she address issues of patriarchy or power.

Despite her tendency to read Scripture symbolically, Habershon's work is everywhere systematizing and analytical. Never in her published material does Habershon work through a book sequentially. Rather, material across large swaths of Scripture is sorted, grouped, and analyzed. Typical of this approach are *The Study of the Parables* (1923) and *The Study of the Miracles* (1911). In the former volume, Habershon examines the parables under chapters such as "Pictures of Men in the Parables," "The Setting of the Parables," and "The Trinity in the Parables." Approaching the material in this way, she sometimes looks at the same passage from several different vantage points. This multiple treatment of Scripture is not at all problematic, however, for her understanding of the depth and divine character of Scripture meant that it could sustain multiple meanings and approaches (*Study of Parables*, 255–57).

Varying degrees of apologetic interest also characterize Habershon's work. In her introduction to *The Bible and the British Museum* (1909), she stresses the goal of providing a guide that would encourage Bible study and strengthen the faith of the reader (viii). To this end, the blackened remains of Ashurbanipal's palace are highlighted as evidence for the dependability of the prophecy concerning the destruction of Nineveh given through Nahum (33; see, e.g., Nah. 3:13, 15). Elsewhere in this work a display of Egyptian deities prompts a discussion of the plagues as attacks on specific Egyptian gods in a way that shows a historical context for the biblical account (51–52).

Apologetic interest is also evident in Habershon's typological works; the manner in which the various types interconnect is evidence for her that the entire system is inspired by the Holy Spirit (*Study of the Types*, iii). As a result, the study of types becomes a "sure antidote for the poison of the so-called 'Higher Criticism'" (21). Habershon's interest in typology was also motivated by a desire to promote "simple truths of God's Word" such as the idea of substitutionary atonement (10)—a doctrine for which she found ample support in the tabernacle and its sacrifices.

Habershon's ordered mind, remarkable knowledge of Scripture, and superb memory are applied to greatest effect in her study of typology. In arguing for Joseph as a type of Christ, for example, she lists no fewer than 129 parallels between the two figures (169–74). For Habershon, typology differs from allegory in that the former is based on historical events reflecting divine intention while the latter is not (11–12). In practical terms, however, her treatment of various narratives shows much of the detailed correspondences characteristic of the allegorical method.

Habershon's treatment of Gen. 24 well illustrates her approach. Here she takes Isaac—the "only" and "well-beloved" son of Abraham, who survives the altar on Mount Moriah—to be a type of Christ, the Son of God, who moves from death to life. With this as the starting point, the search for a bride for Isaac is read christologically; the father's servant sent to procure a bride for the son symbolizes the Holy Spirit, who calls a people to be the bride of Christ. The journey of Rebekah from her homeland to Canaan in turn represents the manner in which union with Christ calls the church out of the world. Along the way, Habershon is not averse to drawing on passages in widely disparate contexts to strengthen the connections she is trying to make. In the case of Gen. 24, for example, she employs John 16:14, "He shall receive of Mine, and shall show it unto you," to draw a parallel between the gifts given by the servant to Rebekah and the blessings of Christ that pass through the Holy Spirit to the church. On occasion, such connections take on an almost rabbinic flavor, exploiting similarities in vocabulary to the exclusion of any connections in context. For example, commenting on the scene in which Rebekah's family asks the servant and Rebekah to remain a while longer ("Hinder me not" [Gen. 24:56]), Habershon cites Heb. 3:7 ("The Holy Ghost saith, 'To-day'") to bolster the connection between the urging of the Holy Spirit and the servant who wishes to depart immediately. In Habershon's use, the two widely separated passages become almost a single sentence—the servant's reply to the family, "Hinder me not" (Gen. 24:56) being completed by "The Holy Ghost saith, 'To-day'" of Heb. 3:7. In this case, there is no connection between the Hebrews passage and the episode of Abraham's servant other than the unconnected appearance of the word "servant" in Heb. 3:5 and the general sense of immediacy (*Study of the Types*, 143–45).

Habershon's interpretative approach and denominational background did not leave her intellectually cloistered. For her context, she shows a remarkable accommodation to the theory of evolution, which by then had firmly taken root in the scientific establishment. In her section on "Creation of Life" in *The Study of the Miracles* (1911), Habershon states, "'Natural selection' and 'the survival of the fittest' may be part of His [God's] method of governing, controlling, and developing the species He has made; but life, fitness, and power to survive come alone from Him" (101). Although this by no means constitutes a wholesale endorsement of Darwinian evolution, it nonetheless affirms in large part the mechanism Darwin had advanced as the means by which evolution took place. Within Plymouth Brethren thinking, this accommodation represented a significant shift from prochronism—the idea that the earth was created with the appearance of age—the position laid out a half century earlier in *Creation-Omphalos* (1857) by the Brethren marine biologist Philip Gosse (1810–88).

Despite her extensive social work and Bible teaching among women, Habershon does not seem to have written with only a female audience in mind. Prefaces to her works, written by leading evangelical figures of the day such as Sir Robert Anderson and James M. Gray of Moody Bible Institute, consistently recommend her books to a broad audience. Furthermore, her own introductions generally avoid the professions of humility found in the works of many other female writers of the era. The fact that as a Brethren woman she eschewed the then-common practice of publishing semi-anonymously under her initials suggests a woman confident in her abilities and willing to share her work with any and all who would consider it. In the United Kingdom, Habershon's books were regularly, if sometimes tepidly, reviewed in publications such as *The Churchman*, *The Expository Times*, and, in one instance, *The Palestine Exploration Fund Quarterly Statement*. Only a few of Habershon's titles remain in print today. While most of her hymn repertoire has been forgotten, her song, "Will the Circle be Unbroken?" became an American gospel favorite when it was reworked by country music pioneer A. P. Carter and is sometimes erroneously attributed to him.

Bibliography

Bettany, G. T., and Kaye Bagshaw. "Habershon, Samuel Osborne (1825–1889)." Page 385 in vol. 24 of *Oxford Dictionary of National Biography*, edited by H. C. G. Matthew and Brian Harrison. Rev. ed. Oxford: Oxford University Press, 2004–11.

Gosse, Philip Henry. *Omphalos: An Attempt to Untie the Geological Knot*. London: J. Van Voorst, 1857.

Habershon, Ada Ruth. *The Bible and the British Museum*. London: Morgan & Scott, 1909.

———. *The Study of the Miracles*. London: Morgan & Scott, 1911.

———. *The Study of the Parables*. London: J. Nisbet, 1904. 6th ed., London: Pickering & Inglis, 1923.

———. *The Study of the Types*. London: Morgan & Scott, [1898]. Repr., Grand Rapids: Kregel, 1957.

Habershon, Ada Ruth, and E. M. Habershon. *Ada R. Habershon: A Gatherer of Fresh Spoil; An Autobiography and Memoir, Compiled by Her Sister (E. M. Habershon)*. London: Morgan & Scott, 1918.

—Brian P. Irwin

Hadewijch of Antwerp (fl. 1250s)

Hadewijch, a great religious thinker and visionary in the Low Countries, was one of the creators of *Minnemystik*, or Love mysticism, and one of the first writers in the Flemish language. Her ideas were a major influence on the fifteenth-century mystic Jan van Ruusbroec (Ruysboeck) and possibly influenced the earlier writer Meister Eckhart as well. Hadewijch wrote two collections of poems, thirty letters, and a collection of fourteen visions. Nothing is known about Hadewijch's personal life, but she was highly educated and probably a member of the beguines, a women's religious movement that flourished in northern Europe from the thirteenth century through the end of the Middle Ages. Hadewijch was one of the greatest representatives of a small group of beguines who acquired reputations for "holiness," primarily through their spectacular visionary experiences.

Hadewijch's letters, visions, and poems demonstrate that she was a bold interpreter of Scripture at a time when only priests were licensed to preach and to interpret the Bible. Like other "unauthorized" biblical interpreters, Hadewijch's heavenly visions provided divine authorization for her work. She recorded her visions in the first-person format and interpreted them by using the Bible and various Christian writers to explain such concepts as hell and the mystery of the Godhead.

Hadewijch's advanced education enabled her to transform her visions into theology and literature. She was proficient in Latin, French, and Flemish. She knew the Scriptures, church liturgy, and the rules of rhetoric. She was also an accomplished poet in the troubadour tradition. Moreover, Hadewijch was clearly familiar with the writings of the early church fathers and also some of the works of famous twelfth-century monastic authors such as Bernard of Clairvaux and William of St. Thierry. Thus she possessed a thorough grounding in both the arts of biblical exposition and Christian theology.

To interpret the meaning of their visions, medieval mystics often turned to biblical models of visionary experiences. As Steven Katz remarks: "Schooled on the Christological rendering of the Song of Songs, Christian mystics quite naturally anticipated such a . . . love encounter, had such an encounter, and subsequently described such an encounter" (11). Hadewijch often turns to Ezekiel's vision of the four heavenly creatures (1:4–25) as a model for her visionary experiences. For example, Vision 10 is described as taking place on the festival of St. John, author of the Gospel of John, who was often represented by the eagle of Ezekiel's vision and associated with mystical divine union. In that vision, she is visited by the eagle, representing St. John, who explains the mysteries of heaven: "Here [in Heaven] is that highest society which wholly lives in love and in the spirit. . . . All the living, both of heaven and of earth, shall renew their life in [your] marriage [of oneness to God]" (Dros 96, 101).

Hadewijch's writing goes much further than description. In Letter 22 she interprets the meaning of the four living creatures as the four attributes of God. Each aspect of God demonstrates how God "is outside all and yet comprises all" (Hart 102).

Hadewijch also theorized that God has a feminine aspect, Love (in Dutch, *Minne*), and that the human soul can thereby be united with God. Indeed, the soul can "become submerged in him [so that] the loved one and the Beloved dwell in one another" (Hart 66). Hadewijch often used other biblical images and texts to explain how and why this union is possible. For example, in Letter 12 she interprets Obad. 18 ("The house of Jacob shall be a fire; the house of Joseph shall be a flame; the house of Esau shall be a stubble") to indicate three ways of loving God—completely ("like a fire"), through moral example ("like a flame"), and poorly ("like a stubble"). In her varied writings that explore the paths by which the soul unites with God, Hadewijch combined the long affective theological tradition of Christianity with the troubadour's lament that love is fickle and demanding complete submission of the lover to the beloved. In Vision 11 she proclaims: "Love is terrible and implacable, devouring and burning without regard for anything. The soul is contained in one little rivulet; her depth is quickly filled up; her dikes quickly burst. Thus the Godhead has wholly engulfed human nature" (Hart 291).

The issue of gender is also pertinent to Hadewijch's works in unexpected ways. Hadewijch does not focus on women figures in the Bible or plead the cause of women. Instead, Hadewijch exploits a feature of the Dutch language—gendered pronouns—to great effect. Because *Minne* (Love) is a female noun, she imagines this aspect of God as female. She also compares herself to a male knight seeking union with the Beloved. Yet Hadewijch also changes male and female pronouns throughout her writing (esp. evident in the poems) so that, in divine union, the soul can be imagined in male and female aspects, and no superiority is assigned to the male gender. Adhering to Christian theology, Hadewijch assumes the absolute equality of each soul before God. For example, Hadewijch states in Letter 2, "Give yourself completely in abandonment to God, to become what He is." The presumed inferiority of earthly women, also a long theological tradition, is simply ignored.

Some of Hadewijch's letters are addressed to women, presumably beguines whom Hadewijch mentored. These letters are full of passionate intensity; Hadewijch has been identified by at least one scholar as a "women-identified woman" (Matter 81–93). The letters are profound meditations, based on the Bible and church writings, on such issues as the nature of the Trinity, the ability of the soul to love God, and the meaning of Christ's sacrifice. Hadewijch clearly had a high regard for her female as well as her male audiences.

Hadewijch's legacy is threefold. First, she was one of the first to shape the Dutch language into a written form, and Belgian schoolchildren still read her works as part of learning their Flemish heritage. Second, Hadewijch is part of a tradition of men and women writers who believed that mystical Love is the defining aspect of the Christian faith. Because she was unusually educated, she was able to place herself in this long tradition of affective mystical Christian writing and to interpret the Bible and Christian theology in a very sophisticated and creative manner. Finally, following the Jesus whom she knew through the Bible and through her own visions, Hadewijch was unafraid to chart her own path. In an era in which women were greatly constrained, she was able to mentor others, follow her vocation of love even through great losses, and through her writings convince men, especially those in positions of authority, that her ideas were worth preserving for the ages. Her theories of the mysticism of Love—combining the ideals of troubadour poetry, biblical exposition, and Christian theology—have become a permanent part of the Christian mystical landscape.

Bibliography

Dros, Imme, trans. *Hadewijch: Visioenen*. Amsterdam: Bert Bakker, 1996.

Hart, Columba, trans. *Hadewijch: The Complete Works*. New York: Paulist Press, 1980.

Katz, Stephen. *Mysticism and Religious Traditions*. Oxford: Oxford University Press, 1983.

Matter, E. Ann. "My Sister, My Spouse: Woman-Identified Women in Medieval Christianity." Pages 152–66 in *The Boswell Thesis: Essays on Christianity, Social Tolerance, and Homosexuality*, edited by Matthew Kuefler. Chicago: University of Chicago Press, 2006.

Newman, Barbara. "*La mystique courtoise:* Thirteenth-Century Beguines and the Art of Love." Pages 137–71 in *From Virile Woman to WomanChrist: Studies in Medieval Religion and Literature*. Philadelphia: University of Pennsylvania Press, 1995.

Petroff, Elizabeth. *Body and Soul: Essays on Medieval Women and Mysticism*. New York: Oxford University Press, 1994.

Simons, Walter. *Cities of Ladies: Beguine Communities in the Medieval Low Countries, 1200–1565*. Philadelphia: University of Pennsylvania Press, 2001.

Suydam, Mary. "Beguine Textuality: Sacred Performances." Pages 169–210 in *Performance and Transformation: New Approaches to Late Medieval Spirituality*, edited by Mary Suydam and Joanna Ziegler. New York: St. Martin's Press, 1999.

———. "Women's Texts and Performances in the Medieval Southern Low Countries." Pages 143–59 in *Visualizing Medieval Performance*, edited by Elina Gertsman. Aldershot, UK: Ashgate, 2008.

Van Baest, Marieke. *Poetry of Hadewijch*. Leuven: Peeters, 1998.

Zum Brunn, Émilie, and Georgette Épiny-Burgard. *Women Mystics in Medieval Europe*. New York: Paragon House, 1989.

— MARY SUYDAM

Hale, Sarah (1788–1879)

Sarah Hale is mainly remembered for her popular nursery rhyme "Mary had a little lamb" and for establishing Thanksgiving as a national holiday. Her legacy as a biblical interpreter and as one of the most influential female editors of her time is less often remembered. She was born in 1788 in Newport, New Hampshire, and educated by her mother at home, eventually finding work as a schoolteacher before marrying David Hale in 1813. With the death of her husband in 1822, she was left to find her own way to support herself and their five children. After a short attempt at dressmaking, she turned to writing as a profession. In 1828 she became the editor of the *Ladies' Magazine*, and in 1837 she assumed the editorial reins of *Godey's Ladies Book*. During her lengthy career, Hale acted not only as an editor but also as a writer, authoring thirty-six books.

Much of Hale's work centered around her role as editor of *Godey's Ladies Book*, an immensely popular periodical among middle-class women. It included not only recipes and needlepoint patterns, but also book reviews, fiction, poetry, and monthly editorials. Prominent authors such as Nathaniel Hawthorne, Harriet Beecher Stowe, and Edgar Allan Poe were among its contributors. Like many of her Victorian counterparts, Hale adhered to a separate-sphere ideology for women. In contrast to those who argued that women's realm of influence was limited to the home, Hale argued for a separate public sphere and created a forum for women's culture within the pages of *Godey's Ladies Book* (Okker 60). Hale also used her prominent role as editor to argue for the rights of women to work as physicians, midwives, postmistresses, and teachers. The disadvantaged of society also figured prominently in her writings, and Hale supported such causes as the Fatherless and Widows' Society and the Seaman's Aid Society.

Hale also published *Woman's Record* (1853), focusing on the lives of women, who had traditionally been overlooked in histories written by men. She began her history with the women of the Bible, and it is in these biographies that one finds her interpretive work. In the general preface, Hale describes her own doctrine of human nature: "WOMAN is God's appointed agent of *morality*, the teacher and inspirer of those feelings and sentiments which are termed the virtues of humanity" (xxxv). She openly disagrees with the theologians of her day and entreats men not to look to Milton or the church fathers for a correct interpretation of Gen. 2–3. Hale offers her own interpretation, arguing that Gen. 2–3 demonstrates the superiority of women rather than their denigration, as advocated by Milton. Chief among her arguments is that woman was created last and therefore is the crown of creation, not only incorporating the best qualities of human nature but also making her the closest link to the angelic world. In her view, woman was created as a complement to man, not simply to help him but to elevate and refine him in the areas in which he is deficient. Hale understands the role of women in relation to men as the following: "She had not his strength of body or his capacity of understanding to grasp the things of earth; she could not help him in his task of subduing the world; she must, therefore, have been above him in her intuitive knowledge of heavenly things; and the 'help' he needed from her was for the 'inner man'" (xxxvii).

Hale also takes issue with the standard interpretation of 1 Cor. 11:9, that woman was created for the sake of man. Against the traditional interpretations of this text, she argues that Paul did not consider women to be inferior to men; instead, she was spiritually superior for "her soul was to 'help' him where he was deficient—namely, in his spiritual nature" (xxxvii).

Hale's view that women are much closer to perfection than are men in the areas of morality and spirituality can be seen in her biographies of women in history. She draws attention to the lives of such prominent biblical women as Eve, Sarah, and Rachel. She also highlights lesser known biblical women such as Dinah, Rahab, Abigail, and Abishag to demonstrate the importance of these women in the biblical record as moral agents. According to Hale, Rebekah is "one of the most interesting female characters in the Bible for the example and instruction of her sex" (*Woman's Record*, 54). Despite her contemporaries' censure of Rebekah, Hale argues that she is morally superior to her husband because she had a higher understanding of God's ways in her deception of Isaac and Esau. Hale argues that Rebekah's actions in favoring Jacob stem from her knowledge that he was the "chosen of God" while Esau despised his birthright. Concerning Rebekah's deception of Isaac, Hale states, "Rebekah must have been either perfectly assured she was working under the righteous inspiration of God, or she was willing to bear the punishment of deceiving her husband rather than allow him to sin by attempting to give the blessing where God had withheld it" (55). Thus, for Hale, Rebekah's example is one that demonstrates the superior nature of woman's knowledge of morality and the divine will.

Hale's legacy is complicated since she advocated for the rights of women but, like many of her contemporaries denied them an equal status among men.

At the same time, in her writing and by her own example she advocated for the advancement of women in many spheres of public life. To her, women were superior in matters of morality and spirituality, but she insisted that politics and policy making were the sole domain of men. She was also a prominent interpreter of the Bible and worked to restore women's importance in the biblical narrative as examples of moral and spiritual superiority. Thus Hale not only highlighted the oft-neglected lives of biblical women but she also corrected the traditional interpretations of her contemporaries who saw them as subordinate and inferior to men.

See also Stowe, Harriet Beecher (1811–96)

Bibliography

Hale, Sarah. *Northwood: A Tale of New England*. 2 vols. Boston: Bowles and Dearborn, 1827.

———. *Woman's Record; or, Sketches of All Distinguished Women from the Creation to A.D. 1854*. New York: Harper & Brothers, 1853.

Okker, Patricia. *Our Sister Editors: Sarah J. Hale and the Tradition of Nineteenth-Century American Women Editors*. Athens: University of Georgia Press, 1995.

Rogers, Sherbrooke. *Sarah Josepha Hale: A New England Pioneer, 1788–1879*. Grantham, NH: Tompson & Rutter, 1985.

— Heather Macumber

Hall, Sarah (Ewing) (1761–1830)

Sarah (Ewing) Hall was born in Philadelphia on October 30, 1761. She was the daughter of the Rev. John Ewing, pastor of the First Presbyterian Church in the same city and provost at the University of Pennsylvania. Despite receiving little formal education, Hall, through exposure to instruction directed at her brothers, became proficient in reading classical literature. Hall also acquired an avid interest in astronomy and would later develop facility in reading Hebrew through her own efforts. She married John Hall in 1782. Together they had eleven children. The family also lived in New Jersey and Maryland. Hall was a frequent contributor to *The Port Folio*, a prominent literary periodical in Philadelphia in the nineteenth century. She died on April 8, 1830.

In her lifetime, Hall published a stream of essays on social issues (female education, the practice of dueling), religious devotion (prayers of thanksgiving, meditations on the Psalms), and works of poetry and fiction. In the last category falls her major work *Conversations on the Bible*, a rehearsal of stories from the Hebrew Bible in the form of a conversation between a mother and her children. While the essays and brief works of fiction are directed at the cultural elite of Philadelphia (the consumers of *The Port Folio*), her major piece addresses children. All of Hall's work, to varying degrees, involve biblical interpretation. Two features stand out in Hall's reading of Scripture: (1) an affinity for filling in gaps in stories, and (2) a search for grounds to support the movement toward egalitarianism between the sexes.

In providing additional detail for biblical narrative, Hall explains the actions of characters in the story. In most cases the intent is to encourage orthodox belief and practice. For example, Aaron's apostasy in forging a golden calf (Exod. 32:1–35) is born of a desire to worship a tangible entity, an impulse cultivated through years of pagan religious practice (*Conversations*, 94). This is a practice to be avoided.

A particular interest of Hall's was reform in the perception of women's roles in nineteenth-century American society. As a rule, Hall adheres to the normative vision of the time: masculine leadership is acknowledged across all areas. Within such a scheme, a woman's role is domestic; her task is to attend to housekeeping and the comfort of her family and guests (*Selections*, 5). However, Hall's commentary on Scripture often suggests equality in capabilities across genders. In assessing Deborah's leadership (Judg. 5:1–31), for example, Hall has young Fanny remark: "The appointment of a woman to the dignity of a ruler and a prophet, by unerring wisdom, is in favour of my opinion, that the mental powers of the sexes are naturally equal" (*Conversations*, 159). The cause of female inferiority in academic achievement, according to Hall's writings elsewhere, is the undue and unfair expectation for women in the household (*Selections*, 9). Hall advocates for men to bear a greater share of domestic duties. The erosion of Hall's perception of limits to a woman's role occurs elsewhere, where she encourages unmarried women to assume various Christian ministries beyond the home (*Selections*, 12–16). Such ministries include the distribution of Bibles and evangelistic tracts, teaching in Sunday schools, and writing on religious subjects and other matters of social and moral concern.

In sum, Hall's work seeks to foster attention to Christian teachings from a careful reading of the Bible, and to challenge unhealthy social trends of her time. An important feature of her perspective on the roles of the sexes is the way it represents a transition from an older interpretation of greater role specification to a more egalitarian point of view. On the one hand, students of biblical interpretation and American social history will find in Hall's writings a wealth of data for analysis. Christians and advocates for social justice, on the other hand, will find in those same works encouragement for their journey.

Bibliography

Hall, Sarah (Ewing). *Conversations on the Bible*. 4th ed. Philadelphia: Harrison Hall, 1827.

———. *Selections from the Writings of Mrs. Sarah Hall*. Edited by Harrison Hall. Philadelphia: Harrison Hall, 1833.

Lee, Bernon P. "Conversations on the Bible with a Lady of Philadelphia." Pages 45–62 in *Recovering Nineteenth-Century Women Interpreters of the Bible*, edited by Christiana de Groot and Marion Ann Taylor. Atlanta: Society of Biblical Literature, 2007.

— BERNON LEE

Hanaford, Phebe Ann (Coffin) (1829–1921)

Born on May 6, 1829, on Nantucket Island, Massachusetts, Phebe Ann (Coffin) Hanaford was a popular preacher, writer, and suffragist. She married Joseph H. Hanaford when she was twenty and she died June 2, 1921. Her works include *Lucretia, the Quakeress* (1853), the first biography of Abraham Lincoln (1865), and a selection of poems and hymns titled *From Shore to Shore and Other Poems* (1870). Although not drawn directly from the Bible, this collection of poems demonstrates a theological thrust aimed at promoting the equality and liberation of women. As one poem, "The Question Answered," declares:

> O God! we'll trust thee for the days to come,
> Thou who hast guided woman in the Past;
> And with a grateful heart thine handmaids sing,
> "The day of righteous freedom dawns at last."
> (*Shore to Shore*, 275)

In 1877, Hanaford published *Daughters of America*, which expresses many of the same beliefs as her poems. Using biblical examples of prominent women, Hanaford argues for the establishment of legal and political equality between the sexes in her contemporary society: "Ever since Deborah judged Israel, there have been women capable of judging and legislating. In our land there are many who are as capable as the men who vote, to legislate for the best good of the community; and within the last twenty-five years there have been great changes in regard to the legal *status* of women in many of our States; and several women have been admitted to the bar as lawyers" (655).

By the 1890s, Hanaford retired from the pulpit but remained heavily involved in women's causes. She was a member on the revising committee and a contributor for the highly controversial *Woman's Bible*. In this work, Hanaford argues in her comment on Num. 20 that the meaning of the Scriptures is not transparent and therefore requires careful reading, criticism, and interpretation. The Pentateuch is particularly suspect since its laws too often advocate the repression of women: "Unjust, arbitrary and debasing are such ideas, and the laws based upon them. Could the Infinite Father and Mother have given them to Moses? I think not" (1:117). As a result, not every Scripture passage needs to be taken literally. "But how thankful we must be that we are no longer obligated to believe, as a matter of fact, of vital consequence to our eternal hope, each separate statement contained in the Pentateuch" (1:121). Passionately believing that Jesus advocated the equality of women, Hanaford alleges that any Old or New Testament texts that degrade women should be reassessed since all such discriminatory rhetoric is "contrary to true Gospel teaching" (1:117).

Undoubtedly, Hanaford read the Bible through the lens of women's rights. An example of this is her assessment of the book of Judges. She contends that the book conveys a great deal of brutality and immorality. Nevertheless, Judges does express an egalitarian view of the sexes and therefore retains some benefit:

> Solemn lessons, and those of moral import, are given in the Book of Judges; yet, as a whole, the book does not leave one with an exalted opinion of either the men or the women of those days. But it certainly gives no evidence that in shrewdness, in a wise adaptation of means to ends, in a persistent effort after desired objects, in a successful accomplishment of plans and purposes, the women were the inferiors of the men in that age. They appear to have been their equals, and occasionally their superiors. (*Woman's Bible*, 2:36)

Hanaford frequently warns against underestimating the prominent role that women played in fulfilling the divine will. Reflecting on Num. 31, Hanaford argues that women's genealogical influence remained strong despite being underestimated:

> The great lawgiver seems to have ignored the fact . . . that transmission of race qualities is even greater through the female line than through the male, and if they kept the women children for themselves they were making sure the fact that in days to come there would be Jewish descendants who might be Jews in name, but, through the law of heredity, aliens in spirit. The freedom of the natural law will make itself evident, for so-called natural law is divine. (*Woman's Bible*, 1:121)

Hanaford's biblical interpretation was radical for her time. Within both her sermons and writings, the line between theology and politics was blurred. Although biblical interpretation was extremely significant to Hanaford, it also served as a powerful platform for advocating women's rightful standing in society.

Bibliography

Hanaford, Phebe. *Abraham Lincoln: His Life and Public Services*. Boston: B. B. Russell, 1866.

———. *Daughters of America; or, Women of the Century*. Augusta, ME: True, 1877.

———. *From Shore to Shore and Other Poems*. Boston: B. B. Russell, 1870.

———. *Lucretia, the Quakeress; or, Principle Triumphant*. Boston: J. Buffim, 1853.

Stanton, Elizabeth Cady, et al., eds. *The Woman's Bible*. Vols. 1–2. New York: European Pub., 1895.

Tetrault, Lisa M. "A Paper Trail: Piecing Together the Life of Phebe Hanaford." *The Historic Nantucket* 51, no. 4 (Fall 2002). http://www.nha.org/history/hn/HNhanaford .htm.

— BETH ROBERTSON

Hands, Elizabeth (bap. 1746–1815)

Elizabeth Hands was born to Henry and Ann Herbert at Harbury, Warwickshire, before the family moved to another town in the same shire, Rowington, where Elizabeth grew up. She had a sister who died in infancy and a brother, Thomas, about whom little is known. Hands was a wife and mother who was employed as a domestic servant for the Huddesford family in Allesley, near Coventry.

Hands was not formally educated, but it is surmised that she honed her knowledge of poetry from reading texts in the Huddesford house. Before her first and only major publication, *The Death of Amnon*, she had written four poems under the pseudonym "Daphne" for the Birmingham and Coventry newspapers. *The Death of Amnon* is an experiment in epic poetry that tackled the difficult subject of the biblical story of the incestuous rape of Tamar by her half brother Amnon (2 Sam. 13). The headmaster of Rugby, Thomas James (1748–1804), and the poet Philip Bracebridge Homer (1765–1838) supported its publication by subscription in 1789. The result was a list of some 1,200 readers that included such well-known figures as Anna Seward and Edmund Burke. Also published in the collection with *The Death of Amnon* was a series of pastoral poems, often of a whimsical nature, that gave an account of Hands's observations of country life. Many of the poems were written in blank verse, including *The Death of Amnon*, while others were simple rhyming verse, such as *The Widower's Courtship*.

The Death of Amnon, the central piece in her published collection, retells the biblical narrative, but diverges from the original story in some key ways. First, it focuses more on the inner thoughts of the characters, particularly Amnon, who is cast not as a selfish rapist, but as a weak man unable to keep his lustful thoughts under control. Amnon's cousin Jonadab is cast as the evil villain who manipulates Amnon to rape his sister. Following the rape, Amnon becomes depressed and removes himself from the room, in Hands's version, whereas in the biblical account he sends Tamar away (2 Sam. 13:15).

Second, Tamar is not portrayed as a passive victim of rape, but is characterized as the heroine of the tale. Each of the men surrounding her fall victim to their own fatal flaws: Amnon is weak and unable to control his desire, Jonadab is calculating and manipulative, and King David is straitjacketed by his love for his firstborn. Even Absalom, the brother of Tamar and Amnon, though noble and generally honorable, seeks vengeance on his sister's behalf not on account of a sense of justice, but with an aim to position himself as the rightful heir to the throne. When he has Amnon killed, Absalom is unable to deliver the blow himself since he is unwilling to involve himself directly in an act he considers to be below him. The subtext of the poem speaks to male inadequacy and vaunting ambition at the expense of the downtrodden.

A final aspect of *The Death of Amnon* is the way Hands vividly describes the horror of rape. This is "one of the few examples in eighteenth-century literature where a woman writer speaks of the social and personal consequences of sexual violation" (Rex 115). Tamar mourns her loss of innocence and imagines how she will be scorned by society for what has been done to her. It is in God that Tamar eventually finds her rest, the one who will be her "all in all" (28). Tamar is the only character who turns to God amid suffering; all the other characters are blinded by their selfish desires. Hands also appears to be subtly critiquing the structures of British society of her day and the requirement of women to be "chaste" in order to gain respect.

Hands was aware that a poem about incestuous rape was a taboo subject for the general public and unlikely to be received positively. With her collections of poems was included *On the Supposition of an Advertisement in a Morning Paper, of the Publication of a Volume of Poems by a Serving Maid* and *On the Supposition of the Book Having Been Published and Read*. In these poems, she presents satirically constructed conversations by high-society people who sneer at a poem published by someone of such "low birth." In this, her poem was prescient: despite the long list of subscribers, it was received with general snobbery and even harshness by such journals as the *Monthly Review*. Nothing is known of what happened to her after the anthology was published. Two centuries later, however, Hands can be lauded as a woman who read Scripture prophetically. Her recasting of the biblical version of Tamar's story in particular brought attention to the evils of rape and called for social change.

Bibliography

Dereli, Cynthia. "Hands, Elizabeth (bap. 1746, d. 1815)." Pages 44–45 in vol. 25 of *Oxford Dictionary of National Biography*, edited by H. C. G. Matthew and Brian Harrison. Rev. ed. Oxford: Oxford University Press, 2004–11. http://www.oxforddnb.com/view/article/45851.

———. "In Search of a Poet: The Life and Work of Elizabeth Hands." *Women's Writing* 8, no. 1 (2001): 169–82.

Hands, Elizabeth. *The Death of Amnon: A Poem with an Appendix Containing Pastorals, and Other Poetical Pieces*. Coventry, UK: N. Rollason, for the author, 1789. http://www.archive.org/details/deathofamnonpoem00handuoft.

Landry, Donna. *The Muses of Resistance: Laboring-Class Women's Poetry in Britain, 1739–1796*. New York: Cambridge University Press, 1990.

Lonsdale, Roger, ed. *Eighteenth Century Women Poets: An Oxford Anthology*. Oxford: Oxford University Press, 1989.

Rex, Michael. *The Heroine's Revolt: English Women Writing Epic Poetry: 1654–1789.* PhD diss., Wayne State University, Detroit, 1998. http://digitalcommons.wayne.edu/dissertations/AAI9915717/.

Steedman, Carolyn. "Poetical Maids and Cooks Who Wrote." *Eighteenth Century Studies* 39 (Fall 2005): 1–27.

— ROBERT KNETSCH

Hayward, Amey (fl. 1699)

What little that is known about Amey Hayward comes from her single work, *The Female's Legacy*, published by Benjamin Harris in 1699. The title page gives her hometown as Limmington, but as Aspinall suggests, such a town does not exist (ix). Neither does any concrete information about Hayward exist in church or public records. It is possible that she married William Pickford in 1730 in Wedmore, a town just north of Limington, Somersetshire (Bell 101); however, since this marriage is more than thirty years after the publication of her book, one cannot be sure that this is the same Amey Hayward (Blain).

What little that is known of Hayward's biography derives from her book and her association with her publisher, Benjamin Harris, a militant Protestant, publisher, and author, best known for his "radical" books on teaching children how to read, spell, and interpret the Scriptures in a "true Protestant" way (Aspinall x). Harris was willing to publish Hayward's work and in his dedicatory poem states that she is among the most important set of divine poets; all this suggests that Hayward and Harris at least shared ideology if not a close friendship. Harris makes several other claims for Hayward's poetic skill and source material in his poem and also promises to defend her should anyone challenge either her authorship or her interpretations of Scripture.

The Female's Legacy appears to be a collection of twenty-six unrelated divine poems, but Hayward sees her work as a narrative whole, following a seventeenth-century tradition of female-authored epic poetry. Her book seems to be modestly priced and has no frontispiece; its dedication to "all Godly Women" on the title page suggests that Hayward saw her work as opening new ways of thinking on women's spirituality:

> Go, little Book, and take thy Rounds,
> And if thou Meet'st with Angry Frowns,
> Then Blame thy Author, and her Quill,
> For having of so little Skill.
> But do not Blame her over much,
> Because that she is one of such
> Which counted is the weaker Sex,
> And wanteth Skill thee to correct.
> Kind Reader, though these Lines are few,
> I pray do not them scorn to view.
> ("The Author on her weak POEMS,"
> in *The Female's Legacy*, title page)

Hayward's Christian epic, starring Christ as her hero, strives to cast the fall of humanity and the redemptive power of Christ in a more personal and direct way than did many of her literary predecessors. She calls on God to be her muse and asks him to fill her with goodness, love, mercy, glory, knowledge, wisdom, and justice. Drawing a direct comparison between God as the fountainhead of the creative process and the classical image of Parneassus Hill, she states that God "is a Fountain that doth Over-flow" (*Female's Legacy*, line 4). Each of God's attributes, as outlined by Hayward, provides her with a point of entry into the epic story of Christ's triumph over evil and his ability finally to bring peace, prosperity, and order to the earth. The first part of the poem chronicles humanity's fall from grace and the introduction of Christ to the world; the second part discusses the issues, problems, and vanity of sin and humanity; the last part explores Christ's victory at the end of the world.

Hayward's presentation of the Christian life differs from her contemporaries. She sets up neither the patriarchal family structure of Milton nor the institutionalized moral ideals of Mary Astell. She does not stray into Christian eroticism like St. Teresa of Avila or even the writer of *Eliza's Babes* (1652; Hobby 56). Instead she describes relationships between Christ and believers as being rooted in logic, friendship, and mutual respect.

Hayward's interpretation of classic concepts such as sin and evil is surprising given her association with seventeenth-century "militant Protestantism." She presents Satan as the necessary evil to God's overwhelming goodness and grace. She also argues against the idea of original sin. Hayward creates several characters who argue for the transmission of sin across generations, but all her authority figures, from Moses to Christ to God himself, speak of sin in monetary terms that cannot be transferred from parent to child: "Mention this thing no more but take good heed, / For of a present he has got no need" (*Female's Legacy*, lines 247–48).

She regards sin, then, as a matter of personal choice for each generation. She also views the fall as fortunate since it allows Christ to reveal himself as the ultimate hero/redeemer of the entire human race. Hayward also counters traditions that place the blame for sin on Eve and, by extension, all women. Unlike Milton and Layner, Hayward's account of the fall has no mention of Eve. Instead, she places the blame for sin squarely on Adam's shoulders, thus challenging one of the foundational arguments used to limit women's roles in church and society:

> And when the Lord did Adam place
> in Paradice upright,
> Oh then the Devil he did rage,
> with all his wrath and spight.
> And then he did purpose to have
> him Captive at his Will,

And for to make of him his Slave,
did try his Hellish Skill.
At length into his wicked Claws
he got this famous Creature,
And made him for to break the Laws
of his own Precious maker.
(*Female's Legacy*, lines 17–28)

The *Female's Legacy* ends with the second coming. Again, however, Hayward shifts the traditional focus away from battles, blood, and conquest. Instead, she depicts face-to-face conversations between Satan, Christ, and the sinners caught in between. In each instance, Christ wins the logical argument, and rather than "killing" Satan, he banishes him from the new realm as only the truly perfect hero can:

God's chiefest end in making of Mankind,
Was to fulfil the pleasure of his mind;
And he by all will Glorified be,
Whether Sav'd, or Lost, to all Eternity:
And seeing God his Pleasure wil fulfil,
Then what is now become of Man's Free-will?
Surely, Free-will was lost in Adam's Fall;
And now to good, Man's Will is very small:
But God out of his matchless Love and Treasure,
Makes Man to will and do of his good Pleasure.
(*Female's Legacy*, lines 1986–95)

Given that there are only two copies of *The Female's Legacy* known to be extant, Hayward's influence is difficult to judge, but she certainly shows an uncommon courage in publishing such a personal remake of the story of salvation.

See also Astell, Mary (1666–1731); Teresa of Avila (1515–82)

Bibliography

Aspinall, Dana. Introduction to *Amey Hayward: The Female's Legacy*, edited by Robert C. Evans. Aldershot, UK: Ashgate, 2003.

Bell, Maureen, George Parfitt, and Simon Shepherd, eds. *A Biographical Dictionary of English Women Writers 1586–1720*. Boston: G.K. Hall, 1990.

Blain, Virginia, Patricia Clements, and Isobel Grundy, eds. *The Feminist Companion to Literature in English*. New Haven: Yale University Press, 1990.

Hayward, Amey. *The Female's Legacy*. London: Benjamin Harris, for the author, 1699.

Hobby, Elaine. *Virtue of Necessity: English Women's Writing, 1649–88*. Ann Arbor: University of Michigan Press, 1989.

— MICHAEL REX

Hemans, Felicia (1793–1835)

Early nineteenth-century British poet Felicia Hemans produced many successful texts touching on themes of national, religious, and gender identity. Her *Female Characters of Scripture: A Series of Sonnets* (1833, 1834), in particular, is currently attracting increased attention from scholars concerned with the overlap between literary history and biblical studies (Clarke 101). This is largely due to the focus of the sonnets series on women's capacity for prophecy, composition, leadership, and loving action.

Felicia Dorothea Browne was born in Liverpool on September 25, 1793, to an Anglican mother of mixed German and Italian lineage and an Irish father. She was taught world literature and biblical narrative from an early age. Hemans's biographer L. H. Sigourney writes:

> Her intellectual training, within the quiet sanctuary of home and under maternal supervision, progressed prosperously. The study of languages aided her development of mind and power of expression. With French and Italian she became early familiar, to which she afterwards added Spanish and Portuguese. She also acquired the rudiments of German, and continued in future years to deepen her knowledge of that noble language, which, it was remarked by critical observers, gave to her own productions an added tone of sublimity. ("Memoir," 30)

Her later poetry contains recurrent images of mothers' teaching their children from Scripture. In "To a Family Bible"—one of her *Sonnets: Devotional and Memorial* (1834)—she writes: "My mother's eyes upon thy page divine, / Each day were bent—her accents grave and mild / Breathed out thy lore" (lines 3–5). Felicia Browne loved her mother dearly; her first poem, written at the age of eight, was titled "On My Mother's Birthday." She began publishing individual poems at the age of fourteen. Her first collection, *Poems*, was published in 1808. When she married Captain Alfred Hemans in 1812, they moved to Northamptonshire, but the captain lost his position, and they began living with Felicia's mother in Wales. In 1818, after the birth of their fifth son, Alfred Hemans left for Italy and never returned. Felicia Hemans turned to her writing as a means to support herself and her children.

From the publication of *The Forest Sanctuary and Other Poems* (1825), Hemans received favorable reviews in British and American journals alike. *The Forest Sanctuary* tells the story of European Protestant dissenters taking refuge in the wilds of America. Even before she composed her *Female Characters of Scripture*, however, Hemans was expressing her faith in verse. "Arabella Stuart," the opening poem of *Records of Woman* (1828), lauds "woman's spirit strong / in the deep faith which lifts from wrong / A heavenwards glance" (lines 32–34). Modern critic Emma Mason refers to the "failure of emotional restraint" in *Records of Woman* and then states: "This failure is absent, however, in Hemans's religious sonnets, marked as they are by a consistent recourse to the Bible" (89). Yet it is important to remember that the Bible itself is not always marked by "emotional restraint"; its scenes are at times full of passion, and Hemans's sonnet series vividly portrays the passionate grief, joy, and love expressed by biblical women.

Female Characters of Scripture: A Series of Sonnets (1833, 1834) begins with two separate "invocations" to the women of the Old and New Testaments and then goes on to dedicate one sonnet each to Miriam, Ruth, Rizpah, the Shunammite Woman, "the penitent at Christ's feet" (unnamed by Hemans, as in Luke 7), and the women of Jerusalem at the cross; two sonnets are devoted to Mary and Martha of Bethany; two sonnets reflect the experiences of Mary Magdalene; and four sonnets contain references to Mary the mother of Jesus. More attention could have been paid to women from the Old Testament: Deborah, Esther, and Rahab are strangely absent. Fascinatingly, Jewish American Rebekah Hyneman responded to Hemans with a more extensive survey of Old Testament women in her own *Female Scriptural Characters* (1853), which takes "the sestet of Hemans's first invocation as its epigraph" (Harris 1030).

Revising the classical invocation of the muses, Hemans's two invocation sonnets seek inspiration in a female cloud of biblical witnesses, sister poet-prophets whom her verse will honor. At the beginning of Hemans's first invocation, she calls on the women of the Old Testament: "Daughters of Judah" (line 10), "Ye of the dark, prophetic, eastern eyes" (line 11). Modern critic Julie Melnyk observes, "The Old Testament women of her 'invocation' sonnet represent a golden age of women's song" (87). In Hemans's second invocation, she turns to the women of the New Testament: "Ye faithful! Round Messiah seen" (line 1). The imagery is much softer in this sonnet: "From *your* hearts subdued / All haughty dreams of power had winged their flight" (lines 6–7). Melnyk argues that Hemans projects Victorian ideals of submissive femininity on to these New Testament women, but they express a paradoxical strength *in* weakness, which Hemans depicts as more sublime than the prophetic grandeur of the Old Testament.

Hemans begins her actual survey of biblical "female characters" with a prophetic Old Testament figure in "The Song of Miriam." In the Bible, Miriam leads the Israelite women, after the triumph at the Red Sea, with the words "Sing ye to the LORD, for he hath triumphed gloriously; the horse and his rider hath he thrown into the sea" (Exod. 15:21). In "The Song of Miriam," Hemans focuses entirely on this female prophet, mentioning neither her brother Moses nor Aaron: "Miriam's voice o'er that sepulchral realm / Sent on the blast a hymn of Jubilee" (lines 3–4). Miriam's ability to sing with joy amid a "sepulchral," or tomb-like, scene inspires Hemans. Addressing "Bright Poesy!" (10), Hemans mourns the loss of sacred themes in contemporary literature: "How hath it died, thy seraph note of praise, / In the bewildering melodies of earth!" (11–12). Within her sonnet on Miriam, Hemans calls for a return to "the life springs" (14) of God-sourced poetry. She next moves chronologically through the Old Testament with the sonnet "Ruth," which draws on imagery from John Keats's "Ode to a Nightingale" (1819). Keats imagines "the sad heart of Ruth, when, sick for home, / She stood in tears amid the alien corn" (66–67). The Bible does not mention Ruth weeping in the fields, but Keats does, and Hemans follows Keats, envisioning a "forlorn" Ruth (line 3). Hemans writes, "I see thee stand / Lone, midst the gladness of the harvest band— / Lone as a wood-bird on the ocean's foam" (4–6). Unlike Keats's Ruth, however, Hemans's Ruth is strong and determined. The sonnet concludes:

> and if thy gentle eyes
> Gleam tremulous through tears, 'tis not to rue
> Those words, immortal in their deep Love's tone
> *"Thy people and thy God shall be my own!"*
> (lines 11–14)

Hemans's description of Ruth ends on an uplifting, soundly biblical note.

Hemans educates her reader by also drawing attention to more obscure women from the Old Testament: Rizpah and the Shunammite woman. "The Vigil of Rizpah" begins with 2 Sam. 21:10 and describes Rizpah watching over the slain bodies of Israelites in a mountainous landscape: "Alone before the awfulness of night" (line 2). In 2 Sam. 21, Rizpah guards the bones of her kinsmen, protecting them from vultures and wild animals. Hemans depicts her as a woman of passionate grief, with "drooping head" (5), who nevertheless "recks not" (7) the "wild rocks" (12) because she is sustained by "mightiest Love" (14). Hemans's final sonnet, focusing on a woman from the Old Testament, "Reply of the Shunam[m]ite Woman," also celebrates love. The sonnet begins with quotation of 2 Kings 4:13 and then celebrates the Shunammite woman's devotion to home, emphasizing her "household love" (12) and cultivation of "home's dear charities" (14). Hemans's Shunammite woman typifies Victorian femininity, challenging Melnyk's thesis that it is only Hemans's New Testament women who embody such ideals.

The first of Hemans's sonnets about a New Testament woman is titled "The Annunciation" and represents the angel Gabriel's call on Mary to bear God's Son. This sonnet does contrast the young Mary with a woman announcing "victory" (line 7) on "her proud lyre" (8), meaning Miriam. However, Hemans's next sonnet, "The Song of the Virgin," celebrates Mary as a prophet-poet whose "calm spirit lightened into song" (4) with words "free and strong" (6). In this sonnet on Mary's "Magnificat," Hemans challenges purely martial definitions of strength, concluding:

> Full many a strain, borne far on glory's blast,
> Shall leave, where once its haughty music pass'd,
> No more to memory than a reed's faint sigh;
> While thine, O childlike virgin! through all time

> Shall send its fervent breath o'er every clime,
> Being of God, and therefore not to die.
>
> (lines 9–14)

Hemans implies that the "Magnificat" is stronger than any national anthem. Mason notes, "Hemans's sonnet serves to rescue Mary from [a] one-dimensional domesticated role as Christ's mother, granting her a clear poetical voice that bears song" (93). Mary's role as composer and prophetess is key for Hemans as a poet.

The next sonnet in the series, "The Penitent Anointing Christ's Feet," adheres to Scripture by leaving the "sinner" of Luke 7:37 nameless. The sonnet begins by envisioning angels mourning over her life of pointless "pleasure" (line 3) and then ends with "a song of joy in Heaven, / For thee, the child won back, the penitent forgiven" (13–14). These last lines recall Christ's parables of the lost sheep and the prodigal son. Hemans follows this with her next sonnet, "Mary at the Feet of Christ," focusing on Mary of Bethany, who sat listening to Christ's teaching, emphasizing progression from repentance to discipleship (Luke 10:38–42). Mary of Bethany appears as a "meek listener at the Saviour's feet" (4), free from "feverish cares" (5) and full of "silent worship" (6). Given a "fresh childhood" (7), she is reborn into childlike wonder. This receptive attitude brings her "quiet" (9), and her "calm soul" (11) is like a well "deep and still in its transparent rest" (12). Hemans's next sonnet, "The Sisters of Bethany after the Death of Lazarus," follows Mary into her time of grief and foreshadows the death and resurrection of Christ (John 11:1–45).

In "The Memorial of Mary," Hemans focuses on the anointing of Christ with perfume before his death. As preface to this sonnet, she quotes Matt. 26:13 and then adds a note: "See also *John*, xii. 3." It is John who identifies the woman by name, recording how "Mary took about a pint of pure nard, an expensive perfume," and "poured it on Jesus' feet" (NIV). Matthew 26:13 contains Jesus's words: "Truly I tell you, wherever this gospel is preached throughout the world, what she has done will also be told, in memory of her" (NIV). Hemans's poetic speaker addresses Mary directly: "Where'er the child /Looks upward from the English mother's knee, /With earnest eyes in wondering reverence mild, /There art thou known" (lines 6–9). Fascinatingly, Hemans places the English child in Mary of Bethany's position, as contemplative learner gazing up in wonder, and Hemans's "English mother" acts as representative of Christ, the teacher. To conclude her sonnet, Hemans asks the rhetorical question: "Oh! say what deed so lifted thy sweet name, / Mary!" (12–13), which she answers in her concluding line: "One lowly offering of exceeding love" (14).

The final three sonnets in *Female Characters of Scripture* trace the central presence of women at the crucifixion, burial, and resurrection of Christ. The first of these sonnets is titled "The Women of Jerusalem at the Cross." John 19:25 records that "there stood by the cross of Jesus his mother, and his mother's sister, Mary the wife of Clopas, and Mary Magdalene." Hemans's sonnet lauds the "bright lingering" (4) of these women who are like "pale stars of tempest hours" (1) as they witness "the death-cloud within the Saviour's eye" (6). The light of their faith is a bright constancy "in the shadow of his agony" (8). Hemans suggests that their faithful courage transcends time to reach women readers of all historical periods: "O blessed faith! A guiding lamp, that hour / Was lit for woman's heart!" (9–10).

"Mary Magdalene at the Sepulchre" moves through grief toward resurrection. The sonnet begins with an image of weeping that recalls Rizpah, Ruth, and the sisters at Bethany: "Weeper! To thee how bright a morn was given / After thy long, long vigil of despair" (1–2). Hemans imagines Mary Magdalene's hearing "that high voice which burial rocks had riven" (3) and falling to her knees, "awed by the mighty gift" won by "tears and love" (14). In these sonnets Hemans returns again and again to the theme of devoted, faithful love. The capstone sonnet of the series is "Mary Magdalene Bearing Tidings of the Resurrection." Hemans presents Mary's spreading the news of the resurrection as her particular "task of glory" (1). She applies a martial word, "glory," to Mary's announcement of resurrected life. For Hemans, this announcement is "nobler" (2) than even the "awful music" (3) of Old Testament prophecy. Mary Magdalene's task was to "wake mankind" (5) to the reality of the resurrection; she was called "to send the mighty rushing wind" (7) with the tidings "*Christ is arisen!*" (9). Like Jesus's conquering of a supposedly shameful death through the resurrection, Mary has herself been "raised from shame to brightness!—*there* doth lie / The tenderest meaning of *His* ministry" (12–13). Hemans concludes her sonnet series by paralleling Christ's facing of death, even the shame of death on a cross, and then rising to the glory of heaven, with each believer rising from the shame of sin to the light of salvation.

Hemans persevered in writing religious sonnets to the end, even dictating a "Sabbath Sonnet" on April 26, 1835, as she was suffering from scarlet fever. On her deathbed, Hemans stated: "I am a tired child, weary, and longing to mingle with the pure in heart. I feel as if I were sitting with Mary, at the feet of my Redeemer" (Sigourney, "Essay," xxii). Hemans died on May 16, 1835. Her brothers installed a memorial at St. Asaph Cathedral that reads: "In memory of Felicia Hemans, whose character is best portrayed in her writings."

Bibliography

Anderson, John. "Icons of Women in the Religious Sonnets of Wordsworth and Hemans." Pages 90–110 in *Fountain Light: Studies in Romanticism and Religion*, edited by J. Robert Barth. New York: Fordham University Press, 2002.

Clarke, Norma. *Ambitious Heights: Writing, Friendship, Love; The Jewsbury Sisters, Felicia Hemans, and Jane Carlyle.* New York: Routledge, 1990.

Harris, Daniel A. "Felicia Hemans: To the Editor." *Publications of the Modern Language Association* 109, no. 5 (Oct. 1994): 1029–32.

Hemans, Felicia. "Arabella Stuart." Pages 323–28 in *The Poetical Works of Mrs. Hemans*. Edinburgh: Nimmo, Hay & Mitchell, 1887.

———. "Female Characters of Scripture." *Blackwoods Magazine* 33 (April 1833): 593–95.

———. "Female Characters of Scripture." Pages 170–84 in *Scenes and Hymns of Life, with Other Religious Poems*. London: T. Cadell, 1834.

———. *Mrs. Sigourney*. Philadelphia: Lea and Blanchard, 1840.

———. *Poetical Works in Two Volumes*. 4th ed. New York: Roorbach, 1828.

———. *Records of Women: A Celebration of Women Writers*. Edited by Mary Mark Ockerbloom. Philadelphia: University of Pennsylvania Press, 1994–2005. http://digital.library.upenn.edu/women/.

———. *Records of Women: With Other Poems*. Edinburgh: W. Blackwood, 1828. http://digital.library.upenn.edu/women/hemans/records/records.html.

Mason, Emma. "Sensibility into Sense: Barbauld, Hemans, and Religious Commitment." Pages 79–95 in *Spiritual Identities: Literature and the Post-Secular Imagination*, edited by Jo Carruthers and Andrew Tate. New York: Peter Lang, 2010.

Melnyk, Julie. "Hemans's Later Poetry: Religion and the Vatic Poet." Pages 74–92 in *Felicia Hemans: Reimagining Poetry in the Nineteenth Century*, edited by Nanora Sweet and Julie Melnyk. New York: Palgrave, 2001.

Sigourney, L. H. "An Essay on the Genius of Mrs. Hemans." Pages vii–xxiii in vol. 1 of *The Works of Felicia Hemans*, edited by H. Hughes. New York: C. S. Francis, 1845.

———. "Memoir." Pages 27–46 in *The Poetical Works of Felicia Hemans: Complete in One Volume, with a Memoir by Mrs. L. H. Sigourney; A New Edition, from the Last London Edition, with All the Introductory Notes*. New York: W. I. Pooley, 1853.

— Natasha Duquette

Herbert, Mary Sidney (1561–1621)

On October 27, 1561, Mary Sidney Herbert was born at Tickenhall, a palace near Bewdley, Worcestershire. Her parents were Sir Henry Sidney (1529–86), a courtier and later lord deputy of Ireland, and Mary Dudley (1531–86), daughter of John Dudley, duke of Northumberland (1504–53). Her birth into the Dudley and Sidney families placed her within an intricate matrix of power and influence. Both families achieved prominence during the reigns of Henry VIII and Edward VI; the subsequent reign of Mary Tudor proved to be more favorable to the family of Henry Sidney, who received the queen's pardon and maintained a certain degree of his previous power, than to the Dudleys. For his role in the succession of Lady Jane Grey, John Dudley was beheaded, his properties and titles forfeited, and his five sons imprisoned. Although Guildford Dudley was executed with Lady Jane Grey in 1554, the four other Dudley sons were released from prison in October 1554, due in part to Henry and Mary Dudley Sidney's intercessions to Queen Mary I.

When Mary Sidney was born in 1561, Queen Elizabeth I had been in power for nearly three years, and the Dudley family's fortunes had begun to improve through the Queen's preferment of Herbert's uncle Robert Dudley (ca. 1532–1588): he was made Master of the Horse upon her 1558 ascension and later a member of the Privy Council, Baron of Denbigh, and Earl of Leicester. Elizabeth was a Protestant queen, but after the religious tumult experienced by her kingdom during the reigns of her father, brother, and sister, she favored moderation and settlement. Yet throughout her reign members of the Dudley and Sidney families formed what has been termed a Protestant alliance, which urged Elizabeth to adopt an ever more active and interventionist Protestantism, including involvement in the Continental religious wars. This nexus of power, prestige, and responsibility shaped Herbert's Protestantism, sense of purpose, relationship to family and monarch, and roles as patron, writer, and noblewoman.

Although Mary was schooled at home, she received far more education than was customary for girls, learning languages (French, Italian, Latin, and possibly even Greek and Hebrew), geography, literature, the classics, patristic writings, and medicine. She played the lute and virginals, studied vocal music, practiced archery, and was skilled at needlework. Accounts from the Sidney household list prayer books specifically for her and "two books of Martirs," likely John Foxe's *Acts and Monuments* (which describes the deaths of a number of Herbert's relatives). As a wide-eyed but worldly wise girl of thirteen, Mary Sidney was invited to Queen Elizabeth's court, where she spent the two years preceding her marriage to Henry Herbert, Earl of Pembroke in 1577. In Queen Elizabeth, Mary met an exemplar of a learned and powerful woman, which deepened her previous experience of educated women, including her mother, her aunt Katherine Dudley Hastings, and the Cooke sisters, friends of her mother who translated religious texts (Hannay, *Philip's Phoenix*, 25): Lady Anne Cooke Bacon translated John Jewel's *Apologie of the Church of England* (1564), Mildred Cooke Burley translated but did not publish a long sermon by St. Basil from the Greek (BL MS Royal 17.B.xviii), and Elizabeth Cooke Russell translated John Ponet's *A Way of Reconciliation of a Good and learned man, touching the Truth, Nature, and Substance of the Body and Blood of Christ in the Sacrament* (1605). More models of learned women were available in print; Mary Sidney had access to publications by her aunt Lady Jane Grey, Margaret Roper, Anne Askew, Anne Lock, and others.

Mary Sidney's marriage to the powerful Henry Herbert, the Earl of Pembroke, brought a great deal of administrative responsibility, and the Pembroke estates also became centers of literary activity. Her brother Sir Philip Sidney was a regular visitor, and the two read and discussed literature together, including Philip's own. Indeed, *A Defence of Poetry*, *Astrophil and Stella*, and his *Arcadia* were all likely written during extended stays with his sister. His dedication to Herbert in the *Arcadia* indicates that the work was "done only for you, only to you," and that he wrote "most of it in your presence, the rest by sheets, sent unto you as fast as they were done." This model of literary encouragement extended to the variety of young poets and courtiers who sought patronage of the earl by means of his young wife, who urged all members of her household to write and even gave writing assignments.

However, Philip Sidney's military death in 1587 while campaigning with his uncle Robert Dudley in the Netherlands dramatically altered Herbert's public role as writer and patron. Poets began to seek her favor through their elaborate praise of Sidney, and Herbert took an active role in promoting the legacy of her brother as a Protestant martyr by contributing to published elegies, such as Edmund Spenser's *Astrophel*. "The Dolefull Lay of Clorinda," although still disputed, is thought by many scholars to have been written in part or entirely by Herbert.

Herbert's public acts of grief for her brother's death included editing and publishing Sidney's work: *Astrophil and Stella* and a heavily revised though incomplete *Arcadia* both came to press through Herbert's efforts. She also prepared translations of texts that had been of particular interest to Sidney and to the cause of the Protestant alliance; by the 1590s, many of the members of the Dudley/Sidney Protestant alliance were dead. Before his death, Sidney had begun translating *De la verité de la religion chrétienne*, a work by his friend Philippe de Mornay, a Huguenot. In 1590 Herbert translated de Mornay's *Excellent discours de la vie et de la mort* (1576) as "A Discourse of Life and Death," a treatise on avoiding the various temptations at each stage of life and on the Christian consolation of a truer life after death. She published "A Discourse" in 1592 along with *Antonius*, her translation of the French Robert Garnier's highly political play *Marcus Antonius*. During the same decade she translated Petrarch's *Il Trionfi* as "The Triumph of Death," which circulated in manuscript. Like "A Discourse," this was a meditation on loss and death.

Herbert's most significant contribution to the history of biblical interpretation and to seventeenth-century English Protestantism was her rendering of the book of Psalms into English poetry. This also was an unfinished project begun by her brother, who had praised the divine poetry of the psalms in his treatise *A Defence of Poetry* and had versified the first forty-three psalms before his death. It was perhaps Herbert's work in editing her brother's psalms that sparked her interest in completing the project, but whatever the reason, the "Sidney Psalter," as it is commonly called, proved to be momentous in the history of women's biblical interpretation. More than a translation, Herbert's psalms relied heavily, but also discerningly, on a wide variety of commentaries, psalm translations, and theological texts in Latin, French, and English: the Geneva Bible; the 1562 French Psalter of Théodore de Bèze (Beza) and Clément Marot, which included varied metrical forms; Bèze's commentaries; Calvin's Psalm commentary; the Psalm translations by Anne Lock, Matthew Parker, and Thomas Wyatt; the Book of Common Prayer; and other works.

First, one may scarcely overstate the importance of the psalms both for the Sidney and Dudley families as well as for the English nation during the sixteenth and seventeenth centuries. Thomas Sternhold, Edward VI's Groom of the Robes, published his small collection of common meter psalm translations in 1549. Perhaps Henry Sidney's and Robert Dudley's closeness to the young king had also brought them into direct contact with Sternhold, who relates in his dedicatory epistle that Edward VI took great pleasure in hearing him sing his metrical psalms. However, during the religious upheavals of the mid-sixteenth century, English Protestants taking refuge in Geneva during the reign of Mary I enlarged and expanded Sternhold's thirty-seven translated psalms into a complete Psalter, which later became the standard text for psalm singing in Elizabethan England. Translating psalms could be a political as well as a devotional activity: Herbert's uncles John and Robert Dudley translated Pss. 55 and 94 while in prison, identifying God's enemies as their own persecutors. By the time Herbert was born, psalm singing had become a ubiquitous practice of everyday life for Protestants: the bishop John Jewel reported in a 1560 letter to Peter Martyr that after services at St. Paul's Cross, one could see "six thousand persons, old and young, of both sexes, all singing together and praising God" (Quitslund 153).

Moreover, the psalms and the medium of translation allowed Herbert to speak frankly as a female poet urging a female monarch to right action and religious devotion. Margaret Hannay suggests that Herbert completed the entire Psalter by 1599, in time to present it along with the pastoral "A Dialogue between two shepherds, Thenot and Piers, in praise of Astrea" to the queen during the monarch's intended (but later canceled) visit to Herbert's estate at Wilton (*Phoenix*, 165; see also 90–91). The two original prefatory poems that she wrote to accompany the Psalter indicate her double dedication to Queen Elizabeth and to her brother Philip Sidney. In "Even now that Care," Herbert adopts standard Elizabethan typology by figuring Queen Elizabeth as a second David: "Thy Rule is painted in his Raigne" (65). The psalms, "Now English denizend" (30), therefore constituted an appropriate gift for such a ruler. Herbert presents the collection of psalms to her monarch as a "liverie robe," a royal garment in the queen's own colors (34), but, continuing the weaving metaphor, it was Philip who "did warpe [frame], I weav'd this webb to end" (27). The other prefatory poem, "To the Angell Spirit of the most excellent Sir Philip Sidney," emphasizes this theme of her dependence on Sidney's invention—but the psalm collection undoubtedly comprises a major work of biblical interpretation by Herbert herself.

The Sidney Psalter was also significant for the development of English poetry, as Barbara Lewalski, Rivka Zim, and Hannibal Hamlin have shown. For the most part, Herbert eschewed the familiar common meter of the metrical psalms, choosing rather to translate her psalms by using an extensive variety of literary forms and meters, many of which were listed in George Puttenham's influential *Arte of Poesie* (1589). The choice of meter contributed importantly to Herbert's autonomy as a translator—her decision to use, for example, the sonnet form, Italian verse forms, rhyme royal, and acrostics is evidence of the artistic freedom available to women within the medium of translation.

Certain patterns emerge from her use of sometimes contradictory sources: she tended to favor those interpretations derived directly from the Hebrew, and she rejected those that contradicted her own experiences as a woman, wife, and mother (see *Collected Works*, 2:11–14, 25). Beth Wynne Fisken has argued that the "private Mary Sidney shines through in her images of birth and child care. . . . Sidney invested a unique tenderness in her use of [such images], which renders those sections of the *Psalmes* softly luminous" (*Silent*, 176). In Ps. 58, Herbert describes a stillborn child, "whose vitall band / Breakes er it holdes and formless eyes to faile / To see the sun, though brought to lightfull land" (lines 22–25). To the psalmist's claim that his mother, when "conceaving me, with me did sinne conceave," Herbert adds the maternal verse "and as with living heate shee cherish me / corruption did like cherishing receave" (Ps. 51:5). God's intimate knowledge of his creation includes knowing "how my back was beam-wise laid, / and raftring of by ribs" (139:44, 50–51). Her translation of Ps. 45 echoes her experiences as a lady-in-waiting and as a bride. As a Christian and as a poet, she declares, "I secure shall spend my happie tymes / in my, though lowly, never-dying rymes, / singing with praise the God that Jacob loveth" (75:25).

The devotional "I" of the psalms allows Herbert to add her own voice to what she understood as a complicated sequence of authorship by which David, inspired by the Holy Spirit, provided material for Philip Sidney, whose translations inspired her to complete the work. Thus John Donne imagines the process in his poem "Upon the translation of the Psalms by Sir Philip Sidney, and the Countess of Pembroke his sister":"The songs are these, which heaven's high holy Muse /Whispered to David, David to the Jews: /And David's successors, in holy zeal, /In forms of joy and art do re-reveal"(lines 31–34). Herbert's psalms are more than a straightforward translation. As her first editor John C. A. Rathmell wrote, she "*meditated* on the text before her" (xx). Perhaps, then, the terms "paraphrase," "metaphrase," "imitation," or "interpretation" would more aptly depict her approach to the biblical text (see Bennett 269n1).

Though the Sidney Psalter was available only in manuscript until the nineteenth century, Herbert's psalms profoundly influenced seventeenth-century poetry, particularly devotional poets such as John Donne, George Herbert (a relative of the Herbert family), and Aemilia Lanyer, who called the Sidney Psalter "The Psalms written newly" (Herbert 1:50). Translation of religious writing was one of the few acceptable avenues for women's writing in the sixteenth and seventeenth centuries, but Herbert worked within these bounds to produce a milestone in Renaissance devotional and lyric poetry.

See also Askew, Anne (ca. 1521–46); Elizabeth I (1533–1603); Lanyer, Aemilia (1569–1645); Lock, Anne Vaughan (1534–ca. 1602); Roper, Margaret More (1505–44)

Bibliography

Bennett, Lyn. *Women Writing of Divinest Things: Rhetoric and the Poetry of Pembroke, Wroth and Lanyer.* Pittsburgh: Duquesne University Press, 2004.

Fisken, Beth Wynne. "Mary Sidney's *Psalmes*: Education and Wisdom." Pages 166–83 in *Silent but for the Word: Tudor Women as Patrons, Translators, and Writers of Religious Works*, edited by Margaret Patterson Hannay. Kent, OH: Kent State University Press, 1985.

Hamlin, Hannibal. *Psalm Culture and Early Modern English Literature.* New York: Cambridge University Press, 2004.

Hannay, Margaret Patterson. *Philip's Phoenix: Mary Sidney, Countess of Pembroke.* New York: Oxford University Press, 1990.

———, ed. *Silent but for the Word: Tudor Women as Patrons, Translators, and Writers of Religious Works.* Kent, OH: Kent State University Press, 1985.

Herbert, Mary Sidney, Countess of Pembroke. *The Collected Works of Mary Sidney Herbert, Countess of Pembroke.* Edited by Margaret P. Hannay, Noel J. Kinnamon, and Michael G. Brennan. 2 vols. New York: Clarendon, 1998.

Lewalski, Barbara Kiefer. *Protestant Poetics and Seventeenth-Century Religious Lyric.* Princeton, NJ: Princeton University Press, 1979.

Quitslund, Beth. *The Reformation in Rhyme: Sternhold, Hopkins and the English Metrical Psalter, 1547–1603.* Aldershot, UK: Ashgate, 2008.

Sidney, Sir Philip, and Mary Sidney Herbert, Countess of Pembroke. *The Psalms of Sir Philip Sidney and the Countess of Pembroke.* Edited by J. C. A. Rathmell. Garden City, NY: Doubleday, 1963.

Zim, Rivka. *English Metrical Psalms: Poetry and Praise and Prayer, 1535–1601.* New York: Cambridge University Press, 1987.

— MEREDITH DONALDSON CLARK

Hildegard of Bingen (1098–1179)

In 1098 St. Hildegard of Bingen was born to a noble family at Bermerseim, about twenty kilometers (twelve miles) southwest of Mainz in what is now Germany. She first began to experience the visions that gave her a unique status among her contemporaries from an early age, about three, and recounted later how at first she did not understand that others could not see the things she saw. From early childhood she was also troubled by illness, including what many modern commentators have taken to be debilitating migraines. In her accounts there is often a connection between periods of illness and intense visionary activity.

Traditionally it has been believed that as an eight-year-old she was enclosed in a cell attached to the Benedictine monastery of Disibodenberg, under the direction of Jutta, a young noblewoman whose reputation for piety attracted others to join her or place their children under her care. Yet there are discrepancies in the sources, and she may first have been entrusted to Jutta before Jutta's own enclosure, with the two entering enclosure together at a later date, when

Hildegard was about fourteen. It was probably under Jutta's direction that she received elementary instruction in reading and writing Latin and church music, at least sufficient for her to take part in regular Benedictine worship, since most enclosures were so constructed as to allow a cell's occupant(s) to at least hear, if not see, the daily offices of prayer and to receive communion at Mass. In either case she remained a part of this small community at Disibodenberg, eventually becoming a nun, until at Jutta's death in 1136 she became the head of what had grown to be a small convent.

In 1141 she experienced a vision of a new kind: in it she was commanded to write down what she saw and heard from God for others to read. It may be significant that this experience came only after she was freed from the oversight of the far more austere Jutta and had assumed control of the community. As a result of the vision, she eventually began to write the first of her major works, *Scivias*, whose title apparently derives from the Latin phrase "Sci [or Scito] vias Domini," "Know thou [or Know ye] the ways of the Lord." She worked with the help of a secretary, the monk Volmar, who would continue in this role until his death in 1173. It appears that he may have worked from Hildegard's rough drafts, smoothing out some of the irregularities of her Latin prose while allowing her authentic prophetic voice to be heard without interference. This is in contrast to what is known of at least some other abbesses and female visionaries of the middle ages, whose secretaries, like Elisabeth of Schönau's brother, seem to have heavily edited the women's work, even at times rewriting or suppressing portions, as well as with the efforts of Hildegard's last secretary, Guibert, who tried to correct and improve her *Life of St. Martin* (of Tours).

So unusual was this step of visionary writing for an enclosed woman religious that the abbot of Disibodenberg informed the archbishop of Mainz, who in turn informed Pope Eugenius III during the Synod of Trier. Eugenius responded by sending a commission to Disibodenberg to investigate Hildegard and her writings. The commission's report included part of *Scivias*, which the pope read aloud to the assembled prelates. As a result of their positive response, Hildegard was commanded by the pope to continue to write and make known what she received from the Holy Spirit, and so she finished *Scivias* in 1151. This almost unprecedented accolade, to which was joined approval from Bernard of Clairvaux, put Hildegard in a strong position in dealing with both civil and ecclesiastical authorities.

During the next two or three decades, Hildegard produced the remainder of her major works, including the other two visionary writings, *Liber vitae meritorum* (a work of moral theology) and *Liber divinorum operum* (a work of exegesis, theology, and spiritual anthropology), as well as her musical compositions, shorter works in theology and medicine, and many letters. It was also the period in which she made preaching tours in the Rhineland area, speaking mostly to clerical or monastic audiences with a strong message of reform and renewal. Judging from the letters in which she describes her preaching, Hildegard (or rather the divine Light speaking through her) prophesied disasters for the church if repentance and reform did not follow. She seems to have regarded God's use of her, a weak woman, as his instrument partly as a sign of the degeneracy of her time, referring to it as a womanish age, in which male prelates and priests had failed, leaving only a woman to do God's will. Thus despite her assumption of such roles as preacher and prophetic teacher, which were usually reserved for male clerics, her attitudes toward the sexes seem to have been quite conventional. In her explication of the creation story in Genesis, for example, she contrasts the greater strength of men with the weaker power of women and emphasizes that man was created first and woman afterward.

During this time she also received a vision that impelled her to move herself and her community, against strong opposition, from the small enclosure at Disibodenberg to a convent at Rupertsberg, about thirty kilometers (nineteen miles) away, at the juncture of the Rhine with the Nahe at Bingen. This required major fund-raising as well as supervision of intensive building activity. The physical move was complete by about 1150, but financial arrangements between the new house and Disibodenberg were not complete until 1158. She died in 1179, shortly after a period of intense conflict over the alleged burial of an unreconciled excommunicated person in the convent's burial ground.

Most of her writing is not directly exegetical, although it reflects her lifelong immersion in Scripture through the rhythm of Benedictine worship, hearing the Psalms and other Scriptures recited on a daily basis as part of the *Opus Dei*. In all that she wrote and in her preaching and other public activity (so unusual for an enclosed female religious), her character as a visionary is preeminent, and her claim to be a conduit for the message of the Living Light is usually at the forefront. Her three most important works reflect her conviction of divine inspiration for her understanding of Scripture and ability to write about it and about God. Although she was not the only exegete of her day to claim to have received a charismatic infusion of knowledge about or understanding of the Bible, no other claimed to have received so much even of the fundamentals in this way or to be imparting directly the very words spoken in visions. Thus she did not so much offer her visions as a way of legitimating or authenticating her preaching and interpretation as claim them as the source of that preaching and interpretation. She claimed to speak not in her own voice but in that of the Living Light she saw in her visions; thus she wrote that in them she saw what she described as "the semblance of the Living Light, and just as the sun, moon, and stars appeared reflected in water, so the Scriptures, sermons, virtues, and some works formed by men shine in it for me" (see CCCM 91A: 258–65, esp. 261).

Her correspondents sometimes posed questions of scriptural interpretation, as in the *Solutiones triginta octo quaestionum* (*Answers to 38 Questions*), which contain queries on a variety of themes, including biblical queries, sent to her by a monk of Gembloux monastery. It might be also said that her three visionary writings are at least partly works of biblical interpretation, since the visions that she recounts are full of such scriptural imagery as the figure of the church as a mother, based on Rev. 12, and recount scriptural themes such as the fall of humankind and its redemption through Christ.

The last of them, the *Liber divinorum operum*, contains two main sections of interpretation, in which she explicates the prologue to John's Gospel (in part 1, vision 4, chap. 105) and the creation stories of Gen. 1–2 (in part 2, vision 1, chaps. 17, 57). Conventional Benedictine commentaries, such as those of her near-contemporary Rupert of Deutz, relied on a tradition of interpretation that reached back into the patristic period. So, for instance, Rupert's commentary on John draws extensively on St. Augustine's sermon series on the Fourth Gospel as well as on a traditional picture of the evangelist as writing to oppose various heresies, which Rupert identifies along with the passages designed to combat them. Hildegard, who did not share the education in the exegetical tradition given to the male religious, neither quotes Augustine or other church fathers nor shows any interest in ancient heresies. Instead, her verse-by-verse and phrase-by-phrase commentary relies on her visionary insights rather than the interpretations passed down in the exegetical tradition. She proceeds mostly by expansive paraphrase, as in her explication of John 1:1, which partly paraphrases it as: "In the beginning of the act of beginning, when the will of God just then opened itself to bring forth the fashioning of creatures, a will that was without a beginning in itself although it had not opened itself, the Word existed without a beginning of any act of beginning. 'And the Word was with God,' just as discourse exists in reason because reason has discourse within it, and discourse is in reason, and these are not divided from themselves" (CCCM 92:250–51). Sometimes in these paraphrases she even writes in the first person as though quoting God's words; for instance, her exegesis of the Johannine prologue begins, "I, Who Am without beginning and from Whom all beginnings procede and Who Am the Ancient of Days, say" (CCCM 92:248).

Respected widely in her own lifetime as a prophet and teacher, judging from the breadth of her correspondence, she nevertheless did not have a wide or long-lasting influence as an interpreter, judging from the manuscript circulation of her works. Certainly her idiosyncratic approach to scriptural exegesis did not influence either monastic or early scholastic writing on the Bible. It would be difficult for any exegete who could not claim to be the recipient of the same kind of revelation to imitate her interpretive style. Her work was widely distributed only in the form of excerpts emphasizing the apocalyptic aspect of her visionary theology, the *Pentachronon seu speculum futurorum temporum* (Five-Time Book, or, Mirror of Future Times [Prophecies]). As Barbara Newman points out, the *Pentachronon* survives in over a hundred manuscripts, while *Scivias* is extant in eleven and the *Liber divinorum operum* in four. Only in recent years has this unique woman become so widely known and popular, although it is not always clear whether the modern picture of Hildegard really bears much resemblance to the complex figure seen in her writings.

See also Elisabeth of Schönau (1129–65)

Bibliography

Davidson, Audrey E., ed. *The "Ordo virtutum" of Hildegard*. 38 pp. of music. Kalamazoo: Medieval Institute Pub., Western Michigan University, 1985.

Finlay, Barbara. "The Origins of Charisma as Process: A Case Study of Hildegard of Bingen." *Symbolic Interaction* 25, no. 4 (2002): 537–54.

Flanagan, Sabina. *Hildegard of Bingen, 1098–1179: A Visionary Life*. 2nd ed. London: Routledge, 1998.

Hildegard, St. *Hildegardis Bingensis Epistolarium*. Edited by Lieven Van Acker. Corpus Christianorum: Continuatio mediaevalis [CCCM] 91, 91A. Turnhout: Brepols, 1991, 1993. To be completed by Monika Klaes.

———. *Hildegardis Causae et curae*. Edited by Paul Kaiser. Leipzig: Teubner, 1903.

———. *Hildegardis Liber divinorum operum*. Edited by Albert Derolez and Peter Dronke. CCCM 92. Turnhout: Brepols, 1996.

———. *Hildegardis Liber vitae meritorum*. Edited by Angela Carlevaris. CCCM 90. Turnhout: Brepols, 1995.

———. *Hildegardis Scivias*. Edited by Adelgundis Führkötter and Angela Carlevaris. CCCM 43, 43A. Turnhout: Brepols, 1978.

———. *Hildegardis Solutiones triginta octo quaestionum*. Cols. 1037–54A in vol. 197 of Patrologia latina, edited by J.-P. Migne. Paris, 1882.

———. *Pentachronon*. In *La obra de Gebenón de Eberbach*. Edited by José Carlos Santos Paz. La tradizione profetica 2. Società Internazionale per lo Studio del Medioevo Latino. Florence: SISMEL, Edizioni del Galluzzo, 2004.

———. *Symphonia: A Critical Edition of the Symphonia armonie celestium revelationum*. Edited by Barbara Newman. Ithaca, NY: Cornell University Press, 1988.

Lerner, Robert E. "Ecstatic Dissent." *Speculum* 67, no. 1 (Jan. 1992): 33–57.

Maddocks, Fiona. *Hildegard of Bingen: The Woman of Her Age*. New York: Doubleday, 2001.

Newman, Barbara. "Commentary on the Johannine Prologue." *Theology Today* 60, no. 1 (April 2003): 16–33.

———. *Sister of Wisdom: St. Hildegard's Theology of the Feminine*. Berkeley: University of California Press, 1987.

———, ed. *Voice of the Living Light: Hildegard of Bingen and Her World*. Berkeley: University of California Press, 1998.

Page, Christopher, ed. *Abbess Hildegard of Bingen: Sequences and Hymns*. 27 pp. of music. Lustleigh, Newton Abbot, Devon, UK: Antico, 1983.

Young, Abigail Ann. "Mission and Message: Two Prophetic Voices in the Twelfth Century." Pages 19–30 in *Essays in Medieval Philosophy and Theology in Memory of Walter H. Principe, CSB: Fortresses and Launching Pads*, edited by James R. Ginther and Carl N. Still. Aldershot, UK: Ashgate, 2005.

— ABIGAIL YOUNG

Hopton, Susanna (1627–1709)

Susanna Hopton (née Harvey) was born in 1627 into a wealthy mercantile family of Westminster in England. Growing up during the English Civil Wars and Commonwealth, she converted by the early 1650s to Roman Catholicism, a move that she later attributed to "the Eclipse of the Church of *England*, and my own Youth" (Hopton, "Letter," 119). She was also greatly influenced by the respect that the priest who instructed her showed for her inquiring intellect. In 1655 she married the barrister Richard Hopton, who devoted considerable efforts to reconverting her to Anglicanism, encouraging her to compare in detail the doctrine, discipline, and liturgy of the two churches. She returned to the Church of England in about 1660, but her engagement with Catholicism remained the defining event in her spiritual life. She retained a lifelong interest in anti-Roman controversy, adapted Roman Catholic devotional works for Anglican use, and continued into her old age in the life of strict spiritual discipline, which she had begun as a Catholic. Although she had little or no understanding of classical or biblical languages and frequently lamented the defects of her education, she was much admired as having "attained to a very considerable Knowledge in Divinity" (Hopton, *Collection*, sig. A4v). After the Revolution of 1688, she allied herself with the nonjuring churchmen, that is, those who refused the oath of allegiance to William and Mary. She died at Hereford in 1709. During her life she anonymously published two popular books of daily prayers and offices, and more of her writings were published posthumously by her nonjuring associates.

Hopton's two biblically inspired works, *Meditations on the Creation* and *Meditations and Devotions on the Life of Christ*, were edited and published in 1717 by the nonjuring bishop Nathaniel Spinckes in a three-part collection of her writings. Both were originally compiled by Hopton at a much earlier date for her own use, and they arise directly from her devotional practices. This accounts for their partly derivative nature, freely adapting excerpts from her spiritual reading in both Catholic and Anglican authors, and for their affective rather than expository style. They are deeply indebted to the meditative techniques of the Counter-Reformation. Hopton's scriptural meditations are rarely concerned with doctrinal issues, even though she was an accomplished controversialist. Here her object is rather "to see the Beauty of the Scriptures, to perform the Duties taught, and to believe the Verities revealed" (213), and she defers in matters of belief to those in authority (240).

Meditations on the Creation, drawing on an hexameral tradition dating from patristic times, consists of six sections of meditations and prayers based on the days of the Genesis account. The purpose of the work is both to express and to prompt praise of God's goodness and power, and thanksgiving for the "Beauty, Profit, and Pleasure" of creation (32), ranging from admiration of the stars to gratitude for bees, whose "Wax maketh us Candles" (60). Wide-ranging scriptural quotations, sometimes combined into a cento of praise, are used to illustrate these themes, as in a reflection on the "wondrous manner" in which angels exercise their ministry (7). Hopton also strongly emphasizes the spiritual lessons to be drawn from applying the events of creation to the individual soul, whether in praying for light to illuminate spiritual darkness, or in learning from the birds to "sing thy Praises early in the Morning" (61).

The Life of Christ consists of devotions on the mysteries of the incarnation and the events of the Gospels. It mainly follows the narrative order of Matthew, supplemented by the other evangelists, but unlike *Creation* it makes little reference to other biblical books. Its aim is "the perfect Conformity of my Life to thine" (93), seeking first to make each incident "as present to my Understanding . . . as it was unto thy Disciples" (118) and then to find its devotional application: Christ was born "in a cold Night, in a poor Stable, . . . to teach us all divine Love and Mortification" (97). Frequently Hopton imagines herself as one of the Gospel characters, needing to be cleansed from leprosy (207), or returning as "thy prodigal Child" (203). Much of the longest section of the work focuses on the passion and combines an intense identification with Christ's suffering with a fervent avowal of personal sin, leading to "an Agony of Love" (243).

Although some sense of Hopton's character, such as her "Rashness and Inconsideration" (206), emerges from these personal devotions, she nowhere claims a specifically female perspective. Her long and celebratory account of "The Creation of Man" scarcely mentions Eve, and while *The Life of Christ* contains extended meditations on many biblical women—including the woman of Canaan (168–69), the woman of Samaria (214–15), and Mary Magdalene (220–22)—she also identifies with male characters such as the centurion (141) and Peter (258). It has been suggested that there are "glimmers" of a female spirituality in Hopton's writing (Wallace 112), but in the current absence of full analysis of her sources, or detailed evidence of the changes made by the male clerics who revised her works for publication, this position is difficult to substantiate.

Creation and *The Life of Christ*, unlike the two works of Hopton's published during her lifetime, were not reprinted, perhaps seeming dated by 1717 when both the devotional ethos of Anglicanism and the intellectual climate of biblical studies had changed radically since they were first drafted. Hopton herself had a flourishing posthumous reputation for learning and piety, and was included in compilations of the lives of celebrated women until the

265

mid-nineteenth century. Subsequently, however, her writings were neglected; during the twentieth century her authorship was questioned, at least in part on the grounds of her gender, and the attribution of *Creation* to the poet and author Thomas Traherne, Hopton's neighbor and contemporary, became widely accepted. More recent scholarship reverses this ascription and, amid emerging evidence of the depth of her theological expertise, Hopton's works are again attracting interest.

See also Eudocia Augusta, Aelia (ca. 400–460); Proba, Faltonia Betitia (ca. 320–ca. 370)

Bibliography

Ballard, George. *Memoirs of Several Ladies of Great Britain, Who have been Celebrated for their Writings or Skill in the Learned Languages Arts and Sciences.* Oxford: For the author, 1752.

[Hopton, Susanna]. *A Collection of Meditations and Devotions, in Three Parts.* London: For D. Midwinter, 1717. *Meditations on the Creation* and *Meditations and Devotions on the Life of Christ* reprinted in Smith, *Susanna Hopton*, I.

———. "A Letter written by a Gentlewoman of Quality to a Romish Priest upon her Return from the Church of *Rome* to the Church of *England*." Pages 118–52 in George Hickes, *A Second Collection of Controversial Letters.* London: For Richard Sare, 1710. Reprinted in Smith, *Susanna Hopton*, I.

Sauls, Lynn. "Traherne's Debt to Puente's *Meditations*." *Philological Quarterly* 50 (1971): 161–74.

Smith, Julia J., ed. *Susanna Hopton*, I and II. The Early Modern Englishwoman: A Facsimile Library of Essential Works; Series II, Printed Writings, 1641–1700: Part 4, vol. 7. Farnham, Surrey, UK: Ashgate, 2010.

———. "Susanna Hopton [née Harvey]." Pages 98–99 in vol. 28 of *Oxford Dictionary of National Biography*, edited by H. C. G. Matthew and Brian Harrison. Oxford: Oxford University Press, 2004.

———. "Susanna Hopton: A Biographical Account." *Notes and Queries* 236 (1991): 165–72.

Wallace, Charles. "The Prayer Closet as a 'Room of One's Own': Two Anglican Women Devotional Writers at the Turn of the Eighteenth Century." *Journal of Women's History* 9 (1997): 108–21.

—Julia J. Smith

Houghton, Louise Seymour (1838–1920)

On November 22, 1838, Louise Seymour was born in Piermont, New York; she married Elihu Reed Houghton in 1856. In addition to publishing books on topics as diverse as the unpublished memoirs of Napoleon I to teaching stories to children, Houghton first served as the associate editor, then editor, of *The Evangelist* and later as associate editor of *Christian Work*. She also contributed articles to many magazines and newspapers. Her time living in Europe and Palestine greatly influenced her writings, as seen by her translation of many German and French works into English, including a biography of St. Francis of Assisi, several Russian folktales, and a series on the life of Christ.

Houghton was educated at home and at the Utica Female Seminary, where she came into contact with critical biblical scholarship. In her writings she adopted some of the viewpoints of critical scholarship, such as the use of chiasmus as a compositional tool, the existence of Deutero-Isaiah, and the Documentary Hypothesis (*Hebrew Life*, 79, 96, 330–31). However, her goal was to harness these perspectives with a desire to make the setting and background of the Bible come alive for laypeople. Houghton emphasizes this value in *Telling Bible Stories* (39), a primer for mothers to help their children apprehend the principles taught in Old Testament stories: "Not the theologian but the mother must restore the Old Testament to the coming age." Her description of the life of Christ is essentially a harmony of the Gospels, intended to serve as a study aid and Sunday school companion, yet it also incorporates details of physical geography and the history of the Galilee region (*Life of the Lord*, 38). Her translation of a German version of a penitential prayer from the time of the Assyrian king Assurbanipal (seventh century BCE) reflects a comparable concern for bridging ancient contexts with the world of her readers. Houghton opines, "That the sense of sin is as old as self-consciousness becomes increasingly evident as history and psychology reveal more and more of the nature of man. The truth is confirmed by archaeology" ("The Penitent," 49). Her concern for using recent scholarly findings to illuminate Scripture peaked with *Hebrew Life and Thought*, where she used data such as the (then) recent discovery of the Mesha Stela and the Black Obelisk of Shalmaneser to construct a chronological framework for the ministry of the prophet Elisha, and the insights of nascent form criticism to discuss the role of folklore in the composition of Israel's historical narratives.

Houghton's reading of the Bible was wedded to a sensitive social conscience. After volunteering at the McAll Mission in France for three years, she became the director of the American McAll Association. Reflecting the influence of W. Rauschenbusch and Social Gospel advocates in New York, she became involved with the Settlement Housing movement, a group seeking to provide housing and education for low-income families.

Houghton's writings also reflect her social conscience, as seen in her exposition of biblical law. With varying degrees of effectiveness, Houghton pointed to a unique, high view of the status of women in the law, as seen in the rules circumscribing divorce, women's ability to inherit property, and the existence of women prophets. She used such biblical precedents to advocate for changes in the status of modern women, like raising the "age of consent" for young women: "From this slight survey it seems evident that the Mosaic code is in advance of any system of laws now in force so far as consideration for women is concerned, as the struggle good women are making in many states of our Union today to get the 'age of consent' raised above sixteen years, fourteen, even ten years, will suffice to indicate" (*Hebrew Life*, 359–60).

Houghton's greatest strength lay in her ability to popularize the writings of other scholars, whether through the work of translation or by harnessing them to her own writings for laypeople. Similarly, her concern for bridging biblical values with the lives of ordinary people evidences itself in her writings and in a lifelong social involvement, most concretely illustrated in her role as a charter member of the King's Daughters' Settlement House, now the Jacob A. Riis Neighborhood Settlement House, a youth and family resource center that continues to provide vital services to the poor in Western Queens, New York City.

Bibliography

Houghton, Louise Seymour. "The Cry of the Penitent. A Babylonian Prayer." *Biblical World* 22 (July 1903): 49–51.

———. *From Olivet to Patmos: The First Century in Picture and Story*. New York: American Tract Society, 1893.

———. *Hebrew Life and Thought: Being Interpretative Studies in the Literature of Israel*. Chicago: University of Chicago Press, 1906.

———. *The Life of the Lord Jesus. An Aid to the Study of the Gospel History of Jesus Christ*. Boston: Bible Study Pub., 1895.

Houghton, Louise Seymour, with T. T. Munger. *Telling Bible Stories*. New York: Charles Scribner & Sons, 1905.

— GORDON OESTE

Hrotsvit of Gandersheim (ca. 935–ca. 975)

One manuscript produced in Saxony late in the tenth century or early in the eleventh, the Emmeram-Munich Codex, provides nearly everything that is known about Hrotsvit. She was a canoness at the imperial abbey of Gandersheim, who in the second half of the tenth century wrote eight religious verse narratives, a brief prayer in verse, six plays, a poem depicting scenes from the Apocalypse, and two biographical/historical verse narratives—all in Latin. (Only one of the biographical/historical narratives is included in the Emmeram-Munich Codex; a third is attested in the sixteenth century but does not survive.) Throughout this manuscript, Hrotsvit introduces and contextualizes her writings with a series of prefaces, prologues, epilogues, invocations, and letters to patrons. She addresses her audience, asking for a sympathetic reading, describing her writing process, even commenting on her sources and purposes; she thanks the teachers, patrons, and critics who have supported her work, and she attributes everything that is good in what she has accomplished to God.

In the first preface Hrotsvit provides some information about her education. She names two teachers, Riccardis and her abbess, Gerberga, who was younger than Hrotsvit but "more advanced in learning." In the same preface, Hrotsvit specifies that Gerberga had introduced her to "the works of those writers whom she herself studied with learned men" (*Florilegium*, 19). To supplement what Hrotsvit says about her education, readers depend on the internal evidence of her writings, which indicate extensive familiarity with the Bible; exegetical writings (esp. commentaries of Augustine, Gregory, Alcuin, and Hrabanus [Rabanus] Maurus); other ecclesiastical writers (such as Tertullian, Venantius Fortunatus, and Cassian); hagiography; pagan and Christian writers (such as Terence [the only one she names], Virgil, Ovid, Seneca, Prudentius, Sedulius, Boethius, and Aldhelm); grammatical and metrical reference books; and pedagogical commentaries and glossaries.

The editorial apparatus that Hrotsvit provides specifies that the order of works in this manuscript is authorial and suggests the ordering mind of an interpreter who sees the Bible, biblical exegesis, and Christian literature as exemplars for her own creative and interpretive writing. Hrotsvit explains in her first preface, written in a rhythmical and rhyming prose:

> However difficult and arduous and complex / metrical composition may appear for the fragile female sex, / I, persisting / with no one assisting / still put together my poems in this little work / not relying on my own powers and talents as a clerk / but always trusting in heavenly grace's aid / for which I prayed, / and I chose to sing them in the dactylic mode / so that my talent, however tiny, should not erode, / that it should not lie dormant in my heart's recesses and be destroyed by slothful neglect's corrosion, / but that, struck by the mallet of eager devotion, / it bring forth a tiny little sound of divine praise / and, thus, if for no other purpose but for this case, / it may be transformed into an instrument of some utility / regardless of the limits of my ability. (*Florilegium*, 19–20)

This passage suggests that Hrotsvit sees herself as enacting the lesson of Christ's parable of the talents (Matt. 25:14–30) in her own life and writings: her talents will not "lie dormant" or be buried and useless as is the talent of the slothful servant in Matthew; rather, "trusting in heavenly grace's aid," she will use her talents to create songs of divine praise (Wilson, *Ethics*, 5, 7). Throughout her writings she invites a comparison of her own words and actions and the words and actions of her exemplary characters with examples in the Bible and in earlier Christian writings. As a whole her works can be described as allegorical interpretations of Scripture: in her writings virtuous Christians enact what is taught in Scripture, and these writings dramatize the promise of future glory for Christians resulting from God's uses of history and Christ's salvific act.

Hrotsvit names herself four times within the poems and plays and three times in the contextual writings. One of these references to herself, in the rhyming prose preface to her dramas, suggests the complexity of her self-identification as a writer and interpreter. She announces that she will imitate

Terence's Roman comedies, but substitute praise for the chastity of sacred virgins where Terence depicts the "shameless acts of lascivious women," and she names herself "Clamor Validus Gandeshemensis," Mighty Voice [Hrotsvit] of Gandersheim, giving the Latin translation of her Saxon name and inviting an identification with the zeal of John the Baptist ("ego vox clamantis," John 1:23), the patron saint of Gandersheim.

Scholars see not only autobiographical elements in the first-person statements that provide the context for the narratives and plays, but also larger order and meaning in the presentation of the texts as she has arranged them. The two stories that open her collection—first "Maria," a lengthy account of the birth of Mary, the incarnation, and the life of Christ through the flight into Egypt, followed by "The Ascension," a brief account of Christ's time with his apostles after his resurrection up to his ascension—in Stephen Wailes's words, "serve as prolegomena to the six that follow, as well as to the rest of her writings, by poetically constructing the age of Grace and of apostleship, the age in which she and her fellows lived" (55). In "Maria," the actions and attitudes of Joachim, Anna, Mary, and Joseph, especially prayers, hymns of praise, obedience to God's will, and faith in God's goodness and omnipotence—all provide models for the Christian behavior celebrated in all the works that follow. Christ's first words in "The Ascension" are closely related to Christ's words to his disciples in the final chapter of Matthew, when Christ tells the disciples what they must do after he leaves them:

> As the Father has sent Me forth, His dearly beloved Son, into the world, so do I also send you, my cherished friends. But you, going speedily to all nations, teach them the commandments of eternal life, purifying forthwith with the sacred water those who believe in the name of the Father, and likewise of the Son, and also of the Holy Ghost, that thus they may put off the stains of ancient guilt; and do ye by My power drive away various diseases and also compel by your authority the savage fiends to leave the cavern of the breast which they have invaded; preserve ever the sweetest charity toward such as would ever injure you in bitter hatred. (*Non-Dramatic Works*, 75–77)

These lessons about Christian behavior and apostolic responsibility permeate all the other narratives and plays, creating a work as a whole that invites readers to see the relevance of Christ's incarnation to their own daily lives and to accept the free gift of grace that can lead to their salvation.

For example, the third narrative tells the story of Gongolf, an eighth-century Frankish nobleman and valiant warrior whose exemplary behavior does not protect him from sorrow resulting from the maliciousness of an unfaithful wife and clerk. Sorrow and kindly justice guide Gongolf's response to their betrayal; when they proceed to murder him, the result is perpetual victory for Gongolf through martyrdom, gifts of healing for believers, and a choice between mercy and divine justice for the betrayers. After a devout man has urged the wife to confess her guilt and ask for pardon, Hrotsvit specifies, "Thus the unfortunate woman, bold deviser of crime that she was, refused to pay heed to these peaceable admonitions, *because she committed herself totally to transitory things and strove not to have any hope in imperishable goods*" (*Non-Dramatic Works*, 119, emphasis added). In a setting and time not very distant from her own, Hrotsvit provides an example of a central lesson of Christianity as articulated in Matt. 6:19–20, that devotion to things of this world results in only short-lived pleasure, while "hope in imperishable goods" leads to salvation. Each of the other verse narratives provides a new example of human choice between good and evil and of the greatness of God's love and mercy for those who trust in him.

Hrotsvit's plays provide a more remarkable context for her interpretation of the Bible. By crafting her narratives in dramatic form, calling the reader's attention to the parallels to Terence's comic drama with their "shameless acts of lascivious women," and selecting plots involving not only prostitution and attempted rape, but even necrophilia—thereby Hrotsvit involves her readers in the danger of thinking about and responding to the delight associated with human beauty and sexuality. Readers, or perhaps actors and audiences of readings or staged performances, then, experience similar choices to those enacted in the plays.

For example, in "Calimachus," Drusiana's beauty motivates Calimachus to try to seduce her and, after her death, to attempt to violate her body. However, after he dies and then is resurrected by St. John the Apostle, Calimachus expresses his new understanding in words reminiscent of Phil. 3:7–9: "All that I have done, I now despise and find appalling / —so much so that no love, no desire for life I find now enthralling / unless, reborn in Christ, I may merit to be transformed into a better man" (*Florilegium*, 61). Yet in Hrotsvit's play, Calimachus has more to learn, for he objects to the idea that Fortunatus should also be raised from the dead, as he and Drusiana were. Therefore he says, "Apostle of Christ, do not deem that traitor, that evildoer, worthy of regaining his breath / of absolving him from the chains of death, / him who deceived me, who seduced me, who prompted me to attempt that horrible deed!" (62). John then teaches him that God's grace is available to all, despite human sinfulness. Fortunatus, however, refuses the gift of grace: "If, as you say, Drusiana revived me and Calimachus is converted, then I renounce life and freely elect to die, for I would rather be dead / than see such an abundant spread / of the power of grace in them" (*Florilegium*, 64). Hrotsvit's play dramatizes the Christian truth that free will and grace are available to all. As Patricia Demers observes, the play's "reliance on scriptural symbology, paralleling of biblical episodes, and emulation of the psalmist's plea lend an undeniable authority to her depictions of conversion, repentance, and martyrdom" (36). All the plays and poetic narratives enact the choices, explain the doctrine, and dramatize the foolishness of denying Christ and worshiping or desiring the things of this world.

Even Hrotsvit's two historical narratives, "The Deeds of Otto" and the "Primordia," include some elements of biblical interpretation inasmuch as in these poems "political history is not significant unless it engages the sacred history of the Church" (Wailes 226). Moreover, Hrotsvit's depiction of women's roles in the historical narratives highlights a quality that runs through her works as a whole: women and men are equally responsible for their life choices. Both women and men are depicted as choosing wrongly *and* as choosing wisely. But very often the women in Hrotsvit's writings cooperate with the men who have political power, with the result that "political power can happily be imbued with spirituality" (226). And Hrotsvit herself uses her creative powers to encourage all Christians to emulate Mary, Jesus, saints, martyrs, and holy men and women with their free will and to join her in praising "the heavenly goodness of Christ, Who does not will to destroy sinners by the punishment they deserve, but rather to convert them and bring them back to eternal Life" (*Non-Dramatic Works*, 193).

Little evidence of Hrotsvit's influence survives between the tenth century and 1494, when German humanists found the Emmeram-Munich manuscript. Since the sixteenth century, she has influenced German and other European literature. However, her main influence has been as a creative writer, especially a playwright, rather than as an interpreter of the Bible.

Helene Homeyer's edition of Hrotsvit's works (*Hrotsvithae Opera*) provides extensive notes on allusions and verbal parallels to biblical, exegetical, and liturgical passages. Essays in Wilson's *Hrotsvit of Gandersheim: Rara Avis in Saxonia?* discuss Augustinian, Boethian, and liturgical elements in Hrotsvit's writings. Although Otten and Pollmann's *Poetry and Exegesis in Premodern Latin Christianity* does not include Hrotsvit among the authors studied, much of the discussion is relevant to an understanding of Hrotsvit as an interpreter of the Bible.

Bibliography

Demers, Patricia. *Women as Interpreters of the Bible*. New York: Paulist Press, 1992.

Dronke, Peter. "Hrotsvitha." Pages 55–83 in *Women Writers of the Middle Ages*. Cambridge: Cambridge University Press, 1984.

Hrotsvit of Gandersheim. *Hrotsvit of Gandersheim: A Florilegium of Her Works*. Translated by Katharina M. Wilson. Library of Medieval Women. Cambridge: D. S. Brewer, 1998.

———. *Hrotsvithae Opera: Mit Einleitung und Kommentar*. Edited by Helene Homeyer. Munich: Schöningh, 1970.

———. *Hrotsvit Opera omnia*. Edited by Walter Berschin. Bibliotheca scriptorum Graecorum et Romanorum Teubneriana. Munich: K. G. Saur, 2001.

———. *The Non-Dramatic Works of Hrotsvitha: Text, Translation, and Commentary*. Edited and translated by M. Gonsalva Wiegand. St. Meinrad, IN: Abbey, 1937.

Otten, Willemien, and Karla Pollmann, eds. *Poetry and Exegesis in Premodern Latin Christianity: The Encounter between Classical and Christian Strategies of Interpretation.* Supplements to Vigiliae christianae 87. Leiden: Brill, 2007.

Wailes, Stephen L. *Spirituality and Politics in the Works of Hrotsvit of Gandersheim.* Selinsgrove, PA: Susquehanna University Press, 2006.

Wilson, Katharina M. *Hrotsvit of Gandersheim: The Ethics of Authorial Stance.* Leiden: Brill, 1988.

———, ed. *Hrotsvit of Gandersheim: Rara Avis in Saxonia?* Medieval and Renaissance Monograph Series 7. Ann Arbor, MI: MARC [Medieval and Renaissance Collegium], 1987.

— PHYLLIS R. BROWN

Hume, Sophia Wigington (1702/3–74)

Sophia Wigington was born in Charleston, South Carolina, and became a Quaker minister, writer, and moral activist. Although brought up in the Anglican tradition of her father (Henry Wigington, a wealthy landowner who was deputy secretary of South Carolina), she was increasingly influenced by the faith of her Quaker maternal grandmother, Mary Fisher (ca. 1623–98), who had been one of the first two Quaker missionaries to arrive in Massachusetts in 1656. After the death of her husband, Robert Hume, in 1737, Sophia converted to the Society of Friends and moved to England to live among a larger Quaker community.

In 1748 Sophia Hume felt a spiritual call to revisit South Carolina. During this trip, she was appalled by what she perceived as pleasure-seeking, iniquitous lives made possible by slavery; hence she reproached the citizens of Charleston in a series of public meetings, calling them to a life of pious simplicity as exemplified in Quakerism. This led to the publication of her major work, *An Exhortation to the Inhabitants of the Province of South Carolina* (1747). In this work, she privileged the self-denial of Christ as a pattern to emulate. She particularly sought to use scriptural language and paraphrased quotations to assert that God desires sobriety and plainness. For instance, to denounce female vanity and pride in fashionable adornments, she quoted Isa. 3:16–24: "*The Daughters of* Zion *are haughty, and walk with stretched forth Necks, and wanton Eyes, walking, and mincing as they go, and making a tinkling with their Feet: Therefore, in that Day* (the Day of his Judgement), *saith the* Lord, *I will take away the Bravery of their tinkling Ornaments from about their Feet. . . . And it shall come to pass, that instead of well-set Hair, Baldness; instead of a Stomacher, a girding with Sackcloth; and Burning, instead of Beauty*" (40). She also reminds readers of Peter's warnings to women against vanity (1 Pet. 3:3–4): "Whose adorning let it not be that outward adorning of plaiting the Hair, and wearing Gold, or putting on of Apparel; but let it be with the hidden Man of the Heart, in that which is not corruptible, even the Ornament of a meek and quiet Spirit, which is in the Sight of GOD of great

Price" (41). Thus Hume selects appropriate sections of the Bible to give God's authority to her ascetic social message, her interpretation of how to live an honorable Christian life. Indeed, her writings aim to encourage holiness and practical piety among all professed Christians.

In later writings Hume continues to speak against pleasure-seeking diversions. In *A Caution to Such as Observe Days and Times* (1760), she warns those who observe holy days and yet still seek worldly pursuits—such as "Feasting, Card-playing, Dancing, Revelling, Wantonness, eating and drinking, rising up to play, foolish Jesting" (8)—that God can bring suffering among them as he did to the Jews who did not fear the Lord's power to judge. To this work, she appends *An Address to Magistrates, Parents, Mistresses of Families, etc.*, putting forward her message that those in positions of authority can reform society if they repent of their sins and enact lives of Christian responsibility by rebuking wayward neighbors, setting good examples, and acknowledging Christ. In this text, she urges magistrates—as well as parents, masters, and mistresses, their analogues in homes and businesses—"to suppress or punish" those who engage in "Drunkenness, Oaths, Prophaneness, Debaucheries of All Kinds" (8). Such lists of "works of the flesh" or "Acts of the Sinful Nature," as listed in Gal. 5:19–21, are a common feature of Hume's writings. At the same time, in her works she also repeats that the Christian soul can come to recognize and enjoy the "Fruits of the Spirit" (Gal. 5:22–23) through denial of earthly pleasures.

In *A Short Appeal to Men and Women of Reason: . . . Who may be walking according to the Course of this evil World, living in the Pleasures thereof, and frequenting THEATRES, BALLS, &c.* (1765), Hume particularly attacks theatergoing. In this text, she paraphrases Phil. 2 to highlight again the self-denying character of Christ, who "for our Sakes, left the Glories of Heaven, and contemning the Glories of Earth, refused, not only all worldly Honours and Emoluments, but deny'd himself the common Accommodations of Life" (4). Consistent with this ascetic philosophy, Hume asserts that Christians are soldiers who must be "sober and vigilant" and "endure Hardness" (7).

In 1766 Hume published a collection of early Quaker writings titled *Extracts from Divers, Antient [Ancient] Testimonies* (1760? 1766?). This was an attempt to promote Quakerism during a time when membership was in decline. Her introductory comments reflect the principal message of all of Hume's writings and urge readers to live upright, nonworldly lives. A year later, she returned to Charleston in a bid to revive Quakerism in the land of her birth. The trip was not fruitful, and she returned to England, where she died in 1774.

Hume's writings call society to repentance and soberness. She urges all Christians to turn away from earthly temptations and gratifications and to live simple lives, as pursued by Quakers. Her works stress the self-denial of Christ, the spiritual benefits of plainness, the universal nature of God's grace, and the dwelling of the Holy Spirit within each human. Although Hume retained a conservative attitude about women's roles, she stepped out of a traditional role, empowered by her religious convictions, and used her knowledge of Scripture to write, publish, and preach publicly about her views on how religion could reform society for the honor of God.

Bibliography

Bowden, J. *The History of the Society of Friends in America.* Vol. 1. London: Charles Gilpin, 1850.

Greene, Dana. "Sophia Hume." In vol. 2, F to Le, of *American Women Writers: A Critical Reference Guide from Colonial Times to the Present in Four Volumes,* edited by Lina Mainiero. New York: Frederick Ungar, 1980.

Hume, Sophia. *A Caution to Such as Observe Days and Times: To which is added An Address to Magistrates, Parents, Mistresses of Families, etc.* [London, 1760? 1763?] 4th ed. Bristol: E. Farley, 1765.

―――. *An Exhortation to the Inhabitants of the Province of South Carolina, to Bring Their Deeds to the Light of Christ, in Their Own Consciences.* Philadelphia: W. Bradford, [1747].

―――. *Extracts from Divers Antient [Ancient] Testimonies.* [London: Luke Hinds, 1760.] [Wilmington, DE: James Adams, 1766.]

―――. *A Short Appeal to Men and Women of Reason: . . . Who may be walking according to the Course of this evil World, living in the Pleasures thereof, and frequenting THEATRES, BALLS, &c.* Bristol: E. Farley, 1765.

Larson, Rebecca. *Daughters of Light: Quaker Women Preaching and Prophesying in the Colonies and Abroad, 1700–1775.* New York: Knopf, 1999.

Spruill, Julia Cherry. *Women's Life and Work in the Southern Colonies.* Chapel Hill: University of North Carolina Press, 1938.

— NANCY JIWON CHO

Hussey, Mary Inda (1876–1952)

On June 17, 1876, Mary Inda Hussey was born into a Quaker family at New Vienna, Ohio. In 1890 the family moved to Richmond, Indiana, where Hussey completed her secondary education. She attended Earlham College in the same town. After graduation, Hussey received a scholarship from the Society of Friends to pursue graduate studies in Semitic languages and the civilizations of the ancient Near East at Bryn Mawr College. Beginning with Hebrew, Hussey's mastery of ancient languages spread to encompass Arabic, Akkadian (Assyrian and Babylonian), Sumerian, Ethiopic, and Egyptian. Through the course of her studies, she came to focus on Sumerian and Assyro-Babylonian studies. Hussey's studies took her to the universities of Pennsylvania, Berlin, and Leipzig, and she received her doctoral degree from Bryn Mawr in 1906.

Hussey accepted an appointment as instructor in biblical history at Wellesley College in 1907, before moving to Cambridge, Massachusetts, to work at the Harvard Semitic Museum in 1911. In 1913 Hussey was appointed to a post in the Department of Biblical History and Literature at Mount Holyoke College. She remained at Mount Holyoke until 1941, retiring with the status of professor emeritus. After she retired, Hussey returned to teach classes in the history of religions at Wellesley College when Gordon B. Wellman died suddenly. Beyond her tenure at these institutions, Hussey also served as annual professor at the American School of Oriental Research in Jerusalem (1931–32), the first woman invited to hold this post. She died of heart failure on June 20, 1952, in Andover, Massachusetts.

The bulk of Hussey's research and writing concerns the collation, translation, and criticism of Sumerian and, to a lesser degree, Akkadian texts. Her interests were largely historical, literary, and religious. In the classroom, however, Hussey's talents were often deployed in the areas of biblical studies and religious studies. During her tenure at Mount Holyoke College, she began to compile a sourcebook on lesser known religious traditions in the world. Sadly, this work was never completed.

The work that Hussey did in the area of biblical interpretation, in keeping with her historical and comparative interests, sought to clarify matters relating to the world of the Bible (see, e.g., "Excavations"). In one article she explains the historical circumstances surrounding the genesis of the appellation "Pharisee" ("Origin"). Hussey argues that the term, derived from a root denoting separation, is used to imply a lack of patriotic fervor. It was coined to qualify the Hasideans, a group promoting a greater degree of separation from non-Jews, for their willingness to be reconciled with a government enjoying the sponsorship of foreigners (the Seleucids) in the second century BCE, because of their willingness to *be separated* from a movement toward a true independence.

A second example of Hussey's contribution to biblical interpretation may be seen in her review of her work on Babylonian historical documents and artifacts for the *Mount Holyoke Alumnae Quarterly* ("Tablets"). Hussey's explorations of the temple of Sin in Ur of the Chaldees (Gen. 11:28; 15:7) reveal that sun-dried bricks were the building material of choice and in abundance on the alluvial plain that is Babylonia. Elsewhere in the review, Hussey speaks of the customary practice of placing a commemorative inscription at the corner of a temple following an act of restoration. The particular document under scrutiny was commissioned by Sin-gashid, king of Erech (Gen. 10:10), who ruled from 2150 to 2110 BCE. In such manner, Hussey's explorations in the cultures and lands of the Hebrew Bible define the historical context of that world, transporting the Bible reader beyond the confines of twentieth-century America.

As observed in her own conclusion to the review, Hussey's scholarship, along with the archaeological research of her time, was ancillary to the practice of biblical interpretation. While not often directly concerned with religious interests in Bible reading, Hussey's scholarship certainly inspired the imagination of the reader in fleshing out the world of, for example, the patriarchs. In her own words, such an approach makes it possible "to think historically about the Old Testament by removing the nation Israel and the Bible from a position of isolation and placing them among the peoples and the literature of the ancient world" ("Tablets," 216). As evidenced by her close association with such prestigious learned societies as the American School of Oriental Research, Hussey stands out as one of the first women to achieve broad recognition in the field of ancient Near Eastern studies.

Bibliography

Hussey, Mary Inda. "Babylonian Tablets." *Mount Holyoke Alumnae Quarterly* 1 (1918): 211–16.

———. "Origin of the Name Pharisee." *Journal of Biblical Literature* 39 (1920): 66–69. http://www.jstor.org/stable/3260113?seq=1.

———. "Recent Excavations in Mesopotamia as Related to the Teaching of the Bible." *Journal of the National Association of Biblical Instructors* 1 (1933): 19–22.

Myers, Jennie. "Mary Inda Hussey." Brown University, n.d. http://brown.edu/Research/Breaking_Ground/bios/Hussey_Mary%20Inda.pdf.

—BERNON LEE

Hutchinson, Anne (1591–1643)

Anne Marbury Hutchinson, born and raised in Alford, Lincolnshire, England, was the second of thirteen children born to Francis and Bridget Marbury (Francis also had three children by a previous marriage). She married merchant William Hutchinson in 1612 and gave birth to fifteen children (1613–36). Because neither she nor any sympathizer kept records of her, and because she came into controversial public notice only in 1636–38, much of what can be said of her education and background must be conjectured. She likely learned to read in her father's household, but it is unclear whether she learned to write; no known document in her handwriting survives. By the 1620s, Hutchinson and her family came under the influence of popular Puritan minister John Cotton in Boston, Lincolnshire. When Cotton (and Hutchinson's brother-in-law John Wheelwright) emigrated to Boston in Massachusetts Bay in 1633, fleeing persecution by Archbishop William Laud, Hutchinson "was much troubled concerning the ministry under which [she] lived" (Ditmore 391). With her family (and biblical encouragement), Hutchinson migrated to Massachusetts Bay in 1634 to be once again under Cotton's ministry. Although her membership was delayed a week, due to suspicion about her opinions, she become a prominent member in the Boston church.

Hutchinson's story is inseparable from the Antinomian or Free Grace Controversy. The entire colony, and the Boston church in particular, became increasingly embroiled in theological and ecclesiastical conflict in the mid-1630s, signaled in part by the election of young newcomer Sir Henry Vane as governor in October 1635. There was considerable tension, and sometimes arcane debate, surrounding soteriology and the nature of church membership, pitting Cotton against several colleagues. Hutchinson became well known among the dissidents; concurrently, she had held conventicles (Bible study and prayer meetings) in her house, attracting at its peak sixty to eighty participants, segregated by gender (with Hutchinson teaching the women). Precisely what transpired at these meetings cannot be established with certainty. They likely began as repetitions and elaborations of sermon outlines, but it seems probable that Hutchinson sometimes diverged, either to offer her own exegesis or to criticize the qualifications of other ministers in the colony.

In October 1636 Hutchinson was invited to share her views with a group of non-Boston ministers. Nothing immediate came of it, but its substance formed the basis of her civil trial a year later. Meanwhile, Wheelwright fomented public passions with an incendiary fast-day sermon on January 19, 1636/37; invited to preach as a conciliatory gesture, Wheelwright only enflamed and divided listeners, and eventually he was charged with sedition and contempt.

Despite several attempts at reconciliation, tensions increased. The civil authorities called for the colony's first synod, held from August 30 to September 22, 1637, to restore order. The synod identified eighty-two errors rampant in the colony and issued resolutions, including a prohibition against Hutchinson's conventicles. But the synod's resolutions did not quell tension, and Hutchinson continued with the meetings. By November 2, the General Court—on the reelection of the old guard—reasserted its authority by arresting, trying, and punishing several dozen dissidents, including Hutchinson. She was charged with disturbing the peace, violating an express order of the "general assembly," and traducing the established ministers for lacking the spirit of Christ. However, she skillfully parried with the court for two days before interrupting with an "immediate revelation," a blistering, Scripture-laden confession that ultimately sealed her fate. In it she quoted—indirectly and directly, sometimes verbatim—from several Bible passages, stemming mostly from the Geneva Bible and its notes. This speech suggests the solitary character of her Bible study and the possibility that she employed the Bible for prognostication; more important, she indirectly confirmed the accusation that she found other New England ministers to be lacking the seal of the Spirit. She ended with a bold prophetic curse on the court and its posterity. The court banished her.

During house confinement in Roxbury, Hutchinson was visited by several ministers, especially Cambridge's Thomas Shepard, who inquired further into her theological and biblical views. By March 1638 Boston church authorities brought her to trial for heterodox opinions. Despite sketchiness and a combative atmosphere, the trial notes give the clearest picture of Hutchinson's exegetical and theological practices and views. Drawing on Eccles. 3:18–21 and other passages, Hutchinson denied the soul's immortality and questioned a bodily resurrection but conceded error when instructed and convinced. The first day ended in a formal admonition against her. A week later, Hutchinson made a retraction but then hedged by saying that her "expression" but not her "judgment" had changed. The result was excommunication for lying.

The Hutchinson family and others moved to Aquidneck (now Portsmouth), Rhode Island; shortly afterward, she experienced a spontaneous menopausal abortion, the graphic description of which was circulated against her. After her husband's death, and fearing that Massachusetts Bay would annex the territory, Hutchinson and other family members in 1642 removed to what is now Westchester County, New York, where they were caught in crossfire between Dutch settlers and Indians in Governor Kieft's War. In late summer of 1643, most of the group was slaughtered by an Indian band.

Because Hutchinson's activities were controversial and covert, it is difficult to reconstruct the extent of her biblical interpretation. She is best known as an example of a Protestant laywoman, excluded from the official channels of interpretation and print but firmly and daringly committed to *sola scriptura*, private and group Bible study, hearing sermons (albeit with a critical ear), and speaking her mind when challenged. Since she left no written record (and almost all the material about her derives from detractors), her influence per se was negligible, except as a martyr on behalf of lay interpretation and practice. But from her two trials, the following generalizations may be gleaned about her practices. First, she was entirely untrained in any language other than English; second, she appears to have had no familiarity with traditions or commentaries other than what she derived from Puritan sermons and the Geneva Bible notes. But from close textual study, she influentially shared insights with other women in her community and possessed a keen, independent mind for close exegesis and theological extraction.

Bibliography

Ditmore, Michael G. "A Prophetess in Her Own Country: An Exegesis of Anne Hutchinson's 'Immediate Revelation.'" *William and Mary Quarterly* 57, no. 2 (April 2000): 349–92.

Hall, David D., ed. *The Antinomian Controversy, 1636–1638: A Documentary History.* 2nd ed. Durham, NC: Duke University Press, 1990.

LaPlante, Eve. *American Jezebel: The Uncommon Life of Anne Hutchinson, The Woman Who Defied the Puritans.* San Francisco: HarperSanFrancisco, 2004.

Winship, Michael P. *Making Heretics: Militant Protestantism and Free Grace in Massachusetts, 1636–1641.* Princeton, NJ: Princeton University Press, 2002.

Winthrop, John. *The Journal of John Winthrop, 1630–1649.* Edited by Richard S. Dunn, James Savage, and Laetitia Yeandle. Cambridge, MA: Harvard University Press, 1996.

— MICHAEL G. DITMORE

279

Hutchinson, Lucy (1620–81)

Lucy Hutchinson, born in 1620 in London, was the daughter of Sir Allen Apsley, lieutenant of the Tower of London. While her father provided her with an excellent education for a woman in the seventeenth century, including extensive training in Latin, her mother encouraged Lucy Hutchinson's later Puritan convictions. She married John Hutchinson in 1638, with whom she had eight children. The majority of her married life was spent in Owthorpe, Nottinghamshire. She and her husband were staunch Republicans, supporting Parliament during the English Civil War (1642–49). After the restoration of Charles II to the English throne in 1660, John Hutchinson was imprisoned for his activities in supporting the Protectorate, including signing the 1649 death warrant for Charles I. The events of the war and his imprisonment are chronicled in her best-known work, the manuscript biography of her husband, "The life of John Hutchinson of Owthorpe." Later published as *Memoirs*, Hutchinson's biography offers both a detailed account of this period of English history and a defense of her husband and his actions. Hutchinson produced an astonishing range of writings, including a translation of Lucretius's *De rerum natura*; a commonplace book authored jointly by her husband and herself; a religious treatise composed for her daughter and published in 1817, titled *On the Principles of the Christian Religion*; manuscript elegies to her husband; a previously lost autobiographical manuscript (compiled by Lucy from her husband's notes) published in 1806; and an epic poem, *Order and Disorder: or, The world made and undone, being meditations upon the creation and fall, as it is recorded in the beginning of Genesis*. Hutchinson died in 1681; her memory as a woman writer lives on largely through the *Memoirs* and Victorian accounts of notable women, which emphasize her devotion to her husband (Norbrook, "Lucy Hutchinson").

While Hutchinson's *Memoirs* offer a providential, biblically inflected narrative of the war and John Hutchinson's Christlike heroism and suffering, Lucy Hutchinson's biblical commentary is clearest in some of her least-known works, including her and John's commonplace book, the treatise to her daughter, and her poem *Order and Disorder*. Although Hutchinson in *Memoirs* describes herself as a mere copyist of the scriptural commonplace book appended to the manuscript biography of her husband, on rare occasions it appears that she may have taken a slightly more active, if still very limited, role in compiling the document. As a source text for understanding the mechanics of scriptural interpretation that underlie the providential and biographical narratives that Hutchinson constructs in *Memoirs* and in some of her elegies, however, the manuscript is an invaluable and understudied resource. By her own testimony, Hutchinson compiled this fifty-seven-page book from the Bible annotations her husband made during his imprisonment in 1663–64. The bulk of the book consists of transcriptions of more than 1,100 Bible verses organized under seventy-one headings and subheadings. While some of these categories engage generic matters of morality or doctrine, a significant number assert typological and quasi-typological correspondences between scriptural history and prophecy on the one hand, and the actors and events of the English Civil War and its aftermath on the other hand.

In some instances, groups of Scriptures memorialize John Hutchinson's immediate reactions to his daily experiences. One collection of verses, for example, records "some Scriptures paralleled to the persecutions of that day." Other groups of verses appear to have been accumulated over time or to have been compiled through retrospective reflections on experiences spanning periods of months or years. One such section, "In reference to an ungratefull Peere & others these might be marked," reflects on John Hutchinson's gracious service to, and subsequent betrayal by, his Nottinghamshire peers. Rather than merely grouping together collections of verses based on a similarity of theme, other sections pursue more complex narrative lines of development. The verses compiled under the head "Upon a Mighty Adversary," for example, construct a genealogy of Old Testament rulers that the Hutchinsons apparently would have their readers map onto the Caroline kings Charles I and II.

The longest and most intricate section of the commonplace book documents the hermeneutic processes supporting John Hutchinson's millenarian beliefs. During the time of his Restoration imprisonment, Hutchinson tells us elsewhere, her husband "discovered" that Christ's second coming would be visible rather than spiritual in nature (*Memoirs*, 286). The first 76 of the 160 total verses transcribed in the commonplace book section titled "Concerning the Glorious kingdome of Christ and the restoration of the seed of Abraham to serve him then these places were markd" alternate, in groups, between the Old and New Testaments in traditional typological fashion; they assert the second coming as the completion of the incarnation and adduce evidence for its visible nature and timing and the portents that will herald it. Taken together, John Hutchinson's reading of Scripture and providential interpretation of his life events combined to convince him and his wife, Lucy, that they and their revolutionary contemporaries were the earthly saints preparing the way for Christ's millennial reign on earth.

On the Principles of the Christian Religion (written ca. 1673) engages less overtly with the history of the English Civil War. Hutchinson humbly presents this work to her daughter as a collection of materials gathered from the Bible and "many [other] bookes already written" (1). Yet the tract's polemical engagement in contemporary religious controversies, its biographical allusions to Hutchinson's own spiritual development, and its consideration of the role of women as scriptural interpreters and teachers all lend political, historical, and social interest to the text. Embracing the conventional Protestant belief that all points of doctrine that are necessary to the individual's salvation are accessible in the Bible, Hutchinson recounts the foundational principles of her Calvinist faith, often citing Scripture in the text and marginalia as authorities. Among the topics covered are the natures of God and man; the respective roles of the Father, Son, and Holy Spirit in the creation; the fall and its consequences; the workings of divine providence, both universal and particular, and the necessity of submitting to it; predestination and the stages of spiritual progress undergone by the elect; the covenants of law and grace; the typological relationship between the Old and New Testaments; the threefold nature of God; the union of humans with Christ; and the role of reason, and its limits, in devotion.

Hutchinson's authorship of the tract appears to have been motivated by her recognition that her own insufficient understanding of essential doctrine had made her susceptible to the sinful "wrest[ing]s" of Scripture by "deviding seducers" (4), or sectarians, of her time. The "stumbling block[s]" (6) that these false professors laid in her way, she testifies, prevented her for a long time from attaining true faith (4), a fact to which she similarly attests in *Memoirs*. Hutchinson calls on her daughter to remain vigilant against such factionalists, whom she claims are now more numerous than at any time in the church's history. Hutchinson particularly attacks the doctrines of Roman Catholicism and Arminianism, but she also offers more general invectives against beliefs held by others of her radical English contemporaries.

Invoking 2 Tim. 3:6–7, Hutchinson notes the particular susceptibility of the female sex, with its inferior capacity for knowledge and judgment, to teachers of false doctrine. Unlike other writers of the time, however, Hutchinson does not counsel her daughter to submit herself wholly in matters of faith to male authority; rather, she urges that "every wise and holy woman ought to watch strictly over herself" (6). Later in the tract, she argues further for the role of women, and herself in particular, as scriptural interpreters and educators. Although she acknowledges that her daughter, as a consequence of her marriage, is now "under another's authoritie" (90), Hutchinson asserts that it is still her duty as a mother to safeguard her children's souls, a duty that she claims the Bible affirms. Although she admits that *Principles* is not as methodically organized as other books she might recommend, she defends the work as a faithful expression of true doctrine. She also urges her daughter to instruct her own children and servants, for in this way her knowledge will be advanced along with theirs.

Lucy Hutchinson's major literary work is her twenty-canto epic poem, *Order and Disorder*, which she describes as "meditations" on Genesis. An unfinished biblical epic, *Order and Disorder* poetically renarrates Genesis up to chapter 31. Only the first five cantos were published in 1679; the bulk of the narrative remained in manuscript until David Norbrook attributed it to Hutchinson in 1999. Written in rhyming couplets, the poem offers a counter to John Milton's own biblical epic, *Paradise Lost*, first published in 1667; Hutchinson's preface seems to explicitly critique Milton's engagement of the Bible in *Paradise Lost*, declaring that she will stay closer to the biblical narrative and substance of the Bible: her preface rejects poetic renderings of other poets who need to "take heed" to "avoid adoring figments of their own brains, instead of the living and true God" (3–4).

Her extensive use of marginal Bible citations in the first five cantos of the poems follows the convention of biblical commentary, though it also gestures to the innovation that will mark her "meditations" on Genesis. Only a small percentage of these (3 out of 129 biblical references) quote a biblical line; the majority underscore a particular theological point through a chain of cited biblical verses with the effect of highlighting Hutchinson's theme. Canto 1 deploys these densely layered references to establish her trinitarian beliefs, a theological concept under increasing pressure by the end of the seventeenth century. In addition to underscoring her theological positions, Hutchinson as poet draws on imagery from cited biblical texts, as in the canto 2 citation of Job 37:18; Hutchinson reworks "Hast thou with him spread out the sky, strong, as a molten looking glass?" into her account of creation, where the "liquid skies the solid world enclosed, / To magnify the almighty hand / That makes thin floods like rocks of crystal stand" (28–30). The spreading skies in Job become the enclosure of the "solid world" by the "liquid skies" in Hutchinson's lines. The reflective aspects of Job's "molten looking glass" become "rocks of crystal" in Hutchinson; the crystal maintains the reflective quality of the looking glass while compounding its strength through the imagery of "rocks." The creation of the world, the most remarkable illustration of God's power, thus resonates with the local and the larger message in the verse and book of Job.

Hutchinson's complex weaving of biblical imagery and themes belies the conservative stance she articulates about using Genesis in her preface; instead, she offers some remarkable innovations on biblical premises. Two of her most radical interventions into Genesis include her representation of the marriage scene between Adam and Eve and her rewriting of maternal authority in the earliest and later chapters of Genesis. As all biblical commentators must, Hutchinson reconciles the Priestly version of creation in Gen. 1, in which undifferentiated "man" is created and given "dominion," with the Yahwist version in Gen. 2, where Adam and then Eve are created. Unlike some of her contemporaries, Hutchinson fuses the two narratives within the marriage scene to clarify that "dominion" is awarded to both Adam and Eve during the marriage ceremony: God jointly gives to them "right to all her fruits and plants, / Dominion over her inhabitants" (3.421–22). This fusion of the account of domination in Gen. 1 with the celebration of marriage in Gen. 2 combines with a maternal authority or "possession" (6.26) that Hutchinson's text asserts over children, one accomplished by conflating the "one flesh" created through marriage with reproduction itself: "When marriage male and female doth combine, / Children in one flesh shall two parents join" (3.415–16). Hutchinson's citations of Matt. 19; Eph. 5; and Gen. 2 actually underscore her significant revision of the account of marriage as "the two shall become one flesh" since all these scriptural references relate the image of "one flesh" to marriage alone, not just to procreation.

Hutchinson's revision of biblical commentary on marriage appears to enable greater maternal authority in the text: Hutchinson specifies that Eve names Cain and Abel, an addition to Gen. 4:1 then expanded in her modification of biblical language identifying children's family lines. Throughout her poem, she introduces mothers who were erased from paternally derived familial lines in the Bible, as here she asserts in the lineage derived through Rebecca: Esau "brings from thence / Bathemath whom Nebajoth's mother bore, / Ishmael's fair daughter" (18.338–40); in this description of descent, the biblical source text had omitted the "mother," whom Hutchinson adds back into her biblical poem.

Hutchinson's production in a range of genres, from theological tract to biography to epic poem, underscores her significance in seventeenth-century biblical interpretation and debate.

Bibliography

Hutchinson, Lucy. *Memoirs of the Life of Colonel Hutchinson*. London: Longman, Hurst, Rees, & Orme, 1806. Repr., London: Everyman Library, 1995.

———. *On the Principles of the Christian Religion, Addressed to Her Daughter; and On Theology*. London: Longman, Hurst, Rees, Orme, & Brown, 1817.

———. *Order and Disorder*. Edited by David Norbrook. Malden, MA: Blackwell Pub., 2001.

———. *Order and Disorder: or, The world made and undone*. London: n.p., 1679.

———. "Scriptural Commonplace Book." Ms. DD/HU4. Nottinghamshire Archives, Nottingham, UK.

Norbrook, David. "'A devine Originall': Lucy Hutchinson and the 'Woman's Version.'" *Times Literary Supplement*, March 19, 1999, 13–15.

———. Introduction to *Order and Disorder*. Malden, MA: Blackwell Pub., 2001.

———. "Lucy Hutchinson." Pages 25–28 in vol. 29 of *Oxford Dictionary of National Biography*, edited by H. C. G. Matthew and Brian Harrison. Rev. ed. Oxford: Oxford University Press, 2004–11.

— SHANNON MILLER AND PATRICIA CROUCH

Jackson, Rebecca Cox (1795–1871)

Rebecca Cox Jackson was born near Philadelphia to free African American parents and raised in the Methodist tradition. She and her husband, Samuel S. Jackson, resided with her widowed brother Joseph Cox, an elder at Bethel African Methodist Episcopal (AME) Church in Philadelphia. Jackson earned money as a seamstress; her husband's occupation is unknown. The couple was childless. In 1830, during a thunderstorm, Jackson had a powerful conversion experience. A year later she felt called to celibacy. She feared violence from her husband, who opposed this decision, and later separated from him.

During the first part of her adult life, Jackson was illiterate, but she credited God with the miraculous gift of literacy. Reasoning that God "learned the first man [Adam] to read," she picked up a Bible and began to read from the book of James (*Gifts of Power*, 108). Jackson reports that she, like Jeremiah and Ezekiel, was chosen to speak to God's people (183).

As an itinerant preacher in Pennsylvania, New Jersey, and New York, Jackson encountered resistance from Methodist, AME, and Presbyterian clergymen. Some opposed women's preaching, but a greater source of contention was Jackson's promotion of celibacy for married persons. Jackson was drawn to the United Society of Believers in Christ's Second Appearing (Shakers), which espoused celibacy and supported women's leadership roles. In 1843 she joined the Shaker community in Watervliet, New York, where she resided on several occasions. She was later appointed as a Shaker eldress.

Between 1831 and 1864 Jackson kept a private journal recounting life events and her thoughts, dreams, and visions. Her memoir frequently employs imagery from the book of Revelation, such as the Lamb, the seven trumpets, and the new Jerusalem. Female figures—apart from Eve, the Virgin Mary, and divine symbolic women like the bride (Rev. 21:2) and Wisdom (Prov. 8:1)—receive strikingly little attention. Abraham's wife, Sarah, appears twice, once wearing a Shaker cap (172). Jackson wrestles with conflicting Bible passages about marriage and celibacy, reconciling the discrepancy between her call to celibacy and the words of 1 Tim. 2:15 that woman "shall be saved in childbearing." She uses Paul's words encouraging unmarried women to be "holy, both in body and in spirit" (1 Cor. 7:34), to argue for the superiority of the celibate state (180). Commenting on Gen. 1:28, Jackson says that God made Eve "Lordess" over the earth, sharing dominion with Adam, for "God blessed them both and gave them one authority" (279). The Lord breathed the breath of life into Adam's two nostrils, rather than his one mouth, in order to breathe two spirits into Adam—the male Spirit and the female Spirit, which dwelt in Eve when she was taken out of Adam's side (279). Woman's subjection to man (Gen. 3:16) no longer applies in Jackson's day, since womankind is now redeemed by the Holy Spirit (279).

Jackson's interpretation of the creation of male and female in God's image (Gen. 1:27) was influenced by the Shaker doctrine of male and female persons of the Deity. Jackson prays to "Heavenly Parents": God the Father and Holy Mother Wisdom, whom she calls "a Mother in the Deity" (154). She draws from the book of Proverbs to speak of Wisdom as the Mother of creation. In Prov. 9:3, Wisdom sends out her maidens to invite people to her feast. Jackson interprets Wisdom's "maidens" not as servants but as daughters. She believes that this prophesies events in her own lifetime, "the day that Solomon wrote of," when women are sent out to preach and teach, supported by a divine loving mother (264). Jackson reports a glorious vision of Mother Wisdom, with wings and a crown like the cosmic woman in Rev. 12 (168).

Despite initial opposition from the Watervliet Shakers, Jackson and her friend Rebecca Perot (d. 1901) founded and led a small predominantly African American Shaker community in Philadelphia. She later received their blessings on this endeavor. The Philadelphia community, founded in 1851, endured for more than thirty years after Jackson's death in 1871. The Shakers preserved Jackson's memoirs, consisting of two original manuscripts in her own hand, as well as copies edited by prominent Shaker leader Alonzo G. Hollister (1830–1911). The memoirs received renewed attention after Jean McMahon Humez edited and published them in 1981. Excerpts from Jackson's writings regularly appear in anthologies of African American women's writings.

Bibliography

Conner, Kimberly Rae. *Conversions and Visions in the Writings of African-American Women*. Knoxville: University of Tennessee Press, 1994.

Jackson, Rebecca Cox. *Gifts of Power: The Writings of Rebecca Jackson, Black Visionary, Shaker Eldress*. Edited by Jean McMahon Humez. Amherst: University of Massachusetts Press, 1981.

Madden, Etta M. *Bodies of Life: Shaker Literature and Literacies*. Westport, CT: Greenwood, 1998.

Schroeder, Joy A. "Wisdom's Voice and Women's Speech: Hrotswitha of Gandersheim, Hildegard of Bingen, and Rebecca Cox Jackson." *Magistra* 13, no. 1 (2007): 41–70.

Williams, Richard E. *Called and Chosen: The Story of Mother Rebecca Jackson and the Philadelphia Shakers*. Edited by Cheryl Dorschner. Metuchen, NJ: Scarecrow, 1981.

— JOY A. SCHROEDER

■ Jacobs, Berta (Sister Bertken) (1426/27–1514)

Berta Jacobs, known as Sister Bertken in her literary work, was the first published female author from the Netherlands. Her father, Jacob van Lichtenberg (d. 1449), played an important role in the politics of his day, and her work demonstrates that she was well-educated, in accordance with her noble birth. When Bertken was thirty years old, she adopted an ascetic life and at her own expense lived in a cell built at the Buurkerk, the largest parish church of Utrecht. A cell typically had a window that opened to the street, through which people could consult the recluses; as a result of their intense relation with God, they were considered to be "mediators of salvation" (Mulder-Bakker 197). Although Bertken lived hidden from the world, she was clearly still well known to the residents, presumably because of her function as spiritual adviser. When she died at the age of eighty-seven on June 25, 1514, an official record was drawn up by three high clergymen of the city to report her death and to describe her way of living. Many Utrecht residents came to pay her the last honors before she was buried in her cell, according to her own wish. Moreover, the bells of the Dom church rang twice over her, an honor that was usually reserved for the highest clergymen.

Bertken's texts were possibly found in her cell after she died; Jan Berntsz, a Utrecht printer, printed them in 1516. They were also printed in Leiden (1516 and 1518) and Antwerp (1520), indications that her audience was substantially larger than that of female authors who had preceded her. Her literary work, focusing on the humanity of Christ, consists of nine songs, four prayers, and three meditation texts (van Aelst, van Buuren, and Tan). Her songs are stylistically simple, in accordance with the oral tradition of the songs of Modern Devotion, which inspired her (Post). These songs are why she became one of the few women with a place in the medieval literary canon of the Netherlands. The meditation texts focus on three major moments in the life of Christ: his birth as a man in the *Christmas Treatise*; his suffering as God and man in the *Passion Book*; and in the *Pious Colloquy*, his final position as the heavenly bridegroom, waiting for union with the loving soul.

The *Christmas Treatise*, generally considered to be Bertken's most beautiful text, is a devotional meditation based on Bertken's visualization of Mary's experiences of the night of Jesus's birth. Bertken presents Mary's experience as a mystical ascent in three phases. From her earthly situation, surrounded and praised by the three highest choirs of angels, Mary ascends on high while continuously experiencing jubilation and finally rests in the highest, "where she tasted that which is impossible to understand for any human heart" (van Aelst, van Buuren, and Tan 99, 110–12). In this lofty place, her jubilation turns into quiet and silence. Then Jesus is born quickly, without bringing any damage to his mother: "like an arrow that is not obstructed or hindered by the air," he appears "like a flash of lightning" (99, 119–25, 141–42). Accompanied by the angels, Mary then descends from heaven to earth, where she resumes her earthly duties and feeds the baby Jesus with her milk. Bertken presents Mary's journey into heaven while giving birth as a reward for her readiness "to be subservient to God" (96, 18–19), and she presents Mary as an ideal example for those who wish to be unified with God.

Bertken's reimagining includes Joseph's experience of the nativity. Bertken places Joseph outside the building where Mary is giving birth, but he has insight into the activities inside. He notices an extension to the house, from which flames are breaking out and smoke is rising. Joseph falls asleep from the heat and the smoke and awakes only after Jesus is born. When he touches the house, it is still warm but not burned, an allusion to the account of Moses and the burning bush (Exod. 3:2–4) and, in Bertken's view, an image of the Immaculate Conception. On a more abstract level, the *Christmas Treatise* can be related to Bertken's life as a recluse. The extension that Joseph observed from the outside can be interpreted as a type of the recluse's cell, and the flames represent the inspiration of the Holy Spirit and the direct contact that recluses were thought to have with God. In this line of interpretation, Mary represents the recluse, who receives special wisdom from above, and Joseph represents the residents of Utrecht, who are enlightened by the advice of the recluse.

The *Passion Book*, Bertken's longest text, was printed as a separate booklet. Like many passion meditations in the late Middle Ages, it is structured after the hours of the Divine Office. Unlike these meditations, however, it opens with a short description of the life of Jesus in which three women from the Gospels figure as exemplary models. The first is Mary Magdalene, who is identified with the sinner who anointed the feet of Jesus (Luke 7:36–50). According to Bertken, her humility evoked God's grace. Second is the Canaanite woman, whose perseverance in faith generated grace so that her prayer was finally heard (Matt. 15:21–28). Finally, the account of the Samaritan woman who offered a drink to Jesus refers to his unquenchable thirst for the salvation of humankind (John 4:1–42). The message of these three women together seems to be that humility and perseverance allow God to be merciful and to quench his thirst to save. At the end of the *Passion Book*, Mary Magdalene is mentioned again, now as "the burning lover Magdalene." In the Middle Ages, two other women were molded with Mary Magdalene into one figure—not only Mary, the sinner who anointed the feet of Jesus (Matt. 26:6–13; Mark 14:3–9), but also Mary of Egypt, a hermit from the fourth century who repented in the desert of Judea for forty-seven years. In her fusion of a lover and a repentant sinner, Bertken follows an established interpretive tradition.

Finally, Bertken's *Pious Colloquy* is a dialogue between the loving soul and the bridegroom, inspired by the Song of Songs. After a long and passionate quest for her bridegroom, the loving soul finally meets him. Their conversation leads to her complete surrender and then to her total submission to him. Her surrender does not result in a carefree enjoyment of love. Instead, the bridegroom teaches the loving soul how she should follow the example of his suffering to the end of her days and to overcome her sinful nature. Bertken relates the suffering Jesus from the Gospels with the bridegroom from the Song of Songs. As long as the soul lives on earth, Christ remains the suffering bridegroom, in whose footsteps she should follow. Only after death will Christ become the glorified bridegroom, with whom the soul will celebrate heavenly glory. At the end of the *Pious Colloquy*, the soul rests in the arms of her bridegroom and speaks the words: "In pace in idipsum dormiam et requiescam [In peace I will lay me down and sleep]" (Ps. 4:8; van Aelst, van Buuren, and Tan 117, 160), words that also occur in the enclosure ceremony of a recluse. The *Pious Colloquy* has been interpreted as a literary presentation of this enclosure ceremony, which symbolizes a funeral (van Aelst 1997). After taking the vows and giving away her life to God, the recluse is guided to her cell, carrying a crucifix in her arms. While singing songs from the requiem Mass, she is enclosed in her cell, which can be regarded as a grave. The recluse would then remain in her cell until her death. The final issue of the *Pious Colloquy* corresponds with that of the enclosure: after her surrender, the loving soul will rest forever in her bridegroom like the recluse will rest forever in her cell.

Bertken's biblical interpretation relates the Bible directly to her own spiritual life, particularly her life and experience as a recluse. She presents the results of her own devotional meditation as biblical interpretation and uses the biblical narrative as a framework to describe her own life.

Bibliography

Aelst, José van. "Sister Bertken: *Pious Colloquy* and a Selection from Her *Songs*." Pages 203–14 in *Late Medieval Mysticism of the Low Countries*, edited by R. van Nieuwenhove, R. Faesen, and H. Rolfson. New York: Paulist Press, 2008.

———. "Suffering with the Bridegroom: The *Innighe sprake* of the Utrecht Recluse Sister Bertken." *Ons geestelijk erf* 71 (1997): 228–49.

Aelst, José van, F. van Buuren, and A. Tan. *Mi quam een schoon geluit in mijn oren: Het werk van Suster Bertken*. Newly edited and explained. Hilversum: Verloren, 2007.

Mulder-Bakker, Anneke B. *Lives of the Anchoresses: The Rise of the Urban Recluse in Medieval Europe*. Middle Ages Series. Philadelphia: University of Pennsylvania Press, 2005.

Post, Regnerus R. *The Modern Devotion: Confrontation with Reformation and Humanism*. Leiden: Brill, 1968.

Vynckier, Henk. "Poetry from behind Bars: Some Translations from the Dutch Recluse Sister Bertken (1427–1514)." *Mystics Quarterly* 14 (1988): 143–53.

— JOSÉ J. VAN AELST

Jameson, Anna Brownell (1794–1860)

Anna Brownell Jameson, a Protestant Irish-born Englishwoman, was educated at home, where she excelled at languages, sketching, and teaching. At age sixteen, in an attempt to assist her family financially and advance socially, she became a governess to the sons of the Marquis of Winchester, who belonged to one of England's great noble families. In 1819 Anna accepted a post as governess with the Rowles family, whom she accompanied to the Continent, and later as governess for the Littleton family, with whom she stayed until her marriage.

In 1825 Anna married Robert Sympson Jameson, who eventually became Upper Canada's first vice chancellor and first speaker of the legislature after the union of Upper and Lower Canada. Their relationship was unstable from the beginning. It deteriorated further while he was away as a colonial administrator in the West Indies, where he turned to drinking to dull his homesickness. He returned home in 1833 but soon left to become attorney general of Upper Canada, while she remained in England and immersed herself in her intense friendships, travel, and highly successful writing career. In 1836 she joined her husband in frontier Toronto, where he had built an impressive house for her, but she found the situation unbearable and left in 1837. They were officially separated soon afterward. He died in 1854, probably owing to his intemperate lifestyle, leaving nothing to Anna in his will. After traveling, lecturing, and writing for several more years, she died in London on March 17, 1860.

Jameson published travel volumes, such as *Diary of an Ennuyeé* (1826), *Visits and Sketches at Home and Abroad* (1834), and *Winter Studies and Rambles in Canada* (1838); works on queens and consorts in British history, such as *Memoirs of Celebrated Female Sovereigns* (1831) and *Memoirs of the Beauties of the Court of Charles II* (1831); volumes of literary criticism, such as *Shakespeare's Heroines: Characteristics of Women, Moral, Poetical and Historical*; and one work that decried the low status of mothers and governesses, *The Relative Social Position of Mothers and Governesses* (1846). Her interpretations of Scripture are found in *The Poetry of Sacred and Legendary Art* (1848), *Legends of the Monastic Orders* (1850), *Legends of the Madonna* (1852), and *The History of Our Lord*, which was published posthumously in 1864. These works later comprised a series that came to be known as *Sacred and Legendary Art*. The series was so popular that it was reissued repeatedly in England and the United States.

Jameson arranged the content of these volumes according to significant people or heavenly beings found in the biblical text, citing biblical and post-biblical legends about them as seen through the history of art. In essence, her work is a kind of reception history: she surveyed the ways that people had made sense of traditions about these figures and made their stories meaningful for the time in which they lived. She also commented on persons of significance within the Christian tradition (e.g., virgin patronesses, Greek martyrs) but not in Scripture.

Jameson's method of interpretation is exemplified in her interpretation of Mary Magdalene in the first volume of *Sacred and Legendary Art* (1850). Although she mentions the debate over the identity of a certain Mary (Luke 8:2) and whether Mary Magdalene is the "woman who was a sinner" (7:36–50) or Mary of Bethany who anoints Jesus (John 12:3), her focus is on the tradition of Magdalene as repentant sinner, who becomes the symbol of pardoning grace (*Sacred and Legendary Art*, 1:202–3). Jameson reviews the popular legend, loosely based on the Gospels, in which Magdalene lived in a castle called Magdalon, was descended from noble or royal race, but lived a dissolute life, squandering her inheritance after her father's death. She is then converted by Jesus and relieved of the seven demons that possessed her (Luke 8:2; Mark 16:9), which symbolize the seven deadly sins. Magdalene later anoints Jesus, washes and wipes his feet with her hair (Luke 7:36–50), ministers to him out of her substance (Mark 15:41; Luke 8:3), attends him at Calvary (Matt. 27:56; Mark 15:40; John 19:25), weeps at his tomb (John 20:11), and is the first person to whom Jesus appears after the resurrection (Matt. 28:1, 8–10; Luke 24:1–12; John 20:1–18). Jameson then discusses the medieval legend that Magdalene subsequently lives and dies in the region of Provence in France. Jameson also analyzes the portrayal of Magdalene in sacred art, in which she is often portrayed as having a box of ointment, a symbol of her conversion and her love (207). Her clothing is usually blue or violet to symbolize penitence and mourning, and she is often found in poses of prayer or penitence (210–11) or Gospel scenes with an ample bosom and long, full hair (215–24). Ultimately, Jameson finds these depictions lacking. The artists may well have represented "the particular situation," but none have truly portrayed Magdalene's noble and powerful faculties, instead relying on "commonplace" and "vulgar" women to portray her (224).

Jameson divided her book *Legends of the Madonna as Represented in the Fine Arts* (1852) into two sections, devotional and historical. In the devotional section, Jameson examines artistic portrayals in which the Virgin Mary stands entirely alone and is glorified as an independent entity. Under the subtitle "Virgin and Child Enthroned," Jameson describes depictions of Mary, the mother of Jesus, as being "enthroned" and wearing a "rich crown as queen of heaven" (149). In her section on the "Coronation of the Virgin," Jameson chooses "to provide sketches of the images that maximize the Virgin's power and status. Four of her six sketches are of the Virgin seated on the same throne as Christ, receiving her crown" (Adams 154). For Jameson, the Virgin Mary is "THE WOMAN of the primaeval prophecy whose issue was to bruise the head of the Serpent; the Virgin predestined from the beginning of the world who was to bring forth the Redeemer of the world, . . . afflicted on earth, triumphant and crowned in heaven; the glorious, most pure, most pious, most clement, most sacred Queen and Mother, Virgin of Virgins" (84).

In the "historical" section of the book, Jameson discusses Mary in biblical accounts. Regarding Jesus's crucifixion, Jameson is especially adamant that Mary should be portrayed as a dignified witness. Jameson states, "Most of the theological writers infer that on this occasion her constancy and sublime faith were even greater than her grief, and that her heroic fortitude elevated her equally above the weeping women and the timorous disciples" (404). Jameson abhors artistic renditions of Mary at the cross in which Mary is depicted as fainting or as prostrate on the ground; she approves of paintings in which Mary is "uniformly standing" (405). Jameson continues, "To suppose that this noble creature lost all power over her emotions, lost her consciousness of the 'high affliction' she was called to suffer, is quite unworthy of the grand ideal of womanly perfection here placed before us" (406).

Jameson's legacy is found in her conviction that the fine arts are an important medium of biblical interpretation and provide insights into how people make sense of biblical traditions throughout the centuries. She is not above criticizing artistic portrayals when they do not meet with her understanding of the protagonists' noble characters. In this way, she provides a window into the thought of nineteenth-century female interpreters who disapprove of traditions that only serve to support conventionally negative societal attitudes toward women.

Bibliography

Adams, Kimberly Van Esveld. *Our Lady of Victorian Feminism: The Madonna in the Work of Anna Jameson, Margaret Fuller, and George Eliot.* Athens: Ohio University Press, 2001.

Jameson, Anna Brownell. *Legends of the Madonna as Represented in the Fine Arts.* London: Longman, Brown, Green, & Longmans, 1852. 2nd ed., London: Unit Library, 1903.

———. *Sacred and Legendary Art.* 2 vols. London: Longman, Brown, Green & Longman, 1850.

Jameson, Anna Brownell, with Lady Eastlake. *The History of Our Lord as Exemplified in Works of Art.* 2 vols. London: Longman, Green, Longman, Roberts & Green, 1864. Commenced by Jameson; completed by Lady Elizabeth (née Rigby) Eastlake.

Johnston, Judith. *Anna Jameson: Victorian, Feminist, Woman of Letters.* Aldershot, UK: Scolar, 1997.

MacPherson, Gerardine. *Memoirs of the Life of Anna Jameson.* London: Longmans, Green, 1878.

Thomas, Clara. *Love and Work Enough: The Life of Anna Jameson.* Toronto: University of Toronto Press, 1967.

—NANCY CALVERT-KOYZIS

Jonas, Regina (1902–44)

Regina Jonas was born on August 3, 1902, to practicing Jews living in Berlin. In 1930 she graduated from an educational institute for rabbis and educators, which recognized her gifts for preaching. As part of her preparation for ordination, Jonas wrote, "Kann die Frau das rabbinische Amt bekleiden?" loosely translated by Toby Axelrod as "Can Women Serve as Rabbis?" Her ordination was delayed when Dr. Eduard Baneth, who had deemed her qualifying work to be good, died prematurely in 1930. She was privately ordained by Dr. Max Dienemann in 1935. Though initial reaction to her preaching was mixed, she continued to preach both to female and to mixed audiences. Commissioned by a countrywide Jewish organization to care for congregations whose rabbis had emigrated or had been arrested, Jonas preached in synagogues throughout northern Germany in the winter of 1940–41. Before being transported to the Theresienstadt/Terezín ghetto in 1942, Jonas left an envelope containing her documents—including a copy of her qualification work, teaching and ordination certificates, manuscripts, correspondence, newspaper excerpts, and two photographs—with the Jewish congregation in Berlin. In the Theresienstadt/Terezín ghetto, Regina both preached and aided the psychologist Viktor Frankl by meeting trains and helping arrivals deal with shock and disorientation. Two years later, Regina was deported to Auschwitz, where she died on December 12, 1944.

In her qualifying work, after outlining the requirements of a rabbi, Jonas presents her defense of the legitimacy of female rabbis based on traditional sources, including the Hebrew Bible, the Talmud, and other Jewish texts. Jonas argues that biblical women were knowledgeable, capable, involved in religious life, and even leaders in Israel. She draws examples from the Torah to show that the law was given to both Israel's sons and daughters at Sinai (Exod. 19–20), that women could bring offerings (Lev. 12:6), and that women received Moses's teaching (Deut. 31:10–13; cf. Neh. 8:1–9). Jonas also highlights examples of women's heroic, sacrificial, spiritual, political, and prophetic roles in the story of Israel. She writes: "To look more closely at the courageous actions of Judith, . . . or the sacrificial spirit and courage of Samuel's mother, Hannah (1 Samuel 1), . . . or at Esther (Esther), would be superfluous." She notes the inspirational singing of Miriam (Exod. 15:20–21); the prophetic work of Huldah (2 Kings 22:14–20); the courage, intelligence, and enterprising leadership of Deborah (Judg. 4:4); the intelligence and determination of Abigail in averting a great disaster (1 Sam. 25:23–35). She concludes:

> By these examples, one can gather, I believe, that as far as women in old times wanted to and could step forward, nothing was placed in their way, if they accomplished something of worth and of genuineness. No religious immaturity, extreme seclusion or false modesty are visible, no carelessness on their part, frivolity or illiteracy; . . . on the contrary, deliverance, bravery, generosity and gentleness crown them. Of course they had defects, but did not even King David sin? It is a question of *human* weaknesses, where both are concerned, men as well as women. (Klapheck, *Fräulein Rabbiner Jonas*, 121)

Jonas also uses examples from the Talmud that systematically illustrate that while women were traditionally discouraged from taking on an active role in religious public life, they were never strictly forbidden, and in practice they did take on such roles. She states that women's opinions were accepted and recorded. For example, Beruria, wife of Rabbi Meir (Babylonian Talmud, *Bracot* [*Berakot*] 10a), on two separate occasions encourages people—her husband reading Ps. 104:35 and a heretic or Sadducee reading Isa. 54:1—to "consider the end of the verse" before commenting about its beginning.

Jonas concludes her work with "may it not be forgotten, that the spirit of freedom speaks" out of the writings and holy precepts of the Jewish people (Klapheck, *Fräulein Rabbiner Jonas*, 301). "Aside from prejudice and unfamiliarity, almost nothing based on religious law precludes a woman from holding rabbinical office" (301).

Jonas's position that women can serve as rabbis is established, then, not by arguments based on ideas about individual equality, but by arguments based on the traditional authorities of the Hebrew Bible and the Talmud.

This work and Regina Jonas's remaining papers were found in the general archives of the German Jews, stored since 1958 in the state archives of the German Democratic Republic (East Germany), and given to the "Centrum Judicum" in Berlin in spring of 1996. With the discovery of Regina Jonas's documents, the general belief that women were not ordained as rabbis until the 1970s needed to be revised.

Bibliography

Klapheck, Elisa. *Fräulein Rabbiner Jonas: Kann die Frau das rabbinische Amt bekleiden? Eine Streitschrift*. 2nd, corrected ed. Teetz: Hentrich & Hentrich, 2000.

———. *Fräulein Rabbiner Jonas: The Story of the First Woman Rabbi*. Translated by Toby Axelrod. San Francisco: Jossey-Bass, 2004.

Von Kellenbach, Katharina. "'God Does Not Oppress Any Human Being': The Life and Thought of Rabbi Regina Jonas." *Leo Baeck Institute Year Book* 39 (1994): 213–25. New York: Secker & Warburg for the Leo Baeck Institute, 1994. http://faculty.smcm.edu/kvonkellenbach/aregina_jonas.html.

— ISA HAUSER

Juana Inés de la Cruz (Sister) (1651–95)

Juana Inés Ramírez de Asbaje was the youngest of three illegitimate children born to Isabel Ramírez and an elusive Pedro de Asbaje in San Miguel Nepantla. She spent her early years on her maternal grandfather's hacienda, some ten miles from Mexico City. Her thirst for knowledge began shaping her life at an early age. Though her mother was illiterate, her grandfather had a library, which the girl absorbed voraciously after being taught the rudiments of reading by an *amiga*, a local teacher of girls. At eight or nine, she went to the capital to live with her aunt María Ramírez, who had married the wealthy merchant Juan de Mata. Sor (Sister) Juana's beauty, precocious intellect, and her gift for writing verses soon made her the favorite of the viceroy's wife, Leonor Carreto, and she received more education at the viceregal court. In 1669, after a brief stay with the Carmelites, she became a professed nun in the convent of Santa Paula of the order of St. Jerome, where she remained until her death in an epidemic in 1695.

Although women rarely wrote in the seventeenth century, Sor Juana was widely published during her own lifetime. She initially published individual works in her native Mexico, and two volumes of her collected works were later printed in Spain in multiple editions (Madrid, Seville, and Barcelona). The four-volume critical edition, *Obras Completas* (OC), edited by Méndez Plancarte and Salceda and completed in the 1950s, includes hundreds of secular and religious poems; five full-length plays; a nine-hundred-line philosophical poem, *First Dream*; two devotional writings, *Exercises for the Incarnation* and *Offerings for the Sorrows of Our Lady*; a theological critique, *Athenagoric Letter*; a political treatise, *Allegorical Neptune*; and her intellectual autobiography, *Response to Sor Philotea*.

Unlike many of her contemporaries, Sor Juana was very familiar with the Bible. Her song cycles (*villancicos*) for feast days, for example, contain many biblical references, one poem of sixty-two lines having more than twenty references (OC 2:203–5, 451). Of her three *autos sacramentales*, or religious dramas, two have biblical settings. *Joseph's Scepter* is a recasting of Gen. 37; 39–50. Her christological play, *Divine Narcissus*, which has as a major focus the temptation of Jesus, includes many quotations or allusions to Scripture, including extensive paraphrases of the Song of Songs, such as this on 1:1–5:

> Following your fragrance, I run quickly.
> Oh, how right that all adore you!
> But you are not expecting
> Me colored by the sun's hot rays.
> See, though I am black, I am beautiful,
> Since your marvelous image I resemble.
> (*Selected Writings* [SW],
> 121; OC 3:51)

When Sor Juana does quote Scripture directly, she uses St. Jerome's Latin translation, the Vulgate, followed by her Spanish translation or paraphrase, in her own way continuing St. Jerome's activity of translating. She refers to Jerome as "my father" six times in her *Response to Sor Philotea* and refers to a decision he had made when translating the Psalms: "Knowing the elegance of Hebrew cannot be pressed into Latin meter; the holy translator [Jerome], more attentive to the importance of the meaning of the text, omitted the meter of the Psalms but retained the number and division into verses" (*SW* 286; OC 4:470).

Though the secular nature of much of Sor Juana's poetry (love poems and an epistemological study, *First Dream*) and drama (a comedy and a mythological tragedy) are obviously atypical for a cloistered nun, her religious writings themselves are unusual from their inception. Whereas most nuns wrote for their convent sisters with the encouragement of their confessor, nearly all of Sor Juana's works were commissioned by the ecclesiastical establishment or by noble patrons. Her *villancicos*, or song cycles for church feasts, were commissioned by the cathedral chapters of Mexico City, Puebla, and Oaxaca. Her political treatise *Allegorical Neptune*, commissioned by the chapter in Mexico City for the arrival of the new viceroy in 1680, also received the encouragement of Archbishop Payo Enrique de Rivera. A song cycle of over twenty poems was commissioned by a wealthy nobleman for the dedication of the convent church in 1690. Her dramas, both secular and religious, were commissioned by noble patrons.

If Sor Juana had admirers, she also had critics: "Who would believe, seeing the general acclaim I have enjoyed, that I have not sailed on a sea of glass with the wind in my sails on a groundswell of universal approbation? God knows that this has not been the case" (*SW* 266; OC 4:452). One of her critics, the bishop of Puebla, Manuel Fernandez de Santa Cruz, was himself a biblical scholar. In 1690, in an ambivalent preface to his publication of her *Athenagoric Letter*, a critique of the sermon of the Portuguese Jesuit Antonio Vieira on the benefits of Christ's love, the bishop berated her for her interest in worldly literature and urged her to "improve her choice of books" and "sometimes read the book of Jesus Christ" (*SW* 250–51; *OC* 4:695). This was a curious accusation since both Sor Juana and Vieira were debating the meaning of Christ's love in reference to John 13, where Christ washes the feet of his disciples. In her critique, Sor Juana uses texts from both the Old and New Testaments to support her points. When debating the issue of tears as a sign of suffering, for example, she analyzes Christ's tears at the death of his friend Lazarus (John 11:35) and the tears of Mary Magdalene at the tomb (20:13).

Within three months of the publication of *Athenagoric Letter*, Sor Juana had written *Response to Sor Philotea de la Cruz*, a remarkable work in which she defends her own accomplishments and enters the debate about women's access to higher education, including the study of the Bible. In her defense of women's rights to study the Bible, she refers to the affirmative answer of the Mexican biblical scholar Juan Diaz de Arce (1594–1653; *SW* 276; *OC* 4:462). She also defends her own secular studies, which she maintains were steps to the highest of studies, "holy theology." She asks: "How could I understand the methodology of the queen of the sciences if I did not know the style of her handmaidens?" (*SW* 261; *OC* 4:447). She deemed that an understanding of such disciplines as music, geometry, astronomy, law, and history was necessary to comprehend the Bible in its context. Curiously, she did not mention philosophy, traditionally considered *the* handmaid of theology.

Sor Juana then takes on the traditional arguments against women's engagement with Scripture that appeal to the writings of Paul. She observes, first of all, that Paul would have experienced the participation of such women as Salome and the sisters Mary and Martha, so his prohibition cannot be considered to apply to all women. She also refers to a later authority, the fourth-century church historian Eusebius, who offers further support of her position when he explains that the term "church" in the Pauline prohibition refers to the building, not to the universal sense of the community of the faithful (*SW* 280; *OC* 4:465). Sor Juana concludes that women may not teach from a university chair or from the pulpit, but "studying, writing and teaching privately are not only permitted, but are very beneficial and useful" (*SW* 277; *OC* 4:462). Furthermore, she argues, if contrary to Eusebius, "church" in 1 Cor. 14:34 was taken to refer to the "universality of the faithful" (*SW* 282; *OC* 4:467) and "being silent" was interpreted "in the most restrictive sense of forbidding women even in secret to write or study," then the church itself was guilty of violating this precept in its tradition of honoring such women writers as "Gertrude, Teresa and Bridget, Maria of Agreda and many others." Similarly, extending this point back to the apostolic tradition, she maintains had "the Apostle . . . prohibited all writing to women, the church would also not permit it as it does today." Therefore the church is following the tradition of the apostles by allowing "women to teach through their writing" (*SW* 283; *OC* 4:467).

Sor Juana draws support for her own writing from the long tradition of women studying and interpreting Scripture, which includes the circle of Jerome's friends and supporters, such as Paula, for whom her convent was named. Identifying herself as a daughter of St. Jerome and St. Paula, she states, "It would be truly disgraceful for such learned parents to have an ignorant daughter" (*SW* 261; *OC* 4:447). Indeed, she recalls that Jerome recognized Paula as a gifted exegete, along with her daughters Blessilla and Eustochium. "I see [that Jerome praised] my most holy mother Paula, learned in Hebrew, Greek, and Latin, and with a gift of interpreting Scripture" (*SW* 276; *OC* 4:461). Other women in her canon include Fabiola of Rome, "also very knowledgeable in Holy Scripture," and "Proba Falconia, a Roman woman, [who] wrote an elegant book with verses from Virgil that illustrated the mysteries of our holy faith" (*SW* 276; *OC* 4:462).

Sor Juana also draws inspiration from outstanding women in the Bible itself: Deborah, as a military and political giver of laws, governing with "many learned men"; the queen of Sheba for her learning; Abigail as a prophetess; Esther for her gift of persuasion; Rahab for her piety; Hannah, mother of Samuel, for her perseverance (*SW* 275; *OC* 4:461). However, the model above all others is Mary, the mother of Jesus, the focus of both her devotional works. The *Exercises for the Incarnation* are structured according to the seven days of creation (Gen. 1), where all creation praises Mary. "In the beginning God created the heavens and the earth, and on the first day God created the beautiful firstfruit of all creatures, saying: 'Let there be light' (Gen. 1:3). . . . This was the first creature he made, and the first to render obedience to his most pure mother, Queen of Light, without the darkness of sin, the most radiant light of all" (*SW* 175; *OC* 4:477–78). The *Offerings for the Sorrows of Our Lady* invite meditation on the Gospel passion narratives through the Stations of the Cross from Mary's perspective, often contrasting the pain she felt at the suffering of her son with the joys of his infancy. "Oh, how different" from "the inert and disfigured body of your holy Son in your virginal arms . . . was that Son, reflection of all beauty, as you took him in your arms to nurse him, your whole soul filled with bliss!" (*SW* 210–11; *OC* 4:511–12). "How different his final resting place from the first! Instead of your pure, maternal womb, the cold, hard stones receive him" (*SW* 211; *OC* 4:512).

Mary is important not just because she brought the Redeemer into the world, but also because, as conceived without sin, she is the perfect representation of humanity. Nonetheless, Sor Juana assiduously avoids the conventional Ave/Eva contrast, referring to Mary as the "daughter of Adam" (*OC* 2:18–19). In her *villancicos*, Sor Juana indeed emphasizes women's strength by characterizing Mary variously as a knight errant, a heavenly choir director, a "doctor of the schools," and even a teacher of rhetoric, greater than Demosthenes and Cicero. As author of the Magnificat, Mary is a poet and thus the ultimate justification for women poets. As mother of the divine Word, her eloquence, skill, and command of the subject matter exceed that of the great teachers of antiquity (OC 1:12–14). Sor Juana is quite aware that through her *villancicos*, the song cycles created to be sung in the church buildings, she is actually "speaking in the church," albeit through her poetry. It is in one such poem, one of over twenty commissioned for the dedication of a convent church of Bernadine nuns, that in a flight of fantasy she allows herself to imagine herself as a preacher, an activity still prohibited to women in the Roman Catholic Church in the twenty-first century:

> The Church, Bernard, and Mary,
> It would be a good occasion
> to bring them into concert
> if I were a preacher.
> But no, no, no, no:
> I'm not cut of such fine cloth.
> But supposing that I were,
> what things would I say,
> moving from text to text,
> searching for connections?
> But no, no, no, no:
> I'm not cut of such fine cloth.
> (OC 2:202–3)

Sor Juana was all but forgotten for nearly two centuries. A groundbreaking biography, published in 1982 by Mexico's Nobel laureate Octavio Paz, renewed interest in her and her work and precipitated a flood of books and articles by Latin American literary scholars, many fascinated by her advocacy for women's intellectual gifts as well as by the beauty of her poetry, drama, and prose. A national icon in Mexico today, her face is on the two-hundred-peso bill. Though Sor Juana interpreted Scripture continuously in her religious poetry, drama, and prose, and even developed a theory of biblical exegesis, her significance as a religious writer has only recently begun receiving attention, and her biblical scholarship is an area waiting to be explored in depth.

See also Birgitta of Sweden (1302/3–73); Gertrude the Great (ca. 1256–1302); Paula (347–404); Proba, Faltonia Betitia (ca. 320–ca. 370); Teresa of Avila (1515–82)

Bibliography

Bénassy-Berling, Marie Cécile. *Humanismo y religión en Sor Juana Inés de la Cruz.* Translated by Laura López de Belair. Mexico City: Universidad Nacional Autónoma de México, 1983.

Gonzalez, Michelle. *Sor Juana: Beauty and Justice in the Americas.* Maryknoll, NY: Orbis Books, 2003.

Juana Inés de la Cruz. *Obras Completas*. Vol. 1, *Lírica personal*; vol. 2, *Villancicos y letras sacras*; vol. 3, *Autos y loas*, edited by Alfonso Méndez Plancarte; vol. 4, *Comedias, sainetes y prosa*, edited by Alberto G. Salceda. Mexico City: Fondo de Cultura Econímica, 1951–57. 3rd repr., 1994.

———. *A Sor Juana Anthology*. Translated by Alan S. Trueblood. Cambridge, MA: Harvard University Press, 1988.

———. *Sor Juana Inés de la Cruz: Selected Writings*. Translated and introduced by Pamela Kirk Rappaport. New York: Paulist Press, 2005.

Kirk, Pamela. *Sor Juana Inés de la Cruz: Religion, Art, and Feminism*. New York: Continuum, 1998.

Scott, Nina. "Sor Juana Inés de la Cruz: Let Your Women Keep Silence in the Churches. . . ." *Women's Studies International Forum* 8, no. 4 (1985): 511–19.

Tavard, George. *Juana Inés de la Cruz and the Theology of Beauty: The First Mexican Theology*. Notre Dame, IN: University of Notre Dame Press, 1991.

—PAMELA KIRK RAPPAPORT

■ Julian of Norwich (ca. 1342–ca. 1416)

The woman known as Julian of Norwich provides little information about herself, her personal circumstances, or her background. She does, however, state that in May 1373, at the age of thirty, when she was gravely ill and on the brink of death, God granted her a series of sixteen visions grounded in a vivid awareness of Christ's passion. She recorded her response to these visions in two texts, now known widely as the Short Text (ST) and the Long (LT), or as, respectively, *A Vision* and *A Revelation*. Although a minority of scholars suggest that Julian used an amanuensis in the composition of these texts, it is now generally accepted that the act of writing was her own. The ST (*A Vision*) can be dated to the 1370s–80s, and it is likely that the LT (*A Revelation*) was composed in the 1390s–1400s. Julian's ST is, as its editorial title suggests, a relatively brief though theologically sophisticated account of her visions, while the LT is a substantial, adventurous, and ruminative expansion on these revelations, composed after a lengthy period of contemplation and after two additional revelations (1388 and 1393) afforded her a more profound understanding of her original 1373 experience.

Julian is known as an anchorite (an enclosed religious solitary), but the point at which she adopted this vocation and her social position before enclosure are the subject of much debate. Some argue that she entered the anchorhold as a professed nun, while others contend that she had been a devout laywoman of some social standing and affluence who assumed the anchoritic life in response to her 1373 "showings." Whichever of these hypotheses is correct, it is possible that Julian originally wrote the ST as part of the procedure of anchoritic enclosure. Anyone wanting to enter the anchorhold in the Middle Ages was required to undergo a process of clerical examination, and Julian may have composed the ST specifically for the scrutiny of an ecclesiastical committee tasked with ascertaining the authenticity of her visionary claims. Such an interpretation would go some way toward explaining the ST's repeated and somewhat defensive insistence on its own orthodoxy. Speculation on the precise purpose and intended audience of the LT is more challenging. The ecclesiastical culture within which Julian operated was informed by Paul's injunction that women should not be permitted to teach, and the LT is anything but straightforwardly instructional. Yet neither is it a purely subjective account of personal experience. Rather, it insists on its relevance not only to Julian but also to all her "evenchristen" (fellow Christians) and adopts a generically adventurous and personally assured voice of literary and theological originality.

Echoes of biblical language and reflections on biblical doctrine permeate both the ST and the LT, but the means by which Julian's scriptural familiarity was gained are much contested. In late fourteenth-century England, the Bible was available principally in its Latin form (the Vulgate), copies of which are likely to have been owned only by churches, monastic establishments, university libraries, and some aristocratic households. For the non-Latinate majority of the population, access to the Scriptures would have been indirect, with knowledge of biblical matters being shaped by clerical intermediaries. It has been argued, however, that Julian was an exception to this rule; Edmund Colledge and James Walsh, who edited her writings in the 1970s, argue that she was a learned nun before she became an anchorite and that she had an intimate knowledge of the Vulgate before her composition of the ST. Such an argument does not, however, take account of the real possibility that, whether Julian was laywoman or nun before her enclosure, her level of Latin was not sophisticated (for further discussion of this matter, see Blamires). Neither does it register the fact that the Vulgate was extremely expensive to produce and to own and that it is difficult to imagine a situation in which Julian would have had sustained personal access to such a text.

However, if we cannot assume that Julian's biblical knowledge was a result of firsthand familiarity with the Vulgate in its entirety, we need to explore other possibilities. It is likely that, as a result of combined education and experience (whether lay or monastic), Julian possessed a degree of Latin, sufficient at least to allow her to understand parts of the liturgy and its biblical lections. Inevitably her sustained exposure to such cyclical and repetitive material (anchorholds tended to be attached to parish churches, enclosing the anchorite within easy earshot of daily liturgical practices) would have left its mark on her. Yet this alone cannot account for her very apparent biblical learning, which might also be explained in part by her knowledge of contemporary devotional and mystical writings, which were informed by biblical allusion and quotation, and by her conversations with clerical advisers, who could be expected to have imparted scriptural wisdom to her. Indeed, in a period when books were costly and reading ability was often extremely limited, we cannot overestimate the importance of aural encounters with the Scriptures in the shaping of an individual's biblical awareness.

When considering the role of the Bible in Julian's writings, we need also to bear in mind that it was in the late fourteenth century that the first English translation of the complete Bible was undertaken by the followers of John Wycliffe. The Wycliffite Bible, as it is now known, survives in two versions, and it has been speculated that Julian might have had access to one or the other of these. This is not impossible, but it is unlikely, for when one considers the suspect reputation of these translations combined with the fact that most of the extant manuscripts are large, evidently designed for public use and possibly available too late to have had a sustained impact on Julian, it seems doubtful that she would have encountered the Bible in such a form. Nevertheless, it remains that Julian lived at a time when the Scriptures were being "Englished," and even if these Wycliffite translations did not have an impact on her, we cannot discount the real possibility that she would have come into contact with other vernacular versions of at least parts of the Bible. The Psalter, in particular, circulated in more than one fourteenth-century English translation, and the existence of material such as this (in conjunction with her aforementioned exposure to Latin) may well have informed Julian's scriptural understanding and the articulation of this in her own writing.

Echoes of biblical vocabulary and meditations on biblical themes inform both Julian's ST and LT, as they do the writings of her devotional contemporaries. Although the breadth of her biblical familiarity is impressive, her prose resounds most strongly with recollections of the psalms (which would have been liturgically familiar to her) and the Pauline Epistles. Yet Julian distinguishes herself from the vast majority of her contemporaries in that she never quotes directly from the Vulgate; all her scriptural allusions are in English. Further, since she tends to embed these persistent echoes within her own ruminative vernacular, it is only on rare occasions that she foregrounds their biblical origins. There are three such occasions in the ST, the first two of which are found in chapter 9, when Julian claims, "And in the tyme of ioye I myght hafe sayde with Paule: Nathynge schalle departe me fro the charyte of Cryste," and then adds, "In payne y myght hafe sayde with saynte Petyr: Lorde, save me, I perysche" (Colledge and Walsh 1.231.33–36). The first of these is clearly an echo of Rom. 8:38–39, while the second sounds like a conflation of Matt. 8:25 and 14:30. The third explicit reference to a biblical authority (this time, Phil. 2:5) occurs in chapter 10 of the ST, when in contemplation of the suffering Christ, Julian writes, "Swilke paynes I sawe that alle es to litelle þat [that] y can telle or saye, for itt maye nought be tolde, botte ylke saule aftere the sayinge of saynte Pawle schulde feele in hym þat in Criste Jhesu" (1.234.23–26). The LT retains the first two of these references to biblical authorities but deletes the third, testament perhaps to Julian's concern that, as a woman, she ought not appear too well-versed in matters scriptural. The LT does allude (chap.

32; 2.424.38–40) to the fundamental importance of "Goddes worde" (a term used more frequently than "Bible" in Middle English devotional literature); yet with the exception of the three instances outlined above, Julian never names any biblical authority as a source of inspiration for her writing.

Despite this lack of signposting, Julian's writings are replete with biblical material. Her scriptural echoes can be very specific, as when she states, "Oure parte is oure lorde" (ST, chap. 14; 1.248.26; and LT, chap. 30; 2.414.20–11), a clear recollection of Ps. 16:5. Or, more striking, when she refers to the "hye depnesse" (LT, chap. 56; 2.572.28–573.29) into which God leads people, a precise rendering of the Vulgate's *alta profunditas* (Eccles. 7:24–25), translated identically in the first version of the Wycliffite Bible. Equally, however, they can be rather more amorphous and general, as on the occasions when she recalls the form and matter of the New Testament parables, such as giving echoes of Matthew's parable of the marriage feast (Matt. 22:1–14; in LT, chap. 14; 2.351.5–7) and of Luke's parable of the prodigal son (Luke 15:11–31; in LT, chap. 79; 2.705.32–706.39). At some moments she seems to depict herself as a character of biblical resonance, as in her retelling of her early illness in language that recalls Christ's own terminology of suffering (ST, chap. 1; 1.204.42–45; and LT, chap. 2; 2.288.36–38). On such occasions, the scriptural recollections are not necessarily conscious and deliberate, but bear witness, instead, to Julian's ruminative familiarity with the Bible and her arguably inevitable adoption of its modes of expression.

Yet what is remarkable about Julian is the extent to which she demonstrates not only fluency in biblical modes of expression, but also a confident grasp of biblical doctrine. This is seen most clearly in her theology of the motherhood of both Christ and God (unique to the LT), in the inception and development of which she draws on the maternal messiah envisaged by the Old Testament prophet Isaiah (specifically Isa. 49:15 and 66:13). However, in presenting her Christ as not merely the caressing and comforting maternal figure envisaged by Isaiah, but also as a mother who feeds his followers "with hym selfe" and leads them for sustenance "in to his blessyd brest" (LT, chap. 60; 2.596.29–598.39), she demonstrates an ability to build imaginatively on scriptural models in establishing her own vivid doctrine. This is also the case in her dealings with the New Testament Epistle to the Hebrews, a text equated with a certain degree of theological complexity and rarely engaged with in contemporary devotional literature. Thus in her presentation of Christ's sacrificial blood as interceding to the Father on one's behalf, she recalls several points in Hebrews (7:25; 9:13–14; 12:24). And in her repeated insistence on the singularity of Christ's passion—"I wate weele he suffrede nought botte anes" (ST, chap. 10; 1.234.27); "The swete manhode of Crist myght suffer but oonse" (LT, chap. 22; 2.385.34)—she borrows a doctrinal point emphasized specifically in Heb. 9:12 and 10:10. Yet in maintaining that such was Christ's love that he would willingly have suffered and indeed died more than the necessary once, she depicts a Christ capable of exceeding (without contradicting) the model of Hebrews. And as in her borrowings from Isaiah, so here again one senses Julian's visionary experience straining at the limits of the very biblical precedent on which it is ultimately founded.

Julian the anchorite certainly had an impact in her late medieval locality; her mystical contemporary, Margery Kempe, refers to her in approving terms, and several wills of the period left bequests to her. Yet it seems unlikely that she cultivated a reputation as an author while she was alive. That her ST survives in only one manuscript and the complete LT in only three seventeenth-century manuscripts of French provenance suggests that the medieval circulation of her writings was neither prompt nor widespread. In the twentieth century, however, she reached a much wider public. Quoted by T. S Eliot in *Four Quartets*, Julian became an important literary figure and was also adopted as model and inspiration by specifically Christian thinkers who understood her devotional practice and divine revelations to be of profound relevance to contemporary society. And as a medieval woman engaging creatively with biblical doctrine and writing in an extraordinarily rich and nuanced vernacular, she continues to command widespread attention in the twenty-first century.

See also Kempe, Margery (1373–1438)

Bibliography

Baker, Denise N. *Julian of Norwich's Showings: From Vision to Book*. Princeton, NJ: Princeton University Press, 1994.

Blamires, Alcuin. "The Limits of Bible Study for Medieval Women." Pages 1–12 in vol. 1 of *Women, the Book and the Godly: Selected Proceedings of the St. Hilda's Conference, 1993*, edited by Lesley Smith and Jane H. M. Taylor. Cambridge: D. S. Brewer, 1995.

Colledge, Edmund, and James Walsh, eds. *A Book of Showings to the Anchoress Julian of Norwich*. 2 vols. Toronto: Pontifical Institute for Medieval Studies, 1978.

Glasscoe, Marion, ed. *Julian of Norwich: A Revelation of Love*. Exeter, UK: Exeter University Press, 1976. Various reprints.

Jantzen, Grace M. *Julian of Norwich: Mystic and Theologian*. New York: Paulist Press, 1987.

McAvoy, Liz Herbert, ed. *A Companion to Julian of Norwich*. Cambridge: D. S. Brewer, 2008.

Sutherland, Annie. "'Our feyth is groundyd in goddes worde'—Julian of Norwich and the Bible." Pages 1–20 in *The Medieval Mystical Tradition: Exeter Symposium VII*, edited by E. A. Jones. Cambridge: D. S. Brewer, 2004.

Warrren, Ann K. *Anchorites and Their Patrons in Medieval England*. Berkeley: University of California Press, 1985.

Watson, Nicholas. "The Composition of Julian of Norwich's *Revelation of Love*." *Speculum* 68 (1993): 637–88.

Watson, Nicholas, and Jacqueline Jenkins, eds. *The Writings of Julian of Norwich: A Vision Showed to a Devout Woman and A Revelation of Love*. Turnhout: Brepols, 2006.

— ANNIE SUTHERLAND

■ Kempe, Margery (1373–1438)

Margery Kempe is known only through *The Book of Margery Kempe*, an account of the devotional life of a prosperous early fifteenth-century East Anglian woman, the daughter of a mayor of King's Lynn, the wife of alderman John Kempe, and the mother of his fourteen children, only two of whom are mentioned in the *Book*. As a record of Margery's actual life, the *Book* offers few details, including her failed ventures as a brewer and miller; her travels throughout England and to Jerusalem, Rome, and Germany; and her unconventional relationship with her husband as well as with some key figures in the ecclesiastical world of the time. The *Book* is a curious mixture of facts that can be verified (the Guild Hall fire in King's Lynn in 1420–21, the death of Henry V in 1422) and events for which there is no record (Margery's conversations with Thomas Arundel, archbishop of Canterbury [1397, 1399–1414], her confrontations with authorities, her preaching tour of London).

The *Book* is not a diary: its sophistication demands that it be seen as shaped by an author, who will be referred to as Kempe in order to distinguish between its maker and its protagonist. Margery's experiences are presented through a narrator, who refers to her in third person, except for one electric instance (chap. 15) when she speaks in first person. The narrative is introduced by two scribal prefaces, both of which testify to the miraculous nature of the life the *Book* recounts. Neither preface is anchored explicitly to a character in the *Book*. On the one hand, by the first third of the fifteenth century, a woman of Kempe's status might have been able to write and certainly able to dictate to a scribe, in which case she would consider herself the author. On the other hand, the authority implicit in a scribal witness would ameliorate the suspicion of heterodoxy in a text about a woman who describes herself as speaking directly to God. Since the threat of being accused of heresy was real during the late Middle Ages, a woman who wished to write about God as criticizing the contemporary church and to offer a private understanding of the divine nature was likely to create a screening device.

Interpretation of Scripture would be included under strictures against unauthorized writing or preaching. Although Margery does not overtly engage in exegetical discussions of scriptural passages, the life that the *Book* recounts suggests Kempe's use of interpretive strategies. She dramatizes texts or repeats interpretations of texts that she has from *private* communication with God or Jesus, such as her personal accounts of events surrounding the nativity (chaps. 6–7) and the passion (chaps. 73, 78–81). During one such interchange (chap. 7), God asks her to ask whatever she wishes, and he will grant it. Margery asks for "mercy and preservation from everlasting damnation for me and for all the world." Margery's request for chastisement but not eternal punishment, for which Kempe records no answer from God, serves as one instance in which orthodox belief is filtered through the voice of Margery.

Both sections exploit the hints for private experience of the Gospels to be found in the thirteenth-century pseudo-Bonaventuran *Meditations on the Life of Christ*, but do so without the directional voice of the male narrator's channeling the devotee's empathetic understanding of a New Testament scene. In the *Book*, Margery herself recounts, focuses, and interprets extrabiblical scenes in which she herself appears, such as the pregnancy of Mary, the birth of Christ, the crucifixion, and the period before the resurrection, when she recounts her own intimate care for Mary—feeding her, taking care of her clothing, encouraging and soothing her. Kempe thus amplifies biblical events, interpreting them in relation to Margery's affective spirituality and presenting Margery's insights as her own rather than as the result of clerical direction.

Her life as it is recounted in the *Book* can be read as a gospel, an attempt to trace out Christ's life in contemporary time and to underline the worldliness and incomprehension of an avowedly Christian England. Margery, who tries to live according to the private commands she receives from the Godhead (to dress in white, abstain from meat and swearing, attend church, and take the Eucharist frequently) and who is sent into outbursts of noisy weeping at mention of the passion, is persecuted for her devotion by her fellow English Christians. Kempe uses her narrative account of Margery's faith and actions as interpretations of the words and life of Jesus in relation to a Christian world alienated by its own rituals of community. In contrast, Margery and those she gathers around her appear as a new type of Christian community, where Margery's gender does not relegate her to silence. Kempe's handling of the strife caused by Margery's gender, travels, weeping, and bold speech underline just how disruptive devotion might be to the settled life of the late medieval townsperson.

The *Book*, written between 1436 and 1438, exists in a unique manuscript from about 1450 (British library, MS Additional 61823). The manuscript was owned by the contemplative and scholarly Carthusian priory of Mount Grace in Yorkshire and has been marked up by Carthusian readers, who were especially interested in highlighting Margery's devotional fervor. The *Book* was discovered in 1934 among the family papers of Colonel William Erdeswick Ignatius Butler-Bowden and was identified and announced in the *London Times* by Hope Emily Allen, the first notable scholar to study the work. At that time it was hailed for the insight it provided into the history of public and private life in late medieval England, yet it was also described by some of its critics as the outpourings of a hysterical woman. The *Book* is now seen as a significant witness to its author's ability to use English prose in creating an account of one woman's attempt to become her own figure of religious authority in a time when authoritative acts of interpretation were the privileges of male figures of church and state.

Bibliography

Atkinson, Clarissa. *Mystic and Pilgrim: The Book and the World of Margery Kempe.* Ithaca, NY: Cornell University Press, 1983.

Gibson, Gail McMurray. *The Theater of Devotion: East Anglian Drama and Society in the Late Middle Ages.* Chicago: University of Chicago Press, 1989.

Lochrie, Karma. *Margery Kempe and Translations of the Flesh.* Philadelphia: University of Pennsylvania Press, 1991.

Meech, Sanford Brown, and Hope Emily Allen, eds. *The Book of Margery Kempe.* EETS 212. Oxford: Oxford University Press, 1940, 1961.

Staley, Lynn, ed. and trans. *The Book of Margery Kempe.* New York: Norton, 2001.

———. *Margery Kempe's Dissenting Fictions.* University Park: Pennsylvania State University Press, 1994.

Stanbury, Sarah, and Virginia Raguin. "Mapping Margery Kempe: A Guide to Late Medieval Material and Spiritual Life." http://college.holycross.edu/projects/kempe/.

— LYNN STALEY

Kenyon, Kathleen M. (1906–78)

Kathleen M. Kenyon was born in London on January 6, 1906, the eldest of two daughters born to Sir Frederic and Amy Kenyon. As the daughter of the director of the British Museum, the position that her father held from 1909 to 1930, Kenyon at an early age gained exposure to the museum and to the national library that it housed. In addition, her father was the first president of the British School of Archaeology in Jerusalem, which was established in 1919. This no doubt gave her exposure to the discipline of archaeology. Her father was also a reputable biblical scholar and a devout man who ensured that his daughters were educated in the Scriptures. However, Kenyon, the most renowned woman archaeologist of modern time, recognized for the archaeological methodology that she introduced to Palestine, explains that she came to archaeology "quite accidentally" ("Digging for History," 1). Fortunately, she did come to archaeology. Her contribution to the discipline of archaeology has forever impacted the method employed in excavations. Her work at Samaria, Jericho, and Jerusalem demonstrates how her method has impacted biblical interpretation.

Kenyon attended Somerville College of Oxford University, where she studied medieval history. While a student there, she served as joint president of the Somerville College Archaeological Society. Her interest in the society, however, was more social than archaeological. She was also a member of the Oxford University Archaeological Society, which at the time had only recently begun to admit women. In an attempt by the society to enlist the support of women, Kenyon was installed as the first female president in 1927. Margery Fry, the principal of Somerville College, was impressed by Kenyon's position in the society and as a result "pushed" her to serve as assistant to Gertrude Caton-Thompson in her excavation for the British Association in Zimbabwe (formerly Southern Rhodesia). Thus, following her graduation from Somerville College in 1928, Kenyon embarked on her first adventure in archaeology. Her assignment on the excavation was to serve as the dig photographer. Although, according to Kenyon, Caton-Thompson was neither a good teacher nor much of an encourager, Kenyon decided that she would like to pursue a career in archaeology as a result of this experience ("Digging for History," 2). Fortunately, Kenyon did receive the encouragement and training that she would need from Sir Mortimer Wheeler, to whom she credits "all of [her] training in field archaeology and constant inspiration towards improved methods" (*Beginning*, 8).

Kenyon first met R. E. M. "Rik" Wheeler in 1930, and later that same year began working with him and his wife, Tessa, on his excavation at the Roman site of Verulamium. She continued on the excavation each season through 1934. The Wheelers believed in the proper training of volunteers; thus at this site Kenyon received the training she desired. Here Kenyon also learned what would later become known as the "Wheeler-Kenyon" method of archaeology. Previous methods focused on architecture; this new method emphasized the careful observation and analysis of stratification in the soil, as well as analysis of contents found in the soil. The observations would then be recorded in detailed section drawings. By making these careful stratigraphic observations and analyses, Kenyon explained, one could understand the history of the time and the area. Wheeler was one of the first to recognize Kenyon's remarkable talent for "dirt archaeology" and her incredible sense of observation, both of which continue to be recognized. According to William Dever, her talent in these areas was not equaled.

During the same years that Kenyon was working with Wheeler at Verulamium, she became a student of the British School of Archaeology in Jerusalem. In 1931 she arrived in Palestine for the first time, joining the Joint Expedition of Harvard University, the British School of Archaeology in Jerusalem, the Hebrew University of Jerusalem, the Palestinian Exploration Fund, and the British Academy to Samaria. Beginning in 1931 and digging for four seasons under the direction of John Crowfoot, Kenyon was able to implement and refine the method she was learning from Wheeler. This was the first time that this distinct approach was used at a Palestinian site. Based on her examination of the stratigraphy and her analysis of the pottery at the summit of the tel, along with a reliance on her knowledge of the biblical text, Kenyon dated the building periods of the site to those found in the book of Kings, beginning with the establishment of Samaria by Omri in 822 BCE and ending with the Assyrian destruction in 722 BCE. Her analysis of the stratigraphy and the Iron Age building structures was published in 1942 in *Samaria—Sebaste I: The Buildings*, but her pottery analysis was not published until 1957 in *Samaria-Sebaste III: The Objects*. By this time, Kenyon was well into her work at Jericho. With this publication in 1957 came much debate concerning Kenyon's method of dating.

She dated the buildings at Samaria based on the latest pottery found in the foundations of the buildings, whereas other prominent archaeologists—such as W. F. Albright, G. E. Wright, Yohanan Aharoni, and Ruth Amiran—dated buildings based on pottery found on the floors. As a result, many disagreed with Kenyon's conclusions regarding the dating of the buildings at Samaria to the beginning of Omri's reign, and argued instead that the buildings should be dated to an earlier period. In more recent studies, Ron E. Tappy also has questioned Kenyon's conclusion. In his dissertation, he reexamined the pottery chronology and stratigraphy of Samaria and also concluded that the pottery indicates an earlier occupation, dating to the eleventh and tenth centuries BCE.

Although Kenyon's method of excavation had been introduced to Palestinian archaeology at Samaria, her application of the method at the famous site of Jericho was "a turning point in Palestinian archaeology and her greatest claim to an enduring reputation in the subject" (Moorey, "Kenyon," 6). Kenyon began her excavations at Jericho in 1952 and continued work there through 1958. Previous excavations had taken place at the site. However, with the improved methods of excavation and pottery-dating since the most recent excavation, Kenyon undertook the Jericho excavation in an attempt to settle some dispute regarding "the date of the entry of the Israelites into Palestine" (*Digging Up Jericho*, 33). It had been generally accepted that the Israelites entered Canaan during the Late Bronze Age (ca. 1550–1200 BCE). Previous excavations showed conflicting conclusions: the excavations in the early 1900s by Sellin and Watzinger indicated that there was no Late Bronze city at Jericho; the excavations by John Garstang during the early 1930s indicated a city at Jericho that had been destroyed during the Late Bronze Age, approximately 1400 BCE. In addition, Garstang's excavations revealed very early remains that Kenyon wanted to explore. While Kenyon was sincere in her Christian beliefs, she also recognized that as an archaeologist she was not obligated to reconcile the evidence with the biblical account. Rather, her obligation was to examine the material evidence and allow archaeology to be the "decisive criterion" (*Digging Up Jericho*, 258). Thus Kenyon set out to examine the stratigraphy of the site in order to obtain "a stratified sequence of archaeological materials at Jericho" (Prag 113). Her findings and conclusions were published in several articles and in her popular book *Digging Up Jericho*. Based on her detailed analysis, Kenyon concluded that there was no fortified Late Bronze city for the Israelites to conquer.

The application of Kenyon's archaeological method at the site of Jericho immediately demonstrated its strengths. As a result of the Jericho excavations, her method was adopted by other well-known archaeologists who reexamined sites previously excavated by employing her method, with some modifications. Most notably, G. E. Wright adopted her method and reexcavated Shechem. The excavations at Jericho also exposed the weakness of Kenyon's method. While the deep trenches provided a chronological sequence at the site, they did not provide comprehensive horizontal exposure to the site, thus providing an inadequate awareness of site-formation processes. Her excavations at Jerusalem would further highlight this weakness.

Kenyon began excavating in Jerusalem in 1961. The purpose of the excavation was to answer particular questions, including the location of the city of David, the dating of the spread of the city to the western ridge, and the authenticity of the traditional site of the Church of the Holy Sepulchre. Excavations continued at Jerusalem through 1967, employing the same stratigraphical method that had been used at Jericho. However, as Kenyon admitted in *Digging Up Jerusalem*, the fallen stones from destroyed buildings made it challenging to arrive at a clean, vertical face from which to analyze the stratigraphy. In addition, excavating in an occupied area also presented certain obstacles. Nonetheless, Kenyon was able to draw some conclusions about the location and size of the city of David. As she had done with Jericho, she also published several articles and a popular book regarding the excavations at Jerusalem. However, Israeli excavations in Jerusalem following Kenyon's, according to Amihai Mazar, "have proved many of Kenyon's conclusions wrong" (Davis 208). The main criticism of Kenyon's work is that her excavation areas were too small and limited and her emphasis on sections "did not prove satisfactory in dealing with monumental architecture" (Dever 535).

In *Digging Up Jericho*, Kenyon explains how she approaches biblical interpretation, specifically interpreting the Old Testament. She views the books of the Old Testament as "true history," which is also "a traditional history, a record of tribal events transmitted verbally," which has been "passed on from generation to generation" (257). The purpose of this written record is to "[show] the relationship of the Israelites to their god Yahweh and his guidance of their destiny" (257). In considering pure history, Kenyon recognizes two limitations of relying on a compilation of traditional history: a traditional history is incomplete, and a traditional history may produce an inflated chronology. Thus, Kenyon concludes, "in attempting to reconcile literary and archaeological evidence, . . . chronology based on the biblical record cannot be taken literally" (258). For Kenyon, archaeology is the deciding factor for determining biblical chronology.

In addition to her work in the field, throughout her career Kenyon held several other influential positions, including lecturer in Palestinian archaeology at the Institute of Archaeology at London University (1948–62); treasurer of the Palestinian Exploration Fund (1948–55); director and/or chairperson of the British School of Archaeology in Jerusalem (1951–76); and principal of St. Hugh's College, Oxford (1962–73). In recognition of her accomplishments and publications, Kenyon was awarded several honorary doctorates from such institutions as the University of London (1951), Oxford University (1964), and Evangelisch-theologische Fakultät der Eberhard-Karls-Universität in Tübingen, Germany (1977). She was also named a Dame Commander of the Order of the British Empire in 1973 for her "services to archaeology," thus becoming Dame Kathleen M. Kenyon.

Kenyon strongly believed in the proper training of those interested in archaeology. Her book *Beginning in Archaeology*, originally published in 1952, was written to provide answers for those interested in pursuing archaeology as a career, as well as information that she wished beginners to have before participating in an excavation. Those who were privileged to work with Kenyon on the Jericho excavations remember her as a demanding yet patient teacher, willing to invest time in her students. Kenyon became a role model for many who participated in her excavations. Kay Prag describes working with Kenyon: "We strove to reach her standards, flowered with her praise, felt her warmth, respected her; where she led, we followed" (122). The Jericho excavation became a type of training ground for generations of archaeologists. According to Peter R. S. Moorey, "Her most enduring legacy may be as much in what she helped others to achieve as in what she achieved herself" ("Women," 99).

Bibliography

Davis, Miriam. *Dame Kathleen Kenyon: Digging Up the Holy Land*. Walnut Creek, CA: Left Coast, 2008.

Dever, William G. "Kathleen Kenyon." Pages 525–53 in *Breaking Ground: Pioneering Women Archaeologists*, edited by Getzel M. Cohen and Martha Sharp Joukowsky. Ann Arbor: University of Michigan Press, 2004.

Kenyon, Kathleen. *Beginning in Archaeology*. London: Phoenix House, 1952. 2nd, rev. ed., 1953. Reprints, New York: Frederick A. Praeger, 1961, 1966.

———. "Digging for History—From Zimbabwe to Jericho via Southwark." Kathleen M. Kenyon Collection, Baylor University.

———. *Digging Up Jericho*. New York: Frederick A. Praeger, 1957.

———. *Digging Up Jerusalem*. London: Ernest Benn, 1974.

Moorey, Peter R. S. "British Women in Near Eastern Archaeology: Kathleen Kenyon and the Pioneers." *Palestine Exploration Quarterly* 124 (1992): 91–100.

———. "Kathleen Kenyon and Palestinian Archaeology." *Palestine Exploration Quarterly* 111 (1979): 3–10.

Prag, Kay. "Kathleen Kenyon and Archaeology in the Holy Land." *Palestine Exploration Quarterly* 124 (1992): 109–23.

— Kathy A. Noftsinger

Kirschbaum, Charlotte von (1899–1975)

Charlotte von Kirschbaum was Karl Barth's assistant, serving as secretary, researcher, critical reader, and likely textual contributor to exegetical and historical sections in his massive *Church Dogmatics* (*CD*). She did not have formal university training (which was still largely restricted to men); however, her theological aptitude was recognized by Barth, whom she met through her pastor in the mid-1920s. As she performed a variety of editorial tasks for him, he came to consider her indispensable to his work. In 1929, certain that she was following a calling, she agreed to move into the Barth household. Barth himself evoked Gen. 2:18 when he thanked her in *CD* for being his true helper.

Von Kirschbaum was given lessons in Latin so that she could read theological texts penned in earlier centuries. From these texts she compiled an extensive file of extracts, which Barth drew on in his lectures and writing; in the process of this ongoing task, she gained her own mastery over the history of theology. She also prepared reports on contemporary theological scholarship for Barth. When Barth's opposition to Nazism resulted in his expulsion from his German university post in 1935, von Kirschbaum accompanied him and his family back to his native Switzerland. She remained his assistant at Basel throughout the difficult war and postwar years until her health seriously declined in 1965.

It is slowly being recognized that von Kirschbaum also did independent and significant work in scriptural interpretation, which she presented in lectures and in published form. Her goal was to begin laying a biblical foundation for a Protestant doctrine of woman. She positioned herself between the radically secular egalitarian feminism of Simone de Beauvoir and contemporary Roman Catholic Mariology, engaging what she saw as strengths and weaknesses in each. Several themes recur in her writings: the image of God as the duality—or twofold unity—of male and female, equally graced with different, complementary gifts; the ways in which the women of Scripture witness to their God-given roles; and insistence that the subordination of women to men in earthly institutions indicates neither women's lesser importance nor men's mediation of women's relationship to God. These institutions include marriage, other male-female relationships, and the church.

In regard to the position of women in the church, von Kirschbaum was responding to another contemporary situation. As World War II continued, German pastors were conscripted, and women, long involved in various kinds of church and parish service, assumed the additional duties of church ministry, including preaching and administration. The women who filled church vacancies were not ordained, and they were expected to renounce their new roles when the war was over. They seem to have done very well in their work, and many of them, with their congregations' support, wished to continue. Directly and indirectly, von Kirschbaum provided much support for their cause.

Von Kirschbaum's lectures were titled "Jesus Christ and the Community [*Gemeinde*]—Man and Woman," "Woman in the Ordering of Life in the New Covenant," "The Role of Woman in the Proclamation of the Word," and "The 'Mother of All Living.'" The lectures, with some additional material on feminism and Mariology, were published in 1949 under the title *Die wirkliche Frau* (*WF*). An expanded version of "The Role of Woman in the Proclamation of the Word" was separately published in 1951.

Von Kirschbaum develops the Barthian motifs of the nonaloneness of the Triune God and the realization of the image of God in male-female encounter in her own way; in turn, Barth cites *WF* in his subsequent discussion in *CD* of the male/female relationship. The essays of *WF* present biblical women in their communal contexts: relationally. In von Kirschbaum's stress on the gifts that women bring to the community of the church, the Pauline conception of gifts of the Spirit (1 Cor. 12:4–12) becomes an important motif for her.

The presentation of motherhood in the old and new covenants—from Eve through the women of Acts, specifically including Mary, Mother of God—demonstrates both human suffering and imperfection *and* women serving as instruments of God's grace. The prophetic women of Israel, such as Rahab (Josh. 2:1–14) and Deborah (Judg. 4), are spiritual mothers, delivering God's vivifying word in times of need. The women surrounding Jesus are part of his witness, as are such women in Acts as Tabitha and Priscilla (Acts 9:36; 18:2–3, 26).

Von Kirschbaum engages the restrictive pronouncements about women in the Epistles. The pronouncements certainly reflect a specific sociohistorical context, as much scholarship of her day declares. Paul enjoins behavioral rules for women of the church in Corinth because, in their overblown understanding of Christian freedom, they have disregarded the apostolic order of church authority. However, von Kirschbaum does not discard the rules as anachronisms. Enforcement of such male/female ordering ensures the inclusion and participation of women. For example, the silence of women in church that Paul prescribes in 1 Cor. 14:34–36 and 1 Tim. 2:11–14 renders them representative of the "Hearing Church" (which receives the Word of God), distinct from the "Teaching Church" and yet essential to the faith and life of the whole church. If man is above woman in the church and other structures in this life, it must be recalled and proclaimed that all of humankind is subordinate to Christ. And if the head of the church is Christ, it must be recalled and proclaimed that Christ subordinated himself to God's will. Hierarchical order is relativized in the new covenant.

In her study of women and proclamation, von Kirschbaum agrees with the growing number of voices in favor of opening the position of ministry to women in peacetime. Von Kirschbaum further argues that women can make a much-needed transformation in the office of proclamation. Men have allowed their ministerial authority to turn into an authoritarianism that separates them from their congregations and obscures the authority of the Word. In contrast, women will speak, not from above, but as an inseparable part of their congregation.

Die wirkliche Frau was reviewed in some sixty journals; almost all the reviews were positive and often enthusiastic. If von Kirschbaum had not dedicated her waking hours to Barth's work, much more of her acute, widely appealing perspective on Scripture would probably be available. However, as Barth's reputation grew and his professional activities widened in the second half of the twentieth century, she seems to have resumed her full-time identity as his assistant. Aptly, the study by Renate Köbler in 1987 that brought her back to scholarly attention is titled *Schattenarbeit: Charlotte von Kirschbaum—Die Theologin an der Seite Karl Barths* (In the Shadow of Karl Barth: Charlotte von Kirschbaum).

Bibliography

Kirschbaum, Charlotte von. *The Question of Woman: The Collected Writings of Charlotte von Kirschbaum*. Translated by John Shepherd. Edited and with an introduction by Eleanor Jackson. Grand Rapids: Eerdmans, 1996.

Köbler, Renate. *In the Shadow of Karl Barth: Charlotte von Kirschbaum*. Translated by Keith Crim. Louisville: Westminster/John Knox, 1989.

Selinger, Suzanne. *Charlotte von Kirschbaum and Karl Barth: A Study in Biography and the History of Theology*. University Park: Pennsylvania State University Press, 1998.

— SUZANNE SELINGER

Konttinen, Helena (1871–1916)

Helena Konttinen, a Finnish Sleep Preacher and the mother of the so-called Uukuniemi Revival, was born on June 18, 1871, to a peasant family of Eronen in eastern Finland. Konttinen was married to a poor farmer, Matti Konttinen, and a mother of four children, and followed in the footsteps of the woman she regarded as her spiritual foremother, Anna Rogel (d. 1784): she delivered sermons and prophecies in a sleeplike state, called to this "office of preaching," she felt, by God. In her own words, she proclaimed nothing in public that was not found in "God's Word." She heard affirmation from Christ: "When the walls of Zion have fallen and the shepherds have degenerated, so the Lord will take care of his herd even through his weak servants. Because if they become silent, then even the rocks will shout. You, Helena, are such a rock" (Konttinen in Sarlin, *Glimpses*, 139).

After having a special dream at the age of seven, Konttinen felt a need to learn about Christ and asked people to read to her from Scripture. Although the only school she attended was a confirmation class, she quickly learned to read the Bible, though she never learned to write. Instead, her life story and many of her sermons were recorded by a local pastor and scholar, Kaarlo Sarlin.

From her youth, Konttinen was known as a devout individual, drawn to prayer and solitude in the woods (a sacred place in Finnish indigenous spirituality, and a place where Konttinen felt the presence of Christ); she shunned merrymaking and vanity and selflessly served others at home and beyond. Her career as an unauthorized lay preacher began in 1895, after her mother-in-law died: she dreamed of God's calling her to wake from the sleep of sin and had a transformative "lightning" experience.

Initially, Konttinen resisted her call since she did not consider it her right as a woman to speak God's word. After a period of suffering and a sense that the "end of times" was approaching, however, Konttinen took to heart the words from Acts 2:17 that "in the last days . . . your sons and daughters shall prophesy." In Scripture she found other support for the preaching ministry that she and other women felt called to against the prohibitions of the "learned men." From the New Testament she argues that Christ himself clearly included women in the work for the kingdom of God; from the Old Testament she points out that the promise that a woman will break the snake's head was given inside paradise (Gen. 3:15). Furthermore, women, particularly wives, are not to be marginal members in Christ's church; they will bring about a "greater blessing":

> Now it has become such a turning point in time that females become persuaded to give speeches, more so than in the past. The Pharisees and the Sadducees would not wish to allow women to speak, but rather prohibit it, with the word of scripture. But the Savior himself has modeled profoundly how women are not forsaken. That women should remain quiet in the church means that they should not strive to become a teacher there, because they are set in the estate of a mother and could not readily and freely be able to take and leave. (*Glimpses*, 49–50)

As a concession to Paul's words in 1 Cor. 11:5, Konttinen, a married woman, covered her head when speaking in public. Each August during her decadelong public ministry, she underwent "changing days," experiencing renewal and receiving new direction from God for her prophetic activity, for which the books of Daniel and Revelation remained central inspirations.

In spite of her worry about the care of her young children, Konttinen felt compelled by her call and traveled widely. She visited individuals with particular messages to them and preached and prophesied in private house gatherings. Before preaching, she would lie down in a semiconscious state with her eyes open and experience being struck by Christ's brightness, the sweetness of the Trinity, and a visitation by particular angels, who gave her words to read from the Golden Book placed in front of her. With a loud voice, sometimes also singing hymns, she proclaimed God's words. She prophesied future events (e.g., wars, catastrophes, private tragedies), revealed unpleasant secrets and crimes, and repeatedly called listeners to repentance and good works. Konttinen emphasized the need to trust in God's mercy and to come to God regardless of one's feelings or failures. At the same time, she maintained the importance of the law in preaching:

> The whore of the Babylon is the fallen church. The other beast is the charismatic spirit. That deception is very powerful as it involves the sweet name of Jesus. That beast's spirit proclaims a gospel that denies the reality of damnation and obliterates God's justice, portraying God only as merciful. That the gospel is being preached without the law is the greatest abomination in the face of the Lord. That kind of wrong teaching shall win most of the people and is thus one

of the signs of the end times. The hell is said to be some hollow place here on earth where all the waste will become burned. This is the worst kind of deception. This spirit shakes people, moves their tongues, and operates in many ways and levels, and causes miracles. (*Glimpses*, 170)

Theologically, she was a Lutheran preacher, even if her venue as a woman was that of a charismatic. Her charismatic gifts allowed her to preach, teach, and interpret Scripture at a time when women were prohibited from carrying out such ministries. Her ministry also included miraculous healings and soul care for troubled consciences.

Konttinen suffered physically until her early death on April 24, 1916, about a year before her country claimed the independence from Russia that she had prophesied. Her preaching activity coincided with the early years of the Finnish nation's struggle for independence and cultural identity. Her work instigated a revival movement in Finland, and her legacy continues in the annual religious convention held in her memory, the work of the Parikanniemi Society, and the orphanage founded in accordance with her careful instructions.

Bibliography

Konttinen, Helena. *A prophet of our times: Her life and teachings, written for the illumination and strengthening of faith for those on the narrow path*. Edited by K. K. Sarlin. Kuopio: n.p., 1918.

Pinomaa, Lennart, ed. *Helena Konttinen, a prophet of our times: life and message*. Ristiina: Parikanniemi Orphanage Association, 1986.

Sarlin, Kaarlo K. *Eräs meidän ajan profeetta*. 3 vols. Puumala, Finland: Tekijä, 1916–19. Repr., Seinäjoki, Finland: Eemil Pulkkinen, 1943.

———. *Glimpses behind the Veil; or, The Seeress of Karelia: Experiences of Helena Konttinen, Reported in Shorthand from the Lips of the Seeress by the Rev. K. Sarlin*. Translated by Justus Bernarder Linderholm. Seinäjoki, Finland: Eemil Pulkkinen, 1948. Topeka, KS: Service Print Shop, 1948.

Stjerna, Kirsi. "Finnish Sleep-Preachers: An Example of Women's Spiritual Power." *Nova Religio: The Journal of Alternative and Emergent Religions* 5, no. 1 (Oct. 2001): 102–20.

Sulkunen, Irma. "Helena Konttinen." Pages 322–23 in vol. 5 of *Finland's National Biography*, edited by Matti Klinge. Helsinki: Suomalaisen Kirjallisuuden Seura, 2005.

— KIRSI STJERNA

▧ Lanyer, Aemilia (1569–1645)

Aemilia Lanyer published one collection of poems, *Salve Deus Rex Judaeorum* (*Hail God, King of the Jews*, 1611), whose centering title narrative in 1,840 lines of ottava rima (the common Renaissance epic stanza, ababab cc) is a description of Christ's passion told entirely from the point of view of women. In addition, the eleven dedicatory poems that precede the narrative and the country house poem, "The Description of Cooke-ham," that follows it, all contain biblical allusion and sometimes direct interpretation. The volume's reception history in its own time (coinciding with the publication of the KJV) is obscure, but it has garnered considerable critical attention since the recovery of early women writers became a serious literary-historical project in the late twentieth century.

She was born Aemilia Bassano, and was baptized on January 27, 1569, in St. Botolph's, Bishopsgate, just outside the city wall of London. She was the daughter of court musician Baptista Bassano, who died when she was seven, and Margaret Johnson, possibly of another family associated with court music, who died when she was eighteen. From sometime after her mother's death until she was twenty-three, she was the mistress of Queen Elizabeth's cousin and Lord Chamberlain, Henry Carey, Lord Hunsdon, forty years her senior. When she became pregnant in 1592, she was married to Alfonso Lanyer, another court musician, who served as father to her son, Henry. It is clear from visits she made to the astrologer Simon Forman in the 1590s that she had difficulty carrying other children to term, was ambitious for her husband's success in serving the Earl of Essex for the Cadiz expedition, and dearly missed the pleasures and privileges she enjoyed in the Elizabethan court, to which her relationship with Lord Hunsdon had given her access.

Lanyer's husband died in 1613, beginning two decades of her effort to gain some income from a hay-and-grain patent he had been granted some years earlier. From 1617 to 1619 she ran a school for girls in the wealthy suburb of St. Giles in the Field. By the end of the 1620s, she was apparently living with her son, Henry, who in due course had become a court musician, and his family in Clerkenwell. He died in 1633, and Lanyer continued to petition her late husband's family for the means to support her son's widow and two young children. She was buried on April 3, 1645, at St. James Clerkenwell.

Lanyer was a member of the minor gentry, but from her early court associations she maintained a friendship with at least one highborn woman who became her patron, Margaret Russell Clifford, countess of Cumberland, and she was acquainted with several others of notable piety or power. These included King James's estranged cousin, Lady Arbella Stuart, and Margaret's daughter, Lady Anne Clifford, who through marriages became countess of Dorset and countess of Pembroke and eventually succeeded to the barony of Cumberland in her own right. Lanyer also apparently served and was probably educated in the household of another of her dedicatees, Susan, countess dowager of Kent, whose mother was Catherine Willoughby, duchess of Suffolk, a Protestant heroine for her resistance during the reign of Catholic Queen Mary. These dedications—and others to such prominent women as Queen Anne, the countess of Pembroke (Sir Philip Sidney's sister and herself a writer of biblical verse), and the countess of Bedford (famously learned and a dedicatee of many poets, including John Donne and Ben Jonson)—suggest that Lanyer hoped to use her volume to extend her sources of patronage and perhaps renew her access to the court. These dedications nonetheless play on the presumed biblical knowledge and piety of the dedicatees.

The poems that begin the volume, therefore, all point to the central narrative poem on Christ's passion and variously announce its protofeminist project of affirming the virtue of women. In the first dedication—properly to the highest among the women, Queen Anne—Lanyer points specifically to a section in the narrative labeled "Eves Apology," and encourages the queen to see it as a valid interpretation:

> Behold, great Queene, faire *Eves* Apologie,
> Which I have writ in honour of your sexe,
> And do referre unto your Majestie,
> To judge if it agree not with the Text.
>> ("To the Queenes most Excellent
>> Majestie," lines 73–76)

This section within the narrative ("Salve Deus Rex Judaeorum," lines 751–840) presents a defense of Eve in the voice of Pilate's wife and has in recent years become easily the most anthologized section of the poem. It expands (and therefore interprets) not only Matt. 27:19, in which Pilate's wife tells him to have "nothing to do with that just man [Jesus]: for I have suffered many things in a dream because of him," but also the whole story of the fall.

The "Eves Apology" section argues that by crucifying Christ, men will abdicate any authority they may claim over women. To set up her startling conclusion in favor of women's "liberty," the speaker (Pilate's wife/Lanyer) insists that

> Our Mother *Eve*, who tasted of the Tree,
> Giving to Adam what she held most deare,
> Was simply good, and had no power to see,
> The after-coming harme did not appeare:
> The subtile Serpent that our Sex betraide,
> Before our fall so sure a plot had laide.
>> (lines 763–68)

However, "surely Adam can not be excused" (777), since "what Weaknesse offerd, Strength might have refused" (779). She continues with this not atypical argument of the time: that Eve was deceived, but Adam was not deceived, and his disobedience effected the fall. She takes it three steps further, though, by emphasizing Eve's simple good intentions, by suggesting that men thereby gained knowledge from women ("Yet men will boast of Knowledge, which he tooke / From *Eves* faire hand, as from a learned Booke"; 807–8), and by laying the crucifixion specifically at the hands of men, "Her sinne was small, to what

317

you doe commit" (818). Pilate's wife claims she "speakes for all" women in not giving "consent" to the crucifixion (833–34), a triumph of gender virtue that should override the curse of servitude from Gen. 3:16 ("Thy husband . . . shall rule over thee"):

> Then let us have our Libertie againe,
> And challendge to your selves no Sov'raigntie;
> You came not in the world without our paine,
> Make that a barre against your crueltie;
> Your fault being greater, why should you disdaine
> Our being your equals, free from tyranny?
> If one weake woman simply did offend,
> This sinne of yours, hath no excuse, nor end.
>
> (lines 825–32)

The pain of childbirth from the same Genesis curse, it seems, remains in place and wields a power of its own.

In addition to this remarkable reading of Gen. 3, Lanyer presents a restrained, empathetic, and even beautiful Christ, more keenly in touch with the weeping women around him than with his male disciples. In a gloss on Luke 23:27–31, Lanyer makes much of the procession to the cross: "The Thieves attending him on either side, / The Serjeants watching, while the women cri'd" (lines 967–68). She gives five stanzas to "The teares of the daughters of Jerusalem," which evoke Christ's sympathy even in his own distress and expose the hard-heartedness of the masculine authority those tears might seek to move. Although the suffering Christ would not "speake one word, nor once . . . lift his eyes / Unto proud *Pilate*, no nor *Herod*, king" (lines 977–78),

> Yet these poore women, by their piteous cries,
> Did move their Lord, their Lover, and their King,
> To take compassion, turne about, and speake
> To them whose hearts were ready now to breake.
>
> (lines 981–84)

Following this section are sixteen stanzas on the Virgin Mary, much of it elaborating on the encounter between Mary and the angel in Luke 1:28–38. Lanyer's feminizing project finds an appropriate topic in Mary, to whom she devotes an extended description and appreciation, but the portrayal falls short of Mariolatry. Mary is the "most blessed Virgin," the "deere Mother of our Lord" (lines 1025, 1031), whose loss is the greatest of all, but she is not herself an object of worship.

Christ's beauty, like his restraint and sympathy, connects him with what were usually considered womanly virtues. Throughout the poem Lanyer praises the "faire Virtues" that give women, and most particularly her patron, the

countess of Cumberland, "everlasting beauty, . . . true grace" (lines 189, 198).
With language from the Canticles, she describes the risen Christ as

> that Bridegroome that appears so fair,
> So sweet, so lovely in his spouses sight,
> That unto Snowe we may his face compare,
> His cheeks like scarlet, and his eyes so bright
> As purest Doves that in the rivers are,
> Washed with milke, to give the more delight.
>
> (lines 1305–10)

The description goes on, notably, to reflect Song 4:3, which describes feminine beauty, now applied to "the Bridegroom": "His lips like scarlet threds, yet much more sweet / Than is the sweetest hony dropping dew" (lines 1314–15).

Here the beauty of Christ becomes compounded with a larger project in Lanyer's volume: her effort to transpose the traditional focus on feminine beauty (with the ritualistic, sometimes implicit Neoplatonic understanding that outward beauty indicates inward virtue) into a focus on feminine virtue, for which beauty may be a secondary signal. The "Salve Deus" poem is itself framed by this emphasis on female virtue as true beauty, particularly as embodied by her patron, but it is also a major theme in many of the dedicatory poems. The theme is most explicit in the poem "To all virtuous Ladies in generall," which begins by addressing "Each blessed Lady that in Virtue spends / Your pretious time to beautifie your soules." These are invited to "put on your wedding garments" as "the Bridegroome stayes to entertain you all" (lines 9–10), presumably in the form of Lanyer's poem on the passion. The biblical allusions to Isa. 62:5 and the story of the wise and foolish virgins (Matt. 25:1–13) and to "*Salomon*" (line 19) and "*Aarons* precious oyl" (line 36; Lev. 8:12) meet companionably with references to Greek mythology, Minerva, Cynthia, Venus. All, in typical Renaissance syncretism, serve to elaborate on the origins of the true "beautie," which is pious virtue:

> In Christ all honour, wealth and beautie's wonne:
> By whose perfections you appeare more faire
> Than *Phoebus*, if he seav'n times brighter were.
>
> (lines 54–56)

A similar coexistence of Christian and pagan suffuses the final poem in the volume, "The Description of Cooke-ham," 210 lines of rhyming couplets that celebrate a summer sojourn with the countess of Cumberland and her daughter Anne in a royal country house owned by the countess's brother. This "delightfull place" (line 32) conjures the *locus amoenus* (or Edenic "beautiful place") of the classical tradition, and she mentions the Muses, Philomela, the Phoenix, and Phoebus, but as part of conventional poetic imagery. The core

319

of the poem is biblical. The setting is Edenic, a garden where the speaker, the countess, and Anne spend innocent hours of pleasurable meditation, reading, and song:

> In these sweet woods how often did you walke,
> With Christ and his Apostles there to talke;
> Placing his holy writ in some faire tree,
> To meditate what you therein did see:
> With *Moyses* you did mount his holy Hill,
> To know his pleasure, and performe his Will.
> With lovely *David* you did often sing,
> His holy Hymnes to Heavens Eternall King.
>
> (lines 81–88)

The spell is broken when "occasions call'd you so away" that even the beauty of this place could not "make you stay" (147–48). The poem suggests that class difference may have played a part in breaking up the idyll as well:

> Unconstant Fortune, thou art most too blame,
> Who casts us downe into so lowe a frame:
> Where our great friends we cannot dayly see,
> So great a difference is there in degree.
>
> (lines 103–6)

As perhaps an extension of Lanyer's radical thinking about gender, she briefly brings a similar awareness to class distinctions as she goes on to ponder the differences "in honour . . . ordain'd by Fate" (108), then pulls herself up short and lets herself speculate a bit:

> But whither am I carried in conceit?
> My Wit too weake to conster of the great.
> Why not? Although we are but borne of earth.
> We may behold the Heavens, despising death;
> And loving heaven that is so farre above,
> May in the end vouchsafe us entire love.
>
> (lines 111–16)

Just as they have enjoyed equally an Edenic world at Cooke-ham, perhaps (in an echo of Gal. 3:28) in heaven they will experience no difference between high and low (as none between Jew and Greek, male and female, slave and free), but all will have "entire love."

Lanyer concludes her volume with a short prose reassurance that places her authority where women writers of the period tended to place it: in the direct call of God. Having long ago dreamed of the words "Salve Deus Rex Judaeorum," then forgotten them, then written her version of Christ's passion, and then suddenly remembering the dream, she thought it "a significant token, that I was appointed to perform this Worke," and so "gave the very same words I received in sleepe as the fittest Title I could devise for this Booke." But what her contemporary audience thought of this claim of biblical authority, or of her book as a whole, is not known. Of the nine known extant copies of the *Salve Deus*, one was a gift from her husband, Alfonso Lanyer, to Thomas Jones, at the time archbishop of Dublin, and another was a gift from the countess of Cumberland to Henry, Prince of Wales. Both copies excluded some of the dedicatory material. There is no recorded reaction from these or any other readers of the time. What does exist is very substantial interest in Lanyer in modern times, with an increasing number of scholars writing and thinking about her work. Her boldness in interpreting biblical texts and her skill as a poet cast new light on the lives and habits of mind of Renaissance Englishwomen.

Bibliography

Callaghan, Dympna, ed. *The Impact of Feminism in English Renaissance Studies*. Basingstoke, UK: Palgrave Macmillan, 2007.

Grossman, Marshall, ed. *Aemilia Lanyer: Gender, Genre, and the Canon*. Lexington: University Press of Kentucky, 1998.

Lanyer, Aemilia. *The Poems of Aemilia Lanyer*. Edited by Susanne Woods. New York: Oxford University Press, 1993.

———. *Salve Deus Rex Judaeorum*. London: Valentine Simmes for Richard Bonian, 1611.

Lewalski, Barbara. *Writing Women in Jacobean England*. Cambridge, MA: Harvard University Press, 1993.

Woods, Susanne. *Lanyer: A Renaissance Woman Poet*. New York: Oxford University Press, 1999.

— SUSANNE WOODS

Leade, Jane (1624–1704)

Jane Ward Leade (or Lead), a seventeenth-century mystic, prophetess, and visionary, became the leader of a religious group in London known as the Philadelphian Society. She wrote at least fifteen books and treatises, including a three-volume spiritual diary titled *Fountain of Gardens*, which spans sixteen years and is nearly 2,500 pages long. Remarkably, nearly all of her works were translated into German and Dutch and published during her lifetime.

Leade was born into a gentry family in Letheringsett, Norfolk, England. She had seven brothers and one sister. Her father, Hamond Warde, served as a justice of the peace. She wrote that during the family's Christmas celebrations in 1640, in her sixteenth year, and without any warning, she heard a voice saying, "CEASE FROM THIS, I HAVE ANOTHER DANCE TO LEADE THEE IN; FOR THIS IS VANITY" (*Wars of David*, 21). This sudden conversion

321

experience plunged her into a spiritual turmoil, and "nothing was able to give her any satisfaction or rest, or to ease her wounded spirit, . . . which continued for the space of three years with very great anguish and trouble" (22). Then she was determined to become a "Bride of Christ." She did, however, eventually marry a cousin, William Leade, whom she described as "pious and godfearing." They lived in London for twenty-five years and had four daughters, two of whom died in infancy.

In the seventeenth century there was intense speculation that the end of the world was fast approaching. Millenarianism, a belief in the imminent second coming of Christ, was widespread and shared by many members of the established church as well as dissenters. Many millenarian authors used biblical images of disorder, drawn from Daniel and Revelation, to predict Christ's second coming; wars, revolutions, and strange sights in the skies were all associated with a change to the new world.

Leade, however, departed from this cataclysmic portrayal of the Apocalypse, believing instead in spiritual regeneration, a quiet revolution that would occur inwardly. Through her emphasis on the spirit, Leade envisioned a future for all through God's love and through personal revelation. Her millenarian expectations were unusual in that she envisioned the future in a highly gendered way: although in common with many people in the seventeenth century in believing that the second coming of Christ was imminent, her millenarian hopes also centered, unusually, as much on Wisdom's return as on Christ's, thus foregrounding the feminine aspect of the divine.

It was in April 1670, two months after the death of her husband, when Leade started to receive a series of visions of Wisdom, or Sophia, whom she witnessed as "an overshadowing bright Cloud and in the midst of it a Woman." Three days later it gently commanded, "Behold me as thy Mother," and six days after came the promise, "I shall now cease to appear in a Visible Figure unto thee, but I will not fail to transfigure my self in thy mind; and there open the Spring of Wisdom and Understanding" (*Fountain*, 1:18–21). From 1670 on, Leade recorded these visionary experiences and her spiritual progression in her diary, titled *Fountain of Gardens*. In a vision, Leade records Wisdom as saying: "[I'm] a true natural mother; for out of my Womb thou shalt be brought forth after the manner of a Spirit, Conceived and Born again; this thou shalt know by a New Motion of Life, stirring and giving a restlessness, till Wisdom be born again within the inward parts of thy soul" (1:18). The vision signaled the beginning of a spiritual relationship with Wisdom, which lasted all of Leade's life.

There was a significant turning point in 1674: Leade met Dr. John Pordage (1607–81), who introduced her to the writings of the German mystic Jakob Böhme (Jacob Boehme, 1575–1624). Böhme's philosophies are extremely complex and involve alchemy, magic, Hermeticism, gnosticism, and the Kabbalah. She was influenced by Böhme's suggestion that Wisdom coexisted with God.

For example, Leade also believed in the trinitarian model of the Godhead, with Wisdom as an integral part—as a mirror of the Godhead. Thus Leade's response to the hypostasis of the Trinity—God the Father, the Son, and the Holy Spirit, three separate identities being one—was to include Wisdom within the Godhead. Leade interpreted the Godhead as "The Tri-une-*Deity*, wherein is included the Virgin-*Wisdom*" (*Living Funeral*, 36). Wisdom was thus "A Virgin hid in Him from all Eternity" (*Wonders*, 31).

Leade also drew directly on biblical imagery and metaphor. In her diary entry for December 13, 1676, Leade describes a vision of the "Woman cloathed with the Sun," from Rev. 12, as a "great Wonder to come forth" (*Fountain*, 3:109). Leade uses "The Woman Clothed with the Sun" as a prophetic declaration of a new age, who provides the key to a new spiritual lineage. She writes: "The Mystery of the Creating Word, shall in the Figure of a Woman, now in this latter Day, in the Earth stand Diversely and in Plurality: as shall be known when the Elected Virgin shall have conceived, and brought forth her First-born Son, that must this strange and marvellous Generation multiply" (3:344). Thus expressed in a feminized way, Wisdom is the new Jerusalem (Rev. 21:1–5).

Apocalyptic marriage and the woman clothed with the sun in the book of Revelation are common metaphors in the prophetic literary tradition. Like Joanna Southcott after her, Leade used this trope for the apocalyptic hope of salvation and ultimate reward in the divine world, and it fueled her belief in the creation of a new spiritual generation. By producing spiritual offspring, Wisdom would lift the curse placed on women by God in Gen. 3:15. Wisdom was thus a creating force in human progress toward a utopia, in which Wisdom would restore humanity to a prefall condition and in which universal harmony would be restored with Christ's return to the new Jerusalem (Rev. 21:1–2).

Elevating Wisdom to the highest realm, Leade goes further in her deification of Wisdom, stating that she is the "eternal Goddess in a high and sober sense" (*Revelation*, 42). Leade writes of her vision of a new Jerusalem, which includes her expectation of Wisdom's return, as explained in *Revelation of Revelations*, published in 1683:

> Oh, great Goddess and Queen of all worlds! Wilt thou, after so long a time of desertion, once appear again! Who is it that hath entreated thy favour, and gained a promise from thee, of a visit, . . . because nothing now will satisfy, unless thou bestow thyself, with all thy divine senses, as a co-deified life, to show that thou art not prevailed upon, to . . . restore thy own Virginity, where thou findest humility and importunity in that personality which is all beloved of the highest Wisdom, and only Spouse of God. (47–48)

For Leade, the expected return of Wisdom was at least of equal importance with Christ. Yet Leade's originality of thought went beyond a christocentric interpretation of millenarianism, to a more gendered nonandrocentric notion of religion. Leade's representations of Wisdom as the second Eve would have more far-reaching repercussions for humanity when Christ returns in Spirit than would his incarnation: "The Birth of Jesus was great and marvellous, but this shall far excell it. . . . The Mother of the Virgin Birth will be more dignified and honoured, than the foregoing Ministration in the Birth of Jesus was" (*Revelation*, 42).

In 1704, however, the death of Jane Leade heralded the death knell of the Philadelphian Society. Although the exact number of the London Philadelphians is not known, Philadelphian circles had already formed in Holland, Germany, and Switzerland, influenced by Leade's published works. That she became such a prolific author was by virtue of the marshaling of loyal followers throughout her publishing years; her writing was a result of male collaboration, and her international reputation came out of sponsored translation. The legacy of her published writings influenced, for example, the eighteenth-century cleric William Law, who wrote *A Serious Call to a Devout and Holy Life* (1729)—one of the central spiritual texts of the eighteenth century.

See also Southcott, Joanna (1750–1814)

Bibliography

Leade (or Lead), Jane. *Fountain of Gardens, watered by the Rivers of Divine Pleasure.* 3 vols. London: P. J. Loutherbourg, or J. Bradford, 1696–1701.

———. *A Living Funeral Testimony; or, Death overcome, and drown'd in the life of Christ.* London: J. Bradford, 1702.

———. *The Revelation of Revelations.* London: A. Sowle, 1683.

———. *Wars of David, and the Peaceable Reign of Solomon.* London: J. Bradford, 1700.

———. *The Wonders of God's Creation Manifested, in the Variety of Eight Worlds.* London: T. Sowle, 1695.

Lee, Francis. *Der Seelig und aber Seeligen Jane Leade Letztere Lebens-Stunden.* Amsterdam: R. & G. Wetstein, 1705.

— JULIE HIRST

Lee, Jarena (1783–ca. 1849)

Jarena Lee was a pioneer preacher/exhorter in the Methodist tradition. Her spiritual narrative, *The Life and Religious Experience of Jarena Lee, a Coloured Lady, Giving an Account of Her Call to Preach the Gospel*, was published in 1836 and in expanded form in 1849. Her book marked the second known publication by an African American woman, and it is the primary source of information about this prophetic preacher. Lee's autobiographical work serves as a historical source, a spiritual biography, a sermonic dialogue with the reader, and an apology for women preachers. Moreover, her book allowed her the legacy of "having her say."

Born in 1783 to free but poor parents in Cape May, New Jersey, Lee was hired out as a maid at the age of seven. Her narrative briefly chronicles her experiences in various households before moving to the first in a series of divine encounters. Her conversion experience is dramatically detailed in her autobiography, followed by her sanctification and call to preach the gospel in 1811. Each of these accounts draws from the rich prophetic tradition in Scripture. Lee's call to preach follows the structure of the call of a Mosaic prophet. Like Moses, Lee experiences disbelief and doubt around her call (Exod. 3:1–4:17). Like the exchange between God and Moses, God reassures, cajoles, and finally insists. Like the exchange between God and Jeremiah, another Mosaic prophet, Lee's call includes God's assurance that "I will put words in your mouth, and will turn your enemies to become your friends," so that Lee finally comes to the place where she can preach with authority (cf. Jer. 1).

Lee's authority as a preacher was very much the result of the Second Great Awakening and the Methodist church. Methodism laid claim to authority that came not from the established institutional church but from Scripture, experience, and the Holy Spirit. It purported to declare a gospel that was so clearly expressed that anyone could understand it, which allowed those with little formal training to base their preaching on the "Word" and their experiences. Lee's writing reflects sensitivity to the power of story, and she was an expert at applying Scripture to her current situation, drawing connections between her own story and that of the stories in the Bible. On one occasion in church, the preacher announced Jonah as the basis for the sermon. During the sermon, Lee was moved to exhort on the spot, identifying with the prophet Jonah: "I told them I was like Jonah; for it had been then nearly eight years since the Lord had called me to preach his gospel to the fallen sons and daughters of Adam's race, but that I had lingered like him, and delayed to go at the bidding of the Lord, and warn those who are as deeply guilty as were the people of Nineveh" (Lee 17).

This was not the first time the Spirit moved Lee, resulting in the interruption of the church service. The first time Lee spoke publicly in church, it was to attest to her salvation. This first declaration was also an interruption. The minister remained silent while she "exhort[ed] sinners." This movement of the Spirit embodied by Lee was literally and symbolically an interruption to the Methodist Church, which, in its desire to be normalized, over time became increasing restrictive and excluded women.

Just as Lee's call to preach interrupted the service, so did it interrupt her life. Lee's call meant that she spent her life engaged in a struggle to respond to God in the face of opposition from her own denomination and her own people. Like other women, she had to navigate the traditional responsibilities of family and children as she sought to preach the gospel, which may explain why she did not answer her call to preach until after her husband's death. Preaching the gospel also meant that she entrusted her children to someone else's care. She experienced bouts of serious illness and most likely depression. What is remarkable is the persistently positive tone Lee's narrative takes:

> I have travelled, in four years, sixteen hundred miles
> And of that I walked two hundred and eleven miles,
> And preached the kingdom of God to the falling sons
> And daughters of Adam, counting it all joy for the sake
> Of Jesus. Many times cast down but not forsaken. . . .
>
> (Lee 36)

This positive tone suggests that Lee's usage of the prophetic motif is not simply a rhetorical device. Rather, she sees herself as a part of a prophetic tradition and line, with a vocation to deliver God's words to God's people who have forgotten how to hear. Jarena Lee's words, like those of the biblical prophets before her, speak to following generations, reminding all of the tension between people's tendencies toward exclusion and the vastness of God's mercy.

Bibliography

Andrews, William L. *Sisters of the Spirit*. Bloomington: Indiana University Press, 1986.

Florence, Anna Carter. *Preaching as Testimony*. Louisville: Westminster John Knox, 2007.

Lee, Jarena. *Religious Experience and Journal of Mrs. Jarena Lee, Giving an Account of Her Call to Preach*. Rev., expanded ed. Philadelphia: The author, 1849.

Marshall, Donald G., ed. *The Force of the Tradition: Response and Resistance in Literature, Religion, and Cultural Studies*. Lanham, MD: Rowman & Littlefield, 2005.

Moody, Joycelyn. *Sentimental Confessions: Spiritual Narratives of Nineteenth Century African-American Women*. Athens: University of Georgia Press, 2001.

— JUDY FENTRESS-WILLIAMS

Leibowitz, Nehama (1905–97)

Nehama (Nechama) Leibowitz was born in 1905 in Riga, Latvia. Her sole sibling, older brother Yeshayahu, went on to become a highly controversial Israeli philosopher. She was well educated in both Jewish and general culture. She was home-tutored up to the tenth grade, when the family moved to Berlin in 1914 and she joined the Berlin Gymnasium to complete her secondary education. She spent the years 1925–30 at the universities of Berlin, Heidelberg, and Marburg, studying English and German philology and literature, and biblical studies, with some of the world's leading scholars, such as Ernst Sellin, Kurt Galling, Hugo Gressman, Rudolf Bultmann, Bruno Meissner, Gustav Hölscher, Eduard Spranger, and Rudolph Otto. Her 1930 doctoral dissertation was titled "Translation Techniques of Judeo-German Bible Translations in the Fifteenth and Sixteenth Centuries, as Exemplified by Translations of the Book of Psalms" (published in German in 1931). At the same time, she advanced her Jewish studies at the Hochschule für die Wissenschaft des Judentums, the Berlin college for the scientific study of Judaism. This resembled an academic department for Jewish studies, but it was not affiliated with a particular university. There she met and studied with Jewish scholars, rabbis, and rabbinical students.

In 1930 she immigrated to Palestine with her husband. She soon established her career, teaching at teacher-training seminaries and at Bar-Ilan and Hebrew universities; she also received a professorship in Bible Education at Tel-Aviv University. She was awarded several prizes throughout her life, including the prestigious Israel Prize in the Field of Education (1957). A staunch Zionist, she remained in Israel, refusing to leave its borders even for brief travel or lecturing purposes.

Leibowitz was first and foremost a teacher. She requested that beneath her name and dates on her gravestone shall appear the sole word "Teacher." Her career was comprised primarily of many thousands of hours in teaching the Bible and its interpretation. She was charismatic, brilliant, and erudite; students flocked to hear her. The impetus for her first major enterprise in print came about through a set of unusual circumstances. During the summer of 1942, although the academic term had finished, a group of students asked Leibowitz for more homework. She accommodatingly sent them her worksheets, comprising a series of questions on various difficulties in biblical texts, accompanied by citations of (primarily rabbinic) Bible commentators; with great enjoyment the students filled them out and mailed their answers back to be checked. Word soon spread, and many strangers asked to be included in the mailings: the number eventually swelled to hundreds of correspondents per week. During a thirty-year period, Leibowitz faithfully checked all the incoming answers—and did it all entirely unpaid. This massive endeavor stemmed solely from her devotion to the study of the Bible and its interpretation.

At some point, it was suggested to Leibowitz that instead of questions alone, she should also include answers. A die-hard educator, she felt that this would hinder the learning of students; however, she eventually reluctantly consented and created pamphlets containing not only questions but also answers. These were eventually published as five books, known as the *Studies* series: *Studies in Bereshit* (1972), *New Studies in Shemot* (1976), *New Studies in Vayikra* (1980), *Studies in Bamidbar* (1980), and *Studies in Devarim* (1980). Extremely popular, they were translated into English, French, Spanish, Dutch, German, and Russian.

These works most concretely express her insights and scholarship. Structurally speaking, each book is divided up according to the traditional weekly portion of Torah readings. Each portion contains approximately seven essays. Each essay begins with the pointed Hebrew text (that is, with vowels) divided into phrases, with key words in boldface. After stating the interpretive difficulty inherent within the text, Leibowitz proposes various solutions, quoting (sometimes at length) from classic and modern interpretations; these interpretations are primarily Jewish, though there are some exceptions, including a small number of biblical scholars, such as S. R. Driver and H. F. W. Gesenius, or writers such as Thomas Mann. She adds her own elucidations and comparisons. The conclusion of each essay consists of either a summary of a commentator's words or her own words bearing some ethical or spiritual message.

The *Studies* series was unique. Many considered it a great work of collation, viewing Leibowitz as having skillfully assembled, organized, and compared the interpretations of others. Leibowitz's activity as an interpreter in her own right, however, was often overlooked. Indeed, even today the question of whether she was a "biblical scholar" or a "biblical interpreter" remains a subject of debate. To the superficial reader, her own words appear as bridging devices between the different opinions presented therein. Her self-effacing style—granting great deference to classical biblical commentators, such as Rashi and Nahmanides (Rambam), and showing far more interest in promoting their words rather than her own—only served to strengthen the appearance of her own words as secondary.

On at least one occasion, Leibowitz was challenged to go beyond the works of others and to write a complete and systematic commentary of her own, suitable for a traditional audience yet updated for the times (Unterman 480), yet she never did. Her primary aim was not to write her own commentary, but to teach her students to think in a different fashion about the text; whether this was achieved through her own insights or those of others was largely immaterial. Her whole approach militated against innovation for its own sake; moreover, she would most likely have been extremely disinclined to take on the mantle of the first acknowledged female commentator on the Jewish Bible (481). Such a role would have brought the unwelcome label "revolutionary," undermining her goal to teach the Bible without ruffling traditional Jewish feathers, a goal that was more or less successfully achieved (298). This was no mean feat for the first Jewish woman ever to teach the Bible to such scope and acclaim, toppling stereotypes as she went.

All the above notwithstanding, a strong argument may be made that she was indeed a scholar and commentator. The fact remains that scattered throughout her writings, sometimes in plain sight and at other times requiring some excavation, are tremendous insights on Leibowitz's part. This was most noticeable in the essays where quotes of other commentators are few or nonexistent and her own ideas make up the lion's share. One such example is her essay "Anatomy of a Blessing" (*Bamidbar*, 290–96), which illustrates her sensitivity to tone and richness of language and involves only a brief mention of midrash and Rashi. Another example may be seen in her essays on the Joseph story.

Such original ideas were often derived from applying a literary approach to the Bible. Decades before the literary approach became popular in biblical studies, Leibowitz had already grasped some of its fundamental tools. From her colleagues Martin Buber and Franz Rosenzweig, she had learned about such things as the *Leitwort* (lead word), a keyword that appears repeatedly within a given passage or unit, and other literary tools. Influences in this direction also included Benno Jacob, a German rabbi, and Umberto Cassuto, an Italian-born rabbi, both of whom held a belief in the essential thematic unity of the Bible and espoused what resembles the literary approach. Leibowitz was also intellectually enriched by her relationships with Aryeh Ludwig Strauss—Buber's son-in-law and the greatest Israeli theoretician of literature in the first half of the twentieth century—and Meir Weiss. The latter, a close friend of Leibowitz's, rejected the historical approach; influenced by the wave of New Criticism sweeping the field of studies in literature, he formulated his own method of biblical interpretation, which he called "Total Interpretation." Buber and Rosenzweig too had anticipated several methodological conclusions of the New Critics, such as the notion of form as content, the unity of the text, and the importance of every word.

All of these influences had their effect on Leibowitz. Many times she spoke of the need for close reading, and she showed herself capable of brilliant literary analysis in a number of instances dispersed throughout her writings. For example, she did some very interesting work in comparing repeated passages and explaining their differences in terms that were not historical (different authors) but ethical-educational—the text's purpose being to highlight two different perspectives. For example, when the Reubenites, Gadites, and half the tribe of Manasseh approach Moses to request possession of land in the Transjordan (Num. 32), their request is repeated by Moses, with emendations. Leibowitz places the passages side by side—the original request and Moses's words—and highlights the phrases *before the Lord* and *against the Lord* (Num. 32:20, 23, 32), then remarking: "The abyss separating their two outlooks stands revealed here. The two and a half tribes saw it in the light of a quid pro quo between themselves and the rest of Israel. . . . Not so Moses. He stated everything in terms of responsibility to and dependence on God, who alone drives out the enemy and apportions the land" (*Bamidbar*, 382–83).

The literary approach allowed Leibowitz to avoid critical biblical scholarship, which she disliked tremendously due to its historicizing nature, its threat to traditional values, and what she viewed as its shoddy and sometimes anti-Semitic scholarship.

Leibowitz also exhibited original scholarship in other genres, writing insightful comments on midrash at a time when only a small minority took seriously this corpus of highly creative rabbinical expositions on biblical verses. She worked hard to demonstrate that midrash was also a commentary on the Bible, its seemingly disjointed and far-fetched thoughts being on occasion fine examples of close reading and sensitivity to anomalies in the text. Although midrash is treated with far more respect today, Leibowitz during her career was a lone voice crying in the wilderness. Some scholars have also identified seeds of postmodern readings in her work, though this can be debated. Leibowitz's ethical philosophy rested at times on her own interpretations of biblical texts and unusual definitions of biblical concepts such "holiness" or "chosenness."

Leibowitz was opposed to feminism and to feminist readings of the biblical text. She was not interested in the female figures of the Bible as females, and she never quoted female scholars in her work. Nonetheless, she did more for the scholarship of Jewish women than almost any other woman in Jewish history. There had been no serious female Jewish Bible interpreter until Nehama Leibowitz. She was the first woman to achieve widespread recognition and acclaim for such scholarship and to take her place among the ranks of the male Jewish biblical interpreters preceding her, whose works she loved. It is impossible to quantify how many doors she opened for women, who previously had not been granted access to high-level Jewish study. Once she proved that it could be done, there was no going back; many Jewish women, as well as men, continue to owe her a debt of gratitude for her dedication, devotion, and the quiet revolution she began, whether intentionally or not.

Bibliography

Amit, Yairah. "Hebrew Bible—Some Thoughts on the Work of Nehama Leibowitz." *Immanuel* 20 (Spring 1986): 7–13.

Leibowitz, Nehama. *Leader's Guide to the Book of Psalms.* New York: Hadassah Education Dept., 1971.

———. *New Studies in Shemot (Exodus).* Jerusalem: WZO [World Zionist Organization], Dept. for Torah and Culture in the Diaspora, 1976.

———. *New Studies in Vayikra (Leviticus).* Jerusalem: WZO, Dept. for Torah and Culture in the Diaspora, 1980.

———. *Studies in Bamidbar (Numbers).* Jerusalem: WZO, Dept. for Torah and Culture in the Diaspora, 1980.

———. *Studies in Bereshit (Genesis).* Jerusalem: WZO, Dept. for Torah and Culture in the Diaspora, 1972.

———. *Studies in Devarim (Deuteronomy).* Jerusalem: WZO, Dept. for Torah and Culture in the Diaspora, 1980.

———. *Torah Insights.* Jerusalem: WZO, Dept. for Torah and Culture in the Diaspora, 1995.

Peerless, Shmuel. *To Study and to Teach: The Methodology of Nechama Leibowitz.* Jerusalem: Urim Pubs., 2003.

Unterman, Yael. *Nehama Leibowitz: Teacher and Bible Scholar.* Jerusalem: Urim Pubs., 2009.

— YAEL UNTERMAN

Lewis, Agnes Smith *See* Gibson, Margaret Dunlop (1843–1920), and Agnes Smith Lewis (1843–1926)

Livermore, Harriet (1788–1868)

Although now more generally and, perhaps, regrettably remembered as an unsympathetic character in J. G. Whittier's 1865 poem "Snowbound," Harriet Livermore was a well-known itinerant preacher, speaking not only in diverse religious and social contexts but also in the Hall of Representatives; she preached to Congress four times over the course of her career, in 1827, 1832, 1838, and 1843. Livermore was a prodigious writer, penning and self-publishing some seventeen volumes of work. Her major motivation to publish such an impressive number of writings, while grounded in her sense of vocation as authoritative interpreter of biblical prophecy, was to fund her preaching activities in the northeastern United States and her multiple journeys to Jerusalem, where she hoped to witness the second coming of Christ. She describes one of her earliest works, *Scriptural Evidence in Favour of Female Testimony, in Meetings for Christian Worship* (1824), as generating enough income to support her traveling expenses as a preacher for an entire year (*Narration*, 189).

Livermore was born in Concord, New Hampshire, on April 14, 1788, to an affluent, influential New England family. Her father, Edward St. Loe Livermore, was associate justice of the New Hampshire Supreme Court and was twice elected to Congress. Her grandfather, Samuel Livermore, was also a congressman as well as a prominent US senator. Little is known about Livermore's mother, who died before Livermore reached the age of five. She received her education at several boarding schools, including Haverhill (MA), Byfield Seminary (Newburyport, MA), and Atkinson Academy (NH). Livermore writes that she was sent away to boarding school because her "volatile" and "impetuous" nature made her difficult to handle at home: "With regard to my natural temper, I was never endowed with any natural equanimity, moderation, or sweetness. I was always called passionate from my earliest remembrance" (*Narration*, 20).

In 1811, at the age of twenty-three, Livermore decided to change her life dramatically: "Tired of the vain, thoughtless life I had led, sick of the work, disappointed in all my hopes of sublunary bliss, I drew up a resolution in my mind to commence a religious life—to become a religious person. . . . Neither fears of hell, nor desires for Heaven influenced the notion. I fled to the name and form of religion, as a present sanctuary from the sorrows of life" (*Narration*, 30–31). Moving between Congregationalist, Presbyterian, Quaker, and Freewill Baptist assemblies, in 1824 she declared herself a "pilgrim stranger," rejecting any formal religious affiliation and unequivocally assuming the role of itinerant female preacher. This role was not easy to adopt, since preaching to audiences of both sexes ("promiscuous" audiences) was not considered proper to the womanly sphere; Livermore therefore describes her public witness as a form of "martyrdom" (*Narration*, 7; *Harp*, 6) and states that she briefly took on a position as a schoolteacher to spare her family and friends the shame of her vocation: "I know that a female preacher was lightly esteemed in this day, therefore thought I . . . I will endeavour to be respectable" (*Narration*, 192–93).

A self-proclaimed "literalist," Livermore grounded her sense of vocation as a female preacher in scriptural revelation; it is the Bible that declares the equal distribution of the rational and spiritual substance in both men and women, and woman therefore cannot be viewed as less than an equal, less than a partner, to man (*Narration*, 202; *Addresses*, 23, 113). Mary Magdalene offers an excellent model for female preachers, Livermore argues, for she was not only the first human to see Jesus after the resurrection; she was also the first to preach that he was risen from the dead: "She knew Him—her eyes were not holden, as we read of the male disciples" (*Tidings*, 3:6). Indeed, women are often represented as more positive figures than men, both in biblical text ("Death reigned from Adam, and not from Eve. Woman presented life to the world; for she brought forth Christ") and in contemporary experience, as she argues that more women than men seek "the path that opens on heaven," the reason being that "humble piety is exceedingly rare among the male sex" (*Tidings*, 3:47, 52).

Although Livermore strongly defends female evangelism and the basic equality of men and women on scriptural grounds, her "literalist" approach leads her to set limits on female authority in the context of the church, and she restricts ordination to men (*Evidence*, 120). Livermore states, "Man takes the lead in authority of all kinds—his responsibility, therefore, is very great. Indeed, man is so gifted with influence, that one like Paul . . . could effect more visible benefit to Christianity, than a host of Phebes [*sic*], because the latter is a weaker vessel" (*Tidings*, 4:51–52). The context of this statement is a discussion of the character of the beast in Rev. 13:11–18; since man "takes the lead in authority of all kinds," Livermore declares that the beast will therefore be a man.

While upholding some conventional views of male authority in the church, Livermore is quite striking in justifying her own authority. She finds numerous female exemplars of preaching in both the Old and New Testaments, but her own sense of authority in preaching is demonstrated most remarkably in her self-presentation in the context of Pauline apostleship. Livermore freely quotes Paul in her depiction of her own vocation: "Of the goodness of God I have a right to boast. I know this long-suffering, merciful, gracious name; it is proclaimed continually in my soul. . . . I know nothing in religion but Christ and Him crucified; for He rose from the dead, which justifies my faith in His blood. . . . The atonement I have received by faith in Jesus Christ: that is the poor sinner's portion. I claim it: it is mine" (*Tidings*, 2:vi–vii).

She emphasizes the authenticity of her calling through recollections of dangers of travel fully resonant with the apostolic struggles of Paul (*Tidings*,

2:iii). Livermore boldly extends this authority of her calling to her interpretation of Scripture, stating that those who do not receive her tidings with faith and who do not adhere to literal interpretation are unprepared to search the sacred Word. Those who have been led astray "by preachers in your pulpits, or by the productions of learned commentators on the Bible, to believe [in] a spiritual reign of the Lord Jesus Christ, . . . will feel a shock like a house falling about your head, when the literal or personal appearing of Emmanuel comes before you" (*Tidings*, 2:58). Livermore may be somewhat ambiguous in her interpretation of male and female roles, but her striking presentation of personal authority in preaching and in biblical interpretation is decidedly unconventional, and it is worthy of further study.

Bibliography

Billington, Louis. "'Female Laborers in the Church': Women Preachers in the Northeastern United States, 1790–1840." *Journal of American Studies* 19, no. 3 (Dec. 1985): 369–94.

Brekus, Catherine A. "Harriet Livermore, the Pilgrim Stranger: Female Preaching and Biblical Feminism in Early-Nineteenth-Century America." *Church History* 65, no. 3 (Sept. 1996): 389–404.

Hoxie, Elizabeth F. "Harriet Livermore: 'Vixen and Devotee.'" *New England Quarterly* 18, no. 1 (March 1945): 39–50.

Livermore, Harriet. *Addresses to the Dispersed of Judah*. Philadelphia: L. R. Bailey, 1849.

———. *The Harp of Israel, to Meet the Loud Echo in the Wilds of America*. Philadelphia: J. Rakestraw, for the authoress, 1835.

———. *Millennial Tidings*. Nos. 1–4. Philadelphia: The author, 1831–39.

———. *A Narration of Religious Experience: In Twelve Letters*. Concord, NH: Jacob B. Moore, for the author, 1826.

———. *Scriptural Evidence in Favour of Female Testimony, in Meetings for Christian Worship: In Letters to a Friend*. Portsmouth, NH: R. Foster, 1824.

— ERIN VEARNCOMBE

Lock, Anne Vaughan (1534–ca. 1602)

Anne Vaughan Lock, daughter of Stephen Vaughan, a London cloth merchant, and Margaret Gwynnethe, both of whom served in the court of Henry VIII and his succession of wives, was inducted early into the fervent Protestantism (in the Church of England) of the London merchant class. Lock's marriage in 1551 to Henry Lock brought her into a more socially prominent family and into contact with the Scottish reformer John Knox, with whom she carried on a multiyear correspondence. During the reign of Mary Tudor, she fled to Geneva and, after her return to England, published her first book in 1560: the translation of four sermons by Calvin, a preface dedicated to another Marian exile, the dowager duchess of Suffolk, and a sonnet sequence on Ps. 51.

After the death of her first husband, she married Edward Dering, a Greek scholar and rising Puritan preacher. With him and the accomplished, well-connected Cooke sisters—including Mildred Cecil, wife of Queen Elizabeth's chief minister, and Anne Bacon, wife of the queen's chief legal officer—Lock produced in 1572 an encyclopedic manuscript dedicated to Robert Dudley, one of the queen's favorite courtiers, to which she contributed a four-line Latin poem. After Dering's death, Lock married Richard Prowse and moved to his home in Exeter, where she continued to be prominently involved with the Reformed wing of the English church. In 1590, following the Marprelate controversy, which pitted Presbyterian-minded reformers against the bishops of the established church and resulted in the increased persecution of Puritans, Lock published a translation of Jean Taffin's *Of the Marks of the Children of God*, again preceded by a courtly dedication (this time to the countess of Warwick) and followed by a long poem on the benefits of affliction. Lock may have died shortly thereafter, but certainly by 1602, when she was remembered by Richard Carew as "a Gentlewoman [surpassing] her rare learning with a rarer modesty and yet expressing the same in her virtuous life and Christian [death]" (White, "Writers," 202).

Lock's biblical interpretation is found in her dedicatory prefaces and poems, where she distinguishes herself with intricate paraphrases and cross-references that create a dense scriptural weave of allusion and admonition. Nowhere can her distinctive style be more clearly seen than in the 1560 dedication to the duchess of Suffolk. Taking as her central motif the weakened state of England newly emerging from the persecutions of Mary Tudor, Lock argues that her country needs "good medicine," the sound doctrine that God himself prescribes, that Calvin "compounds" as skillful apothecary, and that Lock packages into an "English box." She intricately develops this medicinal conceit with reference to three distinctive oils.

Lock first invokes the oil of the wise and foolish virgins in Matt. 25:1–13. The former are welcomed by the heavenly bridegroom because their lamps, fueled by the oil they have saved up for this very purpose, illuminate their persons and their work. The foolish virgins, in contrast, having wasted their oil, now try to "beg and borrow" from their neighbors. Lock equates such borrowing with the Roman Catholic doctrine of supererogation, the attribution of the superfluous good works of the saints to those less godly, and then swiftly converts the foolish virgins' expended lamp oil into bad medicine, the "poisonous potions" that unscrupulous papist physicians administer to their unsuspecting patients.

In contrast to such "unwholesome stuff," true Christians turn to an unlikely cure, oil of scorpion, which provides Lock with a compact image that gains its power from the conjunction of medical, scriptural, and doctrinal discourses. Medically, such distilled oils were part of the avant-garde Paracelsan practices that many sixteenth-century reformers championed. By drawing on the latest medical knowledge of the day, Lock enlarges the traditional trope of medicine that is good for the soul and updates the commonplace notion that only the scorpion can cure its own sting. She also transforms the medical image into concrete biblical exegesis by linking the scorpion to Num. 21:4–9, in which God first punishes the Israelites for disbelief by sending a plague of fiery serpents and then provides their cure in the form of a brass serpent, which Moses constructs and raises on a pole. The conjunction of scorpion and serpent allows Lock to access a long-standing exegetical tradition, beginning with the apocryphal Wisdom 16:5–7 and continuing in John 3:14–15, that identifies the brass serpent with the Messiah. It also provides, however, a contrast between the salvific oil of the scorpion and the spent oil and poisonous potions of the foolish virgins. Furthermore, it anticipates the subject of Calvin's sermons, the translation of which forms the bulk of her volume, because it is King Hezekiah himself who later tears down the brass serpent when the Israelites begin to worship it as an idol (2 Kings 18:4), an account resonant with the reformers who used it to attack Roman Catholic superstition. Lock's introduction of the brass-serpent theme thus adroitly and efficiently incorporates traditional and Calvinist doctrines into her medicinal metaphor.

Lock's portrait of the ailing Hezekiah draws on the humanist conception of poetry as a "speaking picture" and utilizes copious description to evoke a double empathy in the reader: concern over Hezekiah's plight as well as a heightened recognition of and identification with the horror of hidden sin now so graphically revealed in physical symptoms. The reader sees Hezekiah as "sometime chilling and chattering with cold, sometime languishing and melting away with heat, now freezing, now frying, now speechless, now crying out" (preface). The affective rhetoric Lock employs is intended to bring the reader to an empathetic encounter with the sinful and suffering Hezekiah, in preparation for a salvific encounter with the Good Samaritan's anointing oil.

Lock's paraphrase of this familiar parable (Luke 10:30–35) contrasts with Erasmus's rendition of the same text, which emphasizes the role of the apostolic innkeeper and thus of the institutional church. In contrast, Lock draws on Reformed doctrine to highlight not the role of the church hierarchy but rather the dual confrontation of the individual soul with its own sin and the justice of God, followed by the release of receiving "the sweet promises of God's almighty goodness" (preface). Although Calvinists were not alone in acknowledging God's electing, sovereign, and saving work—such was the premise of orthodox Christianity throughout the sixteenth century—Lock's embrace of Reformed doctrine sounds throughout the preface in her profound sense of sin as separation from God and sense of God's Word as sufficient medicine, but most particularly in her complete confidence in God's goodness.

The twenty-one sonnets that comprise the paraphrase of Ps. 51, along with the five-sonnet narrative introduction, draw on the humanist genre of Scripture paraphrase that Lock has utilized in the preface, as well as on Calvinist doctrine and traditional reworkings of this popular penitential psalm. Lock is clearly aware of sonnet conventions as she constructs her introspective narrator. Yet the narrator of the introductory sonnets, a penitent sinner hauled to the very gates of hell by her own conscience and Despair's accusations, displays both a sonnet persona and a psalmic persona. The sonnet persona invokes the courtly rituals of the jousting tournament and is consumed by sighs, trembling limbs, and eyes "full fraught with tears and more and more oppressed / With growing streams of the distilled brine" (introduction to Sonnet 1). The psalmic persona, however, grieves not for an unattainable lover or even for an unattainable God, but rather over sins that seem to be the "marks and tokens of the reprobate" (Sonnet 4). The sins themselves are not enumerated, enabling the narrator's voice to speak not just for herself, but rather for all the individual "I's" who hear or pray the succeeding psalm.

The unexpected and unwarranted mercy the penitent receives is underscored in the introductory sonnets by Lock's allusion to the Syro-Phoenician woman, who is denied access to spiritual food by the disciples but then begs Jesus to give to her the "crumbs" from the master's table (Matt. 15:21–28; Sonnet 5). Lock concludes the psalm sequence with a prayer that Jerusalem "with mighty wall / May be enclosed under thy defense" (Sonnet 20), a prayer that would have resonated with the hopes of returning Marian exiles who hoped to find in their new Queen Elizabeth a resurrected Nehemiah.

Lock may have been influenced in her selection of Ps. 51 by Thomas Wyatt's poetic rendition of Pietro Aretino's penitential psalms, which also include a narrative frame for the psalm paraphrase and pointed political and religious critique. Lock, however, extends Wyatt's reach, particularly by distinguishing between Roman Catholic and Calvinist views of the Lord's Supper. She develops Wyatt's terse two-line comment "Low heart in humble wise / Thou dost accept, O God, for pleasant host" into three separate sonnets. In Psalm Sonnet 18, the "host" is defined not as the consecrated body of Christ offered repeatedly in the Eucharist but as Christ's once-for-all sacrifice in his body on the cross. In the next sonnet, Lock deftly recasts the "host" as the Christian's penitent self, which *is* offered repeatedly as a sacrifice of praise: "I yield myself, I offer up my ghost, / My slain delights my dying heart to thee. / To God a troubled sprite is pleasing host" (Sonnet 19). In the final sonnet, the individual heart is multiplied exponentially as "many a yielded host of humbled hart" gather to praise "The God of might, of mercy, and of grace" (Sonnet 21). Although the vision sounds eschatological, Lock specifies the place of thanksgiving as "thy hill" and "thy walled town," locations that, in the previous sonnet, are tied to the restored English church. By concluding her psalm with a call for national thanksgiving—it is the people who cry, "We praise thee, God our God: thou only art / The God of might, of mercy, and of grace"—Lock, like Wyatt before her, acknowledges that her agenda reaches beyond personal piety to critique the political and religious cultures of her day.

The 1590 translation, dedicatory preface, and concluding poem all explicate Heb. 12:6 and again use biblical exegesis to intervene in the national church during a time when the Puritans were under duress. As Lock argues in her preface, "If God chastise every son whom he receiveth, and every member of Christ's body must be fashioned like unto the head, if the afflictions of this world are manifest tokens to the children of God of his favor and love towards them and sure pledges of their adoption, how can we look, or how can we desire to be exempted from this common condition of God's own children and household?" (Lock 76). While offering a message of hope to Lock's struggling coreligionists, the volume as a whole suggests that the English church hierarchy—and by extension the queen herself—are little better than the papal power England was resisting on the Continent.

The 1590 dedicatory preface makes explicit Lock's expectation that her book could and would intervene in political culture as it urges the countess of Warwick to use her position at court as a "light upon an high candlestick, to give light unto many." Although Lock's famous statement from this preface— "Everyone in his calling is bound to do somewhat to the furtherance of the holy building; but because great things by reason of my sex, I may not do, and that which I may, I ought to do, I have according to my duty, brought my poor basket of stones to the strengthening of the walls of that Jerusalem, whereof (by grace) we are all both citizens and members"—may be read as expressing disappointment with her limited role as a woman, the rhetorical stress of the sentence falls on Lock's claim in the final clause to be both "citizen and member" of God's holy building.

Lock was well known and well regarded in her own lifetime. In 1576, James Sanford acknowledged Lock in a dedicatory preface as a gentlewoman famous for her learning, positioning her as an exemplar to Queen Elizabeth herself. Such high praise paid tribute to Lock's significance as a Reformed writer and public figure. Her first book was reprinted at least twice and her second at least seven times; the latter included her name as translator on the title page in typeset matching that of the author Taffin, suggesting that Lock's imprimatur was as important to the book as that of the French pastor. John Knox wrote letters asking her to intervene at court; Christopher Goodman, another friend from Geneva, arranged to have Lock's sonnet sequence on Ps. 51 set to music. The first psalm sonnet with music is preserved in a set of manuscript partbooks known as the St. Andrews Psalter. Another Scottish Protestant, Lady Margaret Cunningham, imitated the form and content of Lock's writings in a 1607 letter to her erring husband and directly cited Lock's famous "basket of stones" speech.

Although lost to the church for several centuries, Lock's importance to the English Reformed community has been recognized by recent scholars.

See also Elizabeth I (1533–1603)

Bibliography

Collinson, Patrick. "The Role of Women in the English Reformation Illustrated by the Life and Friendships of Anne Locke." Pages 273–87 in *Godly People: Essays on English Protestantism and Puritanism*, edited by Patrick Collinson. London: Hambledon, 1983.

Hannay, Margaret P. "'Unlock my lipps': The *Miserere mei Deus* of Anne Vaughan Lok and Mary Sidney Herbert, Countess of Pembroke." Pages 19–36 in *Privileging Gender in Early Modern England*, edited by Jean R. Brink. Kirksville, MO: Sixteenth Century Journal Pub., 1993.

Lock, Anne Vaughan. *The Collected Works of Anne Vaughan Lock*. Edited by Susan M. Felch. Tempe: Arizona Center for Medieval and Renaissance Studies, 1999.

Schleiner, Louise. *Tudor and Stuart Women Writers*. Bloomington: Indiana University Press, 1994.

Smith, Rosalind. "'In a mirrour clere': Protestantism and Politics in Anne Lok's *Miserere mei Deus*." Pages 41–60 in *"This Double Voice": Gendered Writing in Early Modern England*, edited by Danielle Clarke and Elizabeth Clarke. New York: St. Martin's Press, 2000.

Spiller, Michael R. G. "A Literary 'First': The Sonnet Sequence of Anne Locke (1560)." *Renaissance Studies* 11 (1997): 41–55.

Warley, Christopher. "'An Englishe box': Calvinism and Commodities in Anne Lok's *A Meditation of a Penitent Sinner*." *Spenser Studies* 15 (2001): 205–42.

White, Micheline. "Renaissance Englishwomen and Religious Translations: The Case of Anne Lock's *Of the Markes of the Children of God*." *English Literary Renaissance* 29 (1999): 375–400.

———. "Women Writers and Literary-Religious Circles in the Elizabethan West Country: Anne Dowriche, Anne Lock Prowse, Anne Lock Moyle, Ursula Fulford, and Elizabeth Rous." *Modern Philology* 103 (2005): 187–214.

—Susan M. Felch

Macrina the Younger (ca. 330–379)

Intelligent, capable, and wise, Macrina was elder sister to Cappadocian Basil the Great and Gregory of Nyssa, and the firstborn of Basil the elder and Emmelia. Referring to her as the fourth Cappadocian, Pelikan (ix) ranks her with her brothers for her contribution to fourth-century theological discussion. We know her from two works of her brother Gregory, the *Life* (*Vita*), and the *Dialogue on the Soul and the Resurrection* (*Dialogus*). Both feature her as teacher and leader in female monasticism.

These two works give ample evidence of Macrina's confidence in the Scriptures for life and teaching. The *Dialogue* presents her skillfully confronting materialist and Platonist pagan thought with the truth as she knows it from the Bible. Of course, her portrayal comes through the perspective of her brother Gregory; in that respect, assessment of Macrina is similar to assessing Socrates from the writings of Plato. Gregory's sincere appreciation of her guidance as "my teacher in all things" encourages us to take his presentation seriously (in Migne, *Life*, col. 977; *Dial.*, cols. 12, 20). Her life is depicted as a pursuit of the philosophical ideal of perfection, virtue, and wisdom characterized by ascetic restraint, "reason opposing the passions." After the death of her father, she was joined by her mother, family servants, and other devout women in establishing a religious community on the family estate in Pontus, and she consecrated herself "to the attainment of the angelical life" (*Life*, 969–72).

Her childhood education, given by her own mother, was based on the Scriptures, especially the Psalter and the Song of Songs, thereby avoiding immoral literature of the classical poets. Through her grandmother Macrina she learned of Gregory Thaumaturgus, and thus of his teacher Origen. From the *Philocalia* we know that Origen's approach to Scripture (esp. from *Princ.* 4) was familiar to the Cappadocians. In the *Dialogue*, Macrina reflects Origen's allegorizing approach in discussing the parable of the wheat and the tares (65a–65b), and the rich man and Lazarus in Luke 16:19–31 (80a–88a): "The account [about hell] provides a narration of a bodily nature [*sōmatikōteron*], while at the same time it provides many occasions for those who examine it closely to arrive at a more subtle assessment [*leptoteran theōrian*]" (80b). She reflects Origen's use of words as symbols for the condition of the soul in discussing the scriptural reference to the "bosom of Abraham" (*kolpos*, 84b–d): "Just as we speak metaphorically in referring to the edge of the sea as 'bosom,' so also it appears to me that the word 'bosom' in the account gives a symbol [*endeiksin*] of those unmeasurable good things, for which all who sail through our present life with virtue [*aretē*], anchor their souls [once they are departed] in a quiet harbor, as a good bosom" (84b–c). Origen's influence is clear also in her view of the final restoration as a conquest of good over evil, when God shall be "all in all" (148a; see also 69c on Phil. 2:10).

Even so, her determination not to go beyond the Scriptures on the origin of our world and of the soul may reflect subtle critique of Origen; reflecting on theories of the Greek philosophers and Manichaeans (*Dial.*, 121–24), she affirms, "We should avoid their strange speculation; in the investigation of things that exist, let us accept the account which does not meddle with the 'how' of each of them, according to the instruction of the apostle" (124a–b). Macrina respected the literal meaning of the Scriptures, affirming them as rule of thought and teaching: "Reflection on the soul by secular philosophers has the freedom to accept appearances, but we do not have such freedom to say whatever we want, since we consult the Holy Scripture as rule of all teaching and law [*kanoni pantos dogmatos kai nomō kekrēmenoi tē hagia graphē*]" (49c). She asks, "Who would deny that the truth can only be found in that which bears the seal of the witness of Scripture [*sphragis . . . tēs graphikēs martyrias*]?" (64a–b).

If her words do not evidence the apophatic mystical theology for which Gregory is known (as in his *Life of Moses*), the portrayal of Macrina's death does reveal the impact of Origen's interpretation of the Song of Songs. She approaches death with great joy, anticipating the reunion with the bridegroom, thus coalescing the anticipated meeting of Jesus and reunion with the fiancé of her youth (*Life*, 984). As a true "martyr" (the Greek *martys* means "witness"), her death provides a witness to the centrality of biblical teaching for her life.

Bibliography

Albrecht, Ruth. *Das Leben der heiligen Makrina auf dem Hintergrund der Thekla-Traditionen*. Göttingen: Vandenhoeck & Ruprecht, 1986.

Corrigan, Kevin. *The Life of Saint Macrina*. Toronto: Peregrina, 1987.

Gregory of Nyssa. *Dialogus de anima et resurrectione*. Cols. 11–160 in vol. 46 of Patrologia graeca, edited by J.-P. Migne. Paris, 1863.

———. *The Life of St. Macrina*. Pages 159–91 in *Saint Gregory of Nyssa: Ascetical Works*, translated by Virginia Woods Callahan. Fathers of the Church 58. Washington, DC: Catholic University of America Press, 1967.

———. *Vita Macrinae Junioris*. Cols. 960–1000 in vol. 46 of Patrologia graeca, edited by J.-P. Migne. Paris, 1863.

Maraval, Pierre, ed. and trans. *Vie de Sainte Macrine [par] Grégoire de Nysse: Introduction, texte critique, traduction, notes et index*. Paris: Cerf, 1971.

Meissner, H. M. *Rhetorik und Theologie: Der Dialog Gregors von Nyssa De anima et resurrectione*. Frankfurt: Peter Lang, 1991.

Pelikan, Jaroslav. *Christianity and Classical Culture: The Metamorphosis of Natural Theology in the Christian Encounter with Hellenism*. New Haven: Yale University Press, 1993.

Roth, Catharine P. *Gregory of Nyssa: On the Soul and Resurrection*. New York: St. Vladimir's Press, 1993.

Wilson-Kastner, Patricia. "Macrina: Virgin and Teacher." *Andrews University Seminary Studies* 17 (1979): 105–17.

— WENDY ELGERSMA HELLEMAN

Magnus, Katie (1844–1924)

Katie Magnus was born on May 2, 1844, in Portsmouth, England, one of six children of Julia Moss and Alderman Emanuel Emanuel, a goldsmith and the first Jewish mayor of Portsmouth. Her middle-class Victorian Jewish family provided her with a good education, including the knowledge of the Hebrew language. She married Sir Philip Moses (1842–1933), a high-ranking Jewish aristocrat connected to such families as the Rothschilds and the Montefiores. Sir Philip Moses was also a leading minister for a number of synagogues and Jewish institutes in London from 1866 to 1922. Lady Magnus became a well-respected social activist and religious educator. She was closely affiliated with many Jewish social agencies, and she was actively engaged in the communal life of the Berkeley Street Synagogue, various Jewish schools of London, and the Jewish Deaf and Dumb Home. In 1886, when Magnus was only twenty-two, she founded the Jewish Girls' Club for girls from poor Jewish families in London. Magnus was also a gifted author of such books as *Little Miriam's Bible Stories* (1888), *Jewish Portraits* (1888), *Outlines of Jewish History* (1886), *First Makers of England* (1901), and *Boys of the Bible* (1894), as well as numerous articles in such journals as *The National Review* and *The Jewish Chronicle*.

Magnus viewed the Jewish Scriptures as a source for Jewish history and faith. In her most successful book, *Outlines of Jewish History*, Magnus unfolds the major events in the course of Jewish history from 586 BCE until the late nineteenth century. Many Jewish communities used Magnus's book as a text. It went through several major revisions in Britain, the last in 1963; a revision of *Outlines* by Michael Friedländer in 1890 was the first book published by the Jewish Publication Society of America.

Magnus approached the Hebrew texts as sacred Scripture and held to traditional views about authorship and dating, ascribing, for example, the composition of the Pentateuch to Moses and the Psalter to David (*Outlines*, 3). As a rule, she presents the text's literal meaning (known as *peshat*) and does not engage in contemporary critical debates about the prehistory of the Hebrew Scriptures. Generally speaking, Magnus presents a romantic account of the history of the Jews, stating: "I can only plead that I have told the whole sad, beautiful, 'heroic history' of my race with the keenest sympathy; and I can hope that the moral and the meaning of it all, which are so very clear to me, may be found to shine out between the lines" (viii). However, when Magnus treats the topic of the emergence of Christianity, she adopts a critical view of the portrayal of Jesus in the New Testament (50–52). She compares Jesus's life and work to other Jewish teachers of the time, reporting that "many of the Essenes preached and tended the sick, and the virtues of humility and charity, and contempt of worldliness, were virtues common to all honest Pharisees" (50). She did not trust the New Testament as a historical source, viewing Jesus, who likely denounced neither Pharisees nor Judaism, as a sham: "It was not till long after his death, perhaps fifty years, that ever the first of his biographies . . . came to be written" (51).

Magnus's interest in producing resources for religious educators is also seen in her books for younger readers, *Little Miriam's Bible Stories* and *Boys of the Bible*. In *Boys of the Bible*, Magnus derives moral lessons from the biblical narratives. In the introduction to the book, Magnus explains: "Very dear they are to us for their truth and their hope. . . . I [hope] that the simple stories here retold may lead the children of today to look into the Bible for themselves, and to find in that best and most beautiful of Books the manhood to which these eight boys grew" (*Boys*, 5). Such pedagogical ends are behind Magnus's depiction of Samson as a problematic character, who "fought not God's battles but his own," but who ultimately delivers his people from the Philistines, discrediting the god Dagon and becoming, "in spite of himself, a blessing" (75).

Sabbath Stories from the Pentateuch (1873), written for older readers, shows Magnus's engagement with the biblical text at a more sophisticated level. In her discussion of the birth of Moses (Exod. 2:1–10), she fills out perceived gaps in the story, providing Pharaoh's daughter with motives "for taking Moses home": "partly from pity, and partly perhaps from a girlish fancy for such a nice toy" (48). Moreover, her view of the important role of mothers in educating children influences her supposition that Moses "was always an Israelite, never an Egyptian," at least in part because of his mother's teaching, which "kept him true to his religion and his people" (48).

Lady Katie Magnus was an important author whose work as a Jewish religious educator was valued by Jews and Christians alike. She knew Hebrew and valued Scripture highly as a resource for faith and cultural identity. She did not engage critical scholarship; instead, her readings of texts were shaped by her experiences as a Victorian Jewish woman.

Bibliography

Calisch, Edward Nathaniel. *The Jew in English Literature, as Author and as Subject.* Port Washington, NY: Kennikat, 1969.

Kadish, Sharman. "Magnus, Katie, Lady (1844–1924)." Pages 133–34 in vol. 36 of *Oxford Dictionary of National Biography*, edited by H. C. G. Matthew and Brian Harrison. Rev. ed. Oxford: Oxford University Press, 2004–11.

Magnus, Lady Katie. *Boys of the Bible.* London: Tuck & Sons, 1894.

———. *Outlines of Jewish History.* London: Longmans, 1886.

———. *Sabbath Stories from the Pentateuch.* London: P. Vallentine, 1873.

Scheinberg, Cynthia. *Women's Poetry and Religion in Victorian England: Jewish Identity and Christian Culture.* Cambridge: Cambridge University Press, 2002.

—IGAL GERMAN AND MARION ANN TAYLOR

Makin, Bathsua (ca. 1600–after 1675)

Bathsua Reginald Makin, born in about 1600, was the eldest daughter of Henry Reginald, a schoolmaster in London; her mother's name is unknown. Henry instilled in his daughter a love of languages. Highly skilled in Greek, Latin, French, Italian, and Spanish, she also knew German, Hebrew, and Syriac. At age sixteen she published *Musa Virginea* (*Virgin Muse*), a collection of Greek, Latin, and French poems dedicated to James I and the royal family. She taught at her father's school until her marriage in 1621 or 1622 to Richard Makin (1599–1659), a servant at the royal court. Parish baptismal records suggest that Makin gave birth to eight children, two of whom died in childhood. She tutored Charles I's daughter, Princess Elizabeth, who became proficient in ancient and modern languages. Makin instructed other prominent Englishwomen such as Lucy Davies Hastings, countess of Huntingdon. Though some of her family members had Puritan sympathies,

Makin apparently remained loyal to the royal family during the English Civil War.

Makin was influenced by the educational theories of Bohemian theologian and educator Johannes Amos Comenius, who proposed the simplification of language instruction and developed an experiential method of teaching natural sciences. Makin's contemporaries praised her knowledge of the medical arts. In collaboration with Mark Lewis, who ran a boys' school at Tottenham High Cross, a village near London, Makin opened a girls' school with an innovative curriculum emphasizing languages and science. The date of her death is unknown, but it is after November 1675, when she wrote a letter now preserved at the Royal College of Physicians. Makin is frequently misidentified as the sister of mathematician John Pell, who was actually her brother-in-law. An anonymous pamphlet, *The Malady and Remedy of Vexation and Unjust Arrests and Actions*, is sometimes mistakenly attributed to her.

Makin is best known for *An Essay to Revive the Ancient Education of Gentlewomen* (1673). Though she adopted a male persona and published the essay anonymously, historians universally acknowledge Makin's authorship. The essay refutes objections to educating females, offers biblical and historical examples of notable learned women, proposes a curriculum of study, and concludes with an advertisement for Mrs. Makin's school for young women at Tottenham High Cross. Though the essay discusses the education of "gentlewomen," Makin also recommends educating women of lower social classes. She assumes that women in non-European cultures are particularly oppressed and mistreated by their husbands.

As the essay title suggests, Makin claims that her program for female education is actually a restoration of ancient practice. She argues that women in classical and biblical times received a more comprehensive liberal arts education than women of her own day. Miriam, who sang a victory song after the exodus (Exod. 15:20–21), was "a great poet and philosopher, for both learning and religion were generally in former times wrapped up in verse" (*Essay*, in Teague 114). The queen of Sheba, testing Solomon's wisdom with difficult questions (1 Kings 10:1–13; 2 Chron. 9:1–12), was likewise a philosopher (119). The company of women who greeted David with victory songs (1 Sam. 18:7) was "a great specimen of liberal education," for their ode to David was their own musical composition (114). Huldah dwelt in a college "where women were trained up in good literature" (114; cf. 2 Kings 22:14; 2 Chron. 34:22). Deborah exemplifies a woman's knowledge of legal matters. Makin believes that "extraordinarily enabled" biblical women were "publicly employed" in important roles (114). Since Miriam, Deborah, Jael, Judith, Esther, the Virgin Mary, Anna, Phoebe, Priscilla, Lois, Eunice, and the elect lady (2 John 1, 5) were "eminently employed in the great transactions of the church," no one should forbid women to study arts, languages, history, philosophy, and other subjects, which are "subservient" to religious matters (130).

Countering arguments that Solomon commended the "virtuous woman" for "good housewifery" rather than for learning, Makin asserts that a woman will need knowledge of economics, politics, medicine, arithmetic, geometry, natural sciences, grammar, rhetoric, and logic in order to carry out the extensive list of duties described in Prov. 31:10–31 (142). The villainy of Athaliah and Jezebel illustrates that it is dangerous to deprive women of the moral formation provided by a suitable education (133–34; cf. on Athaliah: 2 Kings 11; 2 Chron. 22–23; on Jezebel: 1 Kings 19, 21; 2 Kings 9). Makin recommends that women should study Greek and Hebrew so that they may better understand Scripture and glorify God (121).

Makin corresponded with another apologist for women's education, Anna Maria van Schurman, a notable scholar residing in Utrecht. Makin's *Essay* influenced Mary Astell's pioneering work in the education of females. Makin was a witty and eloquent advocate for cultivating women's intellectual development. She used female characters as examples to support her arguments for women's education, and in doing so, she shaped or reshaped the biblical characters into scholars, philosophers, and poets. Excerpts from her *Essay* frequently appear in modern anthologies of early feminist writings.

See also Astell, Mary (1666–1731); Schurman, Anna Maria van (1607–78)

Bibliography

Brink, Jean R. "Bathsua Reginald Makin: Most Learned Matron." *Huntington Library Quarterly* 54 (1991): 313–26.

Makin, Bathsua. *An Essay to Revive the Ancient Education of Gentlewomen.* Pages 109–50 in *Bathsua Makin, Woman of Learning*, by Frances N. Teague. Lewisburg, PA: Bucknell University Press, 1998.

———. *An Essay to Revive the Ancient Education of Gentlewomen in Religion, Manners, Arts & Tongues: With an Answer to the Objections against this Way of Education.* London: Parkhurst, 1673.

Salmon, Vivian. "Bathsua Makin: A Pioneer Linguist and Feminist in Seventeenth-Century England." Pages 303–18 in *Neuere Forschungen zur Wortbildung und Historiographie der Linguistik: Festgabe für Herbert E. Brekle*, edited by Brigitte Asbach-Schnitker and Johannes Roggenhofer. Tübingen: Gunter Narr, 1987.

Teague, Frances N. *Bathsua Makin, Woman of Learning.* Lewisburg, PA: Bucknell University Press, 1998.

— Joy A. Schroeder

Marcella (ca. 327–410)

Marcella, a wealthy and aristocratic Roman, was one of the founders of a tradition of biblical scholarship and ascetic living that flourished among well-born women in fourth-century Rome. The daughter of a Roman senator of the illustrious line of the Ceionii Rufii, she renounced position, fortune, and marriage on the death of her husband, just seven months after their wedding, and dedicated herself to a life immersed in the Scriptures. Marcella drew other women into this life, including her mother. When Jerome (through whose letters we know of Marcella) met her in 382, she was the revered head of a circle of women engaged with her in study of the Scriptures at the family palace on the Aventine Hill (home to Rome's rich and famous). They were all vowed to celibacy and committed to an ascetic life of fasting, prayer, and voluntary personal poverty. All of them were virgins or widows; all of them dressed plainly in rough cloth, without ornament or painted face or decorated hair; both individually and together, they devoted their days to serious scholarly reading of the Bible.

Marcella's reading was first of all text-critical. Marcella, like other women of the circle, read Greek, Latin, and possibly Hebrew; with her knowledge of the original languages, she strove to establish the original reading. The women also read extensively in commentaries; Jerome dedicated his *Commentary on Galatians* to Marcella. She was keenly interested in the literal meaning of the text and its historical significance. Marcella noticed discrepancies in Scripture and sought to resolve them; she questioned Jerome relentlessly on the precise significance of untranslated Hebrew words; she tried to establish what exactly "ephod" and "teraphim" were, sending to Jerome a careful and exhaustive study of the use of the terms in the Old Testament, pointing out the apparent discrepancy between the description of "ephod" as a kind of belt for Samuel to wear in 1 Sam. 2:18–19, and as a silver sculpted piece in Judg. 17:4–5. Her concern seems to be biblical consistency. Jerome makes detailed linguistic and exegetical arguments in response. Comparing the Septuagint's Greek with the Hebrew, he points out that where "ephod" is translated into Greek, it is always rendered "garment," and to read "ephod" in Judg. 17 as equivalent to "sculpted piece" is to conflate two different references. His response reveals how thorough her own knowledge of the biblical languages was and how astute her mind.

Jerome treats Marcella with immense respect, noting wryly (*Ep.* 127.28–29, 34) that she drove him to work late into the night, trying to find solutions to the difficult and abstruse problems she raised, and that she felt entirely free to dispute his conclusions. Indeed, in one letter (*Ep.* 59) he avoids responding to a question about the interpretation of the "sheep and goats" in Matt. 25: her reading—that the animals signify the good and the bad generally, and not the Christian and the heathen—opposes his own (exclusivist) reading (cf. *Comm. Matt.* on 25:40–41).

Marcella was also interested in the text's theological implications: Is Jesus's presence after the resurrection and before the ascension limited to earth, or is he present in heaven as well? What is the story's christological import? Jerome engages with her on both the Novatian and Montanist heresies, and in later years she becomes the primary spokesperson for the anti-Origenist movement in Rome.

Marcella's acute mind and enormous intellectual energy are accessible to readers now only "through a glass darkly," in the letters of Jerome. None of her many letters about exegetical matters to Jerome has survived. Jerome, however, found her intellectual companionship in the study of Scripture invaluable; one can assume that his later thought owes something to her influence and to the tradition of exhaustive and precise textual study that she founded among the women of Rome.

Bibliography

Hinson, E. Glenn. "Women Biblical Scholars in Late Fourth Century: The Aventine Circle." Pages 319–24 in vol. 5 of *Augustine and His Opponents, Jerome, Other Latin Fathers after Nicaea, Orientalia*, edited by Elizabeth A. Livingstone. Studia patristica 33. Louvain: Peeters, 1997.

Jerome. *Principal Works*. In vol. 6 of *Nicene and Post-Nicene Fathers*, Series 2, edited by Philip Schaff and Henry Wace. New York: Christian Literature, 1893. Repr., Peabody, MA: Hendrickson, 1995.

Kelly, J. D. N. *Jerome: His Life, Writings, and Controversies*. London: Duckworth, 1975.

Labourt, Jerome, ed. and trans. *Saint Jerome: Lettres*. 8 vols. Paris: Belles Lettres, 1951.

Letsch-Brunner, Silvia. *Marcella—Discipula et Magistra: Auf den Spuren einer römischen Christin des 4. Jahrhunderts*. Berlin: de Gruyter, 1998.

Reuther, Rosemary Radford. "Mothers of the Church: Ascetic Women in the Late Patristic Age." Pages 71–88 in *Women of Spirit: Female Leadership in the Jewish and Christian Traditions*, edited by R. Reuther and Eleanor McLaughlin. New York: Simon & Schuster, 1979.

Yarbrough, Anne. "Christianization in the Fourth Century: The Example of Roman Women." *Church History* 45 (1976): 149–65.

— CATHERINE SIDER HAMILTON

Marguerite de Navarre (Marguerite de Valois, d'Angoulême; Margaret of) (1492–1549)

Marguerite de Navarre was the elder sister of the French King François I (ruled 1515–47) by two years, and grandmother of the suspiciously Protestant King Henry IV (1589–1610), and has often been confused with her Protestant granddaughter-in-law, Queen Margot, wife of Henry IV. Yet her early education—under the direction of her mother, Louise de Savoie, and graced with the same tutors as her brother—introduced her to both orthodox Catholic piety and humanism. Having learned Italian from her mother, Marguerite developed a lifelong interest in Italian literature. In 1507, Marguerite's mother, whose motto was *libris et liberis* (for books and children), commissioned one of the tutors in Latin and biblical history, François Demoulin, to write "a simplified guide to confession and penitence" for Marguerite and her brother (Cholakian and Cholakian 24–25). The popular style of this moral treatise, using allegory and classical allusions in dialogue form, would serve Marguerite as a literary model. Another was Luther's dialogue between the soul and God on the seven articles of the Lord's Prayer, which she translated with amplifications into French at an uncertain date before 1527 (Navarre, Œuvres complètes, 1:28). Apart from her prose *Heptaméron*, written toward the end of her life, Marguerite's preferred mode of expression for religious meditation consisted of rhyming couplets in the vernacular, Middle French. Even her biblical plays and farces followed a similar pattern, conventional for that transitional period between the Middle Ages and the Renaissance.

Marguerite married twice. Her first marriage, arranged with Charles, duke of Alençon, making her duchess of Alençon and of Berry in 1509, was fruitless and allegedly unhappy for sixteen years. Her husband, who shared few of her literary interests, died as a result of the Battle of Pavia (1525), when the French army was defeated and her brother, François (king since 1515) was captured. At that time, Marguerite risked her own life to rally her brother, whose health was failing while imprisoned in Madrid. In 1527 her second marriage, by choice, to the younger Henri d'Albret, king of Navarre, gave her two children: a daughter Jeanne (b. 1529) and a son (b. 1530), who would not survive half a year. Tired of all the intrigues of the court, religious conflict, and marriage negotiations for her daughter, not to mention the conjugal infidelity of a husband ten years her junior and her own poor health, Marguerite retired to the convent of Tusson in Poitou when her beloved brother died on March 31, 1547. When her own turn came at the age of fifty-seven, two years later (Dec. 1, 1549), there is little doubt "that, born a Catholic, [she] died a Catholic" (Cholakian and Cholakian 270, 306).

Marguerite resorted to writing poetry for spiritual consolation from the time of her first marriage until the end of her life. A profound influence was her spiritual director Guillaume Briçonnet, bishop of Meaux, who led a circle of reformers in his diocese with the help of Jacques Lefèvre d'Étaple. The latter shared his commentaries and translations of the Bible with Marguerite until his death in her château at Nérac in 1536. Both Marguerite and her mother even tried to learn Hebrew with the help of these humanists. Marguerite's correspondence with the bishop from 1521 to 1524 introduced her to the Catholic tradition of mystical theology. Briçonnet also encouraged her works for the poor and advised her to read and meditate on the Bible. For the rest of her life, Marguerite in turn would protect reformers from accusations of heresy made by the Parliament and University of Paris.

The correspondence between Marguerite and Briçonnet displays a shared love of poetic imagery and allegorical interpretations of the Bible. For both, God became a purifying and illuminating fire. Among their favored metaphors were the marriage of the Christian soul to Christ the bridegroom (a topos from the Song of Songs), the Pythagorean description of life as a prison, and the Neoplatonic ladder of contemplation, which the eager soul mounts rung by rung to mystical union with God. For both, this mystical ladder was the classical tripartite division of contemplation through purgation, illumination, and perfection (cf. Briçonnet and Marguerite 1:79 [Dec. 22, 1521]). Briçonnet also taught Marguerite to associate the final stage of spiritual ecstasy with Paul's account of being "caught up to the third heaven" (cf. 1:36 [Aug. 1521]; 2 Cor. 12:2). Throughout her life, in response to her own initial barrenness and deaths in the family, Marguerite took consolation in contemplating the essential mysteries through such images.

It is difficult to date most of Marguerite's poems, intended more for private devotion than for publication. Her earliest datable poem is her *Dialogue en forme de vision nocturne* (Dialogue in the Form of a Nocturnal Vision), a theological debate in about 1,260 lines that she wrote shortly after the eight-year-old Charlotte, daughter of François I, died while in her care on September 8, 1524. In the poetic dialogue, the soul of Charlotte highlights the benefits of death and catechizes Marguerite on Briçonnet's evangelical doctrine. The most extended metaphor of the poem is from John 15, where God is the good vine or tree into which individuals are grafted by grace. Likewise, the efficacy of the saints flows directly from God, since "Il est l'arbre, et il[s] sont les rameaulx [He is the tree, and they are the branches]" (Salminen, lines 359–61). The poem also indicates that Marguerite was fully aware of the famous debate of 1524–25 between Luther and Erasmus over free will. The soul of Charlotte advises her aunt:

> Je vous prie que ces facheux debas
> D'arbitre franc et liberté laissés
> Aux grans docteurs, qui l'ayant ne l'ont pas.
> . . . .
> Mais quant à vous, quoy qu'on vous dye ou fac[e],
> Soyés seure qu'en liberté vous estes,
> Si vous ayé de Dieu l'amour et grace.
> (Salminen, lines 925–27, 931–33)

(I beseech you, leave these tiresome debates / over free will and freedom / to the great doctors, who having it [freedom/truth], do not have it. / . . . / But as for you, whatever they say or do to you, / be assured that you are free / if you possess the love and grace of God.)

Marguerite would follow no male school apart from Briçonnet's biblically grounded one. Liberated by Briçonnet's imaginative allegorizations of *Foy*, *Esperance*, and *Charité* (Faith, Hope, and Love; cf. Briçonnet and Marguerite 1:52 [Nov. 11, 1521]; 1 Cor. 13:13), which inspire this poem as well, Marguerite recognized the limits of reason; for example, Charlotte admonishes her not to want to know more about the saints and the afterlife ("Ne desirés plus avant en scavoir"; *Dialogue*, line 829). Two other early works, the *Petit Oeuvre dévot et contemplatif* (Little Work of Devotion and Contemplation) and the *Oraison à nostre Seigneur Jesus Christ* (Prayer to Our Lord Jesus Christ), may likewise be categorized as devotional manuals. Their tone is consistently penitential with few direct citations of Scripture, despite an intimate familiarity with the events of Christ's passion.

In 1531, when Marguerite launched her first publication, her *Miroir de l'âme pecheresse* (Mirror of the Sinful Soul), she did it anonymously and outside the capital in Alençon. Two years later, when it was reprinted in Paris, the little volume was placed on a black list of forbidden books by the faculty of theology in the University of Paris. Much has been made of this incident by Protestants claiming Marguerite's support, but the offense seems to have been a mere legality; the book lacked the imprimatur of the faculty of theology. Marguerite was forced to disclose her authorship, and the university was compelled to apologize to the king for an unintentional attack on his sister.

In this tract, the sinful soul is a persona of Marguerite herself, as well as a kind of universal soul trapped by original sin. By this time, Marguerite possessed the complete Bible translated into French by Lefèvre d'Étaples. In some of the earliest editions, the biblical allusions are cited in the margins of the text by different secretaries who identify them diversely. Apart from the marginal citations, sometimes fully quoted, Marguerite tends to recall the Bible by memory or to paraphrase it. The movement of the soul from sin to reconciliation within 1,500 lines of Marguerite's monologue explores her relationship to God in familial terms that embrace both male and female models. The dominant and most provocative role that she assumes is that of Mary the Mother of God, a role for which she asks God's permission: "Mais, Monseigneur, si vous estes mon pere, / Puis je penser que je suis vostre mere? [But, my Lord, if you are my father, / May I consider myself your mother?]" (Allaire, lines 261–62). The claim seems less audacious, given her relationship to Briçonnet, more than twenty years her elder, who signed his letter of February 12, 1524, as her son (Briçonnet and Marguerite 2:123), to which she responded by repeatedly signing herself his "inutille mere" ("useless mother"; 2:134). In her *Mirror*, Marguerite cites the passage in Matthew stating that whoever does the will of the Father is Jesus's "brother and sister and mother" (Matt. 12:50) to justify her claim. Yet the Mother of God remains exalted above all women (Allaire, line 281) in Marguerite's Marian devotion. From this role, Marguerite's persona shifts to the bereaved prostitute appealing to Solomon for her child (1 Kings 3:16–28), whom the judge has ordered to be split in half ("mys en deux parties"; line 448). As at Solomon's trial, she would rather give the child away than suffer "Jesuschrist divisé" ("Jesus Christ divided"; line 461). Finally, she invokes Paul:

> Parquoy venez, o bieneureux sainct Paul,
> Qui tant avez gousté de ce doulx miel,
> Trois jours sans veoir, ravy jusques au [tiers] ciel,
> Satisfaictes mon ignorance et faulte:
> Qu'avez vous sceu de vision si haulte?
> (Allaire, lines 1,382–86)

349

(So come, O blessed St. Paul, / you who have tasted of this sweet honey / for three days without seeing, caught up to the third heaven; / satisfy my unknowing and lack: / What have you known of such an exalted vision? [*tiers*, "third," added after first ed.].)

Here Marguerite is conflating Paul's own account of the third heaven (2 Cor. 12:2) with the third-person account in Acts of his conversion, when he lost his sight and appetite for three days (9:9). She implies that both Paul's blindness and the three days it lasted were signs that he had come face-to-face with God in mystical union. After invoking the very great gift of faith ("tresgrand Don de foy"; lines 1,413–16), hope, and perfect charity (lines 1,423–26) in Pauline terms, she falls silent (lines 1,423–26). Thus the Virgin Mary and Paul are primary models for Marguerite's contemplative prayer.

In her own time, the *Mirror of the Sinful Soul* was the most influential of Marguerite's works. A copy, probably the 1539 Geneva edition, was sent to the English court of Henry VIII when his daughter Elizabeth was still sister to the future King Edward VI (Prescott 66). Like Marguerite, Elizabeth shared lessons with Edward and outshone her brother, albeit younger. She presented her translation of this treatise, *The Glasse of the Synnefull Soule*, to her stepmother Queen Katherine Parr as a New Year's gift in 1545. Four years later, John Bale, the Protestant polemicist, would publish this English version as *A Godly meditacyon of the christen sowle*, which was reissued from time to time (Prescott 72, 76). In France, however, the events of 1534 would greatly reduce Marguerite's influence in Paris and at court.

In 1534 a sect of Swiss Sacramentarians in the school of Ulrich (Huldrych) Zwingli attacked France in a watershed event of the French Reformation: the Placard Affair. Broadsheets printed in Switzerland were posted in six major French cities, attacking "the insufferable abuses of the papal Mass" and the priesthood (Cholokian and Cholokian 173). François I was henceforth obliged to cooperate with the Parliament of Paris in the persecution of all suspected heretics, and Marguerite was compelled to return to her own domains in southern France to escape being burned herself. Still sheltering some reformers in Nérac while seeking refuge in Béarn, she received a warning from her brother to avoid meddling with religious doctrine. Henceforth she would explore more secular genres like farce and the novella (short story) of the *Heptaméron*.

Nevertheless, she continued to write not for a public audience but to satisfy her own inner needs. Her next publication would not appear until 1547, when she selected poems and plays for her *Marguerites de la Marguerite des princesses* (reprinted in the year of her death and later). The use of *marguerite* here constitutes a wordplay, coined by Briçonnet (cf. Briçonnet and Marguerite 1:55 *et ad passim* [Nov. 11, 1521]), on her own name and its Latin root, meaning "pearl," as in the biblical injunction against casting one's "pearls before swine" (*neque mittatis margaritas vestras ante porcos*; Matt. 7:6, Vulg.). The two volumes begin with the *Miroir* of 1531, include a nativity cycle of four religious plays, *Triomphe de l'Agneau* (The Triumph of the Lamb) and *Chansons spirituelles* (Spiritual Songs), with a host of others too numerous to name. Undaunted, she continued to meditate on her brother's death in her last poems, *La Navire* (The Ship) and *Les Prisons* (Prisons). With her complete works now being published by Champion in Paris, she has achieved the fame she deserves.

Her tetralogy of biblical plays adapted the French tradition of *mystères* (mystery plays) to her evangelical fervor to spread the gospel in French, still influenced by the mystical theology of Briçonnet. Evidence suggests that the plays were performed for her husband and the court of Navarre by her own ladies or Italian actors hired by her husband. Didactic and philosophical in tone, the tripartite path to God is here transferred from the microcosm of a personalized mystical experience to the macrocosm of salvation history; for example, messengers to Mary in the *Comédie du Desert* (traditionally, the "Flight into Egypt") personify Contemplation, Memory, and Consolation.

The same tripartite structure forms the foundation of her two other most appreciated works: *Triomphe de l'Agneau* (1,624 lines) and *Les Prisons* (3,214 lines). The former is an epic of salvation history inspired by the book of Revelation and Paul's Epistles. Here both the individual and history are divided into three parts: the individual is alienated from God by law, sin, and death (*Œuvres*, vol. 3, lines 41–42), but redeemed historically by nature, law, and grace (Ferguson 66–74). The apocalyptic vision omits the disasters of the end time to focus on the incarnation and apotheosis of Christ. The tripartite *Prisons* is an allegorical confession (9) of almost 6,000 lines, her last mirror. Although the protagonist is *Amy* (male lover), his liberation from three prisons—erotic love, worldly ambition, and a thirst for knowledge—seems to be autobiographical (Cholakian and Cholakian 295–96). Likely inspired by reading Marguerite Porete's *Miroir des simples âmes* in the library of the convent of Madeleine-lès-Orléans, Marguerite's protagonist reflects "Le vray Amy qu'elle nommait Gentil / Et son Loing Près" (The true friend whom she named Noble / and her Far-Near; *Prisons*, lines 1,328–29). Porete's anonymous manuscript is described as written by an uneducated woman "Depuys cent ans escript, remply de flame / De charité si tresardentement, / Que rien qu'amour n'estoit son argument . . ." (a hundred years ago, filled with the flame / of charity burning so ardently / That its argument was nothing but love; lines 1,315–18). *Amy* is the Christ who leads *Amye* (female lover/soul) to mystical union. Just as Marguerite aims to transcend words into the immanent silence of God, so also does she transcend gender. A liberated woman in Christian terms, she is not a feminist.

Profoundly nourished on the Bible, the omnipresence of Scripture in Marguerite's work has inspired innumerable taxonomies by which scholars categorize everything from her rarer direct citations to conscious evocations of biblical commonplaces through indirect allusion. Scholars agree that Marguerite's

351

scriptural intertextuality rarely employs expressions from Lefèvre's French Bible; her primary source is the Vulgate. She does not cite the Bible as a proof text but pours out her pearls in a free association (much like St. Bernard of Clairvaux), which she anchors in Pauline Christology and traditional Christian typology. The latter interprets *exempla* (types) from the Old Testament as prefigurations of Christ. Like others of her time, she was uninhibited in her allegorical hermeneutics by humanist philology; her scriptural outpourings arose less from Luther's rallying cry *sola scriptura* (salvation "by Scripture alone") than her own devotion.

See also Elizabeth I (1533–1603); Parr, Katherine (1512–48); Porete, Marguerite (Porette or Margaret Porete; of Hainaut) (d. 1310)

Bibliography

Allaire, Joseph L., ed. *Marguerite d'Angoulême, reine de Navarre, Le miroir de l'âme pecheresse.* . . . Munich: Wilhelm Fink, 1972.

Briçonnet, Guillaume, and Marguerite d'Angoulême. *Correspondance (1521–1524).* Edited by Christine Martineau and Michel Veissière. 2 vols. Geneva: Librairie Droz, 1975. [Only the first instance of Briçonnet's use of any given metaphor is indicated above; the same metaphors are developed repeatedly throughout the letters.]

Cholakian, Patricia F., and Rouben C. Cholakian. *Marguerite de Navarre: Mother of the Renaissance.* New York: Columbia University Press, 2006.

Ferguson, Gary. *Mirroring Belief: Marguerite de Navarre's Devotional Poetry.* Edinburgh: Edinburgh University Press, 1992.

Navarre, Marguerite de. *Les comédies bibliques.* Edited by Barbara Marczuk, Beata Skreszewska, and Piotr Tylus. Geneva: Librairie Droz, 2000.

———. *Dialogue en forme de vision nocturne.* Edited by Renja Salminen. Helsinki: Suomalainen Tiedeakatemia, 1985.

———. *Marguerites de la Marguerite des princesses, tresillustre royne de Navarre.* 2 vols. Lyon: Jean de Tournes, 1547. Facs. ed., New York: Johnson Reprint, 1970.

———. *Œuvres complètes.* Vols. 1, 3–4, 8–9. Gen. ed., Nicole Cazauran. Paris: Honoré Champion, 2001–7. Esp. vol. 1, *Pater Noster et Petit œuvre dévot*, edited by Sabine Lardon (2001); and vol. 3, *Le Triomphe de l'Agneau*, edited by Simone de Reyff (2001).

———. *Les Prisons: Édition et commentaire.* Edited by Simone Glasson. Geneva: Librairie Droz, 1978.

Prescott, Anne Lake. "The Pearl of the Valois and Elizabeth I: Marguerite de Navarre's *Miroir* and Tudor England." Pages 61–76 in *Silent but for the Word*, edited by Margaret Patterson Hannay. Kent, OH: Kent State University Press, 1985.

— JANET RITCH

McAuley, Catherine (1778–1841)

In 1778 Catherine McAuley was born into a middle-class Catholic family in Dublin, Ireland. Although she was well-read, she apparently did not receive formal schooling but was educated at home. For almost twenty years as a young adult, McAuley became a household manager and companion for a Quaker woman, Catherine Callaghan. After Catherine and William Callaghan died, leaving her a considerable inheritance, she established a large house in Dublin for poor servant girls and homeless women. In 1831 McAuley founded the Congregation of the Sisters of Mercy, whose work was to educate poor young girls, protect servants and other distressed women, and visit the sick and dying poor.

McAuley's scriptural interpretation is found in her letters, her sayings, and her congregation's founding documents. Several editions of her letters have been published, most recently Sullivan's *The Correspondence of Catherine McAuley*. A number of collections of her sayings were printed, including *A Little Book of Practical Sayings* (as early as 1868) and *Retreat Instructions*. McAuley is credited by some with writing *Cottage Controversy*, a tract written in the style of "controversy" engaging two women in theological debate. The founding documents that she composed for her community, "The Spirit of the Institute" and the "Rule and Constitutions for the Sisters of Mercy," are published in *Catherine McAuley and the Tradition of Mercy*, by Mary Sullivan.

Scriptural allusions and references were woven throughout McAuley's instructions to her companions. Facing the early deaths of the first sisters, she said, "Without the cross the real crown cannot come" (Rev. 2:10; Sullivan, *Correspondence*, 259). She expressed her desire that her sisters love one another in a witty poem, "If my number full I find / united in one heart and mind, / I'll bless my store" (Acts 4:32; *Correspondence*, 267). She constantly trusted in God's providence, reminding the sisters to "put your whole confidence in God (1 John 3:21). He never will let you want necessaries for yourself or children" (*Correspondence*, 115). She used Scripture to lead the sisters to identify with the example of the first followers of Jesus: "With the Apostle a religious must consider herself a stranger and a pilgrim on earth, having her conversation in heaven" (Phil. 3:20; Purcell 31). Direct citations, modified citations, allusions or echoes of scriptural verses and themes, and mimesis of the literary structure of the ending of Paul's Letters were all among her interpretative techniques.

The tract *Cottage Controversy* presents a series of conversations between Margaret Lewis, a Catholic cottager, and Lady P., the Protestant lady of the manor. It illustrates the two women's understanding of theology, the respect they show toward each other, and their knowledge of the Bible as well as doctrines regarding its authority. These women from different socioeconomic classes and religious traditions converse on theological issues and scriptural texts, activities rarely attributed to women, particularly during the nineteenth century.

For McAuley, scriptural interpretation was primarily about what is named today "praxis" (reflective and reflected action flowing from a theology for liberation and transformation). She sought to influence her sisters to have "the same mind that was in Christ Jesus" (Phil. 2:5). In her most dramatic statement of praxis and by amending Luke 12:49, she described five women who were entering her community as "coming forward joyfully to consecrate themselves to the service of the poor for Christ's sake. This is some of the fire He cast on the earth—kindling" (Sullivan, *Correspondence*, 282).

McAuley did not often refer to texts about women, but when she did, praxis was the focus. She reinterprets the story of Martha and Mary found in Luke by using images from Matthew. "The functions of Martha should be done for Him as well as the choir duties of Mary. . . . He requires that we should be shining lamps giving light to all around us. How are we to do this if not by the manner we discharge the duties of Martha?" (Matt. 5:16; Luke 10:38–42; Purcell 154–55). Psalm 45:13 emphasizes the use of Scripture as a pattern for life: "'All the glory of the king's daughter is within.' Though the life of Jesus Christ was eminent in all virtues, yet poverty, obedience, patience, and humility were those for which He was most remarkable" (Purcell 82). Isaiah 49:15 became a source of comfort for her sisters in their struggles: "God says He will comfort and console us as the loving mother cherishes her child, the greatest example of affection he could give" (51).

McAuley was committed to social action oriented to social change. Although she interpreted Scripture intuitively and without critical self-awareness, she intentionally and authoritatively used Scripture to effect that social change. McAuley's writings have continued to guide and motivate Sisters of Mercy, who today minister in forty-five countries in health care, education, parish work, social services, justice, housing, administration, catechetics, and communications. Her interpretation is a fine example of the interpretation of those "ordinary" persons whose biblical works in nontraditional genres were published and read by communities for whom they were and are instruments for social change.

Bibliography

Harnett, Mary Vincent. *The Life of Rev. Mother Catherine McAuley, Foundress of the Order of Mercy.* Edited by Richard B. O'Brien. Dublin: John F. Fowler, 1864.

McAuley, Catherine. *Cottage Controversy.* New York: P. O'Shea, 1883.

Moore, Mary Clare. *A Little Book of Practical Sayings, Advices and Prayers of Our Revered Foundress, Mother Catherine McAuley.* London: Burns, Oates, 1868.

Purcell, Mary Teresa, compiler. *Retreat Instructions of Mother Mary Catherine McAuley.* Edited by Mary Bertrand Degnan. Westminster, MD: Newman, 1952.

Sullivan, Mary C. *Catherine McAuley and the Tradition of Mercy.* Notre Dame, IN: University of Notre Dame Press, 1995.

———, ed. *The Correspondence of Catherine McAuley, 1818–1841.* Dublin: Four Courts, 2004.

—ELIZABETH M. DAVIS

Mears, Henrietta C. (1890–1963)

Henrietta C. Mears was born on October 23, 1890, in Fargo, North Dakota, the youngest of seven children. Her mother and maternal grandparents were the formative influences in her early Christian experience. Mears graduated from the University of Minnesota with a science degree in 1913. She taught in a number of rural Minnesota high schools before accepting both a teaching job and a principal's position in North Branch, Minnesota. After ten years of teaching, Mears took a sabbatical and traveled to the West Coast; in the fall of 1928, she accepted an appointment as the director of Christian education at the First Presbyterian Church of Hollywood. Under her direction, the Sunday school grew from 450 to 6,500, then the largest in the world. Her teaching ministry continued until her death thirty-five years later, in 1963.

Most of Mears's adult life was spent interpreting and teaching Scripture. She insisted that the Bible be foremost in the Sunday school and all Christian education curricula, with the centrality of Christ and the salvation message the focus of every lesson. For Mears, every portion of Scripture, whether Old or New Testament, had Christ at the heart of the message. She believed that "behind and beneath the Bible, above and beyond the Bible, is the God of the Bible" (Mears 1).

Mears worked from the English text of Scripture rather than the original languages; however, she treated the English translation as the "inspired Word." While she recognized that the text contains difficult passages, she encouraged students to move past the difficulties, advising: "Very early you'll find yourself at a standstill in your spiritual life or separated from it altogether, if you continue 'gagging on the bone.' Lay it aside and go on with the meal!" (Powers 58). Mears read Scripture devotionally; thus her interpretation always focused on the relevance of the passage to life needs and problems, with an emphasis on strengthening the Christian home and building the church. She avoided legalism; as one of her biographers states, "I never heard Miss Mears teach a lesson on what Christians should not do" (60).

As the director of Christian education, Mears had to evaluate available educational resources and, being unhappy with the materials available, she and some colleagues began to prepare their own lessons. Their early endeavors of curriculum writing led to the founding of Gospel Light Press, which became Gospel Light Publications in 1933.

Mears authored many books on the Bible and on Christian education. Her most successful books surveyed the contents of the Bible and the lives of particular biblical characters, considered large questions related to the Christian life and faith, and addressed specific issues related to teaching the Bible in age-appropriate ways. Many of her books went through multiple editions and were translated into other languages. Mears's most successful work, *What the Bible Is All About*, provides students with an understanding of how the various parts of Scripture fit together. An edited version of this book, *What the Bible Is All About for Young Explorers*, is still in use today.

Although Mears's ministry embraced all ages, she focused her work particularly on young adults. She felt that her life's purpose was to challenge young people to always do their best for God in whatever career choice they made: "You should not be content to pump the organ if God wants you to play on it" (Powers 166). She was especially interested in developing strong male leadership in the church. Beginning in 1939 and continuing for twenty-five years, Mears led Forest Home Christian Conference Center in Southern California. Some four hundred young men entered full-time Christian ministry as a result of her teaching.

Mears's views on the role of women in the church were traditional in some ways. She believed in male headship and leadership of the church, although she did not believe in male domination. She believed that women could hold the office of deacon, but not be called to anything beyond the work of missions or assisting in a congregation. Thus the indomitable church leader Mears worked under the authority of a pastor, yet conducted herself as an equal. Vonette Bright suggested that Mears could be impatient with anyone "who did not give her an opportunity to do what she had been called to do" (Leyda 8). Some believe that she would not have accepted ordination if it had been offered to her. Those who did not agree with her position on women in ministry were apparently disarmed by what one biographer called "her respectful attitude, enthusiastic spirit, winsome personality, and disarming sense of humor [which] seemed to render questions concerning gender inconsequential" (8).

One of Mears's greatest contributions to the church was in the area of graded curriculum material for the Sunday school, whereby every person could learn the Scriptures at one's own level. In 1946 she was the only woman to serve on the Lessons Committee of the National Sunday School Association to formulate an alternative curriculum to the existing Uniform Series. Her literal and devotional understanding of the text was never enough if it did not result in practical Christian living. The pledge of the "Fellowship of the Burning Heart" was "to spend 1 hour each day in Scripture and prayer, to maintain Christian 'chastity and virtue' and to 'seek every possible opportunity to witness'" (Turner 147).

Mears's legacy also extends to the personal influence that she had on such key figures as the renowned evangelist Billy Graham; Bill Bright, founder of Campus Crusade for Christ; and Jim Rayburn, founder of Young Life. When she died at the age of seventy-three, more than two thousand people attended her funeral service.

Bibliography

Baldwin, Ethel May, and David Benson. *Henrietta Mears and How She Did It*. Glendale, CA: Gospel Light Pubs., 1966.

Blackenbaker, Frances. *What the Bible Is All About for Young Explorers*. Ventura, CA: Gospel Light Pubs., 1986.

Leyda, Richard J. "Henrietta Cornelia Mears." In Talbot School of Theology's "Christian Educators of the 20th Century Project." http://www.talbot.edu/ce20/educators/view.

Mears, Henrietta C. *What the Bible Is All About: An Easy-to-Understand Survey of the Bible*. Glendale, CA: Gospel Light Pubs., 1966.

Powers, Barbara Hudson. *The Henrietta Mears Story*. Westwood, NJ: Fleming H. Revell, 1957.

Roe, Earl O. *Dream Big: The Henrietta Mears Story*. Ventura, CA: Regal Books, 1990.

Turner, John G. "The Power behind the Throne: Henrietta Mears and Post World War II Evangelicalism." *Journal of Presbyterian History* (2005): 141–57.

—ELAINE BECKER

Mechthild of Hackeborn (von Hackeborn) (1240–98)

Mechthild entered the Benedictine-Cistercian monastery at Helfta in Saxony (modern-day Germany) when she was only seven years old. Here she came under the leadership of her elder biological sister, Gertrude, who was serving as abbess to the thriving mystical and intellectual center. Mechthild gained a sound liberal arts education at Helfta since Gertrude believed that classical study and the pursuit of knowledge were requisite for understanding Scripture and living a devout religious life.

Within this environment, Mechthild lived with and presumably learned from the prolific mystical authors, Mechthild of Magdeburg and Gertrude the Great of Helfta. Mechthild of Hackeborn herself came to be highly regarded for her intellect and religious fervency and eventually assumed the leadership positions of chantress and novice mistress at Helfta.

The mystical and spiritual experiences that Mechthild of Hackeborn enjoyed in her life are presented in the *Book of Special Grace* (*Liber specialis gratiae*), although they are not recorded by her own pen. In 1291, while suffering a serious illness, Mechthild began speaking about her mysticism to two of her religious sisters, Gertrude the Great and an unidentified woman at Helfta. The two women took down Mechthild's words for the next seven years, composing a Latin manuscript of over one thousand pages, concluding the book with a memorial of Mechthild's joyful death, which occurred in 1298.

To illustrate the superabundance of God's grace in her life, Mechthild's book draws attention to a number of themes from Scripture. Various biblical tropes are commonly combined to describe Mechthild's visions of Christ and to provide moral teachings for the women in her community and anyone else who might read her book. In one such visionary account, Mechthild has an encounter with the wounded side of Christ and the water flowing from it. To discuss this water as a symbol of saving grace, Mechthild first draws from Ezek. 47:1: "I saw water flowing out from beneath the threshold of the temple toward the east." She then alludes to John 7:37–39 to interpret these temple waters as the foreshadowing of Jesus, the fountain of salvation. Finally, when Mechthild chants Ps. 51 during Mass, she claims Paul's declaration in Rom. 5:2, 5. Jesus takes her in his arms and says to her: "It is in the love of my divine heart that I have washed you" (Mechthild of Hackeborn, *Liber*, 2.2).

Mechthild's meditation on the Song of Songs contributed to this interpretation of Christ's heart. Within the medieval monastic tradition, it thus was commonplace to apply the words "Come, my dove in the cleft of the rocks, in the hollow places of the wall" (Song 2:14) to the wounded side of Christ. Moreover, Mechthild utilizes the erotic and bridal language of the Song of Songs to speak *literally* of the crucified Christ as the soul's lover:

> His noble couch was the hard cross on which he leapt with such joy and burning love: no bridegroom has ever experienced such delight in his couch of ivory and silk. He is still waiting for you with unutterable and raging desire on this bed of love until he can have full enjoyment of your embraces. But if you wish to be his bride, for your part you must completely renounce all delight and approach him on his bed of sorrow and indignity and join yourself to his wounded side. ("Letters," 174)

The way Mechthild promotes a personal, sensual encounter with the biblical text becomes clearer in book 5 of *Liber*, which includes letters written by Mechthild to an anonymous "laywoman." In the letters Mechthild advises an experiential reading of Scripture for the woman. This entails her appropriating, living, and even physically interacting with the Word. In a highly intriguing instance of such, Mechthild counsels her "dearest daughter in Christ":

> The Lover of your soul holds your hand in his right hand and is touching each of your fingers with his fingers. In this way it will be shown to you how he works in your soul and how you ought to follow him by imitating his example. His little finger signifies his very humble way of life on earth when he "came not to be served but to serve" [Mark 10:45] and to be subject to every creature. Place your finger on his: that is to say, when you are puffed up with pride, recall the humiliation and subjugation of your God, praying that through his humility, you may subdue all pride and self-will, that which springs from the personal love by which humans love themselves. ("Letters," 173)

In the fifteenth century Mechthild's *Liber* was translated into Middle English as the *Booke of gostlye grace*. In its latter version, Mechthild's book became the most widely known and influential piece of Helfta literature. If the Helfta manuscripts and documents had not been destroyed during the tumultuous times of the Protestant Reformation, probably more evidence would be available today of Mechthild's widely appealing sensual interpretation of Scripture.

Nevertheless, the flurry of interest in *Liber* during the last three decades has begun to bring about more awareness of Mechthild's highly emotional and affectionate identification with the Bible.

See also Gertrude the Great (Gertrud von Helfta) (1256–1302); Mechthild of Magdeburg (von Magdeburg) (ca. 1208–ca. 1282/94)

Bibliography

Caron, Ann Marie. "Invitations of the Divine Heart: The Mystical Writings of Mechthild of Hackeborn." *American Benedictine Review* 45, no. 3 (Sept. 1994): 321–28.

Dieker, Alberta. "Mechtild of Hackeborn: Song of Love." Pages 231–42 in *Medieval Women Monastics: Wisdom's Wellsprings*, edited by Linda Kulzer and Miriam Schmitt. Collegeville, MN: Liturgical Press, 1996.

McGinn, Bernard. *The Flowering of Mysticism: Men and Women in the New Mysticism (1200–1350)*. Vol. 3 of *The Presence of God: A History of Western Christian Mysticism*. New York: Crossroad Pub., 1998.

Mechthild of Hackeborn. "Letters from Mechthild of Hackeborn to a Friend, a Laywoman in the World, Taken from the *Book of Special Grace*, Book IV, Chapter 59." Translated by Margot H. King. Pages 173–76 in *Vox Mystica: Essays on Medieval Mysticism in Honor of Professor Valerie M. Lagorio*, edited by Anne Clark Bartlett et al. Cambridge: D. S. Brewer, 1995.

———. *Liber specialis gratiae*. Vol. 2 of *Revelationes Gertrudianae ac Mechtildianae*. Edited by the monks of Solesmes (Louis Pasquelin). Poitiers-Paris: Oudin, 1877.

— ELLA JOHNSON

Mechthild of Magdeburg (von Magdeburg) (ca. 1208–ca. 1282/94)

Mechthild is chiefly known through her book, *The Flowing Light of the Godhead (Fliessende Licht der Gottheit)*. From the *Flowing Light*, one learns that Mechthild had daily mystical experiences from the age of twelve. In her forties she first disclosed these divine encounters to her Dominican confessor, Heinrich of Halle, who advised her to write her experiences down in a book, as if her words came "out of God's heart and mouth" (Mechthild of Magdeburg 144). Her familiarity with the forms and content of German high courtly literature and her lack of knowledge of Latin suggest that she was born into a noble and well-educated family, but received little formal theological training. Never married, in her early twenties Mechthild joined a community of beguines in Magdeburg, Saxony (now in Germany). During her time there, the community was increasingly persecuted due to male clerical control and the group's lack of official ecclesial approbation. This persecution eventually led Mechthild to seek refuge in the nearby flourishing intellectual and mystical center of the Benedictine-Cistercian monastery at Helfta. There she lived and spent the final years of her life among other renowned women spiritual writers, including Mechthild of Hackeborn and Gertrude the Great.

The women at Helfta assisted Mechthild through persecutions, illness, and blindness, and through the completion of her book's last chapters as she dictated its words to them.

Mechthild's *Flowing Light* is divided into seven books and subdivided into 267 sections. The sections vary in style and genre, written in both prose and verse, in the various modes of courtly love poetry, dialogue, drama, folk and wedding song, and allegory. In this way, the book describes Mechthild's visionary experiences, gives counsel and criticism to priests and nuns, offers theological reflection, and provides prayers. To validate Mechthild's religious authority, the book also (re)interprets Scripture in several significant ways.

For example, *Flowing Light* aligns Mechthild with five important figures from the Old Testament: Moses, David, Solomon, Jeremiah, and Daniel. Mechthild declares that these men are the "five lights" the "Lord promises . . . to illumine this book" (126). Mechthild further shifts attention away from her gender and toward God: "And so this book has come lovingly from God and does not have its origins in human thought" (144). She also grants her words clerical sanction by recounting her confessor's command to her to write the book. Finally, Mechthild employs the conventional humility topos, but unconventionally central in her argument is Paul's description of weakness as God's favor (2 Cor. 12:7–10). Mechthild thereby embraces her femaleness to illustrate her lack of worldly power and her possession of divine power.

The accounts of Christ's temptation in the wilderness (Matt. 4:1–11; Mark 1:12–13; Luke 4:1–13) are also important to Mechthild's argument for the authority of her female voice. She dramatically describes Christ's interactions with the devil but replaces the character of Christ in the biblical accounts with herself. In her telling, she is tempted to reject God and to worship the "deceiver with beautiful garments," who promises her great honor instead. Like Christ, Mechthild renounces the devil; however, the remainder of her account does not follow the biblical narrative. Rather than continually rebuke the devil and drive him away as Christ did in Matthew's and Luke's detailed accounts, Mechthild states that the devil's "idle talk annoyed her greatly; nevertheless, she listened to it freely so that she might become more shrewd" (141). Mechthild does not seem to be overly concerned about the devil's powers to entice her to harm her soul; she is considerably more confident in her abilities to use all things—even temptation—for the glory of God. Speaking and writing as a woman, Mechthild's dialogue claims her facility in dealing with the devil: she not only outsmarts his wiles but also uses them to grow in holiness.

Mechthild further validates her religious authority by directly opposing traditional interpretations of Eve's encounter with the serpent in Gen. 3, which held Eve's womanliness as the devil's target for easy seduction. In her inventive (re)interpretation of this text, Mechthild does not focus on Eve. Instead, she is rather ambiguous in assigning responsibility for the fall, either accusing Adam or both Adam and Eve, but never only Eve.

This also leads Mechthild to present an alternative to the traditional Eve/Mary parallel. In the age-old schema, Mary is presented as the new Eve, corresponding to the parallel between Christ and Adam: just as Eve, by her disobedience, brought death upon the human race, so Mary, by her obedience, brought salvation. But Mechthild draws from Prov. 8 and the Wisdom of Solomon to identify Mary as an image of "Eternal Wisdom" rather than as the "New Eve." In contrast to the fallen soul of Adam and humanity, Mary is the bride of God and the mother of Jesus, all persons, and the church. Mechthild reports Mary's words:

> When our Father's *jubilus* was saddened by Adam's fall, so that he had to become angry, the Eternal Wisdom of the almighty Godhead intercepted the anger together with me. The Father chose me for his bride—that he might have something to love; for his darling bride, the noble soul was dead. The Son chose me to be his mother, and the Holy Spirit received me as his beloved. Then I alone was the bride of the Holy Trinity and mother of orphans, and I brought them before God's eyes so that they might not all sink down, though some did. When I was thus the mother of many a banished child, my breasts became so full of the pure, spotless milk of true, generous mercy that I suckled the prophets and sages, even before I was born. Afterward, in my childhood, I suckled Jesus; later, in my youth, I suckled God's bride, Holy Christianity, under the cross when I was so desolate and wretched, as the sword of the physical suffering cut spiritually into my soul. (50–51)

Mechthild's effort to validate her female religious authority provides a snapshot of her (re)interpretations of the Bible. Modern scholarly sources proudly affirmative of Mechthild's visionary experiences and spiritual theology have recently multiplied in number; yet her imaginative biblical interpretation awaits extensive study.

See also Gertrude the Great (Gertrud von Helfta) (1256–1302); Mechthild of Hackeborn (von Hackeborn) (1240–98)

Bibliography

Mechthild of Magdeburg. *The Flowing Light of the Godhead*. In *Mechthild of Magdeburg: The Flowing Light of the Godhead*, translated and introduced by Frank Tobin. New York: Paulist Press, 1998.

Tobin, Frank. "Audience, Authorship, and Authority in Mechthild von Magdeburg's *Flowing Light of the Godhead*." *Mystics Quarterly* 23, no. 1 (March 1997): 8–17.

———. Introduction to *Mechthild of Magdeburg: The Flowing Light of the Godhead*. Translated by Frank Tobin. New York: Paulist Press, 1998.

———. "Mechthild von Magdeburg, the Devil, and Antichrist." In *The Mystical Gesture: Essays on Medieval and Early Modern Spiritual Culture in Honor of Mary E. Giles*, edited by Robert Boenig. Aldershot, UK: Ashgate, 2000.

—Ella Johnson

■ Melania the Elder (ca. 340–ca. 410)

Melania was born in Spain into a wealthy Roman family, and at the age of twenty-two was widowed and lost two of her three children. In 372/73 she sold her property and left her surviving son, Publicola, in Rome. She visited religious communities in Egypt and then traveled to Jerusalem, where she built a monastery for women, was its religious head for twenty-seven years, and provided for its continuation by an endowment. A neighboring monastery for men, probably built at her expense, was led by Rufinus of Aquileia. As an "old woman of sixty" she came back to Rome and her family, but after several years returned to Jerusalem, where she died in about 410, forty days after her arrival.

According to Paulinus (*Letter* 29.13), Scripture was nourishment "like bread" for Melania (Walsh 2:116). She followed the teaching and example of Christ, which she found in Scripture. By the end of her life, obeying Christ's advice to the rich young ruler (Matt. 19:21; Mark 10:21; Luke 18:22), she had given away all of her considerable fortune. Like Christ in the upper room, she dressed in slave's clothing and waited on a group of monks who had been denied servants.

She was remarkable for her influence on women as well as men, who respected her and listened to her. Melania was a "man of God" (Palladius 9, Meyer 43), often named by the masculine form Melanius. She was admired for her serious study of Christian writings. She read so intensely that she was caught up in a controversy over the second-century theologian Origen, in which she was allied with Rufinus (translator of Origen), Palladius, Paulinus, and Evagrius against Jerome.

Two Christian leaders whom she is credited with influencing were Evagrius and her granddaughter and namesake, Melania the Younger. Evagrius came sick to Jerusalem and was convicted by the words of Melania, who addressed him as "son" and told him that the illness from which he was suffering was God's discipline for his sin. In this rebuke she echoed Heb. 12:5, itself quoting Prov. 3:11. As a result, Evagrius adopted asceticism. He corresponded with her and wrote, undoubtedly as a compliment to her, "our Lord arms women too with manliness against the evil spirits" (*Letter* 1.6, Dysinger).

Concern for her granddaughter Melania was her reason for returning from Jerusalem to Rome. The time spent with her family and the example of her life affected her granddaughter, who, like her, adopted asceticism and founded a monastery in Jerusalem, professing that she was "entering into my inheritance of the zeal of my grandmother whose name I bear" (Palladius 61.2, Meyer 142). That the *Life of Melania the Younger* completely ignores the grandmother is best explained by the Origenist controversy (Clark, *Life*, 86).

Jerome had initially praised her, along with Paula, as a model of Christian ascetic behavior (*Letter* 45.4) but later turned against her because of his view of Origen (*Letter* 133.3), making a sour comment on her "black" name (from *melas*, Greek for "black") as bearing witness to "the darkness of her perfidy." According to Rufinus (*Apology* 2.26), Jerome erased her name from his own copy of his *Chronicles* (for 374 CE).

In a quotation preserved by Palladius (54, Meyer 135), Melania borrowed the address used by John (1 John 2:18) as she left Rome for the second time: "Little children, it was written four hundred years ago, it is the last hour. . . . Beware lest the days of the Antichrist overtake you and you not enjoy your wealth and your ancestral property." She was speaking to the senators and their wives who tried to keep her from going back to Jerusalem and whom she had characterized as "wild beasts" against which she had to fight, as Paul had at Ephesus (1 Cor. 15:32). Her warnings were timely: soon after she left, Rome was sacked by Alaric and the Visigoths on August 24, 410.

Melania took positions on doctrinal matters fearlessly, informed by her study of Scripture. She supported the orthodox position against the Arians, hid those who were persecuted, and risked imprisonment. With Rufinus she persuaded four hundred *Pneumatomachoi* monks (who denied the divinity of the Holy Spirit) to give up their heresy.

Her contribution to the formation of Christian leaders as well as her teaching and example within the monastery and beyond were almost forgotten because of the taint of the Origenist controversy. Melania deserves better.

See also Paula (347–404)

Bibliography

Clark, Elizabeth A. *Life of Melania the Younger*. Lewiston, NY: Edwin Mellen, 1984.

———. "Melania the Elder and the Origenist Controversy: The Status of the Body in an Late-Ancient Debate." Pages 111–27 in *Nova et Vetera: Patristic Studies in Honor of Thomas Patrick Halton*, edited by John Petruccione. Washington, DC: Catholic University of America Press, 1998.

Dysinger, Luke. *Evagrius. Letters*. http://www.ldysinger.com/evagrius/11_Letters/00a_start.htm.

Jerome. *Letters*. In vol. 6 of *Nicene and Post-Nicene Fathers*, Series 2, edited by Philip Schaff and Henry Wace. New York: Christian Literature, 1893. Repr., Peabody, MA: Hendrickson, 1995.

Meyer, R. T. (trans.). *Palladius, The Lausiac History: Ancient Christian Writers*, no. 34. New York, NY/Ramsey, NJ: Newman Press, 1964.

Murphy, Francis X. "Melania the Elder: A Biographical Note." *Traditio* 5 (1947): 59–77.

Rufinus. *Apology*. In vol. 3 of *Nicene and Post-Nicene Fathers*, Series 2, edited by Philip Schaff and Henry Wace. New York: Christian Literature, 1892. Repr., Peabody, MA: Hendrickson, 1995.

Trout, Dennis E. *Paulinus of Nola: Life, Letters, and Poems*. Berkeley: University of California Press, 1999.

Walsh, P. G. (trans.). *Letters of Saint Paulinus of Nola*, vol 2: *Ancient Christian Writers*, no. 36. New York, NY/Ramsey, NJ: Newman Press, 1968.

— M. Eleanor Irwin

Meyer, Lucy Rider (1849–1922)

Lucy Jane Rider was born in Vermont to Richard Rider, a New England pioneer, and Jane Child Rider. After attending public schools in New Haven, Weybridge, Middlebury, and Fairfax, she received her college education at Oberlin College. During her tenure as the field secretary of the Illinois State Sunday School Association (1880–84), she became convinced of the need to train women for public ministry. Thus she and Josiah Shelley Meyer, whom she married in 1885, established two institutions that would train women in biblical studies and equip them for service in home and foreign missions: the Chicago Training School, established in 1885, and the Chicago Deaconess Home, established in 1887.

Meyer was a key leader in the establishment of the Methodist order of deaconesses. Part of her effort to establish this order is reflected in her interpretation of Scripture, which is largely confined to two of her publications: her book titled *Deaconesses* (1889) and her article titled "The Mother in the Church" (1901). *Deaconesses* is divided into three parts: the first part considers deaconesses in the Bible, early church, the Reformation, modern Europe, and America; the second part recounts the establishment of the Chicago Training School; and the third recounts the establishment of the Chicago Deaconess Home.

One feature of Meyer's interpretation of the Bible is her defense of the ministry of women in the public domain. First, she highlights examples of women in public ministry in the New Testament. These include Joanna, the wife of Herod's steward; the Marys (the mother of Jesus, Mary of Magdala, and the sister of Martha); Dorcas; Lydia; Priscilla; Philip's four daughters; the unnamed women who host the early church; and the women greeted by name in Paul's letters, Junia, Tryphena, Tryphosa, Persis, the mother of Rufus, and Phoebe (*Deaconesses*, 12–13; cf. Rom. 16).

Second, Meyer argues for the existence of an ancient order of deaconesses. Paul's description of Phoebe is important to that argument (Rom. 16:1–2). Paul calls Phoebe a *diakonos*, which Meyer translates not as "servant" but as "deaconess," and a *prostatis*, a succorer, or as Meyer would translate it, a "president" (13–14). Further, since no definite article precedes *diakonos*, Phoebe is only one among a number of deaconesses in the church for "she is called not *the* Deaconess, the only one, but *a* Deaconess" (14).

The translation of 1 Tim. 3:1–11 is also important to Meyer's argument for the existence of an ancient order of deaconesses. First, while the semantic range of *gynē* (woman, wife) allows the term to be translated as "wives," Meyer contends that the Greek term is better translated as "women." Thus 1 Tim. 3:11 reads, "Even so, the women must be grave." Second, the adverb *hōsautōs* (as, just as), appearing in 1 Tim. 3:8 and 11, was translated into two different English words (in KJV). If *hōsautōs* were translated consistently, Meyer argues that it would be evident that both the deacons and the women, or deaconesses, are being exhorted to be like the bishops described in 1 Tim. 3:1–7. Third, if *gynē* refers to "the wives of the deacons," then the wives of the bishops ought to be exhorted as well. Fourth, the logic of the chapter suggests to Meyer that "Paul, in giving the character of the Deacons, would next most naturally speak of the Deaconesses" (16). Thus she concludes, "There is no intimation that the women spoken of are the feminine complements of the Deacons, their wives; on the contrary, there is strong reason to believe that they are the feminine counterparts of Deacons, Deaconesses" (15).

Another feature of Meyer's interpretation of the Bible is the importance that she places on women's traditional roles as wives and mothers. The Methodist deaconesses did not take vows of celibacy but did remain single. Nevertheless, Meyer argues that they fulfill the traditional roles of women: "The Greek word *diakonos*—of which the English word deaconess is the translation—has at heart the meaning, *prompt and helpful service*. The foundation thought being, thus, that of help, the idea may be traced back to the second chapter of Genesis, in which woman is called by that noblest of titles, a *Help*" (11). The work of the Methodist deaconesses *helped* the pastor and thus fulfilled the proper role of woman as wife. Further, the deaconesses cared for neglected or abandoned children, bringing both food and clothing during their visits and providing manual, moral, and spiritual training. They also cared for the sick in accordance with the biblical injunction to "Heal the sick" (Matt. 10:8; Luke 9:2; 10:9). Thus, by performing the duties typically carried out by the mother, the Methodist deaconesses fulfilled the proper role of woman as mother.

Meyer's desire to justify women's public ministries is evident in her interpretation of the Bible, which not only drew attention to New Testament examples of women in public ministries, but also challenged traditional translations of the Greek New Testament that impacted such important issues as the role of women in the church. At the same time, she sought not to depart from the traditional understanding of women's roles as wives and mothers, but to demonstrate that the Methodist deaconesses fulfilled those roles in new ways.

Bibliography

Choi, Agnes. "From the Mediterranean to America: Lucy Meyer's Biblical Interpretation and the Deaconess Movement." Pages 233–44 in *Strangely Familiar: Proto-Feminist Interpretations of Patriarchal Biblical Texts*, edited by Nancy Calvert-Koyzis and Heather E. Weir. Atlanta: Society of Biblical Literature, 2009.

Horton, Isabelle. *High Adventure: Life of Lucy Rider Meyer*. Women in American Protestant Religion, 1800–1930. New York: Garland, 1928.

Meyer, Lucy Rider. *Deaconesses, Biblical, Early Church, European, American: With the Story of the Chicago Training School, for City, Home and Foreign Missions, and the Chicago Deaconess Home.* 2nd ed., rev. and enlarged. Chicago: Message Pub., 1889.

———. "The Mother in the Church." *Methodist Review* 50 (1901): 716–32.

— AGNES CHOI

■ Montgomery, Helen Barrett (1861–1934)

In 1861 Helen Barrett was born to Amos Judson Barrett and Emily B. Barrows Barrett in Kingsville, Ohio. She majored in classics at Wellesley College, graduating in 1884 when fewer than 2.2 percent of American women attended college. In 1887 she married William A. Montgomery, a business entrepreneur and member of the Lake Avenue Baptist Church, of which A. J. Barrett was pastor.

Montgomery worked in Rochester as a civic leader and member of the school board. She became a well-known speaker in the city and was an associate of Susan B. Anthony in the successful effort to have women admitted to the University of Rochester.

Montgomery went on a national speaking tour in 1910 to promote mission work. In 1921–22 she served as president of the Northern Baptist Convention, guiding the convention through the crucial fundamentalist-modernist controversy, which resulted in the Northern Baptists' rejection of a rigidly Calvinistic creed in favor of "no creed but the New Testament." Poor health resulted in her withdrawal from public life in 1930, and she died in 1934 at the age of seventy-three.

In 1924, Montgomery published a translation of the New Testament that she had originally prepared for her private use. This was called the *Centenary New Testament* because its publication commemorated the one-hundredth anniversary of the American Baptist Publication Society. In this translation, Montgomery offers interpretations of passages that were traditionally used to limit roles of women in the church.

In Rom. 16:1–2 Paul introduces Phoebe to the church at Rome and refers to her as a *diakonos* "of the church at Cenchreae" and a *prostatis* "of many people, including myself." The King James Version (KJV) (among others) translates *diakonos* as "servant" and *prostatis* as "succorer/helper." In contrast, Montgomery translates *diakonos* as "minister" and *prostatis* as "overseer": "I commend to you our sister Phoebe, who is a *minister* of the church at Cenchreae. I beg you to give her a Christian welcome, as the saints should; and to assist her in any matter in which she may have need of you. For she herself has been made an *overseer* to many people, including myself" (emphasis added).

Montgomery also advocated an alternate translation of Rom. 16:7, a greeting to two persons, Andronicus, who is clearly a man, and Junia, taken by translators since Luther to be a man as well (Junian). The early Greek theologians, however, took the name as feminine, and Montgomery agrees, recognizing that Junia was a woman apostle: "Salute . . . Andronicus and Junia, my kinsfolk and fellow prisoners, who are notable among the apostles, and who became Christians before I did."

Montgomery attempts to reconcile two passages in 1 Corinthians, where Paul discusses the proper conduct of women in public worship. In 11:2–16 he regulates the public head coverings of men and women who "pray and prophesy" in worship; in 14:34–36 he appears to command that women "keep silence in the churches." Since in a meeting one cannot prophesy while keeping silent, veil or no veil, these passages need to be reconciled in some way unless Paul is allowed to contradict himself.

Montgomery's translation of 1 Cor. 11:2–16 has interpreted this extremely complex passage to mean that a woman should have authority over her own head and may pray to God without a veil, because her long hair is a glory to her and functions instead of the traditional veil. Nevertheless, a woman may veil while leading worship if failure to do so would dishonor her husband. Men, however, should never cover their heads while praying or prophesying. She takes advantage of the fact that the absence of punctuation in the Greek text allows the sentences usually translated as questions ("Does not nature itself teach you . . . ?") to be translated as statements instead ("Nor does nature itself teach you . . .). This also saves Paul from the embarrassing error of asserting that short hair is "natural" for men.

Montgomery's translation of 1 Cor. 14:33b–36 reads: "In your congregation, [you write], 'as in all the churches of the saints, let the women keep silence in the churches, for they are not permitted to speak, . . . for it is shameful for a woman to speak in church.' What, was it from you that the word of God went forth, or to you only did it come?" Here the prohibition against women's speaking is attributed, not to Paul, but to some Corinthians, whom Montgomery identifies in the footnote as "Judaizers." Paul responds to the prohibition with an indignant "What!"

In 1 Tim. 3:8–13 is a discussion of the qualifications for *diakonoi*, usually translated "deacons" here. In 3:11 *gynaikas* (either "women" or "wives") are included. The KJV, Moffatt, and Goodspeed translate the Greek term as "wives." Montgomery, however, translates it as "deaconesses."

Montgomery recognized the impact of translation on the defining of women's roles in ministry. The interpretations of the passages concerning Phoebe, head coverings in worship, and the silencing of women in 1 Cor. 14 were almost certainly derived from the work of another woman translator, Katharine C. Bushnell (1855–1946). She went further than Bushnell, however, by publishing a translation that incorporates these interpretive ideas into her version. Some of these interpretations of the role of women in church leadership are now widely accepted by New Testament scholars, but Montgomery and her translation remain largely unknown to the scholarly community.

See also Bushnell, Katharine C. (1855–1946)

Bibliography

Bullard, Roger A. "Feminine and Feminist Touches in the Centenary New Testament." *The Bible Translator* 38, no. 1 (1987): 118–22.

Dowd, Sharyn. "Helen Barrett Montgomery's *Centenary Translation* of the New Testament: Characteristics and Influences." *Perspectives in Religious Studies* 19, no. 2 (1992): 133–50.

———. "The Ministry of Women in Montgomery's *Centenary New Testament:* The Evidence of the Autographs." *American Baptist Quarterly* 20, no. 3 (2001): 320–28.

Mobley, Kendal P. *Helen Barrett Montgomery: The Global Mission of Domestic Feminism.* Waco: Baylor University Press, 2009.

Montgomery, Helen Barrett. *Centenary Translation of the New Testament.* Philadelphia: American Baptist Pub. Society, 1924.

— SHARYN DOWD

Morata, Olympia (ca. 1526/27–55)

Olympia Morata was born in Ferrara in 1526 or 1527, the oldest of five children. Her father, Fulvio Morato, was a humanist professor and a tutor to the sons of Duke Alfonso d'Este. Alone of his four daughters, Olympia was taught Latin and Greek. In 1540 she was invited to live at court as the study companion for Duke Ercole's daughter, Anne, under the tutelage of the Sinapius brothers Iohan (John) and Chilian (Kilian) Senf. While at court, Olympia gave public performances of her classical learning, such as lecturing on Cicero's paradoxes.

Fulvio Morato was actively interested in the ideas of Luther, Calvin, Erasmus, and Valdes, an interest cultivated especially during a period in Vicenza and Venice (1532–38). Celio Secondo Curione, a classical scholar familiar with the writings of Melanchthon, Zwingli, Luther, and Calvin, and personally acquainted with Bernardino Ochino, was a friend whom Morata called "my divine teacher, sent to me by God, for my instruction and conversion" (Morata, *Complete*, 13). Olympia's teacher Senf corresponded with Calvin and her patron, the duchess Renée, protected religious reformers.

Morata focused her enthusiastic studies on the classics and paid little attention to religious matters until she found herself beset by a series of disasters. Her father's death in 1548 left the family in financial straits. Meanwhile her position at court terminated abruptly as Anne married and moved away. With Pope Paul III urging the duke to cleanse Ferrara from heresies, both her teachers and Curione left for northern Europe. After two desperate years, Morata married a German medical student and devoted Protestant, Andreas Grunthler, and in 1550 moved with him to Schweinfurt, Germany. There, given her husband's religion, the availability of Protestant books, as well as her feeling that God had reached out to save her, she threw herself fervently into religious studies. She sent some of Luther's writings to her friend Lavinia della Rovere Orsini and urged both Matthias Illyricus and Pietro Paolo Vergerio to translate Luther's work into Italian (117, 133, 167).

In 1554, war destroyed many of her writings, together with the rest of her possessions in Schweinfurt. She moved with her husband to Heidelberg, and died of illness in 1555 at the age of twenty-nine. In 1558 Curione published a first edition of her works, with a dedication to Isabella Brisegna, another Italian who had fled north for religious reasons. Augmented editions were printed and reprinted in 1562, 1570, and 1580, with a dedication to Queen Elizabeth of England.

One of her projects was translating psalms into classical Greek meters, beginning in 1549 with Ps. 46, which clearly expresses her own situation as she saw it: God alone can aid the distressed in times of chaos. Eight of her psalms, in heroic and sapphic meters, were printed in the volume of her works: Pss. 1, 2, 23, 34, 46, 70, 125, 150. The psalms are also the most frequently cited part of the Old Testament in her letters, which make up the bulk of her writing. Her psalm translations are personally felt prayers for God's protection in difficult times and assurances that those who trust in God will be safe while "those who plot wicked things against the good / will not always rule and be strong" (*Complete*, 192). At about the same time, she wrote a paraphrase of Wis. 7–9, attached (intentionally or mistakenly) to her first dialogue to Lavinia, on her shift from classical learning to the pursuit of spiritual wisdom.

Her second dialogue to Lavinia holds up the model of Queen Esther, who "for the salvation of her people . . . ignored even the peril to her own life" (*Opere*, 2:43, my trans.). Having gone with Lavinia to visit the imprisoned Fannio Fanini, an early victim of Ferrara's crackdown on heresy, she encourages Lavinia, living at court like Esther, to make similarly courageous use of her position to defend the victims of unjust religious persecution. Later she urges Anne to defend religious victims in France even against her husband, the duke de Guise.

Olympia Morata did not write explicit commentary on passages of Scripture, but she braided biblical phrases into everything she wrote, especially her many letters. Her favorite writer is Paul. Like Paul, she expects the world to end soon, quoting to Lavinia: "The form of this world is quickly passing" (1 Cor. 7:31; *Complete*, 143). In a reproach to a German preacher, she cites 1 Cor. 3:16–17 about the body as a temple, not to be defiled by drunkenness; Rom. 14:13 about the "stumbling block" of the preacher's offering prideful learning rather than a lived example; and 1 Corinthians, Romans, and Galatians on behalf of "crucifying" the flesh rather than using its weakness as an excuse (*Complete*, 134–36). References to Rom. 6:6 and the Psalms are combined in a letter to Curione, concerning the sinfulness of all and the importance of prayer (140). A letter to her sister references 1 Corinthians, Romans, and Galatians, along with two psalms on the weakness and ephemerality of mortal life, and the importance of prayer and Bible reading as a source of both strength and faith; for "Faith, says Paul, comes through hearing, and hearing through the Word of God" (145; Rom. 10:17).

Her letters to other women continually urge the daily reading of Scripture, if possible its discussion with friends and family, and prayer. Thus she exhorts her sister Vittoria, Lavinia, and Madonna Cherubina to read and discuss Scripture with one another and to govern their life by it "and not the authority of any mere person" (153). The Bible is considered less a source of history or theology than a guide and support to daily life. Morata's emphasis is constantly on faith, sought through Scripture and prayer, rather than on theological issues. Though inevitably aware of the debates violently stirring Europe, she calls herself simply a "Christian." The pope, however, is referred to as "the raging antichrist" (115, 127).

All four Gospels are cited in her letters, but especially Matthew, mined chiefly for Jesus's sayings. So too the citations from Mark, Luke, and John are all Jesus's words. The comfort of Matt. 11:28 is cited repeatedly; Matt. 17:20; 19:26 (Mark 10:27; Luke 1:37); and Matt. 21:22 (Mark 11:24) form a cluster emphasizing the power of faith to do and receive all things. "Ignore the fact that I am a woman when I advise you. Rather be certain that God is graciously inviting you to Himself with words spoken through my mouth" (*Complete*, 152).

The four editions of Olympia's *Opere* indicate a lively interest among contemporary readers. Catherine des Roches, in her "Dialogue de Placide et Sevère [Dialogue of Placid and Severe]" (1583), mentions Morata to demonstrate that education can enhance rather than undermine a woman's virtue. Morata's two homelands produced serious studies of her in the eighteenth century: Georg Nolten's *Dissertationem historicam de Olympiae Moratae . . .* (Historical dissertation on Olympia Morata) in Frankfurt (1731); and Giovanni Andrea Barotti's work on writers of Ferrara, *Memorie, istoriche di letterati ferraresi* (Historical memoirs of Ferrara's writers ["men of letters" would be more literal, but odd with regard to including a female]) (1777, rev. 1792–93). Goethe refers to her correspondence. She continues to be written about in English, German, and Italian by historians of the Reformation and of women.

See also Elizabeth I (1533–1603)

Bibliography

Bonnet, Jules. *Vie d'Olympia Morata, épisode de la Renaissance et de la Réforme en Italie.* 3rd ed., rev. and augmented. Paris: Charles Meyrneis, 1856. On microfilm in History of Women, reel 245, no. 1634. New Haven: Research Pubs., 1975.

Caponetto, Salvatore. *The Protestant Reformation in Sixteenth-Century Italy.* Translated by Anne C. Tedeschi and John Tedeschi. Kirksville, MO: Thomas Jefferson University Press, 1999.

Morata, Olympia. *The Complete Writings of an Italian Heretic.* Edited and translated by Holt N. Parker. *The Other Voice in Early Modern Europe.* Chicago: University of Chicago Press, 2003.

————. *Olympiae Fulviae Moratae foeminae doctissimae ac plane divinae omnia omnia: quae hactenus inveniri potuerunt.* 3rd ed. Basel: Petrum Pernam, 1570. Repr., 1580. On microfilm in History of Women, reel 62, no. 396. New Haven: Research Pubs., 1975.

————. *Opere.* 2 vols. Edited by Lanfranco Caretti. Atti e Memorie, new ser., 11. Ferrara: Deputazione Provinciale Ferrarese di Storia Patria, 1954. [Excludes her translations and letters.]

Smarr, Janet Levarie. "Olympia Morata: From Classicist to Reformer." Pages 321–43 in *Phaeton's Children: The Este Court and Its Culture in Early Modern Ferrara,* edited by Deanna Shemek and Dennis Looney. Tempe, AZ: Medieval and Renaissance Texts and Studies, 2005.

Stjerna, Kirsi. "Olimpia Fulvia Morata, 1526/27–1555—An Italian Scholar." Pages 197–212 in *Women and the Reformation.* Oxford: Blackwell Pub., 2009.

Vorländer, Dorothea. "Olympia Fulvia Morata—eine evangelische Humanistin in Schweinfurt." *Zeitschrift für bayerische Kirchengeschichte* 30 (1970): 95–113.

— JANET LEVARIE SMARR

More, Gertrude (1606–33)

Dame Gertrude More, whose baptismal name was Helen, was a great-great-granddaughter of Sir Thomas More (1478–1535). She was educated by her pious and learned father, Cresacre More, who had once aspired to be a Catholic priest. In adolescence, she responded without enthusiasm to a suggestion that she join a new Benedictine abbey to be founded at Cambrai for English Catholic women. It was not piety, but affection for her spiritual adviser, that moved her at seventeen to try her vocation. Initially she found monastic life uncongenial. Failure to make spiritual progress exasperated her normally cheerful character and left her moody and irritable. At the same time, however, she had a disinclination for worldly satisfactions, as well as a fixed, though apparently impotent, determination to seek after God. She took her final vows at nineteen, full of misgivings. For the next year she remained spiritually desolate, cold, and loveless toward God and rebellious toward her superiors and directors. Then, under the guidance of Father Augustine Baker (1575–1641), she made rapid progress in the interior life. He determined that the methods of prayer and meditation in use at the convent did not suit her personality, which was highly extroverted, vivacious, and emotional, and he developed with her a form of the prayer life better suited to her character. Dame Gertrude More's spiritual about-face was so considerable that she was soon appointed principal assistant to the abbess of the convent, Katherine Gascoigne. Moreover, though one of the youngest sisters in the new abbey, she became a source of guidance and inspiration to the other nuns. Controversies surrounding Baker's spiritual theories and practices triggered a formal inquiry, undertaken by the Benedictine authorities. During the inquiry, in which she testified on Baker's behalf, Gertrude More contracted a fatal case of smallpox. She died in great peace and serenity, to the edification of her sister nuns. More's manuscripts were collected and arranged by Baker. These works were published in 1657 and 1658. The latter volume contains her "Apology" for the spiritual practices of herself and Baker. Baker also wrote a memoir of More, which described her spiritual development in considerable detail.

The bulk of More's writings consists of her "Confessions." These are short meditations on the spiritual life, addressed to God, sometimes prefaced by scriptural texts, interspersed with poetry and prayers, and containing instructions in piety. The major themes are God's excellencies; the desire for and union with God; the necessity of humility, resignation, and obedience; and the benefits of affliction. There are some meditations on special topics reflecting the Christian calendar. Easter, for instance, elicits reflections on the resurrection. There are many "acts" of praise, contrition, confidence, longing for God, and renunciation of worldly attachments. Many profess a very intense and ardent love for Christ. Occasionally the Confessions allude to significant moments in More's life. For instance, Confession 1 seems to refer to her own youthful self-centeredness, rebelliousness, and misused gregariousness. In Confession 37, an allusion to Luke 14:23 ("Compel them to come in") elicits a reference to her own somewhat forced entrance into convent life. Throughout are many references to Baker and his spiritual teachings. Indeed, the Confessions are permeated with his influence, as in More's insistence that it is God the Holy Spirit, moving in the soul, who teaches a method of prayer and serves as the best spiritual director. In addition, More expresses a particular fondness for St. Augustine, whom she quotes frequently, as also for Thomas à Kempis.

Among her "Fragments" are some comments on specific passages of Scripture. Some register her excitement over a particular passage. In response to Ps. 32:8, she writes, "Who is not wholly inflamed with a desire to seek after God alone, to hear such a promise from his own mellifluous mouth?" Psalm 36:9 ("In thy light shall we see light") elicits a short meditation on the cognitive nature of love, or perhaps the relationship between love and cognition, and its superiority to a purely intellectual knowledge of God. Other favorite passages noted and commented on deal with the sinner's dependence on divine mercy, the vanity of all things, and the importance of faith in divine providence. Sometimes her train of thought is difficult to follow. Commenting on Ps. 41:1 ("Blessed is the man that understandeth concerning the needy and the poor: in the evil day our Lord will deliver him"), she rejoices that, even though she has nothing to give the poor, nevertheless she will receive the same blessings as those who consider them. She then cautions her readers to pray for their enemies, and presents Francis de Sales as a model of Christian forgiveness. Both her Confessions and Fragments are sprinkled with citations of Scripture. Her favorite books are the Psalms, Gospels (esp. Matthew and Luke), the Song of Songs, and Proverbs.

More's works, as well as her personal example, have been valued not only as vindicating the spiritual theory and practice of Baker, but also as records of her own interior life. Evelyn Underhill held More in the highest esteem. In her classic study of mysticism, she wrote that Dame Gertrude More's work "exhibits the romantic and personal side of mysticism even more perfectly than St. Teresa [of Avila]" (88).

See also Teresa of Avila (1515–82)

Bibliography

Baker, Augustine. *The Inner Life of Dame Gertrude More.* Edited by Dom Benedict Weld-Blundell. Manchester, UK: R. & T. Washbourne, 1910.

More, Dame Gertrude. *The Writings of Dame Gertrude More.* Edited by Dom Benedict Weld-Blundell. Manchester, UK: R. & T. Washbourne, 1910.

Sandeman, Dame Frideswide. *Dame Gertrude More.* Leominster, UK: Gracewing, 1997.

Underhill, Evelyn. *Mysticism: A Study in the Nature and Development of Man's Spiritual Consciousness.* New York: E. P. Dutton, 1961.

Wekking, Ben. "Re-editing Baker's Biography of Dame Gertrude More." Pages 155–73 in *That Mysterious Man: Essays on Augustine Baker,* edited by Michael Woodward. Abergavenny, UK: Three Peaks, 2001.

— B R A D   W A L T O N

More, Hannah (1745–1833)

For Hannah More, the Bible was the touchstone of her long productive career: a source of inspiration, a repository of allusions and phrases, a catalog of characters, a sustaining guide. Her deep knowledge of the sacred text, a central element of her daily reading regimen, and unwavering belief in its promises suffused her plays, poems, essays, tracts, and novel. She was an evangelical bluestocking and a socially hierarchical but "spiritually egalitarian" (Myers 239) Tory who championed such radical causes as the abolition of the slave trade and the education of the poor. More, a counterrevolutionary par excellence, was also one of the most influential and financially successful women writers in Georgian Britain. As "a progressive rather than a traditionalist," whose vision of social reform extended "from palace to cottage" (Sutherland 52), More continues to defy conventional ideological or class stereotypes. The range and complexity of her writing are critical to understanding literary politics and to enlarging concepts of Romanticism, extending its horizons to embrace the culture of female sensibility and activism. She "celebrated the workings of the rational mind, a mind relocated—in a gesture of revolutionary social implications—in the female body" (Mellor 87).

Hannah More was the fourth of five daughters of schoolmaster Jacob More and farmer's daughter Mary (Grace) More. She was an eager pupil in the family's quarters of the Fishponds free school in the parish of Stapleton, near Bristol. She quickly distinguished herself in Latin and mathematics, so much so that her father, fearful of creating a mere pedant, discontinued the lessons. Thanks to the paroled French officers, prisoners during the Seven Years' War, whom Jacob invited to their home, the More girls spoke French fluently. When the three older girls moved to Bristol to establish a school for young ladies, Hannah and the youngest followed, first as pupils and then as junior teachers.

None of the More sisters married; however, Hannah's canceled engagement became the target of snide comments from male critics who hid behind pseudonyms to attack her as a jilted bride or frustrated prude. Her dilatory suitor, an old bachelor who had postponed the wedding three times in the space of six years, eventually settled an annuity on Hannah and bequeathed her a thousand pounds. Thus he relieved her of the duty of teaching and launched her immensely prosperous career, which brought her to the attention and tutelage of Dr. Samuel Johnson, theater impresario David Garrick, Shakespearean critic Elizabeth Montagu, influential widow Frances Boscawen, and classical scholar Elizabeth Carter, along with a host of bishops and clergymen.

Two outstanding examples of More's ability as a biblical interpreter bookend her career: the four blank-verse plays and one rhyming couplet monologue based on Old Testament stories, *Sacred Dramas: Chiefly Intended for Young Persons* (1782) and *An Essay on the Character and Practical Writings of Saint Paul* (1815). *Sacred Dramas* ran to twenty-four editions, with poet William Cowper maintaining (1788) that these plays had "more verve and energy both in her thoughts and language than half the he rhymers in the kingdom" (3:227). The entire first edition of *Saint Paul* sold out in one day.

More's strong evangelical convictions influence and complicate her attitude toward the stage, her first love. An active participant in "women's ethical spectatorship of governance," she "engaged with the political life of the nation through media suited to forms of sociability deeply tied to the commercialization of culture" (O'Quinn 117)—in her case, initially through theater. She keenly experienced the countervailing influences of dramatic aesthetics and ethical ideas. In her "Preface to the Tragedies" (1801), she admits that "a well-written tragedy is one of the noblest efforts of the human mind" (More 2:127), but acknowledges the problematic opposition between the Christian principles of humility, charity, and peacemaking and tragedy's preoccupation with anger, honor, and revenge. She understands this binarism as the threat posed to "the power of the word, . . . the biblical logos, by the many voices, bodies, and images of the theatre" (Russell 231).

There is a world of difference between More's tragedies—belabored, angst-driven adaptations for the public stage—and her *Sacred Dramas*, designed for private family, closet, or reading-theater enactment. Her well-loved biblical source actually released a creative outpouring: assured versifying, nuanced and poignant characterization, hard-hitting opposition to the order of the state, an acute understanding of the gap separating public acclaim and private integrity, and a humbling, expressive recognition of fallibility. Although most contemporary criticism, when it touches on More's dramatic work at all, concentrates briefly and usually hurriedly on her tragedies, in *Sacred Dramas* the emerging power of Hannah More as a gifted, impassioned artist can be found.

Though in the "Advertisement" she reflects "with awe" on the "holy ground" on which she stands (1:xxv) and defines her aim as being "at once useful and interesting" to a young audience, "in whom it will always be time enough to have the passions awakened" (1:vvvi), More does not shy away from the central concern of Truth, however unfashionable its tenets.

The clear fervor of her address to "undebauch'd," "unsophisticate" youth (1:5) is one indication of More's self-assurance. The twinning of classical and biblical narrative is another indication of her confidence in the power of biblical story "to rouse a holy zeal, / . . . Correct th' irregular, reform the wrong, / Exalt the low, and brighten the obscure!" (1:6).

"Moses in the Bulrushes," "David and Goliath," "Belshazzar," and "Daniel" are well-known stories, to which More brings a subtlety and deftness of character treatment. Pharaoh's daughter—as a voice of solidarity for women, critical of her own father—rescues the infant Moses and understands immediately the dilemma the child's mother must have faced in a time of aggression and ethnic cleansing:

> Who knows but some unhappy Hebrew woman
> Has thus expos'd her infant, to evade
> The stern decree of my too cruel sire.
> Unhappy mothers! Oft my heart has bled
> In secret anguish o'er your slaughter'd sons;
> Powerless to save, yet hating to destroy.
> (*Works*, 1:13)

This position results in a telling rebuke to her less compassionate attendant, Melita:

> How ill does it beseem
> Thy tender years and gentle womanhood,
> To steel thy breast to pity's sacred touch!
> So weak, so unprotected is our sex,
> So constantly expos'd, so very helpless,
> That did not Heav'n itself enjoin compassion,
> Yet human policy should make us kind;
> Lest in the rapid turn of Fortune's wheel,
> We live to need the pity we refuse.
> (1:19)

With her all-female cast in "Moses in the Bulrushes," More makes a considerable effort both to individualize and to render some exchanges, such as these abrupt, tension-filled lines between Moses's mother, Jochebed, and his sister Miriam, flashpoints of anxiety and release:

> *Jochebed.* Come and lament with me the brother's loss.
> *Miriam.* Come and adore with me the God of Jacob!
> *Jochebed.* Miriam!—the child is dead!
> *Miriam.* He lives! He lives!
> *Jochebed.* Impossible!—Oh, do not mock my grief;
> See'st thou that empty vessel?
> *Miriam.* From that vessel
> Th' Egyptian Princess took him.
> *Jochebed.* Pharaoh's daughter?
> Then still he will be slain: a bloodier death
> Will terminate his woes.
> *Miriam.* His life is safe!
> For know she means to rear him as her own.
>
> (1:23)

The predominantly male cast of "David and Goliath"—with the exception of the closing chorus of Hebrew women—also probes the consequences of war and aggression but mainly from the battlefront, the valley of Elah. Although David's opening song praises the shade and humility of his "lowly cot, . . . remote from regal state" (1:37), most of the drama pits critical (Jesse) and vainglorious (Goliath and David's jealous brothers) views against each other. While the description of Goliath's "fearful stature," the "helm of burnish'd brass" on his "tow'ring head," "capacious trunk," and "plaited cuirass . . . of massive iron" (1:53) recalls chapbook details of giants, Goliath's taunting speech to his opponent as "light boy," "stripling," "dainty-finger'd hero," and "insect warrior" (1:70, 72) emphasizes how little he understands David's power. In contrast to his brothers' "glozing speech" (1:50) and Saul's fearful reluctance to let David shine stands the young shepherd's clear declaration of loyalty:

> Far higher views inspire my youthful heart
> Than human praise: I seek to vindicate
> Th' insulted honour of the God I serve.
>
> (1:62)

More's sense of oneness with her text in *Sacred Dramas* means that the doctrinal content is naturally high in a "script" that is both a palimpsest of biblical allusions and a series of comments on the challenges and upheavals of late eighteenth-century British life. The rhetoric of her day, oscillating between revolutionary discontent and reform impulses, supplied a theater of public discourse that deeply engaged More. Not content to be part of a political audience watching "preferably in silence," she was unwilling "to sit back and partake vicariously in action from which [she] had been excluded" (Friedland 12). Through the warning of the prophet Daniel in "Belshazzar," she voices concern about "the still-seeming safety of retreat" (1:117). Whether in ancient Babylon or Georgian Britain, political actors who purport to be working disinterestedly warrant careful scrutiny:

> When selfish politicians, hackney'd long
> In fraud and artifice, affect a glow
> Of patriot fervour, or fond loyalty,
> Which scorns all show of interest, that's the moment
> To watch their crook'd projects.
>
> (1:143)

As an indication of where More's career was headed, it is significant that *Sacred Dramas*, with its strong connections between "the governance of the nation and the regulation of the passions" (Purinton 116), includes the first appearance of her poem "Sensibility." Enshrining sensibility in the home as "thy true legitimate domain" (1:175), the poem concentrates on the quick, intuitive perception of "sweet SENSIBILITY!" as "unprompted moral! sudden sense of right!" and "hasty conscience!" and "prompt sense of equity!" and "eager to serve" and "always apt to choose the suff'ring side" (1:173). Among the corrosive influences that destroy feeling, "Sensibility" catalogs a series testifying to the power of language and gesture: "the look oblique," "the sneer equivocal, the harsh reply," "all the cruel language of the eye," and "the guarded phrase" (1:176). These lessons More could have learned from the theater and from experience.

Just as astringent principles prompted her withdrawal from the public stage, More embarked on prose biblical commentary, a discipline from which her sex was systematically excluded, with equally strong, candid conviction. Admitting "deficiencies in ancient learning, Biblical criticism, and deep theological knowledge," she concentrates on the ways Paul "lets us into the secrets of our own bosoms, . . . discloses to us the motives of our own conduct, and . . . lays bare the moral quality of action" (10:vii, 407). In her positively charged review, Paul is a model stylist and moralist, as well as an accomplished strategist, especially in his pointed reproofs to the church at Corinth: "In no epistle is there more preparatory soothing, more conciliatory preliminaries, to the counsels or the censures he is about to communicate" (10:195). Because she sees Paul "always writing like a man of the actual world" (10:357), she undertakes to defend him on two hugely contentious issues: his treatment of women and of authority. More's Paul is a friend of women (Phoebe, Priscilla, Mary, Julia, Chloe, Tryphena, and "our countrywoman Claudia," whom she contends Paul met when "in all probability [he] preached the Gospel in Britain" [10:244]).

More's Paul is also no hothead or renegade. With his religion characterized by "a peculiar sedateness" (10:225), this Paul appears to have no connection to the apostle who was snubbed by Jews and Christians alike in Jerusalem, whom the Jews of Lycaonia greeted with violent hostility, on account of whom the silversmiths of Ephesus rioted, and for whom the deep hatred of the Jews of Jerusalem resulted in his arrest.

There are glosses and whitewashes in More's essay on Paul. What remains consistent, however, from her earliest to last efforts, is the adherence to biblical doctrines that prompt the cultivation of the civil mind and feeling heart in everyday life and provide the ligature binding private and civic concerns, personal and institutional ethics. Such adherence did not blind More to ironies and shortcomings. In *Christian Morals* (1812), she contemplates why good nominal Christians are not better, drawing her simile from the beloved subject of gardening: "They live, it is true, but it is as the vegetable world lives in the winter's frost, which does not indeed kill it, but benumbs its powers and suspends its vitality" (9:259). Like an expert homilist, she drives home the point about the otherworldly focus she strives to uphold through the simple device of contrasting monosyllabic adverbs: "To suppose that we shall possess hereafter what we do not desire here, that we shall complete then what we do not think of beginning now, is among the inconsistencies of many who pass muster under the generic title of Christians" (9:333).

See also Carter, Elizabeth (1717–1806)

Bibliography

Cowper, William. *The Correspondence, with Annotations by Thomas Wright.* 4 vols. London: Hodder & Stoughton, 1904.

Demers, Patricia, ed. *Hannah More's "Cœlebs in Search of a Wife."* Peterborough, ON: Broadview, 2007.

———. *The World of Hannah More.* Lexington: University Press of Kentucky, 1996.

Friedland, Paul. *Political Actors: Representative Bodies and Theatricality in the Age of the French Revolution.* Ithaca, NY: Cornell University Press, 2002.

Mellor, Anne. *Mothers of the Nation: Women's Political Writing in England, 1780–1830.* Bloomington: Indiana University Press, 2000.

More, Hannah. *The Works.* 11 vols. London: T. Cadell, 1830.

Myers, Mitzi. "'A Peculiar Protection': Hannah More and the Cultural Politics of the Blagdon Controversy." Pages 227–57 in *History, Gender, and Eighteenth-Century Literature*, edited by Beth Fowkes Tobin. Athens: University of Georgia Press, 1994.

O'Quinn, Daniel. *Staging Governance: Theatrical Imperialism in London, 1770–1800.* Baltimore: Johns Hopkins University Press, 2005.

Purinton, Marjorie D. "Gender, Nationalism, and Science in Hannah More's Pedagogical Plays for Children." Pages 113–36 in *Culturing the Child, 1690–1914: Essays in Memory of Mitzi Myers*, edited by Donelle Ruwe. Lanham, MD: Scarecrow, 2005.

Roberts, William. *Memoirs of the Life and Correspondence of Mrs. Hannah More.* 4 vols. London: R. B. Seeley & W. Burnside, 1834.

Russell, Gillian. "Theatre." Pages 223–31 in *Oxford Companion to the Romantic Age: British Culture, 1776–1832*, edited by Iain McCallum. Oxford: Oxford University Press, 1999.

Seward, Anna. "On Visiting the Silvan Cottage Inhabited by Miss Hannah More and Her Sisters, 1791." Page 159 in *The Juvenile Forget Me Not*, edited by Mrs. S. C. Hall. London: F. Westley & A. H. Davis, 1831.

Stott, Anne. *Hannah More: The First Victorian.* Oxford: Oxford University Press, 2003.

Sutherland, Kathryn. "Hannah More's Counter-Revolutionary Feminism." Pages 27–64 in *Revolution in Writing: British Literary Responses to the French Revolution*, edited by Kelvin Everest. Milton Keynes: Open University Press, 1991.

— PATRICIA DEMERS

Murray, Judith Sargent (1751–1820)

Judith Sargent Murray was the oldest child of Winthrop and Judith Sargent, both of whom came from elite merchant families in Gloucester, Massachusetts. Married twice, in 1769 to Gloucester merchant John Stevens and then in 1788 to John Murray, she had one surviving child, Julia Maria Murray, born in 1791. Judith Murray is regarded as the founder of American Universalism.

Murray published poems and essays in the journals that proliferated throughout America in the late eighteenth century; two of her plays appeared in Boston's Federal Street Theater. She is best known for *The Gleaner*, a three-volume "miscellany" published in 1798. Her opus includes her four-part essay "Observations on Female Abilities," which continues to impress scholars with its forthright claim that "*the idea of the incapability* of women, is, we conceive, in this *enlightened age*, totally *inadmissible*" (*Gleaner*, 705).

Murray's insistence on the intellectual equality of men and women was unusual for her time. Although most scholars have attributed her views either to Enlightenment ideology or to the egalitarian language of the American Revolution, it was her Universalist faith that fundamentally shaped her perspective on gender issues. Indeed, Murray may well have remained an obscure figure had it not been for her decision to embrace Universalism. Her first publication—her *Catechism* (1782)—resulted from her determination to promulgate her religious beliefs; without her conviction that she was doing God's work, she would never have had the courage to enter the republic of letters.

Murray's understanding of Universalism stemmed from her interpretation of the Bible. It led her to argue that all humans were assured of salvation. It also provided her with her rationale for gender equality. Universalists believed that all humans had originally been united spiritually with Christ and with one another and that at death they would be as one with Christ once more. Thus every person—of whatever "sect, age, country or even sex"—was part of "one grand, vast, collected family of human nature" (*Gleaner*, 132). The notion that the mind has no sex had special meaning for Universalists.

Murray's theology generally mirrored that of her second husband. Occasionally, however, her understanding of Scripture was her own. Her interpretation of the creation story is a case in point. Murray had grown up with John Milton's rendition of Gen. 1–3, in which Milton placed the responsibility for original sin squarely on Eve's frail shoulders. Eve's weakness had led her to eat the forbidden fruit of the tree of knowledge. She had also persuaded Adam, who was seduced by his partner's wiles, to disobey God's commands. Murray, in a letter to her niece in 1777, and then in public as an appendage to her "On the Equality of Sexes" in 1790, firmly rejected Milton's perspective. She did so by focusing on motives. Eve, she claimed, was moved not by "sensual" appetite, but by the devil's promise of "a perfection of knowledge." It was Adam who was actuated by animal instinct, by carnal lust rather than a desire for mental improvement. "Blush, ye vaunters of fortitude," she wrote, "ye haughty lords of the creation, blush when ye remember, that he was influenced by no other motive than a bare pusillanimous attachment to a woman!" Adam was also the weaker sex. "All the arts of the grand deceiver were requisite to mislead our general mother, while the father of mankind forfeited his own, and relinquished the happiness of posterity, merely in compliance with the blandishments of a female" ("Equality," 224–25; Murray to Miss Goldthwait, June 6, 1777, in Letter Books, 1:63).

Murray is not as well known as Abigail Adams or Susan B. Anthony. Nevertheless, she was a thoroughgoing proponent of women's rights in eighteenth-century America, a leader in the movement to challenge traditional gender constructs. Ignored by many of her contemporaries, forgotten until recently by scholars, she has finally begun to receive the recognition she deserves. Still, even now observers tend to forget that Universalism was what gave Murray the intellectual framework to demand equal rights for all women. Indeed, Murray is an example of a woman who used her religious beliefs and her views of women's nature to challenge traditional interpretations of biblical texts.

Bibliography

Bressler, Ann Lee. *The Universalist Movement in America, 1770–1980*. New York: Oxford University Press, 2001.

Murray, Judith Sargent [Stevens]. *The Gleaner*. Boston: I. Thomas & E. T. Andrews, 1798. Repr., Schenectady, NY: Union College Press, 1992.

———. Letter Books 1–20. Jackson, MS: Mississippi Archives.

———. "On the Equality of the Sexes." *Massachusetts Magazine*, March and April 1990.

Skemp, Sheila. *First Lady of Letters: Judith Sargent Murray and the Struggle for Female Independence*. Philadelphia: University of Pennsylvania Press, 2009.

[Stevens, Judith—later, Mrs. Murray]. *Some Deductions from the System Promulgated in the Page of Divine Revelation, Ranged in the Order and Form of a Catechism.* Norwich, CT: John Trumball, 1782.

— SHEILA L. SKEMP

Murry, Ann (ca. 1755–ca. 1816)

Ann Murry was born in London in about 1755, the daughter of a prosperous wine merchant. Financial misfortune forced her to take up work as a tutor to young girls of the upper classes, and she eventually attained the position of preceptress in the royal nursery (Backscheider 228). Her writings suggest a thorough education and a propensity to read widely; she embraces many Enlightenment principles of morality and reason.

The general objective of all of Murry's work is stated on the title page of *Mentoria*: "to improve young minds in the essential as well as ornamental parts of female education." She intends to "enhance female virtue." Yet her aims extend beyond secular knowledge and morality: in *A Concise History of the Kingdoms of Israel and Judah*, she is actively "confirming and recommending the Christian faith." For Murry, all knowledge is knowledge of God: "At present, I wish sacred and natural history to be the chief objects of your attention; as they both tend to increase your love and admiration of the deity" (*Mentoria*, 101–2).

In 1779, Murry published a volume of poems, many of which are either devotional or celebrate virtues such as fortitude and contentment. On several occasions, however, she ventures into perceptive social satire, including commentary on the relation of the genders. For example, in the poem "Tête à Tête," "Murry implies the benefits of companionate marriage, not to mention the wife's importance when she is more intelligent and principled than her mate" (Kairoff 285). Although she shares many of the values and attitudes of her society, Murry has a high opinion of the intelligence and character of women, which she seeks to develop in her students.

The popularity of *Mentoria*, first published in 1778, motivated her to produce the *Sequel* in 1799, both of which appeared in multiple editions. These texts deal with topics as diverse as grammar, science, and music but also contain an extended section dealing with the significance of church services and a discussion of parables. The book uses a dialogue between a governess and her two highborn female students as a vehicle of conveying knowledge, always with appropriate "moral reflections." Her largely allegorical interpretation of the parable delivered to David by Nathan is introduced thus: "I shall first recite the Parable, explain each particular branch of it, and then endeavour to find how we can apply it to ourselves" (*Mentoria*, 132). Following her detailed analysis, Murry concludes: "The moral is briefly this, and may be applied to every state and condition of life. It shews how blind we are to our own failings, and how quick-sighted to those of others. It also instructs us, when we are passing sentence, never to inflict a punishment disproportionate to the offence committed; or what, in the same situation, we should think unreasonable to undergo ourselves" (138). Her students invariably express gratitude for her insights.

In *Mentoria*, the feminine environment is diversified when the girls' brother arrives home from Eton. Mentoria asks, "I hope you will not think it lessens your consequence as a man, to be taught by a governess, and have young Ladies for your school-fellows and companions." Murry has him respond, "Not in the least, madam: I shall esteem myself much obliged to you, for permitting me to partake of your instructions" (60). Although her egalitarianism is not without its limits—she states that geometry is not a part of female education—she believes that science and history, particularly sacred history, are appropriate areas of study for women (174).

In 1783, Murry published a major two-volume work, *A Concise History of the Kingdoms of Israel and Judah*. The first volume covers the events from creation to the exile, synthesizing the biblical narratives into chronological order and incorporating events from the Prophets and Writings. Murry has a high view of Scripture, privileging revelation over philosophical speculation. Her work is a lively summary of Old Testament events viewed from a christological and dispensational perspective. The second volume is an overview of the intertestamental events from the exile to the birth of Christ, based on the Apocrypha and other extrabiblical primary sources. Murry makes occasional references to other biblical scholars in her footnotes, even venturing to disagree with them in several instances. Her evaluation of both women and men in the Bible is based on their character and behavior. Her historical sense is well developed, her narratives are engaging, and her "moral reflections" often challenge or refine conventional mores.

Murry's usual method of interpretation is to quote a passage, often at length, and then provide a general explanation and moral application. She tends to take a literal approach but uses symbolism and typology when she analyzes a text more deeply. In relating Nathan's parable in *Mentoria*, Murry comments, "By this we find Uriah had but one wife; and by her being compared to a lamb, we are naturally led to suppose, she was a woman of an amiable disposition, and exemplary conduct; as a lamb is an emblem of innocence" (135). In *A Concise History of the Kingdoms of Israel and Judah*, Canaan is a figurative type of heaven (xii), Isaac is a type of the Savior (xvii), and the priestly rituals such as the Day of Atonement prefigure Christ: "It was on this day, the high-priest entered the most holy place dressed in his rich garments, and sprinkled the blood of a peculiar sacrifice before the mercy seat to make atonement for the sins of the people, and offered incense on the golden censer; which was a striking type of the blessed effects of Christ's expiation, and intercession on our behalf" (lxxvi). Murry's interpretive method is also illustrated in the *Mentorian Lectures on Sacred Subjects* of 1808.

Murry's legacy is more as an educator than an exegete; however, she organized and popularized Scripture in a format that young women found accessible and meaningful.

Bibliography

Backscheider, Paula R. *Eighteenth-Century Women Poets and Their Poetry*. Baltimore: Johns Hopkins University Press, 2005.

Kairoff, Claudia Thomas. "Gendering Satire: Behn to Burney." Pages 276–92 in *A Companion to Satire: Ancient and Modern*, edited by R. Quintero. Oxford: Blackwell, 2007.

Murry, Ann. *A Concise History of the Kingdoms of Israel and Judah: Connected with the history or chief events of the neighbouring states and succeeding empires to the time of Christ*. 2 vols. London: Frys & Couchman, for Charles Dilly, 1783.

———. *Mentoria; or, The young ladies instructor, in familiar conversations on moral and entertaining subjects*. London: J. Fry, for Edward & Charles Dilly, 1778. Dublin: Price, Sheppard, et al., 1779.

———. *Mentorian Lectures on Sacred Subjects*. London: Longman, Hurst, et al., 1808.

———. *Poems on Various Subjects*. London: The author, 1779.

———. *The Sequel to Mentoria; or, The young ladies instructor*. London: Charles Dilly, 1799.

— MARY CONWAY

■ Narducci da Paradiso, Domenica (1473–1533)

Domenica Narducci, renowned preacher in Florence, was born on September 8, 1473, in the suburb of Florence called Paradise, daughter of Francesco, a market gardener. The fifth of seven children, she was left orphaned at the age of six and soon afterward needed to work in the home and in the fields.

It took Narducci a long time to find her own particular place among the varied forms of religious life of the period. She entered the Augustinian monastery of Santa Maria de' Candeli (Jan. 17, 1492), but subsequently alternated between lay and religious life. From 1495 to 97 she regularly visited the Brigidine Convent, Santa Maria, until she was accused of being a follower of Savonarola, the Italian Dominican religious and political reformer who was executed in 1498.

In December 1499 Narducci moved to Florence to escape her family, who wanted her to marry, as well as those who were suspicious of her charismatic gifts. Yet her difficulties continued: in 1500 she was tried for being a scandalous heretic accused of abandoning her paternal home, of not having a regular confessor, and of preaching illicitly. She was also asked to explain the content of her revelations. Health problems prevented her examiners from forcing her to enter a monastery so that they could examine her more closely.

Narducci became increasingly aware of the role that she could play in fulfilling Savonarola's vision that women could be leaders in spiritual and social renewal, the so-called women's reform. With other laywomen, she formed a group of women devoted to prayer and service. A number of important people supported her work, though she continued to have strained relationships with the Dominicans. Encouraged by the new spiritual direction of the priest in charge of San Lorenzo, Francesco Onesti da Castiglione, she asked for protection from the archbishop Cosimo dei Medici.

Narducci soon found it necessary to define her own position as a leader within her community; she consolidated her small community of fifteen women at the monastery of the Crocetta. On May 27, 1515, the community received canonical status through a papal bull of Leo X and was placed under the jurisdiction of Bishop Giulio de' Medici. Narducci's authoritative and charismatic role over the community was formalized, although she refused solemn vows until just before her death.

Narducci's influence extended far beyond her own community. Through her letter writing, she established relationships with other religious communities. Many recognized her visionary, prophetic, and preaching gifts and asked to read her "sermons," which circulated well beyond the cloister walls. Many people, both lay and ordained, turned to her for counsel, for doctrinal clarification, and for scriptural interpretation. The Episcopal vicar Pietro Andrea Gammaro, the canonist Niccolò Ardinghelli, and the duchess Caterina Cibo are just a few of the prominent figures who gravitated to the monastery. Narducci's "spiritual children" included those identified with orthodoxy, those who were sympathetic to the teachings of Savonarola, and those from the tormented context of Italian evangelism.

Narducci was a significant though controversial interpreter of Scripture. On several occasions, Onesti had to defend her against those who accused her of interpreting the Bible without authorization. One such case was launched on August 19, 1519, and revolved around the Dominican Tommaso Caiani, who accused Narducci of erroneous interpretation of the Bible. Yet the verdict was favorable toward Narducci, who enjoyed the cardinal's favor. Both her orthodoxy and the conformity of her thought with Scripture and tradition were recognized.

Many of Narducci's extant writings are found in the Archivio del Monastero della Crocetta in Florence, including the "Epistolary" (130 letters, 1506–48), "Sermons" (ca. 20 works, 1507–45), "Dialogue" (1503), "The Vision of the Tabernacle" (1508), "Revelations and Visions" (1507–45), and several spiritual treatises.

Narducci's sermons and letters reveal her complex approach to the task of biblical interpretation. Savonarola had taught her the importance of the study of Scripture in the Christian life. The Dominican Sante Pagnini, who directed her biblical study and was recognized as the best translator of Hebrew after Jerome, influenced her strongly biblical approach to the spiritual life. Narducci interpreted Scripture by using the traditional medieval fourfold approach to Scripture: literal, allegorical, moral, and eschatological. She easily moved from the literal sense of a text to its allegorical and moral sense. Often she used typology to show how the Old Testament prefigured Christ. She was especially drawn to a few passages and such key figures as Adam and Eve, Noah, Abraham, Isaac, and Moses, as well as the most important events in the life of Christ: the annunciation, birth, circumcision, presentation in the temple, passion, death, and resurrection. Narducci also made use of the monastic custom of *lectio divina*, reading Scripture and listening to it being read, meditating on its significance, and praying for a contemplative encounter with God. Further, Narducci's mystical and visionary experiences informed and lent authority to her interpretations of Scripture.

Narducci's writings reveal a confident, well-informed, and often inspired biblical interpreter and preacher, roles traditionally denied to women. Narducci preached that the Word of God was not just for clerics and academics but was for all and must be proclaimed. On the evenings before she preached, she would prepare her sermons, beginning with a verse or a story from Scripture and explaining it by making references to other parts of Scripture and drawing examples from everyday life. Although prophetic inspiration was a part of her interpretive process, her sermons were not improvised.

Narducci's exposition of Paul's words to the Corinthians that "women be silent in the assembly" (1 Cor. 14:34) illustrates her method and her theology. In 1507, Narducci preached on this historically important text and explained that this passage was "not understood properly by many" (Riconesi 158). She challenged the traditional interpretation of this text as prohibiting women from preaching by appealing to a direct revelation allowing her to understand that God gave women permission to speak, to preach, and to prophesy in order to confound the proud. Narducci used an earlier text from Paul to support her case for women's preaching and teaching: "God does not choose knowledge or riches but rather goodness and simplicity" (1 Cor. 1:27–29). She explained that Paul had prohibited *only the women of Corinth* from speaking because they made too much noise, and she argued that Paul could not have limited the freedom of the Spirit, who calls whomever the Spirit chooses. Thus Narducci judged traditional ecclesial exegesis of this classic text to be in error (159).

Narducci was particularly drawn to the Gospels, which in a particular way constitute the lifeblood of her sermons. The Synoptics, among which Matthew receives prominence, are used to sustain the moral exhortations and the spiritual directions she offered to her disciples: prayer (Matt. 7:7), good works (7:16, 21), humility (23:12), shrewdness (10:16), vigilance (25:1), active and strong concern (11:12), poverty (19:24), and sanctifying grace (Luke 7:36–50; Valerio, "Le prediche").

Narducci's letters also contain frequent allusions to Scripture, usually to stories and figures from the Old and New Testaments. These became the lens through which she read events in her own time. For instance, she used the story of the flood (Gen. 6–9) and the story of the prophet Jonah to exhort her readers to repent in order to placate the anger of God.

Domenica Narducci was a woman who used her mystical and visionary experiences, as well as more traditional interpretive methods, to open up Scripture for her contemporaries. Her messages often challenged the status quo, most notably her reinterpretation of the traditional understanding of Paul's mandate for women to be silent in the assembly. She did not intend to offer an academic knowledge of Scripture, but an understanding of faith based on a direct relationship with God.

Bibliography

Librandi, Rita, and Adriana Valerio. *I sermoni di Domenica da Paradiso*. Studi e testo critico. Florence: SISMEL, Edizioni del Galluzzo, 1999.

Riconesi, Anton Maria. "Annali della vita della ven. . . . . Domenica da Paradiso." MS in 4 vols. Archivo della Crocetta, Florence, 1637–40. Chap. 386v from vol. 2 (1638), in *I sermoni di Domenica da Paradiso*, edited by Rita Librandi and Adriana Valerio. Studi e testo critico. Florence: SISMEL, Edizioni del Galluzzo, 1999.

Valerio, Adriana. "La Bibbia nell'umanesimo femminile (secoli XV–XVII)." Pages 73–98 in *Donne e Bibbia: Storia ed esegesi*, edited by Adriana Valerio. Bologna: EDB [Edizioni Dehoniane Bologna], 2006.

———. *Domenica da Paradiso: Profezia e politica in una mistica del Rinascimento*. Spoleto: Centro italiano di studi sull'alto Medioevo, 1992.

———. "'Et io espongo le Scritture': Domenica da Paradiso e l'interpretazione biblica: Un documento inedito nella crisi del rinascimento fiorentino." *Rivista di storia e letteratura religiosa* 26 (1994): 499–534.

———. "Le lettere di Domenica da Paradiso tra Bibbia e profezia." *Hagiographica* 6 (1999): 235–56.

———. "Le prediche di Domenica da Paradiso tra esperienza mistica e Riforma della Chiesa." Pages 46–49 in *I sermoni di Domenica da Paradiso*, edited by R. Librandi and A. Valerio. Studi e testo critico. Florence: SISMEL, Edizioni del Galluzzo, 1999.

— ADRIANA VALERIO

■ Nightingale, Florence (1820–1910)

Nightingale is remembered by most as nurse in the Crimean War (1854–56); however, that was only a small part of this remarkable woman's life. Nightingale was born into a wealthy family, was a lifelong member of the Church of England, and led a very privileged life. She received the equivalent of a Cambridge education at home; traveled abroad to Italy, Egypt, and Greece; and was friends with many leaders in politics and the arts. Privilege also had its limitations. She could neither work nor manage her own time. Her frustration at the limitations imposed on her because of her class and gender are reflected in her classic work *Cassandra*, an exploration of the oppression of women within the family (*Works*, vol. 11). Finally, when she was thirty, Nightingale's father bequeathed on her a small allowance, giving her independence. She became the superintendent of a home for indigent governesses, and from this position she was called to serve her country by leading a group of nurses to Crimea. When she returned to England after the war, although often sick with an illness contracted in Crimea, she began her work of reform in many areas of public life, as well as studying and writing on the Bible, the classics, medieval mysticism, philosophy, and theology.

Nightingale's interpretation of Scripture is reflected in the annotations she made in her personal Bible; in the journals and sermons that she wrote; in her correspondence with Dr. Benjamin Jowett, the Regius Professor of Greek at Oxford University; and in her treatise on philosophical theology, *Suggestions for Thought for Searchers after Truth* (*Works*, vol. 11). Her reflections reveal her brilliance: she was fluent in many languages, including Greek, German, French, Italian, Latin, and some Hebrew, and was widely read. Her biblical annotations include comments connecting biblical themes with the Greek classics, the Talmud and Jewish mysticism, the philosophy of Kant, as well as the latest in German scholarship: J. G. Eichhorn, G. H. A. Ewald, and J. G. Herder (2:91–321). She understood the Documentary Hypothesis, dated Second Isaiah to the Babylonian exile, and dated Daniel's visions to the Greek period.

Nightingale worked with Jowett, the author of the controversial essay "On the Interpretation of Scripture," on a new version of Plato's *Republic*, as well as a revision of the *School and Children's Bible* (*Works*, 3:521–624). The correspondence connected with these two projects reveals that Jowett incorporated many of her suggestions and that they agreed in their views on Scripture. Both held that within Scripture there was development from a more primitive to an enlightened understanding of God, morality, evil, God's people, and the presence of God. Nightingale traces the trajectory from a local religion to a universal religion, from a chosen people to including all, from a religion steeped in ritual to a spiritual religion. For example, in her biblical annotations, she comments on the rending of the temple veil at the time of Jesus's death (Matt. 27:51): "Influence of Christ's death in substituting a spiritual for a ritual worship is here symbolized" (2:245). The primitive science found in Scripture is understood to be a product of its time, and this accounts for the belief in miracles found in the Bible. Nightingale did not believe in miracles, including the bodily resurrection of Jesus, nor could she believe that the God of love and justice whom she worshiped would order the extermination of the Canaanites. She concludes that Scripture sometimes reflects the primitive morality of its ancient authors. Both Jowett and Nightingale assert that Scripture should be read as any other book; they made use of the results of science, the discoveries of archaeology, and the knowledge of ancient cultures.

Nightingale did not engage the biblical text in order to reflect on her life and faith as a woman. In her biblical annotations, she nowhere identifies with a biblical woman, or comments on the life or sayings of any woman. In fact, in the correspondence on the *School and Children's Bible*, she wrote disparagingly of the women in Scripture: "The stories about Andromache and Antigone are worth all the women in the Old Testament put together, nay, almost all the women in the Bible" (3:550).

Although Nightingale's interpretive legacy does not further the study of the women in the Bible, it does display how a brilliant woman in the nineteenth century read Scripture in dialogue with the best of critical scholarship as well as the classics of Western civilization.

Bibliography

de Groot, Christiana. "Florence Nightingale: A Mother to Many." Pages 117–34 in *Recovering Nineteenth-Century Women Interpreters of the Bible*, edited by Christiana de Groot and Marion Ann Taylor. Atlanta: Society of Biblical Literature, 2007.

Dossey, Barbara Montgomery. *Florence Nightingale: Mystic, Visionary, Healer*. Oxford: Springhouse, 1999.

Jowett, Benjamin. "On the Interpretation of Scripture." Pages 330–433 in *Essays and Reviews*. London: John W. Parker & Son, 1860.

Nightingale, Florence. *Collected Works of Florence Nightingale*. Vols. 1–3, 11. Edited by Lynn McDonald. Waterloo, ON: Wilfred Laurier University Press, 2001–2, 2008.

Webb, Val. *Florence Nightingale: The Making of a Radical Theologian*. St. Louis: Chalice, 2002.

— CHRISTIANA DE GROOT

▧ Nogarola, Isotta (1418–66)

As the daughter of parents descended from the nobility of Verona and Padua, two subject states of Venice in northern Italy, Isotta Nogarola had learned ancestors on both sides and thus inherited both high social rank and a rich cultural heritage. Unusually, her widowed mother hired a humanist tutor to instruct the adolescent Nogarola and her sister. (The foremost intellectuals of Renaissance Italy were humanists, who pursued the revival of classical thought and literature and had no kinship with modern humanism and its characteristic rejection of Christian theism.) The young women exchanged letters in polished Latin with a circle of Venetian nobles and privileged students at the University of Padua.

After her sister's marriage, Nogarola returned to Verona to live with her mother as an unmarried woman, adopting the lifestyle of a *pinzochera*, an uncloistered "holy woman," a social category not uncommon in urban Italy. At the same time, her intellectual focus shifted from the secular to the Christian classics. Her holiness of life and her learning won the notice of prominent men, including Lauro Quirini, who encouraged her philosophical studies in a letter written between 1445 and 1452; Ludovico Foscarini, who engaged in an extensive correspondence with her from 1451 and was her opponent in the debate of that year on Adam and Eve (see below); and Ermolao Barbaro, bishop of Verona, for whom she wrote a celebratory oration in 1453. Distressed by her mother's death in 1461, she apparently took refuge in Foscarini's household until her own death in 1466.

Of Nogarola's many works in classic humanist genres, extant are some thirty letters: the dialogue on Adam and Eve (1451/53); three orations (to Bishop Ermolao Barbaro in 1453; on St. Jerome in 1453; to Pope Pius II on the crusade against the Turks in 1459); and a consolatory treatise to Venetian nobleman Jacopo Antonio Marcello (1461). It is in the pivotal dialogue on Adam and Eve that Nogarola engages in the interpretation of Scripture.

Recording the arguments put forward in the debate held publicly in Verona in 1451, Nogarola's "Dialogue on the Equal or Unequal Sin of Adam and Eve" features the interlocutors Nogarola and Foscarini grappling with Gen. 1–3, the former defending Eve on the charge of responsibility for original sin, the latter condemning her. There is no analysis of biblical texts; the debate takes the form of a disputation or dialogue, typical for the era, in which the authors reason their own cases, bringing in useful quotes from authoritative texts.

This issue of the responsibility for original sin could not have been more important. Eve's role as the temptress who corrupted Adam and thus brought condemnation on all later generations was the central argument of the Western misogynist tradition: woman's essential malevolence was here displayed, and she could never be free of its burden.

Nogarola attacks circuitously: Eve could not be responsible because she was the inferior being; being weak and suggestible, she was no match for the clever serpent. Thus it was Adam, whose force of mind and spirit was greater, who bears the greater responsibility for succumbing to temptation. Each time Nogarola raises this argument, Foscarini counters. Both display their extensive learning, citing Ambrose; Aristotle; Gregory the Great; Peter Lombard; especially Augustine's commentary on Genesis (*De Genesi ad litteram*), which had posited that Adam and Eve had sinned differently but bore equal responsibility for original sin; and quoting the Bible (Gen. 1:26; 2:15–18, 23; 3:4–6, 12, 16–19; Ps. 69; Rom. 5:12; 1 Cor. 1:27–29; 14:38; 15:22; and all four Gospels: Matt. 15:24, 26; 19:16–17; 26:63; Mark 10:17–27; 14:61; Luke 18:18–27; 22:67, 70; John 11:47; 15:22). Each correspondent adduces quotations from these texts in defense of his or her own arguments: Foscarini's are drawn from the long tradition that views Eve as instrumental in the downfall of humankind; Nogarola's are nimble and original in asserting Eve's innocence. Nogarola argues, for instance, that God's instructions to care for the garden of Eden but not to eat the fruit of the tree of knowledge was directed, in the singular, to Adam alone (Gen. 2:15–17). Elsewhere, alluding to 1 Cor. 15:22, she argues that it was Adam's sin, not Eve's, that brought death to all humankind. In closing, Foscarini declares himself the victor yet admires Nogarola's rhetorical and intellectual mastery.

Although a few women had previously resisted the message about Eve, especially in Gen. 3, Nogarola's work is historic: it is the first known major defense of Eve by a woman author, refuting a tradition of biblical interpretation profoundly hostile to the dignity and advancement of women.

Bibliography

King, Margaret L. "Book-Lined Cells." Pages 66–90 in *Beyond Their Sex: Learned Women of the European Past*, edited by Patricia H. Labalme. New York: New York University Press, 1980.

———. "Isotta Nogarola." Pages 313–23 in *Italian Women Writers: A Bio-Bibliographical Sourcebook*, edited by Rinaldina Russell. Westport, CT: Greenwood, 1994.

———. "The Religious Retreat of Isotta Nogarola (1418–1466)." *Signs* 3 (1978): 807–22.

Nogarola, Isotta. *Dialogue on Adam and Eve*. Pages 145–58 in *Complete Writings: Letterbook, Dialogue on Adam and Eve, Orations*, edited and translated by Margaret L. King and Kiana Robin. Chicago: University of Chicago Press, 2004.

———. *Isotae Nogarolae veronensis opera quae supersunt omnia, accedunt Angelae et Zenevrae Nogarolae epistolae et carmina*. Edited by Eugenius Abel. Critical edition of the Latin text. Vienna: Gerold et socios; Budapest: Fridericum Kilian, 1886.

— MARGARET L. KING

Palmer, Phoebe (1807–74)

The American holiness revivalist Phoebe (Worrall) Palmer was born in New York City to devout Methodists Henry Worrall and Dorothea Wade Worrall. Palmer was the fourth of sixteen children, only nine surviving to adulthood. The family lived in some degree of material prosperity and abided by a strict Methodist piety, following an intense spiritual regimen of Scripture reading as well as morning and evening family prayers. Palmer's pious upbringing guided her development of a sensitive conscience and intelligent, religious sensibilities.

Lacking in the record of Palmer's childhood are details regarding her education. Even though these details are not known, it is clear from her writing that she was well educated and possessed a bright intellect. It is also evident that she had access to the writings of such figures as John Wesley, William Bramwell, Mary Bosanquet Fletcher, Hester Ann Rogers, Nancy Cutler, John Fletcher, John Nelson, Lady Maxwell, William Carvosso, and Susanna Wesley.

Although raised in a devout Methodist family, Palmer did not experience a traditional conversion experience that involved a deep conviction of sin, a turning to God, and assurance of salvation. She came to the conclusion that her lack of emotional experience was an indicator of spiritual weakness and furthermore that she did not have the guaranteed assurance of salvation. She remained unsure of her spiritual state into her twenties.

In 1827, Phoebe Worrall married Dr. Walter C. Palmer, a homeopathic physician, who, like her, was a committed second-generation American

Methodist. Walter supported his wife on her spiritual journey, which eventually led to her success as the first female American revivalist to promote the pursuit of "holiness." He eventually quit his profession so that they could work together in a ministry that involved speaking, writing, and publishing. The first ten years of the Palmers' marriage, however, were marked by great tragedy. Of the six children born to the Palmers, only three survived. The deaths of three of their first four children prolonged Palmer's religious struggle and turmoil. She understood these losses as purposeful acts of God to teach her not to love anything or anyone more than or even as much as she was to love God.

In time, Palmer resolved her interior religious struggle through reason: she set aside the expectation of strong religious feelings and experiences typical of nineteenth-century American Methodism and claimed assurance of her salvation not in the "witness of the Spirit" but rather in the act of believing, which relied on nothing but the Bible. Palmer became involved in and later headed the well-known "Tuesday Meetings," which became a meeting for people of all denominations, ages, and gender to gather together for the promotion of Christian perfection and holiness. Knowledge of Palmer's gifts of teaching and preaching grew as she traveled all across the United States and to parts of Canada and the British Isles to ignite revivals for holiness and complete sanctification. She was also involved in humanitarian work and published a number of books including *The Way of Holiness* (1843), *Entire Devotion to God* (1845), *Faith and Its Effects* (1848), *Incidental Illustrations of the Economy of Salvation* (1855), *The Promise of the Father* (1859), and *Four Years in the Old World* (1865). She was also the editor of *The Guide to Holiness* from 1864 to 1874 and of *Pioneer Experiences* (1868).

During Palmer's revival meetings, she developed three "new measures" that would contribute to her career and the "Holiness Movement," which grew largely from her work. First, the "holiness altar invitation" was extended to converted Christians who desired a second experience of "complete sanctification." Second, Palmer began the "believing meeting," where people were brought to the point of believing God for present holiness and given the opportunity to take action: to seek, pray, receive instruction, and to believe. Third, Palmer pioneered the "altar testimony," which involved a compulsory testimony to saving and sanctifying grace *immediately* upon receiving it.

Palmer's theology grew out of her own spiritual struggles and her deep engagement with Scripture. Her "altar theology" and her "shorter way" to spiritual perfection in particular are tied to her interpretation of key biblical texts. Using the Bible as her sole "textbook," Palmer came to understand her own salvation assurance from reading Matt. 23:19, which asks: "Which is greater, the gift or the altar that sanctifies the gift?" This verse was foundational for her "altar theology" as she interpreted the altar as a type of Christ and the gift as that which the believer placed on the altar: one's entire devotion. Palmer argued that what is desired (holiness, perfection, and complete sanctification) comes about at the very moment that the offering touches the altar. The immediacy of this experience challenged the traditional Methodist teaching about Christian perfection and established a "shorter way" to holiness, which Palmer grounded solely on the biblical teaching "Be ye holy" (Lev. 11:44–45; 20:7, 26; Deut. 26:19; Matt. 5:48; 1 Pet. 1:15–16). In this way, Palmer rejected the emotionality in traditional Methodism—more specifically, a waiting for the feeling of conviction—arguing that knowledge alone was enough for conviction (*Way of Holiness*, 19). Holiness then required action based on this knowledge.

Palmer's writing and teaching were laced with references to Scripture. Often she followed the typical style of proof-texting. However, in her book *The Promise of the Father*, Palmer employs a sophisticated approach to biblical interpretation to support her argument for the full involvement of women in teaching, preaching, and service ministries. Her approach to the subject shows that she is aware of the wider world of biblical scholarship and of the work of contemporaries' advocating for equality for women in ministry and in general American culture. Palmer begins her argument by asserting that the present age is the age of the "dispensation of the Spirit," which gives the power to preach and proclaim the good news of Christ to all, both men and women. This leads into her discussion of Pentecost, where both male and female "disciples" were present when the Holy Spirit descended (Acts 1:12–2:12). She also observes how, in the Gospels, Jesus gives his female followers the privilege of first bearing the news of his resurrection (*Promise*, 18–19). Palmer then proceeds to treat some difficult passages of Paul: she insists that 1 Cor. 14:34–35 must be interpreted in its historical context and set alongside all other passages that concern women's ministering: Rom. 16:1–2 (Phoebe); Acts 18:26 (Priscilla); Luke 2:36–38 (Anna). With this support, Palmer argues that God has used many women to do his work throughout history. She then identifies inconsistencies in church practices (e.g., why was it acceptable for women to speak with the congregation in congregational responses, when it was unacceptable for women to speak at all?) and appeals to the authority of tradition, past and present, to support accepting women in ministry. Finally, Palmer argues that God is now using women to bring about change in the world. She sees "the promise of the Father" (Joel 2:28–29; Acts 2:17–18) as being fulfilled by the Holy Spirit, who is being poured out on God's daughters, enabling them to prophesy (*Promise*, 71).

Palmer's legacy also includes the many individuals she influenced through her writings, her speaking, and her personal example. Her writing and revival campaigns profoundly influenced the theology and pastoral practice of Catherine Booth. Following Palmer's lead and in her defense, Booth published a vigorous response to those opposing women's right to preach. The authorization for women to preach has remained a core doctrine for the Salvation Army.

Palmer is remembered primarily for her innovative understanding of Christian perfection and complete sanctification, but it was her reading of Scripture that fueled her holiness theology. Her interpretive method of using Scripture to understand Scripture led her to the insight that each person needs to undergo a "personal Pentecost"; this idea was eventually adapted by Pentecostalism and separatist holiness organizations. Palmer's thoughts on "Spirit baptism" and the "second blessing" or the "second work" of God's grace helped to shape the thoughts of those who understand the day of Pentecost as a model of religious experience. Ironically, Palmer herself would not have been comfortable with such a model. She came to her "shorter way" and "altar theology" through the exercise of reason and her personal study of Scripture. Her own journey made her suspect of emotional, religious experience; rather, she grounded her religious convictions on knowledge as presented in the Bible. She would not have supported any promotion of holiness that led to schism or emotional religious experience independent of the rational logic of her "textbook," the Bible (*Way of Holiness*, 20). In the end, it was Palmer's knowledge and study of Scripture that informed her preaching, teaching, and theology.

See also Booth, Catherine Mumford (1829–90); Wesley, Susanna (1669–1742)

Bibliography

Palmer, Phoebe. *The Promise of the Father*. Boston: H. V. Degen, 1859. Repr., Salem, OH: Schmul Pub., 1981.

———. *The Way of Holiness, with Notes by the Way*. New York: Piercy & Reed, 1843. New ed., New York: W. C. Palmer & Hughes, 1867.

Raser, Harold. *Phoebe Palmer: Her Life and Thought*. Studies in Women and Religion 22. Lewiston, NY: Edwin Mellen, 1987.

Wheatley, Richard. *The Life and Letters of Mrs. Phoebe Palmer*. Edited by Donald W. Dayton. The Higher Christian Life: Sources for the Study of the Holiness, Pentecostal, and Keswick Movements 31. New York: Garland, 1984.

White, Charles Edward. *The Beauty of Holiness: Phoebe Palmer as Theologian, Revivalist, Feminist, and Humanitarian*. Eugene, OR: Wipf & Stock, 2008.

— RENEE KWAN MONKMAN

Parr, Katherine (1512–48)

Katherine Parr, King Henry VIII's sixth wife and widow, was the first known woman to publish her own work under her own name in English and in England: *Prayers or Medytacions* (1545). Due to the absence of written source material, her life before her marriage to Henry remains largely obscure (Susan James and Linda Porter have provided the authoritative biographies to date). Her parents, Sir Thomas and Maud Parr, were professional courtiers in service, respectively, to Henry VIII and Catherine of Aragon. Katherine was the eldest of three children; together with her sister, Anne (later the wife of

William Herbert, Earl of Pembroke), and her brother, William (later marquis of Northampton), she received a solid humanistic education, although its specifics must be inferred (James 22–39). While Katherine's siblings followed their parents in making careers as courtiers, Katherine was steered by her widowed mother toward social advancement through marriage—first, at the age of sixteen, to Edward Borough of Gainsborough, who died in his early twenties. Katherine's second husband was John Neville, Lord Latimer, a ranking magnate of the north of England, who bore a heavy weight of service in Crown affairs in the aftermath of the conservative religious uprising known as the Pilgrimage of Grace. When Lord Latimer died at the age of fifty during the 1542–43 session of Parliament in London, the thirty-year-old Katherine evidently sought a place of service for herself in the household of Princess Mary Tudor. What she instead found was her primary place in the affections of Henry VIII, who precipitously married her in July 1543 (James 59–70, 77–90). Only from this point does Katherine Parr's life become legible, in the annals of court history and in her own literary activity, which commenced after she became queen.

Queen Katherine's eventual literary output comprised four volumes. (1) Her translation of Bishop John Fisher's *Psalmi seu precationes* (1525; repr., 1544) was issued anonymously as *Psalmes or prayers* (1544). (2) Her boldly reordered and reworded assemblage of excerpts from book 3 of Richard Whitford's *The Following of Christ* (ca. 1531), an English translation of Thomas à Kempis's *De imitatione Christi*, appeared as *Prayers or Medytacions* (1545), explicitly ascribed to her authorship. (3) Her remarkable hybrid prose composition—one part a narrative of her own sinfulness and ignorance climaxing in her experience of justifying faith, one part an affective meditation on the crucified Christ and the marvel of human redemption, one part an envisioning of England's potential to become a truly Christian commonwealth—was published late in 1547, after Henry's death, with another explicit ascription of authorship as *The lamentacion of a sinner* (Mueller, "Tudor Queen," 18–33). (4) Written entirely in her own hand, her eclectic compilation of prayers and portions of Scripture drawn from a spectrum of devotional sources, including John Fisher and Thomas More but weighted most heavily with material from English Lutheran editors and publishers, survives in the British Library (MS Harley 2342). This manuscript, which was still being added to at the time of Parr's death in 1548, has now been identified as her work and published as *Queen Katherine's Personal Prayerbook* (in *Works*).

During the three-and-a-half years of her queenship, the period that saw all of her documented literary activity except for the continuing project of her personal prayer book, Katherine Parr's spirituality underwent a reorientation from traditionalist Catholicism to emergent Protestantism. This is most plausibly attributed to the influence of Archbishop Thomas Cranmer, with whom she consulted daily while she served as Regent of England (July–Sept. 1545), entrusted by Henry VIII to exercise his royal authority while he conducted a military campaign in France. Yet despite the traces of this confessional shift that emerge in Queen Katherine's work—notably in her account of the onset of justifying faith in her *Lamentacion* and in her preference for Lutheran devotional sources in her *Personal Prayerbook*—the gamut of her literary activity is most consistently marked by her intense absorption in portions of Scripture that speak resonantly to or for her soul, whatever the confessional label of her source. Precluded by her gender, lay status, and historical moment from expounding or interpreting the Bible in any formal sense, Parr nonetheless infuses her accessible, expressive quotations and allusions throughout a considerable range of prayers, devotions, and meditations, "spreading the Word" as she pursues and drives home its implications for the soul. Her authorial intent chiefly takes shape in compilations of first-person utterances whose biblical vocabulary and themes could be employed by all Christians in praying to the God and Savior whom they share, whatever their other disagreements and differences.

Thomas à Kempis and John Fisher have been widely acknowledged for the prominence given to biblical allusion and quotation in their affectively charged christocentric strain of late medieval devotion. Queen Katherine's attraction to Fisher's *Psalmi seu precationes* as the text she would translate as her first work and to à Kempis's *Imitatio* in Whitford's English translation as the quarry from which she would extract and compose her second work demonstrates how strong an impetus to her literary activity arose from her immersion in vernacular Scripture. Along the trajectory of that activity, Parr draws most heavily on the book of Psalms, both as thematic source and as compositional model. Comprising fifteen "Psalms"—in fact, phrases and verses excerpted mainly from prophetic, prescriptive, and Wisdom literature in the Old Testament and Apocrypha (the Psalms preeminently, but also Job, Lamentations, Ecclesiastes, Isaiah, Daniel, Exodus, Deuteronomy, Ecclesiasticus [Sirach], Wisdom of Solomon, Tobias, Judith, and others) and melded into new lyric wholes—Fisher's compositions in *Psalmi seu precationes* may well have established the archetypal status of the psalm as a first-person lyric form for Parr, as she worked closely through his text in translating it as *Psalmes or prayers*.

In general, Parr translates Fisher's Latin so closely that it cannot be ascertained from her English phrasing whether she recognizes that he has recast Vulgate wording or spliced together phrases from disparate places in Scripture. (No source references appear anywhere in either volume.) As an example (*Psalmi*, sig. Ci r; EEBO image 20), nearing the close of his lengthy first Psalm, Fisher splices recast phrases from the Vulgate texts of Ps. 144:8–9 [145:8–9E] and Ezek. 18:32 into a verse of his own composition: "Quoniam deus es tu, bonus et misericors, ac paciens erga nos nolens aliquos perire, sed omnes ad poenitentiam reverti." Parr duly renders Fisher's Latin as "For Thou art God, gracious and merciful, and patiently dost suffer us; and wouldest that no man should perish, but that all men should return to penance." Does she recognize as recastings the phrases from Ps. 144, "misericors Dominus: patiens. . . . Bonus Dominus omnibus" (the Lord is merciful, patient. . . . The Lord is good to all) and the phrases from Ezekiel, "nolo mortem morientis, dicit Dominus Deus, revertimini, et vivite" (I do not wish the death of a mortal, saith the Lord God, turn yourselves and live)? Evidently not in this case: Parr's faithfulness to Fisher appears not only linguistic but also theological, for she reproduces his "ad poenitentiam reverti" as "return to penance"—a traditionalist twist given to the Vulgate's "revertimini, et vivite" (turn yourselves and live). At other points, however, Parr's English tallies more closely with the Vulgate reading than Fisher's Latin adaptation does. In Ps. 5:3 (2E) (*Psalmi*, sig. Eviii v; EEBO image 44), Parr translates, "Open my lips and my mouth, that I may speak and show forth the glory and praise of Thy name"—rendering Ps. 50:17 (51:15E) in Fisher's minor recasting, "Aperi labia mea et os meum, ut nunciem laudes nominis tui" (Open my lips and my mouth, that I may declare praises of Thy name). But Parr's "may . . . show forth" is closer to the Vulgate's "adnuntiabit" (will make known) than is Fisher's "nunciem" (may declare). She could well have recognized the source text and made fidelity to it a priority in translating Fisher.

Parr's next work, *Prayers or medytacions*, reveals a considerably more assertive authorial design in the many minute interventions made in the text of book 3 of à Kempis's Latin original as translated by Whitford. She aims at a fresh universalizing of the Christian imperative "Take up your cross, and follow Me" by effacing the explicit masculinist and monastic norms of her source text. Parr does away with dialogue between a gender-marked pair of intimates identified as "Jesus," "Lord," "sir," or "sire" on the one hand, and invariably as "my son" on the other. Elimination of this dialogue dispenses with a dynamic in which the monk of the source text is brought, by instruction and exhortation, through stages of moral and spiritual proficiency to the privilege of mystical rapture in a relation of ever-closer male bonding. Parr replaces dialogue with monologue: the "I," "me," and "my" of an erring, needy human speaker whose psychology is characterized only in terms of a generic heart, mind, and will. *Prayers or medytacions* consists of the soul's personal addresses to God, yearning for grace in various guises—consolation, patience, strength—to be enabled to follow Christ and be united with God as Christ is (Mueller, "Devotion," 180–87).

Parr's universalizing design operates as a selection mechanism on the densely scriptural weave of her source text. She consistently selects lyric and affective verses couched in the first person (or restyles them in this form). The repeated result is to bring into prominence utterances of David in the Psalms and utterances of Jesus in the Gospels, which then are blended into a rich resource for the soul's self-expression. A sequence from the middle of *Prayers or medytacions* (sig. Biv v; EEBO images 12–13) will illustrate: "May it, therefore, please Thee to deliver me: . . . help me, Lord God. . . . And now, what shall I say but that Thy will be done in me. . . . But would to God that I might suffer gladly, . . . that when I am clearly delivered by Thee, I may with gladness say, The right hand of Him that is highest, hath made this change." The first phrases draw conjointly on Ps. 40:13, "Let it please Thee, O Lord, to deliver me; make haste, O Lord to help me"; on excerpts from the Lord's Prayer in Matt. 6:10, 13, "Thy will be done. . . . Deliver us from evil"; and on Jesus's repeated prayer in Matt. 26:39, 42, "O my Father, . . . let this . . . pass from me: nevertheless, not as I will, but as Thou wilt." The next phrase alludes to Mark 8:31 and Luke 9:22, "He began to teach them, that the Son of man must suffer many things." The final phrases combine excerpts from Ps. 34:6, "The poor man cried unto the Lord, and He . . . delivered him out of all his troubles"; and from 76:11 (77:10E) in the unique Vulgate reading: "Et dixi . . . haec commutatio dexterae Excelsi" (And I said, . . . This change [has been made] by the right hand of the Most High).

Parr's one nondevotional composition, *The lamentacion of a sinner*, exhibits the most versatile, innovative handling of Scripture to be found in her work. As is typical of many tracts and treatises of the Reformation era, the page margins of the *Lamentacion* feature a steady procession of biblical references intermixed with message-oriented alerts to the reader, such as "The judgment of man is corrupt in all things," and "The Word of God is only the doctrine of salvation." The scaffolding (so to speak) of these clustered marginalia supports Parr's varied utilization of Scripture within her main text by assuring that an allusion can be traced to its source and a passing mention can be clarified. In the first section of the *Lamentacion*, she effectively evokes her willfulness and sinfulness as states of mind and heart wholly contrary to Scripture. This section climaxes in a series of antitheses that locate the first-person speaker in diametric opposition to the Christ of the New Testament, as focused in specific marginal references such as these (*Lamentacion*, sig. Avii r-v; EEBO images 14–15): "Christ was obedient unto His Father, even to the death of the cross [mg., Phil. 2]; and I disobedient and most stubborn, even to the confusion of truth." "Christ came to serve His brethren [mg., Matt. 20]; and I coveted to rule over them." "Christ prayed for His enemies [mg., John 12], and I hated mine."

A dramatic hermeneutical turn occurs in the second section of the *Lamentacion*, where Parr's first-person speaker now finds herself enabled by God's grace to speak with and through Scripture as she meditates on Christ crucified and the marvel of human salvation (sigs. Dii v, Diii v-D iv r; EEBO images 33, 35–36):

Truly, it may be most justly verified that to behold Christ crucified, in spirit, is the best meditation that can be. . . . Such be the wonderful works of God, to call sinners to repentance [mg., Matt. 9], and to make them to take Christ, His well-beloved Son, for their Saviour [mg., Rom. 6]. This is the gift of God [mg., John 15]. . . . For in Christ is all fulness of the Godhead, and in Him are hid all the treasures of wisdom and knowledge [mg., Col. 2]. Even He is the water of life, whereof whosoever shall drink shall nevermore thirst; but it shall be in him a well of water, springing up into everlasting life [mg., John 4]. Saint Paul saith, . . . "If when we were enemies we were reconciled to God by the death of His son, much more, seeing we are reconciled, we shall be preserved by His death" [mg., Rom. 5]. It is no little or small benefit we have received by Christ, if we consider what He hath done for us.

Continuing to speak with and through Scripture in the third and final section of her *Lamentacion*, Parr breaks further new ground by extending her range of discourse beyond meditation to what looks and sounds at points like preaching—an office unavailable to any woman of that day, even a dowager queen. Yet the reader-alert rubrics in this final section emphasize the boldness and forthrightness of Parr's social and moral critique of England as being far from a model Christian commonwealth: "Contentions in religion," "Persecutors of the Word," "Christian liberty," "Traditions of men," "The Word of God the only sure doctrine," "Self-love," "Weaklings mislike all things," "Wicked men mislike good things," "Vain gospellers," "Evil living slandereth the best profession," "This age requireth learning," "Prerogative of the Scripture."

Parr's modulations into prayer in this final section of the *Lamentacion*, moreover, reaffirm the conviction fundamental to her devotional practice, that immersion and absorption in Scripture can transform the receptive soul into a living expression of its saving truth (*Lamentacion*, sigs. Div r-Dv v; EEBO images 36–37):

I pray the Lord that this great benefit of Christ crucified may be steadfastly fixed and printed in all Christian hearts, that they may be true lovers of God and work, as children, for love [mg., 1 Pet. 1]. . . . The sincere and pure lovers of God do embrace Christ with such fervency of spirit, that . . . they be not wise in their own opinion, neither high-minded in their prosperity, neither abashed in their adversity [mg., Rom. 12], but humble and gentle, always to all men. For they know by their faith they are members all of one body [mg., 1 Cor. 12], and that they have possessed, all, one God, one faith, one baptism [mg., Eph. 4], one joy, and one salvation. . . . Well, I shall pray to the Lord to take all contention and strife away: . . . with sending also a godly unity and concord amongst all Christians, that we may serve the Lord in true holiness of life [mg., Luke 1].

The handwritten manuscript preserved in the British Library (Harley 2342) appears in print as *Queen Katherine's Personal Prayerbook* (in *Works*), and its source annotations confirm its character as a counterpart to the irenic aspirations that conclude her *Lamentacion*. In her prayer book, a project of exploration and integration pursued out of the public eye, Parr positions herself reflectively with regard to the widening divide but, even more, the extent of common ground in Catholic and Reformed strains of lay devotion. The Primers and Psalters of the 1530s and her other sources from this decade made the developments that concerned her traceable. Whatever their confessional orientation, Parr's prayer book sources all share an introspective turning from the world and a concomitant focus on Christ as the sole Savior of humankind. This inward turn and this christocentrism constituted notable common denominators in the devotionalism of her contestatory age. As elsewhere documented in her *Psalmes or prayers* and *Prayers or medytacions* published in her lifetime, such commonality profoundly engaged Katherine Parr's hope and interest as she immersed herself in the text of Scripture and found it expressing as well as addressing the yearnings of her spirit. A corresponding engagement will be found to animate and inform the personal prayer book left unfinished at her death from puerperal fever after giving birth to her only child, a daughter, borne to her fourth husband, Thomas Seymour, Baron Seymour of Sudeley, younger uncle of the boy-king Edward VI, in September 1548 (James 294–303, 327–33).

Bibliography

Fisher, J. *Psalmi seu precationes ex variis Scripturae locis collectae.* [London]: Thomas Berthelet, April 18, 1545. Revised Short-Title Catalogue 2994. Early English Books Online, http://eebo.chadwyck.com/.

James, Susan E. *Kateryn Parr: The Making of a Queen.* Aldershot, UK: Ashgate, 1999.

Mueller, Janel M. "Devotion as Difference: Intertextuality in Queen Katherine Parr's *Prayers or Meditations* (1545)." *Huntington Library Quarterly* 53 (1990): 171–97.

————. "A Tudor Queen Finds Voice: Katherine Parr's *Lamentation of a Sinner.* Pages 15–47 in *The Historical Renaissance: New Essays on Tudor and Stuart Literature and Culture,* edited by Heather Dubrow and Richard Strier. Chicago: University of Chicago Press, 1988.

Parr, Katherine. *Katherine Parr: Complete Works and Correspondence.* Edited by Janel M. Mueller. Chicago: University of Chicago Press, 2011.

————. *The lamentacion of a sinner, made by ye most vertuous Ladie, Quene Caterin.* [London]: Edward Whitchurch, November 5, 1547. Revised Short-Title Catalogue 4827. Early English Books Online. http://eebo.chadwyck.com/.

————. *Prayers or Medytacions, wherein the mynd is stirred: . . . Collected out of holy woorkes by the most vertuous and graciouse Princesse Katherine quene of Englande.* [London]: Thomas Berthelet, November 6, 1545. Revised Short-Title Catalogue 4919. Early English Books Online, http://eebo.chadwyck.com/.

————. *Psalmes or prayers taken out of holye scripture.* [London]: Thomas Berthelet, April 25, 1544. Revised Short-Title Catalogue 3001.7. Not in Early English Books Online. A modern-spelling, annotated text is in *Katherine Parr: Complete Works and Correspondence.*

Porter, Linda. *Katherine the Queen: The Remarkable Life of Katherine Parr.* London: Macmillan, 2010.

— JANEL MUELLER

Paula (347–404)

Paula began her life at Rome amid wealth and privilege and ended it at Bethlehem in a spare monastic cell, amid utter poverty but next to the cave where her beloved Jesus was born and surrounded by the monastic women she led and taught. Paula was a Roman aristocrat, descended from the Gracchi and Scipios (and even, Jerome claims, from Agamemnon himself [*Ep.* 108.4]). By her own account, she enjoyed the silks and linen and whitened face of a patrician Roman in her youth; she and her husband, Toxotius, had five children. After her husband's early death, when she was only about twenty-six, she determined to devote herself entirely to Christ, following the example of Antony and the desert monks, in a life of poverty, chastity, and constant prayer and Bible study. She studied with Marcella, and like Marcella she gathered around her in her home in Rome other women attracted by her life of scholarly devotion and celibacy.

Unlike Marcella, however, Paula left Rome in the mid-380s, accompanied by her daughter Eustochium and a company of dedicated women, to travel with her friend and mentor Jerome via Portiae and Cyprus to Egypt and the Holy Land, in the footsteps of contemporary saints and the ancient heroes of Scripture. She finally settled in Bethlehem, where with her own funds she built a double monastery beside the Cave of the Nativity—one for women, which she directed; another for men, directed by Jerome; as well as a hospice for travelers. There she trained her women, who were divided into three houses on the basis of social rank, in a life of rigorous Bible study and prayer, accompanied by material poverty. They wore rough cloth, ate mainly bread and vegetables, bathed only rarely, and made their own clothes. Paula herself would not even take oil with her bread and slept on a mat of goats' hair on the ground.

To this life of asceticism and pilgrimage, the Bible was central. In her reading of Scripture, Paula combines two emphases. The first is "spiritual." In an exegetical conversation preserved in a letter of Jerome (for we have access to Paula only through Jerome's few surviving letters to her), she seeks the meaning of the acrostic psalms (e.g., Ps. 119). On the basis of the spiritual meaning of each letter of the alphabet, Jerome explains that *alef* means "doctrine"; *bet*, "house"; *gimel*, "plenitude"; and *dalet*, "tablets"; hence the first four letters together (thus the first four groups of verses beginning with these letters [119:1–32]) signify that "the doctrine of the church, which is the house of God, is found in the plenitude of the divine books" (Jerome, *Ep.* 30.5–6).

Yet Paula also insists on the literal, historical meaning of the scriptural texts. She read the New Testament in Greek and mastered Hebrew so that she could read the Old Testament in the original language. She traveled to the Holy Land to find there the very place where each event of Scripture occurred. Her literalism was extreme: when she arrived at the place of the cross and tomb (as Jerome reports), she threw herself down in adoration, kissed the stone of the sepulchre, and licked the ground where Jesus had lain. In this pilgrimage to the places where the scriptural stories occurred, she found not just a historical record, however, but also an intense spiritual experience in which the scriptural story became present for her. In Jerome's letter on her behalf to Marcella, she describes the experience: Here on this crag, she says, she will "see" Amos blowing his shepherd's horn; she will see Lazarus come forth bound with grave clothes; she will weep in the sepulcher of the Lord with his sister and with his mother. Here in the Holy Land, above all in the cave where Jesus was born, she will find "him whom [her] soul seeks" (Jerome, *Ep.* 46.13). The instinct is spiritual, the soul's communion with Christ. But it is anchored in the biblical stories taken literally, relived at the very place where (she believes) they occurred. Exegesis merges into pilgrimage; pilgrimage becomes the outworking of exegetical inquiry.

Paula became, for her monastics as well as for Jerome himself, a beloved spiritual mentor. When she died, denying herself all physical comforts to the end, Jerome was bereft; he had lost not only a dear sister but his conversation partner and spiritual mate. As she died the entire monastic community as well as the surrounding clergy—three bishops among them—gathered to do her reverence and sing her on her way.

See also Marcella (ca. 327–410)

Bibliography

Campbell, Mary. *The Witness and the Other World: Exotic European Travel Writing, 400–1600*. Ithaca, NY: Cornell University Press, 1988.

Clark, Elizabeth. "Authority and Humility: A Conflict of Values in Fourth Century Female Monasticism." *Byzantinische Forschungen* 9 (1985): 17–33.

Elm, Susanna. *"Virgins of God": The Making of Asceticism in Late Antiquity*. Oxford: Clarendon, 1994. ACLS Humanities E-book ed., 1996. http://www.humanitiesebook.org/.

Hinson, E. Glenn. "Women Biblical Scholars in the Late Fourth Century: The Aventine Circle." Pages 319–24 in *Augustine and His Opponents, Jerome, Other Latin Fathers after Nicaea, Orientalia*, edited by Elizabeth A. Livingstone. Studia patristica 33. Louvain: Peeters, 1997.

Jerome. *Principal Works*. In vol. 6 of *Nicene and Post-Nicene Fathers*, Series 2, edited by Philip Schaff and Henry Wace. New York: Christian Literature, 1893. Repr., Peabody, MA: Hendrickson, 1995.

———. *Saint Jerome: Lettres*. Edited and translated by Jérôme Labourt. 8 vols. Paris: Belles Lettres, 1951.

Kelly, J. N. D. *Jerome: His Life, Writings and Controversies*. London: Duckworth, 1975.

Palladius. *The Lausiac History*. Translated and annotated by Robert T. Meyer. Ancient Christian Writers 34. Westminster, MD: Newman, 1965.

—CATHERINE SIDER HAMILTON

Penn-Lewis, Jessie (1861–1927)

Jessie Penn-Lewis was born in Neath, South Wales, as the second of nine children. Though plagued with ill health throughout her life, she was always a quick and voracious learner. Her father, a civil engineer, died when she was only sixteen, forcing her mother into business to provide for her large family. Jessie's paternal grandfather, the Calvinistic Methodist minister Samuel Jones, brought the family into regular contact with prominent ministers of that denomination.

Despite her upbringing in the church, it was not until age twenty-one, after her marriage to William Penn-Lewis, an auditor's clerk, that she had a conversion experience. A few years later, Penn-Lewis began working with the YWCA, and in her ministry to young women displayed her gifts for evangelism and discipleship. As her ministry expanded, opportunities to speak took her all over the British Isles and abroad to Continental Europe, North America, India, and Egypt. Her connections with leading ministers also led to her involvement in the Welsh Revival of 1904–5.

Penn-Lewis wrote over eighty published works, mostly in the form of short booklets. While they all display her deep grounding in Scripture, only a few are directed specifically toward biblical interpretation. These include studies of Joshua, the Song of Songs, and Job, which reveal her fundamental approach. First, she was convinced that Scripture interprets Scripture. She frequently quotes other biblical passages to illuminate the text at hand and often uses the New Testament as an interpretive grid for understanding the Old Testament. Second, she saw the goal of biblical interpretation as personal spiritual growth. Although her treatment of Scripture reflects deep study, illustrated by occasional references to Septuagintal readings and underlying Greek or Hebrew words, her primary aim is not to explain exegetical details but to address the charges and challenges of the Christian life.

In *The Conquest of Canaan*, Penn-Lewis examines the Joshua narrative in light of Eph. 6, reading the story as a "type" of the church's call to fight a spiritual battle. In this regard, Jericho portrays a spiritual victory gained through prayer, while Ai illustrates the lesson that Christians cannot proceed in their spiritual journey until they have retaken ground lost to the enemy. She addresses the issue of spiritual warfare elsewhere as well, most notably in *War on the Saints*, written with the help of Evan Roberts, a leading figure of the Welsh revival. In this work she argues that evil spirits are able to deceive and even, to some extent, possess Christians who are unaware of the spiritual battle they face and who are not fully grounded in the truth. Penn-Lewis also attributes the death of the Welsh revival to evil spirits who sought to counterfeit the work of the Holy Spirit, thus subtly leading people astray.

Penn-Lewis also uses a typological approach in *"Thy Hidden Ones,"* interpreting the Song of Songs as a portrait of the soul's journey from its initial acceptance of salvation toward a full union with Christ. When the Lover compares the Beloved's eyes to doves (Song 1:15; 4:1; 5:2), she takes this as signifying that the Beloved "has been enabled [by the Holy Spirit, represented by a dove in the Gospels] to yield herself wholly to her Lord, . . . becoming single-eyed in her choice of Christ" (19). Similarly, to be "in the clefts of the rock" (Song 2:14) is to be "hidden in [Christ's] wounded side," since the rock symbolizes Christ crucified (29; cf. Exod. 17:6; 1 Cor. 10:4).

Penn-Lewis's treatment of *The Story of Job* includes some discussion of historical issues, such as the historicity of Job and the nature of his physical malady. Yet she is primarily interested in examining the theological outlooks of the various characters and exploring how Job portrays the role of suffering in the lives of Christians. Through Job we learn that an "innermost knowledge of God is given only when the soul has been stripped of all that may—even unknowingly—dim its inner vision" (194). A refining suffering leads Christians to die to themselves, so that they may be raised again to a new life in Christ, in which they seek the will of God above all else. This theme of being crucified with Christ, leading both to victory over sin and to effective ministry, reappears in many of Penn-Lewis's writings and is clearly an important feature of her thought (cf. *The Pathway to Life in God*). Her focus on the cross also dominates her most widely distributed booklet, *The Word of the Cross*, which sold millions of copies and was translated into at least one hundred languages.

In response to a published letter calling women in Christian ministry to defend their actions biblically, Penn-Lewis wrote *The "Magna Charta" of Woman*, summarizing and simplifying Katharine Bushnell's reinterpretations of difficult "women" passages, based largely on lexical and syntactic argumentation and examinations of historical background. Penn-Lewis, following Bushnell, argues that rabbinic influence on the church in the centuries following the apostolic period led to a misunderstanding of Paul and Gen. 3 on the status and role of women. She contends that, rightly understood, Paul (1) argues against the Judaizing claim that women must be silent in church, which he quotes in 1 Cor. 14:34; (2) claims that women have freedom in regard to head coverings (1 Cor. 11:13); and (3) calls uneducated women to learn the truths about God (1 Tim. 2:11), while at the same time giving a temporary injunction against women teaching in the church, due to the church's precarious situation in that era of persecution and threatening heresy (1 Tim. 1:8–11; 4:1–4; 6:20–21; 2 Tim. 3:1–10). Furthermore, in Gen. 3 Eve should be viewed as a deceived but redeemed figure, who laudably takes her stand against the serpent, marking him as her enemy (v. 13) and leading the Lord to prophesy her ultimate vindication over him (v. 15). The statement that her husband will rule over her (v. 16) is given as a warning, not a mandate prescribing the universal subjection of women. Thus Penn-Lewis calls Christian women to a new understanding of Scripture that restores their God-given freedom and dignity and is compatible with a call to ministry.

Although her beliefs about demonic activity have sparked controversy, Jessie Penn-Lewis illustrates the tremendous impact that one woman can have on the spiritual formation of her own generation. Moreover, she leaves behind a legacy of piety and engagement with the Scriptures.

See also Bushnell, Katharine C. (1855–1946)

Bibliography

Garrard, Mary N. *Mrs. Penn-Lewis: A Memoir.* London: Overcomer Book Room, 1931.

Jones, Brynmor Pierce. *The Trials and Triumphs of Jessie Penn-Lewis.* North Brunswick, NJ: Bridge-Logos, 1997.

Penn-Lewis, Jessie. *The Conquest of Canaan: Sidelights on the Spiritual Battlefield.* 4th ed. London: Overcomer Book Room, 1945.

———. *The "Magna Charta" of Woman: "According to the Scriptures": Being Light upon the Subject Gathered from Dr. Katherine Bushnell's Text Book, "God's Word to Women."* 2nd ed. London: Overcomer Book Room, 1929.

———. *The Pathway to Life in God.* 4th ed. London: Overcomer Book Room, 1925.

———. *The Story of Job: A Glimpse into the Mystery of Suffering.* London: Marshall Brothers, 1902.

———. *"Thy Hidden Ones": Union with Christ Traced in the Song of Songs.* 5th ed. Leicester, UK: Excelsior, 1939.

———. *The Word of the Cross.* Madras: Mission, 1903.

Penn-Lewis, Jessie, and Evan Roberts. *War on the Saints.* 9th ed. New York: Lowe, 1973.

— BRITTANY KIM

▓ Petersen, Johanna Eleonora (1644–1724)

Johanna Eleonora Petersen is one of the most important women of early Lutheran Pietism. Born in 1644 in Frankfurt-am-Main, the daughter of the impoverished noble von Merlau family, she experienced childhood during the last phase of the Thirty Years' War. As was common for daughters of the lesser nobility, she was sent to the courts of the greater nobility to work as a lady-in-waiting. In 1661, Johanna Eleonora von Merlau began to work in the service of a branch of the family of the dukes of Schleswig-Holstein who resided in Schloss [Castle] Wiesenburg in Saxony. Her interest in a deeper piety began during this period, and she made contact with leading representatives of the fledgling Pietist movement. In 1675 she moved to Frankfurt, the center of German Pietist activity.

In 1680 she married Johann Wilhelm Petersen (1649–1727), a Lutheran theologian from Schleswig-Holstein, who was also inclined toward Pietism. From 1680 to 1692 they lived in North Germany, where their son was born in 1682. After J. W. Petersen was dismissed from his church position in 1692, the family lived on two different estates near Magdeburg, first in Niederndodeleben and then in Thymer, where they concentrated on their writing. They moved in Pietist circles, entertained many guests, traveled, and corresponded extensively. Johanna Eleonora Petersen died on their estate in 1724.

In addition to her letters, fifteen of Petersen's printed writings remain. The most well-known work is her autobiography, which is available in a new German edition as well as in an English translation. One of the distinguishing features of Pietism is the high value that Pietists placed on engagement with the Bible. Biblical texts were understood as instructions for daily life; academic exegesis played only a subordinate role. Petersen's earliest writings, letters from the years 1672 to 1684, reveal that she saw her work as following "the dearest Saviour's teachings" (Matthias 78). Inspired by her Pietist milieu, she learned Greek and Hebrew to better work with biblical sources. Her early publications, *Gespräche des Hertzens mit Gott* (Conversations of the Heart with God), 1689 and *Glaubens-Gespräche* (Faith Conversations), 1691, take the form of prayers and interpret the mystical sense of individual biblical verses. During this period, the writings of both J. E. and J. W. Petersen featured the theme of the imminent coming of God's thousand-year reign on earth, or millennialism. In her main theological work, *Anleitung zu gründlicher Verständniß der Heiligen Offenbahrung Jesu Christi* (Guide to the Thorough Understanding of the Holy Revelation of Jesus Christ), 1696, Petersen focuses on millennialism. Her *Guide* is loosely styled after a classic commentary, a genre traditionally reserved for academically educated male theologians. Yet Petersen's commentary is limited to texts that, in her view, refer to end-times issues. Using verses from Revelation, Petersen charts out the passage of time until the completion of Christ's thousand-year reign.

In her later publications, Petersen moved away from millennialism and focused instead on the idea of universal salvation, the *Apokatastasis*. Here also she took great pains to base her work on a biblical foundation. Yet no longer was her method commentary; instead she wove together verses from various biblical books. In *Die verklärte Offenbahrung* (The Transfigured Revelation), 1706, Petersen interprets Revelation in relation to the *Apokatastasis*. She develops her own interpretive method: adding to Revelation by continuing sentences and thereby changing meaning. She identifies her additions to the biblical text. Christ's statement in Rev. 1:8, for example, is expanded as follows: "I am Alpha and Omega, the beginning and the ending, says the Lord, which is, and which was, and which is to come, the Almighty (who has with the Father the same Honor, Name, and Glory, through whom all will come in the beginning and all will be completed, through whom all was created and through whom all will be restored and established)" (4–5). In this expansive interpretative text, Christ himself, and not only the author Petersen, refers to the restoration in the end-times. Petersen's claim to divine authority, especially with regard to a teaching rejected in Lutheran confessional writings, was met by the majority of her contemporaries with disapprobation. Indeed, both J. E.

and J. W. Petersen were attacked far more strongly for their views on universal salvation than for their teachings on the millennial kingdom, even by those on the side of Pietism.

Strengthened through Pietism, Johanna Eleonora Petersen was a self-confident interpreter of Scripture. She insisted that she, as a woman, most certainly had the right to interpret the Bible authoritatively and thereby to teach. She believed that all the passages generally brought to bear on this subject supported her position. In the introduction to her *Guide*, she states:

> Some will reproach me with the words of Paul in 1 Cor. 14:34 and 1 Tim. 2:12 that it is not becoming for a woman to teach in the congregation of God. But these should know that these same words do not apply to me. I respect what the Holy Spirit testified through Paul, and I presume to teach nothing in the congregation of God that is against proper womanly submission. This, however, I truly know, that just as in Christ Jesus according to the giving of grace and the Spirit, neither man nor woman count (Gal. 3:28), so also grace and the gift of God are not to be dampened or suppressed in a female person, according to the admonition of Paul (1 Thess. 5:19); all gifts of God, whether they show themselves in men or women, are worthy to be disclosed and employed (1 Cor. 12:7). (*Anleitung*, Vorwort, b4vf)

Writing as a Pietist theologian, Petersen endeavored to wed the truest possible observance of biblical teachings with her own ideas about gender. Her attempts to reclaim for women the right to theological discourse had no far-reaching effects at first, but she did show that such a position, based on a Pietist point of view, was possible.

Although various places in her writings demonstrate that Petersen was thoroughly acquainted with the exegetical debates of her time, she rarely referred to the arguments and positions of her contemporaries. Instead, she tried to present her understanding of Scripture as divinely inspired and as the only correct one. For the opponents of Pietism, this claim, as well as the contents of her interpretations, caused her to be regarded as the negative embodiment of all of the forms of the early modern church reform movement. The positions represented by Johanna Eleonora and Johann Wilhelm Petersen were, nevertheless, widely accepted. Yet in the long run they became associated with the male rather than with the female theologian. Johanna Eleonora Petersen's legacy lies not in the historical impact of her writings, but rather in that she belongs to the group of women of the late seventeenth and early eighteenth centuries who helped to define the field of exegetical debate. Pietism provided a foundation on which women, who were not trained in the academy, could advance their insights and have them be considered as theologically relevant.

Bibliography

Albrecht, Ruth. "Johanna Eleonora Petersen in the Context of Women's and Gender Studies." Pages 71–84 in *Pietism in Germany and North America, 1680–1820*, edited by Jonathan Strom, Hartmut Lehmann, and James Van Horn Melton. Farnham, UK: Ashgate, 2009.

———. *Johanna Eleonora Petersen: Theologische Schriftstellerin des frühen Pietismus.* Göttingen: Vandenhoeck & Ruprecht, 2005.

———. "Pietistische Schriftstellerin und Theologin: Johanna Eleonora von Merlau-Petersen (1644–1724)." Pages 123–96 in *Weisheit—eine schöne Rose auf dem Dornenstrauche,* edited by Elisabeth Gössmann. Munich: Iudicium, 2004.

Matthias, Markus. "Mutua Consolatio Sororum: Die Briefe Johanna Eleonora von Merlaus an die Herzogin Sophie Elisabeth von Sachsen-Zeitz." *Pietismus und Neuzeit: Ein Jahrbuch zur Geschichte des neueren Protestantismus* 22 (1996): 69–102.

Petersen, Johanna Eleonora. *Anleitung zu gründlicher Verständniß der Heiligen Offenbahrung Jesu Christi.* . . . Frankfurt: Johann Daniel Müller, 1696.

———. *Gespräche des Hertzens mit Gott.* . . . Ploen: Siegfried Ripenau, 1689.

———. *Glaubens-Gespräche.* . . . Frankfurt: Michael Brodthagen, 1691.

———. *Leben, von ihr selbst mit eigener Hand aufgesetzet: Autobiographie.* Edited by Prisca Guglielmetti. Leipzig: Evangelische Verlagsanstalt, 2003.

———. *The Life of Lady Johanna Eleonora Petersen, Written by Herself: Pietism and Women's Autobiography in Seventeenth-Century Germany.* Edited and translated by Barbara Becker-Cantarino. Chicago: University of Chicago Press, 2005.

———. *Die verklärte Offenbahrung Jesu Christi.* . . . [Büdingen]: Regelin, 1706.

— Ruth Albrecht

Phelps, Elizabeth Stuart (1844–1911)

American writer Elizabeth Stuart Phelps wrote some 47 books, 17 works of children's fiction, 142 short stories, and 95 essays over the course of her career, almost all of which deal with moral questions relating to social issues and the status of women. In her autobiography, *Chapters from a Life,* Phelps states that her literary interests and talent spring wholly from the circumstances of her personal biography, meaning her New England clerical and literary ancestors (3). Both grandfathers were Congregational ministers, one of whom (Rev. Moses Stuart, 1780–1852) introduced the first German lexicon to the United States as chair of sacred literature at Andover Theological Seminary in Massachusetts; the other (Rev. Eliakim Phelps, 1789–1880) is remembered for his work on the Underground Railroad.

Phelps took on several different names over the course of her writing career, but she was given the name Mary Gray Phelps at the time of her birth in a parsonage in Boston. Phelps took on not only the name of her mother, Elizabeth Stuart, after her death in 1852, but she would also take on her profession: her mother was a popular writer at the time, best known for her novel *The Sunny Side; or, A Country Minister's Wife* (1851) as well as *The Angel over the Right Shoulder* (1852)—works that confront the tension for women between professional and domestic self-fulfillment. Her mother's struggle to be both mother and professional writer deeply affected Phelps: many of her works are framed around this question of the "dual nature" of women and the "civil war" of professional versus domestic life (*The Story of Avis*, 1877; *Doctor Zay*, 1882). In 1902, under the pseudonym of Mary Adams, Phelps published *Confessions of a Wife*, a bleak presentation of married life. Phelps took on the last name of her husband, Herbert Dickinson Ward (1861–1932), upon their marriage in 1888. Ward, seventeen years Phelps's junior, was a successful journalist and writer, and the couple penned several biblical romances together, including *Come Forth* (1891).

While her mother's fiction conveyed an implied critique of marriage and the social status of women, the views of Phelps's father, Rev. Austin Phelps (1820–90), were, as Phelps calls them, "feudal" (*Chapters*, 60), and he penned several anti-women's rights essays in the 1880s. Her father was also a minister and professor of sacred rhetoric and homiletics at Andover Seminary, a "heavily masculine place" (133). Phelps attended a private school for girls in Andover, and despite the general doubt at Andover of the intellectual capacity of women, she published her first short story at the age of thirteen in the children's journal *Youth's Companion*. Her second publication soon followed, a story for which she received payment: $2.50. Phelps recalls the sense of dignity she felt on receiving this sum, stating, "I felt that I had suddenly acquired value—to myself, to my family, and to the world" (*Chapters*, 22).

Phelps is best known as a religious writer, especially in the context of her spiritualist novels *The Gates Ajar* (1868), *Beyond the Gates* (1883), and *The Gates Between* (1887). These novels were written for women who had lost loved ones in the Civil War and who were unable to find comfort in a heavily masculine church. In *The Gates Ajar* she creates a strong female leading character who interprets the Bible from the "original Greek" on her own terms, not only to herself and to her family, but also to the whole community, including the minister, who realizes that his generalizing statements about God and Christianity meant to provide comfort to others in fact provide little consolation for him upon the unexpected death of his wife. While her spiritualist novels were extremely popular, Phelps was accused of blasphemy since the series constructs a vision of the afterlife based on the realities of everyday existence, complete with firesides, puppies, and gingersnaps.

Her most explicit work of biblical interpretation remains largely unknown and unnoticed. In *The Story of Jesus Christ: An Interpretation* (1897), Phelps creates her own interpretive method, distancing her work from male-dominated realms of discourse and expressing a real impatience with traditional biblical scholarship. Instead, she claims to write narrative, thus gaining greater freedom by moving outside those modes whose principles had been laid out exclusively by male scholars. In her introduction to the work, Phelps writes: "This book is not theology or criticism, nor is it biography. It is neither history, controversy, nor a sermon. It makes none of the claims, it assumes none of the pretensions, of any one of these. It is not a study of Jewish life or Oriental customs. It is not a handbook of Palestinian travel, nor a map of Galilean and Judean geography. It is not a creed; it speaks for no sect, it pleads for no doctrine. It is a narrative, and will be received as such by those who understand the laws of narrative expression" (vii–viii). Thus Phelps creates a narrative space for her biography, space outside the masculine principles of the aforementioned mode of discourse. In this narrative space, Phelps presents a uniquely feminine portrait of Jesus; he is the ideal friend of women but displays many conventionally "womanly" virtues himself; he is humble, nurturing, craving love and loyalty, and uniquely sensitive to the needs of others, particularly those of women. Christlike behavior therefore becomes associated with female behavior, forging an intimate connection between Christ/Christianity and women. Jesus, for Phelps, is a revolutionary not in terms of social conditions, but rather of character: Jesus worked to show women their identities as "true women," individuals worthy of self-respect, attentive to individual personality and character rather than societal ideals.

In her interpretation Phelps's constant focus is on female characters in the life of Jesus; she writes from their points of view and encourages her readers to actively participate in their stories. Phelps invites women to respond authentically to the biblical narrative, creating a community not only of women readers but also of women interpreters. Her interest in biblical interpretation therefore cannot be separated from her interest in the status of women, since in all of her work she strove to combine narrative with moral responsibility. As she affirms in her autobiography, "I believe in the Life Everlasting, which is sure to be. . . . I believe in women; and in their right to their own best possibilities in every department of life" (*Chapters*, 20).

Bibliography

Kessler, Carol Farley. *Elizabeth Stuart Phelps*. Twayne's United States Authors Series 434. Boston: Twayne Pub., 1982.

Phelps, Elizabeth Stuart. *Chapters from a Life*. Boston: Houghton, Mifflin, 1896.

———. *The Gates Ajar*. Boston: Fields, Osgood, 1868. Repr. in *Three Spiritualist Novels by Elizabeth Stuart Phelps*. Introduction by Nina Baym. Urbana: University of Illinois Press, 2000.

———. *The Story of Jesus Christ: An Interpretation*. Boston: Houghton, Mifflin, 1897.

Privett, Ronna Coffey. *A Comprehensive Study of American Writer Elizabeth Stuart Phelps, 1844–1911: Art for Truth's Sake*. Studies in American Literature 61. Lewiston, NY: Edwin Mellen, 2003.

— ERIN VEARNCOMBE

Porete, Marguerite (Porette or Margaret Porete; of Hainaut) (d. 1310)

In 1946 Marguerite Porete was identified by Romana Guarnieri as the author of *Miroir des simples âmes* (The Mirror of Simple Souls), as it is popularly known, but the full title continues: *brought to nothing, who live only in the will and desire for Love (anéanties et qui seulement demourent en vouloir et désir d'amour)*. Apart from this one mystical treatise, most of our information concerning Porete comes from her inquisitorial trial, at which she was named a beguine. If she was a beguine, she was not living in a fixed community in harmony with her sisters when apprehended. In a lyric passage toward the end of her book, she laments:

> The Beguines say that I am all astray,
> and priest, and clerics, the Preachers,
> . . . Because of what I write of the being
> of Perfect Love.
> (*Mirror*, 152–53)

The fact that more manuscripts of *The Mirror* are extant in Latin, Italian, and English translations than in the original Old French is explained by the burning of her book in Valenciennes in 1306, when Porete was forbidden to disseminate it further. After continuing to circulate it with the cautious but significant endorsement of Godefroid de Fontaines (d. ca. 1309), she was imprisoned for over a year while she refused to defend herself before her Dominican inquisitor and twenty-one theologians from the University of Paris. Like Jesus, she faced her inquisitors in silence. The original Latin translation of *The Mirror* was likely made for her trial, but all extant manuscripts present an unstable text, showing signs of corruption. Although fifteen articles were lifted straight out of context from *The Mirror*, they were judged heretical, and on June 1, 1310, she was burned at the stake in Paris as a relapsed heretic. At her death, she is said to have moved the audience to tears.

Porete's treatise describes the path to union with God in seven stages, following the way of negation (*via negativa*) of the Neoplatonic tradition as reflected in the mystical theology of pseudo-Dionysius (6th century), and in terms similar to those found in the work of contemporary Flemish mystics, notably that of the Beguine Beatrice of Nazareth (fl. 1230–50). *The Mirror*'s 139 chapters in over 100 folios (ca. 60,000 words) develop an allegorized debate in which Love and Reason, among others, externalize the soul's inner psychomachia (lit., "soul struggle" in Greek). Porete's mysticism is further grounded in the Johannine principle that "God is love" (1 John 4:7–16), complemented by the famous precept "Love and do what you want" (*Dilige et quod vis fac*) of St. Augustine (13.52), Pauline Christology's placing the spirit before the law, and the refined love (*fin amor*) of the troubadours, which likewise inspired her Italian contemporary Dante Alighieri. For her part, Porete audaciously challenges the androcentric model of both the courtly love tradition and her patriarchal Christian heritage by proposing a partially feminine Trinity made up of *Dame Amour* (Lady Love), *Dame Âme* (Lady Soul), and *le gentil Loinpres* (the noble Far-Near), of which only the third person projects masculinity on to God (Müller 125).

Porete rarely cites the Bible directly; her allusions are implicit and christo-centric. For example, her exegesis of the seraphim in Isaiah's beatific vision (Isa. 6:2) as the simple soul associates the first two sets of wings with which the seraphim covers itself with the soul's inability and yet aim to know Jesus:

> With two wings she hides her face from Jesus Christ our Lord. . . . / With the next two wings she covers her feet. That is to say that the more she knows of what Jesus Christ suffered for us, the more perfectly she knows that she knows nothing of it, compared with what he did suffer for us, for he is not known except by himself alone. / With the other two wings the Soul flies . . . and she hovers, for she is always in God's sight; and she is at rest, for she dwells always in the divine will. (*Mirror*, 15)

Ultimately what the pure soul shares with the highest angels in the hierarchy is the ability to see God face-to-face (1 Cor. 13:12). Jesus is the *speculum Scripturae*, the only true "mirror," whose example of goodness and innocent suffering draws the soul back to the simple unity of God. It is precisely this privileged proximity to God, without intermediary, that renders the annihilated soul simple (cf. Müller 26, 32–43). Exemplary of such a soul are Mary Magdalene (chaps. 74, 76, 93, 124) and the Virgin Mary (chaps. 93, 126), who both found Christ within themselves, the former (confused in Porete's time with the sister of Martha) through contemplation, the latter through divine insemination.

The significance of Porete's life and *The Mirror* is still being explored. No one has yet adequately explained her apparent literacy and familiarity with traditional male theology. *The Mirror*'s allusions to an audience suggest that it was meant to be read aloud, thus rendering it accessible to the illiterate. Her trial may have provided new fodder for the backlash articulated by the Council of Vienne (1311–12) against beguines and the Free Spirit movement, but ecclesiastical prohibitions did little to dampen enthusiasm for *The Mirror*; copies of it were disseminated throughout Europe up to the seventeenth century. Disadvantaged by *not* being male, university educated, and armed with biblical proof texts, Porete's call to salvation "by faith alone" (*sola fide*), not surprisingly, earned her a more severe excommunication than that of Martin Luther.

See also Beatrice of Nazareth (ca. 1200–1268)

Bibliography

Lerner, Robert E. *The Heresy of the Free Spirit in the Later Middle Ages*. Berkeley: University of California Press, 1972.

Müller, Catherine M. *Marguerite Porete et Marguerite d'Oingt de l'autre côté du miroir*. Currents in Comparative Romance Languages and Literature 72. New York: Peter Lang, 1999.

Porete, Marguerite. *The Mirror of Simple Souls*. Translated from the French with an introductory essay by Edmund Colledge, J. C. Marler, and Judith Grant. Notre Dame, IN: University of Notre Dame Press, 1999.

———. *Speculum simplicium animarum: Le mirouer des simples âmes*. Presenting the Middle French text of the late 15th c. with Latin, in the custody and library of Paul Verdeyen, SJ. Edited and introduced by Romana Guarnieri. Corpus Christianum: Continuatio Mediaevalis 69. Turnhout: Brepols, 1986.

Verdeyen, Paul. "Le procès d'inquisition contre Marguerite Porete et Guiard de Cressonessart (1309–1310)." *Revue d'histoire ecclésiastique* 81 (1986): 47–94.

— JANET RITCH

Proba, Faltonia Betitia (ca. 320–ca. 370)

Proba, the author of *Cento Virgilianus*, is generally identified with Faltonia Betitia Proba, who was born to a distinguished Roman family. From the *Cento* we learn that the author was named Proba (line 12); that she had written an earlier poem on a military campaign (3–8, 47–49), usually identified with that of Constantius and Magnentius in 353 CE; and that she was married, had children, and hoped for grandchildren (lines 689–94). Her familiarity with Virgil (which indicates that she had had a traditional classical education) and her change of poetic subject from war to the Bible suggest that she became a Christian as an adult.

A cento is a patchwork of lines and half lines from a poet, combined so as to be different in content and sometimes in tone from the original (Meconi). It was not exclusively a Christian genre, nor did Proba invent it. But Proba's is the earliest example of a Christian cento, and she is the earliest known female Christian poet.

Proba's cento consists of 694 lines composed of lines and half lines from Virgil. She begins by renouncing previous war themes and praying that the Holy Spirit will assist her (1–55). The presence of sin in the world and the need for a savior is developed through creation, fall, and flood (56–317). The rest of the Old Testament receives sketchy treatment (318–32); the life of Christ occupies more than half the poem (346–688) and is introduced (333–45) by the announcement of a "greater work" (*maius opus*). Proba personalizes her poem by thanking Christ for removing her "hardened stain [*concretam labem*]" and promising to follow him through fire, exile, misfortune, and "a thousand flying darts" (415–27).

Proba calls herself *vates*, Latin for both "poet" of lofty poetry (not a mere versifier) and "prophet" (line 12). She prays not to the classical muses but to the one true God, asking to be inspired like an Old Testament prophet.

A possible spur to composition was the decree of the Roman emperor Julian (the Apostate) who in 362 forbade Christians to teach in schools. (This suggests a date of composition for the cento later than 362.) Even after Julian's death in 363, it has been argued that continuing concern for the education of children of Christian parents would have made the cento valuable. It introduces children to Virgilian language and meter without the elements of betrayal and immorality unsuitable for young minds (Clark and Hatch 99–100). Her cento was read and used as a school text for generations and was highly regarded; she was the only woman to be named among the illustrious men of the church (*inter viros ecclesiasticos*) by the seventh-century biographer Isidore of Seville (*De viris illustribus* 22 [18]; Clark and Hatch 97–98). The manuscript copies and early printed texts show that the cento continued to be widely known until at least the end of the eighteenth century (Stevenson 532–35).

Her poem was not universally admired. Jerome (*Letter* 53.7) is assumed to mean Proba when he refers slightingly to a "chatty old woman" (*garula anus*) who presumed to teach the Bible. He criticizes those who call Virgil a Christian because some of his lines could be applied to Christ and God, giving as examples lines found in Proba's *Cento*.

In the *Cento*, Eve is cast as the temptress, made more dangerous by her entitlement as Adam's wife. Adam takes Eve by her right hand (a sign of Roman marriage) to signify that they are husband and wife and embraces her, a more physical response than the Genesis account (line 135). When Eve offers the fruit to Adam, the serpent encourages her, "You are his wife. It is right for you to test his will by pleading" (194; Clark and Hatch 35); Eve then uses her wiles, appealing to her husband "with sudden sweetness" (line 205). Though the woman is not made subject to the man as God's punishment for her disobedience, in general Proba aligns Eve with Virgilian female figures of evil (Clark and Hatch 153–54).

Mary, who was often contrasted with Eve in patristic writings, is unremarkable in the *Cento*. She is a "virgin" (line 341), in acknowledgment of Christ's miraculous birth, and Joseph is absent. The child is the center of the narrative, but a spotlight rests briefly on Mary when, juxtaposed with the horrendous slaughter of the innocents, "under the beams of the narrow roof, she nursed her son, bringing her breasts to his tender lips" (375–76), a scene that has no counterpart in the New Testament but will be picked up by later writers. This may reflect Proba's own experience of the protective tranquility of nursing mother and baby.

Proba crossed cultures between the Bible and the classical world and presented Bible material in a classical meter and language to enrich the education of Christians. It is easy to underestimate the skill involved in weaving Virgilian lines into a narrative, particularly when these lines bring with them a memory of their original context and color the narrative.

Bibliography

Clark, Elizabeth A., and Diane F. Hatch. *The Golden Bough, the Oaken Cross: The Virgilian Cento of Faltonia Betitia Proba.* Pages 12–94 present the Latin text and English trans. Chico, CA: Scholars Press, 1981. The Latin text is from *Poetae christiani minores*, edited by Michael Petschenig, Karl Schenkl, et al. Corpus scriptorum ecclesiasticorum Latinorum 16. Vienna: Tempsky, 1888.

Disse, Dorothy. http://home.infionline.net/~ddisse/proba.html. This website (maintained by Dorothy Disse) includes an article on Proba, "That I May Find All Mysteries within My Power to Relate," and an annotated bibliography.

Green, Roger P. H. "Proba's Cento: Its Date, Purpose, and Reception." *Classical Quarterly* 45, no. 2 (1995): 551–63.

———. "Proba's Introduction to Her Cento." *Classical Quarterly* 47, no. 2 (1997): 548–59.

Matthews, John F. "The Poetess Proba and Fourth-Century Rome: Questions of Interpretation." Pages 227–304 in *Institutions, société et vie politique dans l'Empire romain au IVe siècle ap. J.-C.*, edited by Michel Christol. Rome: École Française de Rome, 1992.

Meconi, David Vincent. "The Christian Cento and the Evangelization of Christian Culture." *Logos: A Journal of Catholic Thought and Culture* 7, no. 4 (2004): 109–32.

Pavlovskis, Zoja. "Proba and the Semiotics of Virgilian Narrative." *Vergilius* 35 (1989): 70–84.

Schnapp, Jeffrey. "Reading Lessons: Augustine, Proba, and the Christian Détournement of Antiquity." *Stanford Literature Review* 9 (1992): 99–124.

Stevenson, Jane. "Proba." Pages 64–71 in *Women Latin Poets: Language, Gender, and Authority, from Antiquity to the Eighteenth Century*. Oxford: Oxford University Press, 2005.

—M. Eleanor Irwin

■ Pulci, Antonia (1452/54–1501)

Antonia Pulci was the daughter of Francesco d'Antonio Tanini, a Florentine merchant, and Jacopa Torelli, his Roman wife. She was perhaps educated at home; her mother was literate. Antonia probably learned to write poetry only after marrying Bernardo Pulci, a poet and member of a family of prominent writers. He and his brothers Luigi and Luca belonged to the circle of poets and scholars who frequented the household of Lorenzo de' Medici and enjoyed Medici patronage. Antonia, like her husband, was the author of *sacre rappresentazioni*, one-act miracle and mystery plays, written in verse (octaves). She wrote at least three plays on biblical subjects: the *Play of the Prodigal Son*, the *Play of the Destruction of Saul and the Lament of David*, and a *Play of Joseph, Son of Jacob* (this play has not been identified). Her other known plays are hagiographical and treat the lives of the virgin martyr St. Domitilla; St. Guglielma, a wife and queen, falsely accused but eventually vindicated; and St. Francis of Assisi. Her work was clearly influenced by that of members of the Pulci family. Lorenzo de' Medici's mother—Lucrezia Tornabuoni, a patron of Luigi Pulci and author of biblical stories in verse on Judith, Esther, Susanna, John the Baptist, and Tobias—may also have been an inspiration to her. Antonia's plays were published during her lifetime and again often throughout the sixteenth and seventeenth centuries. Widowed in 1488, she became a nun and founded the convent of Santa Maria della Misericordia.

The *Play of the Prodigal Son* (*Rappresentazione del figliuol prodigo*) was probably one of the first she wrote, since her text closely follows that of an earlier play written by Piero di Mariano Muzi, and both vary little from the biblical parable (Luke 15:11–32). Her innovations consist of an opening scene in which the prodigal son plays cards and loses money to a bad companion, a foreshadowing of his future misfortunes, a lively opening to the play that demonstrates Antonia's talent for engaging her audience through believable contemporary scenes and conversation. She also lengthens the episode in which the prodigal son encounters the seven vices, only an octave in Muzi's play, but seven octaves in Pulci's. Finally, she gives a more believable rendering to the relationships among family members. While in Muzi's version the prodigal son is rude, his father angry, his brother unforgiving, Pulci's version has a loving family: the father is sorry to see his son leave and worries for him, the elder son first resents but then welcomes his reformed brother, and the returned prodigal son expresses remorse, humility, and gratitude. In both plays the religious message, proclaimed in the conclusion, is, "Repent and you will be forgiven; humble yourself and you will be exalted in heaven."

In the *Play of the Destruction of Saul and the Lament of David* (*Distruzione di Saul e il pianto di Davit*), Pulci's treatment of the death of Saul and his sons in their war with the Philistines and of David's sorrow and his punishment of the wayfarer who brings him the news (1 Sam. 31; 1 Chron. 10:10, 13–14; 2 Sam. 1) shows that she is a quite original interpreter of the biblical account. She gives the story an unusual connection with the present by identifying the Philistines as Turks, the enemy of Christendom in the fifteenth and sixteenth centuries, especially feared in the 1480s, when she was writing, since they had recently besieged and destroyed the city of Otranto in southern Italy. Her depiction of the court of the Philistine king, with its barons, queen, and ladies-in-waiting, is reminiscent of medieval romance literature and is also anachronistic. These transformations of the story are clearly meant to bring the Old Testament account closer to the experience of her Florentine audience. There is also an episode of her invention that stages the martyrdom of Saul's widow, a portrait of female heroism. This character, only a name in the biblical account, is given prominence in the play equal to that of Saul and of David. Saul's widow is interrogated by the Philistine king, who wants her to reveal her husband's whereabouts; neither knows at this point that Saul has died. There is lively repartee in which the widow holds her own against the king; she is condemned and taken to be hanged by her hair and beaten until she dies. The invention of this episode seems to be another appeal to the author's contemporaries, for whom the stories of female martyrs were especially popular theatrical subjects at the time. It also reflects her interest, revealed in other plays as well, in portraying women, such as Domatilla and

Guglielma. Even in the *Play of St. Francis*, she includes among the very few episodes of the saint's life his deathbed encounter with the Roman woman Jacopa (da Settesoli), undoubtedly homage to her own mother. Finally, it seems that with three of her plays Pulci intends to present the three canonical statuses of women, the virgin (Domitilla), the wife (Guglielma), and in this play the widow; and she proposes her heroines as models of religious faith for the women in her audience at performances in churches and local convents.

Pulci's plays are still read, especially two of them: the *Play of St. Guglielma*, which is included in the two major anthologies of *sacre rappresentazioni*; and the *Play of St. Francis*, largely because of the fascination, even today, with the figure of St. Francis of Assisi. Recently scholars have expressed interest in Pulci's work: there have been two dissertations devoted to her, and there has just appeared a bilingual edition of her collected plays.

See also Tornabuoni, Lucrezia (ca. 1427–82)

Bibliography

Pulci, Antonia. *Saints' Lives and Bible Stories for the Stage*. Edited by Elissa B. Weaver. Translated by James Wyatt Cook. Toronto: Toronto Centre for Reformation and Renaissance, 2010.

Weaver, Elissa. "Antonia Pulci (c. 1452–1501), the First Published Woman Playwright." Pages 75–85 in *Teaching Religious Women Writers*, edited by Albert Rabil Jr. and Margaret King. Chicago: University of Chicago Press, 2007.

———. "Antonia Tanini (1452–1501), Playwright, and Wife of Bernardo Pulci (1438–88)." Pages 23–37 in *Essays in Honor of Marga Cottino-Jones*, edited by Laura White, Andrea Fedi, and Kristin Phillips. Florence: Cadmo, 2003.

—ELISSA B. WEAVER

Ramabai, Pandita (1858–1922)

Ramabai Dongre was born into an orthodox Brahmin family near Mangalore, in southwestern India. Unusual at that time, Ramabai's father firmly believed in women's education, so at the age of eight Ramabai began to memorize and learn prodigious amounts of Sanskrit texts. The family made its living as *puranikas*, Sanskrit specialists who traveled extensively around the country reciting, reading, and expounding on Hindu scriptures. When Ramabai was sixteen, a severe famine claimed the lives of most of her family, forcing her and her brother to wander all over India in poverty. They ended up in Calcutta in 1878, where Hindu priests and other scholars were astounded at her learning and quickly proclaimed her "Pandita," or Teacher, and then "Saraswati," the Goddess of Learning. However, due to the hardships she had experienced, her faith in her inherited religion grew cold (Kosambi 302). Sponsored by Anglican nuns, who had given her English lessons in Pune, at the age of twenty-five she went as a young widow with an infant daughter to England for further studies, and four months after her arrival she and her daughter were baptized as Christians.

After six years in England and the United States, Ramabai returned to India. First in Mumbai, then in Pune, and finally in a village named Kedgaon, she established institutions for sheltering and promoting the welfare of Indian girls and women. A Pentecostal revival occurred in her Mukti Mission—literally, "Salvation Mission"—in Kedgaon in 1905. That same year Ramabai began work on translating the Bible from the original languages into Marathi, the language used in her region of India. She had studied Greek and Hebrew in England, and she renewed her study of these languages in Kedgaon (Sengupta 295). She also planned to produce Hebrew and Greek vocabularies and grammars, interlinear English translations, and a Bible commentary (Ramabai, quoted in Adhav 199). This project became the great consuming work of her life until she died. While she did finish the Marathi translation of the Bible with assistance from various Indians and foreigners, her other work was only partially completed.

Ramabai is rather unique in that she had been a professional reciter and interpreter of scriptures since childhood. First she first dealt with Hindu texts, and much later with the Bible. In her writings, two general reasons surface for the production of a new Bible translation and of biblical interpretive tools. The first is that she sees the Bible as providing an alternative worldview to the dominant one propounded by Hinduism. She avers that Hindu scriptures provide the rationale for oppressing women and low-castes and out-castes; do not produce morality; are blatantly false; encourage idolatry; and encourage rote recitation of scripture rather than a right relationship with God ("Religious Consciousness"). The Bible, however, provides a different consciousness, a different philosophy for the Indian people, one that is spiritually and socially liberative. For this reason, she objects to the contemporary Marathi Bible produced by the Bible Society, which used Sanskrit terminology; she insisted on producing her own Bible translation, employing Marathi words of her own choice. For example, she criticizes the Bible Society's choice of a word for "created" in Gen. 1:1, because it means "begotten or produced" and refers to the union of the "Supreme Being *Brahman*" with "*Maya*, a coeternal female deity," who "begat of her a golden egg, of the same substance as *Brahman* [and] called Brahmand." The maker of all of creation was hatched from this egg, "and he made all things out of the same substance as himself. . . . So then all creation, being of the same substance as *Brahman*, is the manifestation of the Brahman, and can therefore be worshiped as God. This teaching is at the root of all idolatry" ("Vernaculars of India," 6). For Ramabai, the biblical worldview is opposed to the Vedic worldview, and a translation is itself an interpretation of the world and humans' place in it.

The second reason for Ramabai's biblical work is her belief that the Bible is meant for the ordinary people of India. One of the problems of the Marathi

Bibles of the day, she argues, is that they use a very sophisticated language, full of Sanskrit, Persian, and Arabic words understood only by scholars: "The object of translating the Bible in [the] vernacular is that it may be understood by all, and all may be enlightened by it and find the way of Salvation. . . . The common men, women and children, especially those living in villages, should have the Bible given them in the language which they will easily understand" (Ramabai, quoted in Adhav 201).Thus she produced her own simple translation, along with hermeneutical and exegetical tools to interpret that translation—for Bible women, preachers, and catechists with an elementary education who were working with common people, mostly those in villages. "The object of the work is to give help to Bible-women, catechists and preachers, who have very elementary and ordinary education," she explains. "The study of the Bible becomes very difficult and tedious without the help of a commentary, a good concordance and references" (Ramabai, quoted in Adhav 200). Thus when Ramabai died, her life had come full circle: once again, she was an interpreter of Scripture for the Indian masses who were seeking salvation.

Bibliography

Adhav, Shamsundar Manohar. *Pandita Ramabai: Introduced by Shamsundar Manohar Adhav*. Madras: Christian Literature Society, 1979.

Frykenberg, Robert Eric. "Pandita Ramabai Saraswati: A Biographical Introduction." Pages 1–54 in *Pandita Ramabai, Pandita Ramabai's America*, edited by Robert Eric Frykenberg and translated by Kshitija Gomes. Grand Rapids: Eerdmans, 2003.

Kosambi, Meera, ed. and trans. *Pandita Ramabai through Her Own Words: Selected Works*. New Delhi: Oxford University Press, 2000.

Ramabai, Pandita. "The Holy Bible in the Vernaculars of India." In *Mukti Prayer-Bell* 4, no. 3 (Nov. 1909): 4–15.

———. "Religious Consciousness of the Hindus." *Mukti Prayer-Bell* 3, no. 3 (Jan. 1907): 26–30; no. 4 (Sept. 1907): 24–40.

Sengupta, Padmini. *Pandita Ramabai Saraswati*. New York: Asia Pub. House, 1970.

— Arun Jones

Roberts, R. (ca. 1728–88)

Although neither her first name nor the details of her life are known, Roberts, a sermon writer, translator, and poet, likely lived in Gloucester or Bristol in England, two cities her father was associated with. She may have known Hannah More and her circle: a niece, Margaret, was More's literary executor, while Margaret's brother William produced a four-volume encomium on More's life (1834). The bulk of Roberts's literary output consists of translations from French of works by Marmontel, Millot, de Graffigny, and de la Villette, and of moral tales in verse, some of which were intended for the stage.

Roberts's exegetical contribution is limited to a single volume titled *Sermons Written by a Lady, the Translatress of Four Select Tales from Marmontel*

(London, 1770; reissued as *Seven Rational Sermons* in Philadelphia, 1777). She reports the specific occasion of her writing as a challenge from a clergyman of her acquaintance that "he would preach any sermon which I would write. An agreement was made, and I sat down to compose" (iii–iv). Roberts defends her work by contending that when most contemporary preaching concerns politics and *public* virtue, "it is no wonder that a Woman should take the lower department, and write moral essays" (xi). In keeping with this assessment, the bulk of her sermons concern what Roberts terms "a steady adherence to Christian virtue" (36), inspired by a conviction that "religion is the base on which all virtue is built" (139) and "the best stock on which to engraft the moral virtues" (142).

Most of the seven homilies begin with a consideration of the biblical text. The first, citing Matt. 19:24, appeals to narrative and historical context (the circumstances of the rich young ruler), then quotes ancillary texts both directly and indirectly to support her argument. Sermon 2 concerns Matt. 6:15, on forgiveness: its argument is chiefly ethical and theological, appealing for imitation of Jesus's example, and again adducing Scripture (e.g., "Vengeance is mine, I will repay"; Rom. 12:19) as support rather than expounding details of the primary text. Sermon 3 sets Job 19:26 in its narrative context, quoting, conflating, and explaining related passages (e.g., 19:25, "I know that my Redeemer liveth"). Job serves as moral exemplar, directing the attention of the reader toward eternal consolations and drawing into consideration additional passages on the same topic. Sermon 4, on Prov. 14:13, begins by discussing the intent of the biblical author, evaluating it in context and by comparison with Eccles. 2:2, before turning to a thematic treatment of "recreation" and the service of God. Sermon 5, on Matt. 7:1 ("Judge not, that ye be not judged"), was commended in its day for its eloquent (and pointed) defense of fallen women:

> Surely I may be pardoned when I say that, among those unhappy females, who by one false step have for ever forfeited any claim to the world's good opinion of their past or future actions, there are some who, had they not been possessed of the most amiable qualities that can adorn the mind, would never have fallen. Tenderness of disposition, attachment, an open unreserved confidence, an unsuspecting innocence, have been the sources of that fatal error, which has unfitted them for chaste society, and made them the scorn of those who have either escaped through want of solicitation, or owed their preservation to the frigidity of their constitutions, and the prudent selfishness of their hearts. (103–4)

Elsewhere the sermon's biblical content serves primarily to buttress and illustrate its thematic argument. Of the two concluding sermons (on Exod. 20:12 and Prov. 22:6, respectively), Roberts writes, "Having already treated on the subject of the duty owing from children to parents, I proceed, in the next place, to explain what I think is the real duty from parents to children"

(137). Although without benefit of direct exegesis, both articulate a generally biblical and natural theology ("the great law of Nature," 115) concerning filial duty and parental obligation. The concluding sermon in particular addresses the question of appropriate education for girls and young women:

> I am far from thinking that women should be taught no kind of literature, or believing they will make worse mistresses of families for having more learning than their cookmaid: on the contrary, I think they are the fitter for the office, as I imagine every man of sense will wish his wife to be not merely a domestic, but a friend and companion; for which reason I would recommend such studies as tend to enlarge the understanding, improve the ideas, and entertain the soul with the beauties of nature and virtue. (155–56)

While rooted in orthodox theological convictions, Roberts's interpretive method assumes that Scripture, natural law, and (for the most part) contemporary social mores are of one voice on questions of both private and public virtue. Scriptural interpretation serves this end, although without neglecting authorial purpose, narrative context, and historical setting.

See also More, Hannah (1745–1833)

Bibliography

Rizzo, Betty. "Roberts, R." Page 269 in *A Dictionary of British and American Women Writers, 1660–1800*, edited by Janet Todd. Totowa, NJ: Rowman & Allan Held, 1985.

Roberts, R. *Sermons Written by a Lady, the Translatress of Four Select Tales from Marmontel*. London: J. Dodsley, 1770. Reissued as *Seven Rational Sermons*. Philadelphia: Robert Bell, 1777. Eighteenth Century Collections Online. Gale Group. http://galenet.galegroup.com/servlet/ECCO. Gale Document Number: CW3318335123.

Sherbo, Arthur. "Roberts, R. (c. 1728–1788)." Pages 180–81 in vol. 47 of *Oxford Dictionary of National Biography*, edited by H. C. G. Matthew and Brian Harrison. Rev. ed. Oxford: Oxford University Press, 2004–11.

— MICHAEL P. KNOWLES

Roper, Margaret More (1505–44)

Margaret More was born to Sir Thomas More and his wife, Joanna, in 1505, and lived to become one of sixteenth-century Europe's foremost learned women, the "ornament of Britain," according to Erasmus (quoted in Lamb 90). Although most of her writings have been lost to time—including poems, Latin speeches, letters, translations of patristic writings, and a treatise on the *Four Last Things*—her two most well-known surviving works are indicative of the two enduring aspects of her life and reputation: her remarkable and exemplary humanist scholarship, and her close relationship with her father. These works consist of an English translation, published anonymously in 1524, of the More family friend and correspondent Erasmus's *Precatio dominica* and a lengthy letter to her stepsister detailing, in a dialogue, her failed attempt to convince her father to take the Oath of Succession (1534) and save himself from execution. Roper's intellectual achievement was made possible by her father's firm conviction that a humanist education was beneficial for both sons and daughters. For his household school, where often the female pupils outnumbered the male, More recruited the top tutors, and all his children were schooled in Greek and Latin, the writings of the patristics, philosophy, theology, geometry, arithmetic, and astronomy.

The method and the success of More's home school were clear. Upon receiving letters written to him in 1521 by Roper and her fellow students (which now included her new husband, William Roper), Erasmus praised the pupils' proficiency and the achievement of More's school in a letter to Guillaume Budé: "I never saw anything so admirable. In what they said there was nothing foolish or childish. . . . There you never see one of the girls idle, or busied with the trifles that women enjoy; they have a Livy in their hands. They have made such progress that they can read and understand authors of that class without anyone to explain them, unless they come upon some word that might have held up even me" (Erasmus 8:296).

Erasmus's affectionate letter details how Roper became capable of tackling, three years later, a translation of his *Precatio dominica*. Around the same time that she translated Erasmus's devotional treatise, Roper was also working through Erasmus's edition of St. Cyprian: she not only noticed but also solved a typographical error, overlooked by Erasmus, which rendered a particular sentence nonsensical. She also determined that the letter was not St. Cyprian's at all, but rather composed by Novatian (Guy 141–42). Erasmus had surmised that Roper could be stumped only by "some word that might have held up even me," but Roper was actually able to elucidate thorny transcription errors that eluded even Erasmus himself. Roper's proficiency in Latin was honed by a pedagogical method of translation from Latin to English and back to Latin again, and much of Roper's highly praised individual style emerged from this emphasis on mastering the parameters of prose composition for two distinct languages.

That Roper published her translation at all is the first surprising and remarkable fact about her as an interpreter of Scripture. In a letter written to her a year before her publication of *A Deuoute* (Devout) *Treatise*, More praised her: being "content with the profit and pleasure of the conscience, in your modesty you do not seek for the praise of the public, nor value it overmuch even if you receive it, but because of the great love you bear us, you regard us—your husband and myself—as a sufficiently large circle of readers for all that you write" (quoted in Lamb 84). Something evidently later changed in More's attitude. Perhaps it was the wholly positive and amazed reaction he received from colleagues whenever he happened to show them a composition of his daughter's.

421

Perhaps, as Lamb suggests, the publicizing of Roper as a virtuous learned woman "served a larger humanist project: to gain access to the power of the king by displacing an aristocratic elite legitimated by wealth with a humanist elite legitimated by learning" (84). Roper's published translation was one of several of her appearances in print: Erasmus included an ornate dedication to Roper in his *Commentary on the Christmas Hymn of Prudentius* (1523) and also modeled the character of Magdalia after her, in his colloquy "The Abbot and the Learned Lady." Goodrich suggests that the translation had political significance, particularly in the context of the early years of the Reformation. Perhaps the title page's anonymous authorial attribution to "a young, virtuous, and well learned gentlewoman of nineteen year of age" sufficiently concealed Roper's identity. Or perhaps Roper's decision to translate Erasmus's work was due to the inclusion of Erasmus, through mutual familial affection, into the "circle" More imagined as a sufficient audience for his daughter's work.

For a female translator, particularly in the early sixteenth century, the decision of what to translate was as much an interpretive act as any changes she made to the original source in the process of translation. Erasmus's *Precatio dominica*, published in 1523, is a multifaceted text. On one level it is a commentary on the Lord's Prayer, a scholarly exercise of catechetical explanation and interpretation. On another level, however, it is an expansion of the Lord's Prayer itself, a devotional work divided into seven prayers for seven days, and meant to be used itself as a prayer book. As a published female translator, Roper had few antecedents, the most well-known one being Lady Margaret Beaufort. Unlike Beaufort, Roper was young, largely unknown, and, since she did not belong to the royal family, her credibility was established by her virtue, her academic accomplishments, and her father's reputation. Yet like Beaufort, Roper's choice to translate a devotional text from Latin to English made the text available to a significantly wider readership, including women and those unschooled in Latin.

Roper follows Erasmus's organizational structure and content, with a number of noteworthy alterations. She demonstrates particular skill in embellishing, amplifying, condensing, and intensifying Erasmus's original text into readable English, often in accordance with what Erasmus outlines as principles for effective prose, in his *De copia*, a handbook for composition. She often doubles what were originally single nouns or adjectives: for example, "terrible and fearful" for Erasmus's "*timoris* [fear]," or "diseases and sickness" for "*morbis* [diseases]" (C1r, C4r). Such amplifications, as Verbrugge observes, were advocated by Erasmus in *De copia* "not only for the writing of general compositions but also for the translation of foreign languages" (40). Demers notes that "Roper's most successful expansions are those which reinforce the scriptural foundations of Erasmus's commentary" (5), and she cites as an example Erasmus's "Accordingly, it is shameful now for any one of us to prefer our will to yours" (69.69), rendered by Roper as

"So that then needs must man be ashamed to prefer and set forth his own will if Christ our master was content to cast his own will away and subdue it to thine" (E1r). Roper expands the original "with an additional subordinate clause that emphasizes the Biblical example" (Demers 5). In "a sensitive rethinking of the Latin in the light of her native English," Roper frequently translates the same Latin word differently to fit the context (McCutcheon 663). She also recognizes that she was writing for an English audience, and occasionally she deviates from Erasmus's text in order to make any obscure terms clear: for instance, "*Abba pater*, which in English is as much to say as O father father" (B4v; see Verbrugge 39). This passage is also an example of Roper's tendency to intensify vocatives and nouns (see McCutcheon 665). In this intensification, a single word is often made superlative: for example, Erasmus's "*filii tui corpus* [body of your son]" becomes "the most holy body of thy son" (B4v). Such amplifications are particularly noteworthy when they occur with respect to God as Father. When Roper expands "father" into "good father" (for example, E3v), she almost gives the sense as if she were "writing to or talking with her own father" (McCutcheon 665). This personal voice appears also in Roper's addition of "our": "*patre spirituum* [spiritual father]" becomes "our spiritual father" (E3r). Roper subtly reinterprets Erasmus's original by augmenting and intensifying the familial aspects of the Lord's Prayer, "magnif[ying] states of feeling and relationships, heightening them emotionally and making them more overt and more personal" (McCutcheon 665). Such changes reveal Roper not only as a proficient translator but also as an independent interpretive voice.

Roper's translation was popular—A Deuoute Treatise Upon the Pater Noster was issued in 1524, 1526, and 1531—but instead of the qualities of her translation being praised on their own merits, the text was read as an argument in favor of educating women, and Roper herself was held up as an exemplar for the humanist learned woman. Roper's *Deuoute Treatise* appeared at a time when there was a fierce debate in England and the Continent over whether women should be educated (see Beilin 3–15). Yet even as Roper stood for an exemplar of female learning in Richard Hyrde's preface to her translation, his fierce support of education for women never ventured so far as to suggest that women could serve as biblical interpreters: he recognized them only as readers and translators. Yet Roper's *Deuoute Treatise* balances on this thin fulcrum between public and private, speaking and silence. Her identity was only partially concealed by Hyrde's attribution of the work to a learned nineteen-year-old girl; the dedication to Roper's cousin Frances Staverton, and his mention of Staverton's education "among your honourable uncle's children" (B2r), would have revealed Roper's identity to anyone with even passing knowledge of More, one of Henry VIII's closest advisers. Roper's translation demonstrates how, while faithfully working within such strictures, learned women during the early modern period could craft and shape their own voice.

The last word on Roper as a biblical interpreter should be with respect to her relationship with her father. It was from More that readers learn of Roper's proficiency in composing the now-lost work on the *Four Last Things*: as an observer noted, More insisted "most solemnly that the treatise of his daughter was in no way inferior to his own" (quoted in Guy 73). What does remain of Roper's writings is a letter from 1534, likely written by her (although authorship is highly debated), in which she records her attempt to convince her father to save himself from execution at the hands of his former close ally, Henry VIII. While the letter is a reminder that, as More's daughter, Roper lived at the forefront of Henry VIII's tumultuous reign, it also shows that all of Roper's education in theology, logic, and rhetoric converged and focused at the end of her father's career in an effort to preserve his life. Roper urged More to follow the example of "so many so good men and so well learned" who already took the oath, and that "since it is also by a law made by the parliament commanded, they think that you be upon the peril of your soul, bounden to change and reform your conscience, and confirm your own, as I said, to other men's" (More 524). After More's execution in 1535, Roper devoted herself to preserving his legacy and writings; within her own family, she educated her own children with the lessons she had been taught. Her eldest daughter, Mary Roper Basset, became a noteworthy translator in her own right, producing English versions of Eusebius's *Ecclesiastical History* and her grandfather More's *History of the Passion*.

In the history of feminist scholarship, Roper has not received enough critical attention due largely to a view that she deferentially played the role of dutiful daughter to her powerful and at times overbearing father. Yet scholars have recently argued that to recognize the significance of Roper's writings, one must first recognize how they contested the boundary between private and public and read them with a more nuanced consideration of what she achieved in the context of the opportunities available to non-noblewomen in the first decades of the sixteenth century.

See also Beaufort, Margaret (1443–1509)

Bibliography

Beilin, Elaine V. *Redeeming Eve: Women Writers of the English Renaissance*. Princeton, NJ: Princeton University Press, 1987.

Demers, Patricia. "Margaret Roper and Erasmus: The Relationship of Translator and Source." *Women Writing and Reading* 1, no. 1 (Spring 2005): 3–8.

Erasmus, Desiderius. *The Collected Works of Erasmus*. Edited by William Barker et al. 84 vols. Toronto: University of Toronto Press, 1974–.

Goodrich, Jaime. "Thomas More and Margaret More Roper: A Case for Rethinking Women's Participation in the Early Modern Public Sphere." *Sixteenth Century Journal* 39, no. 4 (Winter 2008): 1021–40.

Guy, John. *A Daughter's Love: Thomas More and His Dearest Meg.* Boston: Houghton Mifflin Harcourt, 2009.

Lamb, Mary Ellen. "Margaret Roper, the Humanist Political Project, and the Problem of Agency." Pages 83–108 in *Opening the Borders: Inclusivity in Early Modern Studies; Essays in Honor of James V. Mirollo*, edited by Peter C. Herman. Newark: University of Delaware Press, 1999.

McCutcheon, Elizabeth. "Margaret More Roper's Translation of Erasmus' *Precatio dominica*." Pages 659–66 in *Acta conventus neo-latini Guelpherbytana: Proceedings of the Sixth International Congress of Neo-Latin Studies; Wolfenbüttel 12 August to 16 August 1985*, edited by Stella Revard and Fidel Rädle. Binghamton, NY: Center for Medieval and Early Renaissance Studies, SUNY, 1988.

More, Sir Thomas. *The Correspondence of Sir Thomas More.* Edited by Elizabeth Frances Rogers. Princeton, NJ: Princeton University Press, 1947.

Roper, Margaret More. *A Deuoute Treatise Upon the Pater Noster.* London: Thomas Berthelet, 1526. Short-Title Catalogue 10477.

Verbrugge, Rita M. "Margaret More Roper's Personal Expression in the Devout Treatise upon the Pater Noster." Pages 30–42 in *Silent but for the Word: Tudor Women as Patrons, Translators, and Writers of Religious Works*, edited by Margaret Patterson Hannay. Kent, OH: Kent State University Press, 1985.

— MEREDITH DONALDSON CLARK

Rossetti, Christina Georgina (1830–94)

Christina Rossetti was born in London on December 5, 1830. By the time of her death in December 1894 she was recognized as one of the century's most important poets. Memorial tributes stressed her importance as a religious voice in what was beginning to be described as an age of doubt. Throughout her life, her poetry reflected her Christian beliefs, often employing the language of Scripture. In 1874 she began contributing to the field of biblical study with the publication of *Annus Domini: A Prayer for Each Day of the Year, Founded on a Text of Holy Scripture.* Five more devotional books followed: *Seek and Find: A Double Series of Short Studies of the Benedicite* (1879); *Called to be Saints: The Minor Festivals Devotionally Studied* (1881); *Letter and Spirit: Notes on the Commandments* (1883); *Time Flies: A Reading Diary*, the most personal of these works (1885); and her most ambitious work, *The Face of the Deep: A Devotional Commentary on the Apocalypse* (1892). In three of these volumes she mingles devotional poetry with prose commentary. In 1893, Rossetti gathered these poems into one volume, arranging them under biblical headings. This volume, simply titled *Verses*, published not long before her death from breast cancer, can be read as a series of religious meditations, telling a story of spiritual pilgrimage.

Rossetti was the youngest of four children born to Gabriele Rossetti, an Italian poet and political exile, and his wife, Frances (née Polidori), a governess of English and Italian descent. Both parents encouraged their children to engage in literary and artistic endeavors. The eldest, Maria Francesca, became known for her work on Dante's *Divine Comedy*. Rossetti's two brothers were important figures in the Pre-Raphaelite Movement. Gabriel Dante (later Dante Gabriel) became one of its leading poets and painters. William Michael served as its historian, becoming a literary critic in his own right. While Rossetti's development as a poet should be viewed within the context of the whole of this talented family, it was the women who most influenced her religious development. Although Rossetti's father had been raised as Roman Catholic, in matters of religion he deferred to his wife, a devout member of the Church of England. Along with her mother, sister, and two maternal aunts, Rossetti became involved in the religious life of the Anglican Church. Influenced by the Oxford movement, they associated themselves with practices and beliefs of the High Church. For example, they supported the establishment of religious sisterhoods. In 1875 Maria became a fully professed sister of All Saints' Sisterhood.

In the preface to *The Face of the Deep*, Rossetti refers to a "dear saint," identified as Maria, who once pointed out to her that patience was the lesson in the book of Revelation. Clearly the sisters engaged in biblical study together; however, it was Rossetti's mother who most shaped her faith. Not only was Rossetti educated at home by her mother, but until her mother's death in 1886 she was hardly ever separated from her. Rossetti often dedicated her books, both poetry and prose, to her mother. This loving relationship had a strong influence on Rossetti's understanding of divine love. In a letter to her friend Caroline Gemmer, Rossetti writes, "Mother's love patient, forgiving, all-outlasting, cannot but be the copy & pledge of Love all-transcending" (*Letters*, 2:40).

Despite this reverence for her mother, Rossetti did not see becoming a wife and mother as necessary for a woman to find fulfillment. Contrary to the prevailing cultural views of her time, she did not elevate the wife over the unmarried woman. In *Letter and Spirit*, she argues that these "contrasting figures" both represent holy estates, for the virginal heart has "Her Maker as her husband" (91). Associating the virgin with the First Commandment, and the wife with the Second, Rossetti cautions the wife not to worship the creature more than her Creator. Indeed, the thematic thread that unifies these notes on the Ten Commandments is love of God: the filial love owed to God comes before all else.

While Rossetti's views on marriage might be seen as liberal for her time, her views on female suffrage were conservative. Finding in Genesis evidence that in this world men and women are assigned different roles, she does not support parliamentary votes for women. A woman need not marry, but she is nevertheless to serve as a "helpmeet" in society. Although Rossetti considers the days of creation as possibly representing vast stretches of time, she views Eve as an actual historical person, who diverts her mind from God. As a consequence, "Eve's lapse" means that "weakness and shame devolved on woman as her characteristics, in a manner special to herself and unlike the corresponding heritage of man" (*Face of the Deep*, 310). Rossetti's depictions of Eve, however, are always sympathetic. For example, observing that at the foot of the cross Mary Magdalene stands beside the Virgin Mary, Rossetti expresses her hope that "amongst all saints of all time will stand before the Throne, Eve the beloved first Mother of us all" (310–11). For Rossetti, Eve is always "our mother." One of her most sympathetic depictions of Eve can be found in her poem "Eve," in which the first mother appears as grieving over the body of Abel and blaming herself, not Cain, for his death. For Rossetti, Eve is never the seductive temptress.

Although Rossetti depicts Eve sympathetically, she follows the tradition of highlighting Eve's weaknesses by contrasting her with the mother of Jesus: Eve exhibits "disbelief and disobedience," while Mary displays "faith and submission" (*Face of the Deep*, 310). Yet Rossetti's depictions of Mary are always measured in their praise. After affirming a belief in the perpetual virginity of Mary, Rossetti reminds her readers that the Virgin Mother is a "shut gate, not a gate of access: Christ is our open door" (*Called to be Saints*, 181). Rossetti's statements regarding Mary should be viewed in part as a response to the immaculate conception, made Roman Catholic doctrine by Pius IX in 1854. Quite possibly, Rossetti viewed this doctrine exempting Mary from original sin as dangerously approaching a deification of Mary. However, although many in Victorian England held strong anti-Catholic sentiments, there is no evidence that Rossetti ever shared that prejudice.

Rossetti's depiction of Mary Magdalene is also worth noting, as are her comments on Esther. Although many Victorians viewed Magdalene as the penitent whore, never does Rossetti refer to this saint as a fallen woman; rather, alluding to Luke 7:47, Rossetti typically describes Magdalene as simply the "manifold sinner" whose love for Christ has led to forgiveness (*Seek and Find*, 174). Though Magdalene is depicted as a genderless figure serving to represent all sinners, Queen Esther functions as a distinctly feminine figure to inspire other women. Such a role is apparent in Rossetti's poem "A Royal Princess," in which the princess, courageously deciding to leave her protective tower in order to help the starving poor, echoes Esther 4:16: "I, if I perish, perish; in the name of God I go." The female speaker of Rossetti's sonnet sequence *Monna innominata* also desires to resemble Esther, and in *The Face of the Deep*, "trembling Esther" again appears as the heroic woman who has overcome fear "to the saving of her people" (493).

While Esther's story was inspirational, it could not serve to justify Rossetti's authorship of biblical commentary. For such justification, Rossetti turns to Lois and Eunice. Doing so allows her to use Paul's own words to qualify the limits he places on women in his First Epistle to Timothy: "St. Paul has written: 'Let woman learn in silence with all subjection. But I suffer not a woman to teach.' Yet elsewhere [2 Tim. 1:5] he wrote: 'I call to remembrance the unfeigned faith . . . [Rossetti's ellipsis] which dwelt first in thy grandmother Lois, and thy mother Eunice.'" By alluding to these women of faith, Rossetti suggests that the origins of Timothy's faith are maternal; thus it is lawful for women along with men to study Scripture: "To expound prophecy lies of course beyond my power, and not within my wish. But the symbolic forms of prophecy being set before all eyes, must be so set for some purpose: to investigate them may not make us wise as serpents; yet ought by promoting faith, fear, hope, love, to aid in making us harmless as doves" (*Face of the Deep*, 195). Not only does Rossetti use one Pauline text to modify another but she also alludes to Jesus's message to his apostles when sending them out to preach: they must have the wisdom of serpents and the harmlessness of doves (Matt. 10:16). Thus Rossetti associates her investigation of Scripture with the work of the apostles in spreading the gospel.

In all of Rossetti's devotional writings, she moves seamlessly from one Bible verse to another, with the result that one text often comments on another. Such an approach reflects Rossetti's reading of the Bible as a unified poetic text, inspired by the Holy Spirit. Not only could one read the Old Testament as prefiguring the New, but one could also trace image patterns to learn of God's love. For example, associating the dove that brings the olive branch to Noah (Gen. 8:11) with the dove as symbol of the Holy Spirit (Luke 3:22), Rossetti reminds her readers that one of God's gifts to us is peace (*Seek and Find*, 99). Although Rossetti often assumes the voice of the teacher and at times even that of the preacher, she distinguishes her devotional work, even her commentary on the Apocalypse, from biblical interpretation. When considering whether "delay" should be substituted for the word "time" in Rev. 10:6, she defers to others: "As this alternative word would have to do with the interpretation of the sense, not with simple meditation, I leave it to my betters" (*Face of the Deep*, 277).

All of Rossetti's devotional work can be viewed as the result of a Christian meditation; her slow careful reading of Scripture has as its main goal the worshiping of a loving God. For Rossetti, the greatest sign of that love is the incarnation. Not surprisingly, therefore, although she occasionally cites a sermon read or commentary consulted, praise is reserved for Thomas à Kempis: he is "one of our holiest of writers" (*Seek and Find*, 92). Rossetti often turned to the *Imitation of Christ* for spiritual guidance. The dominant tone of all her devotional work is that of the humble Christian who seeks to follow Christ. Never placing herself above her readers, she speaks as a pilgrim to fellow pilgrims. Indeed, it is not unusual for Rossetti to allude to her own "failings" and her own "feeble eyes." Her farewell letter to Frederick Shields, friend and artist who shared her religious beliefs, captures her evaluation of herself and her work as she neared death: "Let me beg your prayers for the poor sinful woman who dared to speak to others and is herself what God knows her to be" (*Letters*, 4:389).

Today Rossetti's place in the faith community seems assured. Many of her poems, having been set to music, such as "A Christmas Carol" and "Christmastide," are regularly sung as hymns. Her devotional prose is now being given serious scholarly attention. In 1996 she was included in the Common Worship Calendar of the Church of England. The date chosen on which she is to be commemorated is April 27, for on that day in 1842 she wrote her first poem, a birthday poem for her mother.

Bibliography

Arseneau, Mary. *Recovering Christina Rossetti: Female Community and Incarnational Poetics.* New York: Palgrave, 2004.

Benckhuysen, Amanda W. "The Prophetic Voice of Christina Rossetti." Pages 165–80 in *Recovering Nineteenth-Century Women Interpreters of the Bible,* edited by Christina de Groot and Marion Ann Taylor. Atlanta: Society of Biblical Literature, 2007.

D'Amico, Diane. *Christina Rossetti: Faith, Gender, and Time.* Baton Rouge: Louisiana University Press, 1999.

Larsen, Timothy. "Christina Rossetti, the Decalogue, and Biblical Interpretation." *Journal for the History of Modern Theology* 16 (2009): 21–36.

Palazzo, Lynda. *Christina Rossetti's Feminist Theology.* New York: Palgrave, 2002.

Roe, Dinah. *Christina Rossetti's Faithful Imagination: The Devotional Poetry and Prose.* New York: Palgrave, 2006.

Rossetti, Christina. *Called to be Saints: The Minor Festivals Devotionally Studied.* London: SPCK, 1881.

———. *The Face of the Deep: A Devotional Commentary on the Apocalypse.* London: SPCK, 1892.

———. *Letter and Spirit: Notes on the Commandments.* London: SPCK, 1883.

———. *The Letters of Christina Rossetti.* Edited by Antony H. Harrison. 4 vols. Charlottesville: University Press of Virginia, 1997–2005.

———. *Seek and Find: A Double Series of Short Studies of the Benedicite.* London: SPCK, 1879.

———. *Selected Prose of Christina Rossetti.* Edited by David A. Kent and Paul G. Stanwood. New York: St. Martin's Press, 1998.

— Diane D'Amico

Rowe, Elizabeth Singer (1674–1737)

Elizabeth Singer Rowe was born in Somersetshire, the daughter of a dissenting preacher. She was a prolific writer, poet, and correspondent. The publisher John Dunton took an interest in her endeavors and steadily ensured a circulation of her work, culminating with *The Miscellaneous Works in Prose and Verse of Mrs. Elizabeth Rowe,* a two-volume edition published in 1739.

Apparently not wanting for suitors—Isaac Watts reportedly angled for her hand—Elizabeth eventually married Thomas Rowe in 1710, though Thomas was thirteen years younger. Only five years later Thomas died of consumption, and Elizabeth was inconsolable. Despite such adversity, her literary output continued until the end of her life, with her work published in several editions and languages. In terms of biblical interpretation, her best-known work is the 1736 poem titled *The History of Joseph*, approximately 15,000 words and stretching to 10 books in its final version. For the contemporary reader interested in literary approaches to Scripture and the history of interpretation, Rowe's poetic reimagining of the story is a powerful performance on a number of levels.

The plot is episodically based on the Genesis material, with most of the key incidents from chapters 37–45 included in some form: sibling jealously, sale into slavery, false imprisonment, audience with Pharaoh, forecasting of seven years of famine, the brothers' journey, accusation of espionage, and eventual reconciliation of the family. At the same time, the poem is ambitious and far-reaching, with shifting points of view and focalization, and an interweaving of narrational discourse with direct speech from the dramatis personae. The reader travels to exotic locales such as the pyramids in Egypt ("Here ancient kings, embalm'd with wond'rous cost, / A long exemption from corruption boast") and is privy to a congress of infernal powers plotting against the Hebrew family at a temple of Molech. Indeed, the supernatural activity is a striking component of the poem, ranging from angelic visitations (archangel Gabriel appears to Joseph in prison) to a tour of a sorcerer's den. All of this, however, is equally fraught with more ordinary human volition, as evidenced from this sample in book 3, where the fury of Joseph's brother is first aroused against him when he hears of his dream, "The shepherds hear his story with surprise: / Must we thy vassals be? proud *Ashur* [Asher] cries, / With rage and threat'ning malice in his eyes."

A notable literary technique is to present "stories" as told by one character to another. So Jacob—in response to his sons' vengeance on Shechem for the rape of Dinah—tells his sons the account of Abram's victory over the coalition of foreign kings, featuring a cameo on the mysterious Melchizedek. In the darkness of prison, Joseph the dreamer receives a panoramic vision of Israel's enslavement and liberation from Egyptian bondage, complete with Aaron's rod and obdurate Pharaoh, capped off with some schematics for the "curtain'd *Tabernacle*," as Rowe paints it. One can contrast that future Pharaoh of Exodus with the Pharaoh of Joseph's dream, who is more stately and discerning, willing to turn to a sage prisoner for wisdom. The king of Egypt is impressive in his robe, and Rowe seems acquainted with the clothing motif that marks various stages of Joseph's journey in the biblical text.

The characterizing dimension of the poem is intriguing. Potiphar's wife, in Rowe's poem, is *Sabrina*, famous for her ravishing beauty and dangerous deportment. The "secret fire" is kindled in her breast on noticing her husband's new employee:

When first she saw the charming *Hebrew's* eyes,
She felt, but well dissembled the surprise;
But thro' her various arts an inward care,
The languors of her pensive looks declare.

After Gen. 39, when Joseph is wrongly thrown into prison, Potiphar's wife is not mentioned again. But where the biblical text is silent, Rowe's *Sabrina* is fraught with sorrow and remorse for her actions, even to the point of confessing her treachery to her husband. At the same time, it is curious that Rowe does not include the episode of Judah and Tamar in Gen. 38: one suspects that it could have been incorporated into her theme in a creative way. Similarly, Reuben is far more noble in Rowe's poem than in the Genesis material. In the biblical text Reuben is a figure of shame for defiling his father's couch (Gen. 35:22), and thus when he speaks, it is under this cloud of guilt. Rowe's Reuben, though, is a noble firstborn son, more moved by Joseph's tender beauty than the dual trajectories of his own sin and shame. Reuben's view of Joseph, one guesses, is far closer to the poet's own vision. As exemplified in this passage from book 4, Rowe has a highly romantic view of Joseph, even Homeric in proportion:

His hair, like palest amber, from his crown
In floating curls and shining waves fell down.
Young *Paris* such surprising charms display'd,
When first in gold and *Tyrian* silks array'd,
He laid his crook aside, forgot the swain,
And bid adieu to *Ida's* flow'ry plain.

As the poem ends with the moving reconciliation scene familiar to readers of Genesis, the demonic plan to destroy this sacred family is evidently foiled, and the aged Jacob is given the last words. With a remarkable work of imagination, Rowe has bequeathed a poetic achievement worthy of recovery in our age.

Bibliography
Pritchard, J. "Rowe, Elizabeth (1674–1737)." Pages 995–96 in vol. 47 of *Oxford Dictionary of National Biography*, edited by H. C. G. Matthew and Brian Harrison. Rev. ed. Oxford: Oxford University Press, 2004–11.
Rowe, Elizabeth Singer. *The Miscellaneous Works in Prose and Verse of Mrs. Elizabeth Rowe: The greater part now first published, by her order, from her original manuscripts, by Mr. Theophilus Rowe; To which are added, Poems on several occasions, by Mr. Thomas Rowe; And to the whole is prefix'd, an account of the lives and writings of the authors. . . .* 2 vols. London: R. Hett and R. Dodsley, 1739.

— KEITH BODNER

■ Ruoti, Maria Clemente (1609/10–90)

Suor (Sister) Maria Clemente Ruoti was born in the Mugello region, north of Florence, one of seven children of Prospero di Santi Ruoti; her baptismal name was Ottavia. In 1621, together with her sister Margherita, she entered the Franciscan convent of San Girolamo, situated on the Costa di San Giorgio in Florence, where they had lived as boarders since 1619. In the seventeenth century San Girolamo was known for its theater and music; indeed, the renowned singer Margherita Signorini, the daughter of Francesca Caccini, was a nun in that convent. Ruoti wrote at least two plays for convent productions. In 1637 she published the *Giacob patriarca* (*Jacob, the Patriarch*), which was performed that year at San Girolamo in the presence of the young grand duchess of Tuscany, Vittoria della Rovere (1622–94), to whom the published work is dedicated. Ruoti also wrote *Il natal di Cristo* (*The Birth of Christ*), dated 1657 [1658 Florentine Style] on the manuscript; it contains a publishing privilege, but no printed edition has yet been found. It is likely that she wrote other plays in the intervening years. Ruoti's talents came to the attention of prominent Florentine literati, and in 1649 she was named to the Florentine Academy of the Apatisti, the first woman and only nun to be a member. As an enclosed nun, it is unlikely that she ever attended the academy gatherings; in a letter to her "Cortese lettore" (kind reader) that prefaces the *Natal di Cristo*, she claims never to have left her convent since entering there at the age of nine. Her works demonstrate a high level of literacy, exceptional even in Florence's elite religious institutions.

The *Giacob patriarca* is a five-act sacred comedy in verse (primarily unrhymed hendecasyllables) with musical *intermedi* and occasional musical accompaniment of the action in the play. Based on the story of Jacob in Gen. 27–34, the play dramatizes only a portion of the story, beginning with Jacob's flight from Mesopotamia with his family and ending with his return to Canaan and reunion with his brother Esau (Gen. 31:23–34:31); narrating characters tell the rest of the patriarch's experiences. This story provides the overall structure of the play, yet most of the action instead involves Jacob's wives, Leah and Rachel; his daughter Dinah; and Norminda, a character invented by the playwright, a Mesopotamian princess in love with Jacob's son Reuben. Although Jacob must make peace with Esau in order to return home, this problem and its resolution occupy very little of the action; instead, the story of the rape of Dinah by Shechem and the love of Norminda for Reuben are the main focus of the play. The rape of Dinah is given a happy matrimonial solution, quite different from the biblical account of deceit, revenge, and slaughter; the story of Norminda, a pastoral subplot, is interwoven with it; and the competition between Leah and Rachel for the love of Jacob is a motif that accompanies most of the action. The addition of the pastoral love story adds entertainment value to the play and has a certain logic, since Jacob and his sons are shepherds, but the happy ending to the rape of Dinah, while it conforms to theatrical conventions for a love story, shows a curious indifference on the part of the playwright to the authority of the biblical text. The women in the play are weak, flawed characters who are shown to need the guidance of men: Leah and Rachel are unable to get along, and Dinah and Norminda wander far from home, too curious about the world and careless with their honor. The message that the play offers to the women of the audience is to work to overcome the frailness of their sex, to appreciate the protection their enclosure ensures, and to learn to live peacefully together in their community. The playwright, however, also voices an objection to the misogyny implicit in the play: Leah complains about the subjection of women to the will of men throughout their lives, and Norminda protests the double standard that accuses women and excuses men for similar behavior.

Il natal di Cristo (*The Birth of Christ*), like *Giacob patriarca*, is about much more than the title suggests. It is a three-act play, written in prose and verse, with three intertwined plots (two main plots and a subplot) whose connection becomes clear only at the end of the play. The story that opens the play is that of Noemi, a virtuous widow, falsely accused by her lecherous brother-in-law, whose offer of illicit love she has rejected. She is sent to be punished but is saved by the Tibertine sibyl and two heavenly virtues, disguised as beautiful women, who come to her aid and try to reform the Pharisee and his friends; unsuccessful, they have the evil men swallowed up by the earth. Parallel to this story is a comic subplot involving shepherds: one, named Veggio, speaks a language of errors and malapropisms; like Noemi, he is falsely accused, condemned, and finally vindicated. Meanwhile, intertwined with the above plots, is that of Mary and Joseph's finding shelter for the night. Christ is born, and all plots come together for a finale of adoration of the Christ child. Pharisees and shepherds are converted by the vision, a good Pharisee marries the widow, and Veggio begins to speak eloquently. There is music throughout the play, building to a crescendo at the end, with competing choirs of angels and shepherds. The biblical story itself is minimal, but Mary and Joseph have long conversations that are meditations on the miracle of the birth of Christ. In this play, unlike the earlier one, all the women are strong and virtuous.

In both plays, Ruoti felt free to rework the biblical narratives and use her work to address contemporary issues regarding women. The difference in the portrayal of women in the two plays suggests that the first was written with only a convent audience in mind; after publishing that play and intending to publish *Il natal di Cristo* as well, she here had a larger audience to address. By portraying women as virtuous, strong, and capable of playing an active role in salvation, she had become a confident spokesperson to the world for her convent sisters and her sex.

Bibliography

Rescia, Laura. "Giacobbe nel Dramma di formazione europeo tra XVI e XVII secolo: Gioventú, libertà e Problemi di genere." Pages 33–50 in *Contatti, passaggi, metamorfosi: Studi di letteratura francese e comparata in onore di Daniela Dalla Valle*, edited by G. Bosco, M. Pavesio, and L. Rescia. Rome: Edizioni di Storia e Letteratura, 2010.

Weaver, Elissa. *Convent Theater in Early Modern Italy: Spiritual Fun and Learning for Women.* Cambridge: Cambridge University Press, 2002.

———. "Suor Maria Clemente Ruoti, Playwright and Academician." Pages 281–96 in *Creative Women in Medieval and Early Modern Italy: A Religious and Artistic Renaissance*, edited by E. Ann Matter and John Coakley. Philadelphia: University of Pennsylvania Press, 1994.

— ELISSA B. WEAVER

Sayers, Dorothy Leigh (1893–1957)

Into a world of general biblical illiteracy and widespread suspicion about the biblical text, Dorothy L. Sayers strode with vigor and passion, reshaping an entire generation's understanding of the gospel and story of Jesus.

The daughter of a clergyman, Sayers grew up surrounded by the rhythm and language of the Anglican Church. Her parents provided her with a stimulating intellectual background that included a grounding in music and Latin. Fluent in both French and German at an early age, she made up stories and put on plays at home. As an undergraduate at Oxford, she maintained not only her studies but also continued to write prolifically.

Sayers had no intention of becoming a writer of theology; in fact, she is most well known for her detective stories. However, due to the success of her 1937 Canterbury Festival play, *The Zeal of Thy House*, Sayers became increasingly sought after as an authority on Christian faith and dogma.

As her letters and speeches show, Sayers had a quick wit, a firm grasp of the issues at hand, and an extremely engaging way of speaking. She became sought after for radio broadcasts and speeches. Sayers's contribution as a biblical interpreter is most evident in her two radio plays: *He That Should Come* and *The Man Born to Be King*. In the first of these, Sayers's intention is "to show the birth of Christ against its crowded social and historical background" (5). In doing this she was entirely successful: the context of empire and its bearing on the story of Jesus's birth, the multifaceted character of first-century Judaism, and the rich intertextual nature of the gospel story in relation to the Jewish Scriptures are all brought alive. This play, broadcast by the British Broadcasting Corporation (BBC) on Christmas Day 1938, was met with an overwhelmingly positive response.

Sayers was increasingly frustrated by the general biblical illiteracy of those who wrote to her with questions about Christian faith. She became determined, at the very least, to tell the basic story of the gospel. To that end, *The Man Born to Be King*—a series of twelve radio plays on the life of Jesus, broadcast on the BBC from December 1941 to October 1942—portrays the gospel story as something that really happened in history, "all mixed up, like other events, with eating and drinking and party politics, and rates and taxes, and working and sleeping and gossiping and laughing and buying and selling and coping with life in general" (*Letters*, 2:355).

To reflect this historical period accurately, she read widely in the theology of her day, listing her debt to Archbishop Temple's *Readings in St John's Gospel*, Sir Edward Hoskyns's *The Fourth Gospel*, R. A. Edwards's *The Upper Room*, Frank Morison's *Who Moved the Stone?*, and Ronald Gurner's *We Crucify!* (*Born to Be King*, 36). She also consulted Josephus and other ancient historians. The plays are based on her own translations of the Greek text.

In her writings, Sayers clearly indicates her dismissal of the "higher criticism" and its suspicions of the historical reliability of the Gospel accounts. This is why, against general scholarly opinion, Sayers gives primacy to the Gospel of John in her plays; rich detail, realistic conversation, and plausible chronology gave this Gospel the ring of authenticity.

Sayers insisted that the characters in the plays speak with accents that demonstrate their social status in the first century (Matthew, for instance, was portrayed with a Cockney accent). No one, not even Jesus, would be allowed to "talk Bible" (*Letters*, 2:282). This strategy created extensive controversy before the plays were even aired, resulting in widespread protests against the broadcasts. The resulting publicity inevitably ensured a large audience for the plays, which were met with an outpouring of gratitude from many listeners. She had sparked an interest in the Gospels among young and old alike, unchurched and churched.

Her essays are not specifically exegetical. However, in her attempts to make Christian dogma and teaching clear to the average layperson, Sayers drew widely on the biblical text, specifically Gen. 1–3 and the Gospel accounts. Her influential book *The Mind of the Maker* explores human creativity as a reflection of the Trinity. In various essays and letters, she unpacks the meaning of the crucifixion and of suffering. She shows an incredibly wide grasp of the biblical text and biblical theology in her writings on work, women, the image of God, the incarnation, the problem of evil, and the death and resurrection of Jesus. Sayers wanted to show that these beliefs mean "something quite concrete and relevant. [They apply] in the most matter-of-fact way to my everyday experience" (*Christ of the Creeds*, 7).

In particular, she felt that it was of utmost importance for people to grasp that this story took place in history, and that in history God was arrested, roughed up, and brutally killed. She was appalled that so many people felt that Christianity meant an escape from suffering. On the contrary, "Christians should never be astonished by evil and suffering because that is what the story is about—how humanity killed God" (77). Her writings on the crucifixion and resurrection try to demonstrate that in the face of evil, God does not strive to return to some paradise where there is no evil. Rather, God transforms evil into good: death leads to resurrection.

In a time when discussion concerning Christian faith was vigorous and varied—as seen in the work of C. S. Lewis, G. K. Chesterton, T. S. Eliot, and Charles Williams (all of whom Sayers knew and admired)—Dorothy L. Sayers had an overwhelming impact on an entire generation's understanding of the Gospels. Her plays anticipated later Gospel scholarship, especially the emphases of those in the "third quest" of Jesus scholarship. In her hands, the text came alive, against the grain of much biblical scholarship of the time. It is no wonder that her work continues to be read and discussed today.

Bibliography

Sayers, Dorothy L. *The Christ of the Creeds: And Other Broadcast Messages to the British People during World War II*. With an introduction and notes by Suzanne Bray. Hurstpierpoint, West Sussex: Dorothy L. Sayers Society, 2008.

———. *Creed or Chaos?* New York: Harcourt, Brace, 1949.

———. *He That Should Come: A Nativity Play in One Act*. London: Victor Gollancz, 1939.

———. *The Letters of Dorothy Sayers*. Vol. 2, *1937–1943: From Novelist to Playwright*. Edited by Barbara Reynolds. Cambridge: Dorothy L. Sayers Society, 1997.

———. *The Man Born to Be King: A Play-Cycle on the Life of Our Lord and Saviour Jesus Christ*. London: Victor Gollancz, 1959.

———. *The Mind of the Maker*. London: Methuen, 1941.

———. *Unpopular Opinions*. London: Victor Gollancz, 1946.

———. *The Zeal of Thy House*. London: Victor Gollancz, 1937.

—Sylvia C. Keesmaat

■ Schimmelpenninck, Mary Anne (1778–1856)

Mary Anne Schimmelpenninck was born and raised in England in a wealthy and intellectual family. Her father was a scholar and a member of several learned societies. His influence and the family's social circle introduced Schimmelpenninck to various streams of scientific and religious thought, which shaped the hermeneutic of her adult life. Her mother was her childhood spiritual guide, daily teaching her the Scriptures. In her paternal grandfather's Quaker home, she participated in meetings where she first "felt the influence of that holy presence of God" (*Life*, 1:55). After intense inquiry, she came to Christian faith in her early twenties through the influence of Moravian evangelicals. She joined the Moravian church in her forties and remained there throughout her life, albeit with continued interaction with Roman Catholic, Anglican, and dissenting Christians that marked her life and work with a generous Christian ecumenicity.

Schimmelpenninck's education and interests were broad, including the classics, physiognomy and phrenology, aesthetics, social justice, geography, and biblical languages and history. A work on Christian aesthetics—*Theory on the Classification of Beauty and Deformity* (1815); *Biblical Fragments* (1821–22); and *Psalms according to the Authorized Version* (1825)—mark her turn to more explicitly biblical topics.

Schimmelpenninck's primary biblical works, *Fragments* and *Psalms*, were written for women "of high mental cultivation and Christian profession" and their children (Dedication, in *Fragments*, 2:2). Schimmelpenninck was committed to women's education, which involved preparing women for the societally prescribed role of helpmeet to her "husband, her father or her brother" and to the "calls of the sick-room, the school-room, the dispenser to the poor; or the claims of the social or domestic circle" (*Life*, 2:131).

Although living during the paradigm shift to historical-critical interpretive methods, Schimmelpenninck (like many contemporary male interpreters) did not use this approach. Her childhood experiences in reading the new historical-critical methods were deleterious to her early faith, and she wholly eschewed such methodologies as an "unhappy teaching" (*Life*, 1:306). She was not unconcerned with historical inquiry, however, and used it to illuminate the Bible, considering historical inquiry legitimate if it illuminated the "peculiar customs, manners, or facts which constitute the literal sense of Scripture" (*Fragments*, 1:72). *Fragments* and *Psalms* demonstrate Schimmelpenninck's interpretive commitments and methods. Essays in *Fragments* explore a wide variety of texts and topics, from the prophet of Bethel (1 Kings 13) to the Samaritan woman (John 4). Each essay seeks to throw "light upon the text" and arises from her personal study notes that record "a fact, a custom, or a verbal criticism . . . [but] more frequently . . . memoranda of ideas, or trains of thought, suggested either by books, conversation or arising in any other way" (*Fragments*, 1:vii). *Psalms* sets each psalm into its historical context and provides interpretive work on the titles (or superscriptions) to unfold each psalm's literal and spiritual meaning. For instance, the common title *lamnaṣṣēaḥ* (as for Ps. 18), an obscure musical term difficult to render with certainty and often now translated as "To the Chief Musician," is interpreted by Schimmelpenninck christologically as "To the Giver of Victory," that is, to God in Christ (*Psalms*, 100). To *Psalms* is appended an essay first published in *Fragments* on the proper interpretation of the psalms.

Schimmelpenninck held to an authoritative, inspired text (*Fragments*, 1:xxxii) and prophetic authorship, particularly of the Psalms (*Psalms*, xii–xiii). Yet her most determinative interpretive assumption is that Scripture is fully read only christologically. Christological interpretation arises out of the literal meaning of the text and is "definitely intended," "literally and solidly true," and "as capable of a fixed interpretation as the literal sense" (*Psalms*, xx). In both *Fragments* and *Psalms*, Schimmelpenninck first illuminates the literal (i.e., historical) and then the spiritual (i.e., christological) meaning of the text.

Schimmelpenninck equates the literal meaning with historical referentiality. The biblical text, including the Psalms' superscriptions, is the primary

437

avenue to biblical history. Other sources also illuminate biblical history. For instance, Herodotus is a source of knowledge of Babylonian forms of worship at the time of Daniel (*Fragments*, 1:166), and the extensive accounts of travels in the Sinai by Father Sicard, an eighteenth-century Jesuit missionary to Egypt, illuminate the historical reality of Israel's passage through the Red Sea (*Fragments*, 1:175–231).

Further evidence of her historical concern is her extensive use of Hebrew morphology and syntax to determine the literal meaning of the text. Schimmelpenninck was self-taught in Hebrew and appears proficient in its use. Although the Hebrew word *wᵉw* is traditionally literally translated as "and" in Judg. 11:31 ("[it] shall surely be the Lord's, *and* I will offer it up . . ."), Schimmelpenninck argues that it should be translated as "or" ("[it] shall surely be the Lord's, *or* I will offer it up . . ."; *Fragments*, 1:216). This translation opens up the possibility that Jephthah's daughter was not sacrificed. More frequently, however, her Hebrew exhibits the contemporary fascination with etymological work. She uses etymology as an avenue to christological interpretation. For instance, the Mountains of Ararat are etymologically "Mountains of a curse and of a trembling" (from *'rr*, "he cursed," and *rṭṭ*, "he trembled"). By this reading, Ararat is a type of Calvary, "that mountain of *a curse of trembling*" (*Fragments*, 1:118). Similar etymological work supports christological readings throughout her writings, particularly in her commentary on the psalm titles (*Psalms*, passim; cf. Wray Beal, 91–92).

Schimmelpenninck's christological interpretive goal is served by the allegorical methods so common to precritical interpreters. Thus Christ's mother at the wedding of Cana is the Jewish church, "which was, till the resurrection, the true one,—that church who had received the promises, who was present at the marriage, but . . . was not herself the person married" (*Fragments*, 1:240). Much of her work on the psalms follows this allegorical method and draws on the many precritical commentators whom she acknowledges as helpful to her own devotion but does not cite in each instance (*Fragments*, 1:xxxiii, 114–15; *Psalms*, xvii).

Schimmelpenninck's work does not focus on texts particularly concerning women, and her interpretive methods and assumptions differ little from her male precritical colleagues. Her reading of Jesus's mother, however, may reflect the cult of domesticity, a social construct holding that women by nature are the perfect embodiment of virtues such as purity, domesticity, and piety. The exercise of these virtues in women's God-given roles as wives and mothers makes them the center of the home, their proper sphere of influence. Schimmelpenninck devotes a whole chapter to Mary, whom Jesus addresses as "Woman" (John 2:4; 19:26). As Woman, Mary represents the church, the mother of the faithful and the bride of Christ (*Fragments*, 2:253–78). The chapter elevates woman's roles of wife and mother, but the cult of domesticity is subsumed under Schimmelpenninck's ultimate goal. Her concern is christological reading that calls the whole church to faithfulness, and she holds this as the spiritual goal of interpretive work.

Schimmelpenninck's interpretive work exemplifies those who chose to remain within the historic interpretive traditions of the church when new interpretive models were supplanting older approaches. Additionally, her *Fragments* and *Psalms* incorporate both Catholic and Protestant sensibilities, reflecting her ecumenical commitments. For instance, as a Protestant her writing was informed by the great Catholic writers of the then-dissolved Port Royal convent in France. She presented their work to her audience as one of unexcelled learning and unequalled spirituality (*Fragments*, 1:114–15). Schimmelpenninck engaged in a spiritual reading that was overshadowed by the historical-critical paradigm in scholarship. The work of some contemporary scholars demonstrates some continuity with the theological reading exemplified in Schimmelpenninck's work.

Beyond her biblical interpretive work, Schimmelpenninck's published scholarship in other areas is also being rediscovered. An available republication of *Select Memoirs of Port Royal*, her commentary on her travels to Port Royal, demonstrates renewed interest in her ecumenical writings. Her *Theory on the Classification of Beauty and Deformity* and the outworking of those principles in her lifelong social action is also the subject of ongoing scholarly interest (see Duquette).

Bibliography

Duquette, Natasha. "'Dauntless Faith': Contemplative Sublimity and Social Action in Mary Anne Schimmelpenninck's Aesthetics." *Christianity and Literature* 55 (2006): 513–38.

Schimmelpenninck, Mary Anne. *Biblical Fragments*. 2 vols. London: Ogle, Duncan, 1821–22.

———. *Life of Mary Anne Schimmelpenninck*. Edited by her relation, Christiana C. Hankin. Vol. 1, *Autobiography*. Vol. 2, *Biographical Sketch and Letters*. London: Longman, Brown, Green, Longmans, & Roberts, 1858.

———. *Psalms according to the Authorized Version: With Prefatory Titles, and Tabular Index of Scriptural References, From the Port Royal Authors, Marking the Circumstances and Chronologic Order of Their Composition; To Which Is Added, An Essay upon the Psalms, and Their Spiritual Application*. London: J. & A. Arch, 1825.

———. *Select Memoirs of Port Royal: To Which Are Appended Tour to Alet, Visit to Port Royal, Gift of an Abbess, Biographical Notices, etc.; Taken from Original Documents*. 3 vols. London: J. & A. Arch, 1829. Repr. in 2 vols. Whitefish, MT: Kessinger Pub., 2006.

———. *Theory on the Classification of Beauty and Deformity*. London: J. & A. Arch, 1815.

Wray Beal, Lissa M. "Mary Anne SchimmelPenninck: A Nineteenth-Century Woman as Psalm-Reader." Pages 81–98 in *Recovering Nineteenth-Century Women Interpreters of the Bible*, edited by Christiana de Groot and Marion Ann Taylor. Atlanta: Society of Biblical Literature, 2007.

—Lissa M. Wray Beal

Schurman, Anna Maria van (1607–78)

Anna Maria van Schurman was widely recognized in her own time as an extraordinarily learned woman. Born in Cologne to Calvinist parents Frederick van Schurman and Eva von Harff, she could read German and recite parts of the Heidelberg Catechism at the age of three. Her father tutored her along with her brothers in Latin classics while also emphasizing the study of Scripture. Her artistic accomplishments included scissor-cuttings, painting, embroidery, and calligraphy, as well as vocal and instrumental music. As a young woman, she corresponded with leading Dutch writers Jacob Cats, Daniel Heinsius, and Constantijn Huygens.

It was through her theological contacts, however, that she attained international recognition. In 1636 she was invited by Gisbert Voetius to write congratulatory poems for the opening ceremony of the university in Utrecht, of which he was to be the first rector. Subsequently, he arranged for her to attend his lectures in Near Eastern languages, even though she had to be concealed from the male students in a separate cubicle. She thereby became unofficially the first female student at a Dutch university.

Her willingness to advocate for women's education developed out of her correspondence on the subject with André Rivet, professor of theology in Leiden. The exchange of letters led to the 1638 publication of her logic exercise on the question of *Whether a Christian Woman Should Be Educated*, which was reprinted in 1648 along with her letters to learned men and women throughout Western Europe and also published in French (1646) and English (1659).

During the 1650s van Schurman faded from the public eye, devoting her time to charitable activities and the care of two elderly aunts. Far from resenting her caregiving obligations, she experienced with her aunts and brother Johan Godschalk a sense of Christian community that she found lacking in the church. When the aunts died in 1661, she and her brother turned to the reform ideas of Jean de Labadie, then a preacher in Geneva. Through their influence, Labadie came to the Netherlands, but his reform efforts did not find acceptance in the state church. When Anna Maria followed him in the formation of a religious community outside the established church, she renounced her earlier absorption in the academic study of languages and theology. Choosing a life of love and faith within a Christian community that strove to imitate the early church was for her "the better part" (Luke 10:42 NRSV).

Van Schurman's approach to the study of the Bible clearly changed over the course of her lifetime. In her defense of the education of Christian women, she argues that many fields of knowledge contribute to the better understanding of

Scripture: first are grammar, logic, and rhetoric; next are physics, metaphysics, and history; then come Hebrew and Greek languages. She was not content with these languages, but also studied rabbinic Hebrew, Aramaic, Syriac, Arabic, Persian, and Samaritan. She read the Qur'an and copied it by hand. Perhaps her greatest linguistic accomplishment was to write an Ethiopian grammar. In her study of Semitic languages, she was following Voetius's belief that this knowledge was important to understanding the Bible and also to the ultimate goal of conversion of Jews and Muslims.

In later life she regarded the linguistic approach to the Bible as insignificant in comparison with spiritual understanding. Grammatical explanations are of no use, she wrote in her autobiography, if the reader of Scripture is not illumined by God's Spirit: "For either the Scripture is read in the light of the Holy Spirit, or it is not. If not, it is futile to employ a grammatical explanation of one word or another in order to grasp its innermost spiritual meaning" (*Eukleria* 1.2.15). Van Schurman regarded the state church as insufficiently reformed and sought the true church in the community of the regenerate led by Labadie. Because of her sectarianism, she may be classified at this stage as a radical Pietist, yet she differed from others in this category who appealed to inspiration independent from Scripture. The Bible remained the basis of van Schurman's beliefs, and she remained essentially Calvinist, defending the doctrines of predestination and atonement against the visionary Antoinette Bourignon. Against those who, after her affiliation with Labadie, charged that she had little regard for Scripture, she responded that she would not want to compare it or replace it with any treasure on the whole earth (*Eukleria*, 2.167).

Van Schurman's most explicit work of biblical interpretation is her *Amplification of the First Three Chapters of Genesis* (*Uitbreiding over de drie eerste capittels van Genesis*). In this thirty-eight-page poem, van Schurman tells the story of creation and moves from the fall of Adam and Eve to the new covenant in Christ and eternal redemption. The covenant theology of the Reformed tradition provides the framework for her biblical interpretation, yet her description of redemption as loss of self and union with God reflects the Pietist approach of her later phase of life. Aside from the absence of reference to the dominion of Adam over Eve as part of the curse (Gen. 3:16b), there is little to suggest her female identity. Her paraphrase of Adam's excuse for eating the fruit charges him with being unfaithful to God and his spouse, seeking to lay the blame on the woman, and holding her in low esteem. The primary focus of the poem, however, is neither gender relations nor original creation, but the restoration of God's designs for creation through the coming reign of Christ, a theme she pursues in another poem, *Considerations on the Future of Christ's Kingdom* (*Bedenckingen over de toekomste van Christi Koninkrijk*). These works, probably written in about 1660, express her longing for a pure community of believers, which was to be fulfilled for her among the followers of Labadie.

441

While biblical interpretation was only one aspect of van Schurman's wide-ranging interests and accomplishments, the shifts in her approach to the Bible are a significant reflection not only of her personal search for genuine Christianity but also of the broader transition from scholastic orthodoxy to Pietism during the course of the seventeenth century.

Bibliography

Baar, Mirjam de, et al. *Choosing the Better Part: Anna Maria van Schurman (1607–1678)*. Dordrecht: Kluwer Academic Pub., 1996.

Beek, Pieta van. *De eerste studente: Anna Maria van Schurman (1636)*. Utrecht: Matrijs, 2004.

———. *Verbastert Christendom: Nederlandse gedichten van Anna Maria van Schurman (1607–1678)*. Houten: Den Hertog, 1992. Pages 79–92 include Bedenckingen over de toekomste van Christi Coninkrijk (1675).

Irwin, Joyce. "Anna Maria van Schurman: From Feminism to Pietism." *Church History* 46 (1977): 48–62.

Schurman, Anna Maria van. *Eukleria, seu melioris partis electio*. Part 1, Altona: Meulen, 1673. Part 2, Amsterdam: Jacob vande Velde, 1685. Dutch trans., *Eucleria, of Uitkiezing van Het Beste Deel*. Amsterdam: Jacob vande Velde, 1684. Repr., Leeuwarden: De Tille, 1978.

———. *Opuscula hebraea, graeca, latina, gallica: Prosaic et metrica*. Leiden: Johannis à Waesberge, 1648.

———. *Uitbreiding over de drie eerste capittels van Genesis: Beneffens een vertoog van het geestelyk huwelyk van Christus met de gelovigen*. Groningen: Jacobus Sipkes, 1732.

———. *Whether a Christian Woman Should be Educated and Other Writings from Her Intellectual Circle*. Edited and translated by Joyce L. Irwin. Chicago: University of Chicago Press, 1998.

— JOYCE IRWIN

Scott, Mary (1751–93)

Mary Scott was born the daughter of a well-to-do dissenting linen merchant in Somerset, England. A number of her early hymns suggest that she adhered to "a broad Anglicanism that accepted some Calvinist ideas and language" (Ferguson, "Mary Scott," 361). She lived with her parents and in 1788 married her longtime suitor, Unitarian John Taylor, following the death of her parents. Scott was encouraged to become a Unitarian by her husband, and his decision to become a Quaker several years later caused marital discord. Scott struggled with health issues throughout her life and died at forty-one, three weeks before her third child was due. She is perhaps best known as an epistolary friend of both Anna Seward and Anne Steele, to whom she dedicated *The Female Advocate*; details of Scott's life are primarily derived from her letters to Seward.

Scott published two major poetic works, in addition to a few pieces in local magazines. Her first work, a 522-line poem titled *The Female Advocate* (1774), expands John Duncombe's poem *The Feminead* (1754), in praise of the accomplishments of female writers. Scott's poem lauds the talents and accomplishments of women writers from the time of the Reformation through the eighteenth century and argues indirectly for women's education (Ferguson, *Women Poets*, 27–28).

Scott's *Messiah* (1788) is a 791-line epic poem of two parts written in blank verse. She published *Messiah* in response to William Hayley's call to write a national epic poem. In *Messiah*, Scott presents Christ as the ultimate hero, "thou Prince of Peace, thou Friend of human kind!" and as "*the Perfect Man!*" (1.6.10). Her epic begins with Old Testament prophecies of Christ's birth and "the peaceful glories of [his] promis'd reign" (1.20). She follows the birth account in Luke, highlighting the responses of Mary, Simeon, and Anna to "The holy babe" (1.64). She includes the visit of the Magi (Matt. 2), taking the opportunity to compare the "new-born King" with the "haughty" Jewish tyrant Herod (1.101–18), her antihero, whom she chastises: "Check, haughty tyrant! Check thy causeless fear! / He shall not from thy hand the sceptre tear. / 'Tis o'er the soul *his* empire shall extend!" (1.109–11). Scott moves beyond description of the events of Jesus's early life to instruct readers: she suggests that the obedience of Jesus's parents to "a vision all divine," which informed them of "the fierce monarch's black design," teaches "The all-victorious pow'r of truth divine, / The human soul t'ennoble, and refine!" (1.137–44). She continues her dark depiction of Herod, the "Blood-thirsty monster! Scandal to a throne!" (1.179). Drawing on Josephus, Scott embellishes the circumstances surrounding Herod's tortuous and deserved death:

> Then, to the vision of his tortur'd brain;
> Appears the slaughter'd white-rob'd infant train:
> The strangled pledges of connubial love,
> 'Midst the pale band, in solemn silence move.
> Mark! Mark his fiery eye-balls, how they glare
> In all the wildest horrors of despair!
> (1.199–204)

Scott continues her narrative of her hero's life, including his baptism, temptation in the wilderness, and the beginning of his ministry as "God's chosen messenger of love," whose purpose is to bring "Glad news of life eternal . . . With lore divine to meliorate the heart" and to bring nations together (1.264–68). In her construal of Jesus as the ultimate hero, Scott challenges the traditional heroic code and condemns pagan and non-Christian moral philosophy: "Did e'er your Socrates, your Zeno. Teach / A moral code, so pure in every part, / So form'd to elevate the glowing heart?" (1.288–90). Scott stresses Jesus's uniqueness, cataloging his miracles (1.306–26) as proof of the truth of his mission: "Jesus, of teachers Thou supremely blest, / Stupendous deeds thy mission's truth attest!" (1.307–8).

Scott's Jesus insists that he comes from God and directs glory to God: "To God alone, then all the glory give" (1.338). At the same time, Scott calls attention to Jesus's humanity, recalling the tears he sheds at Lazarus's tomb before he raises him from the dead (1.341–54). Jesus is exalted as the healer, "messenger of love divine," and teacher of "hallow'd precepts to impart / Peace to the world, and pleasure to the heart!" (1.358–62). Scott moves beyond theological reflection to preach as she calls the lost to hear Jesus's message and to find peace, hope, and eternal bliss in heaven (1.363–68). In this way, Scott reinterprets the epic project in terms of spiritual and Christian renewal.

The second part of Scott's epic focuses on Jesus's teachings, passion, resurrection, and postresurrection appearances and suggests their significance. She highlights women in the passion narrative: Scott contrasts the fleeing disciples with "*Judea's* matrons [who] his steps attend, / And mourn the fate of man's *unwearied friend*" (2.206–7); she amplifies Jesus's instructions to Jerusalem's daughters not to cry for him but for themselves as they face the coming desolation (Luke 23:28–31); she recasts the scene at the foot of the cross where John is told to care for Jesus's "gentle mother, weeping near his side" (2.246). Scott boldly suggests that "matrons" alone understand Mary's pain:

> Ye tender matrons, whose fond bosoms prove
> The softest meltings of maternal love,
> 'Tis your's, kind spirits, your's alone to know
> Her agonizing bitterness of woe.
>
> (2.258–61)

Scott speaks words of comfort and hope to Mary: "Thy son shall rise triumphant from the tomb" and conquer death (2.262–73). She stresses Jesus's message of hope beyond the grave in his postresurrection appearances to his disciples and the mission of Jesus's followers to "spread felicity through ev'ry clime, / And bid hope look beyond the bounds of time" (2.322–53, 366–71).

In her epic, Scott argues that the creation of a national epic hero is unchristian and unnecessary. She portrays Christ as the perfect hero, heroic yet passive, tried, convicted, and brutally executed and resurrected for the eventual good of all. She criticizes Roman imperialism and implicitly denounces British imperialism: "Tyrannic Man, shall then no more control / God's undivided empire o'er the soul" (2.9–10). Her critique of empire includes an anti-Catholic polemic as "Gaunt *Superstition* rear'd his giant head" (2.372), manifesting itself in such practices as the selling of indulgences. In the final lines of her epic, Scott prays for the end of war, intolerance, and empire:

Hasten, great God! the long predicted time
When Jesus shall be known in every clime,
When the red torch of war no more shall burn,
Nor feeling hearts o'er slaughter'd millions mourn;
And when, malignant scourge of every age,
Shall bigot fury cease its dreadful rage;
When ever-smiling concord's golden chain
Shall bind each clime through nature's fair domain;
When man his destiny divine shall prove
By all the tender charities of love;
When to the child of virtue shall be given,
To find e'en earth the blissful porch of heav'n!
(2.412–23)

A contemporary reviewer of Scott's *Messiah* judged her theology heterodox but lauded her poetry, suggesting, "Her poem might probably have been more beautiful, and more sublime, had her religious principles been less heterodox" (*Monthly Review*). Still, her heterodoxy makes her work as a biblical interpreter significant. As another reviewer cogently observes: "[*Messiah*] is, however, perhaps the first poem on the subject written by a Unitarian" (*Analytical Review*).

Bibliography
Anon. "Art. 43, Messiah: A Poem, in Two Parts." *Monthly Review; or, Literary Journal* 79 (1788): 277–78.
———. Review of *Messiah: A Poem*, by Mary Scott. *Analytical Review* 1 (1788): 460.
Blain, Virginia, Isobel Grundy, and Patricia Clements. *The Feminist Companion to Literature in English*. New Haven: Yale University Press, 1990.
Ferguson, Moira. "'The Cause of My Sex': Mary Scott and the Female Literary Tradition." *Huntington Library Quarterly* 50 (1987): 359–77.
———. *Eighteenth-Century Women Poets: Nation, Class, and Gender*. Albany: State University of New York Press, 1995.
Mullan, John. "Scott, Mary (1751/52–1793)." Pages 444–45 in vol. 49 of *Oxford Dictionary of National Biography*, edited by H. C. G. Matthew and Brian Harrison. Rev. ed. Oxford: Oxford University Press, 2004–11.
Rex, Michael. "The Heroine's Revolt: English Women Writing Epic Poetry, 1654–1789." PhD diss., Wayne State University, Detroit, 1998.
Scott, Mary. *The Female Advocate: A Poem; Occasioned by Reading Mr. Duncombe's Feminead*. London: Joseph Johnson, 1774.
———. *Messiah: A Poem, in Two Parts; Published for the Benefit of the General Hospital at Bath*. Bath, UK: R. Cruttwell, 1788.

— MICHAEL REX

▧ Sengers, Justitia (fl. 1585)

History remembers Justitia Sengers of Braunschweig (Germany) as the blind author of a commentary on Ps. 69. Sengers's 1585 publication was titled the

445

Little Book of Comfort on the Subject of the Sixty-Ninth Psalm (*Trostbüchlein, über den Neun und Sechzigsten Psalm*). "Little Book" is a misnomer, for the work contains more than four hundred pages, with only every second page numbered. Its long subtitle describes its contents well: *About the Suffering and Death of Our Lord Jesus Christ and about Our Cross and Suffering, as We Must Step in the Footprints of Christ, and What a Wonderful Reward We Will Receive, Ornamented with a Few Beautiful Prayers.* The 1586 edition, printed in Magdeburg, does not give the name of the author but adds a description ("By a female servant of Jesus Christ, briefly pulled together out of the Holy Scriptures") and a quotation ("'And call upon me in the day of trouble: I will deliver thee, and thou shalt glorify me.' Psalm 50[:15]"). The title of the 1593 reprint of Sengers's work reveals much of what is known about her: *From the Holy Ghost's Description of the Suffering and Death of Our Lord Jesus Christ, by a Maiden Who Was Born Blind, Justitia Sengers in Braunschweig.* Historian Susan Karant-Nunn has reconstructed the broad strokes of Sengers's life via information gleaned from the publication history of her book, as well as information in the book's foreword, dated December 14, 1585, and dedicated to King Frederick II of Denmark, the son of Christian III (225–26). Karant-Nunn suggests that Sengers, who refers to herself as a person blessed with "spiritual and material goods," possibly belonged to the upper burgher classes of Braunschweig. It is not known how she managed her disability, but her work demonstrates that she knew the Scriptures and devotional literature and was familiar with Luther's life and teaching.

In the foreword of her book, Sengers narrates that she felt compelled by the Holy Spirit to author her work and only reluctantly penned it, expecting that most would not approve. She believed that God would deal with those who criticized either her or her "little book" (226). She speaks of her own blindness as a "heavy cross" that she has had to bear and at the same time expresses her gratitude to God for his goodness to her. As a female author, Sengers places herself alongside Miriam, Mary (the mother of Jesus), and Monica (the mother of Augustine of Hippo), who, like her, praised God and authored songs.

Sengers's commentary includes a German translation of Ps. 69 and follows a traditional verse-by-verse format. A personal responsive prayer follows her commentary on each verse. Sengers divides the psalm's thirty-six verses into three sections: 1–22, 23–30, and 31–36. She adopts a threefold approach to interpretation: she assumes the psalm's literal/historical sense as it relates to David's life; she explains the psalm's christological sense, hearing its words as Jesus's own words; and she explores the spiritual meaning of the psalm as it relates to her life and the lives of her readers. Her comments on verse 1 illustrate her technique of weaving the various senses of Scripture together seamlessly:

In this first verse of the psalm the Lord Christ laments about his great spiritual and inner suffering, which he suffered in his soul. This psalm is justly called a psalm of prayer, for dear David begins it with a prayer, as he says, "Save me, O God; for the waters have come in unto my soul." When just such a prayer is uttered; [it is uttered] by one whose soul is experiencing great fear and despair, as is also found with us when we are in need, and particularly when we have fear in our soul, that at times our misery is so great, the fear is so severe, that we cannot even utter many words [Matt. 6:7]. Indeed we probably cannot pray anything at all. So also the Son of God shows here that he was in such fear, that he also could not pray a lot. (*Trostbüchlein*, 8–9)

Sengers also reads the psalm intertextually, making references to passages from both the Old and New Testaments. For example, Sengers begins her comments on Ps. 69:3 by using John 5:39 to justify her christological reading of the psalm: "Our Lord Christ says in John 5[:39] 'Search the scriptures; for . . . they . . . testify of me.' With these words he, Christ the Lord, directs us" (14). She continues in the next paragraph to speak of Jesus's experiences of suffering and rejection: "How distant and harsh the heavenly Father opposes his dearest Son, so that he gives him no answer at all, as he says in Psalm 22[:2] 'O my God, I cry in the daytime, but you do not hear . . . ,' so that it appears as if the Son of God can expect no help from his heavenly Father. . . . In Psalm 88[:4] He says, '. . . I am as a man who has no strength'" (14).

When Sengers reads Ps. 69 in light of her personal experiences of suffering, especially her sense of being ostracized and maligned because of her blindness, she reveals much about her own life and about attitudes toward disabilities in the sixteenth century. She also discloses her understanding of the gospel, humanity's inadequacies, and sin. In her prayerful response to verse 11, Sengers personalizes Jesus's parable of the seed and the sower (Matt. 13:1–23), identifying herself as a little seed, sprinkled by Jesus's blood, but in peril of destruction by the ungodly who ridicule her. Still, she expresses hope for the future:

O Lord Jesus Christ, I am also a little seed that you have sprinkled with your precious blood; therefore do not let me be destroyed under the stones of the cross or under the weeds of the godless, but grant that I might encase my soul with patience, so that I might gladly take the bread of affliction and the draft of tears with which I am fed and given to drink by you, although I will be mocked by the godless world because of it, so that I overcome everything with patience according to your example, so that I, who also sow here in tears, shall once reap in joy. (102)

Justitia Sengers's unique commentary on Ps. 69 was popular in her day but has been forgotten. It awaits the careful attention of biblical scholars, theologians, and historians, who will find that her extensive commentary provides an important example of sixteenth-century Protestant exegesis and insight into Sengers's life of faith, knowledge of Scripture, and theology of disability.

Bibliography

Karant-Nunn, Susan C. *The Reformation of Feeling: The Shaping of Religious Emotions in Early Modern Germany*. Oxford: Oxford University Press, 2010.

Sengers, Justitia. *Trostbüchlein, uber den Neun und Sechzigsten Psalm: Von dem Leiden und Sterben, unseres Herrn Jhesu Christi, und von unserm Creutz und Leiden, wie wir in die Fußtapfen Christi treten müssen; Und was wir für einen herrlichen Lohn bekommen warden; mit etlichen schönen Gebeten gezieret*. Magdeburg: Donat, 1586.

—Isa Hauser and Marion Ann Taylor

Simpson, Mary E. (ca. 1821–84)

Mary E. Simpson was born in England in about 1821. In 1856, at the age of thirty-five, she moved with her clergyman father to his new parish in the village of Boynton, East Yorkshire (Freeman 9). Her interest in biblical interpretation grew out of a desire to provide night classes for the young farm laborers living in this agricultural parish, whose lives she felt could be improved by a rudimentary education (Simpson, *Ploughing*, xii). Although her night school covered "secular" topics, such as reading, history, and geography, Simpson firmly believed that the Bible was "the foundation of all knowledge" and a timeless guide to living a good Christian life (18). Her primary goal was thus to ensure that her students learned to read and understand it. She was impelled to begin writing her own commentaries, however, when she realized that the already-published biblical notes written for the "unlearned," such as those by Sarah Trimmer, were not sufficiently simple for her students, whom she confessed were "all very ignorant" (*Scripture lessons* [1861], ix).

Simpson published two biblical commentaries, *Scripture lessons for the unlearned* (1861), a commentary on the books of the Pentateuch, and *Plain words on the Psalms of David* (1869). In each work she addresses a given text, one or more verses at a time, expounding its plain sense and clarifying its meaning within the original historical context of ancient Israel. Her commentary style is detailed but simple, including explanations of any words or phrases that she thinks readers might not understand. Thus, for example, in her commentary on Gen. 1:1–5, she writes, "At first, we are told, it [the earth] was 'without form' (there was nothing in it that had any shape or form,) 'and void' (that is empty,) 'and darkness was over the face of the deep,'—everywhere a dark empty sea, and nothing else—no living creature, even in the sea" (*Scripture lessons* [1861], 22). Similarly, she ensures that the readers understand allusions in the texts to ancient traditions or practices. Thus in her commentary on Ps. 51:7—"Purge me with hyssop, and I shall be clean"—she explains, "Hyssop was dipped in water, and the unclean person was sprinkled with it" (*Plain words*, 177). Simpson also makes extensive use of intertextual references, inviting her students to look up other Old Testament passages that she thinks have a similar meaning to the text in question or help clarify its significance.

In addition to these plain readings, Simpson's commentaries also stress the homiletic and theological significance of the biblical traditions. She believed that together the Old and New Testaments provide a guide to proper Christian faith and practice, with the Old Testament revealing God's working in human history and looking forward prophetically to the coming of Christ. Her interpretations therefore contain frequent intertestamental references, through which she expounds the meaning of an Old Testament passage in light of traditional Christian doctrine. For example, after explaining the significance of hyssop for purifying ritual uncleanliness in Ps. 51:7, she adds, "The washings and cleansings of the Jewish Law were a sign or figure of the cleansing power of the Blood of Christ, as we read in Hebrews ix.13, 14" (*Plain words*, 177). In addition, Simpson emphasizes the practical application of Scripture within her interpretation, using biblical passages to provide homiletic lessons in "right living" for her pupils. Thus Joseph's willingness to interpret the dreams of his fellow prisoners in Gen. 40:1–8 becomes an occasion to remind her students of the Christian virtue of helping others: "True Christians will 'bear one another's burdens and so fulfil the Law of Christ' (Galatians, vi.1.), not only helping one another, but feeling for one another; ready to rejoice with them that rejoice, and weep with them that weep. (Romans, xii.15)" (*Scripture lessons* [1861], 80).

In addition to her commentaries, Simpson composed other theological works for her pupils, including an address warning them against Nonconformist churches and a book titled *Short prayers for the hard working* (1862). In addition, she also wrote other genres of religious writing, which she aimed toward a wider audience. These included three works of religious fiction—*Little Molly* (1871); *Janetta* (1872); *The Shadow: How it came and went away; A temperance tale* (1879); and a book explaining the significance of Holy Week (1864). Although Simpson is perhaps a lesser-known figure in the history of women interpreters, her work nonetheless deserves attention and admiration, rooted as it was in her genuine desire to educate and thus enrich the lives of those whom conventional education had failed to inspire. Although she appreciated the traditional interpretative approach taken by scholars, preachers, and theologians, she also saw the importance of popularizing interpretation in order to reach a wider audience, and she utilized this tactic to significant effect. The success of her approach is perhaps best illustrated by the fact that both of the biblical commentaries that she wrote in the 1860s were republished as a second edition the following decade, while *Short prayers for the hard working*, initially published in 1862, reached its eighth edition by 1870. It is therefore fitting that Simpson's editor, F. Digby Legard, makes the following comment with regard to her involvement in religious education: "Woman's sphere is wider than we think and woman's influence is perhaps stronger than we like to allow" (*Ploughing*, vi).

See also Trimmer, Sarah (1741–1810)

Bibliography

Freeman, Clifford B. *Mary Simpson of Boynton Vicarage: Teacher of Ploughboys and Critic of Methodism.* York, UK: East Yorkshire Local History Society, 1972.

Simpson, Mary E. *An address to farm servants who had been confirmed, many of whom had soon after joined the Primitive Methodists or Ranters.* London: J. & C. Mozley, 1862.

———. *Gleanings: A sequel to Ploughing and sowing, by a clergyman's daughter.* Edited by F. Digby Legard. London: n.p., 1876.

———. *The Holy Week.* London: Mozley, 1864.

———. *Janetta; or, The little maid of all work.* London: SPCK, 1872.

———. *Little Molly.* London: n.p., 1871.

———. *Plain words on the Psalms of David, as translated in the Book of Common Prayer.* London: J. T. Hayes, 1869.

———. *Ploughing and sowing; or, Annals of an evening school in a Yorkshire Village, and the work that grew out of it: From letters and private notes by a clergyman's daughter.* Edited by F. Digby Legard. Editions 1–3. London: J. & C. Mozley, 1861.

———. *Scripture lessons for the unlearned; or, Notes on the Pentateuch.* 2nd ed. London: J. & C. Mozley, 1873.

———. *Scripture lessons for the unlearned, to be read with the Bible.* London: J. & C. Mozley, 1861.

———. *The Shadow: How it came and went away; A temperance tale.* London: SPCK, 1879.

———. *Short prayers for the hard working, and for those who have but little time to pray.* London: J. & C. Mozley, 1862.

———. *A simple commentary, or plain words on the Psalms of David as translated in the Book of Common Prayer: For use in Sunday or other schools.* 2nd ed. London: J. T. Hayes, 1875.

— CAROLINE BLYTH

Smith, Amanda Berry (1837–1915)

Amanda Berry Smith, African American evangelist, missionary, and moral reformer, was born a slave in Maryland. After purchasing their freedom in the early years of Amanda's life, her family moved to Pennsylvania, where she learned to read at home, briefly attended school, and eventually took a job as a household servant at age thirteen. In 1854 she entered the first of two unfortunate marriages. Her first husband never returned after enlisting in the Union Army during the Civil War; the second, James Smith, died in 1869. Only one of Amanda's five children, a daughter, survived to adulthood. It was during these years of marriage that Smith converted to Christianity (1856), experienced a later "blessing of holiness" (1868), and sensed a call to public ministry. Just before the death of her second husband and while living in New York City, Smith began testifying in local African Methodist Episcopal (AME) churches and attending Phoebe Palmer's weekly Tuesday Meeting for the Promotion of Holiness. In 1870 Smith preached her first sermon at an AME church in New Jersey. For the next several years she spoke at camp meeting revivals hosted by predominately white advocates of the burgeoning holiness movement and at the conventions of Frances Willard's newly organized national Women's Christian Temperance Union (WCTU). Smith created a small scandal in the AME church, which debarred women from public ministry, when she tried to participate in the denomination's 1876 national conference. With a growing reputation as an outspoken promoter of holiness and temperance, Smith embarked on a speaking tour through England, Ireland, and Scotland that initiated with the 1878 Keswick Convention. Between 1879 and 1890, she worked as a missionary in India and Liberia. After returning to the United States, Smith founded an orphanage for African American girls in Illinois (1899) and graduated from the Chicago Training School for Deaconesses (1906). She retired to Florida a few years before her death in 1915.

The lack of African American primary sources is an impoverishment of the history of biblical interpretation; this reality makes the available records so invaluable. The chief sources of information on Smith's method of interpreting the Bible are her autobiography, published in 1893, and excerpts from sermons that appeared in contemporary newspapers. They reveal two types of biblical interpretation: (1) meanings of scriptural texts given in association with spiritualized understandings of events that occurred in Smith's own life, and (2) explanations offered through the course of her preaching ministry. Since the most substantial body of Smith's writing is her autobiography, the former is significantly predominant over the latter in the surviving literature.

A major aspect of Smith's approach to biblical interpretation is her promotion of a Wesleyan-influenced doctrine of entire sanctification. She understood the holiness commended in 1 Thess. 4:3 to be freedom from sin. Smith saw the sixth beatitude in the Sermon on the Mount, "Blessed are the pure in heart" (Matt. 5:8), and its immediate context (esp. 5:11–12), as the standard of full sanctification. Smith rejected the notion that one could achieve the "blessing of holiness" through personal effort, though she admitted to having understood such passages as John 13:15 to this effect at one time (Smith 90). Romans 12 was a key text for Smith in her dual mission to preach holiness and advocate temperance. The only sermon by Smith that has been preserved in its entirety, one that she preached frequently, is on Rom. 12:1 (reproduced in Israel 159–61). For her, the Christian's "reasonable service" of setting oneself apart to God as a "living sacrifice" is both keeping the body pure from "depraved appetites" and cultivating "perfect faith" (160–61). In support of this interpretation of the temporal and spiritual aspects of sanctification, the sermon draws from biblical passages that speak of the body as a temple (1 Cor. 3:16–17; 6:19–20) and point to the standard of God's holiness (Isa. 6:3; 1 Pet. 1:16; Rev. 4:8). The exhortation concludes: "Let us sanctify our lives through perfect faith, real living faith. . . . Nothing is absolutely perfect but God. Let Him be your standard" (Israel 161).

Another prominent issue related to biblical interpretation in Smith's autobiography and public ministry—one that she shared with contemporary women preachers—was the struggle to have her work as a gospel minister rendered legitimate. Smith associated her charge with the divine commissioning of Moses in Exod. 33:1–2 and Jesus's disciples in Matt. 28:20, appropriating them as calls that she had personally received from God (Smith 132, 135). Similarly, she recounts that the biblical text of the first sermon that she preached, "Have ye received the Holy Ghost since ye believed?" (Acts 19:2), came to her as a direct revelation (156). Perhaps the most fascinating use of Scripture in Smith's defense of her public ministry, however, comes from two accounts of her engagement with 1 Cor. 14. On one occasion, she claimed the right to speak on the ground of exemption: "As I had no husband at home to ask [1 Cor. 14:35], I thought according to my orders in John [15:16], I had my authority from the words of the Master" (Smith 431). In the other instance, Smith simply observed that there was a time for men to refrain from speaking as well (1 Cor. 14:28) and applied this to her reading of 1 Cor. 14:34: "Let your 'men' keep silence in the church." She recalled: "Oh, what a stir it made" (Smith 321).

Smith's interpretation of the Bible was profoundly shaped by her religious and social circumstances. Like other black women preachers of her day, Smith endeavored to validate her ministry by correlating events in her life with specific biblical texts, creating an identity that imitated the Bible's prophetic tradition. The remarkably wide hearing that she achieved in the United States and abroad marks her significance as one of the most recognized African American female biblical interpreters of the nineteenth and early twentieth centuries.

See also Palmer, Phoebe (1807–74); Willard, Frances Elizabeth (1839–98)

Bibliography

Haywood, Chanta M. *Prophesying Daughters: Black Women Preachers and the Word, 1823–1913*. Columbia: University of Missouri Press, 2003.

Israel, Adrienne M. *Amanda Berry Smith: From Washerwoman to Evangelist*. Lanham, MD: Scarecrow, 1998.

Smith, Amanda. *An Autobiography: The Story of the Lord's Dealings with Mrs. Amanda Smith, the Colored Evangelist*. Chicago: Meyer & Brother, 1893.

— ERIC BRANDT

▨ Smith, Elizabeth (1776–1806)

Elizabeth Smith was born at Burnhall near Durham. In her short life of twenty-nine years, she lived in poverty as the ward of family and friends. As a child she received a limited education from a governess and gained the reputation of being "a living library" by teaching herself French, Italian, Spanish, German,

Latin, Greek, Hebrew, Syriac, Arabic, and Persian, as well as other subjects. She was encouraged to read broadly by such learned contemporaries as Hannah More, Elizabeth Hamilton, and Henrietta Maria Bowdler. Although she wrote extensively, her works were not published during her lifetime. Instead, friends and admirers edited and published her works after her death. *Fragments in prose and verse* (1808), a collection of Smith's poems, letters, and reflections, was so popular that it went through several editions.

Smith's *The Book of Job* is a translation of Job. It was completed in 1803 but not published until 1810. Compared to the majestic rhetoric and archaic syntax of the King James Version (KJV), Smith's translation captures well the vivid images and dramatic effects of the Hebrew poetry, while preserving the clarity of the English language. Her proficiency in Hebrew and elegance in the poetic rendering of Job were applauded by her generation.

Smith's translation of the difficult Hebrew in this book reflects not only her superior knowledge of Hebrew but also her willingness to reinterpret the biblical text. For example, the portrayal of the moral character of God in the book of Job has long been problematic: How could a just God initiate a wager with the evil one concerning the integrity of his devout servant? At the scene of the divine counsel (Job 1:6–12), Smith presents an innocent God who is challenged by a group of ill-intentioned angels led by Satan. The KJV translates 1:6 as follows: "Now there was a day when the *sons of God* came to present themselves *before* the Lord, and Satan came also among them" (see also 2:1). In contrast, Smith took the liberty of reconstructing a hostile scene in the divine council, where the tempting angels initiate the challenge against God and Job: "And the day was, and the *sons of perdition* came to set themselves *against* Jehovah, and the Satan [enemy] also came among them." In this way, she successfully explains away God's problematic morality and eliminates his cruelty by placing him in a passive position in the wager.

Smith also recasts the character of Job in a more orthodox light. For example, at the end of Job's trial, Smith emphasizes Job's portrait as a submissive believer. The KJV translates 42:7b as "For ye have not spoken *of* me *the thing that is right*, as my servant Job hath." Although the KJV and many other modern translations emphasize that the content of Job's remarks about God are correct, Smith stresses the rightness of Job's attitude (42:7): "Jehovah said to Eliphaz the Temanite, my wrath is kindled against thee and against thy two friends, for ye have not spoken *to* me *respectfully*, like my servant Job" (Smith's version of 42:8: Speak *to* me "*submissively*"). In Smith's translation, Job neither accuses God for his undeserved ordeal nor doubts the divine purpose behind the tragedy. Instead, Job firmly believes in God's compassion.

Smith also offers an alternative presentation of Job's wife. The KJV supports the traditional negative reading of her as a second Eve or "the devil's helpmeet" (Augustine). For example, the KJV translates Job 2:9–10 as, "Dost thou still retain thine integrity? Curse God, and die!" Smith, however, translates these verses as, "Dost thou still hold fast thy integrity, *blessing God, and dying?*" Smith's translation softens the dishonorable image of Job's wife by literally translating the Hebrew verb "to bless" (*bārēk*), going against the traditional interpretation, in which the verb was understood to be a euphemism for "to curse." Smith also took the imperative of the Hebrew verbs "bless" and "die" as participles—"blessing" and "dying"—which describe Job's reaction and state of suffering: he still blesses God in the process of dying. Through her fresh rendering, Smith refashions the character of Job's wife. Job's wife is not tempting him to curse God and to suffer death, as if she has lost her patience and faith in the face of divine attack. On the contrary, she is simply describing Job's reaction to his suffering and destitution.

The second mention of Job's wife occurs in Job's debate with his friends, to whom he laments his alienation from those around him (19:13–19): brothers have left him, servants ignore him, children despise him, friends abhor him. Job's wife's attitude of repulsion is assumed when Job wails: "My breath [*rûwaḥ*] is strange [KJV; NRSV: repulsive; NASB, NIV: offensive] to my wife!" (v. 17a). Discontented with this negative view of Job's wife, Smith offers a reading that softens her attitude toward her husband: "My *voice* becomes strange to my wife." Smith did not discuss why she challenged traditional negative portrayals of Job's wife; however, one can surmise that her own experiences of pain and poverty and her confidence as a woman made her a very empathetic reader of Job's wife.

The foundation of Smith's translation endeavor was laid as early as the age of seventeen, when she developed a list of Hebrew words and their Arabic and Persian cognates, a work that reveals her linguistic genius. A contemporary judged her remarkable systematic collation of these languages "not only useful and interesting but . . . like her translation of Job, a wonderful performance" by a young woman "adorned with all the accomplishments of her sex and distinguished by the various talents of Poetry, Metaphysics and moral observation" (*A Vocabulary*, viii).

Although Smith's life as a scholar was cut short, her work as a translator, philologist, and interpreter of Scripture deserves to be remembered. Her translation of the book of Job especially provides an important example of the development of the English Bible. As the English language evolves and the knowledge of ancient Hebrew continues to grow, the project of translating the Bible continues, and Smith's translation of Job has left an indelible footprint in the history of the English Bible. Smith's translation provides an important example of a woman's interpretation. Through her daring alterations and loose rendering of the original text, one gains a glimpse of her theological understanding of the book of Job and of God, and a glimpse of her empathetic interpretation of the suffering Job and his wife.

See also More, Hannah (1745–1833)

Bibliography

Anon. "Smith's (Miss) Translation of Job, with a Preface and Annotations by Dr. Randolph." *Eclectic Review* 7, no. 2 (1811): 657–71, 768–80.

Hawley, Judith. "Smith, Elizabeth (1776–1806)." Pages 94–95 in vol. 51 of *Oxford Dictionary of National Biography*, edited by H. C. G. Matthew and Brian Harrison. Rev. ed. Oxford: Oxford University Press, 2004–11.

Smith, Elizabeth. *The Book of Job: Translated from the Hebrew by the late Miss Elizabeth Smith, with a Preface and Annotations by the Rev. Francis Randolph*. Bath: Richard Cruttwell, 1810.

———. *Fragments in prose and verse: By a young lady lately deceased (Elizabeth S—); With some account of her life and character*. Edited by Henrietta Maria Bowdler. Bath: Richard Cruttwell, 1808. Other editions at Bath, 1809, 1810, 1811–12; Boston, 1810; Burlington, NJ, 1811; London, 1814, 1818, 1824–26, 1842.

———. *Memoirs of Frederick and Margaret Klopstock: Translated from the German, by the author of "Fragments in Prose and Verse."* Bath: Richard Cruttwell, 1808. Other editions at Philadelphia, 1810; Bath, 1812.

———. *A Vocabulary, Hebrew, Arabic, and Persian: To which is Prefixed, a Praxis on the Arabic Language, by John Frederick Usko*. London: A. J. Valpy, 1814.

—SOPHIA H. Y. CHEN

Smith, Julia Evelina (1792–1886)

Julia Evelina Smith was one of five daughters born into a Congregational family in Glastonbury, Connecticut. From her father, Zephaniah Smith—who left the ministry for law and later explored the teachings of the end-times Baptist preacher William Miller—Smith learned to appreciate diverse thinking. Her mother, Hannah Hickok, helped lay the foundation for the extraordinary journey that Smith would later take in life by teaching her and her four sisters French, Latin, and Greek and advocating for the freedom of slaves.

In 1810 Smith attended a boarding school in New Haven, where she studied French. By 1823, at the age of thirty-one, she was offered a position at the Troy Female Seminary in New York; that lasted about a year. For whatever reasons, her health or homesickness, she returned to Glastonbury and lived on the family farm with her sisters until, at eighty-seven, she married Amos H. Parker.

Prompted by the failed teachings of Miller that the world would end in 1842, Smith decided to search the Bible herself for clues about the present and the future. In 1874 she wrote that her goal in translating the Bible was "to see whether no new light and clearer light might not thus be thrown upon passages whose meaning is ambiguous and whose construction is disputed" (Shaw 147). She translated the Greek New Testament, the Septuagint, and the Latin Vulgate before she mastered Hebrew so that she could translate the Old Testament from its original language. She translated the Bible five times over the span of eight years (1847–55), sharing the results of her work with family and friends. In 1876 Smith decided to publish her translation of the

Bible in response to her treatment by men in government, who insisted on taxing the family farm even though she and her sisters could not vote. Thus a campaign to challenge the government's right to levy taxes on disenfranchised people began. This decision was her way of proving that women were not second-rate citizens.

Smith's translation surprised scholars like Professor Edward James Young of Harvard, who was astonished that she had "translated so correctly without consulting some learned man" (Stanton 151). She translated each Greek and Hebrew word with the same word in English wherever possible and had an unusual conception of the Hebrew tenses, often rendering the Hebrew imperfect tense with the English future. Smith defended the literalness of her work, arguing that "exactness" rather than "smoothness" was her intent (151). Smith's often mechanical translation opened up a number of new interpretive possibilities. For example, Lillie Devereux Blake expressed a new sense of sympathy for Potiphar's wife, who was a wife only in name, based on Smith's understanding that Potiphar was Pharaoh's eunuch, not his officer, for Smith translated the Hebrew term as "eunuch," rather than "officer" (Stanton 65).

Smith's translations of texts related to women also challenged traditionally accepted views of women. For example, instead of following the King James Version (KJV) of 1 Tim. 2:11–12 ("Let a woman learn in silence with all subjection") or the American Standard Version (ASV; "Let a woman learn in quietness with all subjection"), Smith translates the Greek text: "Let the woman, in freedom from care, learn in all subjection." Moreover, instead of "I suffer not a woman to teach, nor to usurp authority over a man" (KJV) or "I permit no" (RSV), Smith's "I trust not" seems to make it Paul's individual preference that a woman learn in submission and not a command. Smith's translation suggests that a woman may have authority over a man, though the writer prefers that women do not exercise that option if they are not in a state of "freedom from care."

History remembers Julia Smith as the woman who published a translation of the Bible in English and as a suffragist who with her sister Abby (1797–1878) gained national and international attention for their protests over their lack of property and voting rights. Selections of Smith's translation were used by the revising committee for *The Woman's Bible* (1895, 1898), by Elizabeth Cady Stanton, but in general most researchers do not refer to her monumental efforts.

See also Stanton, Elizabeth Cady (1815–1902)

Bibliography

Samson, Emily. *With Her Own Eyes: The Story of Julia Smith, Her Life, and Her Bible*. Knoxville: University of Tennessee Press, 2006.

Selvidge, Marla J. *Notorious Voices: Feminist Biblical Interpretation, 1500–1920*. New York: Continuum, 1996.

Shaw, Susan J. *A Religious History of Julia Evelina Smith's 1876 Translation of the Holy Bible: Doing More Than Any Man Has Ever Done*. San Francisco: Mellen Research University Press, 1993.

Smith, Julia E. *The Holy Bible Containing the Old and New Testaments: Translated Literally from the Original Tongues*. Hartford, CT: American Pub., 1876.

Stanton, Elizabeth Cady, ed. *The Woman's Bible*. 2 vols. in 1. New York: European Pub., 1898.

— MARLA SELVIDGE

Smith, Louise Pettibone (1887–1981)

Louise Pettibone Smith, born in Ogdensburg, New York, was a biblical scholar, professor, author, translator, book reviewer, and social activist. "Politics" was no strange word to Smith since her family had strong ties to the Republican Party: her grandfather was one of the founders of the Abolition Society in central New York State, and her father was an editor of the Republican paper in northern New York. Yet later in her life her social consciousness led her to campaign against some of the Republican policies.

Smith attended Bryn Mawr College, receiving her bachelor's degree in 1908, her master's degree in 1912, and her doctorate in Semitic languages and Palestinian archaeology in 1917, with her thesis titled "The Messianic Ideal of Isaiah." From 1908 to 1911 she taught English and Latin at Hardin College in Mexico, Missouri. From 1913 to 1914 she held the Thayer Fellowship of the American School of Oriental Research in Jerusalem. In 1915 she joined the faculty at Wellesley College as a member of the Department of Biblical History, a position she held until 1953, when she was appointed professor emerita.

Smith, a gifted linguist, translated and made available to the English-speaking world the works of some significant German scholars. Her translations include Rudolf Bultmann's *Jesus and the Word* (1934) and *Faith and Understanding* (1969); Hans Hofmann's *The Theology of Reinhold Niebuhr* (1956); and Karl Barth's *Theology and Church* (1962). In 1958 she and Joseph Haroutunian cotranslated *Calvin: Commentaries* from Latin into English. Smith later acknowledged these great theologians for their influence on her thinking and teaching.

Smith's academic publications were dispersed in the pages of journals, reviews, and commentaries. In many of her works, she employed historical and literary criticism of the Bible. She also consulted other ancient Near Eastern literatures and Jewish literature, such as the Talmud and Midrash Rabbah. She did not show any "feminine trait" in her work. In "The Book of Ruth," on which Smith collaborated with James T. Cleland, it was almost impossible to distinguish her work from that of her male counterpart. She was profoundly influenced by Calvin, whose social ethics, she claimed, "were more demanding than even the 'Social Gospel' at its best" (*Diamond Jubilee*, 5). Her article "The Book of Micah" (1952) demonstrates how Calvin's ethics had shaped her perspective on issues such as social injustice and civil liberty. At times her exposition of the prophetic messages in Micah led to criticism of her own government's policy. For example, commenting on Mic. 2:8–11, Smith accused the US government of using extreme measures to silence the voices of Cold War dissidents: "In a time of peace the nation's actions are those of war, an indictment which is especially timely with the death penalty for espionage, the denial of the right of reasonable bail, and the suppression of free speech and free assembly" (219).

Recognized as a distinguished biblical scholar by her peers, Smith did graduate work at the Divinity School of the University of Chicago, at Radcliffe College, and in Germany at Halle, Bonn, and Marburg. From 1944 to 1945 she took a brief break from her academic profession to join the American Association for Greek War Relief, working for the UN Relief and Rehabilitation effort at a Greek refugee camp in Palestine for six months and teaching English at Pierce College in Athens for four months.

Her involvement in the civil liberties struggle in the United States began when Smith saw similarities between what was happening in her own country and what she had experienced in 1936 while she was in Germany, studying the relation of the German churches, the "Confessional Church" in particular, to the Hitler regime. Her social advocacy was deeply rooted in the teachings of the Pentateuch and especially in the Holiness Code of Leviticus, which teaches justice for all (Lev. 24:22) and love for the sojourners (Lev. 19:33–34). In 1951 she was elected cochair of the American Committee for Protection of Foreign Born, which served to protect many innocent naturalized American citizens from injustice and deportation. After her retirement, Smith worked tirelessly, traveling throughout the country and speaking to numerous groups, seeking to instill the hope and promise of a just and free society in which there is one law for the sojourner and for the native. Smith wrote *Torch of Liberty: Twenty-Five Years in the Life of the Foreign Born in the U.S.A.* (1959) to document the twenty-five years of the committee's history and struggle.

Smith was a long-standing member of the Society of Biblical Literature (SBL). In 1915 she joined the SBL, and in 1917 she was the first woman to publish an article in the *Journal of Biblical Literature*. From 1950 to 1952 she served as secretary of the society (the second woman holding an executive committee position in the SBL) and in 1951 represented the society at the Conference of the United Nations Educational, Scientific and Cultural Organization in New York. Her dedication and achievements in the field of biblical studies were honored by the SBL during its centenary celebration in 1980.

Bibliography

Lehmann, Paul. "Louise Pettibone Smith, Rudolf Bultmann, and Wellesley." Pages 91–101 in *Bultmann Retrospect and Prospect: The Centenary Symposium at Wellesley*, edited by Edward C. Hobbs. Harvard Theological Studies 35. Philadelphia: Fortress, 1985.

Louise Pettibone Smith Birthday Committee. *Louise Pettibone Smith Diamond Jubilee Testimonial Dinner, October 12, 1962*. New York: Louise Pettibone Smith Birthday Committee, 1962.

Saunders, Ernest W. *Searching the Scriptures: A History of the Society of Biblical Literature, 1880–1980*. Chico, CA: Scholars Press, 1982.

Smith, Louise Pettibone. "The Book of Micah." *Interpretation* 6 (1952): 210–27.

———. "The Messianic Ideal of Isaiah." *Journal of Biblical Literature* 36 (1917): 158–212.

———. *Torch of Liberty: Twenty-Five Years in the Life of the Foreign Born in the U.S.A.* New York: Dwight-King, 1959.

Smith, Louise Pettibone, and James T. Cleland. "The Book of Ruth." In vol. 2 of *The Interpreter's Bible*. New York: Abingdon-Cokesbury, 1953.

— GRACE KO

Southard, Mabel Madeline (1877–1967)

Tenacious and determined, Mabel Madeline Southard composed her life as a response to God's call for her to preach. She was born July 29, 1877, in Kansas near the small town of Rock. Southard and her sister, Stella, were reared by their mother, Madeline Delaphina Rogers Southard (born 1848), and grandmother Almira Santee Rogers (born 1823). This matrifocal situation—grandmother, mother, and two girls making their life together on the Kansas prairie—had an enduring influence on Madeline's sense of self.

Southard's progressive nature manifested early when she became a preacher and evangelist in her teens. Graduating with a bachelor's degree from Southwestern College in 1899 and a master's degree from Garrett Biblical Institute, Northwestern University, in 1919, she diligently worked for ecclesial suffrage, serving as a delegate to the General Conferences of the Methodist Episcopal Church in 1920 and 1924. After a brief stint with prohibitionist Carry Nation, including the famous saloon-smashing raid in Topeka, Kansas, in 1901, she lectured briefly for the Woman's Christian Temperance Union (WCTU) circuit before settling into a life of itinerant preaching and evangelism. Her long peripatetic career extended beyond Kansas and the United States to the Philippines and India; she founded an organization for women ministers, the International Association of Woman Preachers (IAWP), and served as its first president and esteemed editor of its journal, *The Woman's Pulpit*. In addition, she wrote *The White Slave Traffic versus the American Home* (1914); *The Attitude of Jesus toward Woman* (1927), a revision of her master's thesis (1919); and *The Christian Message on Sex* (1931). She lived to be ninety, maintaining a personal diary from the time she was fourteen years old—a voluminous record now located at the Schlesinger Library, Radcliffe Institute, Harvard University.

Southard's most extensive hermeneutical project was *The Attitude of Jesus toward Woman*, her master's thesis, in which she concentrated on how Jesus interacted with women as reported in all four Gospel accounts. While William T. Noll, author of three articles on women and Methodism, remarked in his *Methodist History* article (1992) that Southard's thesis was an "early feminist classic," it has received scant scholarly attention to date.

Influenced by nascent historical criticism and cultural studies, Southard emphasized the importance of cultural context while seldom relying on analyses of New Testament Greek or literary structures. Sketching the historical standards prevailing in Jewish and Roman societies during the first century, she accentuated Jesus's contrary actions. For example, in the context of addressing Jesus's reproofs of women, Southard claims women in Roman society were required to worship the deities of one's husband, and "even the Hebrew did not trust the woman to make her own religious decisions" (52), while Jesus required women to take full control of their spiritual lives, reprimanding even his own mother when she apparently did not understand his full calling. In Southard's view, Jesus was a reforming figure, one who treated women as persons in their own rights and not people simply by virtue of their relationships as mothers, sisters, wives, and so forth; thus Jesus's actions were decidedly different from his culture and its patriarchal reality.

Southard's conclusion that Jesus treated women with respect and equality confirmed the rightness of her childhood calling to the ministry and propelled her to work for women's ecclesial equality in the Methodist Episcopal Church. Indeed, her legacy continues in the ordained ministries of Methodist women and the sustained presence of the IAWP—now the American Association of Women Ministers.

Bibliography

Noll, William T. "A Welcome in the Ministry: The 1920 and 1924 General Conferences Debate Clergy Rights for Women." *Methodist History* 30, no. 2 (January 1992): 92.

Southard, M. Madeline. "The Attitude of Jesus toward Woman." MA thesis, Northwestern University, 1919.

———. *The Attitude of Jesus toward Woman.* New York: George H. Doran, 1927. Repr., Stroudsburg, PA: International Association of Women Ministers, 1999.

———. M. Madeline Southard Papers. Schlesinger Library, Radcliffe Institute for Advanced Study, Harvard University. Processed Oct. 2010. http://oasis.lib.harvard.edu/oasis/deliver/deepLink?_collection=oasis&uniqueId=sch01306.

———. "Woman and the Ministry." *Methodist Review*, Nov.–Dec. 1919.

Weddle Irons, Kendra. "M. Madeline Southard on Ecclesial Suffrage." *Methodist History* 45, no. 1 (Oct. 2006): 16–30.

———. *Preaching on the Plains: Methodist Women Preachers in Kansas, 1920–1956.* Lanham, MD: University Press of America, 2007.

—KENDRA WEDDLE IRONS

Southcott, Joanna (1750–1814)

Joanna Southcott was born near Ottery St. Mary, in Devon, England. She was the daughter of a tenant farmer and had little formal education. In 1792 she claimed to have heard the Spirit of God warning her that the coming of Christ was imminent. She then prophesied about meteorological and other local events and attracted interest in the Exeter region. From the start of her prophetic ministry until her death she claimed to be the "Woman clothed with the Sun" of Rev. 12:1 and the bride of Christ (Rev. 19:7). Southcott spoke publicly only on rare occasions. Her ministry was primarily in print: she produced sixty-five publications from 1801 to 1814. She did not think that her prophecies were to replace the Bible but to supplement it, offering its true meaning, especially with regard to the imminent establishment of God's kingdom on earth and her eschatological role in that process. According to Southcott, some prophecies in Scripture are sealed up (cannot be understood) until the time of the end (Dan. 12:4). Her conviction that she had authority to reveal the true meaning of the Bible was derived from her claim that the time of unsealing (revealing) had now come, and that she was the second Eve, the Lamb's bride. The bridegroom (Christ) revealed to his bride how his kingdom would be established and the events that would precede its establishment. She in turn fulfilled the purpose of God in creating woman—to be a true "helpmeet for man" (Gen. 2:18). She believed that when John had seen the woman in his vision, it was she, Joanna Southcott, whom he was seeing. For much of her life she interpreted this passage figuratively of herself as the mother of her spiritual children, whom she understood as her disciples. She believed that to be the bride of Christ was open to all who joined with her in her eschatological mission. Although women had led prophetic movements previously (such as Sarah Flaxmer, Ann Lee, Dorothy Gott), it was unusual for a woman to attract many supporters. The number of her followers was claimed to approach 100,000, her publications were widely read, and reports of her claims appeared in national newspapers in the early nineteenth century.

In early 1814 she changed her understanding of Rev. 12 from a figurative to a literal interpretation. In February she received a communication from the Holy Spirit that she was to give birth to a real child, Shiloh (Book 61). The rest of her life was spent preparing for the birth of the child. Southcott was pronounced pregnant by several reputed physicians. She died two days after Christmas Day 1814, allegedly in the process of giving birth. An autopsy showed no signs of a child or any clear cause of death. Her followers interpreted the events in different ways. Some believed that the child was caught up to God, as in Rev. 12:5, to return at some point in the near future. Others believed that she would return to give birth, or that the child was to be incarnate in another living person, possibly one of her followers.

Southcott's theology was based on her interpretation of the fall in Gen. 3. She relays the words of the Spirit:

> The answer he (Adam) gave for his disobedience was, "The woman *thou* gavest me, gave me the evil and I did eat!" Here he cast the blame upon his frail partner,

461

whereas the man and woman, being the perfect man, ought not to have been divided against themselves, but ought to have been one in spirit, and one in perpetual unity and innocence. (Book 7)

Here was Paradise lost. The man copied after the woman in disobedience, and cast the blame on his MAKER. Now here let Paradise be regained. The woman you shall all see stands in perfect obedience to ME, and in her writings hath told you what is MY mind and will. Now bring forth your arguments, show your strong reasons, *why you refuse to hear her.* (Book 14)

The woman, Eve, had told the truth, that Satan had beguiled her, but the man had wrongly blamed her and ultimately blamed God for giving her to him. God's purposes in redemption were to be fulfilled in the advent of a second Eve, who would complement the salvation begun by Christ. Since there was still evil in the world, Southcott believed that the promise made in Eden concerning the crushing of the serpent's head had not yet been fulfilled, though the bruising of the heel of the woman's seed was fulfilled in the death of the woman's seed, Christ (Gen. 3:15). This had come about by men's petitioning Pilate for his death. The crushing of the serpent's head had to come through the petitioning of God by Joanna Southcott, the "Second Eve," together with followers who would join with her in her petition to God to bring the downfall of Satan.

The movement around Southcott did not disappear with the nonappearance of Shiloh. Many Southcottians were happy to await further developments. New prophets claimed to be Shiloh or his herald (e.g., John Wroe; John [alias Zion] Ward; Mabel Baltrop, founder of the Panacea Society), resulting in several religious groups, some of which continue to this day. A great contribution to world thought was her interpretation of the fall, putting woman in the right and man in the wrong, which laid a foundation for later feminist thinking.

See also Gott, Dorothy Newberry (1747/48–1812)

Bibliography

Allan, Gordon. "Southcottian Sects from 1790 to the Present Day." Pages 213–36 in *Expecting the End: Millennialism in Social and Historical Context*, edited by K. C. Newport and Crawford Gribben. Waco: Baylor University Press, 2006.

Brown, Frances. *Joanna Southcott: The Woman Clothed with the Sun.* Cambridge: Lutterworth, 2002.

Harrison, John F. C. *The Second Coming: Popular Millenarianism, 1780–1850.* London: Routledge & Kegan Paul, 1979.

Hopkins, James K. *A Woman to Deliver Her People.* Austin: University of Texas Press, 1982.

Southcott, Joanna. Her books (1801–14) and manuscripts are online at http://www.joannasouthcott.com.

—CHRISTOPHER ROWLAND

Sowernam, Ester (fl. 1615–17)

Ester Sowernam's biography is brief: in 1617 she wrote a pamphlet titled *Ester hath hang'd Haman*, in response to Joseph Swetnam's 1615 *Araignment of lewd, idle, froward, and unconstant women*. "Sowernam" was probably an acidic pseudonym, punning on the adversary's "sweet name," and "Ester" connects the author with the biblical queen who saved her people and caused their would-be destroyer, Haman, to be hanged. On her title page, Sowernam proclaims herself "neither Maide, Wife, nor Widdowe, yet really all, and therefore experienced to defend all." Wayne argues that this denial of the standard categories marks her as a single, experienced woman; Purkiss concludes that the author rejected "compulsory heteronormativity" (84). Internal evidence persuades commentators to agree that, whatever the gender, Sowernam was a highly educated and sophisticated rhetorician.

In her two prefaces, one addressed to women and the other to "worthy youths," Sowernam explains that she is responding to Swetnam because a recent rebuttal by "a Minister's daughter . . . of tender . . . years" (Rachel Speght) was inadequate. She then outlines her attack: she herself will prove the worthiness of women by studying references to their depictions in the Bible, then turn to classical writers and to everyday life. Finally she will bring the woman-hater to justice. (The 132 lines of jingling rhymes that conclude the pamphlet are signed "Joane Sharpe" and were probably not written by Sowernam.)

Sowernam starts with Swetnam's misinterpretation of Genesis: "*Woman was made to bee an helper to Man: And so they are indeed, for they helpe to consume and spend*" (B1). In an uncannily contemporary voice, she retorts: "Was the end of Gods creation in Woman to spend and consume? Is *helper* to be taken in that sence, to helpe to *spend*? Is spending and consuming, *helping?*" (B2). She playfully rebuts Swetnam's joke, that women are crooked because they were formed from Adam's rib, with an equally old feminist joke—that women were made from a higher substance than "durt," and that if ribs do cause crookedness, well, Adam had more ribs. More seriously, she observes that both received their "souls and dispositions" from God's breath. In a chapter devoted to reading Genesis as pro-woman, some of her arguments are poetic. Thus ribs are symbols: solid, substantial, and located near the heart. Eve first blossomed in a paradisal garden and retains the odor of paradise. Other arguments foreground Adam's responsibility for Eve, Eve's fruitfulness, the seed of redemption, and the idea that Eve is to practice obedience because obedience is God's dearest virtue. A few are self-consciously partisan. After a casuistic claim that Adam sinned first because he ate first, and "there was no sinne till the fruit was eaten," Sowernam admits that she is "taking all advantages I may, to defend my sexe" (B4).

Chapter 3 consists of eighteen one-sentence tributes to "helpful" Old Testament women, each with book, chapter, and verse marginally noted. (Shepherd points out that she uses the Geneva, Douai, and Bishops Bibles [119].) Nine named women—Sarah, Rebecca, Deborah, Jael, Malchal (Michal?), Abigail, Judith, Hester (Esther), and Susanna—taken together demonstrate women's capacity for direct action as well as for necessary deception. The unnamed are simply identified by their helpful actions: Hebrew midwives, Pharaoh's daughter, the Samarian widow. Chapter 4 briefly notes a dozen virtuous New Testament women, further proving the "impudencie" of Swetnam's attacks.

Later chapters argue with less "gravitie" that women have military skill (Boadicea), intelligence (the Muses), even the approval of Plato, and that they deserve better than the double standard, which condemns them for acts deemed acceptable in men. These chapters prove that Sowernam knows the classics; moreover, by imitating Swetnam's analogy-making style and using the logician's technical vocabulary to prove him illogical, they demonstrate Sowernam's superior rhetorical skills.

In her "arraignment" of Swetnam, Sowernam specifically equates Haman's evil edicts with Swetnam's blasphemous pamphlet, implicitly comparing her own writings with those of Queen Esther (Carruthers, "Neither"). After convicting Swetnam on charges of blasphemy against God's handiwork, Sowernam returns to Genesis, reminding her readers that the serpent was masculine, and that Eve is a victim of the poor role modeling given her by a disloyal husband, who tried to save himself by shifting blame onto her (F, F1).

As Carruthers demonstrates, "Ester Sowernam" is as dangerous a writer as the arguably biblical queen whose name she shares or claims ("Neither," 337). Her reasoning skills are many, her humor apparent, and her lack of sectarianism hinted by the fact that she uses Catholic, Lutheran, and Anglican Bibles. That she subverts the current rhetoric of female chastity and passive obedience is clear from her tributes to Old Testament women, tributes that only partially erase problematic actions. Thus "Rahab the harlot" is just a helpful woman from Josh. 2:6. Jael (Iahell) merely slew a general; for the rest of that story, Sowernam directs readers to Judg. 4. She notes that a woman preserved Joash when "the bloud-Royall of Judah had been all murthered," but sends readers to 2 Kings 11 to learn that the murderer was Joash's powerful grandmother. She generally mutes women's capacity for violence, yet leaves traces visible. And she scoffs at Swetnam for blasphemously listing Judith as a lewd rather than virtuous woman. For Ester Sowernam, devaluing active women is sinful. One reads the fate of Haman's followers, scripted by biblical Esther (Esther 9–10), as Sowernam's subtext for those who echo Joseph Swetnam's blasphemies.

Whoever Sowernam was, her writing stands as an important reminder that women of her period resisted misogynist interpretations of Scripture.

See also Speght, Rachel (ca. 1597–ca. 1661)

Bibliography

Carruthers, Jo. *Esther through the Centuries.* Malden, MA: Blackwell, 2008.

———. "'Neither Maide, Wife or Widow': Ester Sowernam and the Book of Esther." *Prose Studies* 26, no. 3 (2003): 321–43.

Eastwood, Adrianne L. "Controversy and the Single Woman in *The Maid's Tragedy* and *The Roaring Girl*." *Rocky Mountain Review* 58, no. 2 (2004): 7–27. http://rmmla.wsu.edu/ereview/58.2/articles/eastwood.asp.

Purkiss, Diane. "Material Girls: The Seventeenth Century Woman Debate." Pages 69–100 in *Women, Texts and Histories 1575–1760.* Edited by Clare Brant and Diane Purkiss. New York: Routledge, 1992.

Schnell, Lisa. "Muzzling the Competition: Rachel Speght and the Economics of Print." Pages 57–77 in *Debating Gender in Early Modern England, 1500–1700,* edited by Cristina Malcolmson and Mihoko Suzuki. New York: Palgrave Macmillan, 2002.

Shepherd, Simon. *The Women's Sharp Revenge: Five Women's Pamphlets from the Renaissance.* New York: St. Martin's Press, 1985.

Sowernam, Ester. *Ester hath hang'd Haman; Or, An Answere to a lewd Pamphlet, entituled, the Arraignment of Women.* London: Nicholas Bourne, 1617. Pages A1–H4 in *Defences of Women: Jane Anger, Rachel Speght, Ester Sowernam and Constantia Munda,* selected by Susan G. O'Malley. Early Modern Englishwoman: A Facsimile Library of Essential Works; Series 1, Printed Writings, 1500–1640; Part 1, vol. 4. Aldershot, UK: Scolar, 1996.

Wayne, V. "The Dearth of the Author: Anonymity's Allies and Swetnam the Woman-Hater." Pages 221–40 in *Maids and Mistresses, Cousins and Queens: Women's Alliances in Early Modern England,* edited by S. Frye and K. Robertson. Oxford: Oxford University Press, 1999.

— BETSY DELMONICO

Speght, Rachel (ca. 1597–ca. 1661)

Rachel Speght, born in about 1597, was the daughter of the Calvinist minister James Speght. Her two published works, *A Mouzell for Melastomus* (1617) and *Mortalities Memorandum* (1621), illustrate her extensive biblical knowledge and solid education. Though Speght was probably not provided a classical education that included training in Greek and Latin, she does deploy Latin in her two publications. In 1621 she married William Procter, a Calvinist cleric.

She is best known for her 1617 publication titled *A Mouzell for Melastomus,* one of a number of responses to Joseph Swetnam's highly popular attack on women, *Araignment of lewd, idle, froward, and unconstant women.* Speght's *Mouzell for Melastomus* refutes in detail his attack on womankind while simultaneously mounting a sustained argument for women based on the Genesis fall account. In a twenty-one-page tract, followed by a fourteen-page appendix titled "Certaine Quaeres to the bayter of Women," Speght offers a reinterpretation of Scripture that includes marginal notions directing the reader to biblical citations either quoted or referenced within the body of the text.

The most extensively glossed book is Genesis, but her use of 1 Corinthians and Galatians produces a reconfiguration of Protestant marriage doctrine with "considerable subversive potential" to "affirm categorically the moral and spiritual equality of women" (Lewalski, introduction, xxiii).

A Mouzell for Melastomus is structured around the refutation of four main attacks derived from the Bible by Swetnam: that women "brought death and misery upon all her posterity"; that woman "was in the transgression" (1 Tim. 2:14); that "It were good for a man not to touch a woman" (1 Cor. 7:1); and that among a thousand women, no good one is to be found (Eccles. 7:28). Her refutation of these four biblically based attacks allows her to argue for radical equality between men and women. She begins by positioning men as more culpable for the fall than women: since man was the "stronger vessel" (15), he should have been able to resist the temptation more so than Eve. Her punishment is consequently the lesser, applied only to women, while "for the sinne of man the whole earth was cursed" (14–15). Speght's use of Gal. 3:28, "male and female are all one in Christ Jesus," is her "most radical claim" according to Lewalski (xxv); here through the promise of salvation, Speght asserts the "good"-ness of women, countering centuries of attacks on women in the *querelle des femmes* dispute, attacks from antifeminist tradition, in which women's flaws are enumerated.

Arguing that Eve meant no harm in offering Adam the fruit, a frequent argument in the early seventeenth century, Speght diminishes Eve's sin. This works in concert with language of greater equality between husband and wife. Made from Adam's side, not his foot, Eve is "to be his equall, . . . their authority equall, and all creatures to be in subjection unto them both" (18). Made for man by God, Eve cannot be "bad work from that workman" (Ps. 100:5). The defense of women offered by Speght allows her to argue for marriage, consequently countering the third and fourth main claims from Swetnam's *Araignment*. Deploying the language of "mutuall participation" as a couple, Speght invokes the language of "Flesh of his flesh, bone of his bone" to make woman a "copartner" (21) in marriage. For Speght, the status of woman in marriage is elevating to both men and to women. Speght's biblical subtext appears to be Paul's statements about marriage and, given her public engagement of the Bible, Paul's assertions of women's necessary silence. Both statements by Paul are aggressively disputed in her *Mouzell*.

In the 1621 *Mortalities Memorandum*, Speght produces a dream-vision poem in which the author is positioned within an Eden-like garden space, followed by the poem "Mortalities Memorandum." Ostensibly an elegy for her mother, "Mortalities Memorandum" sustains the textual apparatus of marginal biblical references. Filled largely with "religious commonplaces" (Lewalski xxvii), the poem stays close to its biblical sources, leading the reader through meditations on death to the acceptance of salvation. Its opening three stanzas return to the story of the fall in Genesis, offering the reader a mutual portrait of Adam and Eve's action at the heart of *Mouzell*. Their "joint" sin, and thus exposure to death, is emphasized in lines like "Thus eating both, they both did jointly sin. . . . Thus on them, and their off-spring thenceforth seaz'd / *Mortalitie*, because they God displeas'd" (13, 17–18).

Speght's two early seventeenth-century publications thus offer examples of quite radical reinterpretations of the biblical narrative that enable a sustained defense of women's goodness, the value of marriage, and women's ability to preach through print.

Bibliography

Lewalski, Barbara Kiefer. Introduction. In *The Polemics and Poems of Rachel Speght*, edited by Barbara Kiefer Lewalski. Women Writers in English, 1350–1850. New York: Oxford University Press, 1996.

———. "Rachel Speght." Pages 778–79 in vol. 51 of *Oxford Dictionary of National Biography*, edited by H. C. G. Matthew and Brian Harrison. Rev. ed. Oxford: Oxford University Press, 2004–11.

Speght, Rachel. "Mortalities Memorandum." In *The Polemics and Poems of Rachel Speght*, edited by Barbara Kiefer Lewalski. Women Writers in English, 1350–1850. New York: Oxford University Press, 1996.

———. *A Mouzell for Melastomus: The Polemics and Poems of Rachel Speght*. Edited by Barbara Kiefer Lewalski. Women Writers in English, 1350–1850. New York: Oxford University Press, 1996.

—Shannon Miller

▪ Spurrell, Helen (1819–91)

Helen Spurrell was the first English woman to publish a translation of the entire Old Testament from Hebrew into English. She learned Hebrew after turning fifty years of age, and she acknowledges that her translation work "almost entirely occupied her time for many years past" (H. Spurrell, preface).

A musician and artist (painting and sculpture), she was the second daughter of Edward Wigan, a hop merchant in North London. In 1839 she married James Spurrell (1815–92), the son of a brewer and hop merchant, who in the early years of their marriage was himself a brewer. James was ordained in 1847 and is remembered for his pamphlet (1852) against the work of Priscilla Lydia Sellon, founder of the Society of the Sisters of Mercy of Devonport, a monastic-like group associated with the Oxford Movement within the Anglican Church. From 1852 onward, James no longer had charge of a parish, and he and Helen lived out their days in the town of Hove, near Brighton, on the south coast of England.

Spurrell's major work, *A Translation of the Old Testament Scriptures from the Original Hebrew*, was published in 1885. Her brief preface and her translation work show a confluence of higher criticism and an evangelical trust in the power of the Holy Spirit to convert the reader of Scripture. She wrote (speaking of herself in the third person): "To Him does she commit it, beseeching Him to illuminate with His Own Light the following pages, and to bless them to the convincing and converting [of] sinners, and to the building up of His saints. May very many exclaim, as the Translator has often done when studying numerous passages in the original: I have found the Messiah!" (preface). An example of such discovery comes in a note to the introduction of Ezekiel's heavenly guide, who leads him through his vision of the new temple (Ezek. 40:3)—a note that reads: "The Second Person in the Trinity seems clearly indicated, the Man Christ Jesus."

Such piety accompanies her desire to attain a proper translation. To this end, she worked explicitly from the unpointed Hebrew (i.e., a Hebrew text without vowels), which she considered to be "the Original Hebrew." Spurrell's translation is eclectic, including emendations from the Samaritan Pentateuch, the Septuagint, and the Vulgate, as well as notes addressing variations in Aramaic, Syriac, and Arabic manuscripts and Jewish Targumim. Among the handful of scholars to whom she gives credit in the notes throughout the volume, Spurrell acknowledges her indebtedness to the text-critical work of Benjamin Boothroyd (1768–1836), an independent minister and scholar of Hebrew whose two-volume *Biblia Hebraica* provided access to a range of the text-critical work done up to the early nineteenth century. An example of her attention to other versions is her inclusion of lengthy additions from the Samaritan Pentateuch after Exod. 20:19 and 21. She occasionally corrects the received Hebrew text by rearranging verses and smoothing internal contradictions (e.g., changing the number of horsemen in 2 Sam. 8:4 from 1,700 to 7,000 to reflect the number in 1 Chron. 18:4). The Song of Songs receives the most comment on her part in the form of section headings suggesting that this *is* Solomon's song, a clear contrast to the Revised Version, the Old Testament portion of which was also published in 1885 and clearly states that the Song is about Christ and the church.

Other marks of her translation are italicized print for words not in the Hebrew text, the use of JEHOVAH for the Tetragrammaton, notations of variant readings of the Hebrew text, poetic arrangement of Hebrew verse likely following her self-expressed appreciation for the work of Bishop Lowth (1710–87), Protestant ordering of the Old Testament books, grammatical attention to texts that include potential messianic expectations (e.g., explanation of "Mine iniquities" in Ps. 38:4), and a peculiar and pervasive attention given throughout the work to marking all emphatic uses of the Hebrew particle and definite article with a symbol, and so forth.

In addition to her translation of the Old Testament, Spurrell also authored two pamphlets now extremely rare: *The Real Presence of the Holy Ghost; or, The dispensation of the Spirit*; and *The Deluge; or, The Mosaic Accounts of the Flood corroborated by the writings of Antiquity*—both published in London in 1873 (by Hatchards).

Outside of works on the history of the Bible in English (Price 293), little scholarly attention has been given to Spurrell's work. When her work is cited by these historians, it is often viewed as a poor example, with occasional derision directed at Spurrell herself, suggesting that her late entry into the language and translation enterprise caused the work to suffer. Thus one historian suggests, "The translation has no real value for future translators, except as a warning [of] what not to do" (Robertson 49). Spurrell's translation, however, is a monumental achievement; as a published translation of the Old Testament from Hebrew into English by a woman, it is second only to the very wooden, note-like translation of the American Julia Smith (Hartford, CT: American Pub., 1876).

See also Smith, Julia Evelina (1792–1886)

Bibliography

Boothroyd, Benjamin. *Biblia Hebraica; or, the Hebrew Scriptures of the Old Testament, Without points, after the text of Kennicott, with the chief various readings, selected from his collation of Hebrew mss. from that of De Rossi, and from ancient versions, accompanied with English notes, critical, philological and explanatory, selected from the most approved, ancient and modern, English and foreign biblical critics.* 2 vols. Pontefract, UK: B. Boothroyd, 1810–16.

Price, Ira Maurice. *The Ancestry of Our English Bible: An Account of Manuscripts, Texts, and Versions of the Bible.* Edited by W. A. Irwin and A. P. Wikgren. 3rd ed. New York: Harper & Brothers, 1956.

Robertson, Edwin Hanton. *The New Translations of the Bible.* Studies in Ministry and Worship. Naperville, IL: Alec R. Allenson, 1959.

Spurrell, Helen. *A Translation of the Old Testament Scriptures from the Original Hebrew.* London: James Nisbet, 1885 (corrected from MDCCCCLXXXV [1985] in the original). Facsimile repr., Grand Rapids: Kregel, 1987.

— SAMUEL D. GIERE

■ Stanton, Elizabeth Cady (1815–1902)

Elizabeth Cady Stanton was the leading intellectual light of the first wave of feminism in the United States and a formidable writer and speaker on women's rights. A well-educated daughter of a judge, she experienced firsthand in her marriage the daily drudgery of woman's work as a housewife and mother of seven children while living in Seneca Falls, New York. She first came to public view when she, along with her friend Lucretia Mott and a few other women, helped to plan the infamous women's rights convention, held in Seneca Falls in 1848. For the convention, Stanton spearheaded the formulation of the Declaration of Sentiments and Resolutions, modeled on the Declaration of Independence, which, among other significant issues, included a resolution on female suffrage, specifically inserted by Stanton. For five decades, she championed female suffrage, including her term as president of the National

Woman Suffrage Association in the 1890s. She also worked to pass the Married Women's Property Act, for which she gave several speeches before the New York State Legislature.

Stanton believed that the supreme impediment to women's advancement was the widespread, long-standing belief that women's subordination was divinely ordained by an infallible Bible. To counteract this reigning opinion, advocated by clergymen and sanctioned by church tradition, she organized the publication of *The Woman's Bible* so that women, in particular, would be able to assess critically the most influential and highly regarded text in Western civilization. Her guiding hermeneutical assumption, greatly influenced by the claims of historical criticism, was that biblical texts were written and edited by men, not by God; therefore these texts are open to interpretation, criticism, and even rejection. For this two-volume project, she recruited only female biblical and classical scholars to write comments on every biblical reference about women in general, individual women, female animals—in short, anything remotely related to the female sex.

In her autobiography, *Eighty Years and More*, Stanton recalled the family gathering at which she proposed the exercise that eventuated in the compilation and publication of *The Woman's Bible*. "I had long heard so many conflicting opinions about the Bible—some saying it taught woman's emancipation and some her subjection—that, during this visit of my children, the thought came to me that it would be well to collect every biblical reference to women in one small compact volume, and see on which side the balance of influence really was" (389–90). Of critical importance to her was the formation of an all-female editorial board because it was time, in her opinion, for women to do the interpreting. Then the women went to work. "We found that the work would not be so great as we imagined, as all the facts and teachings in regard to women occupied less than one-tenth of the whole Scriptures. We purchased some cheap Bibles, cut out the texts, pasted them at the head of the page, and underneath, wrote our commentaries" (391). Part 1 of *The Woman's Bible* (1895) addresses the Pentateuch; part 2 (1898) deals with the remainder of the Old Testament and the entire New Testament. The format of *The Woman's Bible* is to quote a biblical text, generally a portion of a chapter or portions of several chapters from the same biblical book, followed by a comment on the text by one of the scholars who identifies herself by her initials. Stanton wrote more than half the comments. The editorial board even used a translation of the Bible written by a woman, Julia Smith. In a lengthy appendix to the first edition, Stanton introduces Smith and praises the painstaking work evidenced in her translation, "the only one ever made by a woman." Stanton then makes this ironic comment: "King James appointed fifty-four men of learning to translate the Bible. . . . Compare this corps of workers with one little woman performing the Herculean task without one suggestion or word of advice from mortal man!" (149–50).

470

Many of the comments, even on seemingly inconsequential biblical passages, bring to light female subordination in various arenas. On rules regarding the sex of sacrificial animals in Lev. 4 and 6, Stanton makes this observation: "There seems to have been some distinction of sex even in the offerings of male and female animals. For rulers, priests and people of distinction male animals were required, but for the common people a female lamb or goat would do" (1:90). On the topic of vows made to God, she observes that a woman's vow was always dependent on the approval of the male authority in her life (her father, brother, or husband). In contrast, a man's vow did not require the approval of another party. Even a brief reference to a priest's daughter marrying a stranger in Lev. 22:12 did not go unnoticed by Stanton in terms of its gender connotations: "These restrictions on the priests' daughters would never be tolerated by the priests' sons should they marry strangers. The individuality of a woman, the little she ever possessed, is obliterated by marriage" (94). In addition, she observes the inequality in punishment in Num. 12:1–15 between Miriam and Aaron, who were chastised by Moses for speaking against his marriage to an Ethiopian woman. While Miriam was afflicted with leprosy and banished from the camp for seven days, Aaron escaped with impunity. Stanton opines that Aaron was treated thus because of his priesthood. "Had he been smitten with leprosy, his sacred office would have suffered and the priesthood fallen into disrepute." And Miriam's punishment, she observes, was solely due to her gender: "As women are supposed to have no character or sacred office, it is always safe to punish them to the full extent of the law. . . . As a class, women were treated among the Jews as an inferior order or beings, just as they are to-day in all civilized nations. And now, as then, men claim to be guided by the will of God" (102).

The Woman's Bible provides interpretations of pivotal passages that were frequently cited as directly relating to the status of women. To that end, its first pages offer not a commentary on Gen. 1:1, as one might expect of a biblical commentary, but instead on Gen. 1:26–28, where Stanton underscores the passage's depiction of a "simultaneous creation of both sexes, in the image of God" (1:14). In her lengthy commentary on the passage, she interprets the "consultation in the Godhead" as occurring not between the traditional three persons of the Trinity—Father, Son, and Holy Spirit—but rather between a Heavenly Father, Mother, and Son. To emphasize this, she put in italics several critical words in Gen. 1:27: "So God created man in his *own image*, in the image of God created he him; *male and female* created he them." From this, she further extrapolates that there exists a feminine element in the Godhead, which, by virtue of her existence, not only negates woman's subordination but also holds up male and female equality as the biblical model. With this interpretation of the first creation account of male and female, Stanton then dismisses the second creation account in Gen. 2 as "mere allegory," specifically intended by "some wily writer . . . to effect woman's subordination in some way" (1:21).

In Stanton's comments on Gen. 3:1–24, she declares the fall to be an allegory and considers Eve's demeanor in the passage as that of a heroine exhibiting "courage, dignity, and lofty ambition." Eve is ambitious, according to Stanton, not for riches or trivial luxuries, but for knowledge and wisdom. Stanton manages to elevate Eve and denigrate Adam by stating that the tempter "roused in the woman that intense thirst for knowledge, that the simple pleasures of picking flowers and talking with Adam did not satisfy. Compared with Adam she appears to great advantage through the entire drama" (1:24–25). In her comment on the curse that follows Eve's consumption of the forbidden fruit, Stanton simply states, as she does on the creation account in Gen. 2, that it was added to justify woman's subordination.

In a brief introduction to the New Testament, Stanton denounces the common opinion that woman is exalted more in these texts than in the Hebrew Bible and claims that if anything, it is the opposite. "In fact, her inferior position is more clearly and emphatically set forth by the Apostles than by the Prophets and the Patriarchs. There are no such specific directions for woman's subordination in the Pentateuch as in the Epistles" (2:113). Stanton's attitude is quite dismissive of passages in the Pauline Epistles that relate to women. She refers to the custom of women's wearing head coverings (1 Cor. 11) as "very frivolous" in Paul's day, and even more so in her own day (2:157). Therefore her exhortation to women is to rebel against such a custom supposedly based on divinely ordained subordination. On the command for women to keep silence in the churches (1 Cor. 14:34), Stanton concludes that considering the wide-ranging opinions on this passage, it is preferable to allow women to interpret its meaning for themselves, "guided by their own unassisted common sense" (2:159). Finally, on 1 Tim. 2:9, a passage about women's dress and hair, she seems to poke fun at the writer's obsession with women's braided hair when there is much more important work to accomplish.

The publication of *The Woman's Bible* brought a vociferous reaction from many directions. One clergyman derided it for being "the work of women, and the devil." To that comment, Stanton cleverly retorted, "His Satanic Majesty was not invited to join the Revising Committee, which consists of women alone" (2:7). The Women's Christian Temperance Union, one of the largest women's organizations in the late nineteenth century, denounced *The Woman's Bible*. However, the most personally painful censure emerged from Stanton's own suffrage organization, which, despite a moving plea by her longtime friend and associate Susan B. Anthony, passed a resolution denouncing it.

The methods that Stanton and the editorial board employed in *The Woman's Bible*—such as focusing on texts about women, interpreting the Bible as a text like any other piece of literature, and adopting a "hermeneutics of suspicion" about traditional interpretations that subordinate women—have been adopted by feminist biblical scholars in the second and third waves of feminism in the twentieth century. Certainly in this respect, as well as others, Stanton was a century ahead of herself.

See also Smith, Julia Evelina (1792–1886)

Bibliography

Banner, Lois W. *Elizabeth Cady Stanton: A Radical for Women's Rights.* Boston: Little, Brown, 1980.

Griffith, Elisabeth. *In Her Own Right: The Life of Elizabeth Cady Stanton.* New York: Oxford University Press, 1984.

Kern, Kathi. *Mrs. Stanton's Bible: Elizabeth Cady Stanton and the Woman's Bible.* Ithaca, NY: Cornell University Press, 2001.

Stanton, Elizabeth Cady. *Eighty Years and More, Reminiscences, 1815–1897.* Introduction by Ellen Carol Dubois. Boston: Northeastern University Press, 1993.

Stanton, Elizabeth Cady, and the Revising Committee. *The Woman's Bible.* Part 1, *Comments on Genesis [to]* ... *Deuteronomy.* Part 2, *Comments on* ... *Joshua to Revelation.* New York: European Pub., 1895–98. Repr., Seattle: Coalition Task Force on Women and Religion, 1974.

—PRISCILLA POPE-LEVISON

Starr, Lee Anna (1853–1937)

A women's rights activist, minister, and biblical scholar, Starr has been considered second in importance only to Anna Howard Shaw among women in the Methodist Protestant Church in America. An early member of the Woman's Christian Temperance Union (WCTU), Starr served a brief time in prison for her participation in the "Woman's Crusade" of 1873–74. After graduating from Allegheny Theological Seminary in 1893, she was ordained in the Methodist Protestant Church; she went on to pastor a succession of small Midwestern churches, and in 1900 she served as a ministerial delegate to her church's general conference. That same year she published *The Ministry of Woman*, a scholarly booklet outlining a biblical justification for women's right to preach that drew on the work of the Baptist minister Adoniram Judson Gordon (1836–95). She also developed a biblical defense of woman's suffrage and lectured across the nation under the auspices of the WCTU. In the 1920s Starr headed the committee on biblical and historical research for the Association of Women Preachers, and she continued to work for women's rights in her denomination.

In 1926 she published her major work, *The Bible Status of Woman*, in which she insisted that both the King James Version and the Revised Version of the Scriptures are tainted by masculine bias. Rejecting "destructive" modern criticism, she draws instead on her knowledge of Hebrew and Greek, as well as on modern theological and anthropological writings, to argue that the Scriptures, rightly translated, mandate the emancipation of women. Influenced by the work of Katharine Bushnell, Starr contends that Gen. 1 and 2 establish the original equality of men and women. She takes issue with traditional arguments for male superiority based on the order of creation, pointing out that creation order appears to be ascending rather than descending. "If priority of creation is a proof of superiority," she explains, "the monkey has advantage over man, for the monkey was on the scene first" (22). She also insists that Gen. 3:16 should be interpreted as a prophecy rather than penalty. Subsequent history has amply demonstrated the suffering of women at the hands of men, and Starr contends that a proper understanding of the Old Testament makes clear that the development of patriarchy contradicts God's will for humankind. In the New Testament she turns to 1 Tim. 2:15 to establish her claim that Jesus Christ is the emancipator of woman, and to the Gospel accounts of the Samaritan woman (John 4:4–42), Mary and Martha (Luke 10:38–42), and the woman taken in adultery (John 7:53–8:11) to demonstrate how Christ has rejected the debasement of women in both word and deed. She analyzes the writings of Peter and Paul that seem to undermine women's rights (1 Pet. 3:1–7; 1 Cor. 11:3; Eph. 5:21–33; Col. 3:18–19; and 1 Tim. 5:14) in terms of their historical context and in light of Christ's teachings. She argues, for example, that Paul himself considers some of his comments on women to be "uninspired" (1 Cor. 7:12, 25) and therefore contingent on historical circumstances. Yet Starr observes that the church has tended to clothe the apostle Paul with infallibility, elevating his teachings above those of Christ. "Expositors tug and wrench" at the teachings of Jesus in order to bring them into accord with the writings of Paul; "why not reverse the process?" she asks (239).

Starr was concerned with practical issues such as legal and educational equality for women, equal pay for equal work, and expanding women's opportunities beyond the domestic realm. Based on her reading of the Scriptures, she utterly rejected the notion of a "woman's sphere": "We have heard much in the past about woman's sphere, and it is a trite saying that 'Woman's sphere is home.' Woman's God-given sphere is as wide as the earth's circumference, as high as the firmament and as deep as the sea. Talk about a woman getting out of her sphere! She would have to get off the earth in order to do that. Every foot of this globe has been deeded to her as much as to man" (21).

A few years after her death in 1937, *The Bible Status of Woman* came into the hands of the translation committee for the American Standard Bible, who committed themselves to guarding against the sort of unfairness she describes. Its ongoing significance is further evidenced in its republication in 1955.

See also Bushnell, Katharine C. (1855–1946)

Bibliography

Bushnell, Katharine C. *God's Word to Women: One Hundred Bible Studies on Woman's Place in the Divine Economy.* Oakland, CA: The author, 1923. Many reprints, such

as Mossville, IL: God's Word to Women Pub., n.d. http://godswordtowomen.org
/gwtw.htm.

Davis, Lyman. *Democratic Methodism in America: A Topical Survey of the Methodist Protestant Church.* New York: Fleming H. Revell, 1921.

Du Mez, Kristin Kobes. *The Forgotten Woman's Bible.* Louisville: Westminster John Knox, 2012.

Starr, Lee Anna. *The Bible Status of Woman.* New York: Fleming H. Revell, 1926. Repr., Zarephath, NJ: Pillar of Fire, 1955.

———. *The Ministry of Woman.* Chicago: Keen, Aitken, 1900.

— Kristin Kobes Du Mez

Stewart, Maria W. Miller (1803–79)

Maria W. Miller Stewart, African American abolitionist, moral reformer, and educator, was born to a free family in Hartford, Connecticut. Orphaned at the age of five, Maria Miller was raised in a clergyman's family and worked as a domestic servant, receiving only a rudimentary education in local Sabbath schools. In 1826 she married James W. Stewart, a black veteran of the War of 1812 and successful businessman from Boston. Tragedy soon disrupted this life of relative comfort. James died of illness in 1829, and Maria was defrauded out of a sizable inheritance. Several months later she experienced a religious conversion and, as she put it, was "brought to a knowledge of the truth, as it is in Jesus" (Stewart, *Meditations*, iv).

The five years that followed were remarkably productive. Shortly after her conversion, Stewart wrote an essay titled "Religion and the Pure Principles of Morality, the Sure Foundation on Which We Must Build" (1831) and published it in the radical abolitionist William Lloyd Garrison's nascent newspaper, *The Liberator*. Soon afterward Garrison published a small pamphlet of Stewart's religious reflections and prayers, *Meditations from the Pen of Mrs. Maria W. Stewart* (1832). For the next year and a half she lectured openly on the injustices of slavery, the humiliation and irreligion of her fellow African Americans, and women's rights. Garrison published each of her four lectures. Through these addresses, Stewart became the first documented woman, black or white, to speak publicly on political themes in America (Richardson in Stewart, *Essays*, xiii).

By late 1833 Stewart had lost the support of her circle of black Bostonians. Her lectures, in which she criticized the decadence and indolence of her own people more than that of their oppressors, proved agitating. In her farewell address, Stewart attributed the growing hostility to "contempt of my moral and religious opinions," admonishing her audience, "Let us no longer talk of prejudice till prejudice becomes extinct at home" (*Meditations*, 79). This lecture marked the conclusion of Stewart's public speaking career. After relocating to New York, she committed herself to working toward the ideals she had advocated, training to be a public schoolteacher while republishing her writings as *Productions of Mrs. Maria W. Stewart* (1835). She taught for several years in New York City, actively participated in the Female Literary Society, and attended the first Women's Anti-Slavery Convention in 1837. Sometime in the 1850s Stewart moved to Baltimore, then to Washington in 1859. In the last two decades of her life, she held regular prayer meetings in her home and established a Sunday school under the care of her native Episcopal church. In 1871 Stewart was appointed the matron of the Freedman's Hospital and Asylum (later Howard University Hospital). Due to new legislation, in 1878 she became eligible for her late husband's military pension. Several months before her death, Stewart used a portion of this new income to fund the publication of a second edition of her works, with a new autobiographical sketch and letters of recommendation, under the title of her first pamphlet, *Meditations from the Pen of Mrs. Maria W. Stewart* (1879).

The dominant theme of the addresses that Stewart delivered during her brief venture as a public lecturer was the social degradation of African Americans, slave and free. While she called for the abolition of slavery and fiercely opposed colonization, Stewart's primary ambition was the uplift of her people. Acknowledging that white culture was largely set against them, she argued that their social elevation "must be effected between God and ourselves" (*Meditations*, 80). Stewart personified an Old Testament prophet in her essays and speeches, calling the people back to God (what has been termed the "black jeremiad"). Admitting at one point, "I have borrowed much of my language from the Holy Bible," her writings created a nearly seamless blend of biblical passages or phrases and original thoughts (36). For instance, in her first essay, Stewart immediately follows an accusation that slavery and ignorance were the result of the collective sins of African Americans by exclaiming the words of Isa. 59:1 and Jer. 3:22—without attribution—that God is willing to return to and save the people (29). On numerous occasions Stewart confesses how she was inclined to despair that her fellow African descendants would ever value righteousness or rise above their lowly position if it were not "that the King Eternal has declared that Ethiopia shall stretch forth her hands unto God," quoting Ps. 68:31 (*Meditations*, 57). Similarly, her brief meditations and prayers are filled with exhortations to holiness, drawn principally from Exodus, the Major Prophets (chiefly Isaiah and Jeremiah), Job, the Psalms and Proverbs, the Gospels (she favors Matthew), 1 Corinthians, and Revelation.

Another significant theme in Stewart's lectures, albeit subordinate to the first, is the advocacy of women's rights, especially the biblical grounds for speaking publicly. Regarding her own authority to speak, she appeals to her spiritual calling. On consecrating herself to God's service, Stewart assumed the posture of a disciple, claiming the ability to share Jesus's cup and baptism (Matt. 20:21–23). Likewise, when faced with being ostracized, she identified with the Messiah personally, quoting Matt. 8:20 to indicate that she had nowhere to lay her head either (74, 79). On the right to speak as a woman,

Stewart in her final address asks, "What if I am a woman; is not the God of ancient times the God of these modern days?" Listing several major biblical heroines, including Deborah, Esther, and Mary Magdalene, she finally points to the Samaritan woman, who publicly speaks of Christ (John 4:28–29, 39). While conceding that Paul opposed women speaking in public (1 Cor. 14:34; 1 Tim. 2:12), Stewart responds that Jesus does not condemn the Samaritan for a worse offense, and neither would he condemn her. She concludes that if Paul had known the plight of African American women, "I presume he would make no objection to our pleading in public for our rights" (76).

Maria Stewart is a remarkable figure in the history of women interpreting the Bible, one of the first American female lecturers to present a biblical vision of social justice and women's rights.

Bibliography

Bassard, Katherine Clay. *Transforming Scriptures: African American Women Writers and the Bible.* Athens: University of Georgia Press, 2010.

Stewart, Maria W. *Maria W. Stewart, America's First Black Woman Political Writer: Essays and Speeches.* Edited and introduced by Marilyn Richardson. Bloomington: Indiana University Press, 1987.

———. *Meditations from the Pen of Mrs. Maria W. Stewart: Presented to the First African Baptist Church and Society, in the City of Boston.* Boston: Garrison & Knapp, 1832. 2nd ed. Washington, [DC]: Enterprise Pub., 1879.

— ERIC BRANDT

Stoddart, Jane T. (1863–1944)

Jane T. Stoddart was born on All Souls' Day (Nov. 2) in 1863 in Kelso, Scotland. She obtained her early education at an all-girls school near her home, receiving instruction in history, language, arithmetic, and Bible. A diligent student, Stoddart quickly took to reading and writing, with one of her earliest memories being her introduction to the English classics *Macbeth* and *Oliver Twist*. In her memoirs, Stoddart recalls her first attempt at authorship, preserved in her penny exercise books, as a collection of the lives of the German reformers. She also tried her hand at verse writing, and though she felt that her skill was greatly lacking, she persisted in improving and received encouragement to develop her craft. Stoddart acquired facility in French, Italian, and German through formal and informal study, then secured her first post as a teacher in the summer of 1879. Her placement lasted two years, at which time she went to Germany to improve her language skills as a complement to her grammar skills. When she completed her year, she was competent to teach the German language and relocated to Clifton, having secured a post as a teacher in a private school.

Coinciding with her return from Germany, she revived a friendship from her childhood that would influence her future career dramatically. At the age of thirteen, Stoddart had made the acquaintance of William Robert Nicoll, a young minister who had come to take over pastoral responsibilities of her family's church in Kelso. His deep love of literature was evident. His heavy use of literary quotations in sermons and Bible studies, in addition to his hosting of public readings of select poetry and prose, impressed young Stoddart. She attended his studies and shared with him her verse writing. He was ever an encouragement to her and instilled in her the belief that a sound education was critical to properly preparing herself for life. When Stoddart returned from Germany, Nicoll employed her to do some German translation for him. Additionally, he invited her to produce accounts of church services and sermons she had attended for a small publication he was overseeing, *The Contemporary Pulpit*. This arrangement persisted until 1885, when Nicoll was forced to leave Kelso due to health concerns. He moved to London, where he founded and acted as editor of a penny weekly that focused on religion and politics, the *British Weekly: A Journal of Social Progress*. With this, he made his official transition from pastoral ministry to journalism, and it was not long before Stoddart joined him in London. She agreed to help Nicoll prepare and edit a series of homiletic volumes and would research in the British Museum Reading Room during her weekends and days off. At this same time, Stoddart was making preparations for the Cambridge Higher Local examination in order to adequately credential herself for teaching high school. She passed with honors and was posted at Maida Vale High School. Teaching provided her with financial stability, but her passion for research and writing captured every moment of her spare time. In the summer of 1890, she was asked to write unsigned articles for the *British Weekly* in the series "Life among the Close Brethren," and at the conclusion of this successful series of articles, she was asked to join the staff of the *British Weekly* full time.

In the beginning, Stoddart wrote unsigned articles on religious thought from a Christian perspective and conducted personal interviews with notable public figures. She became involved in a women's monthly publication *Woman at Home*, for which she was the primary editor and was also an original member of the Society of Women Journalists. She attended the Women's Writers Dinner in London every year and met many influential female writers of her day. In 1893 she began to publish under the pen name Lorna, or simply "L." Her responsibilities at the paper grew, and before long she was Nicoll's most trusted employee. When he was out of town on business, he would leave the paper in her capable hands. Stoddart established herself as a key member of the staff and devoted herself to the *British Weekly* for the better part of her life. She retired from the paper in 1937 and died on December 15, 1944.

Alongside her work for the paper, Stoddart published her own books. Some of the most notable titles include *The Earl of Rosebury* (1900), *The Life of the Empress Eugenie* (1905), *The New Socialism: An Impartial Inquiry* (1908–9), *The Girlhood of Mary Queen of Scots* (1908), and *Against the Referendum*

(1910). These works covered a range of interests, but they evidenced her commitment to sound research and the need for stimulating public discourse. In addition to her political and historical investigations, Stoddart also contributed to the life and work of the church through a collection of volumes intended for the enhancement of daily devotions and pulpit ministries. She published works related to this interest, including *The Expositor's Treasury of Children's Sermons* (1912), *The Old Testament in Life and Literature* (1913), *The New Testament in Life and Literature* (1914), *The Christian Year in Human Story* (1920), *Private Prayer in Christian Story* (1927), *Great Lives Divinely Planned* (1930), *A Book of the Golden Rule* (1933), and *The Psalms for Everyone* (1939).

Stoddart's approach to biblical interpretation grew out of two sensibilities that guided her reading of Scripture. The first was her belief that the Bible functions as the divine Word of God in the life of the church and in the life of the believer (*Old Testament*, vii). The Bible is authoritative, and thus it is important for the devout reader to seek its wisdom and apply its directives. The second was her conviction that the intersections between the biblical narrative and literature in general play a key role in bringing to light the meaning of the sacred text. Stoddart's immersion in poetry and prose in conjunction with her knowledge of scriptural tropes and images allowed her to identify these key points of connection. These connections, in turn, allowed her to establish a creative space where the words of Scripture and the expressions of human reflection come into productive conversation.

The Old Testament in Life and Literature was built around Stoddart's private reading of domestic and foreign literature, historic writings, and modern biographies. It came into being through the encouragement of Nicoll, and its purpose was to provide ministers and laity with a resource for preaching and devotion that supplied them with fresh illustrative material as they grappled with the deeper meaning of the text. Stoddart did not wish to replicate the many encyclopedic works that already existed, but to contribute something new. The result was a volume filled with poetry, quotations, and the personal experiences of believers throughout history, a reference work with source material drawn explicitly from "life and literature." It touched on each book of the Old Testament, though limitations of space required that each book consist of only a select sampling of verses.

By way of example, Stoddart's treatment of Gen. 32:24–32, Jacob's wrestling with the angel, highlights her sensibilities regarding Scripture (*Old Testament*, 71–73). Her belief that Scripture is authoritative and that it must impact daily practice is addressed through two examples. The first, included under Gen. 32:24, speaks to the difficult lesson of submission to God. The reflections of a doctor who had lost his wife to death offer this insight: "I have been thinking much lately of Jacob's wrestling with the Angel, finding his weakness and his strength at the same time, and going on through the rest of his life halting and rejoicing. I believe this is the one great lesson of life—the being *subdued by God*" (71). The second, included under Gen. 32:26, speaks to the hallowed and urgent nature of time spent in communion with God. A soldier recollects that his general would place a handkerchief outside his tent every morning to communicate to the entire camp that he was spending time alone with God and was not to be disturbed. This request for privacy was honored by all: the entire camp took seriously the importance of time spent in prayer. In both of these snapshots from daily life, Stoddart draws attention to individuals who have studied Scripture, submitted their lives to the authority of the truth, and now serve to illustrate the transformative work of the divine Word.

Her second conviction—that Scripture inspires literature, and literature in turn engages in an ongoing dialogue with Scripture—is evident through her inclusion of two poetic passages, one by Alfred Lord Tennyson and the other by Christina Rossetti. The poem by Tennyson draws on the character qualities of the angel in Jacob's encounter to describe the integrity and tenacity of a dear friend whom he greatly respected. Tennyson writes:

> Like that strange angel which of old,
> Until the breaking of the light,
> Wrestled with wandering Israel,
> Past Yabbok brook the livelong night,
> And heaven's mazed signs stood still
> In the dim tract of Penuel.
> (quoted in *Old Testament*, 71)

This perspective on the angel informs the simile he constructs for his friend, which in turn provides the reader with a literary interpretation of the encounter that sheds new light on the angelic figure who came to wrestle with Jacob. The lines by Rossetti are an allusion to Gen. 32:26 and are taken from a longer poem intended for Advent. They read:

> Weeping we hold Him fast Who wept
> For us, we hold Him fast;
> And will not let Him go except
> He bless us first or last.
> (quoted in *Old Testament*, 72)

This plea, originally on the lips of Jacob as he begs the angel for a blessing, is now placed in the mouths of those anxiously awaiting the coming of Christ and begging the One who wept to have compassion on his children, who now wait and weep for him. Here a narrative of the Old Testament is infused with a christological interpretation, not only informing the poem crafted by Rossetti, but also expanding the reader's understanding of the original story.

The New Testament in Life and Literature, a companion volume to Stoddart's work on the Old Testament, was published soon afterward and retained the same purpose and approach. In her dealing with the nativity story in Luke 1–2, Stoddart again draws attention to the impact the divine Word has in the life of the believer. One example is taken from the private memoirs of Queen Mary II of England, who suffered great sorrow because she had not been blessed with a child. Stoddart includes the queen's personal reflections under Luke 1:13, the angel's promise to Zechariah:

> "Thy prayer is granted, and thy wife Elisabeth shall bear a son." Those are the angel's words (wrote Mary) to Zacharias. Joyful words certainly, and the accomplishment of which was much more so. . . . Though I have been married about thirteen years, I know that the Lord can still give me one, or several, if He finds it right; while in the interval of waiting I must have patience, I must even remember that humanly speaking there is no probability that I should be thus blessed after such a long sterility, and that I should be contented, knowing that man does not see as the Lord sees. (136)

These words reveal a deep longing and a deliberate choice to find both comfort and hope in the story of Elizabeth. The faithful God of Luke's Gospel remains the same God who has power and wisdom to intervene in present-day affairs. It is in wrestling with Scripture that direction for daily life is found. Stoddart also persists in her use of poetic expression, including a stanza from Richard Crashaw under Luke 2:7, the birth of Christ:

> That he whom the Sun serves, should faintly peepe
> Through clouds of Infant flesh; that he the old
> Eternall Word should be a Child and weepe;
> That he who made the fire, should feare the cold;
> That Heaven's high majesty his Court should keepe
> In a clay cottage, by each blast control'd;
> That glorie's self should serve our griefs and feares;
> And free Eternity, submit to yeares.
> (quoted in *New Testament*, 140)

Crashaw draws on the story of Luke's Gospel to create a poem infused with an articulated view of Christ's omnipotence and omnipresence. Echoes of John's Gospel, the "Eternall Word," and the ensuing ministry of Jesus that would attend to "griefs and feares" invite the entire story of Jesus's life into this one moment. The poem provides a thoughtful engagement with the implications of Christ's birth and invites the reader to see the baby in the manger as all-powerful God.

Stoddart's contribution to biblical interpretation could perhaps be more fully investigated under the umbrella of reception history. The interplay between literature and Scripture and the circular influence that one has on the other provide a window into her methods and motivations. Her deep commitment to the biblical text and her relentless pursuit to find interpretive inspiration in the realm of the creative arts suggest that there is more to study in her works than simply her understanding of texts and their original meanings. As her legacy she leaves a challenge to immerse oneself in the beautiful and tragic expressions of the human condition, and in doing so to discover the transformative power of the divine Word.

See also Rossetti, Christina Georgina (1830–94)

Bibliography

Stoddart, Jane T. *Against the Referendum*. London: Hodder & Stoughton, 1910.

———. *The Earl of Rosebury K. G.: An Illustrated Biography*. London: Hodder & Stoughton, 1900.

———. *The Girlhood of Mary Queen of Scots from Her Landing in France in August 1548 to Her Departure from France in August 1561*. London: Hodder & Stoughton, 1908.

———. *The Life of the Empress Eugenie*. 1905. 3rd ed. London: Hodder & Stoughton, 1906.

———. *My Harvest of the Years*. London: Hodder & Stoughton, 1938.

———. *The New Socialism: An Impartial Inquiry*. [1908?] 2nd ed. London: Hodder & Stoughton, 1909.

———. *The New Testament in Life and Literature*. London: Hodder & Stoughton, 1914.

———. *The Old Testament in Life and Literature*. London: Hodder & Stoughton, 1913.

—SHERRI TRAUTWEIN

Stowe, Harriet Beecher (1811–96)

Harriet Beecher Stowe, author of the internationally acclaimed *Uncle Tom's Cabin* (1852), was the seventh of nine children born to Roxanna and Lyman Beecher. Four other children were born to Lyman's second wife, Harriet Porter, following Roxanna's death when Harriet was four. Yale-educated Lyman Beecher was a Presbyterian minister, theologian, and seminary president. The Beecher children were raised with the expectation that they would influence the world, their father making sure that all his children could launch into any sort of exegetical debate, essay, or sermon. Beecher's seven sons became preachers; Catharine, the eldest daughter, was a pioneer in female education and a significant female theologian and philosopher; the youngest daughter, Isabella, was a founder of the national Women's Suffrage Association; and Harriet, the author of more than thirty books, interpreted Scripture and preached with her pen.

Harriet Beecher Stowe's religious formation took place primarily under the tutelage of her father, who also ensured that his children received a fine education. Stowe's gift for writing was evident from a young age; at twelve she won an award at Litchfield Academy for her essay "Can the Immortality of the Soul Be Proved by the Light of Nature?" At thirteen she began attending Hartford Female Seminary, a girls' school founded by her sister Catharine, where she was first a student and later a teacher. In 1832, when her father was appointed president of Lane Theological Seminary, Stowe moved with the family to Cincinnati, where she became friends with a number of writers, including Eliza Stowe, the wife of Lane's biblical scholar, Calvin Ellis Stowe. Harriet Beecher taught at her sister's new school and began to write professionally, coauthoring a geography textbook with Catharine and publishing several stories. In 1836 she married widower Calvin Stowe. Harriet had seven children and continued to write to supplement her husband's meager salary. The family moved to Bowdoin College in Maine in 1850, where Stowe wrote the best-selling antislavery novel *Uncle Tom's Cabin; or, Life among the Lowly* (1852). Two years later, they moved to Andover Theological Seminary. Stowe continued to write articles for newspapers and magazines, as well as fiction and poetry; she traveled extensively in North America and Europe, speaking about *Uncle Tom's Cabin* and issues related to slavery. Her biblical interpretation is embedded in many of her fictional writings and is the focus of her later prose writings.

Stowe's interpretation of the Bible brings together the distinctive male world of the academy and church that she accessed through her father and later her husband and the distinctive women's culture of nineteenth-century America. On the one hand, Stowe constantly relied on the literary and scholarly judgment of her husband, whom she affectionately called "Rabbi," who kept up with the latest developments in Continental biblical scholarship. She skillfully incorporated many of his scholarly insights into her writing, adding another dimension to the exegetical and practical homiletical skills that she had learned from her father. On the other hand, Stowe read the Bible through the lens of her life as a woman. Her experiences at Hartford Female Seminary and then marriage and motherhood pushed her to explore how gender, race, and class shape biblical interpretation. Stowe had a special interest in women in Scripture and questions related to women's roles in the church and society.

Stowe's works of fiction feature biblical interpretation and theology. She uses her characters to debate such contentious issues as women's place in God's economy and the interpretation of biblical texts on marriage and slavery. In *The Minister's Wooing* (1866), for example, Stowe uses the novel's dialogue to make a case for women's priestly and prophetic ministries. She names her young heroine Mary Scudder, one of God's real priests, "whose ordination and anointing are from the Holy Spirit; and he who hath not this enthusiasm is not ordained of God, though whole synods of bishops laid hands on him" (131). Her character Dr. Hopkins makes a biblical case for women to exercise prophetic gifts, arguing that holy and inspired women "such as Deborah, Huldah, and Anna, the prophetess" have exercised prophetic ministries throughout history (364–65). At times Stowe felt that she herself was imbued with God's Spirit to write.

Stowe's embedded exegesis also shows her awareness of the complex hermeneutical issue of how gender, race, and class influence interpretation. In *The Minster's Wooing*, she discusses 1 Pet. 3:7, which mandates that "the weaker vessel" give honor to her husband. She problematizes the verse by having Candace, a black slave, respond to a deacon's criticism of her "ordering" of her husband:

> "I de weaker vessel?" said Candace, looking down from the tower of her ample corpulence on the small, quiet man whom she had been fledging with the ample folds of a worsted comforter, out of which his little head and shining bead-eyes looked, much like a blackbird in a nest,—"I de weaker vessel? Umph!"
>
> A whole woman's-rights' convention could not have expressed more in a day than was given in that single look and word. (178–79)

Similarly, Stowe raises the hermeneutical problem of the use of the Bible in the debate over slavery. When Zebedee Marvyn, a slaveholder, asks, "Was there not an express permission to Israel to buy and hold slaves of old?" Dr. Hopkins points to the complexities of biblical literalism, advocating the interpretation of a text within its historical context and the notion of progressive revelation. He declares: "Many permissions were given to them [the Israelites] which were local and temporary; for if we hold them to apply to the human race, the Turks might quote the Bible for making slaves of us" (173).

Stowe's later prose writings, *Woman in Sacred History* (1873) and *In His Footsteps* (1877), contain her most mature work as a female exegete. They blend her distinctive female-centered reading of Scripture with a scholarly approach that draws on traditional and contemporary resources and methods. In the introduction to *Woman in Sacred History*, Stowe advocates viewing biblical figures with "the same freedom of inquiry as the characters of any other history" (12). By bringing to readers the real "flesh and blood" of biblical personages, Stowe "takes them out of a false, unnatural light, where they lose all hold on our sympathies" (13). Thus Stowe's Vashti (Esther 1) is read in light of the nineteenth-century debate over women's rights. She also views the king's adviser's fear that Vashti's defiance "might infect other wives with a like spirit and weaken the authority of husbands" as "a most delightful specimen of ancient simplicity" (151). The notion of development undergirds her view that the "history of Womanhood Under Divine Culture" climaxes in "that high ideal of woman which we find in modern Christian countries" (11).

Miriam's story, with its many gaps, both intrigued and inspired the intuitive Stowe, who tries to recover her story by using clues in the text and information gleaned from ancient and modern sources. Stowe embellishes Miriam through her imaginative construal of Scripture and tradition, encouraging readers to see her experience of bondage through the lens of "the anguish" and "the ignominy" of the American slave (63–64). She highlights Miriam's leadership qualities, describing her as Israel's future leader "in miniature" (64–65). Stowe wonders what happened to Miriam when the focus of the story turns to Moses; she fills in the story's perceived gaps with traditional materials found in Josephus (*Antiquities* 2–4) and more contemporary scholarly resources (e.g., Sir John Gardner Wilkinson's books on Egypt and William Smith's *Dictionary of the Bible*, 1863). Stowe suggests Miriam's influence on Moses and envisages Miriam as being instrumental in Moses's "peculiar and almost feminine tenderness" for the "helpless and defenseless" (*Woman*, 65). Stowe cites Mosaic laws (e.g., Deut. 22:6–7; 24:14–17) that reflect Moses's compassion for the "downtrodden" members of society, observing that some laws "sound more like the pleadings of a mother than the voice of legal statutes" (66). Stowe's unique exploration of the female influence on Moses and on the Mosaic laws and institutions is a striking example of her gendered exegesis.

Stowe gives considerable attention to the story of the crossing of the Red Sea (Exod. 14:1–15:21). She focuses on Miriam's prophetic leadership in song and dance, finding in the combined spiritual and cultic leadership of Moses and Miriam proof for "the equality given to women by the Divine Being in all that pertains to the spiritual and immortal" (75). She then infers that Miriam continued to exercise shared leadership in other contexts, citing as evidence the prophet Micah (6:4). Stowe argues that Miriam shared administrative duties with Moses during the time of the crystallization and consolidation of the laws and religious rituals: "We infer from a passage in the prophet Micah, that it was not in mere brotherly fondness that Moses would have consulted this sister, who had been to him as a mother, . . . and that he was thus justified in leaning upon her for counsel" (75).

Stowe was troubled by the narrative silence on Miriam (Num. 13:1–20:13) following the account of her rebellion and punishment (Num. 12). She used Jewish tradition to fill in the narrative gaps and redeem Miriam (81–82). First, there is Josephus's account of her glorious funeral (*Antiquities* 4.4.6). Second, the rabbinic legend of the spring of living water that dried at her death reflects Miriam's bravery and devotion in preventing her brother's death at the Nile. Third, the long-standing veneration of her tomb suggests to Stowe that Miriam's "one fault and punishment" ended neither her brother's love for her nor the nation's high regard for her. Relying on information from Josephus (*Antiquities* 3.2.4), Stowe comments on Miriam's marital status. That Miriam is a wife and a mother is important to Stowe's larger thesis that all Hebrew women called to be prophetic leaders "were literally, as well as metaphorically, mothers in Israel" (*Woman*, 81). Here Stowe's attitude reflects a significant tenet of the cult of domesticity, that women, ideally mothers, exercise leadership from within the family. Stowe also accepts that Miriam's silencing is typical of many great women (82). Nevertheless, she brings Miriam out from the shadows of the text by highlighting once again the noble and womanly influence she had on Moses's heart, which indelibly shaped Israel's laws and institutions: "The nation identified her with the MAN who was their glory, and Miriam became immortal in Moses" (82). Although Stowe seems to accept the subordination of Miriam to Moses, her attempt to fill out Miriam's story, by recourse to Jewish tradition and legend, suggests her deep dissatisfaction with the biblical story. In praising Miriam as prophet and singer, courageous public leader, and shaper of national laws and institutions, Stowe presents in Miriam a model for faithful women everywhere to emulate; but in so doing, Stowe brings herself into the nineteenth-century debate about the proper place of women in society and the roles considered acceptable for them.

Stowe includes chapters on Judith and Mary, "the Mythical Madonna," in *Woman in Sacred History*. While conceding to the views of "competent scholars" that Judith is fiction, Stowe argues that her tale "illustrates quite as powerfully as a true story the lofty and heroic type of womanhood which was the result of the Mosaic institutions and the reverence in which women were held by the highest authorities of the nation" (159). Similarly, Stowe is intrigued by the reception history of Mary in art and literature. She sets traditional and aesthetically appealing views of Mary against what she views as the simple story of the New Testament: "It is our impression that the true character will be found more sweet, more strong, more wonderful in its perfect naturalness and humanity, than the idealized, superangelic being which has been gradually created by poetry and art" (181). Using Scripture, scholarship, intuition, and presuppositions about women, Stowe presents "the lineaments of the real Mary," a woman whom "we may not adore, but we may love" (198).

Harriet Beecher Stowe was one of the most popular writers of her time. In 1862 Abraham Lincoln called her "the little woman" whose book started the Civil War. Although her writings continue to be studied by scholars of American literature, her work as a biblical interpreter deserves more attention. Her intermingling of the world of biblical scholarship with women's culture produced sophisticated, relevant, and often novel readings of texts, which merit careful study as a unique source for the history of the interpretation of Scripture in nineteenth-century America.

Bibliography

Stowe, Harriet Beecher. *In His Footsteps*. London: Samson Low, 1877.

———. *The Minister's Wooing*. Boston: James R. Osgood, 1866.

———. *Uncle Tom's Cabin; or, Life among the Lowly*. Boston: John P. Jewett, 1852.

———. *Woman in Sacred History*. New York: J. B. Ford, 1873. Repr., New York: Portland House, 1990.

Taylor, Marion Ann. "Bringing Miriam out of the Shadows: Harriet Beecher Stowe and Phyllis Trible." Pages 263–72 in *From Babel to Babylon: Essays on Biblical*

History and Literature in Honour of Brian Peckham, edited by Joyce Rilett Wood, John E. Harvey, and Mark Leuchter. London: T&T Clark, 2006.

———. "Harriet Beecher Stowe and the Mingling of Two Worlds: The Kitchen and the Study." Pages 99–115 in *Recovering Nineteenth-Century Women Interpreters of the Bible*, edited by Christiana de Groot and Marion Ann Taylor. SBL Symposium Series 38. Atlanta: Society of Biblical Literature, 2007.

— Marion Ann Taylor

▪ Sullivan, Kathryn Lois (1905–2006)

Kathryn Sullivan, a pioneer in modern Catholic biblical studies, was born in Philadelphia in 1905 and in 1928 entered the Society of the Sacred Heart, a Catholic religious community of women. In 1937 she received a doctorate in history at the University of Pennsylvania, but as a woman she was not permitted to enter graduate programs in Scripture study. She studied privately with John E. Steinmueller, founder of the Catholic Biblical Association, and coauthored many works with him. Sullivan was the first woman to be accepted into the Catholic Biblical Association (1947) and the first woman to hold a major post in the association when she was elected its vice president in 1958. She taught history, religion, and Sacred Scripture at Manhattanville College in Purchase, New York (1938–84), and was one of the first women to lecture at major Catholic seminaries in New York, Philadelphia, and Rome. Sullivan authored some of the first Catholic biblical manuals and textbooks of the second half of the twentieth century and was a regular contributor to the journals *Worship*, *Theological Studies*, and *Catholic Biblical Quarterly*. She was a founding editorial board member of the *Catholic Biblical Quarterly* and *The Bible Today*. Between 1967 and 1976, following the Roman Catholic Church's Second Vatican Council, she lectured in more than thirty countries on a renewed Catholic appreciation of Scripture.

Sullivan studied, taught, and wrote at a pivotal time in the life of the Roman Catholic Church and its approach to the Bible. In 1943, Pope Pius XII's encyclical *Divino Afflante Spiritu* (Inspired by the Divine Spirit, often called the Magna Carta of Catholic biblical scholarship) allowed Catholic biblical scholars to apply historical-critical methodology to the understanding of Scripture for the first time, thus providing the stimulus for the development of modern biblical scholarship within Catholicism. In 1965 this movement was further strengthened by Vatican II's Dogmatic Constitution on Divine Revelation (*Dei Verbum*). Sullivan was one of a number of Catholic biblical scholars (e.g., John Steinmueller, Augustin Bea, Roland de Vaux, Raymond Brown, Joseph Fitzmyer, Barnabas Ahern, David Stanley, R. A. F. MacKenzie) who provided leadership in that development. Like most biblical scholars of this era, she believed that the Bible was the inspired Word of God and that, to be complete, its study must include a spiritual understanding. Thus her critical studies were supplemented by attention to biblical theology, liturgy, and religious education.

As a biblical-historical critic, Sullivan authored or coauthored commentaries and scholarly articles on books from the Old and New Testaments and translated the works of French biblical scholars. In her work she affirmed and used tools and methods of modern scholarship: archaeology, philology, exegesis, biblical languages, literary criticism, textual criticism, and the study of Semitic psychology. In commenting on any Old Testament book, she always identifies the place of that book in the Hebrew Bible and any difference in name or place with the Protestant Bible (e.g., the Paralipomena, so named in the Septuagint, are the last books of the Hebrew Bible and are called Chronicles in English Protestant Bibles). She cautiously identifies challenges to the historicity of some Old Testament books, as with respect to the writer of Job ("Did he write about an imaginary hero or of someone whose memory was venerated in his day? Opinions are divided" ["Job," 454]) or the writer of Judith ("Scholars ask whether it is history or fiction or a combination of both" [God's Word, 132]). In both her critical and pastoral works, she always returns to the theme of love: "The message of the last book of the Old Testament [for Sullivan, 2 Maccabees] repeats the teaching of the first: God made us to love and serve Him" (157). She explores the diverse words for this inexpressible love in the Old Testament: 'ahăbâ, meaning love that unites, endures, and never flinches; and raḥûm, meaning love that is merciful, affectionate, compassionate, friendly, and trusting. In her commentary on the book of Ruth, she says, "When God so blessed a Moabite, the ḥesed, the loving-kindness He showed to a woman of a neighboring enemy tribe, prefigured the love He would one day pour out on all men, and prepared them to welcome Gentile as well as Jew into His kingdom" (79).

Sullivan did not specifically choose texts about women, but she was careful to notice the women who were present in the texts on which she was commenting. In a commentary on Genesis, Sullivan writes about the three matriarchs: Sarah, who "loyally shared the great patriarch's trials; with him she left the comforts of Mesopotamian culture; with him she endured the hardships of a semi-nomad life; with him she prayed that God would send her a son"; Rebecca, who was commended for her prudence, her courteous reserve, her fine courage, and her modesty and tact; and Rachel, whom Jacob loved dearly until her dying day and whose love for her children and their many descendants played a prominent part in the history of Israel (11–12).

Although Jewish history makes no mention of Judith, Sullivan counts her among the great women of the Old Testament. She compares Judith with Jael, "the intrepid Israel of the north whose praises Deborah sang," and with Esther, "who set aside her humble garb and in queenly robes dazzled all beholders and won mercy for her people from a hostile Persian king" (133). However, she adds, "Today from an objective point of view our judgment might be more severe. The inspired writer recorded Judith's conduct but this does not necessarily imply his approval. Nor can we conclude that because she was praised for her heroic patriotism she was blameless in everything she did" (134). Of Esther, Sullivan writes, "Grace, beauty, queenly dignity and power of intercession make Esther a worthy figure of our Blessed Mother. . . . Like Mary she is one of Yahweh's loved ones, 'a poor little one of Israel'" (143). In the *Catholic Biblical Encyclopedia*, biblical women are described in this way: "The Hebrews honored women and treated them with greater kindness than did some of their western neighbors, because the dignity of woman was one of the lessons taught in Sacred Scripture. In the story of creation it is related that God, who had made man according to his image, created them male and female and blessed them both" (Steinmueller and Sullivan 2:671; cf. Gen. 1:27–28).

In a commentary on the book of Job, Sullivan observes that although Job's wife speaks only once in the book, commentators have not neglected her throughout the centuries. She concludes that usually the commentaries have been negative (in early Christian inscriptions she is called "the blasphemer," and many have commiserated with both Adam and Job because of their wives), but "it is pleasant to find some exceptions to these expressions of almost universal disapproval": William Blake portrays her "with tenderness and sympathy" and illustrates the Lord's blessing both Job and his wife. Sullivan was not without humor in her writing. She comments that the church fathers argue "with more charity than logic" that the attitude of Job's wife finally becomes one of perfect submission, adding cynically, "They find much to admire in a woman who is silent." In reflecting on the proverbial patience of Job, she says, "To be perfectly frank: Job's patience lasts for two chapters" ("Job," 456–57).

At the beginning of a review of Lécuyer's *Le sacrifice de la nouvelle alliance* (*The Sacrifice of the New Covenant*), Sullivan writes: "Scholarly exegesis of scripture texts used in the liturgy is imperative if scriptural advances are to influence the total life of the Church and if liturgical studies are to be solidly grounded. Too often exegete and liturgist work along parallel rather than converging lines. Only when experts in each field are concerned about what has been accomplished in both fields will their work be fully enriched and enriching" (190). Between 1955 and 1957, she wrote a series of commentaries in the journal *Worship*, exploring individually all the books of the Old Testament. Although written from a scholarly basis, these articles were intended for a nonacademic audience. Using the benefits of biblical criticism and archaeology, she addresses historical-critical aspects of the books, including explanations of key Hebrew words like 'āmēn (which she translates as "truly"), ḥesed ("loving-kindness"), and 'ĕmet ("faithfulness"). To help the reader appreciate the richness of the biblical books, she uses the works of a variety of writers (e.g., Aristotle, Josephus, Origen, the church fathers, Rabbi Hillel, Jerome, Julian of Norwich, John of the Cross, Thomas Aquinas, Paul Claudel, Thomas Merton) and artists (e.g., T. S. Eliot's "Ash Wednesday,"

Dante's *Divine Comedy*, Milton's "Paradise Regained," Michelangelo's *Ezekiel*, Handel's *Messiah*, Longfellow's *Judas Maccabaeus*, Rembrandt's two artistic representations of the sacrifice of Isaac). In her words, "There is no better way to grow in our love of the Scripture than to study it in the liturgy" ("Scripture in Worship," 192).

Sullivan anticipates the postmodern understanding of the dialogue between the reader and the text when she argues, "Very often, we do not fully understand the Word of God until we have been shaped and conditioned by life, according to the words of St. John (3:21): Only 'he who acts according to the truth comes to the light'" (195). As an educator, she believed that one of the primary purposes of reading and studying Scripture was formation for what she called "the social apostolate." In an article titled "Sacred Scripture and Race," Sullivan argues against those who co-opt Scripture to justify segregation, strongly criticizing their misuse of passages such as Gen. 9:18–28 and 11:1–9 to support segregation. She challenges their use of Lev. 19:19 to advocate for racial purity and refers to the names of Rahab and Ruth in Matthew's genealogy of Jesus as "offending racial purists" (Matt. 1:1–17). In her thinking, passages such as Gen. 16:3; 38:2; 41:50; and Num. 12:1 show biblical support for marriages between Hebrews and non-Hebrews. In this article and indeed in many of her works, she presents a strong Scripture-based defense of the core biblical teaching of both Old and New Testaments as "You shall love your neighbor as yourself" (Lev. 19:18; Matt. 22:39). About segregation she concludes, "Opponents of interracial justice can find no support for their claims in the Bible. Religious education incorporating the findings of modern Scripture scholarship can easily show that there is no divine sanction for the superiority of one race, or for racial segregation, or against interracial marriage" (12).

Sullivan was one of several biblical scholars in this time period who were concerned about Jewish-Christian relations. She endeavored to move away from the religious notion of the Jews as a people to be condemned by Christians for their treachery and wickedness. To do so, she cited scriptural references on God's election of the Jewish people (e.g., Exod. 19:4–6; Deut. 7:7–8; Josh. 1:2; Hosea 2:16–18; Isa. 54:10), with Gen. 12:2–3 as "the first chapter opened in the long love story of the chosen people" ("God of Israel," 27). She was adamant that there was no dichotomy between the "Old Covenant and the New" since "love, God's love for man and man's answering love for God, is at work from the first page of Genesis to the last page of the Apocalypse" (25). For her significant accomplishments in this field, Sullivan received the Edith Stein Medal for Judeo-Christian Relations.

Sullivan was a biblical scholar, an exegete, an author, a translator, a teacher, a lecturer, a leader, and a woman committed to using her learning, her skills, and her opportunities to strengthen the place of Scripture in the lives of Roman Catholics and to restore respectful relations between Jews and Catholics. She began her journey at a time when women were not welcomed or supported in such work; yet she persevered, overcoming all obstacles with tenacity and grace and inspiring two generations of Catholic female scholars who have followed in her footsteps. In her 101st year, the Song of Solomon was her constant meditation, and the last words read to her in the moments before her death were, "Arise, my love, my beautiful one, and come, for . . . the time of singing has come" (Song 2:10–12; Osiek 105).

See also Julian of Norwich (ca. 1342–ca. 1416)

Bibliography

Osiek, Carolyn. *Kathryn Sullivan, RSCJ (1905–2006): Teacher of the Word.* St. Louis: Society of the Sacred Heart, 2011.

————. "In Memoriam: Kathryn Sullivan, R.S.C.J." *Catholic Biblical Quarterly* 69, no. 1 (Jan. 2007): 104–5.

Steinmueller, John E., and Kathryn Sullivan. *Catholic Biblical Encyclopedia: Old and New Testaments.* 2 vols. New York: J. F. Wagner, 1950–59.

————. *A Catholic Companion to the Old Testament and the New Testament.* 2 vols. New York: J. F. Wagner, 1946.

Sullivan, Kathryn. "Biblical Theology and Christian Education." *Religious Education* 52, no. 1 (Jan./Feb. 1957): 8–12.

————. "The Book of Job." *Worship* 29, no. 8 (Sept. 1955): 449–61. This is one example of the series of commentaries on every book of the Old Testament published in *Worship* from 1955 to 1957.

————. "The God of Israel, God of Love." Pages 23–43 in vol. 4 of *The Bridge: A Yearbook of Judaeo-Christian Studies,* edited by John M. Oesterreicher. New York: Pantheon Books, 1961.

————. *God's Word and Work: The Message of the Old Testament Historical Books.* Collegeville, MN: Liturgical Press, 1958.

————. Review of *Le sacrifice de la nouvelle alliance,* by Joseph Lécuyer. *Catholic Biblical Quarterly* 25, no. 2 (1963): 190–91.

————. "Sacred Scripture and Race." *Religious Education* 59, no. 1 (Jan./Feb. 1964): 10–13.

————. "Scripture in Worship." *Worship* 29, no. 4 (March 1955): 189–97.

—Elizabeth M. Davis

■ Tarabotti, Arcangela (1604–52)

Elena Cassandra Tarabotti was one of eleven children born to Maria Cadena and Stefano Tarabotti, a Venetian chemist. Since she was lame and unlikely to obtain a husband without a substantial dowry, her father sent her to the Benedictine convent Sant'Anna in Venice when she was eleven. She took initial vows as a nun in 1620, adopting the religious name Arcangela. Forced to make final vows in 1623, she protested by refusing to cut her hair or wear a habit.

She was later compelled to conform to convent rules for dress. Tarabotti was highly educated and well versed in Italian literature. Though she could read Latin, most of her knowledge of classical literature came from studying Greek and Latin works translated into Italian. A female teacher provided her with a rudimentary education, but Tarabotti was largely self-taught. She may have obtained private instruction from male humanist scholars visiting the convent. She received correspondence and visits from members of the Incogniti, a Venetian literary academy notorious for libertine views. Though she claimed that her writings were printed without her permission, she eagerly sought opportunities for publication. Several of her works circulated pseudonymously under anagrams such as Galerana Barcitotti or Baratotti. Tarabotti remained in the convent, which she regarded as a prison, until her death in 1652.

Tarabotti's published works, written in Italian, include *Antisatira* (a response to a satire by a leader of the Incogniti, 1644), *Lettere familiari e di complimento* (a collection of correspondence, 1650), *Che le donne siano della spezie degli uomini* (*Women Are of the Human Species*, 1651), and *La semplicità ingannata* (*Innocence Betrayed*, published posthumously in 1654), which was originally entitled *Tirannia paterna* (*Paternal Tyranny*). Two writings were inspired by her favorite author, Dante: *Il paradiso monacale* (*Convent Paradise*, 1643) and *L'inferno monacale* (*Convent Hell*), which she was not permitted to publish. She mentions a work titled *Il purgatorio delle malmaritate* (*Purgatory of Mismatched Wives*), which has not been found.

Tarabotti quotes the Latin Vulgate Scriptures extensively in *Paternal Tyranny*, a protest against women's involuntary enclosure in convents. This work argues that women are frequently the victims of men's violence. Defying centuries of traditional Christian interpretation, Tarabotti insists that Shechem's lust, not Dinah's curiosity, causes the rape narrated in Gen. 34 (115). She observes the substantial power differential between King David and Bathsheba, whom he exploits (2 Sam. 11). The murder of Uriah is caused not by any fault of Bathsheba but by "David's savage nature, his overweening ambition" (118). Tarabotti's treatment of the story of Jephthah's daughter is perhaps the earliest extant female-authored interpretation of Judg. 11. Though she condemns Jephthah's rash vow to sacrifice his daughter, Tarabotti says he is less blameworthy than the men of Venice. Jephthah sacrifices his daughter because of an inviolable religious vow and a military victory, but Venetian men's miserly unwillingness to pay marriage dowries causes them to offer unwilling daughters to the convent as perpetual living sacrifices. Tarabotti does criticize Judah's daughter-in-law Tamar (Gen. 38) and the prostitute Rahab (Josh. 2; 6) for being willing to "sell their honor" (118), but she normally praises the women of Scripture, especially the females present at the crucifixion. She says that Jesus treats women as men's equals (132). Tarabotti protests that male interpreters "persist in burdening us innocents with all the guilt of Eve's sin" (122). Instead, "Adam's sweet innocent wife" was a victim of the devil's treachery, for he falsely promised her wisdom (124). Eve's desire to eat from the tree of knowledge is proof of women's innate, praiseworthy "thirst for knowledge" (108).

Women Are of the Human Species responds to an anonymous sixteenth-century pamphlet, which was probably written by a Roman Catholic satirizing Anabaptists for their reliance on Scripture alone. He claims that it cannot be proved from Scripture that women are human. Tarabotti apparently misunderstood the work's satirical nature. She takes the author to task for his interpretation of the stories of Eve, the Canaanite woman, Mary Magdalene, and other women. Accusing the author of twisting Scripture to suit his own purposes, she defends Eve as a "reasoning creature" who was made of "nobler material" than was Adam (93–99).

Tarabotti's writings, well-known in Venetian circles, were lively contributions to the *querelle des femmes*, the early modern literary debate about the nature of women. In 1661 *Paternal Tyranny* was placed on the Roman Catholic Church's *Index of Prohibited Books* for discouraging religious vocations and criticizing church leaders. Historians and literary scholars frequently celebrate Tarabotti as an early feminist forerunner.

Bibliography

Barcitotti, Galerana [Arcangela Tarabotti]. *Women Are of the Human Species: A Defense of Women*. Pages 89–159 in *"Women Are Not Human": An Anonymous Treatise and Responses*, edited and translated by Theresa M. Kenney. New York: Crossroad, 1998.

Costa-Zalessow, Natalia. "Tarabotti's *La semplicità ingannata* and Its Twentieth-Century Interpreters, with Unpublished Documents Regarding Its Condemnation to the *Index*." *Italica* 78 (2001): 314–25.

Tarabotti, Arcangela. *Paternal Tyranny*. Edited and translated by Letizia Panizza. The Other Voice in Early Modern Europe. Chicago: University of Chicago Press, 2007.

———. *La semplicità ingannata: Edizione critica e commentata*. Edited by Simona Bortot. Padua: Poligrafo, 2007.

Weaver, Elissa B., ed. *Arcangela Tarabotti: A Literary Nun in Baroque Venice*. Ravenna: Longo, 2006.

— JOY A. SCHROEDER

■ Teresa of Avila (1515–82)

Teresa was born on March 28, 1515, in the Castilian city of Avila to Alonso de Cepeda, a widower with two sons, and Beatriz de Ahumada. Alonso descended from converted Jews (*conversos*, or New Christians), while Beatriz came from a peasant, or Old Christian, family. Teresa was the third child and first daughter born to the couple. Teresa writes of learning to read at home with her siblings, instructed by their mother. Lacking a formal education, Teresa did not know Latin, but she read Spanish with facility and pleasure.

493

In 1535 Teresa entered the Carmelite Convent of the Incarnation in Avila, where she took vows two years later, adopting the name Teresa of Jesus. Soon afterward she developed an unidentified illness that left her almost completely paralyzed for three years. On resuming her vocation as a Carmelite nun, she began to experience spiritual sensations so unusual and troubling that some of her confessors judged the source to be the devil. Teresa found no reliable guidance or relief from her wrenching spiritual trials until 1554 when, in two experiences that she narrates as conversions, God identified himself and the angels as her spiritual guides.

Later mystical experiences, including a vision of herself in hell, motivated Teresa to follow a more rigorous spiritual practice than what she found in Carmelite convents, which accommodated varying degrees of religious commitment. Teresa's need for more discipline led her to found a Carmelite convent in Avila based on the stricter, so-called primitive, rule of the original twelfth-century Carmelites. She developed this convent into a nationwide movement known as the Barefoot, or Discalced, Carmelites, since they wore sandals without socks. They became an independent jurisdiction in 1581 and a separate order in 1593. In 1582, shortly after consecrating the seventeenth of the Barefoot Carmelite convents and monasteries in Spain, Teresa died.

Teresa's book-length writings include *The Book of Her Life* (1562–65), *The Road to Perfection* (1566), *The Interior Castle* (1577), and *The Book of Her Foundations* (1582). In addition, Teresa wrote hundreds of letters, a small body of poetry, manuals on governance and visitation of Discalced Carmelite establishments, accounts of her spiritual experiences, and *Meditations on the Song of Songs* (1566–71), the only work in which she attempts something like biblical exegesis.

Jerónimo Gracián, a protégé of Teresa, published the first edition of the controversial *Meditations* in Brussels (1611). In 1580 a theologian for the Inquisition, who was also a confessor to Teresa, ordered the work to be destroyed because reading Scripture linked her to Protestant heresy and because writing a book defied the proscriptions that Paul imposed on women's participation in the church. Teresa is said to have burned the manuscript of the *Meditations* in his presence, but numerous copies survived in her convents. Teresa had tried to protect this work by claiming divine permission to study the Song, which she compares to a beautiful fabric that adorns the spiritual meaning: "I hold it as certain that we do not offend Him when we find delight and consolation in His words [Scripture] and works. A king would be happy and pleased if he saw a little shepherd he loved looking spellbound at the royal brocade and wondering what it is and how it was made. Just so, we women need not entirely refrain from enjoyment of the Lord's riches. . . . I am just like this little shepherd-boy" (1.8; trans. Peers).

Teresa's *Meditations* resembles biblical exegesis only superficially, however. She takes her translations of the Song from the Daily Office of the Virgin, rather than from a text of the Bible. Gracián imposed the exegetical format on the work, organizing it with quotations of and commentary on five verses from the Song (1:1, 2; 2:3, 4, 5). He also gave it a euphemistic title, *Conceptions of the Love of God*. Teresa acknowledges knowing about an exegetical tradition, but she places her work outside it by pleading a weak memory and citing God as her only source. Besides, she complains, the explications by "doctors of the Church," probably a reference to Bernard of Clairvaux, have not satisfied her desire for the true meaning of the Song. Teresa identifies two philological problems in the biblical text addressed by many commentators but declines to try to resolve them, preferring instead simply to delight in the experience of God's presence through the Song. Rather than commenting on the details of the text, then, Teresa uses her *Meditations* to draw an analogy between the marriage of the bride in the Song and her own mystical marriage to God.

Teresa's access to Scripture was limited in that she did not read Latin, and vernacular translations were prohibited (Andrés Martín 1:322). Her writings show that she assimilated Scripture through the liturgy, sermons, and devotional books not placed on the Index until 1551. Misspelling and variations in her biblical quotations point to her reliance on paraphrase and her writing from memory, rather than transcribing them from a text. In a few instances she quotes a phrase in Latin, but she attributes any knowledge of that forbidden language to spiritual gifts from God: "while in this [state of] quietude, and understanding hardly anything of the Latin prayers, especially of the Psalter, I have not only understood how to render the Latin verse in the vernacular but have gone beyond to rejoicing in the meaning of the verse" (*Life*, 15.8). Given Teresa's extraordinary verbal acuity, as well as the many cognates in Spanish and Latin, it seems likely that she assimilated the Latin version of biblical passages she heard in oft-repeated church rituals.

Teresa recognized the importance of using Scripture to validate her experiences and ideas: "I was told without seeing anyone, but I understood clearly that it was Truth itself telling me: '. . . all the harm that comes to the world comes from its not knowing the truths of Scripture; not one iota of Scripture will fall short'" (*Life*, 40.1). By invoking God as the source of her interpretation, she sometimes overrode ecclesiastical interpretations. When church officials invoked Paul's Letters to thwart what she considered to be her divine mandate, God gave her a hermeneutic principle for correcting their flawed interpretations: "[God] told me, 'Tell them [unnamed priests] that they shouldn't follow just one part of Scripture, but that they should look at other parts, and ask them if they can by chance tie my [God's] hands'" (*Spiritual Testimony*, 15). Teresa's mystical experience occasionally gives her a warrant for qualifying the revelation of Scripture. She quarrels with Christ's description of the road to God as narrow in Matt. 7:14 because she has found it to be broad and secure (*Life*, 35.13), and she quarrels with Ps. 119:32 based on her experience that the center of the soul, not the heart, expands when one follows God's commandments

(*Interior Castle*, 4.2.5). In contradicting church interpretations with privately received instructions and considering Scripture as sometimes fallible, Teresa challenged an important plank of Roman Catholic doctrine.

Teresa was particularly interested in the phenomenon of prophecy in the Old Testament, especially figures who received divine communication or intervention: Jacob, Moses, Joshua, Solomon, and Elijah. In her writings she places herself in their lineage and compares their interactions with God with her own. Thus—based on the distinction she makes between imaginative and intellectual visions from God, the former involving images, which she can remember, and the latter concepts, which she usually cannot articulate—she posits that Jacob receives divine communication beyond his imaginative vision of a ladder (Gen. 28:12). She also maintains that Moses sees more in his vision of the burning bush (Exod. 3:2) than he is able to describe.

Teresa also presses references from the Hebrew Bible into didactic and political service. She finds numerous analogies for explaining the nature of the soul and exhorting her followers to diligently prepare themselves for spiritual enlightenment. For example, she refers to Gen. 1:26 to account for the difficulty of understanding one's own soul: "Since this castle [the soul] is a creature and the difference between it and God is the same as that between the Creator and His creature, His Majesty in saying that the soul is made in His own image makes it impossible for us to understand the sublime dignity and beauty of the soul" (*Interior Castle*, 1.1.1). She uses the story of the transformation of Lot's wife into a pillar of salt (Gen. 19:26) as a caution against looking at the world rather than at one's own soul. For Teresa's argument on behalf of women's active participation in the church, most significant is her interpretation of the bondage of the Israelites in Egypt as an analogy for the confinement of women to home and cloister. For suffering these restraints, she maintains, women warrant rescue comparable to the exodus led by Moses (Exod. 14:21–23): "A woman in this stage of prayer . . . has great envy of those who have the freedom to cry out and spread the news abroad about who this great God of hosts is. . . . You have the power, Lord, to make the great sea and the large river Jordan roll back and allow the children of Israel to pass" (6.6.3–4). She frequently calls the priests who have tried to impede her work "sons of Adam," but she does not even mention Eve or the forbidden fruit in any of her writings.

Teresa identifies most closely with the figure of Mary Magdalene. Following Jacobus de Voragine's *Golden Legend* (ca. 1260), Teresa considers the woman who bathes Christ's feet with fragrant oil in the home of Simon the Pharisee (Luke 7:36–50) as Mary Magdalene and conflates her with Mary of Bethany (10:38–42). In this way she dispenses with Mary Magdalene's reputation as a prostitute. This Magdalene's dutiful performance of domestic labors demonstrates the injustice of the gossip about her, which Teresa, using biographical details that appear in the *Legend*, attributes to envy of her wealth and high social rank. Teresa follows the *Legend* and the Gospel of John in making Mary Magdalene apostle to the disciples. John 20:1–18 identifies her as the first person to speak with the resurrected Christ, who dispatches her to spread the good news, an evangelical function that Teresa yearns to assume.

Teresa often invokes the Letters of Paul, usually looking beyond his subordinating women in the church to identify with his conviction that Christ lives within him (Gal. 2:20) and that he has a life hidden in Christ (Col. 3:3–4). Teresa compares Paul's mystical experience on the road to Damascus and his three days of blindness (Acts 9:1–9) with Mary Magdalene's conversations with Jesus. In Teresa's view, Paul is much slower than the Magdalene to realize what has happened to him: "Look at St. Paul, or the Magdalene: in three days the former began to understand that he was sick with love; that was St. Paul. The Magdalene knew from the first day, and how well she understood!" (*Way of Perfection*, 40.3). Teresa also refers to Paul's claim in 2 Cor. 12:2–4 to having been caught up into the third heaven in connection with a phase of her mystical experience (*Interior Castle*, 6.5.8). Most insistently and importantly, she identifies with Paul's role as a founder of Christian communities and evangelist for the faith.

Teresa was beatified in 1614 and canonized in 1622. In 1970 Pope Paul VI named Teresa and Catherine of Siena the first female doctors of the church. As of December 2011 the Discalced Carmelites numbered 3,997 monks in 612 monasteries and 9,552 nuns in 890 convents in over one hundred countries worldwide (General House of the Discalced Carmelites).

See also Catherine of Siena (1347–80)

Bibliography

Andrés Martín, Melquíades. *La teología española en el siglo XVI.* 2 vols. Madrid: Biblioteca de Autores Cristianos, 1977.

Bertini, Giovanni M. "Interpretación de *Conceptos del Amor de Dios* de Teresa de Jesús." Pages 545–56 in vol. 2 of *Congreso internacional Teresiano, 4–7 octubre 1982*, edited by Teófanes Egido Martínez, Victor García de la Concha, and Olegario González de Cardenal. Salamanca: Universidad de Salamanca, 1983.

Boucher, Teresa. "Craving Credibility: Teresa de Avila's Shifting Discourse in *Meditaciones sobre los Cantares*." *Romance Languages Annual* 11 (1999): 417–23.

Bultman, Dana. "Comparing Humanist and Mystical Understanding in Luis de Leon's 'Noche serena' and John of the Cross's 'La noche oscura.'" Pages 232–39 in *Approaches to Teaching Teresa of Ávila and the Spanish Mystics*, edited by Alison Weber. New York: Modern Language Association, 2009.

General House of the Discalced Carmelites. Personal communication, January 2012.

Howe, Elizabeth Teresa. "St. Teresa's *Meditaciones* and the Mystic Tradition of the Canticle of Canticles." *Renascence* 33, no. 1 (1980): 47–64.

Hunter, M. J., Geoffrey Sheperd, Henry Hargreaves, W. B. Lockwood, C. A. Robson, Kenelm Foster, and Margherita Morreale. "Vernacular Scriptures in Spain." Pages

465–91 in *The West from the Reformation to the Present Day*, edited by G. W. H. Lampe. Vol. 2 of *The Cambridge History of the Bible*, edited by S. L. Greenslade. Cambridge: Cambridge University Press, 1963.

Kavanaugh, Kieran, and Otilio Rodríguez, trans. and eds. *The Collected Works of St. Teresa of Avila.* 3 vols. Washington, DC: Institute of Carmelite Studies, 1976–85.

Pietro della Madre di Dio. "La sacra scrittura nelle opere di S. Teresa." *Rivista di vita spirituale* 18 (1964): 41–102.

Slade, Carole. "Saint Teresa's *Meditaciones sobre los Cantares*: The Hermeneutics of Humility and Enjoyment." *Religion and Literature* 18, no. 1 (Spring 1986): 27–44.

——. *St. Teresa of Avila: Author of a Heroic Life.* Berkeley: University of California Press, 1995.

Teresa of Avila. *Conceptions of the Love of God* [*Meditations on the Song of Songs*]. Pages 359–90 in vol. 2 of *The Complete Works of Teresa of Avila*, translated and edited by E. Allison Peers. London: Sheed & Ward, 1946.

— CAROLE SLADE

◼ Thérèse of Lisieux (1873–97)

Marie-Françoise Thérèse Martin was born in Alençon, France, in 1873 as the youngest of five surviving children (all girls) of Louis Martin, a watchmaker, and Azélie-Marie (Zélie) Guérin, a highly successful lace maker. Mme Martin died when Thérèse was four, and later that year the family moved to Lisieux, a prosperous industrial town in Normandy. Thérèse was educated at home by her sisters and attended a local Benedictine abbey school as a day student. The family was close-knit, devoted, and devout; though Thérèse was a highly sensitive child, she was also extraordinarily secure and confident, with a deep awareness of being loved—a conviction that would come to form the core of her spirituality and message. Eventually all her sisters entered religious life, three of them at the Carmelite convent of Lisieux, which Thérèse herself entered by a special dispensation of the bishop, being then, at fifteen, still underage.

As Sister Thérèse of the Child Jesus and of the Holy Face, she lived in Carmel for the nine remaining years of her life, assisting in the duties of sacristan, portress, and novice mistress, the latter a challenging ministry in which she was highly effective. In 1895, at the request of her sister Pauline (Mother Agnès of Jesus, the prioress at the time), Thérèse composed a memoir of her early life, intended as a family souvenir. The following year her eldest sister, Marie (Sister Marie of the Sacred Heart), asked her to record some of her insights regarding her spirituality and vocation. Then in the last year of her life, in her last illness, Thérèse was asked to bring her memoirs up to date. Together these three texts were published in 1898 as the *Story of a Soul*, exactly one year after her prolonged and agonizing death from tuberculosis at the age of twenty-four.

St. Thérèse of Lisieux lived a hidden life, spent entirely in the chosen obscurity of an enclosed religious order. Yet her influence to this day cannot be measured. The *Story of a Soul* went into a second edition almost immediately after publication and since then has never been out of print. Widely available in English in a number of translations and now in its ninetieth French edition, it has sold millions of copies and has been translated into over fifty languages. This popularity is due in great part not only to the resonance and accessibility of her message but also to its powerful witness to the truth of the gospel. Her spirituality, sometimes called the Little Way, or the Way of Spiritual Childhood, affirms the same unshakeable trust in the love of God that Jesus taught his disciples when he told them to be "as a little child" (Mark 10:15). Beatified in 1923 and canonized in 1925, Thérèse was declared a doctor of the church in 1997, the centenary of her death, becoming one of only three women to carry this title, in the company of such figures as St. Augustine, St. Jerome, and St. Thomas Aquinas. All this reflects the reality that her teaching has impacted the life of the church as no other saint of modern times.

Thérèse wrote as a woman speaking within and to a community of women, yet she wrote not as one on the margins, but as one dwelling within the very heart of God's love, trusting completely in the knowledge of God's faithfulness. This is nowhere more apparent than in her great manifesto in which she confessed to Jesus: "To be Your Spouse, to be a Carmelite . . . No doubt, these privileges sum up my true vocation, . . . and yet I feel within me other vocations: . . . the vocation of the warrior, the priest, the apostle, the doctor, the martyr. . . . O my Jesus! what is your answer to all my follies?" (192–93). The answer she was given in prayer formed the crux of her faith, her thought, and her life—a powerful yet stunningly simple intertwining of Scriptures, from Deuteronomy, Proverbs, Wisdom, the Song of Songs, the Psalms, Isaiah, the Gospels, 1 Corinthians, and Revelation—bursting into an illumined cry of indescribable spiritual energy: *"My vocation is Love!"* (194). Concerning 1 Cor. 12 and 13 in particular, she writes:

> Considering the mystical body of the Church, I had not recognized myself in any of the members described by St. Paul, or rather I desired to see myself in them all. Charity gave me the key to my vocation. I understood that if the Church had a body composed of different members, the most necessary and most noble of all could not be lacking to it, and so I understood that the Church had a Heart and that this Heart was burning with Love. I understood it was Love alone that made the Church's members act, that if Love ever became extinct, apostles would not preach the Gospel and martyrs would not shed their blood. I understood that Love comprised all vocations, that Love was everything, that it embraced all times and places—in a word, that it was eternal! (194)

Thérèse's was an intensely biblical spirituality, which engaged Scripture as a profoundly transformative encounter with the living God—an unveiling of God's face in the person of Jesus, and a window into God's heart through the events of his life. To read the Bible as she did means to embrace the complete surrender that brings forth, from the fire of God's love, a new creation.

Bibliography

Thérèse of Lisieux, St. *Story of a Soul: The Autobiography of St. Thérèse of Lisieux.* Translated by John Clarke, OCD. 3rd ed. Washington, DC: ICS [Institute of Carmelite Studies] Pubs., 1996.

— LISA WANG

Tonna, Charlotte Elizabeth (1790–1846)

Charlotte Elizabeth Tonna was born on October 1, 1790, in Norwich, England. Her father, Michael Browne, was an Anglican clergyman and canon of Norwich Cathedral. Tonna lost her hearing at the age of ten. She turned from music, an early interest, to imaginative literature, particularly Shakespeare, though later in life she regretted her passion for this kind of reading. Tonna communicated with others by using signs.

After the death of her father in 1812, Tonna married Captain George Phelan (d. 1837) and traveled with him to his post in Nova Scotia, where they remained for two years. In 1819 they moved to Ireland, where Phelan left his wife at a country estate and spent his time in Dublin, engaged in a lawsuit. Tonna spent her time engaged in research for her husband's legal affairs. During this time she had a conversion experience. The remainder of Tonna's life was devoted to her God-given vocation, "the responsible duties of Christian authorship" (Tonna, *Recollections*, 391).

When Phelan returned to North America on military duty, Tonna separated from him. She joined her brother's household in England. Because of her separation from her husband, Tonna wrote using only her given names, Charlotte Elizabeth, so that Phelan would have no claim on the income from her published works. Following Phelan's death in 1837, Tonna married Louis Hippolytus Joseph Tonna (1812–57), who supported her writing vocation. Tonna was diagnosed with cancer in 1844; she continued to write throughout her remaining two years, dying in July 1846.

Following her conversion experience in the early 1820s, Tonna was invited to write for the Dublin Tract Society. She understood this invitation as a call from God and continued writing throughout her life. Tonna was a prolific author, producing short and long fiction, poetry, and essays. For the last three years of her life, she felt she could no longer write fiction in good conscience, though she continued to write essays and editorials until her death. Tonna edited the *Christian Lady's Magazine* from 1834 to 1846 and the *Protestant Magazine* from 1841 to 1846. Many of her longer works were first published serially, then collected into book form.

Tonna's writing is both didactic and political. She bases her view of the world on her reading of the Bible. Her writing is infused with the certainty of her Protestant evangelical convictions. In the spirit of Protestantism, Tonna interprets the Bible according to its plain-sense meaning. In her autobiography,

Personal Recollections, Tonna repeatedly assured her readers that she is not influenced by a particular political party or by any theological writers but only by the Scriptures as illuminated by the Holy Spirit. For example, she states, "I frequently wondered . . . at the ease with which, aided by the Bible alone, I settled so many disputed points; and as it really was by the Bible I settled them, man's teaching has never yet on any subject altered my views" (133).

The Church Visible in All Ages (1844) is an example of Tonna's didactic and political fiction. It contains a discussion between a mother and her children on the interpretation of the Bible as it relates to the history of the church. Mrs. Willis, the mother character, bases all that she teaches her children on the Bible, claiming, "Whatever man teaches me I must bring to the blessed Bible, to examine and compare it with what God has spoken" (13). The central issue discussed in *Church Visible*, whether the Roman Catholic Church could be considered the true church, is a major theme of Tonna's writings.

Principalities and Powers in Heavenly Places (1842) examines the biblical evidence for angels and demons. Tonna tries to correct "the prevailing error" of Christians who understand spiritual beings to be "grotesque devils and namby-pamby angels" (155). Tonna thinks that the cultural caricature of both demons and angels is dangerous, so she examines the Bible for teaching on these spiritual entities and presents her findings. As in her other works, Tonna uses a literal plain-sense understanding of the Bible. This leads her to question the identification of the "Angel of the LORD" in the Old Testament with Jesus. She thinks this interpretation is a dangerous error, which can be avoided by "receiving in its most obvious sense what the Holy Spirit has moved his servants to write for our learning" (187–88).

Tonna finds examples for conduct in biblical characters. An example of this can be found in her description of Hannah More, an inspiring and encouraging friend. Tonna writes of More's political involvement that "she had been a Deborah when many a Barak shrunk from the post of honour, and skulked behind a woman" (*Recollections*, 224). Tonna urges other women to be like Deborah, not in leading an army, but in serving as "instruments of the word of God" (Krueger 138).

Tonna was a political and opinionated writer, often virulently anti-Catholic. Because of this, people either loved or hated her writing. In her introduction to Tonna's collected works (1844), Harriet Beecher Stowe observes that it is not necessary to agree with all of Tonna's opinions in order to admire her writing. Stowe calls Tonna's *Personal Recollections* the key to understanding and appreciating "the woman as she appears in all her writings." Clara Lucas Balfour's assessment of Tonna's opinions is similar to Stowe's, though Balfour adds that Tonna's "habit of going to the Scriptures for direction" safeguards her against her impetuous tendencies.

Stowe's and Balfour's notice of Tonna's work indicates that she was influential in her own time. As interest in woman writers has grown in the last twenty years, some reassessments of Tonna have appeared. Christine Krueger's analysis of Tonna's writings on social problems clearly sets these books in their nineteenth-century context and argues that Tonna was a social prophet who preached by using her pen. Krueger places Tonna in a succession of woman preachers along with Hannah More, Elizabeth Gaskell, and George Eliot and argues that Tonna developed a particularly religious way of discussing social issues, based on her understanding of the Bible.

See also More, Hannah (1745–1833); Stowe, Harriet Beecher (1811–96)

Bibliography

Balfour, Clara Lucas. *Working Women of the Last Half Century: The Lessons of Their Lives*. London: W. & F. G. Cash, 1854.

Krueger, Christine L. *The Reader's Repentance: Women Preachers, Women Writers, and Nineteenth-Century Social Discourse*. Chicago: University of Chicago Press, 1992.

Tonna, Charlotte Elizabeth. *The Church Visible in All Ages*. London, 1844; New York: Dodd, 1845.

———. *Personal Recollections*. London, 1841. 3rd ed., London: Seeley, Burnside & Seeley, 1847.

———. *Principalities and Powers in Heavenly Places*. London, 1842. 2nd ed., London: Seeley, Burnside & Seeley, 1844.

———. *The Works of Charlotte Elizabeth, with an Introduction by Mrs. H. B. Stowe*. 3 vols. New York: M. W. Dodd, 1844–45. 7th ed. in 2 vols., New York: Dodd, 1849.

—HEATHER WEIR

■ Tornabuoni, Lucrezia (ca. 1427–82)

Lucrezia Tornabuoni de' Medici was probably born in Florence on June 22, 1427, though one historical record suggests a birth year of 1425. The wealthy Tornabuoni family was comprised of merchants and landholders descended from nobility. In 1444 Tornabuoni married Piero de' Medici (1416–69), who later became de facto ruler of the Republic of Florence. Tornabuoni was mother to seven children, five of whom survived past childhood: Maria, Bianca, Lucrezia (Nannina), Lorenzo, and Giuliano. Maria may have been Piero's illegitimate daughter, raised together with the other children. Tornabuoni played an active role in her children's education, helping to select prominent humanist scholars to be her sons' tutors. She periodically conducted business on her husband's behalf, including a diplomatic mission to Pope Paul II.

After Tornabuoni was widowed, her son Lorenzo "the Magnificent" (1449–92) ruled Florence. Tornabuoni actively worked behind the scenes to influence Florentine civic affairs. Professors and clergymen sought her help in securing academic and ecclesiastical posts. Tornabuoni was especially admired for her charitable activities. She served on the city's dowry committee (one of the few public committees open to female membership), which distributed funds to impoverished young women. Tornabuoni also managed her considerable landholdings and rental properties. In 1478 her younger son Giuliano was assassinated in a plot instigated by a rival family. Throughout her life, Tornabuoni suffered from various ailments, including eczema, arthritis, and gout.

No extant historical sources describe Tornabuoni's education. Biographers believe that she received private tutoring. She knew some Latin and was highly proficient in writing Italian verse. She engaged in intellectual conversations with noted humanist scholars, including Lorenzo's tutor Gentile Becchi, who wrote to her: "You have always studied so much, your study is filled with books, you have listened to the letters of Saint Paul, you have spent all your time with illustrious men" (*Lettere*, 122). Tornabuoni owned several Greek manuscripts, including a treatise by Ptolemy, but it is unknown whether she could read Greek.

Tornabuoni's surviving writings, all in Italian, include correspondence, nine *laudi* (devotional poems), one sonnet, and five *storie* (histories), which were versified retellings of biblical stories about Susanna, Tobias, Judith, Esther, and John the Baptist. She probably also wrote a *Life of the Virgin*, which has been lost. During her lifetime her works circulated privately among family members and acquaintances. Most biographers believe that, in her study of Scripture, Tornabuoni relied on one of the medieval Italian translations circulating in Florence at that time. She may have used the Tuscan *Diatessaron*, a translation of a compilation of the Gospels into the Tuscan dialect. She may also have consulted the Vulgate. Her poem about John the Baptist, Florence's patron saint, includes details absent from Scripture but found in popular tales. For instance, drawing on legends that contradict Luke 1:56–57, Tornabuoni states that the Virgin Mary remains with Elizabeth for the birth of John. Tornabuoni also exercises creative license, adding subplots and scenes not contained in Scripture, such as Elizabeth and Zechariah's tearful farewell when John departs for the desert. She offers a poignant and sympathetic portrayal of Adam and Eve's perplexity immediately following their banishment from Eden: "And they stand still knowing not what to do" (*Sacred Narratives*, 284).

Tornabuoni had a gift for vivid description of narrative settings. For instance, her poems contain rich detail about Susanna's lush garden (Sus. 1:7) and Ahasuerus's lavishly decorated palace (Esther 1:5–6). She introduces courtly themes into biblical stories, highlighting the beauty of female protagonists and the chivalry of male heroes. Tornabuoni appreciated biblical stories of female heroism. She writes about Judith: "I found her story written in prose, / and I was greatly impressed by her courage" (*Sacred Narratives*, 123). She also speaks of Judith's "manly heart" (145). Nevertheless, she critiques female characters, including Eve, "that ambitious woman," when she feels it is warranted by the biblical text (284).

Tornabuoni's poems reveal her understanding of Florentine culture and gender relations. When Elizabeth wants to name her son John (Luke 1:60), her family members initially refuse to accept her decision, for "in such affairs, we should not trust the mother" (*Sacred Narratives*, 232). Tornabuoni's treatment of Esther and Herodias (Matt. 14:1–12; Mark 6:17–28) reflects the challenges faced by wellborn women who involve themselves in public affairs, negotiating the boundaries between the public and private spheres. Echoing the ways that Tornabuoni and the women in her family influenced their powerful male relatives, she writes at length about how prudent Esther and wicked Herodias resort to indirect means to further their interests by working behind the scenes to persuade their husbands.

In her poem on Esther, Tornabuoni offers advice to female readers. Vashti's public flouting of her husband's wishes, refusing to appear at Ahasuerus's banquet "dressed in her regal vestments" (*Sacred Narratives*, 174), illustrates the need for women to be more cautious: "Women, learn nothing from this queen: / be prudent, and listen to my words / with great care and discretion" (177). As she paraphrases the counsel of the king's advisers, Tornabuoni omits the statement that husbands should be "masters" in their own houses (Esther 1:22). Instead, she softens their assertion of male authority, as the counselors say that wives should be "courteous, wise, and respectful, / so that their husbands have no reason to leave them" (176).

On two occasions Tornabuoni adds narrative details illustrating her concern for poor women's dowries. After Judith beheads Holofernes, she gives her faithful servant woman "bountiful treasures, / with which she could marry well" (160). When Esther is chosen to be Ahasuerus's wife, the other virgins under consideration are showered with "expensive gifts and presents, / so that they would have dowries and be able to wed" (181).

Tornabuoni died in Florence on March 25, 1482. She was grandmother to two popes (Leo X and Clement VII) and great-grandmother to Catherine de' Medici (1519–89), queen consort of France. Tornabuoni has always been better known for her progeny than her poetry, but in recent years her writings have begun to receive critical attention.

Bibliography

Kent, Francis W. "Sainted Mother, Magnificent Son: Lucrezia Tornabuoni and Lorenzo de' Medici." *Italian History and Culture* 3 (1997): 3–34.

Pernis, Maria Grazia, and Laurie Schneider Adams. *Lucrezia Tornabuoni de' Medici and the Medici Family in the Fifteenth Century*. New York: Peter Lang, 2006.

Russell, Rinaldina. "Lucrezia Tornabuoni (1425–1482)." Pages 431–40 in *Italian Women Writers: A Bio-bibliographical Sourcebook*, edited by Rinaldina Russell. Westport, CT: Greenwood, 1994.

Tomas, Natalie R. *The Medici Women: Gender and Power in Renaissance Florence*. Burlington, VT: Ashgate, 2003.

Tornabuoni, Lucrezia. *La istoria della casta Susanna.* Edited by Paolo Orvieto. Bergamo: Moretti & Vitali, 1992.

———. *Lettere: Con una scelta di lettere a lei inviate.* Edited by Patrizia Salvadori. Florence: Olschki, 1993.

———. *I poemetti sacri di Lucrezia Tornabuoni.* Edited by Fulvio Pezzarossa. Florence: Olschki, 1978.

———. *Sacred Narratives.* Edited and translated by Jane Tylus. Chicago: University of Chicago Press, 2001.

—JOY A. SCHROEDER

Trimmer, Sarah (1741–1810)

Sarah Trimmer was born Sarah Kirby on January 6, 1741, in Ipswich, England, the daughter of John Joshua Kirby (1716–74) and Sarah Bull Kirby (d. 1775). Trimmer was educated at Mrs. Justiner's School for Young Ladies in Ipswich and by her father. Following Joshua Kirby's career, the Kirbys moved to London in 1755. After this move, Kirby took on sole responsibility for directing his daughter's education. In addition to theology, Trimmer read and memorized English poets, including John Milton (1608–74). Trimmer's education also included meeting and conversing with her father's friends, "people of eminence in the literary world" (*Some account*, 1:8); one of these people was Samuel Johnson (1709–84). Trimmer drew the attention of Johnson in particular when, at her father's request, she produced a copy of *Paradise Lost* from her pocket to settle a disputed point in a conversation (1:8).

Joshua Kirby was appointed Clerk of the Works of the Royal Palace at Kew, so the Kirbys moved to Kew, where they met the Trimmer family. Sarah Kirby married James Trimmer (1739–92) in 1762 and moved across the Thames from Kew to Brentford, where she lived the rest of her life. James and Sarah Trimmer had twelve children, six daughters and six sons, nine of whom survived into adulthood. Sarah Trimmer's energy was focused on providing an education to all her children; this led her to read widely on the subject. In 1780, on the encouragement of her friends, Trimmer wrote her first educational book, *An Easy Introduction to the Knowledge of Nature and the Reading of the Holy Scriptures*, drawing on the experience she gained from teaching her own children. For the rest of her life, Trimmer pursued a vocation of writing to teach others, especially about the Bible.

In June 1786 a Sunday school began in Brentford; Trimmer and her children were volunteers at the school. Trimmer's experience while teaching poor children in the Brentford Sunday school set the direction for her future work. She continued to write, but instead of writing only for her peers and their children, she also wrote works to be used for teaching poor children in Sunday schools, schools of industry, and charity schools. In November 1786 Trimmer met with Queen Charlotte at the queen's request in order to advise the queen on starting a Sunday school at Windsor (*Some account*, 1:120). After this

505

meeting, Trimmer began work on *The Economy of Charity* (1787), in which she encouraged her peers and their daughters to sponsor and volunteer in local Sunday schools. Trimmer also campaigned to have her books placed on the list of approved texts by the Society for Promoting Christian Knowledge; she achieved this goal in June 1793, ensuring wide use of her works in schools (*Some account*, 2:36). When Trimmer died in December 1810, she was working on a revision of her *Essay on Christian Education*, one of more than forty works that she published in the last thirty years of her life, all in some way devoted to religious education.

Many of Trimmer's works contain biblical interpretation, but two in particular are devoted to that task. Her six-volume *Sacred history*, first published in 1782–85, provides a chronological edition of the historical portions of the Bible for use in teaching children in families and schools. *A help to the unlearned*, first published in 1805, is a one-volume commentary on the Bible, written to aid literate adults in their understanding of Scripture. Trimmer's interpretation of Scripture as seen in these two works will be the focus of the analysis that follows.

Both Trimmer's identity as an Anglican woman and her setting in eighteenth-century England shaped her understanding and interpretation of the Bible. As an Anglican, she heard Scripture in a liturgical setting; as a woman, her experiences provided her with a particular lens through which to view the Bible; and as an eighteenth-century woman, she was concerned with what was proper for her students to know. Trimmer also was an eighteenth-century biblical interpreter and thus, along with other English interpreters of the time, was concerned with a rational and historical approach to the Bible. Reason was the measure of truth in the eighteenth century, and so it was also the measure of what was true in the Bible and the Christian religion. The interest in history was particularly manifested in England and English-speaking countries with focus on the chronology represented in the biblical text and on what really happened during the events described in the Bible.

Trimmer's concern for history, especially chronology, is most clearly seen in *Sacred history*. Its first four volumes contain selections from the historical books of the Bible, which follow the chronological narrative thread of the Old Testament from the creation story to the intertestamental period. The final two volumes cover the narrative thread of the New Testament, ending with a discussion of the book of Revelation and the future "consummation of all things" (6:477). Each volume is divided into a number of sections, each section having two parts: first, an excerpt from the Authorized Version of the Bible; second, "Annotations and Reflections," in which Trimmer explains the passage to her reader. Trimmer's selections from the Bible are not in canonical order but follow a chronological order determined by marginal dates (1: preface). For example, in Trimmer's treatment of the book of Judges, Judg. 17–21 are paraphrased and placed between the accounts of Othniel and Ehud in Judg.

2 (2:253–59). Further, the book of Ruth, which occurs during the time of the Judges, is placed following the story of Deborah (2:272–76). Parallel accounts of the same events, such as those found in the four Gospels, are harmonized into a single account.

The "Annotations and Reflections" in *Sacred history* show Trimmer's esteem for reason. She often warns her readers against "enthusiasm," which in the context of the late eighteenth century means fervent yet misplaced religious emotion. For example, her annotations on the conversion of Paul make it clear that this event is extraordinary and thus not to be viewed as a model for other conversions. Instead of expecting grace to pour down like a torrent, as it does for the apostle, her readers may avail themselves of the means of grace and find that grace "will descend into our hearts *insensibly* like drops of rain into the thirsty earth, exciting us to what is right, and deterring us from what is sinful, by informing our *reason*; but *our own will* must co-operate with it to render it effectual" (6:369). For Trimmer, divine grace informs human reason; it does not inflame human emotions.

In producing the chronologically ordered *Sacred history*, Trimmer was also concerned with propriety; she did not want to include anything that would be improper for her younger readers, thus she omits or paraphrases verses that refer to details of childbirth and sexuality. In the account of the annunciation, for example, Trimmer's version of Luke 1:34 omits the last phrase of Mary's question, "seeing I know not a man?" Further, when Mary visits Elizabeth (Luke 1:39–45), any mention of either woman's womb and the babies in them is omitted (5:18). A similar concern for propriety may be behind Trimmer's dismissal of the Song of Solomon in her commentary *A help to the unlearned*. Though Trimmer comments on every other book of the Bible extensively, the Song merits only a single sentence: "This book is understood to relate to Christ and his church, but being all figurative language it is not easy to explain it; you may therefore pass it over, without puzzling yourself to understand it, as all which it is designed to teach us is taught in plainer words in the other parts of Scripture" (387).

The influence of Trimmer's experiences as a wife and mother on her interpretation of the Bible can be seen in *A help to the unlearned*. For example, Trimmer's remarks on Gen. 21:8–21, when Hagar and Ishmael are sent away from Abraham's household, give a practical and pastoral application to young people who may need to move away from home to earn a living. Because "the Lord showed that he had not forsaken Ishmael though he had sent him away from his father's house," young people who leave home should take comfort because "they may be under the protection and care of their heavenly Father in every place" (25). Trimmer's words to young people could also be comforting to parents as they sent their children from home to earn a living. Trimmer's own children had moved away to earn a living; she was not speaking without experience.

Trimmer's immersion in the Anglican liturgy is evidenced in many ways through her commentary, but particularly in the way she heads the book of Psalms. These psalms are read through each month according to the Anglican prayer book; Trimmer partitions them by day of the month and morning and evening prayer (*Help*, 270–340). In other places in *A help to the unlearned*, she points out biblical sources for the Apostles' Creed (583, 587), which was an important part of most Anglican services. The liturgy served both as an organizing guide for Trimmer's interpretive work and as the atmosphere within which she heard and understood the Bible.

Both *Sacred history* and *A help to the unlearned* are careful works of scholarship, showing that Sarah Trimmer studied the Bible carefully, read relevant scholarship on the Bible, and wrote as a confident scholar and interpreter of Scripture. *Sacred history* proved to be a popular and influential work. Following the success of the first edition (1782–85), Robert Raikes, the founder of the Sunday school movement, printed the second, revised edition in Gloucester in 1788. By 1801 a fourth edition was being sold in London. An eighth edition was printed in London in 1824, fourteen years after Trimmer's death and forty years after the first edition. Although *Sacred history* was initially intended for use by school-age children learning about the Bible in a family or school setting, many adults also found Trimmer's work attractive, and at least part of its popularity came from adult use of the work as an edition of the Bible. *A help to the unlearned* also went through several editions, with one print run as late as 1850. Trimmer's life was also included in volumes of women's biography both in the United Kingdom (in Clara Lucas Balfour's *Working Women of the Last Half Century*, 1854) and the United States (Sarah Josepha Hale's *Woman's Record*, 1855).

Despite the popularity of her work within her lifetime and for half a century afterward, Trimmer's reputation began to suffer in the latter part of the nineteenth century. Her published and personal works in Christian religious education were all but forgotten. With regard to children's literature, Trimmer was remembered, though not always with sympathy. In this field she is particularly remembered for her pioneering reviews of children's books, published in the periodical *The Guardian of Education* (1802–6), which she founded and edited. Trimmer the children's writer is not, however, widely understood as a biblical interpreter.

As interest in the reception history of the Bible has grown, so Trimmer's work has gradually been rediscovered. She is included in Patricia Demers's survey of *Women as Interpreters of the Bible* (1992) and is analyzed as an interpreter representative of the early nineteenth century in Stephen Prickett's *Origins of Narrative* (1996). While the work of analyzing and understanding Sarah Trimmer's work on the Bible has begun, much more work remains to be done on both her *Sacred history* and *A help to the unlearned*.

See also Hale, Sarah (1788–1879)

Bibliography

Demers, Patricia. *Women as Interpreters of the Bible*. Mahwah, NJ: Paulist Press, 1992.

Prickett, Stephen. *Origins of Narrative: The Romantic Appreciation of the Bible*. Cambridge: Cambridge University Press, 1996.

Trimmer, Sarah. *A help to the unlearned in the study of the Holy Scriptures: Being an attempt to explain the Bible in a familiar way; Adapted to common apprehensions, and according to the opinions of approved commentators*. London: F. C. & J. Rivington & J. Hatchard, 1805.

―――. *Sacred history selected from the Scriptures: With annotations and reflections, particularly calculated to facilitate the study of the Holy Scriptures in schools and families*. 6 vols. London: J. Dodsley, 1782–85.

―――. *Some account of the life and writings of Mrs. Trimmer*. 2 vols. London: F. C. & J. Rivington, 1814.

Weir, Heather E. "Helping the Unlearned: Sarah Trimmer's Commentary on the Bible." Pages 19–30 in *Recovering Nineteenth-Century Women Interpreters of the Bible*, edited by Christiana de Groot and Marion Ann Taylor. Atlanta: Society of Biblical Literature, 2007.

— HEATHER WEIR

Truth, Sojourner (née Isabella Baumfree) (ca. 1791–1883)

Sojourner Truth was a well-known abolitionist, activist for women's rights and freed slaves, and itinerant evangelist. She was born into slavery and experienced in and on her body the brutality of that system. On July 4, 1827, the New York State Legislature granted her (and all slaves in the state) emancipation, and she promptly moved with her son to New York City, where she worked as a live-in domestic. The turning point in her life came on June 1, 1843, when she adopted a new name, Sojourner, and traveled to the east coast for the purpose of "exhorting the people to embrace Jesus, and refrain from sin" (*Narrative*, 101). She preached at camp meetings, lived for a period in a utopian community, and toured the country on the lecture circuit, speaking on behalf of abolition and women's rights. She also devoted herself to working for a colony for freed slaves in the west, where they could become self-supporting and self-reliant.

Sojourner believed that God was an "all-powerful, all pervading spirit" who spoke to her directly, thus this inner voice was for her as authoritative as Scripture. This voice helped her to interpret Scripture. For that reason, she, being illiterate, preferred children to read Scripture aloud to her rather than adults because the latter often added, much to her dislike, their own comments along with the text. She concludes that "the spirit of truth spoke in those records, but that the recorders of those truths had intermingled with them ideas and suppositions of their own" (109).

Sojourner references biblical figures and stories in her most famous speech, "Ain't I a Woman?" given at the Woman's Rights Convention in Akron, Ohio, in 1851. The first biblical figure she mentions is Eve, particularly her role in the

509

fall in Gen. 3. She acknowledges that "Eve caused man to sin," but she then issues this ironic retort, "Well if woman upset the world, do give her a chance to set it right side up again" (Mabee 82). Both statements about the Gen. 3 story suggest that women have the power and the capability not only to disturb, but also to amend; therefore her appeal is, in the spirit of the conference, to let women get on with the latter by supporting women's rights. Her attention then turns to Jesus's welcome for women, such as Mary and Martha, who beg him to raise their brother, Lazarus, from the dead (John 11:17–27). She makes this simple, declarative comment about Jesus's treatment of women: "He never spurned woman from him" (82). Further, although she does not explicitly give Mary's name, Sojourner reminds the audience that Jesus himself came "through God who created him and woman who bore him" (82). Again Sojourner provides an ironic epitaph when she queries, "Man, where is your part?" (82). What is apparent in her interpretation of these biblical references is the agency that women possess and have to employ.

Sojourner also utilizes biblical figures and themes in her vigorous comments denouncing slavery and white racism. Appealing to the book of Esther, she likens the oppression of the Jews, who are helpless against the intended slaughter by Haman, to that of African American slaves. Only with Esther's intervention is the situation reversed. By referencing this biblical book, Sojourner addresses the oppression of two groups in her context—women and slaves: there was triumph not only for the intended victims, the Jews, but also for the liberator, Esther, a woman (Mabee 91).

She seemed to have an affinity for the book of Daniel because she draws on several stories from its pages. While speaking to a group who espoused what she called "Second Advent" doctrines, or the imminent return of Jesus, she likens herself to the young men who withstand the fiery furnace in Dan. 3:19–30:

> You seem to be expecting to go to some parlor *away up* somewhere, and when the wicked have been burnt, you are coming back to walk in triumph over their ashes—this is to be your New Jerusalem!! Now, *I* can't see any thing so very *nice* in that, coming back to such a *muss* as that will be, a world covered with the ashes of the wicked! Besides, if the Lord comes and burns—as you say he will—I am not going away; *I* am going to stay here and *stand the fire*, like Shadrach, Meshach, and Abednego! And Jesus will walk with me through the fire, and keep me from harm. Nothing belonging to God can burn, any more than God himself; such shall have no need to go away to escape the fire! No, *I* shall remain. Do you tell me that God's children *can't stand fire*? (Gilbert 111–12)

In another reference to the book of Daniel, she compares then-president Abraham Lincoln to Daniel because both have survived the "lions' den," thanks to God's mighty hand (Mabee 121).

Sojourner Truth remains one of the most recognized women of the nineteenth century, particularly for her relentless work on behalf of women and

African Americans. Less well known is the mission for which she changed her name and traveled eastward, for the purpose of "'testifying of the hope that was in her'—exhorting the people to embrace Jesus and refrain from sin" (Gilbert 101).

Bibliography

Gilbert, Olive, recorder. *Narrative of Sojourner Truth: A Northern Slave, Emancipated from Bodily Servitude by the State of New York, in 1828.* Introduction by Harriet Beecher Stowe. Boston: William Lloyd Garrison for Sojourner Truth, 1850. http://xroads.virginia.edu/~hyper/TRUTH/toc.html. Many editions, such as the one edited and introduced by Margaret Washington. Vintage Classics. New York: Vintage Books, 1993.

Mabee, Carleton. *Sojourner Truth: Slave, Prophet, Legend.* New York: New York University Press, 1993.

Painter, Nell Irvin. *Sojourner Truth: A Life, A Symbol.* New York: W. W. Norton, 1996.

Pope-Levison, Priscilla. *Turn the Pulpit Loose: Two Centuries of American Women Evangelists.* New York: Palgrave Macmillan, 2004.

Robinson, Marius. "Editorial." *Salem (Ohio) Anti-Slavery Bugle,* 21 June 1851. Cited in Mabee, *Sojourner Truth,* 81–82.

—Priscilla Pope-Levison

Tucker, Charlotte Maria (A. L. O. E.) (1821–93)

Charlotte Maria Tucker was born in Barnet, Hertfordshire, England, to Henry St. George Tucker (1771–1851) and Jane Boswell (d. 1869). The year after her birth, the family moved to the London house that was Tucker's home until her mother's death. Tucker's father achieved his goal of becoming a director of the East India Company in 1826 (Cutt 80). The family's fortunes and connections thus improved during Tucker's early years.

Henry St. George Tucker disapproved of schools for women; all five of his daughters were therefore educated at home. Her education allowed Tucker to follow her natural inclinations toward drawing, music, dance, and teaching her younger siblings. Tucker's father published a volume of plays in 1835 (Giberne 12), and Tucker followed his example by writing plays for her brothers and sisters to perform at home. Any other inclination Tucker might have had to write and publish was held in check until after her father's death in 1851. In 1852 she published her first work as A. L. O. E. (A Lady of England), *Claremont Tales.* Following this, Tucker produced at least two and as many as seven books per year between 1853 and 1875 (Giberne 515–17).

Tucker was raised in the Church of England; from the time of her confirmation, she took her religious life quite seriously. In an undated letter to a niece preparing for confirmation, Tucker recalled that at age fifteen, preparing for her own confirmation, she had had a religious experience that informed her faith throughout her life (Giberne 28). Tucker's evangelical Church of England sensibilities can be clearly seen in her writings.

Tucker's mother and older sister both died within months of each other in 1869. Following her mother's death, Tucker lived with her younger brother and his family. Eventually she decided to go to India as a self-supporting missionary. In 1875 Tucker traveled first to Canada to see her nephew living near Toronto; then, after briefly returning to England, she went to India, where she remained for the rest of her life. Tucker worked as a missionary visitor and teacher in Amritsar and Batala, in the north of India, near the present border with Pakistan. After serving for eighteen years in India, she died in Amritsar in 1893 and was buried in Batala. A plaque to her memory can still be seen in the cathedral in Lahore, Pakistan.

Tucker's books were mostly for children. The tales can primarily be classified as moral: they taught children how best to act and the kinds of attitudes they should cultivate. Some were principally allegorical; others were stories of nineteenth-century families and children. In some of her books, Tucker engages directly with the Bible, interpreting it and teaching it to her readers. Tucker's method of interpretation and application of the Bible is largely analogical: she tries to draw parallels between the biblical texts and contemporary life.

The most obvious example of Tucker's directly teaching the Bible can be found in *House Beautiful; or, The Bible Museum* (1868). This book, not directed specifically to children, is intended to aid the Christian reader in general in "holy musings on the past" (vi). The book contains forty-one meditations on objects found in the Bible and one concluding meditation on the names of the twelve tribes listed in Rev. 7. Some of the applications presented are more suited to adults than children, including an admonishment to the reader who might be "an active and useful member of the church" (15) and a reflection for "a mother's eye" (45). Because the book does not engage subjects unsuitable for children, it could have been used in family worship.

The reflections in *House Beautiful* illustrate both Tucker's attitude toward the Bible and her method of interpreting and applying the Scriptures to life. The chapter titled "Jehoiakim's Knife" first tells the story of Jehoiakim's use of his knife to destroy the scroll dictated by the prophet Jeremiah (Jer. 36). This episode is named as the first attempt to "mutilate the Scriptures, and stop the free course of the Word of God" (179). Superstition and Heresy are personified as active agents who employ the knife to destroy Scripture throughout church history (179–80). Skepticism is finally named as the most recent destroyer of the Bible (180). Readers are exhorted to "receive—honour—and keep the Bible in its integrity, deeming no portion superfluous which God hath thought fit to preserve; waiting for more light from above to reveal its hidden mysteries, and being assured that though heavens and earth may pass away, yet *the Word of the Lord endureth forever*" (182).

Tucker also taught the Bible by using stories, both short and long. In *Precepts in Practice; or, Stories Illustrating the Proverbs* (1875), a verse from Proverbs serves as the epigram for each chapter, and the story in that chapter illustrates the proverb. Each story is independent of the others, though the characters all seem to live in the same village or neighborhood, so some appear in more than one story. Throughout each story the proverb being illustrated is often repeated so the point of the tale is not easily missed. For example, Prov. 27:10, "Thine own friend, and thy father's friend, forsake not," is the epigraph for chapter 4, titled "The Friend in Need" (43). This proverb is repeated in whole and part throughout the story, and then in each of the three stanzas of the poem that concludes the chapter. The story itself deals with a young man who visits an old friend of his father's each week, bringing him what food he can and keeping him company. When the young man falls gravely ill, he tries to get up to make this visit, and the doctor asks his mother what he is trying to do. On hearing of his habit of visiting the old man, the doctor is shamed, since the old man was a former servant to the doctor's family. The doctor rectifies his neglect of his father's former gardener through the example of his patient (55). Through the stories readers are taught how to understand and apply the wisdom of Proverbs to their own lives.

Exiles in Babylon; or, Children of Light (1864) is an example of a children's novel that teaches principles from a Bible story. In this work, the story of Daniel is put into the mouth of a clergyman holding cottage meetings. The clergyman, Mr. Eardley, gives seven lectures on the book of Daniel, each illustrated with a print. The prints are included in the book for the reader to see. The lectures not only recount the story of Daniel and his friends but also include historical details from secular histories of the ancient Near East. Mr. Eardley does not dwell long on these details but clearly puts each episode into its setting. For example, at the beginning of the fifth lecture, he briefly summarizes Nebuchadnezzar's successors to introduce his hearers to Belshazzar, the current Babylonian ruler. Similarly, at the beginning of the sixth lecture, Darius and his place in the Persian Empire are introduced to the hearers. These details show that Tucker uses history to understand the Bible, a practice that became common in the nineteenth century.

In *Exiles in Babylon*, the cottage-meeting lectures are embedded into a frame story that reflects the story of Daniel and his friends in many ways. For example, just before the story of Daniel and the lions' den (Dan. 6), the steward who hosts the cottage meetings loses his job by refusing to work on a Sunday. This obviously reflects the situation of Daniel, condemned for praying despite the law against it. To add to the parallel, the servants encourage their employer to require the Sunday work, thus precipitating the steward's dismissal. These servants parallel the courtiers around Daniel, who look for a way to discredit him. The point of the Bible story is thus made twice—once directly in the lecture, and once indirectly in the parallel story surrounding the lecture.

As already noted, Tucker was a prolific writer; the quantity of her publications alone means that she left an impression on her time. The release of a biography two years after her death and her inclusion in a retrospective of women novelists in the Victorian era indicate that her work was recognized as significant in her lifetime and immediately afterward. Neither Giberne, Tucker's biographer, nor Marshall, the essayist in *Women Novelists of Queen Victoria's Reign*, are enthusiastic about Tucker's writing. They see her as too didactic, with a tendency to indulge in "long and discursive 'preachments,' which interrupted the main flow of the story, which were impatiently skipped that it [the story] might flow on again without vexatious hindrances" (Marshall 294). Despite the didacticism in Tucker's stories, both Marshall and Giberne recognize that she was a good writer, whose stories show flashes of brilliance.

Tucker's moral stories have not been widely examined by more recent scholars. They are primarily seen as standard period children's works with a religious and moral message, popular because Sunday reading at the time required that kind of book (Cutt xi). Tucker's work has received no attention in the theological disciplines; any insight her work might bring to understanding how the Bible was read by, and taught to, laypeople in her own lifetime requires further study.

Bibliography

Cutt, Margaret Nancy. *Ministering Angels: A Study of Nineteenth-Century Evangelical Writing for Children.* Wormley, UK: Five Owls, 1979.

Giberne, Agnes. *A Lady of England: The Life and Letters of Charlotte Maria Tucker.* New York: A. C. Armstrong & Son, 1895.

Marshall, Mrs. "A. L. O. E. (Miss Tucker)." Pages 293–97 in *Women Novelists of Queen Victoria's Reign: A Book of Appreciations by Mrs. Oliphant, Mrs. Lynn Linton, Mrs. Alexander, Mrs. Macquoid, Mrs. Parr, Mrs. Marshall, Charlotte M. Yonge, Adeline Sergeant and Edna Lyall.* London: Hurst & Blackett, 1897.

Tucker, Charlotte Maria [A. L. O. E.]. *Exiles in Babylon; or, Children of Light.* London: T. Nelson & Sons, 1864.

———. *House Beautiful; or, The Bible Museum.* London: T. Nelson & Sons, 1868.

———. *Precepts in Practice; or, Stories Illustrating the Proverbs.* London: T. Nelson & Sons, 1875.

— HEATHER WEIR

Warner, Susan Bogert (1819–85), and Anna Bartlett Warner (1827–1915)

Anna and Susan Warner were patriotic American authors whose biblical interpretation was woven into their seventy novels, hymns, and devotional works. Susan Warner was born in New York City in 1819 to Henry Whiting Warner, a prominent lawyer and businessman, and Anna Marsh Barlett Warner, who died a year after their second daughter, Anna, was born in 1827. After their father suffered tremendous losses during the 1837 economic panic, the sisters moved to the family's country home, a Constitution Island farmhouse on the Hudson River. The family's financial distress pushed the sisters to write as a source of income.

The Warners' works, specifically Susan's, gained immense popularity, resonating with women who empathized with their characters. In her best-selling novel, *The Wide, Wide World* (1850), Susan gives voice to her own experiences of financial hardship, loss of a parent, and helplessness in the face of the restrictions placed on women; her protagonist, Ellen, learns the importance of faith through suffering and self-abnegation. Her fiction also taught religious and moral values, functioning as advice manuals for the ideal American woman. When the wise grandmother speaks in *Walks from Eden* (1866), the characters "always reverently listened" (*Walks from Eden*, 16). Susan Warner also elevates the position of women in Christianity, arguing that a woman in a non-Christian society "is in a dark place indeed" (50). Her novels popularize the domesticated moral woman.

Anna Warner, Susan's younger sister, was also an author. Her hymn "Jesus Loves Me," originally written in the sisters' novel *Say and Seal* (1860), was later published as a children's song for missionaries. Anna's hymn elevates weakness, something many women at the time felt was a Christian virtue. The theme of power through weakness is also featured in her devotional commentary, *The Melody of the Twenty-Third Psalm* (1869). She argues that a position of weakness, like that of Jesus their "Master, despised and rejected," can "give glory" (18). Anna Warner reads the Psalms on multiple levels: literal, christological, and spiritual as applied to the life of the Christian. She also reads Scripture intertextually. Commenting on Ps. 23:1, Anna uses verses from other psalms—as well as Isaiah, Ezekiel, Matthew, John, and 1 Peter—to fill out the meaning of the first verse of Ps. 23. Thus "The Lord is my shepherd" becomes a consolation for those who are "sheep going astray, but are now returned unto the Shepherd and Bishop of [their] souls" (1 Pet. 2:25). Susan Warner also engages the biblical text in a similar fashion. Describing her interpretive approach, she writes that one must "patiently [put] words together," never leaving them at a surface level, but "noting carefully the blanks as well" (*Tired Christians*, 6).

Anna Warner's devotional commentary on men and women of the Old Testament, *What Aileth Thee?* (1881), showcases her ability to engage the resources of the academy and the church and, at the same time, read through the lens of her own experiences. In her commentary, she references such classic authors as Matthew Henry and Samuel Rutherford and seamlessly weaves into her work details regarding history, physical geography, and even her own knowledge of gardening. When Hagar is abandoned by Abraham and Sarah (Gen. 16), for example, Warner suggests that her lonely journey is accompanied by scarlet tulips and crimson anemones (4). When she writes of Sarah's death (Gen. 23), she mentions that the distance between Kirjath-arba and Beersheba (Sarah's death and Abraham's location) is twenty-four miles, a journey she estimates at eight hours (16). When Warner discusses the Egyptian oppression of the Israelites, she describes the scene through the eyes of the colossal figures that would have towered over the Israelites: Ip-Sambul and Rameses II gaze over the desert at a height of "sixty feet," their persecuting stare embodying the cruel dictatorship of Egypt (134). She also expands on the lives of characters who are given little attention in Scripture. Thus she pays special attention to Deborah, Rebekah's nurse in Gen. 35:8, elevating her to a position of Christlike servanthood and humility. For Warner, Deborah is a type of those who "get no share in our successes, who are used, paid, turned off" (48). And the reward for these unknown servants is nothing less than entrance into the kingdom, where at last all men and women are equal (50). Her traditional views of the woman question are also expressed in her essay on Esther, whom she holds up as a prime example of modesty, patience, and self-control, modeling how a woman can change culture by "working within her confines to change her situation" (345). The book of Esther ends with Esther's writing the decree to save her people. Warner comments with "delight" on Esther's "writing with all authority" because "women can certainly write letters" (352).

Susan and Anna Warner, descendants of the Puritan Pilgrims, were patriotic Americans. In *What Aileth Thee?* Anna describes America as the new Jerusalem, viewing her country as "the best that the sun shines on" (317). She implores her readers to "take up Ezra's confession [Ezra 9:5], and 'spread out their hands,' and make it for America" (317). Susan Warner's prize-winning essay, "How May an American Woman Best Show Her Patriotism?" (1850), written under her early pseudonym, Elizabeth Witherell, expresses similar patriotic sentiments and fleshes out her traditional view on women's roles. The sisters' zeal for their country and their deep religious convictions also found a home at the West Point Military Academy, where they developed Sunday school material and implemented Bible studies for the cadets. Their weekly sessions were very popular; when Anna died, many of her former Bible study cadets attended her funeral.

Susan Warner died in 1885, leaving Anna to live out her remaining thirty years while writing works of fiction and Susan's biography. Though their writings of fiction, devotion, and commentary were popular in their time, they are relatively unknown today. The influence of Anna Warner's hymn "Jesus Loves Me," however, has continued. When asked what was his greatest thought, Karl Barth quoted the first lines of Anna's hymn: "Jesus loves me! this I know, / For the Bible tells me so" (Bence 87). The Warners were traditional women who asserted their voice and their theological authority through their writing. Their interpretation of Scripture blended traditional approaches with an experientially based approach that reads texts through a female Protestant lens that many American women shared. The sisters understood their writing as their way of fulfilling the call of the Great Commission in Matt. 28:19. Anna

Warner died in 1915, never seeing a penny from her hymn, "Jesus Loves Me." The sisters are buried in the government cemetery at West Point, New York.

Bibliography

Bence, Evelyn. *Spiritual Moments with the Great Hymns: Devotional Readings That Strengthen the Heart*. Grand Rapids: Zondervan, 1997.

Pritchard, Peggy Kulesz. "God of Our Mothers: Hymns and Nineteenth-Century American Women (Anna Warner, Elizabeth Prentiss, Phoebe Cary)." PhD diss., University of Texas at Arlington, 2000.

Warner, Anna. *Gardening by Myself*. New York: Edward Jenkins, 1872.

———. *The Melody of the Twenty-Third Psalm*. London: James Nisbet, 1869.

———. *What Aileth Thee?* London: James Nisbet, 1881.

Warner, Anna, and Susan Warner. *Say and Seal*. Philadelphia: J. B. Lippincott, 1860.

Warner, Susan. "How May an American Woman Best Show Her Patriotism?" *Journal of History, Criticism, and Bibliography* 19 (2009): 219–32.

———. *My Desire*. New York: Robert Carter & Brothers, 1879.

———. *Tired Christians*. London: James Nisbet, 1881.

———. *Walks from Eden*. New York: Robert Carter & Brothers, 1866.

———. *The Wide, Wide World*. New York: George P. Putnam, 1850.

—Rebecca Tait

Wedgwood, (Frances) Julia (1833–1913)

Julia Wedgwood was born in England in 1833 to barrister and philologist Hensleigh Wedgwood and Francis Emma Mackintosh. Surrounded by intellectuals from childhood, including her famous cousin Charles Darwin, Wedgwood became well acquainted with emerging scientific, philosophical, and theological ideas. Although not formally educated, she taught herself Latin, Greek, French, and German and familiarized herself with various ancient texts. Resisting the marital ideal, she was employed as a research assistant and became a popular novelist, biographer, historian, and literary critic (Taylor and Weir 93, 173).

Wedgwood approached the Bible intellectually and rationally. In analyzing the Bible, she frequently employed her extensive knowledge of Darwinian naturalist theories, biblical criticism, literature, church history, and gnosticism, as well as Aristotelian and Platonic philosophy. Although she regularly signed her name to her work, Wedgwood only intermittently mentioned her gender throughout much of her writing. In "The Boundaries of Science," Wedgwood assumes the persona of a man. She successfully avoids referencing her sex in *The Moral Ideal* and "Greek Mythology and the Bible." Similarly, in "Plutarch and the Unconscious Christianity of the First Two Centuries," Wedgwood does not indicate her gender. Nevertheless, she does emphasize Plutarch's egalitarian view of woman: "Plutarch is the first to protest against that theory which is allotting the woman a lower standard. . . . The claim for one half of the race to participate in the duties of another implies a much nobler kind of equality than does any claim to participate in equal rights" (53–54).

Despite this apparent reluctance to showcase her identity as a woman, however, Wedgwood does forcefully express her feminine voice throughout some of her writings. In "A Word for Women by One of Themselves," Wedgwood employs the rhetoric of maternal feminism to encourage women to be more active in the faith development of others (279). In her article "Male and Female He Created Them," Wedgwood takes this one step further. In this piece, she argues that according to science, women lay claim to a longer moral inheritance than men due to the necessities of motherhood, which emerged before the conception of fatherhood. Although temporarily dethroned from this moral superiority, women once more became humanity's moral guardians through the Virgin Mary and the legacy of her son Jesus: "The worship of the Virgin expresses the new development of female influence after its long classic eclipse. . . . Evangelical Christianity dethroned Mary only to make way for an idea of Christ which differs from the historic Jesus precisely by lack of manliness" (132).

In *The Message of Israel in the Light of Modern Criticism*, Wedgwood uses the theories of source criticism to compare the priestly and Jehovist (Yahwist) creation accounts. Notably, she identifies the priestly writers' more egalitarian views in the relation they draw between sex and the Divine. According to these priestly writers, Wedgwood indicates that "sex in some mysterious form, would seem embodied in the divine nature." She continues by asserting that in this particular account of creation (Gen. 1), "Woman is no afterthought, no postscript, as it were, to the work of creation, but shares with man the first thought of God, and derives her being directly from Him" (261–62). Likewise, Wedgwood criticizes male figures such as Abraham for their improper treatment of women. According to Wedgwood, Abraham lacks "the physical courage to protect Sarah against Pharaoh [Gen. 12:10–20], and the moral courage to protect Hagar against Sarah [16:6; 21:9–10]. He surrenders the beloved mother to the most miserable death rather than encounter the anger of a woman; he is willing to surrender this woman to what he should have dreaded more than any death, in order to avert an imaginary danger to himself" (157).

Although constrained by the patriarchy of her time, Wedgwood rose above such limitations and interpreted the Bible for the intellectual and moral benefit of both women and men. Her capacity to master the languages of ancient texts and effectively grasp the biblical criticism of her time led to an astute interpretation of Scripture. Her insights at the very least matched and perhaps even exceeded those of her male contemporaries.

Bibliography

Taylor, Marion A., and Heather Weir, eds. *Let Her Speak for Herself*. Waco: Baylor University Press, 2006.

Wedgwood, Julia. "The Boundaries of Science: A Dialogue." *MacMillan's Magazine* 2 (June 1860): 134–38.

———. "Greek Mythology and the Bible." *Contemporary Review* 61 (March 1892): 368–81.

———. "Male and Female He Created Them." *Contemporary Review* 56 (July 1889): 120–33.

———. *The Message of Israel in the Light of Modern Criticism*. London: Isbister, 1894.

———. *The Moral Ideal: A Historic Study*. London: Trübner, 1888. 2nd ed., 1889.

———. "Plutarch and the Unconscious Christianity of the First Two Centuries." *Contemporary Review* 39 (Jan. 1881): 45–60.

———. "A Word for Women by One of Themselves." *Catholic World* 19 (May 1874): 277–80.

— BETH ROBERTSON

Weld, Angelina Grimké *See* Grimké, Sarah (1792–1873), and Angelina Grimké Weld (1805–79)

Wesley, Susanna (1669–1742)

The writings of Susanna Wesley reveal a deeply felt but rigorous piety, an exacting conscience, and a searching, well-informed intelligence. Her writings, including even her private journals, generally aim at moral and religious persuasion. Her purposes are well served by an accomplished and frequently powerful prose style that emphasizes clarity of ideas and an orderly progression of thought.

Wesley wrote in three genres, none of which were designed for circulation much beyond her immediate circle. Her journal was intended for her own use. She wrote a series of substantial letters and a dialogue intended for the moral, spiritual, and theological instruction of her children; these documents are a more formal extension of the daily education of her children, which she conducted at home (ten of her nineteen children survived infancy). Her letters, many of which were written to her children as adults, were intended for the circle of her family and friends, but also include interesting discussions with bishops and clergy on ecclesiastical and theological matters. For a brief period in 1711 and 1712, when her husband was at convocation in London, Susanna Wesley expanded the circle of family prayers and religious instruction to include groups of parishioners as large as two hundred people in her Sunday evening prayers. When her husband heard of these meetings, he protested, citing the Conventicle Act of 1664. Wesley, however, refused to discontinue them unless her husband explicitly commanded her to cease, lest it be on her conscience (Wesley 13–14, 78–83), and Samuel Wesley relented.

A fire destroyed almost all of her writings in 1709, including an autobiographical sketch and some catechetical writings, but an excellent recent collection is available of all her extant writings between 1709 and 1742, and some letters written before 1709 (Wesley).

Susanna Wesley writes on the Bible in all of her genres, but she does not write in genres devoted to biblical interpretation. She does not set out to write disinterested commentary on Scripture. And though in a precritical way she fully accepts the historical reference of the biblical narrative, she does not dwell on its merely historical reference. Most of her references to Scripture and her meditations on Scripture are devoted to its theological, moral, and spiritual meanings and are embedded in discussions of divinity, theoretical and practical ethics, and the Christian spiritual life. Wesley had a sophisticated understanding of these disciplines. Since her reading of the Bible conforms to her doctrines in these disciplines, knowledge of certain turning points in her intellectual life sheds light on her reading of the Bible.

Susanna was the twenty-fifth child of her father, Dr. Samuel Annesley, a famous Puritan pastor and divine of the seventeenth century. Her mother may have been Mary White, Dr. Annesley's second wife, but it is practically certain that both her parents were directly involved in her religious, moral, and intellectual formation (Newton 45). What is known of Annesley's home points to something like a model Puritan home, with biblical instruction as the foundation of education, the model that Susanna adapted for her own household. Judging by the quality of her writing, her broad knowledge, and her treatment of difficult books, she had an excellent education.

As a precocious thirteen-year-old, she made a momentous conversion from the dissenting Puritanism of her parents to communion in the Church of England. Unfortunately, her own account of the reasons for this conversion, written in a letter to her son Samuel, was lost in the 1709 fire before it was sent. She does state that it proceeded from a carefully considered study of arguments on both sides of the ecclesiastical and theological questions. Between the ages of thirteen and her early twenties, when she married the Anglican priest Samuel Wesley, she made an intellectual journey into "Socinianism," or Unitarianism, which many Puritan dissenters and Anglicans also made in the seventeenth and eighteenth centuries, only to return quite decisively during that same period to orthodox trinitarianism, in which she remained and through which she read the Bible for the rest of her life (Wesley 356).

In civil and ecclesiastical politics, Susanna and her husband were High-Church Tories. But Susanna was aligned with the nonjurors, who refused to recognize the right of the Protestant William of Orange to be the king with his coregent, Mary, after the Glorious Revolution of 1688, in which the Catholic James II was deposed. Susanna was not sympathetic with his Catholicism but believed that the English nation was bound by its prior oath of allegiance to James. She held to the divine right of kings: even when kings abuse their power, they are responsible only to God, from whom they derive their power, and not to their subjects (Wesley 204). For this reason, she omitted to pray for William as the king of England for fear that such a prayer made her complicit in the removal of King James, and she refused her husband's demand to pray for the king when Samuel noticed the omission in 1702. In consequence, Samuel left for London to look for an appointment as a naval chaplain. Susanna maintained her position on principle at great personal cost, appealing to nonjuring leaders for support (35–39); the six-month separation was finally resolved through the intervention of others after the death of William and a fire at their home.

Wesley takes the theological meaning of the Bible as entirely consistent with her own hard-won orthodoxy, her particular Anglican and Puritan inheritance, and her strict conscience. The most momentous changes in her intellectual life were in large part changes in theology and in ecclesiastical polity.

From her childhood Wesley read widely in English divinity. Her learning in divinity and her drive to know her own mind on important controversies inform her understanding of Scripture. Wesley frequently recommends Bishop Pearson's *Exposition of the Creed* on a variety of questions; she follows it as a model and source for her own exposition of the Apostles' Creed, in the form of a letter to her daughter Sukey (Wesley 379–97). In this exposition her understanding of the orthodox rule of faith guides her reading of Scripture, and she defends the rule of faith through her reading of Scripture. Each page consists of dense references to Scripture as warrant for each of the main points of orthodox Christian doctrine, including a defense of the apostolic rule of faith resident in the church catholic (393).

Wesley reads the Bible according to the distinction between natural and revealed religion, one of the main principles of her thought, which she makes a foundation of her discussions of Christian belief (381, 384, 396) and her discussions of what one might call her philosophy of religion (427–54; esp. 447–54). She allows a great deal of scope to natural religion but holds that central Christian doctrines—such as original sin, the incarnation, and the Trinity—require revelation and are revealed in the Scriptures (447–51). Thus, in an undated journal reflection, Wesley considers the Socinian denial of Christ's divinity, the Arian assertion that Christ was created, and the question of whether the doctrine of the Trinity is discoverable by natural reason without revelation. She follows Beveridge in a discussion of the divine names in the Scriptures, the names for Christ in the New Testament, and the conjunction of "Father," "Son," and "Spirit" as names for God in the New Testament. She concludes that, without accepting the authority of the Scriptures, God could not be proved to be "three persons or subsistencies (call them as you please)" in "one Jehovah or essence or being," but that with the Scriptures "this is not hard to do" (314–15).

Yet she considers that the doctrine of the Trinity and even the biblical revelation truly name in words what is in reality well beyond words:

521

What is it to have a just sense of Almighty God as he is distinguished into three subsistencies; namely, Father, Son, and Holy Spirit? Indeed I cannot tell. After so many years of inquiry, so long reading, and so much thinking, his boundless essence appears more inexplicable, the perfection of his glory more bright and inaccessible. The farther I search, the less I discover. . . . It is impossible to speak of God without impropriety, or to think of him without ecstasy. The subject is too vast, the matter too important. His sublimity transcends all thought; words cannot express what is so far above their nature; therefore, the simplist and plainest are the best. There is more significancy in that awful name by which he condescended to manifest himself to the Israelites, "I AM," than can be comprehended or expressed by any or all the words that are comprised in all languages on earth. (Wesley 351)

Wesley ties this teaching on the limits of words about God to the classic teaching of Christian theology that God cannot be known in his essence, but nevertheless has made himself known, and is known most directly in Christ, "in whom 'dwelleth the fulness of the Godhead bodily.'" She concludes this section of her journal, which combines her theological and biblical reasoning and an examination of her own soul, with an expression of worship: "I adore, O God! I adore!" (352).

Wesley takes an informed moral philosophy broadly in the Christian Aristotelian tradition and coordinates it with her reading of the moral sense of the Scriptures. Among other sources, her journal demonstrates a careful reading of the philosophical and religious ethics of Richard Lucas and frequent interactions with John Locke's *Essay* and Pascal's *Pensées*. For an outline of her moral philosophy, see her "religious conference," written as a dialogue, with her daughter Emilia as the interlocutor (433–54). Wesley coordinates her moral philosophy with her reading of practical biblical ethics as she exposits the Ten Commandments, in a letter to her daughter Sukey (409–19). For example, her comment on the commandment "Thou shalt have no other gods before me" (Deut. 5:7) weaves rich biblical reasoning together with an adjudication of competing definitions of love in Christian Platonism and the Christian Aristotelian tradition, and with a sensible application of an informed moral theory of the human will (413–14). She reads the commandment in light of the "greatest commandment," the commandment to love God (Deut. 6:5; Matt. 22:37–38). In one statement of the basic principle of her moral reasoning about love, both in this passage and as a foundation for her ethics, she asserts: "Nothing can be plainer than that love is a simple act of the soul, a pleasing motion towards union with the person beloved. And whether we shall wish well to or have a complacence in and press toward a union with what we love is wholly to be determined by the nature and circumstances of the object" (Wesley 414).

Thus, since God's being comprises all perfections, he is the proper object of the fullest love, worship, and adoration one can offer in body, mind, or soul, and the love of God implies the love of neighbor and of all creatures that somehow reflect God's image:

Since his infinite perfections and essential happiness supersedes all our wishes and desires of the kind, our love to him is determined in a high estimation of him, in adoration, praise, profound reverence, perfect resignation of ourselves to him, complacency in and desire of union and communion with him, zeal for his glory, delight in thinking or speaking of him, love of his name, day, word, sacraments, works, *in fine* of all his ordinances and all his creatures in which we perceive the smallest ray of his divinity. (414)

In a journal reflection on the nature of a godly soul, Wesley admits that it is a human duty to keep the body "in tenantable repair," but insists that a rightly ordered human soul aims for "the nearest union and communion with God that it is capable of and vigorously aspires to a divine resemblance" (Wesley 264–65). Her acceptance of this pious standard, with her frequent meditations on it as a theological, moral, and religious idea, best explains Wesley's life of great moral and religious seriousness, including her lifelong intellectual achievement. While the aspiration to divine resemblance requires natural moral goodness and Christian holiness, it is most fully realized in the life of worship and prayer, as "the one thing needful" (309).

As one would expect, then, she reads the Bible not only in its doctrinal and moral senses but also in its spiritual sense. This is seen most intensely and frequently in her private journal. In extended sections of her journal, she interacts with Lucas's work *Religious Perfection* or Beveridge's work on holiness, but does so with constant reflection on biblical sentences and themes. The following quotation, for example, is a condensed personal meditation on many passages, but especially on "the greatest of all the commandments":

If comparatively to despise and undervalue all [that] the world contains, which is esteemed great, fair or good, if earnestly and constantly to desire thee, thy favour, thy acceptance, thyself, rather than any or all things thou hast created [shall] be to love thee—I do love thee! . . . If to feel a vital joy overspread and cheer the heart at each perception of thy blessedness, at every thought that thou art God and that all things are in thy power, that there is none superior or equal to thee [shall] be to love thee—I do love thee! (Wesley 356)

Susanna Wesley is most widely remembered in Methodist traditions. Methodists have honored her as the mother and teacher of her children, among whom were John Wesley and Charles Wesley, the founders of Methodism; indeed, many have called her "the Mother of Methodism."

Bibliography

Newton, John A. *Susanna Wesley and the Puritan Tradition in Methodism.* 2nd ed. London: Epworth, 2002.

Wesley, Susanna. *Susanna Wesley: The Complete Writings*. Edited by Charles Wallace Jr. New York: Oxford University Press, 1997.

— MARK MEALEY

Wharton, Anne (1659–85)

Anne Wharton was orphaned shortly after birth, was raised by her pious grandmother, and was coheiress (with her sister) to a fortune consisting of extensive properties in Oxfordshire and around London. Anne was married at age fourteen to the twenty-six-year-old Thomas Wharton, a future leader in the Whig party (a faction of Covenanters opposing the Catholic duke of York), who would prove to be a neglectful and unfaithful husband. When Anne was only twenty-six, she died childless of a "pox" contracted from her husband.

Even though only one of her poems appeared in print before her death, Wharton was one of the most highly praised English poets of the Restoration (the period following the return to monarchy after the end of the Protectorate in 1660). Though known for her piety, many of her poems display religious uncertainty, and one of her poems (now lost) was even criticized by a bishop.

Shortly after her death, several of her works were published, including *The Lamentations of Jeremiah*, a paraphrase of the biblical book of Lamentations. One could read her work as simply a pious paraphrase of the biblical book, but Wharton skillfully used the biblical story of Jerusalem's destruction to speak to issues of her day. Some hold the work to be a direct attack on both the moral and political failures of the English monarch Charles II and on social institutions like marriage.

The Lamentations of Jeremiah is comprised of a dialogue between the male voice of Jeremiah, the feminine voice of the city of Jerusalem, and the God whom they view as faithless and capricious. Her first chapter begins with Jerusalem's female voice lamenting both her loss of freedom and the death of her citizens. The following two chapters resound with Jeremiah's male voice, reprimanding Jerusalem for her sin. The final two chapters again return to Jerusalem's voice.

Politically, Wharton supported the Whig and Protestant camps and was involved in national politics throughout her upbringing (though she could not actively participate due to her gender). A Royalist who was committed to having a Protestant monarchy, Wharton focuses on three events that devastated London and occurred shortly after Charles II was restored to the English throne: the Great Fire of London (1666); a year of plague (1665); and the War with the Dutch (1665–67). Fearing that the monarchy could return to Catholicism, Wharton blames these events on Charles's refusal to remove his Catholic brother James from the succession (as well as on Charles's military failures).

Through the voice of Jeremiah, Wharton castigates Charles for breaking God's commandments and incurring divine retribution. Just as Jerusalem could not prevent Babylonian destruction, so London will not escape the punishment of defeat. By casting London as Jerusalem, Wharton further criticizes the monarch by having the city sentenced to death by fire on account of the sins and arrogance of her king and his court:

> Her swift Destruction, is from Heaven sent,
> The Lord hath purpos'd, and will not relent,
> Her People languish round her sinking Walls,
> Her Strength decays, and all her Glory falls,
> Her Bars are broke whereon her Strength depends,
> So sure his Ruin which the Lord intends.
>
> *(Letters to the Lady Wharton and Several
> Other Persons of Distinction*, 71–72)

Her use of Jerusalem's destruction is apparently meant to bring to mind the fire of London and the attack of the Dutch navy. Wharton's casting of then-current events in biblical terms allows her to blame the monarch for these events without great legal or political risk.

Wharton's use of Lamentations also takes aim at the institution of marriage. By casting Jerusalem as an abandoned wife, Wharton attacks the monetary motives behind many aristocratic marriages of her day. This polemic may have been fueled by her own experience in marriage (which mainly functioned to allow her husband to gain the necessary monetary means to pursue politics). In order to denounce the loveless arranged marriages of the aristocracy, Wharton emphasizes Jerusalem as an abandoned wife in an unfair, one-sided marriage in which the husband (God) has inexplicably left his wife. Wharton thereby attacks the typical marriage of her class where the husband holds all the power, and the wife is at his mercy.

Despite being recognized for her poetical genius, only eighteen of her works were printed in the years following her death, though twenty-four of her poems can be identified. Though her biblical work was not as well known, *The Lamentations of Jeremiah* stands as a striking example of biblical interpretation by a woman. Wharton uses a perceived analogy between Jerusalem's fall and the deterioration of London and the fortunes of England to criticize both political and social institutions of her day. In some ways, it stands as a prophetic attempt to empower the disadvantaged women of her day who, despite their aptitudes and abilities, were at times trapped in loveless relationships with both their husbands and the wider society, which excluded them from full participation.

Bibliography

Clark, J. Kent. *Whig's Progress: Tom Wharton between Revolutions.* Madison, NJ: Fairleigh Dickinson University Press, 2003.

Gould, Robert. *A Funeral Eclogue to the Pious Memory of the Incomparable Mrs. Wharton.* [London:] Joseph Knight & Francis Saunders, 1685.

Rex, Michael. "The Heroine's Revolt: English Women Writing Epic Poetry. 1654–1789." PhD diss., Wayne State University, Detroit, 1998.

Wharton, Philip, et al. *Letters to the Lady Wharton and Several Other Persons of Distinction.* Vol. 2 of *Whartoniana; or, Miscellanies: In Verse and Prose.* London: H. Curll, 1727.

—PAUL S. EVANS

■ White, Ellen Harmon (1827–1915)

Ellen Harmon White was a charismatic cofounder of the Seventh-Day Adventist (SDA) Church, a well-known temperance speaker, and a prolific author. She was born in 1827 in Gorham, Maine, and her poor health ended her formal schooling at grade three. She and her family were drawn to William Miller's preaching of the imminent return of Jesus. After the Great Disappointment (Oct. 22, 1844), she was among those who believed that God had been leading them. Her first vision (Dec. 1844) encouraged the "little flock," and continuing visions established her in Adventism as one who had the gift of prophecy (cf. Eph. 4; 1 Cor. 12).

In 1846 she married James White, another Adventist pioneer; both of them played key roles in the formal organization of the SDA Church in 1863. She also contributed significantly to important developments in Adventism: publications, from the late 1840s; health reform, from the 1860s; education and missions, from the 1870s. White remained active after James died in 1881, spending time in Europe (1885–87) and Australia (1891–1900). In addition to her church work, White became an effective temperance lecturer, addressing crowds as large as five thousand and working closely with the Women's Christian Temperance Union.

White's writings are roughly of three kinds: autobiographical, counsel ("testimonies"), and devotional commentaries on Scripture. She published over five thousand articles in Adventist journals. At her death some twenty of her books were still in print. All her published writings are available on disc from the Ellen G. White Estate (check this CD-ROM for works not listed in the bibliography).

Among her writings are several multivolume sets. The 4,738 pages in nine volumes of the *Testimonies for the Church* (1855–1909 [*TC*]) were originally addressed to individuals and various church entities. Precisely dated up through 1889 (vols. 1–5) but more thematically ordered thereafter, the *Testimonies* are a rich resource for the study of early Adventism.

More popular among modern Adventists, however, is the five-volume Conflict of the Ages series (1888–1917), White's 3,600-page devotional commentary on Scripture. Two Old Testament volumes, *Patriarchs and Prophets* (1890 [*PP*]) and *Prophets and Kings* (1917 [posthumous]), and two New Testament ones, *The Desire of Ages* (1898 [*DA*]) and *The Acts of the Apostles* (1911 [*AA*]), are augmented by a final historical volume, *The Great Controversy* (1888, 1911

[*GC*]), that moves from the fall of Jerusalem (70 CE) to Eden restored. The Conflict series revises and expands two earlier four-volume series, *Spiritual Gifts* (1858–64 [*SG*]) and *The Spirit of Prophecy* (1870–84 [*SP*]).

Though not as obviously so as the "testimonies," her commentaries are also shaped by time and place. This becomes clear when late passages are compared with the antecedent parallels from 1858 and 1877. John the Baptist, for example, moved from a life "without pleasure" (1858) to one in which he at least had "joy" at work (1877), to a simplicity that he actually "enjoyed" (1897; see Thompson, *Escape*, 143–44).

White also helped move Adventism from its early Arian Christology to full orthodox trinitarianism (cf. Knight 110–17). Though she never polemicized against the Trinity, as her husband did—"that old trinitarian absurdity" was his rhetoric—an incipient Arianism is evident in her earlier writings. A key sentence in *DA* (1898) marks her mature theology: "In Christ is life, original, unborrowed, underived" (530).

A full Christology allowed her to use simple bookends for the Conflict series: "God is love" are the first words in *PP* and the last in *GC*. The buoyant commentary on the "law of love" that opens *PP* (33–34) is absent from the earlier series. Indeed, neither "God is love" nor "God of love" appears at all in *SG*, her first published account of the "great controversy" story (cf. Thompson, *Escape*, 137–50).

Her new vision of Jesus as God incarnate reordered her writing priorities. Instead of simply completing the Conflict series with *DA*, she wrote four more books about Jesus: *Steps to Christ* (1892), *Thoughts from the Mount of Blessings* (1896), *Christ's Object Lessons* (1900 [*COL*]), and *Ministry of Healing* (1905).

White's successive narratives of the story of Jesus's mother also illustrate her changed perspective. In 1877, Jesus's response to his mother at Cana— "Woman, what have I to do with thee?" (John 2:4)—is a rebuke; in 1898, it is simply a polite "Oriental custom." In 1877, the "pride" of Mary's heart leads her astray, but in 1898 she experiences a "fond mother's natural pride" (*SP*, 2:101–2//*DA*, 145–46).

White's understanding of her own role as a woman leader calls for further exploration. Generally ignoring male condescension, she wrote no apology for women's rights, no polemic against male privilege. Children of both genders should be educated so that they would be "qualified for any position in life" (*TC*, 3:134 [1872]). The vibrant view of humanity in *Education* (1903) has been seen by some as a mandate for Christian humanism.

White was eager for Adventists to grow in their knowledge of Scripture. In the aftermath of the 1888 "righteousness by faith" crisis, she warned that when believers "rest satisfied" with their knowledge of Scripture, they tend to "discourage any further investigation of the Scriptures. . . . They become conservative and seek to avoid discussion" (*TC*, 5:706–7 [1889]).

Given that SDAs hold to a so-called high view of Scripture, White's role as an "inspired" writer has led to significant turmoil within Adventism (cf. Thompson, *Inspiration*, 267–76). Though many SDAs intuitively grant her "final" authority in the interpretation of Scripture, she herself refused it. In the context of the 1888 crisis (noted above), she emphatically denied having the last word. She defended the right of E. J. Waggoner, one of the protagonists in the debate, to "honestly" hold views of Scripture differing from hers. Such differences do not make him a "dangerous" man, she declared (*1888 Materials*, 1:163 [1888]).

Distinguishing between her role and that of Scripture, White compared her "inspiration" to that of the noncanonical prophets who spoke for God, but "in matters no way relating to the giving of the Scripture" (*GC*, viii). Comparing Scripture with the incarnate Christ, she spoke of the mysterious blending of the human and divine in "inspiration" (cf. *GC*, vi). Referring to Jesus's two great commands (Matt. 22:35–40), she argued that the "unity of the church" could not consist "in viewing every text of Scripture in the very same light." "None need make a mistake," she argued. When one loves God supremely and one's neighbor as oneself, then "oneness in Christ" will be the "natural result" (*1888 Materials*, 3:1092–93 [1892]). Her views on inspiration were clearly influenced by Calvin E. Stowe's *Origin and History of the Books of the Bible* (1867).

White's extensive use of undocumented sources has been a vexed issue in Adventism, yet it has yielded significant insights into her methods of interpreting Scripture. Walter Rea, an Adventist pastor who had published compilations of White's quotations, became a vocal critic over the issue of sources. As a result the general conference asked Fred Veltman, a New Testament scholar from Pacific Union College, in Angwin, California, to do source analysis.

Analyzing fifteen chapters from *DA*, Veltman concluded that in her writings on the life of Christ, White had used at least twenty-three sources of various types, including fiction. She was especially drawn to "Victorian lives of Christ," which in Veltman's view are a genre much like "historical fiction" today (2:13). Her favorites were William Hanna, *The Life of Christ*, and two books by Daniel March, *Night Scenes of the Bible* and *Walks and Homes of Jesus*. Her chronology came from the harmony in Samuel Andrews's life of Christ.

White was ambivalent about nineteenth-century biblical scholarship. The King James Version was her pulpit Bible, and she preferred it in writing. Nevertheless, she welcomed and valued new Bible translations, using the English Revised Version (1881, 1885) and the American Standard Version (1901) as soon as they appeared. On the negative side, however, an 1893 incident at a New Zealand camp meeting troubled her. A Wesleyan minister's sermon in support of higher criticism of the Bible was circulating. In White's view, he was undermining the Bible's divine inspiration. Thus in *Education* (227 [1903]) and again in *AA* (474 [1911]), this cryptic comment appears: "The work of 'higher criticism,' in dissecting, conjecturing, reconstructing, is destroying faith in the Bible as a divine revelation; it is robbing God's word of power to control, uplift, and inspire human lives."

White's convictions about a personal God, supernaturalism, and Scripture as a divine revelation put her at odds with key elements in higher criticism. Yet her critical side was very much alive. In a Methodist-style appeal to experience, for example, she did an about-face on the doctrine of eternal hell fire, describing it as "repugnant to every emotion of love and mercy, and even to our sense of justice" (*GC*, 535; cf. Thompson, *Escape*, 70–82).

As for difficult matters in the Bible itself, Calvin Stowe had given her two choice nuggets: (1) "Men will often say that such an expression is not like God"; and (2) "It is not the words of the Bible that are inspired, but the men that were inspired" (*Selected Messages*, 1:21 [*SM*, 1886]). But she never published those words in her lifetime. So she would idealize—God did not send serpents, but "permitted" them (*PP*, 429, on Num. 21:6)—or she would skip stories like the dismembered concubine (Judg. 19–21) and the bloodguilt for Saul (2 Sam. 21). She could leave two quite different interpretations in place. In *COL* (405–21), for example, the parable of the ten virgins (Matt. 25:1–13) refers to Jesus's second coming. But in *GC* (393–408) she uses the same parable as a road map of the 1844 experience, a traditional Adventist "historicist" interpretation. She does not try to correlate the two views. Though she does not employ allegory or typology, her occasional use of the "historicist" method does represent a departure from the obvious meaning of the text, perhaps analogous to the New Testament's use of midrashic method in interpreting the Old Testament.

Finally, in *PP* (515 [1890]), White begins to make an explicit case for "radical divine accommodation," an approach to Scripture often resisted by devout conservatives. Commenting on Num. 35, she argues that the cities of refuge were a "merciful" and "necessary" provision in light of the "ancient custom" of blood vengeance: "The Lord did not see fit to abolish this custom at that time, but he made provision to insure the safety of those who should take life unintentionally." Defenders of divine sovereignty would not be pleased. But White was simply developing her free-will theodicy: God must win, not coerce.

In that connection her remarkable use—and nonuse—of Calvin Stowe may be understandable. Caught between believers who opposed the revision of the *Testimonies* (1884) and the scorn of the ex-Adventist preacher D. M. Canright, who mocked the changes (in 1889; cf. Thompson, *Inspiration*, 267–76, 285–98), White apparently discovered a copy of Stowe in J. N. Andrews's library in Switzerland in 1886. Perhaps out of deference to the needs of conservative believers, she never published her revision of Stowe during her lifetime. Only in 1958 did it appear in print (*SM*, 1:19–21). But not until Yale Old Testament scholar Brevard Childs articulated his "canonical criticism" would there be the needed academic muscle for a view that allows the devout believer to be honest with Scripture, using critical tools in its study, while being wholehearted in belief—concerns to which Ellen White seemed to have been drawn intuitively.

Given White's prodigious literary production, her understanding of inspiration, especially as reflected in her revision of Calvin Stowe (*SM*, 1:19–21) and in the introduction to *GC* (v–xii), allows the researcher and the believer much latitude in exploring her dynamic approach to the Bible. And there is much to explore, for though her goal was always to provide soul food for her audience, she never explicitly commented on the striking changes in her own perspective over time.

Bibliography

Canright, Dudley Marvin. *Seventh-Day Adventism Renounced*. New York: Fleming H. Revell, 1889.

Knight, George. *A Search for Identity: The Development of Seventh-Day Adventist Beliefs*. Hagerstown, MD: Review & Herald, 2000.

Rea, Walter T. *The White Lie*. Turlock, CA: M&R Pubs., 1982.

Thompson, Alden. *Escape from the Flames: How Ellen White Grew from Fear to Joy and Helped Me Do It Too*. Nampa, ID: Pacific, 2005.

———. *Inspiration: Hard Questions, Honest Answers*. Hagerstown, MD: Review & Herald, 1991.

Veltman, Fred. "The Desire of Ages Project: Part 1, The Data." *Ministry*, Oct. 1990, 4–7. "The Desire of Ages Project: Part 2, The Conclusions." *Ministry*, Dec. 1990, 11–15.

White, Ellen. Conflict of the Ages [series with various titles]. 5 vols. Mt. View, CA: Pacific, 1888–1917. Revision and expansion of *Spiritual Gifts*, 4 vols. (1858–64); and *The Spirit of Prophecy*, 4 vols. (1870–84).

———. *The Ellen G. White 1888 Materials*. 4 vols. Washington, DC: Ellen G. White Estate, 1987.

———. *Ellen G. White Writings*. CD-ROM. Silver Spring, MD: Ellen G. White Estate, 2009.

———. *Testimonies for the Church*. 9 vols. 1855–1909. Repr., Mt. View, CA: Pacific, 1948.

— ALDEN THOMPSON

Wild, Laura Huldah (1870–1959)

Laura Huldah Wild was born on December 22, 1870, in Greensboro, Vermont, and was never married. At age fifteen, Wild spent one year at Mount Holyoke College in South Hadley, Massachusetts (1887–88); in the fall of 1888, she transferred to Smith College in Northampton, Massachusetts, where she graduated in 1892 with her bachelor of arts degree. During her time at Smith College, Wild became interested in the Bible and was exposed to higher criticism of the Bible. Because of her piqued interest in the Bible, she went on to Hartford Theological Seminary (1893–96), where she acquired a bachelor of divinity (completing her thesis in 1906).

From 1896 to 1901 Wild worked for the YWCA, first as a YWCA city missionary in Lincoln, Nebraska, and then as national secretary of the YWCA (based in Chicago). In 1901 Wild was ordained in the Congregational church and became the pastor at Butler Avenue Congregational Church of Lincoln, Nebraska. She served in this capacity until 1905, when she was called to serve as a teacher of biblical literature at Doane College in Crete, Nebraska. After four years at Doane, Wild spent the next seven years in teaching at Lake Erie College in Painesville, Ohio. In September 1917, Wild returned to Mount Holyoke College, where she served as the chair of the department of the history and literature of religion until she retired in 1937. During her tenure at Mount Holyoke, she was a visiting professor at Ginling College for women in Nanking, China, for the school year 1923–24. Throughout her life, Wild held memberships and high-ranking positions in a number of societies and associations, including memberships in the American Association of University Women, the American Association of University Professors, and the Palestine Oriental Society. She also served as the president of the National Association of Biblical Instructors. Wild retired in California, where she taught informal Bible classes for women from 1949 until sometime before her death on September 18, 1959.

As a teacher, Wild felt that the Bible held a "central place in the minds of the students and in the curriculum of the College [Mount Holyoke] because it is the book of supreme religious import" (*Alumnae Quarterly*, 208). As a practitioner of historical criticism, she sought to alter the way the Bible had been traditionally taught. Wild did not feel that the classroom was the place for theological or homiletical discussions of the Bible, but rather a place for focused study on the Bible's literary and historical value as a book. In her own words, Wild thought that the purpose of the biblical department was fourfold: "first, to help a student to get her bearings toward a world classic; second, to help her to develop strong mental and moral integrity; third, to help her to take her place in the world with a vital social and religious message; fourth, to help any with a scholarly bent to become specialists in the subject" (210). Her desire for her female students was that they embrace the new scientific methods and apply them to Bible study, thereby "training the student in intellectual and moral integrity" (210). Her interests in contemporary scholarship continued throughout her retirement.

Wild wrote and taught during the new scientific and rationalist period of the late nineteenth and early twentieth centuries. She saw in the new scientific era a chance to embrace scholarship and discover the Bible anew. Beyond her obvious Darwinian sympathies, Wild moved away from the traditional consensus about the authorship and history of the Bible and embraced the historical-critical approach. In this vein, Wild comments, "To the naturally conservative this change has sometimes seemed to indicate destruction, whereas really the historical method has meant a nearer approach to the original meaning, and advancement in our understanding of the messages of the Bible" (*Literary Guide*, 109). She downplayed the supernatural, using rational explanations for many miracles in the Old Testament. Wild explains the development of the Israelite nation in purely anthropological terms, often eliminating the direct intervention of Yahweh in the process (*Evolution*, 190–91; *Literary Guide*, 203). Common to the era, Wild often betrays her biased evaluation of "white" culture over other races. She states, "The red race and the black race, while very interesting to the ethnologist, have not had so much to contribute to the progress of our world" (*Evolution*, 37).

Along with a number of dictionary entries and articles, Wild authored at least seven books on a range of biblical topics. Although her textbooks were primarily used for the classroom setting in the women's colleges where she taught, her writings appealed to a wider audience. Wild's works cover a wide range of themes, including ethical and devotional guidance for modern-day Christians; the geography, topography, and flora and fauna of Palestine; sociological development of the Hebrew people; and literary/genre studies of the Bible. Generally, Wild's writing does not betray her gender. While she addresses female figures in the Bible, she does not stress these passages over other texts. However, on occasion Wild does reflect traditional ideals for women. For example, she finds Jael's murder of Sisera in Judg. 4 to be unacceptable behavior for women of her enlightened era (*Evolution*, 110).

Two of her best-known works, *The Evolution of the Hebrew People* and *A Literary Guide to the Bible*, showcase Wild's methodological approach to the Bible. In these books, she embraces the historical-critical method by observing the "composite" nature of many Old Testament books. For example, she espouses Wellhausen's theory of the four sources of the Pentateuch, accepts the notion of First and Second Isaiah, and speaks of earlier and later material in the book of Daniel (*Evolution*, 164–67, 246; *Literary Guide*, 65–67, 77).

Wild, a biblical scholar in her own right, spent her life as a popularizer of modern critical and literary approaches to the study of the Bible. Her primary audience was women, though female figures in Scripture were never the focus of her scholarship. She was active in the academy and remained on the cutting edge of modern scholarship until her death.

Bibliography

Anon. "Bible Class Continues Strong for Six Years." *The Progress-Bulletin* [Pomona, CA], Monday Evening, Sept. 19, 1955.

———. "Department of Biblical History and Literature." *Mount Holyoke Alumnae Quarterly* 1, no. 4 (Jan. 1918): 206–16.

———. "Dr. Laura Wild, Ex-Mount Holyoke Professor, Dead." *Holyoke Transcript-Telegram*, Friday, Oct. 2, 1959.

———. "Prof. Laura H. Wild Will Leave after Long Service." *Holyoke Transcript-Telegram Centennial Supplement*, May 1937.

Mount Holyoke College Archives and Special Collections. 8 Dwight Hall, 50 College St., South Hadley, MA.

Wild, Laura H. Books online: http://www.onread.com/writer/Wild-Laura-Hulda -1870-111989/.

———. *The Evolution of the Hebrew People.* New York: Charles Scribner's Sons, 1917.

———. *Geographic Influences in Old Testament Masterpieces.* Boston: Ginn, 1915.

———. *A Literary Guide to the Bible.* New York: George H. Doran, 1922.

— Brian Peterson

Willard, Frances Elizabeth (1839–98)

On September 28, 1839, Frances Elizabeth was born in Churchville, New York, to Josiah and Mary Willard. In 1841 the family relocated to Oberlin, Ohio, home of Oberlin Collegiate Institute, where both parents attended classes. In 1845 the family moved farther west, to Wisconsin. When she and her sister, Mary, enrolled in Northwestern Female College in Evanston, Illinois, in 1858, the whole family moved there. It became her home until her death on February 17, 1898.

Willard taught school for a few years. From 1865 to 1866 she helped the American Methodist Ladies Centenary Association raise money to build Heck Hall (in honor of Barbara Heck, who helped to found Methodism in both the United States and Canada) at her brother's alma mater, Garrett Biblical Institute, in Evanston. After a grand tour of Europe and the Middle East, she became president of Evanston College for Ladies in 1870, and thus the first female college president to confer degrees. However, when the Chicago fire dried up contributions, her college was subsumed into Northwestern University, and she was named dean of the Women's College and professor of aesthetics.

As a delegate to the first national conference of the Woman's Christian Temperance Union (WCTU) in Cleveland in 1874, Willard was named corresponding secretary. She had found her calling. In 1879 she became its president, a post she held until her death. In 1891 she was elected president of the World's WCTU as well.

Willard grew up in a deeply religious family. She had a conversion experience during a bout of typhoid fever when she was about twenty years old and became a member of Evanston's First Methodist Church on May 5, 1861. In 1866, when Holiness advocate Phoebe Palmer visited First Methodist, Willard claimed the "second blessing," or entire sanctification.

Her family had daily family prayers and Bible readings, a practice she continued throughout her life. However, her diary shows that her frequent resolutions to read the Bible herself more often were crowded out by other activities. Yet it also reveals frequent quotations from, paraphrases of, and allusions to Scripture—references to twenty-four of the sixty-six books in excerpts edited by Gifford (447). For example, when her brother, Oliver, decided to become

533

a Methodist minister, she wrote that he would be sharing "the story of One who so loved [the world] that He gave His Son to die for its redemption [John 3:16]; . . . of One who 'knoweth our frame—who remembereth that we are dust' [Ps. 103:14]; who is 'touched with the feeling of our infirmities,' 'who was tempted in all points like as we are' [Heb. 4:15b], who 'was wounded for our transgressions, who was bruised for our iniquities'" [Isa. 53:5] (Gifford 61).

The WCTU was a thoroughly Christian organization. Meetings always included Bible readings and usually hymns. Women ministers were given prominence in the organization. Willard's writings and speeches are liberally sprinkled with biblical references. The WCTU members knew well the biblical arguments for and against both temperance and woman's suffrage. They depended on such verses as Eph. 5:18: "Be not drunk with wine, wherein is excess; but be filled with the Spirit." Their opponents preferred the example of Jesus's turning water into wine in John 2 and 1 Tim. 5:23, where Timothy is instructed to "use a little wine for thy stomach's sake." In arguing for woman's suffrage, Willard often contrasted humanity's original sinful state to the salvation brought by Jesus Christ. For example, in her 1887 presidential address to the WCTU, she first notes that "under the curse, man has mapped out the state as his largest sphere, and the home as woman's largest," but "women are tired of this unnatural two worlds in one." Instead, they would "ring out in clear but gentle voices the oft-repeated declaration of the Master whom they serve: 'Behold, I make all things new,'" quoting Rev. 21:5 (Hardesty 132).

Although a devoted daughter of the Methodist Church, Willard had a tumultuous relationship with it. In 1880 she was sent by the WCTU to Cincinnati as a "fraternal delegate" to simply bring greetings to the Methodist General Conference, staunch supporters of temperance. Her presence evoked a contentious discussion of the "woman question." Although the all-male body eventually voted to let her speak, the rancor was so deep that she simply left a written message for a male friend to deliver. The conference went on to deny ordination to two women and to withdraw preaching licenses from all women. In 1888 Willard was back at the general conference in New York City as one of five duly elected female lay delegates. After another lengthy and vicious debate, the women were denied seats. Long an advocate of women's rights and women's suffrage, Willard published *Woman in the Pulpit* (expanding her article in the *Homiletic Review*, Dec. 1887), the only works in which she makes a biblical argument on behalf of women.

Despite numerous previous nineteenth-century exegetical justifications for women's ministry to draw on (Hardesty 143–45), or perhaps because of them, Willard does little in-depth biblical analysis. Her first two chapters are titled "The Letter Killeth" and "The Spirit Giveth Life." In the first she points out the numerous inconsistencies in two arguments used by opponents of women's ministry: the "literal" method and the "playing fast and loose" method (Willard, *Pulpit*, 19). For example, some male ministers preach fervently on the literal veracity of 1 Tim. 2:12, "I suffer not a woman to teach," while at the same time ignoring the fact that many women in the congregation are in violation of verse 9, which tells women not to adorn themselves with "braided hair, or gold, or pearls, or costly array" (20). They hold 1 Cor. 14:34, "Let your women keep silence in the churches," to be absolute truth while ignoring Paul's previous injunctions in the Corinthian letter against taking church members to court, against marriage and remarriage, and in favor of celibacy (19). In opposition to temperance advocates, some ministers argued endlessly in pulpit and print that at the Last Supper Jesus used real wine—yet they remained totally indifferent to the fact that he also used unleavened bread (19). With regard to 1 Cor. 11:3 ("The head of every man is Christ; and the head of the woman is the man; and the head of Christ is God"), Willard says that many exegetes play fast and loose. In order to argue that this verse teaches woman's subordination to man, many are willing to assert—against trinitarian orthodoxy—that Christ is subordinate to God. She concludes that people interpret Scripture on the basis of their cultural biases.

Willard also notices that interpretations change. Earlier in her own lifetime, many upheld the several New Testament injunctions of "Servants, be obedient to them that are your masters" (Eph. 6:5; cf. Col. 3:22; 1 Pet. 2:18) as evidence that slavery was an institution acceptable to God. But wiser understandings made literal interpretations of these passages obsolete. She also points out that early church fathers buttressed with Bible verses their belief in many scientific "facts" now proved to be erroneous (*Pulpit*, 24).

Turning to "The Spirit Giveth Life," she declares that "Christ, not Paul, is the source of all churchly authority and power" (40). She then points out that Jesus draws from Martha the same affirmation as from Peter that Jesus is the Messiah (John 11:27; Mark 8:29) and that Jesus discloses his own commission to the Samaritan woman (John 4:1–42). While he "called" the Twelve, women followed without being "called" (*Pulpit*, 41). "No utterance of his marks woman as ineligible to any position in the church he came to found" (41). "Christ's commission only is authoritative" (42), says Willard, and it was women whom Christ commissioned to announce his resurrection (Matt. 28:10; Mark 16:7; Luke 24:10; John 20:17). She observes that women as well as men received the Holy Spirit at Pentecost (Acts 1:13–14; 2:1–2). And Peter, in explaining what has happened, quotes the prophet Joel: "It shall come to pass in the last days, saith God, I will pour out my spirit upon all flesh; and your sons and your daughters shall prophesy" (Acts 2:17).

As a good Methodist, Willard was undoubtedly familiar with the Methodist Quadrilateral. For Wesley, the Bible was the primary authority, but it was also to be balanced by Christian tradition, human experience, and reason. Willard declares, "A pinch of common-sense forms an excellent ingredient in that complicated dish called Biblical interpretation, wherever it is set forth at the feast of reason, especially if it is expected at all to stimulate the flow of soul!" (*Pulpit*, 26). Later she declares, "And the truth of God, a thousand times repeated by the voice of history, science, and every-day experience," is that "it is not good for man to be alone" (45, alluding to Gen. 2:18). She argues that both men's and women's perspectives on the Bible are necessary to understand God's message fully.

She looked forward to the day when "women share equally in translating the sacred text" and urged "young women of linguistic talent . . . to make a specialty of Hebrew and New Testament Greek in the interest of their sex" (*Pulpit*, 31). She initially supported Elizabeth Cady Stanton's *Woman's Bible* because it was to be a new translation made entirely by women. But when Stanton could not find the resources to do that, she instead published polemical commentary on selected passages. Stanton's own contributions expressed some rather unorthodox opinions, which offended many WCTU members. Willard withdrew her support (Bordin 172–73).

Willard preferred to point out the positive examples of women's ministry in the Bible. She reported that thirty to forty passages in the Bible illustrate women's public work while only two speak against it. Those two would presumably be 1 Cor. 14:34, "Let your women keep silence in the churches," and 1 Tim. 2:12, "I suffer not a woman to teach, nor to usurp authority over the man, but to be in silence." She cites in particular 2 Tim. 2:2, "The things that thou hast heard from me among many witnesses, the same commit thou to faithful *men*." But in rebuttal, she observes that "the word translated 'men' is the same as that in the text 'God now commandeth all *men* every where to repent' [Acts 17:30, *anthrōpoi*]," a text that even the most literal would also apply to women (*Pulpit*, 34). She lists women from both Testaments who did God's work and shared the gospel: "Miriam, the first prophetess, and Deborah, the first judge; . . . Esther, the deliverer of her people; . . . Lois and Eunice, who trained Timothy for the ministerial office; . . . 'Tryphena and Tryphosa and the beloved Persis'" (the last three from Rom. 16:12; *Pulpit*, 33–34).

Although Willard rarely offers any systematic biblical interpretation, her work shows that she was thoroughly grounded in the Bible and constantly used it in her life's work on behalf of all women.

See also Palmer, Phoebe (1807–74); Stanton, Elizabeth Cady (1815–1902)

Bibliography

Bordin, Ruth. *Frances Willard: A Biography*. Chapel Hill: University of North Carolina Press, 1986.

Gifford, Carolyn De Swarte. *Writing Out My Heart: Selections from the Journal of Frances E. Willard, 1855–96*. Urbana: University of Illinois Press, 1995.

Hardesty, Nancy A. *Women Called to Witness: Evangelical Feminism in the Nineteenth Century*. 2nd ed. Knoxville: University of Tennessee Press, 1999.

Willard, Frances E. *Glimpses of Fifty Years: The Autobiography of an American Woman*. Chicago: Woman's Temperance Pub. Association, 1889.

———. *Woman in the Pulpit*. Boston: D. Lothrop, 1888. Repr., Chicago: Woman's Temperance Pub. Association, 1889. http://lincoln.lib.niu.edu/file.php?file=fewpulpit.html.

— NANCY A. HARDESTY

▪ Witter, Mary L. T. (1818–ca. 1900)

Mary L. T. Witter, wife of Baptist merchant James Samuel Witter and mother of a daughter, Mary (b. 1858), was a well-educated Canadian author from Berwick, Nova Scotia. She wrote three books: *A Book for the Young: Being a History of the Kings Who Ruled over God's Ancient People* (1870); *The Edomites: Their History as Gathered from the Holy Scriptures* (1888); and *Angels* (1900). Witter intended children and youth as her primary audience. She interpreted the Bible literally, providing readers with a very material perspective of biblical events. Given her geographical isolation, her knowledge of archaeological discoveries and biblical criticism seemed limited. Nevertheless, she did demonstrate knowledge of the geography and cultural customs of the Middle East (*Kings*, vii–viii). Drawing lessons from a sometimes fragmented biblical record, she collected instances from the lives of Israelite kings, the Edomites, and angels to offer instruction and guidance.

Witter interpreted the Bible through her experience as a woman. Notably, she clung to traditional gender roles, claiming that women were intellectually and physically inferior to men: "To me it seems absurd to claim for woman intellectual equality with man; that she is greatly his inferior in physical strength is too apparent" (*Kings*, 40). She attributes incidents proving otherwise as either inherent wickedness or extraordinary circumstances. Jezebel and Athaliah were unusual for they "both possessed the intellect of man and almost infernal wickedness united to their womanly tact" (40). Deborah normally would have "clung to her husband for support," but needed to assume leadership in the midst of chaotic circumstances (*Angels*, 17).

This being said, Witter often expresses deep compassion for female biblical characters and frequently extends to them the benefit of the doubt. In Witter's view, Sarah's request to cast Hagar and Ishmael out into the desert was not a command to her husband (Gen. 21:10), but rather a "humble entreaty" (*Angels*, 4). Similarly, Witter views Job's wife as acting uncharacteristically when she spoke harshly, as was evidenced by Job's surprised response (Job 2:9–10; *Angels*, 106). In like manner, Witter attributes women with several virtues, including unselfish love, resilience, and tenderness. Witter also emphasizes God's love for women. In her view, Christ consistently treated women with dignity, asserting that obedience is the only prerequisite for communion with God. "How much to comfort her, and raise her in the estimation of the other sex is there in the gracious words: 'whosoever shall do the will of God, the same is my brother, my sister and mother.' Matthew 12:50" (*Kings*, viii). By promoting a heightened view of women, Jesus emancipated them by denouncing demeaning practices like polygamy. He rescued women from debilitating illness and harsh domestic circumstances. An example of this is Witter's characterization of a demon-possessed man as an abusive husband whose wife had to endure until rescued by Christ's divine intervention: "The mother, mother-like, says nothing of the abuse she has suffered, but . . . expresses the hope that . . . 'There is one who casts out demons'" (*Kings*, 115).

Although Witter's brand of feminism was maternal and subtle in nature, she did make several poignant statements regarding the plight of women. Identifying women's long history as steadfast followers of Jesus, Witter offers reason for women to be liberated from past prejudice: "Did not Christ first appear to woman? And did she not receive the first commission to tell of his resurrection? Are not women the warmest and most steadfast adherents of Christianity at the present day? . . . If all this be true, has not woman in part wiped off the stain of being the first transgressor?" (*Kings*, 58). While observing improvement in women's rights, Witter also laments the "disabilities, which at times press heavily upon her, and she longs for that state where character forms the only distinction" (84).

Her "womanly" modesty served as a means to placate male audiences. She berated women for flaunting claims of male inferiority, arguing that "every true woman shuns every act that could be construed as implying that her husband is her inferior" (*Edomites*, 41–42). At the same time, Witter also recognizes women's feminine strength, which could at times exceed men's: "morally and spiritually, she is his equal; and as far as her emotional nature is concerned, his superior" (*Kings*, 40). Like many other women interpreters of the Bible in her time, Witter remained largely unnoticed by prominent male writers of the period. Her writings nevertheless stand out as an example of Victorian feminism, which strove to identify women's place within the family of God.

Bibliography

Taylor, Marion, and Heather Weir, eds. *Let Her Speak for Herself: Nineteenth-Century Women Writing on Women in Genesis*. Waco: Baylor University Press, 2006.

Witter, Mary L. T. *Angels*. Glasgow: William Asher, 1900.

———. *A Book for the Young: Being a History of the Kings Who Ruled over God's Ancient People*. Halifax, NS: A. & W. MacKinlay, 1870.

———. *The Edomites: Their History as Gathered from the Holy Scriptures*. Halifax, NS: S. Seldon, 1888.

— BETH ROBERTSON

■ Wollstonecraft, Mary (1759–97)

Mary Wollstonecraft was born at Primrose Street, Spitalfields, London. She was an educator, writer, and advocate of women's rights. Mary married the philosopher and novelist William Godwin; their daughter was the novelist Mary Wollstonecraft Shelley. Wollstonecraft's most celebrated work is *A Vindication of the Rights of Woman*, published in 1792. Although a staunch defender of the French Revolution, Wollstonecraft felt that the revolution had not gone far enough in establishing equality between the sexes and in defending the rights of women. It is this flaw that *A Vindication* seeks to expose. For Wollstonecraft, inequality of all kinds disturbs the proper moral development of humankind. For her, human beings will fulfill their higher purpose and achieve harmony only if equality is achieved at all levels and, principally, if equality between the sexes becomes the norm. "There must be more equality established in society," Wollstonecraft contends, "or morality will never gain ground" (5.211).

Mary Wollstonecraft was an Anglican, but in the mid-1780s she became acquainted with what was then termed radical dissent. Richard Price, the minister, and Joseph Johnson, the publisher, belonged to this circle and were instrumental in helping Wollstonecraft set herself up as an author. Her writings evidence an individualistic faith characterized by a strong belief in rationalism and human perfectibility. In *Vindication*, Wollstonecraft contends with Scripture and its representation of women. Although she does not approach Scripture directly, she critiques the biblical narrative of creation as appropriated by the two most influential male thinkers of her intellectual milieu: John Milton and Jean-Jacques Rousseau.

Politically, Rousseau and Milton belong to the same radical tradition as Wollstonecraft: all three were committed republicans. Yet she chiefly objects to their gender politics; her glowing admiration for these two authors is complicated by her outright rejection of their views on women. Before directly addressing their arguments, Wollstonecraft dismisses the story of Adam and Eve as it appears in Genesis, deeming it "Moses' poetical story" (5.95), which cannot be accepted as the literal truth but as a "childish" allegory of women's subordination. "Few, it is presumed, who have bestowed any serious thought on the subject," Wollstonecraft informs readers, "ever supposed that Eve was, literally speaking one of Adam's ribs." As a matter of fact, the meaning of this "story" must be searched for elsewhere. "From the remotest antiquity," she continues, "[man] found it convenient to exert his strength to subjugate his companion, and his invention to show that she ought to have her neck bent under the yoke, because the whole creation was only created for his convenience or pleasure" (5.95). Wollstonecraft thus summarily removes Genesis, as such, from the center of her discussion and directs her critique at Milton's *Paradise Lost* instead. During this period, Milton's epic retelling of Genesis arguably had superseded its scriptural model in poetic, religious, and political authority. It is therefore Milton's Eve that Wollstonecraft finds unacceptable, specifically those verses where Milton intimates that God is Adam's law, while Adam is Eve's law. Eve is the suspect creation of a Milton who, "in true Mohametan strain meant to deprive us of souls," placing women in the midst of creation only "to gratify the senses of men" rather than to achieve "virtue or happiness" in their own right (90).

Both Milton and Rousseau used Scripture to assume a prophetic voice and thus legitimate their works. In his highly influential treatise on education, *Émile*, Rousseau rewrites the story of Adam and Eve for his contemporary secular audience. Wollstonecraft objects to the character of Sophie, Rousseau's Eve, in much the same way she has objected to Milton's Eve. It is sensuality and not reason, she contends, that has inspired these two Eves. For an audience of the Enlightenment, the primary readers of her work, Wollstonecraft eschews a direct engagement with Scripture and shapes a mediated feminist critique of it by addressing two key appropriations.

Bibliography

Acosta, Ana M. *Reading Genesis in the Long Eighteenth Century: From Milton to Mary Shelley*. Aldershot, UK: Ashgate, 2006.

Wollstonecraft, Mary. *A Vindication of the Rights of Woman*. London: J. Johnson, 1792. Reissued as vol. 5 of *The Works of Mary Wollstonecraft*. Edited by Janet Todd and Marilyn Butler. 7 vols. New York: New York University Press, 1989.

— ANA M. ACOSTA

Wordsworth, Elizabeth (1840–1932)

Elizabeth Wordsworth, great-niece of the famous poet William Wordsworth, was born on June 22, 1840, in Harrow, Middlesex, England, to Susannah Hatley Frere and Christopher Wordsworth, Anglican clergyman and later bishop of Lincoln. Although she did not receive a formal education (except for one year at a girls' boarding school), she nevertheless received a fine classical education at home. She was well versed in Hebrew, Greek, Latin, French, German, Italian, history, Bible, theology, music, and art. Although she was mostly self-taught, her father had the most profound influence on her, teaching her the Bible and theology. She assisted with his multivolume commentary on the Bible (a work that took twenty years to complete). Her work of editing her father's commentary gave her a solid foundation for understanding Scripture, and this in turn shaped her own interpretation of the Bible.

When Lady Margaret Hall was established, the first residential hall for women in Oxford, Wordsworth became its founding principal, where she served thirty-one years (1878–1909). In 1886 she also founded St. Hugh's Hall, another hall for women in Oxford. She published twenty-seven books as well as a number of articles and essays. Many of these were based on her lectures and addresses to her students. For her tireless work for women's education, she received two honorary degrees, a master's and a doctorate, both from Oxford University.

Wordsworth was both traditional and modern in her interpretations of the Bible, reflecting the influences of her father, Anglican tradition, upper-class Victorian ideals, and her classical and modern education, which made her open to developments in science, philosophy, theology, and biblical criticism. She always analyzed the Scriptures in Hebrew and Greek, setting a high standard and example for her readers.

In her approach to the Psalms, Wordsworth argues that there are two levels of meaning in the Psalms, a natural (original) meaning and a spiritual meaning (*Psalms*, 70). She begins her study of a psalm by discussing historical-critical questions related to authorship, date, and original context, being fully aware of current scholarly debates (70–71, 109–14); she then proceeds to its spiritual meaning and application. Wordsworth often read the Psalms typologically, arguing for their universal appeal: "Whatever their origin may have been—their meaning never could have been tied down and limited to one person, or one generation, or even one set of events" (xi).

In her book *The Decalogue*, Wordsworth adopts the concept of development as an important interpretative key. For example, in comparing the first command, "Be fruitful, and multiply," in Gen. 1:28 with the Decalogue, she argues that the Ten Commandments represent a higher stage of development, something that natural science has demonstrated in the concept of evolution (x). She believes that this notion of progress distinguishes the Bible from other literature (109). "The Law and the Prophets are throughout *prospective*. They breathe not regret for a vanished past—but progress. . . . 'Development' is the watchword of the Old Testament" (110, her emphasis).

Adopting an understanding of progressive development within Scripture was not an unusual approach at this time; what was unique was how she applied this notion to the actual Ten Commandments themselves. For example, the ninth commandment, "Thou shalt not bear false witness against Thy neighbour," takes humanity to "a stage higher up in civilization than the four which have preceded it. . . . The ninth goes higher still, and looks upon man as belonging to some kind of political organization" (210). Here one sees the popular nineteenth-century concepts of development, progress, and evolution influencing her interpretation of the Ten Commandments.

Wordsworth's interest in the education of women often shapes her reading of texts. She explains that parents should be honored "because a father is a type of the Father of all, Almighty God" (142) and the mother is a type of Christ: "The full beauty of motherhood was never realized till the Incarnation of our Lord. . . . He hallowed the office of maternity. . . . By giving us an example of self-sacrifice, by laying down His life for us, He has given a new beauty to that most mysterious and affecting relation between mother and child, and has made us feel that not only is fatherhood typical of God as our Creator, but that motherhood is to be reverenced as setting forth, as no other human type can do, both the pain and the joy of our redemption" (*Decalogue*, 143). Because of the self-sacrifice of mothers for their children, by the very act of bringing forth life through pain, motherhood becomes a type of Christ. Thus Wordsworth claims that motherhood changed after the coming of Christ; it was now "peculiarly *Christian*" (*Psalms*, 143–44, her emphasis).

In her writings Wordsworth also addresses the concept of the ideal woman. For example, she understands Ps. 45 typologically, describing the ideal wife as being unselfishly devoted to her husband, "exquisite perfection," giving of her best, and so forth (17). She extends her application of the psalm to both married and single women: "Is not the lesson for us all to strive in everything to be as pure, as complete, as perfect as we can? No room for carelessness, slovenliness, half-done work, ugliness, bad taste. The ideal woman's life ought to show exquisite finish in every detail. Dress, handwriting, good manners, refined speech—none of these things should be beneath her care" (17). Wordsworth's views of the ideal woman are drawn more from traditional Victorian ideals and her specific context of teaching privileged, upper-class, young women in a women's college, than from Ps. 45.

Wordsworth was one of the most influential pioneers in women's education at Oxford. As a biblical interpreter, she blended a traditional approach to Scripture, including the use of typology and traditional attitudes toward women's roles in the family, with insights derived from science, evolutionary notions of development, and biblical criticism. Shaped by her educational context, she often read Scripture through a distinctively female lens. Wordsworth set an example by her own desire to learn and to share that knowledge with others through her teaching and writing.

Bibliography

Barta-Smith, Nancy A. "Elizabeth Wordsworth." Pages 313–27 in *Modern British Essayists*, vol. 98 of *Dictionary of Literary Biography: First Series*, edited by Robert Beum. Detroit: Gale Group, 1990.

Battiscombe, Georgina. *Reluctant Pioneer: A Life of Elizabeth Wordsworth*. London: Constable, 1978.

Idestrom, Rebecca G. S. "Elizabeth Wordsworth: Nineteenth-Century Oxford Principal and Bible Interpreter." Pages 181–99 in *Recovering Nineteenth-Century Women Interpreters of the Bible*, edited by Christiana de Groot and Marion Ann Taylor. Atlanta: Society of Biblical Literature, 2007.

Wordsworth, Elizabeth. "Colleges for Women." Pages 14–28 in *Ladies at Work: Papers on Paid Employment for Ladies*, edited by Lady Jeune. London: A. D. Innes, 1893.

———. *The Decalogue*. London: Longmans, Green, 1893. http://catalog.hathitrust.org/Record/008415329.

———. *Glimpses of the Past*. London: Mowbray, 1912.

———. *Psalms for the Christian Festivals*. London: Longmans, Green, 1906.

—Rebecca G. S. Idestrom

Yonge, Charlotte Mary (1823–1901)

Charlotte Mary Yonge was born at Otterbourne, near Winchester, Hampshire. She remained in the area throughout her life, educated at home by her parents and a tutor in the classical languages, French, Spanish, and mathematics—and teaching in the local Sunday school mornings and afternoons from her childhood and throughout her life. From John Keble's (1792–1866) arrival in the nearby parish at Hursley in 1836, Yonge came under the strong influence of and worked closely with this Tractarian priest until his death. She was the author of over two hundred volumes of fiction, biblical reflections, historical studies, and a variety of works for Christian education.

Her first published novel, *Abbeychurch; or, Self-Control and Self-Conceit*, appeared in 1844 and was followed by some fifty other novels in her lifetime; her most popular one was *The Heir of Redclyffe* (1853). Committed to the Tractarian doctrine of reserve, she tended to avoid the explicit treatment of religious topics in her novels, a pattern less in evidence in her four-volume *The Pillars of House* (1873). Thus in her *Heir of Redclyffe*, the only significant reference to the Bible occurs when the protagonist tries to comfort a child at the death of a loved one, but is restricted in his endeavor by the limits of "the poor child's religious knowledge. She hardly ever had been at church and though she had read one or two Bible stories, it seemed to have been from their having been used as lessons at school." A similar reference to the comfort of scriptural words for those suffering grief or worry is also in Yonge's almost equally popular *Daisy Chain; or, Aspirations* (1856).

Encouraged in her educational writing by a friend and local teacher, from 1842 to 1875 Yonge was engaged in writing for Anne Mozley's (1809–91) *Magazine for the Young*, a London monthly. From 1851 to 1899 she also edited the *Monthly Packet of Evening Readings for Younger Members of the English Church*, a semiannual published by John and Charles Mozley. Because of her primary orientation in teaching, most of her more than twenty volumes directly treating the Scriptures are written as school manuals and were widely reprinted. These writings fall into two general categories: retellings of biblical narratives and compilations of biblical readings, with questions and directives for reading the biblical text. In the retelling category there are four that are the most important. The first is *Aunt Charlotte's Stories of Bible History for the Little Ones* (1875), short renditions of biblical stories with questions from Septuagesima Sunday through the fifty-fourth Sunday of Trinity, beginning with the creation and following through the Old and New Testaments to the ascension. The second is *Book of Worthies* (1869), reviewing the lives of Joshua, David, Nehemiah, and Judas Maccabeus, among other characters from the classics. The third is *The Chosen People* (1859), thirty-four short chapters from creation to the Reformation, with additional pieces on the later spread of the gospel, chronological charts, and an extensive series of questions for each chapter. The fourth is *The Pupils of St. John the Divine* (1878), an outline of the New Testament Greek world, the beloved disciple (John), his work as an evangelist, his visions on Patmos, his theology of love, Ignatius of Antioch, Quadratus, Polycarp, Papias, Melito of Sardis, Irenaeus, and others, with final sections on the churches of St. John.

Examples of her work from the biblical-readings category include *Key-notes of the First Lessons for Every Day in the Year* (1869); *Scripture Readings for Schools and Families* (1871–79); *Questions on the Gospels* (1874); *Questions on the Epistles* (1874); *Questions on the Psalms* (1881); her 1884 four-volume edited series *Faith, Hope, Charity, Mercy and Peace*—each with the subtitle *Scripture Texts and Sacred Songs*; and her *Chimes for Mothers: A Reading for Each Week in the Year* (1893).

In her one work directly concerned with the lives of women, *Womankind* (1876), written as Yonge indicates at "middle age" (1), she is certain that the Judaic and Christian traditions have "uplifted" the role of women, and Christianity in particular has raised women beyond the mere status of a "help-meet" (3). Clearly reflecting on her own situation, she interprets wifehood, motherhood, and maidenhood hierarchically: "[Wifehood is] a faint type or shadow of the Union of the Church with her Lord. Motherhood [is] . . . ennobled by the Birth that saves the world. And Maidenhood [is] acquir[ing] a glory it never had before, . . . which taught the unmarried to regard themselves . . . as pure creatures, free to devote themselves to the service of their Lord; for if His Birth had consecrated maternity, it had also consecrated virginity" (3). She understands the Roman vestal virgins analogically as types of the later virgin martyrs, deaconesses, and nuns dedicated to serve as "help-meets" to the man, Christ (3), a "change mak[ing] less visible difference to the married woman" (4), but allowing the maiden to "feel herself responsible to the one great Society of which she is a part, and let her look for the services that she can fulfil by head or by hands, by superintendence or by labour, by pen or pencil" (7). The same view of the unmarried woman is made in Yonge's chapters on early religious training (14–19), religion (72–80), and Sunday school (90–99), although direct references or allusions to Scripture are not at all notable in the work; when women are admonished to study and read Scripture, it is, not surprisingly, framed within the wider context of ecclesial religious observances generally. Thus in a section on daily devotion, Yonge urges: "Make some Scripture reading, *however brief*, a daily obligation; and likewise some endeavour at meditation, if only for five minutes; also some portion of devotional reading, such as [à Kempis and others,] . . . or *a portion of some comment on* the Psalms or Gospels" (77–78, emphasis added).

What stood first in all of Yonge's biblical interpretation was the Christian education of the young. The best introduction to her pedagogy is her *How to Teach the New Testament* (1881). The volume appeared in the same year and in the same Religious Knowledge Manuals series of the National Society as did William Benham's (1831–1910) *How to Teach the Old Testament* (1881), directing the reader to Benham's recommendations for teaching young children (the use of illustrations for "ear and eye"), his succinct summary of Old Testament history and themes, and above all, the Old Testament themes prefiguring the life of Christ. But whereas Benham focuses primarily on the content of the Old Testament, Yonge directs the teacher's attention to the developmental needs of students. Although insisting that the New Testament must remain the central focus of all biblical instruction, Yonge expresses her concern that it is not to be reduced to the Gospels alone or taught outside the context of the entire Scripture. Of the three stages in the educational program for children, Yonge expects the first to begin at four (for the very precocious) or five years of age, the second at eight or nine, and the third (to last for three to four years) at ten or eleven. At each stage she provides advice on the primary content for instruction: first stage, the life of Jesus, with concluding lessons on Pentecost and the final judgment for infants; second stage, a single Gospel (Mark preferably), with emphasis on the parables and memorization, Luke, the first twelve chapters of Acts, the opening of John, the first Epistle of John; third stage, the function of types and prophecies as well as practical guides. For all levels she provides specific references to pictures (esp. suited for the infant stage), maps (to which the second-stage students are introduced), illustrative guides, and books for both students and teachers. At all stages she expects that scriptural lessons will be directed to the liturgical life of the church through the church year and supported by appropriate hymns and, as students mature, poetic passages from her master, John Keble's much reprinted *The Christian Year: Thoughts in Verse for the Sundays and Holydays throughout the Year* (1827).

As in many of her biblical guides, a major section of *How to Teach the New Testament* is devoted to suggestions regarding study and preparation on the part of instructors. First among the virtues she assigns to a teacher is diligence in preparation: examining parallel scriptural passages, and as befits her Anglo-Catholic orientation, reading the section in the context of the Epistle and the Gospel of the day. For a teacher without Greek, Yonge suggests extensive use of *The Sunday School Centenary Bible . . . ; With Various Renderings and Readings . . .* (1880) and close readings of the Revised Version (1881) of the New Testament, always taking care not to attack the Authorized Version (KJV) when differences appear since one "does not really know how authorities have been balanced, and meanings weighed, or how much there is to be said on either side for passages where there are important alterations or omissions, beyond the frequent change in tenses which, though important to the learned, hardly strike an ordinary reader" (*How to Teach*, 51). Thus she tells readers of Acts 21:15 that the word "carriages" in its older usage "expressed what a traveller carried," and that on the story of the woman taken in adultery (John 8), "the doubt is whether the narrative was really first written by St. John the Evangelist, not whether the event happened" (52). After five pages of extensive bibliographic recommendations for teachers' aids, Yonge mentions some historical difficulties regarding Scripture that are "really perplexing to some persons, and occasionally suggested to a child by some shrewd caviler at home as a question wherewith to puzzle a teacher. Such are the name of the priest who gave David the shewbread," the identity of "the Zacharias who was slain between the temple and altar, why St. Stephen spoke of Abraham's sepulchre as at Shechem, and what is meant by being baptized for the dead" (57).

As to Yonge's general view of Scripture and her interpretive method, perhaps the best insights are available in her short volume *The Chosen People* (1859), a work also concerned with the instruction of children. Opening the book with Heb. 1:1, she compares this author's depiction of the voice of God "at sundry times and in diverse manners" with a passage from John Keble's *Lyra Innocentium* (1846), in which Keble takes up his ongoing Tractarian theme of the analogy between nature and supernature and its implications for understanding scriptural types and figures. Yet any such analogies, Yonge insists, must be rooted in "facts," and therefore "prophecy, the course of types, has been passed over, lest the plain narrative should be confused, since types are rather subjects of devotional contemplation than of history" (*Chosen People*, iii). Despite the significance she places on "devotional contemplation," in this work she is concerned with "the Scripture narrative treated historically," making extensive use of Humphrey Prideaux (1648–1724), *An Historical Connection of the Old and New Testaments* (new ed., 1758), "thus filling up the interval between the New and Old Testaments" (*Chosen People*, iii). As part of her interest in biblical "facts," Yonge attaches a detailed chronology chart for "older and more critical persons" (iv). Based roughly on Ussher's chronology, her special interest is the dating of the Psalms, sketching their individual compositions within a wide range (respecting traditional titles) between Ps. 88, ascribed to Heman the Ezrahite, written before Exodus and Leviticus in 1491 BCE, and Pss. 74, 76, 77, 80, by the younger Asaph, in or after 713 BCE. Her New Testament dating is highly conservative: Matthew, 37 CE; Luke, 54; Mark, 64; John, 97; all the Pauline pieces between 52 (1 and 2 Thessalonians) and 66 (2 Timothy); the Petrine Epistles, 64 and 66; the Johannine Epistles, 68–69; and Revelation, 96; she claims Hebrews to be undateable.

Although a number of Yonge's novels continued to be published with fair regularity in the twentieth century, interest in her books tended to fade at the close of the decade following her death. By the beginning of World War I, little attention was given to her books on Scripture, except for some Anglo-Catholic circles.

Bibliography

Battiscombe, Georgina. *Charlotte Mary Yonge: The Story of an Uneventful Life*. London: Constable, 1943.

Hayter, Alethea. *Charlotte Yonge*. Plymouth: Northcote House, 1996.

Jay, Elisabeth. "Charlotte Mary Yonge." Pages 808–10 in vol. 60 of *Oxford Dictionary of National Biography*, edited by H. C. G. Matthew and Brian Harrison. Rev. ed. Oxford: Oxford University Press, 2004–11.

Mare, Margaret, and Alicia C. Percival. *Victorian Best-Seller: The World of Charlotte M. Yonge.* London: Harrap, 1948.

Yonge, Charlotte M. *The Chosen People: A Compendium of Sacred and Church History for School-Children.* London: J. & C. Mozley, 1859.

———. *How to Teach the New Testament.* London: National Society's Depository, 1881.

———. *Womankind.* London: Mozley & Smith, 1876. New ed., London: Walter Smith & Innes, 1889.

— PETER C. ERB

Zell, Katharina Schütz (ca. 1498–1562)

Katharina Schütz Zell, one of the most prolific women or lay writers of the early Protestant Reformation, demonstrates the remarkable biblical literacy and teaching ability that an intelligent person of the "common people" (educated only in the vernacular) could achieve. Born to middle-rank citizens of Strasbourg in about 1498, Katharina Schütz was a devout girl who dedicated herself to God to live a celibate life in her own home, following the medieval ideal of chastity, prayer, and good works. But she was unable to feel sure of her salvation until she heard the "gospel" teaching of Martin Luther as preached by Matthew Zell. Freed by this word proclaiming justification by faith and grace alone through the sole Savior Jesus Christ and the power of the Holy Spirit, made known through Scripture alone, Katharina Schütz believed she was called to be a "fisher of people," an assistant to the (male) reformers, and what she would eventually term a "church mother" (Zell 439–76). Marriage to Matthew Zell in December 1523 was an initial step in her pastoral ministry, and the home they established became a center of hospitality for refugees, reformers, relatives, and more. Katharina continued this ministry after Matthew's death in 1548, until her own death in 1562, although in this second generation of more strictly defined confessionalism, her open welcome to all who "followed the gospel" led to accusations of heresy (McKee, *Life and Thought*, 48–49, 66–70, 80–82, 104–9, 130–37, 171–73, 188–93, 211–26; chaps. 6–7 for second generation).

Schütz Zell's biblical knowledge came from a number of sources: hearing frequent sermons, personal Bible study, talking with preachers, and reading the German writings of reformers, especially Luther but also many others. Her knowledge was extensive, including the Old Testament as well as the more familiar New Testament; biblical allusions are pervasive in all her works, and her conscious citations rest on a wide foundation of scriptural images and phrases. This was not merely rote proof-texting but usually informed by scholarly exegesis (e.g., how she refers to a passage of Ps. 119 shows that she knew that Hebrew letters also represented numbers; Zell 247). Unlike most lay writers who, lacking university training and Latin, appealed to inspiration for their authority, Schütz Zell claims her right to teach based on her knowledge of the Bible aided by the "first and best books" (289) of the Reformers. She is clearly Protestant in her interpretation of Scripture but also more theologically sophisticated than the great majority of lay writers: she not only appropriated ideas from the clergy but also constructed her own arguments. (For a full discussion of Schütz Zell as biblical scholar, see McKee, *Life and Thought*, chap. 9.)

Her biography is an important factor in the manifestation of Schütz Zell's biblical knowledge as well as its origin, since what she wrote was her scripturally informed response to particular circumstances. Her first pamphlet (1524) was prompted by receiving Protestant male refugees fleeing Catholic persecution; after welcoming the men, Schütz Zell wrote *A Letter to the Suffering Women of the Community of Kentzingen*. With a tapestry drawn mostly from the New Testament, though with some effective use of various Old Testament texts such as Isa. 49:15, she encourages the women to see themselves as witnesses to the gospel, including a distinctive paraphrase of Matt. 10:27; 19:29; and Luke 14:26: "So also to you, believing women beloved by God, Christ says, 'Whoever does not want to leave father and mother, wife, husband, and child, and all that he has, for my sake and the Gospel's, that one is not worthy of me. Whoever, however, for my sake leaves father and mother, wife, husband, and child, farm and field, to that one I will return them a hundredfold here, and in the age to come eternal life'" (Zell 51–52). (Luke lists the "wife," but this woman interpreter addressing women adds the "husband" to fit their situation.) In 1524 Schütz Zell used the Vulgate numbering of the Psalms, since there were no German Protestant translations of the Old Testament until the 1530s (Zurich 1531; Luther 1534). This *Letter* was reprinted a few months later and received warm notice from a number of Protestants (Schütz Zell 47–56).

Also in 1524 Schütz Zell published an *Apologia for Master Matthew Zell*, a polemical letter defending clerical marriage on biblical grounds (e.g., 1 Tim. 3:2). She emphasizes the authority of Scripture alone above all others (e.g., church traditions of clerical celibacy) and offers a fascinating argument for the obligations of lay Christians to "speak out" for the truth. Matthew had been attacked for breaking his priestly vows by marrying her, but Katharina says that she is defending him not because he is her husband, but because he is her brother in the faith (Gal. 3:28). Scripture teaches that people should love their neighbors as themselves (Lev. 19:18; Matt. 22:37–39), and if she were attacked, she would want to be defended. But she is speaking out not simply because the attacks on her husband are false but because she is concerned for those who are deceived by the lies and may therefore turn away from the gospel that he is preaching; love for these neighbors requires setting the story straight. Suffering for the gospel (Matt. 5:11–12) is right, but Schütz Zell distinguishes suffering from silence; Jesus did not keep silent when the high priest's servant struck him (John 18:22–23), and he also admonished his disciples not to put stumbling blocks before others (Luke 17:1–2). Thus it is her duty as a Christian to love her neighbors by telling them the truth so that they will not stumble over the lies; she is willing to suffer for speaking out, but not to keep silence. Since "faith comes by hearing" (Rom. 10:17), she must act to undeceive those who are rejecting Matthew's preaching and losing their salvation. She hopes her truth-telling may be helpful to the authors of the lies since they are also neighbors who should be loved. In this text, she mentions a number of biblical women as models, including Judith, Esther, the queen of Sheba, Mary, and Elizabeth (Schütz Zell 36–82; cf. McKee, "Speaking Out").

In the early 1530s, Schütz Zell produced several didactic texts. The first was an exposition of the Lord's Prayer (1532) for two women of Speyer. The preface makes a number of contrasts between the Old and New Testaments and employs some feminine language for Jesus Christ, especially maternal images, such as "laboring" on the cross (Schütz Zell 151–73). The preface for a hymnbook of the Bohemian Brethren that Zell published in 1534 employs the Old and New Testaments in complementary fashion to argue for the appropriateness of singing the faith and for the character and organization of the hymns. The focus is the priesthood of believers, who should engage in mutual edification, and much of the imagery is feminine; when they sing their faith while they "keep house, obey, cook, wash dishes, wipe up and tend children," or sing a lullaby to a wailing baby in the night, they are serving God ("better than any priest, monk, or nun," 95). By this time Schütz Zell is using the Hebrew-Protestant numbering of the Psalms, evidence for her increasing awareness of "academic" study of the Bible (82–96; cf. McKee, "Our Father"; *Life and Thought*, 239–47).

As time passed, Schütz Zell's grasp and interpretation of the Bible grew in complexity and sophistication, but it never became less personal. *The Lament* at her husband's grave in 1548 was remarkable first because it happened. A woman's preaching in public, even if it was not in the pulpit, was startling, though Katharina presented her words as speaking for Matthew and as unpremeditated, like Mary Magdalene's message of Christ's resurrection to the apostles (Matt. 28:8; Mark 16:10; Luke 24:10; John 20:18). *The Lament* includes another brief exposition of the Lord's Prayer, but there is much more theological reflection, based on Scripture and the creeds, because her sorrow was more than private grief. Emperor Charles V had recently defeated the Protestant forces, and soon the Augsburg Interim would be imposed, bringing Catholic practice back to Strasbourg and generally threatening the survival of the gospel that Luther and Matthew Zell had preached and that Katharina Zell believed was vital for salvation (Schütz Zell 96–123).

During the next several years, as she struggled with personal grief and religious adversity, Katharina wrote some very private journals of meditations on the Psalms. In 1558, as part of a composite work, she published a few of these private prayers (short and long versions of Ps. 51 and one of Ps. 130), which reveal her own wrestling with God. She concludes her first and longer version of Ps. 51:19 with the hope that what she has said "may not be contrary to the meaning of David and of his thoughts" (145). It is unclear whether this phrase dates from the time of first writing or was added for later publication, but it reflects the lay theologian's growing exegetical sophistication (Schütz Zell, 136–50).

Increasing confessional struggles led to more narrow definitions of theology, and Schütz Zell's writings in the 1550s were shaped by having to defend her own orthodoxy and that of the departed first generation. These exchanges with various reformers demonstrate her breadth of biblical knowledge as it had become woven into her theology. The 1553 letter to Caspar Schwenckfeld offers a finely developed scriptural pattern of her understanding of the relationship between God's sole saving work and the instrumental role of human beings. It also includes a spirited reference to those who mockingly call her "Doctor Katrina" and her own identification with the prophetess Anna (Luke 2:36; Zell 191, 196; see Schütz Zell 180–215).

The largest and most impressive of Schütz Zell's publications is the set of letters addressed to Ludwig Rabus, her erstwhile foster son and Zell's successor, who led the attacks on her. (Her dedication to Strasbourg appears as *A Letter to the Whole Citizenship of the City of Strasbourg . . . concerning Mr. Ludwig Rabus*, 1557, in Schütz Zell, 215–31; along with Rabus's vitriolic response to her letters, in 233–34. The whole exchange, which is not yet translated, can be found in McKee, *Writings*.) It began as private correspondence, but when Rabus accused Schütz Zell of being a heretic who had troubled the church in Strasbourg from the beginning, and essentially damned her, she decided that she must set the record straight—again, truth-telling as an act of love for her neighbors. She reminds Rabus that she was there when he was not yet born, and she proceeds to unfold a remarkable history of the early Reformation. Along with quotations from Luther and Matthew Zell, whom Rabus claims as his heroes but whom Schütz Zell knows better, his foster mother with a long memory answers his accusations word by word with precise facts. She also includes some very pungent comments about how Rabus measures up to the scriptural standards for ministers as set by Pastor Matthew Zell (e.g., Rabus brushed the dust from his feet even though the city not only did not cast him out but even begged him to stay; Matt. 10:5–15).

Schütz Zell's final writing was a letter to a man afflicted with "leprosy," for whom she had been a faithful pastor when everyone else had abandoned him. Published along with the exposition of the Lord's Prayer and mediations on the Psalms as *The Miserere Psalm . . . Sent to the Christian Man Sir Felix Armbruster* (1558), this beautiful letter of consolation shows the deeply biblical spirituality of the mature Christian woman. Here Schütz Zell clearly expresses both her recognition of the power of the Holy Spirit and her own humble role of showing her love for her neighbor by sharing the biblical comfort with which God had comforted her (cf. 2 Cor. 1:4; Schütz Zell 123–36).

The impression Katharina Schütz Zell made on her contemporaries was remarkable, given her sex, social status, and education; a woman, from the middle ranks, who did not know Latin and had never been a nun. As a woman and biblical exegete, she had to wait until the twentieth century for real recognition, but Schütz Zell's legacy as a voice for the Reformation was clearly important to at least a number of people both in her own day and later. Not only her printed texts but also various manuscript letters were preserved. Her *Lament* was recopied (its earliest form exists in an eighteenth-century hand, which has slight modifications, showing that it was intended to be understood in that age and not simply kept as a relic). And her correspondence with Rabus was republished in 1753 in Zurich, contributing to the history of the Reformation in Strasbourg.

Bibliography

McKee, Elsie Anne. *Katharina Schütz Zell*. Vol. 1, *The Life and Thought of a Sixteenth Century Reformer*. Vol. 2, *The Writings, a Critical Edition*. Leiden: Brill, 1999.

———. "Katharina Schütz Zell and the 'Our Father.'" Pages 210–18 in *Oratio: Das Gebet in patristischer und reformatorischer Sicht*, edited by Emidio Campi et al. Göttingen: Vandenhoeck & Ruprecht, 1999.

———. *Reforming Popular Piety in Sixteenth-Century Strasbourg: Katharina Schütz Zell and Her Hymnbook*. Princeton, NJ: Princeton Theological Seminary Press, 1994.

———. "'Speaking Out': Katharina Schütz Zell and the Commandment to Love One's Neighbor as an Apologia for Defending the Truth." Pages 9–22 in *Ordenlich und Fruchtbar: Festschrift für Willem van't Spijker*, edited by Wilhelm H. Neuser and Herman J. Selderhuis. Leiden: J. J. Groen en Zoon, 1997.

Zell, Katharina. *Church Mother: The Writings of a Protestant Reformer in Sixteenth-Century Germany*. Translated and edited by Elsie Anne McKee. Chicago: University of Chicago Press, 2006.

— Elsie McKee

List of Entries

Chronological List
of Women Biblical Interpreters

ca. 320–ca. 370	Faltonia Betitia Proba
ca. 327–410	Marcella
ca. 330–379	Macrina the Younger
ca. 340–ca. 410	Melania the Elder
347–404	Paula
fl. 380s	Egeria
ca. 400–460	Aelia Eudocia Augusta
fl. 841	Dhuoda of Septimania
ca. 935–ca. 975	Hrotsvit of Gandersheim
1098–1179	Hildegard of Bingen
1129–65	Elisabeth of Schönau
1193/94–1253	Clare of Assisi
ca. 1200–1268	Beatrice of Nazareth
ca. 1208–ca. 1282/94	Mechthild of Magdeburg (von Magdeburg)
1240–98	Mechthild of Hackeborn (von Hackeborn)
ca. 1248–1309	Angela of Foligno
fl. 1250s	Hadewijch of Antwerp
ca. 1256–1302	Gertrude the Great (Gertrud von Helfta)
1302/3–73	Birgitta of Sweden
d. 1310	Marguerite Porete (Porette or Margaret Porete; of Hainaut)
ca. 1342–ca. 1416	Julian of Norwich
1347–80	Catherine of Siena
ca. 1364–ca. 1430	Christine de Pizan
1373–1438	Margery Kempe
1407–58	Magdalena Beutler
1418–66	Isotta Nogarola
1426/27–1514	Berta Jacobs (Sister Bertken)

ca. 1427–82	Lucrezia Tornabuoni
1443–1509	Margaret Beaufort
1452/54–1501	Antonia Pulci
1473–1533	Domenica Narducci da Paradiso
1492–1549	Marguerite de Navarre (Marguerite de Valois, d'Angoulême; Margaret of)
1492–ca. 1563/68	Argula von Grumbach
1495–ca. 1561	Marie Dentière
ca. 1498–1562	Katharina Schütz Zell
1505–44	Margaret More Roper
1512–48	Katherine Parr
1515–82	Teresa of Avila
ca. 1521–46	Anne Askew
ca. 1526/27–55	Olympia Morata
1533–1603	Elizabeth I
1534–ca. 1602	Anne Vaughan Lock
1555–92	Moderata Fonte
1561–1621	Mary Sidney Herbert
1569–1645	Aemilia Lanyer
fl. 1585	Justitia Sengers
fl. 1589	Jane Anger
1590–1652	Eleanor Davies
1591–1643	Anne Hutchinson
ca. 1597–ca. 1661	Rachel Speght
1599–1672	Marie Guyart (Marie of the Incarnation)
ca. 1600–after 1675	Bathsua Makin
1604–52	Arcangela Tarabotti
1606–33	Gertrude More
1607–78	Anna Maria van Schurman
ca. 1608–ca. 1664	Sarah Cheevers (Chevers)
1609/10–90	Maria Clemente Ruoti
1612–72	Anne Bradstreet
1614–1702	Margaret Askew Fell
fl. 1615–17	Ester Sowernam
fl. 1616–53	Katherine Chidley
ca. 1618–92	Katherine Evans
1620–81	Lucy Hutchinson
b. 1620/21, fl. 1647–53	Mary Cary
1624–1704	Jane Leade
ca. 1624–1710	Anne Docwra
1627–1709	Susanna Hopton
1629/30–97	Hester Biddle
1644–1724	Johanna Eleonora Petersen
1648–1717	Jeanne-Marie de Chesnoy Guyon
1651–95	Juana Inés de la Cruz (Sister)

ca. 1653	An Collins
1659–85	Anne Wharton
1666–1731	Mary Astell
1669–1742	Susanna Wesley
1674–1737	Elizabeth Singer Rowe
fl. 1678–85	Elizabeth Bathurst
ca. 1692–1765	Anne Dutton
fl. 1699	Amey Hayward
1702/3–74	Sophia Wigington Hume
ca. 1717–97	Elizabeth Stuart Bowdler
1717–1806	Elizabeth Carter
ca. 1728–88	R. Roberts
1738–1800	Ann Francis
1741–1810	Sarah Trimmer
1743–1825	Anna Barbauld
1745–1833	Hannah More
bap. 1746–1815	Elizabeth Hands
1747/48–1812	Dorothy Newberry Gott
1750–1814	Joanna Southcott
1751–93	Mary Scott
1751–1820	Judith Sargent Murray
ca. 1755–ca. 1816	Ann Murry
1755–1831	Hannah Adams
1758–1836	Mary Cornwallis
1759–97	Mary Wollstonecraft
1761–1830	Sarah (Ewing) Hall
fl. 1774–97	Mary Deverell
1776–1806	Elizabeth Smith
1778–1841	Catherine McAuley
1778–1856	Mary Anne Schimmelpenninck
1783–ca. 1849	Jarena Lee
1786–1851	Esther Beuzeville Hewlett Copley
1788–1868	Harriet Livermore
1788–1879	Sarah Hale
1790–1846	Charlotte Elizabeth Tonna
b. 1790, fl. 1846	Zilpha Elaw
ca. 1791–1883	Sojourner Truth (née Isabella Baumfree)
1792–1873	Sarah Grimké
1792–1886	Julia Evelina Smith
1793–1835	Felicia Hemans
fl. 1794–1816	Elizabeth Dawbarn
1794–1860	Anna Brownell Jameson
1795–1871	Rebecca Cox Jackson
1800–1866	Francis (Harriet Catherine) Egerton
1801–87	Gracilla Boddington
1803–79	Maria W. Miller Stewart

1805–79	Angelina Grimké Weld
1807–74	Phoebe Palmer
1811–96	Harriet Beecher Stowe
1812–83	Marie Françoise Catherine Doetter (Fanny) Corbaux
1815–1902	Elizabeth Cady Stanton
1816–47	Grace Aguilar
1818–ca. 1900	Mary L. T. Witter
1819–85	Susan Bogert Warner
1819–91	Helen Spurrell
1820–1910	Florence Nightingale
ca. 1821–84	Mary E. Simpson
1821–93	Charlotte Maria Tucker (A. L. O. E.)
1821–1910	Mary Baker Eddy
1823–1901	Charlotte Mary Yonge
1825–1921	Antoinette Louisa Brown Blackwell
1827–1915	Anna Bartlett Warner
1827–1915	Ellen Harmon White
1828–96	Elizabeth Rundle Charles
1828–1906	Josephine Elizabeth Grey Butler
1829–90	Catherine Mumford Booth
1829–1921	Phebe Ann (Coffin) Hanaford
1830–94	Christina Georgina Rossetti
1833–1913	(Frances) Julia Wedgwood
1837–1915	Amanda Berry Smith
1837–1926	Elizabeth Baxter
1838–1920	Louise Seymour Houghton
1839–98	Frances Elizabeth Willard
1840–1932	Elizabeth Wordsworth
1843–1920	Margaret Dunlop Gibson
1843–1926	Agnes Smith Lewis
1844–1911	Elizabeth Stuart Phelps
1844–1924	Katie Magnus
1847–1933	Annie Wood Besant
1849–1922	Lucy Rider Meyer
1852–1930	Elizabeth Bowerman (Madame Cecilia)
1853–1937	Lee Anna Starr
1855–1946	Katharine C. Bushnell
1856–1940	Briet Bjarnhjedinsdottir
1858–1922	Pandita Ramabai
1861–1918	Ada Ruth Habershon
1861–1927	Jessie Penn-Lewis
1861–1934	Helen Barrett Montgomery
1861–1935	Mary Louisa Georgina (Petrie) Carus-Wilson
1863–1944	Jane T. Stoddart
1867–1944	Emilie Grace Briggs
1870–1959	Laura Huldah Wild

1871–1916	Helena Konttinen
1873–97	Thérèse of Lisieux
1876–1952	Mary Inda Hussey
1877–1967	Mabel Madeline Southard
1886–1972	Margaret Brackenbury Crook
1887–1973	Mary Ellen Chase
1887–1981	Louise Pettibone Smith
1890–1963	Henrietta C. Mears
1891–1981	Suzanne de Dietrich
1893–1957	Dorothy Leigh Sayers
1899–1975	Charlotte von Kirschbaum
1902–44	Regina Jonas
1903–98	Beatrice Laura Goff
1905–97	Nehama Leibowitz
1905–2006	Kathryn Lois Sullivan
1906–78	Kathleen M. Kenyon
1921–95	Joyce Baldwin
1921–2007	Mary Douglas
1926–2002	Elizabeth Rice Achtemeier

Subject Index

Scripture Index